OCR Classical Civilisation

GCSE

ROUTE 2

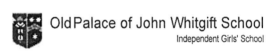

Old Palace of John Whitgift School
Independent Girls' School

Tel: 0208 688 2027

Date of Issue	Student name	Form

OCR Classical Civilisation

GCSE

ROUTE 2:
Women in the Ancient World

ROBERT HANCOCK-JONES

DAN MENASHE

JAMES RENSHAW

GENERAL EDITOR:

JAMES RENSHAW

Bloomsbury Academic

An imprint of Bloomsbury Publishing Plc

B L O O M S B U R Y
LONDON · OXFORD · NEW YORK · NEW DELHI · SYDNEY

Bloomsbury Academic

An imprint of Bloomsbury Publishing Plc

50 Bedford Square	1385 Broadway
London	New York
WC1B 3DP	NY 10018
UK	USA

www.bloomsbury.com

BLOOMSBURY and the Diana logo are trademarks of Bloomsbury Publishing Plc

First published 2017

© Robert Hancock-Jones, Dan Menashe and James Renshaw, 2017

Robert Hancock-Jones, Dan Menashe and James Renshaw have asserted their right under the Copyright, Designs and Patents Act, 1988, to be identified as Authors of this work.

British Library Cataloguing-in-Publication Data

A catalogue record for this book is available from the British Library.

ISBN:	PB:	978-1-3500-1503-6
	ePDF:	978-1-3500-1505-0
	ePub:	978-1-3500-1504-3

Library of Congress Cataloging-in-Publication Data

A catalogue record for this book is available from the Library of Congress.

Cover design by Terry Woodley and Olivia D'Cruz
Cover image © Getty/Universal History Archive

Typeset by RefineCatch Limited, Bungay, Suffolk
Printed and bound in Great Britain

To find out more about our authors and books visit www.bloomsbury.com. Here you will find extracts, author interviews, details of forthcoming events and the option to sign up for our newsletters.

ACKNOWLEDGEMENTS

The authors divided the text between them as follows:

'Women in the Ancient World' by Robert Hancock-Jones
'The Homeric World' by Dan Menashe
'Roman City Life' and 'War and Warfare' by James Renshaw.

The authors would like to thank the many anonymous reviewers at universities, schools and OCR who read and commented on drafts of this text. All errors remain their own.

CONTENTS

INTRODUCTION

Welcome to your textbook for OCR GCSE Classical Civilisation.

This book has been created to support the new OCR GCSE (9–1) specification with the Thematic Study option 'Women in the Ancient World'. You will study this section followed by a choice of one out of the three Literature and Culture sections, 'The Homeric World', 'Roman City Life' and 'War and Warfare'.

Through your reading of this textbook and your wider study in class, you will be able to gain a broad knowledge and understanding of a range of literary and cultural materials from the classical world. As well as learning about the culture, history and ideas of the ancient Greeks and Romans, you will read ancient texts in translation and study ancient art and objects from the classical world, together with the surviving remains of religious and domestic architecture.

The specification requires you to respond to the prescribed source material and assess content through analysis and evaluation. The box features (see pp. x–xi) are designed to build up your skills and knowledge, while exam tips, practice questions, and chapters on assessment will prepare you for taking your final examinations.

A Companion Website, available at www.bloomsbury.com/class-civ-gcse, supports this textbook with further information, resources and updates. If you have any suggestions for improvement and additional resources please get in touch by writing to contact@ bloomsbury.com.

We hope you will enjoy this wide-ranging and fascinating GCSE course, and that it will inspire you to go on to further study of the ancient world.

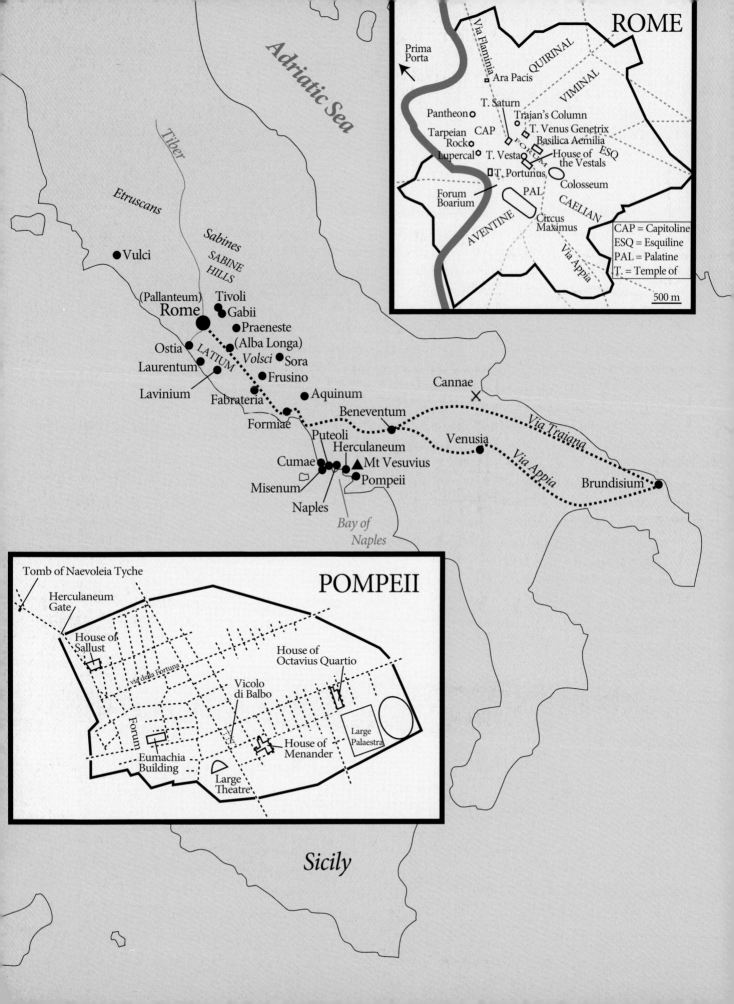

ROME

Prima Porta

Via Flaminia

QUIRINAL

Ara Pacis

VIMINAL

T. Saturn

Pantheon

Trajan's Column

T. Venus Genetrix

CAP

Basilica Aemilia

Tarpeian Rock

ESQ

House of the Vestals

Lupercal

T. Vesta

FORUM

T. Portunus

Colosseum

Forum Boarium

PAL

CAELIAN

AVENTINE

Circus Maximus

Via Appia

CAP = Capitoline
ESQ = Esquiline
PAL = Palatine
T. = Temple of

500 m

Adriatic Sea

Tiber

Etruscans

Sabines

SABINE HILLS

● Vulci

(Pallanteum)   Tivoli
● **Rome**   ● Gabii

● Praeneste

Ostia ●   (Alba Longa)

LATIUM   *Volsci*   ● Sora

Laurentum

● Frusino

Lavinium

● Aquinum

Fabrateria

Cannae ✕

Beneventum

Via Traiana

Formiae

Puteoli

Herculaneum

Venusia

Via Appia

Cumae   ▲ Mt Vesuvius

● Pompeii

Misenum

Brundisium ●

Naples

Bay of Naples

Sicily

POMPEII

Tomb of Naevoleia Tyche

Herculaneum Gate

House of Sallust

Via della Fortuna

House of Octavius Quartio

Vicolo di Balbo

Forum

Large Palaestra

Eumachia Building

House of Menander

Large Theatre

GAUL

Comum   Padua

Forum Iulii

Dacians

Danube

Black Sea   (Colchis)

(Amazons)

THRACE   BITHYNIA
PONTUS

ASIA   Persians   PARTHIA
MINOR   Hittites   Tarsus

MAGNA
GRAECIA

Carthage

Knossos   Ulu Burun

Crete

Mediterranean Sea

Alexandria

EGYPT   *Nile*

ATHENS

Kerameikos

Panathenaic Way

Bouleuterion   Agora
Areopagus   Erechtheion

Pnyx   Parthenon

Acropolis   Theatre of
Dionysus

Long Walls   Temple of   Sanctuary of
Athena Nike   Dionysus

MACEDON

Philippi ✕

Hellespont

Hisarlik (Troy)

Mt Olympus ▲

THESSALY

Cape
Artemisium

(Lapiths)

Aegean Sea

Actium ✕

Thermopylae ✕

Delphi   Thebes

Plataea   Eleusis

Ithaca   Patras   ATTICA ✕ Marathon
Megara   Brauron

ELIS   Corinth   ✕   Athens
Olympia   Argos   *Salamis*
Pisa   Mantinea   Mycenae
    Dendra
    ✕   Tiryns   Troezen
Bassae   Epidauros   Miletus

MESSENIA   *Naxos*

Pylos   Sparta

LACONIA   Akrotiri

Santorini

(Taenarus)

PELOPONNESE

HOW TO USE THIS BOOK

The layout design and box features of this book are designed to aid your learning.

COLOUR

Box features that focus on assessment preparation and exam skills are coloured in blue.

Box features with Stretch and Challenge material are coloured in yellow.

All other box features are coloured in red.

ICONS

The Prescribed Source icon **PS** flags a quotation or image that is a source prescribed in the specification.

The Stretch and Challenge icon **S&C** indicates that an exercise extends beyond the core content of the specification.

The Companion Website icon **CW** highlights where extra material can be found on the Bloomsbury Companion Website www.bloomsbury.com/class-civ-gcse.

BOX FEATURES

In the margins you will find feature boxes giving short factfiles of key events, individuals and places.

Other features either **recommend** teaching material or highlight **prescribed** content and **assessment** tips and information.

Recommended teaching material is found in the following box features:

Activities
Debates
Explore Further
Further Reading
Modern Parallels
Study Questions
Topic Reviews

Prescribed content and assessment-focused tips and information are found in the following box features:

Exam Overviews
Exam Tips
Practice Questions
Prescribed Sources

Material that extends beyond the specification is found in the Stretch and Challenge box features. Remember that the specification requires students to study extra sources and material not listed in the specification, so S&C information and exercises will provide a good place for you to start.

NOTE ON QUESTIONS

Discussion prompts found in Topic Review boxes and Study Question boxes are not worded in the form you will find on the exam papers. They are intended to encourage investigation and revision of the material, but do not reflect the questions you will answer in the exam. Practice Questions at the end of each topic, and the questions found in the 'What to Expect in the Exam' sections do mirror the format and wording you will encounter in the exam.

GLOSSARY

At the back of the book you will find a full glossary of key words. These words are also defined on pages in margin features.

Spellings of names and texts are formatted in line with the OCR specification.

On the Companion Website you will find a colour-coded glossary that highlights which components the words come from.

IMAGES

Illustrations give you the opportunity to see the ancient visual material you are required to study. Images of the prescribed visual/material sources are flagged with the **PS** icon, but other images illustrate other relevant aspects of the ancient world. Often what survives from the ancient world does not provide us with ways to illustrate what we study. Thus, art, drawings and reconstructions from later periods and the modern day may be used to illustrate this book. Don't forget that these are not sources like your prescribed texts and visual material – they are later interpretations of aspects of antiquity and do not represent evidence for analysis.

TRANSLATIONS

If not otherwise specified, translations are copyright OCR. Documents of translations covering the prescribed sources for each component are available from the OCR website and include OCR and other translations of the texts.

COMPANION WEBSITE

Resources will include:

- links to the text of Prescribed Literary Sources
- further images and information on Prescribed Visual/Material Sources
- annotated further reading
- links to websites that give useful contextual material for study
- quizzes on key topics and themes
- worksheets to supplement Activity box features in the book

DON'T FORGET

Look out for cross references to other pages in the book – this is where you will find further information and be able to link concepts or themes.

PART 1
THEMATIC STUDY:
WOMEN IN THE ANCIENT WORLD

Introduction to Women in the Ancient World

Half of your GCSE in Classical Civilisation involves a Thematic Study. This component provides the opportunity to study both Greece and Rome, looking at literature and visual/ material culture. You will also be expected to draw informed comparisons between Roman and Greek ideas, including the characteristics of the different societies, and the impact of the different cultural contexts on the theme studied.

OCR offers the choice between two options:

Myth and Religion	J199/11
Women in the Ancient World	J199/12

This textbook includes the content for the option Women in the Ancient World.

EXAM OVERVIEW   J199/12

Your assessment for the Thematic Study option will be:

    50% of the GCSE   1 hr 30 mins   90 marks

58 marks will test AO1: demonstrate knowledge and understanding of:

- literature and visual/material culture from the classical world
- how sources reflect their cultural contexts, and
- possible interpretations of sources by different audiences and individuals.

32 marks will test AO2: analyse, interpret and evaluate literature and visual/material culture from the classical world, using evidence and producing coherent and reasoned arguments.

The Thematic paper is divided into three sections:

Section A	Greece	30 marks
Section B	Rome	30 marks
Section C	Greece and Rome	30 marks

In Section C you will be expected to draw comparison between the two cultures.

In this component learners will explore the lives and representations of women in the ancient world. By studying a range of ancient sources, learners will be able to come to their own conclusions about the varying roles of women in the ancient world, and how they were perceived and treated by men and by each other.

The focus of the study will be on the city of Athens in the fifth century BC (Greece) and on Republican Rome (late-6th-century to 1st-century-BC Rome), although other societies will be considered where appropriate. For example, the experiences of Athenian girls, wives and mothers will be contrasted with the experiences of women in Sparta to give a more rounded understanding of the lives and roles of women in Greece. So too, some sources for the Rome portion of the component are taken, not from the city of Rome itself, but from other Roman towns including Pompeii.

This component is divided into eight sections, each of which includes content from Greece and from Rome. In this way, learners are invited to make direct comparisons between these societies throughout the course of study.

Daily life is an important aspect of this component, and learners will be able to trace the experiences of Greek and Roman women from birth to death, focusing on their roles within their households. The role that women played in public life is also examined, including their involvement in religious worship and in the world of politics. Learners will also investigate the experiences of 'improper' women in both societies and be able to discuss what these stories suggest about attitudes towards women and 'proper' female behaviour.

Just as important as daily life are the stories that the ancients told about women. Learners will study some of the most famous individual women from the Greek and Roman worlds, from Pandora and Helen of Troy to Camilla the warrior princess and Cleopatra.

1.1 Women of Legend

TOPIC OVERVIEW

Depiction of women in myths and legends of Greece and Rome, including the presentation of these women, and what this says about each culture's views on the nature of women and female virtue.

Greece

- Pandora
- Helen of Troy

Rome

- The Sabine Women and Tarpeia
- Lucretia

The prescribed sources for this topic are:

- Hesiod, *Works and Days,* 54–105
- Homer, *Iliad*, Book 3, 121–80
- Euripides, *Helen*, 1–67
- Livy, *History of Rome*, 1.9–10; 1.12–13; 1.57–59

Don't forget that you will be given credit in the exam if you study extra sources and make relevant use of them in your answers.

In this topic you will study famous female figures in Greek and Roman legends. The stories that societies tell about their own culture's past can reveal much about the values and beliefs of the society itself. So by studying how women were presented in legends, you will be able to understand a lot about how each society viewed women. Our Greek examples, Pandora and Helen of Troy, were usually thought of as bad women. Their presentation and behaviour was not to be admired or copied. On the other hand, our Roman examples include admirable women (the Sabine Women and Lucretia) and the opposite: Tarpeia was seen by most Romans as a very bad woman indeed.

GREECE

Pandora

The Greeks believed that, in the beginning, the human race was only men. They did not grow old or die and there was no disease or hardship. The first woman was created to punish mankind for receiving a stolen gift of fire (see p. 6). She marked the end of this time of ease and plenty. Now humans experienced old age, suffering and death.

The Greek poet Hesiod narrates this myth in his poem *Works and Days*. He uses the episode to explain how and why evils exist in the world.

Zeus (king of the Olympian gods; see Figure 1.1) asked Hephaestus (god of the forge and of craftsmen) to shape a woman out of earth and water. Zeus' plan is to punish mankind by giving them something that they will welcome, but that will lead to their destruction. Many of the gods contributed to her creation by giving her gifts that would make her appealing, and this is how she came to be called Pandora (which means 'all gifts').

Goddesses teach her handicrafts and make her graceful and full of desire. Finally, Zeus asks the god Hermes to give her a shameless mind and deceit. According to Hesiod, Pandora's gifts are varied indeed – some make her attractive, others make her dangerous.

FIGURE 1.1
Statue of Zeus.

> The bright-eyed goddess Athena clothed her and styled her; both the godly Graces and lady Persuasion put golden trinkets upon her skin; and the lovely-haired Seasons put a garland around her, made from the flowers of springtime. With all kinds of decoration Pallas Athena adorned her body. It was then that the messenger, the giant slayer, put lies and crafty words and a thievish nature into her heart
>
> Hesiod, *Works and Days*, 72–79

PS

Apart from Hermes' gifts of a thievish nature and crafty words, Hesiod's narration of Pandora's 'birth' focuses mostly on beauty and fine clothing. This passage could suggest that, for a Greek woman to be attractive, she had to be physically beautiful.

Zeus sent her down to earth and gave her as a bride to the **titan** Epimetheus as a bride. Epimetheus had been warned not to accept gifts from Zeus, but he forgot, and took her for his wife. Although Hesiod does not state why Epimetheus forgot, a reasonable interpretation would be that he was so attracted to Pandora that he did not stop to think.

Pandora brought with her to earth a pithos (jar). In it were all the evils that plague mankind. Pandora opened the jar as soon as she reached earth and let them out. Only Hope remained in the jar, because that was Zeus' will. Hesiod does not suggest why Pandora did this – the audience is left to make their own guesses.

Later versions of the story say Pandora had a pyxis (box), and so the popular story of Pandora's Box was born. Another later addition to this myth is the detail that Pandora was given the box but forbidden to open it. Eventually, Pandora's curiosity was too great and she opened the lid of the jar to see what was inside, unleashing the evils by mistake. This later version makes Pandora's character more complex, demonstrating her curiosity, disobedience and lack of self-control.

The Greeks, then, saw the dangerous and seductive power of Pandora in one of two ways. Either she was a double-agent, working for the gods against humanity, or she was

---

PRESCRIBED SOURCE

***Works and Days*, 54–105**

Date: *c.* 700 BC

Author: Hesiod

Genre: didactic poetry

Significance: narrates the story of the creation of the first woman

Read it here: OCR source booklet

---

didactic Something that is meant to teach or instruct.

titan The generation of gods before Zeus and the other Olympian gods.

ACTIVITY

Compare the story of Pandora to the biblical story of Adam and Eve using a Venn diagram to help organise the similarities and differences.

How does this comparison impact your understanding of the story of Pandora?

KEY INDIVIDUALS

Pandora the first woman of Greek mythology

Zeus the king of the Greek gods

Hephaestus the god of the forge and craftsmen

Epimetheus a titan whose name means 'hindsight'

Hermes messenger of the gods, sometimes called Giant-Slayer or Argus-Slayer

an uncontrolled slave to her own curiosity. Both interpretations are damning of Pandora and indeed of the women who came after her. In another poem called the *Theogony*, Hesiod describes the inherent evil of women, made worse by the fact that men need women in order to have children.

> For from [Pandora] is the race of women and female kind: of her is the deadly race and tribe of women who live among mortal men to their great trouble . . . Zeus who thunders on high made women to be an evil to mortal men, with a nature to do evil. And he gave them a second evil . . . : whoever avoids marriage and the sorrows that women cause, and will not wed, reaches deadly old age without anyone to tend his years, and . . . when he is dead, his kinsfolk divide his possessions amongst them.
>
> Hesiod, *Theogony*, 590–608

S & C

Why did the gods punish mankind?

The Olympian gods of Greek myth did not always rule. They came to power by overthrowing the previous generation of immortals, known as the Titans. One titan known as Prometheus (whose name means 'forethought') sided with Zeus and his Olympian siblings in the war to overthrow the previous gods. As a reward, Prometheus was not banished after the war.

As his name suggests, Prometheus was inventive and one day he played a trick on Zeus and the Olympian gods to help mankind, of whom he was particularly fond. He presented Zeus with two offerings. The first disguised the finest cuts of beef inside the stomach of a cow. The second disguised the cow's bones in a layer of fat. Because the second offering looked more appealing, Zeus chose it. From that day, humans would keep the edible parts of an animal sacrifice and burn the inedible bones and the attractive fat.

Zeus was angry with Prometheus and mankind, and punished them by hiding fire. Without fire, mankind could not keep warm or cook food, and so Prometheus devised another trick. He stole a spark of Zeus' fire from Olympus and brought it down to earth. When Zeus discovered what had happened, he was even more angry and devised a trick of his own: Pandora.

Discussion question: How does the story of Pandora mirror Prometheus' first trick with the sacrificial offerings?

FIGURE 1.2

The creation of Pandora by the Olympian gods. Pandora stands stiffly in the centre, passive, like a statue. To her left is Aphrodite, about to give her a wreath or necklace. Ares stands to the right in full armour.

EXPLORE FURTHER

See the story of Pandora in motion as part of the Panoply Vase Animation Project. Real artefacts form the basis of a short video with accompanying commentary, http://www.panoply.org.uk/pandora.html.

Study questions

Read the complete prescribed passage of Hesiod's *Works and Days* (54–105) and answer the questions below.

1 List Pandora's gifts. For each one, explain how it would have made her appealing to Epimetheus.
2 What do we learn about Pandora's inner mind or personality?
3 How similar is Hesiod's depiction of Pandora to the version in Figure 1.2?
4 What can we learn about Hesiod's opinion of women based on his two versions of the Pandora myth, from *Works and Days* (prescribed source) and from *Theogony*.
5 Why do you think Hope is the one thing left in Pandora's jar once all the other evils have escaped?

Helen

Helen of Sparta was the daughter of Zeus and the mortal woman Leda (wife of Tyndareus, King of Sparta). She was renowned for being a princess, a demi-god and the most beautiful woman in the world. Every eligible prince and noble from across the Greek world wanted Helen to be his queen.

In order to make sure that none of the disappointed suitors sought revenge against Helen and her future husband, Tyndareus made all suitors swear an oath that they would go to war against anyone who threatened the marriage. Helen then chose Menelaus (a prince of Mycenae) to be her husband. The pair continued to live in Sparta and had a daughter, Hermione.

KEY INDIVIDUALS

Helen daughter of Zeus and the mortal woman Leda. The most beautiful woman in the world

Menelaus Helen's first husband, a prince of Mycenae and king of Sparta

FIGURE 1.3
Helen (left) seated holding a mirror or fan and inspecting the contents of a box. Paris stands to the right.

KEY PLACES

Sparta a town in the Peloponnese area of Greece

Mycenae a town in the Peloponnese area of Greece. During the time in which the *Iliad* is set, Mycenae was the most powerful state in the region

KEY INDIVIDUALS

Paris prince of Troy

Aphrodite goddess of love and beauty

One day a Trojan prince named **Paris** visited Sparta and disrupted Menelaus and Helen's stable marriage. Paris was one of the favourite mortals of **Aphrodite** (goddess of love) and she had promised to give him a gift: the love of the most beautiful woman in the world. So when Paris left Sparta, he secretly took Helen with him back to Troy. By agreeing to go with Paris, Helen was agreeing to live in Troy as his wife. By being unfaithful to Menelaus she brought ultimate shame upon herself.

The poet Homer shows how Helen came to regret her decision:

PS

"I respect and reverence you, dear father-in-law," the lovely Helen replied: "I wish I had chosen death rather than following your son, leaving behind my bridal chamber, my beloved daughter, my dear childhood friends and my kin. But I did not, and I pine away in sorrow."

Homer, *Iliad*, 3.173–177

So why did Helen go with Paris? One version of the story is that she was blinded by her newfound love. However, there are competing versions in which Helen was either overcome by the irresistible power of Aphrodite or carried off by force. These interpretations make Helen a victim rather than a villain.

The Athenian playwright Euripides gives an imaginative version of the story. He writes that Hera, angry with Paris, made a phantom of Helen for him to take back to Troy. The real Helen was whisked away to Egypt, where she stayed for the duration of the war that ensued. In this interpretation, Euripides removes the question of Helen's guilt altogether. She is neither victim nor villain, just a pawn in a game played by the gods.

In your prescribed lines of Euripides' *Helen*, we see her give a speech that tells how she came to be in Egypt. The theme of female beauty is prominent in these lines, as Helen mentions the divine beauty pageant as well as her own beauty. She seems bitter that beauty has been the cause of so much suffering.

PRESCRIBED SOURCE

Iliad, **3.121–180**

Date: (unknown) first written down *c.* 8th century BC

Author: Homer

Genre: epic poetry

Significance: the oldest story in the Western literary canon

Read it here: OCR source booklet

S & C **The judgement of Paris**

When the mortal Peleus married the sea nymph Thetis, the only goddess not invited was Eris (whose name means 'strife'). She decided to wreck the wedding and threw a golden apple among the guests with the words 'for the fairest' written on it. Immediately, three goddesses claimed the apple. Zeus did not want to judge between them, and ordered them to find an honest mortal instead. They chose Paris, a Trojan prince.

No goddess wanted to lose and so they each offered Paris a bribe. Athena (goddess of wisdom and war, also known as Athene) offered Paris victory in war, Hera (queen of the gods) offered him power, and Aphrodite (goddess of love and beauty) offered Paris the love of the most beautiful woman in the world. Paris was most tempted by Aphrodite's offer, and awarded her the golden apple. This story suggests that 'beauty' in ancient Greece meant what was beautiful to male onlookers. The story might also show that beautiful women and love were valued more highly than military victory or power in ancient Greece. This seems unlikely, however, as Paris is often criticised for being shallow and superficial because he preferred Aphrodite's bribe.

FIGURE 1.4
In this relief sculpture, Helen is seated to the left in conversation with the goddess Aphrodite whose arm is around her shoulder. The figure top left is believed to be Peitho, goddess of persuasion. On the right Paris and the god Eros stand rather casually.

Three goddesses came to Paris in the hollows of Mount Ida for the sake of beauty;
Hera, Aphrodite, and the virgin daughter of Zeus;
who wanted a judgement of their appearances to be decided upon.
Aphrodite promised my beauty, if misfortune is beautiful, for Paris to marry:
she won.

Euripides, Helen, ll. 21–26

Helen's beauty is about to cause even more trouble, as the local ruler Theoclymenus wants to force her to marry him. For this reason, we see Helen seeking sanctuary (safety) at a sacred tomb. Although the whole world believes she is guilty of adultery, she refuses actually to commit the crime. This version of Helen's story reverses the more common tale, making it clear that Helen should be viewed as innocent of any wrongdoing.

Once Menelaus realised that Helen had left with Paris, he set about the business of getting her back. Invoking the oath that all of Helen's suitors had made, he assembled

PRESCRIBED SOURCE

***Helen*, 1–67**

Date: *c.* 412 BC

Author: Euripides

Genre: tragic drama

Significance: a creative reimagining of the Helen story by one of Athens' preeminent tragedians

Read it here: OCR source booklet

Study questions
Read the prescribed lines of Euripides' *Helen* (ll.1–67) and answer the following questions.

1 Helen recounts the story of the rape of her mother Leda by Zeus. What can you tell about Greek attitudes towards non-consensual sex based on the way she speaks?

2 What is Helen's primary concern at this point in the play? How do you know? What does this imply about feminine virtue?

xenia hospitality given unconditionally to a traveller, involving the giving of any help needed; known as 'guest friendship'

S & C What really caused the war?

Scholars have traditionally agreed that Menelaus went to war to retrieve Helen. But this is not the only possibility. The Homeric world placed great value on the relationship between guests and hosts and had a set of regulations to ensure that guests and hosts treated each other well. This was known as **xenia**. There were a rigid set of practices that must be followed and, as xenia was overseen by Zeus, a violation of it was blasphemous. Because Paris took Helen when he was a guest in Menelaus' home, it is reasonable to think that Menelaus went to war to avenge a breach of xenia.

The ancient poet Semonides suggested that Helen had been sent to earth by her father Zeus to start a war that would reduce the number of people in the world, which had become overpopulated.

More modern interpretations, for example the 2004 film *Troy*, have suggested that the Greeks merely used Helen's infidelity as an excuse to go to war for money and power.

the greatest force of Greek soldiers that the world had ever known to set out for Troy and retrieve his wife. This is why Helen is sometimes described as having a 'face that launched a thousand ships'.

What followed is known as the Trojan War, a ten-year siege of the city of Troy in which many great heroes were killed and, ultimately, the city and its people destroyed. Homer's epic poem the *Iliad* tells the story of a brief part of this war. It takes place in the tenth year of the siege, and includes Helen as a minor character.

The prescribed lines of Homer's *Iliad* show Helen living as Paris' wife in the city of Troy. At the start of the scene, she is weaving. Women in Homeric society were expected to weave – for poorer women this was a way of contributing to the household and for richer women it was a way of demonstrating their virtue. The Helen of the *Iliad* deeply regrets her choice to leave Sparta with Paris. Her presence in Troy is the reason for the war and she regrets the suffering she has caused. The Trojan elders are impressed by her beauty, but wish that she would leave. Only king Priam is kind to her.

Homer gives us another glimpse of Helen during the war in the Book 6 of the *Iliad*:

EXPLORE FURTHER

Read Book 4 of Homer's *Odyssey* for a picture of Helen and Menelaus' life after the Trojan War.

> Brother, I am indeed that wicked she-dog whom all abhor. I wish that on the day of my birth, some vile blast of wind had blown me to the mountains, or into the waves of the echoing sea, where the waters would have drowned me, and none of this would have come about. But since the gods ordained this fate, I wish that I had a better man for husband, who felt the reproaches and contempt of his fellow men. But this man of mine is fickle, and ever will be so, and will reap the harvest of it hereafter.

> Homer, *Iliad*, 6.343–353

It is clear that Helen regrets leaving with Paris, whom she refers to as her 'husband'. She bemoans her situation, but avoids taking any blame herself, rather saying it is the fault of the 'gods' and 'fate'.

FIGURE 1.5
This vase painting depicts Helen fleeing from Menelaus during the sack of Troy. He is in full armour but has dropped his sword behind him, possibly stunned by Helen's beauty as she glances back at him.

Study questions

Read the prescribed lines of Homer's *Iliad* (3.121–180) and answer the following questions.

1 What do the Trojan elders admire about Helen?
2 Why do the elders not wish for Helen to stay in Troy?
3 How does Priam's speech to Helen differ from the words of the old men?
4 Why does Helen wish that she had not left Menelaus?
5 How does Homer convey the depth of Helen's sorrow?

Based on your understanding of the story of Helen and of all the sources you have read answer the following.

1 What is the biggest difference between Homer's and Euripides' Helen?
2 Are there any similarities between these two portrayals of the same woman?
3 How do the sources on Helen convey her beauty? Make specific reference to Figure 1.2, Figure 1.3 and at least one of the prescribed literary sources.
4 Who do you think was to blame for the Trojan War? Justify your response.

PRACTICE QUESTIONS: GREECE

1. a. List any **two** gifts that Pandora was given by the gods. [2]
  b. Why were the gods' gifts significant? [1]
2. 'Helen should take the blame for starting the Trojan War.' Using the extract from the *Iliad*, Book 6 (quoted opposite) and your own knowledge, discuss how far you agree with this statement. [8]

ROME

The Sabine women

Sabine a person belonging to the Italian race of Sabines

patrician Rome's elite/noble class (determined by family not money)

Roman citizenship a high privilege with various rights and protections, normally reserved for the children of two Roman citizens

According to legend, the founder of Rome and its first king was a man called Romulus. Romulus grew the fledgling city by inviting refugees from all over Italy to resettle in Rome. Soon, however, he realised that they had a shortage of women and the first generation of Romans was at risk of becoming the last. So he went to his neighbouring kingdoms to arrange marriages between his citizens and theirs. Romulus' idea was not welcomed by many outside his city. Rome was a new and untested kingdom and fathers did not want to give their daughters away when Rome's future was so uncertain. So Romulus devised a plan. The Roman historian Livy tells the story of what happened next in a work called *The History of Rome*. Despite the title of his work, Livy is very open about the fact that he based several of his episodes (including the sections prescribed in this topic) on myths and folklore, not proper historical investigation.

Livy tells how Romulus sent invitations to neighbouring towns to attend a festival. A large number of **Sabines** attended the celebration. When the formal part of the festival was about to begin, Romulus gave a signal and the Roman men seized and carried off as many Sabine women as they could carry. Livy states that particularly beautiful maidens had been marked out for the **patrician** Roman men.

Afterwards, in the homes of their new Roman 'husbands', the Sabine women were outraged. They claimed that the bond of hospitality between the Romans and Sabines had been broken. Romulus disagreed, blaming the arrogance of the girls' parents for refusing to consent to inter-marriage. Romulus decreed that each was now married to the man who had taken her and would enjoy the privileges of **Roman citizenship**, as would their children. This gesture went some way to soothe the anger of the Sabine women.

Livy tells us that the Sabine's new husbands tried to soothe the women's anger by speaking loving words to them and giving excuses:

> This was supported by the men's efforts to charm the maidens; they justified their deed with love and longing, which is the most effective way of appealing to a woman's heart.
>
> Livy, *History of Rome*, 1.9

PS

Livy's own opinion of women is clear here, when he implies that appealing to vanity is most effective in winning over a woman's heart. He suggests that women are ruled by feelings of pride and that they will easily be swayed, not by logic and reason, but by flattery.

FIGURE 1.6
Iconic image of Rome's legendary first king Romulus and his twin brother Remus being suckled by a she-wolf after having been abandoned and left to die.

PRESCRIBED SOURCE

***The History of Rome,
1.9–10; 1.12–13***

Date: 1st century BC

Author: Livy

Genre: History

Significance: an important
work of history to the
Romans, as it told their
national story

Read it here: OCR
source booklet

S & C This episode of Roman myth/history is referred to as the 'Rape of the Sabine Women'. This title implies that the Roman men sexually assaulted the Sabines, but this is not necessarily the case. The Latin verb 'rapere' means 'to carry off/to seize' and, although it is the root of our modern word 'rape', it does not carry a specifically sexual connotation. The Roman men did, however, forcibly abduct the Sabine women to be their wives.

Discussion question: What does the behaviour of Romulus and his followers imply about Roman morals?

Tarpeia

Although the Sabine women were content, and in time Romulus granted their parents Roman citizenship too, the Sabine king Tatius was still angry. He made one final attempt to retrieve the stolen women, entering the city in secret to launch a surprise attack. At this time Rome was protected by city walls and these would have blocked the Sabine warriors, had it not been for the actions of a young Roman girl called Tarpeia.

Tarpeia was the daughter of the general Spurius Tarpeius. Whilst she was outside the city, collecting water for a religious ritual, King Tatius managed to bribe her to give him and his men entry to the city. Having betrayed her own people and given them access, Tarpeia was then killed by the Sabines. Livy says the Sabines used to wear heavy gold bracelets and jewelled rings. Apparently, Tarpeia said that she would let the men into Rome in exchange for what they had on their arms. The men agreed, but rather than give her their jewellery, they crushed her to death underneath their shields.

The story of Tarpeia is normally read quite simply as an example of a 'bad woman'. She gives in to her own greed and is justly punished for doing so. Livy does, however, allow for the possibility that Tarpeia was not a traitor but a trickster. After telling the normal version, he offers an alternative:

> Some say that in bargaining for what they had in their left hands, she expressly asked for their shields, and being suspected of wishing to betray them, fell a victim to her own bargain.

Livy, *History of Rome*, 11

FIGURE 1.7
A sixteenth-century statue portraying the rape of the Sabine Women.

In this version of events, Tarpeia could be viewed not as a traitor, but as a heroine. Seeing that the Sabines were about to invade the city, and knowing that she could not stop them from getting inside, she tried to take their shields away once they had got in and so make them weaker in the upcoming fight.

Regardless of this possible interpretation, Romans had no problem labelling Tarpeia as a traitor. The cliff from which Roman traitors were thrown to their deaths was known as the 'Tarpeian Rock'.

After the Sabine soldiers had entered the city, a fierce battle ensued in the Roman Forum. The day could have ended in tragedy, were it not for the intervention of the

KEY INDIVIDUALS

Tatius the king of the Sabines

Tarpeia a young Roman girl

FIGURE 1.8
A Roman coin, depicting Tarpeia on the reverse side, buried up to her waist in circular shields.

Sabine (now Roman) women. The women made their way to the centre of the fighting and pleaded with their husbands and with their fathers to end their fighting. They argued:

> "If you regret," they said, "the alliance between you; if you regret the marriages, then turn your anger against us. We are the cause of war."
>
> Livy, *History of Rome*, 1.13

Their appeal worked and an end was put to the fighting. The leaders even agreed that the Sabines should join the Romans, and form a single people.

The intervention of the Sabine women is remarkable because it shows women having a great impact in government by influencing their male relatives. It also clearly demonstrates the vital role women played in politics through marriage.

Study questions

Read the prescribed sections of Livy's *History of Rome* (1.9–10 and 1.12–13) and answer the following questions.

1 Make a storyboard of what happens to the Sabine women. Annotate your storyboard with an explanation of what each moment suggests about how the Romans viewed women.

2 Based on the story of the Sabine Women and Tarpeia, how much freedom did women have in the history of Rome? Support your answer with specific references to the story and sources.

3 Why do you think the most popular version of Tarpeia's involvement in Rome's war with the Sabines shows her as a traitor?

KEY PLACE

Roman Forum a public square in the centre of Rome which, over time, became an important centre for businesses, government and the law

FIGURE 1.9
The 'Tarpeian Rock' in Rome can still be seen today.

Lucretia

Many generations after Romulus founded Rome, there was a patrician woman named Lucretia. She was married to Collatinus, the son of a respected general and a distant relative of the current king Tarquinius Priscus. Lucretia was regarded by the Romans as a perfect example of female virtue. Her story is retold by Livy.

Livy first mentions Lucretia when some leading Roman men, including Collatinus and the king's sons, are enjoying a drinking party and discussing their wives. Each man ardently claimed that his wife was the most virtuous woman alive. To settle the matter, Collatinus suggested that the men make a surprise visit to each woman. Surely the way the women behaved in the absence of her husband would be the best test of virtue:

> . . . Lucretia was found rather differently from the king's daughters-in-law, who they had spotted at a sumptuous banquet, passing the time with their peers. Lucretia, on the other hand, was completely occupied by her spinning, even though it was late at night, and her maids toiled by lamplight around her as she sat in the hallway of her house. And so, the prize in the contest of feminine virtue was awarded to Lucretia.

Livy, History of Rome, 1.57

While the wives of the princes had been found selfishly enjoying themselves, Lucretia was working at her loom long into the night. Even noblewomen worked with wool, and skill with textiles was seen as a sign of obedience and hard work. The contest of virtue had been decided and so Collatinus and his companions, weary from their own night of drinking and horse-riding, ate at the house of Collatinus and Lucretia.

Sextus Tarquinius Superbus, Priscus' son, was so impressed by Lucretia's beauty and virtue that he resolved to sleep with her. A few days later, while Collatinus was away, Superbus returned to Collatinus' house alone. After dinner, Superbus was shown to a guest bedroom for the night. Livy's account of what happened next is telling of Roman attitudes towards women:

KEY INDIVIDUALS

Lucretia wife of Collatinus

Collatinus a leading Roman and distant relative of the king, Tarquinius Priscus

Tarquinius Priscus king of Rome

PS

KEY INDIVIDUAL

Sextus Tarquinius Superbus the king's son

PRESCRIBED SOURCE

The History of Rome, 1.57–59

Date: 1st century BC

Author: Livy

Genre: history

Significance: an important work of history to the Romans, as it told their national story

Read it here: OCR source booklet

pudicitia the Roman idea of sexual modesty shown through a woman's chastity or fidelity to her husband, but also by how she behaved in public and by dressing modestly

PS

He was burning with passion, and waited until it seemed that everyone was asleep, and everything around him was suitably secure, before he drew his sword and went to the sleeping Lucretia. He held the woman down with his left hand on her breast, and said: "Keep silent, Lucretia. I am Sextus Tarquinius, and my sword is in my hand. If you say a single word, you will die. She awoke with a start, and saw nothing which could help; only imminent death. Then Tarquinius began to declare his love, to beg, to mix prayers with threats, to attempt to turn her womanly heart by every means he had. When he found she was unmoved, and not even touched by the fear of death, he added disgrace to his threats, and said that when she was dead he would slaughter his servant and lay him, naked, beside her; so it could be said that she was put to death on a count of adultery with a lowly slave. Her steadfast chastity was overcome at this terrible prospect, as if by force, but in fact by his victorious lust. Tarquinius left, revelling in his successful conquest of a woman's honour.

Livy, *History of Rome*, 1.58

Despite Superbus' initial threats to her life, Lucretia refused to have sex with him – she would prefer death. To a Roman reader, this clearly demonstrated Lucretia's **pudicitia** and thus her virtue. The only way Superbus was able to make Lucretia relent was to threaten not only her life but her reputation. It would have been truly shameful for a noble Roman matrona to have sex with a slave, and so Superbus' final threat succeeded.

After the attack, Lucretia sent messengers to her father and her husband, asking them to come immediately. When they arrived, each with a trusted friend, Lucretia resolves to die:

PS

". . . Collatinus, there is the mark of a strange man in your bed, but only my body has been violated; my heart is innocent, as death will be my witness! But swear with your right hands that the adulterer will not go without punishment . . . It is your job," she said, "to decide what he deserves; as for me, although I absolve myself of the sin, I do not relieve myself of punishment. No shameless woman will ever live by the example of Lucretia." She took out a knife which was hidden beneath her clothes, she thrust it into her heart and died as she fell forward, sinking into the wound.

Livy, *History of Rome*, 1.58

ACTIVITY

Explain why Lucretia was declared the winner of the contest of virtue. *Remember that explaining is not the same as telling. You need to think of reasons why Lucretia's actions were deemed to be more virtuous, not just retell the story.*

Writing frame: When the men arrived at her house Lucretia was . . . which they thought was virtuous because . . . This was deemed to be more virtuous than the actions of the other women because they . . . which was thought to be less virtuous because . . .

Lucretia's actions were held up as an example of excellent female behaviour. Although she was innocent, she could not bear the thought that her reputation would suffer. Indeed, she could not bear the thought of being an excuse for future unchaste women to live despite their lack of pudicitia. In a way, this suggests that Roman society valued the perception of a woman by others more highly than it valued the woman herself.

Immediately after Lucretia's suicide the men present swore an oath, by the blood of Lucretia herself, that they would seek revenge. They took Lucretia's body to the Forum and immediately a crowd gathered. They announced what had happened, and urged all men present to do their duty by raising an army against the king. When the king became aware of an uprising in the city, he immediately gathered his family and escaped into exile.

Although Lucretia is generally seen as an example of great womanly virtue, some Romans thought that she showed some masculine characteristics. The poet Ovid called her a 'matrona with a manly spirit' and the public speaker Valerius Maximus called her a 'leader', but the Latin word he uses for leader (dux) is usually only used to describe men. Lucretia's suicide would also have been seen as manly by a Roman audience. In Greek and Roman literature, whenever women kill themselves it is usually by hanging or poison. Using a sword or a knife and dying a bloody death was usually what men did.

FIGURE 1.11
Lucretia in a medieval stained-glass window.

Roman Family Law

S & C

In Republican Rome, adultery was not a crime. If a woman was discovered having an affair, she would be given a trial by four of the male members of her household, including her father and husband. Livy's story mirrors this practice as Lucretia tells her story to four men (including her husband and father) who then pass judgement on her. Livy uses legal terms 'guilty' and 'acquit' to remind the reader of this custom. The men tell Lucretia that 'where there has been no consent, there is no guilt', meaning that she is officially innocent of any wrongdoing and her pudicitia is intact.

Discussion question: Why do you think Livy made reference to this aspect of Roman law in this scene?

Study questions

1 What can we learn about 'proper' womanly behaviour from the contest of the wives?
2 What can we learn about the value placed on a woman's chastity by the Romans based on this story?
3 What does it say about Roman attitudes towards women if Lucretia, a role model for Roman women, behaved in such a 'masculine' way?

Read the prescribed sections of Livy's *History of Rome* (1.57–9) and answer the following questions.

1 How does Livy convey Lucretia's emotional state during and after her assault by Superbus? Support your answer with specific reference to the text.
2 Why do you think Lucretia is concerned that no Roman woman be able to 'plead Lucretia's example' as an excuse for willing adultery?

PRACTICE QUESTIONS: ROME

1. What was the name of Lucretia's husband? [1]
2. Why did Lucretia kill herself? [1]
3. How important were the bonds of marriage in Roman legends? Use Livy's *History of Rome* 1.9 and your own knowledge in your answer. [8]

TOPIC REVIEW

You should be able to:

1. Describe:
   • how Pandora was created, came to earth and her role in bringing evils to the world
   • the story of Helen's marriage to Menelaus, how she met prince Paris of Troy and the two versions of her role in the Trojan War
   • how Romulus and his followers abducted the Sabine Women and how the Sabines attempted to retrieve their women
   • the story of Tarquin's rape of Lucretia and her suicide.

2. Explain:
   • what the story of Pandora suggests about Greek views regarding women
   • why Helen was so desirable to Greek men
   • how Homer and Euripides' versions of the story of Helen differ, and the impact these differences have on how Helen would have been viewed
   • why Romulus needed to abduct the Sabine women and how Livy's audience would have viewed the abduction
   • why Lucretia was so desirable to Roman men.

PRACTICE QUESTIONS: COMPARING GREECE AND ROME

These questions are based on two stimulus sources, one from Greece and one from Rome. The sources could be extracts from prescribed sources or unseen.

Source A (Greek): *Relief sculpture depicting a scene from the story of Helen*

Source B (Roman): *Livy, History of Rome, 1.58*

They found Lucretia sitting in sorrow in her chamber. The arrival of her loved ones made tears spring from her eyes, and when her husband asked her "Is everything alright?" she replied: "Not in the slightest. How can it be, for a woman who has lost her virtue? Collatinus, there is the mark of a strange man in your bed, but only my body has been violated; my heart is innocent, as death will be my witness! But swear with your right hands that the adulterer will not go without punishment. It was Sextus Tarquinius who last night exchanged hospitality for hostility, and, armed with force, brought ruin upon me and (if you are men) himself, as he claimed his disgusting pleasure."

Study **Source A** and **Source B**.

1. Explain how each of these sources show the powerlessness of women in Greek and Roman legends.　　[6]
2. Was female monogamy more important in Greek or in Roman legends? Refer to at least one Greek and one Roman story in your response.　　[15]

1.2 Young Women

TOPIC OVERVIEW

Typical experiences of young women in Greece and Rome, and what these imply about the status of women in each society.

Greece: Athens

- Education in the home in preparation for marriage
- Typical Athenian wedding rituals and arrangements

Greece: Sparta

- The Spartan system of education and marriage

Rome

- Education in the home in preparation for marriage
- Evidence of academic education for some Roman girls
- Varieties of marriage in Roman society:
    - o *coemptio, confarreatio* and by *usus*
    - o difference between *cum manu* and *sine manu* marriages

The prescribed sources for this topic are:

- 'Sappho' fresco of an educated upper class Pompeiian woman

Don't forget that you will be given credit in the exam if you study extra sources and make relevant use of them in your answers.

In this topic you will study the lives of young women in Greece and Rome, from birth and early upbringing, through education to marriage. For both, marriage was the point when a woman entered adulthood, so weddings were important rites of passage in Greece and Rome. In order to get a fuller picture of different customs that existed across the Greek world, you will have the opportunity to study the upbringing, education and marriage in both the city-state of Athens, and Sparta, the premier warrior culture of antiquity.

GREECE

Upbringing and education of Athenian girls

From the moment she was born until the day she died, an Athenian woman was under the direct control of her **kyrios**. When a baby was born, it was the responsibility of the kyrios to decide whether the baby would be welcomed into the household or subjected to **exposure**. This was seen neither as illegal nor immoral because the baby was left 'in the hands of the gods' and it was believed that, if the gods wished, they would save it. Baby girls were at greater risk of being exposed than boys, mainly because raising a girl would be a greater strain on the family's resources than raising a boy. A boy could grow up to work in the family business and inherit the family estate, helping to boost the family's wealth and reputation. A girl, on the other hand, would be married into another household. What's more, her kyrios would need to give an expensive **dowry** to her husband's family. Sources suggest that an average dowry could have been between five and twenty per cent of the kyrios' total wealth. Some poorer Athenian families therefore exposed baby girls.

Athens had no state education system. Each family had to arrange education for their children, which would normally involve employing a range of subject-specialist tutors to teach literacy and numeracy, music and physical education. This kind of education would normally only have been received by male children.

Young girls would be educated at home, usually by their mothers. They could expect to learn a range of practical skills that they would need to be a good **kyria** in later life. Probable 'subjects' include spinning wool, weaving, cookery, managing the household finances and managing the household slaves.

There is evidence, such as Figure 1.13, that some women knew how to read. It is unlikely, however, that this was the case for all or even most women. The Athenian comic playwright Menander wrote:

> a man who teaches a woman to write should recognize he is providing poison to an asp.
>
> Menander, fourth-century BC fragment

This seems to suggest that teaching girls to read and write was not the norm. Moreover, it suggests that some men viewed literate women as dangerous. We should remember, however,

kyrios the male head of a Greek household, with responsibility for and authority over his wife, children and any unmarried female relatives

exposure the ancient practice of leaving an unwanted baby outside the city to die

dowry an amount of money paid to a prospective groom by the bride's family

DEBATE

Scholars debate how common the practice of exposure actually was in the Classical period, but there is no doubt that it did occur.

kyria the wife of the kyrios, under the direct control of her husband

FIGURE 1.12
This mid-fifth-century red-figure hydria (water jar), now in the Harvard Art Museums, shows a mother (seated) passing her baby to a **wetnurse**.

wetnurse woman who looks after and breastfeeds another woman's baby. Common in Athens, wetnurses were usually slaves, foreigners or poorer citizens who charged for their services

FIGURE 1.13
A red-figure hydria depicting a seated woman reading. The presence of three attendants, presumably slaves, suggests that she is from a wealthy household.

Study questions

1 How much control did the kyrios have over his daughter's life until marriage?
2 How useful was the education given to Athenian girls?

that Menander was a comic playwright and so this could be a joke and therefore not representative of general Athenian views.

Again, it is worth noting that class differences certainly impacted what sort of education a girl was likely to receive. Lower-class girls, who may have taken an active role in running a family business, might have had more extensive training in finances and record-keeping than their upper-class counterparts.

Athenian marriage customs

Matchmaking and betrothal

Marriage for an Athenian girl would have been arranged by her kyrios as soon as she reached puberty, around the age of fourteen.

Making a marriage match was handled like a business deal, with no room for romance. The girl's kyrios would select an appropriate groom and they would agree a dowry. They would then swear a solemn oath in front of witnesses, as this extract from a play by Menander shows:

> [Pataikos] Listen to what I say: I give you this girl for the plowing of legitimate children
> [Polemon] I take her
> [Pataikos] And a dowry of three talents

Menander, *Perikeiromene*, 1012–14

From the moment of this betrothal (engagement) ceremony, the couple were considered legally married. However, betrothals could happen at any age and it was common for years to pass before the actual wedding ceremony. The primary concern of the kyrios, when making a match, was that the relationship be beneficial to both families. For example, it would be common for a kyrios to give his daughter in marriage to one of his friends or business partners.

The significance of the dowry

The dowry was an important part of negotiating an Athenian marriage. A kyrios who could not offer a dowry would have difficulty in arranging the marriage of his daughters. It is probable that the dowry was intended to compensate the groom's family for the expense of providing for the bride. The dowry could also help to protect the bride. If a husband wanted to divorce his wife, he would have to return the dowry. This could encourage men not to mistreat their wives or to seek a divorce without good reason. Indeed, if the dowry were large enough and the husband had spent the money, he would not be able to divorce his wife at all and she might be able to use this fact to influence him.

The wedding ceremony

Athenian weddings lasted three days. On the first day, the bride would be joined by her female relatives and friends and they would share a feast. The bride would make sacrifices to Artemis in her capacity as goddess of childhood and virginity. The bride would offer a lock of hair as well as her childhood toys. This was to thank the goddess for her protection during childhood, and to ask for continued favour as the bride was entering the sphere of adult womanhood. The bride may also have made offerings to Hera (goddess of marriage) and Aphrodite (goddess of love).

The second day began with a ritual bath for the bride. This was intended to purify her and enhance her fertility. After her bath, she would be dressed in the finest clothes and jewellery available. The most symbolically important part of the bride's costume was the veil. This would have covered her face and symbolised her modesty.

When the bride was ready, her kyrios would host a wedding feast in their home for both families as well as close friends. This would involve fine food, plenty of wine, music and entertainment. As citizen women were usually excluded from drinking parties (see p. 39), wedding feasts were one of only a small range of social occasions that women could attend. After the feast was over, the torchlight procession would commence. A highly symbolic act, the procession involved the groom literally dragging the bride away from her mother, putting her in a cart, and taking her to his house. This represented the bride officially stopping being a member of her childhood household, and becoming a member of her groom's household, with him as her new kyrios.

The procession itself was a real spectacle. Torches lit the way to ward off evil spirits. The men would sing wedding songs accompanied by musicians. The women would throw fruit and flowers at the couple, symbolizing fertility. At the end of the procession, the bride would be taken to the hearth of her groom's house, the symbolic centre of the home.

ACTIVITY

Make a storyboard of Athenian wedding ceremonies. Explain the significance of the procession, the burning of the cart's axle and the gifts given on the third day.

FIGURE 1.14
This mid-sixth-century black-figure lekythos (oil flask) depicts a wedding procession. The couple are seated on the cart facing forwards. Behind the face of the bride (painted white to show her fair skin), a dark red sheet is visible, probably her veil.

At the end of the procession, the wooden axle of the processional cart was burned. This represented the fact that the bride could not now return to her previous home.

What happened next was a central part of the wedding ritual. The couple would retire to their bedroom, decorated with flowers, and they would spend the night together. Their friends would stand guard, singing songs and banging on the door. This may have been to prevent evil spirits from cursing the marriage, or it could have been to offer moral support to the bride, about to lose her virginity.

On the final morning of the wedding ceremony the bride's female attendants would still be outside their room, with some of the male guests. The celebrants would sing wedding songs and the bride would be given gifts by the members of her new family. Gifts would have been intended to help the bride in her new life and probably included clothing, perfumes, jewellery and cosmetic tools.

Because the Athenian government did not keep a record of married couples (like the modern wedding registry), eyewitnesses were very important to the wedding ceremony. If someone ever claimed that the couple were not married (as could happen in the Athenian law courts), then the eyewitnesses would be called to give evidence.

DEBATE

Although the three-day wedding ceremony outlined here represented an ideal celebration, scholars have wondered how practical it would have been for poorer Athenians to devote three whole days, with expensive celebrations, to a wedding.

S & C Married to death?

Scholars have noted similarities between Athenian marriage rituals and Athenian burial rites. Both involve a symbolic bath for purification, dressing in fine clothes and a procession to a new 'home' (see pp. 78–9 for more information on Athenian burial rites).

This similarity may not be a coincidence. It could relate to the idea that, in her marriage, the young girl disappeared from her household. Surely her parents would have felt an amount of grief at their loss, but less than the grief for a loved one dying. It could also be a reference to the myth of the goddess Persephone's abduction by Hades. Hades was god of the Underworld and so his abduction of Persephone could be understood both as her marriage and as her funeral.

Activity: Research the myth of Persephone's abduction by Hades. How similar is it to an Athenian wedding?

Study questions

1 Why were eyewitnesses important in Athenian wedding ceremonies?
2 Why did Athenian brides make offerings to Artemis, Hera and Aphrodite?
3 Imagine you are an Athenian kyrios. What qualities would you look for in a potential husband for your daughter? Explain your decisions.

Upbringing and education of Spartan girls

Sparta is famous for having been the 'warrior society' of antiquity. Every adult male was a professional soldier. Spartan laws and customs were designed to produce elite soldiers that would enable Sparta to achieve and maintain total military dominance.

Although Spartan women did not go to war, they played a vital role in ensuring the success of their militaristic system. Laws and customs governing the upbringing and education of Spartan girls were intended to help them to bear healthy children and to encourage the men of Sparta to excel in their training.

In Athens, it was the kyrios who decided whether a newborn baby would be accepted into the household, or if it would be exposed. In Sparta, this decision rested with the Spartan elders. If the baby was deemed to be sturdy and not weak or in any way deformed, they would order it to be raised. If not, it would be left to die.

In Sparta, it seems as though there was no preference for raising boys over girls. The only criterion seems to have been the health of the baby. This suggests that the Spartan elders (all of whom would have been men) valued the contribution women made to Sparta.

Spartan girls engaged in physical training, just like the boys. According to the biographer Plutarch, this was so that they might:

> withstand childbearing because of their strength and struggle smoothly and easily
> with the pains of childbirth.

Plutarch, Life of Lycurgus

Similarly, the historian Xenophon gives us evidence of how Sparta rejected traditional Greek customs regarding women, establishing ones that would develop their strength:

> With other people, girls who are intending to become mothers and who are
> respectable girls are raised on a completely modest diet and with the smallest
> possible number of delicacies. . . . Other Greeks think that girls ought to sit alone

The reason behind Spartan militarism: the Second Messenian War

The 'Spartan System' arose in response to a war that devastated early Spartan society, and was designed to prevent anything similar from ever happening again.

In *c.* 670 BC, the citizens of Sparta were outnumbered 10:1 by their slave-class. Years before, Sparta had conquered a neighbouring people known as Messenians and had enslaved all the survivors, calling them Helots, which means 'captives'. Now, the Messenian Helots rose up against their Spartan masters. This began a seventeen-year conflict known as the Second Messenian War. The Messenians massively outnumbered the Spartans, but eventually the Spartan forces were victorious and the Helots were enslaved again.

The war had been long, bloody and had cost Sparta dearly. Shortly after the end of the war, Spartan society experienced a radical change in organisation. This change is often attributed to a man called Lycurgus, a lawgiver. Modern scholars do not know if Lycurgus ever truly existed, but it is certain that, around that time, Sparta changed into a 'warrior state'.

Study questions

1 What evidence do we have that Spartan society valued excellence in sports and physical activities for its women?
2 Explain how a Spartan girl's education was designed to produce healthy offspring.
3 What was the biggest difference between the upbringing and education of a Spartan girl from that of an Athenian girl?

doing their wool-working. . . . How, then, can they expect that girls raised like this will bear strong children? But Lycurgus thought that slave women produced clothing that was sufficient, and thinking that producing children was the most important function of free women he established physical exercise for the female no less than for the male sex. Then he set up competitions in speed and strength just as there were for the men. In this way, he also set up contests for females to compete with one another, thinking that the offspring from parents of two fit parents will be stronger.

Xenophon, *Constitution of the Spartans*

The Spartan system of education encouraged physical excellence from its women as much as its men. In fact, the very first woman to be a victor at the ancient Olympic Games was a Spartan named Cynisca. The Olympic Games were held every four years (like the modern Olympics), and any freeborn male Greek could compete. Cynisca got around this rule by entering the games as a trainer of horses. She did not attend the games, but her team of horses won first place in the chariot race. That Cynisca was able to enter the games openly, representing her city, is clear evidence that the Spartans valued physical prowess in their women.

Spartan marriage customs

Matchmaking

In Sparta, unlike Athens, young men and women would have had plenty of opportunities to interact. Boys and girls would have exercised outside in full view of each other, and the girls were actively encouraged to heckle the boys. If a boy was seen to be lazy or inept, they would insult him. If another boy excelled in his training, they would loudly praise him to motivate others.

This means that it is highly unlikely that Spartan brides would be strangers to their grooms. It is unclear exactly how Spartan marriages were arranged. The girl's parents would probably have had a hand in arranging a suitable match. A key difference in Spartan culture was the lack of a dowry. There was no financial aspect to Spartan marriages. The main purpose was to produce strong Spartan children.

Another key difference between Athens and Sparta was the age at which a girl would marry. Whereas in Athens the usual age was fourteen, as soon as she had gone through puberty, Spartan girls did not marry until much later, probably in their late teens or early twenties. This was because older girls who were in their physical prime were thought to be able to produce stronger children and were more likely to survive childbirth.

The wedding ceremony

syssition communal mess hall in which Spartan warriors dined and for which each man had to contribute food

On her wedding night, a Spartan bride would have her hair cut short, like a man's, and wear a man's clothes and sandals. The she would lie waiting for her husband on the floor of her bedroom. The groom, meanwhile, would have had dinner as normal in his **syssition** and have gone to bed in his military barracks. At some point that night, the groom would sneak out of his barracks, trying to avoid being caught. He would go to his bride's house, carry her to the bed and they would consummate the marriage. He might stay with her for a short while, but before morning he would return to his barracks to sleep alongside his comrades. This arrangement would continue indefinitely, with the couple only meeting secretly at night.

Nobody is entirely sure why Sparta's wedding ritual took this form. One suggestion is that, by sneaking around, the couple would be excited to see each other. As a result, their sex would be more energetic (it was believed that vigorous sex would lead to healthier offspring). Another theory is that, as this custom prevented husbands and wives from spending too much time together, it ensured that a Spartan warrior's first allegiance was always to his comrades and not to his family. It was not until he reached the age of thirty and retired from the full-time army that a Spartan man would move out of his barracks and into his wife's home to live with her and his children.

Study question

Imagine you are the father of a Spartan girl. What qualities would you look for in a potential husband for her?

ACTIVITY

Imagine you are a Spartan girl about to be married. Write a diary entry detailing your hopes and fears for the future. Refer to specific aspects of Spartan marriage customs.

PRACTICE QUESTIONS: GREECE

Source A: *Greek lekythos showing a wedding procession*

1. Describe why dowries were important in Athens. [2]
2. Do you think an Athenian bride would have enjoyed her wedding?
   Use **Source A** and your own knowledge in your answer. [8]

ROME

Upbringing and education of Roman girls

paterfamilias the male head of a Roman family

patria potestas the power or authority held by the paterfamilias over members of his household

As in Athens, when a Roman child was born it was under the control of the head of household, called the **paterfamilias**. He held complete control over all dependents in his family – the Romans called this power **patria potestas**. A Roman woman would spend her entire life under the authority of her paterfamilias. The paterfamilias was responsible for deciding if a child would be accepted into the family or rejected. When a baby was born, a midwife would check it for physical deformities and then leave it at the paterfamilias' feet. If he picked it up and lifted it into the air, then it had been formally accepted into the family. If he did not do this, then the baby would be given to the family slaves or the midwife to expose. Scholars debate how common it was to expose a child. While it certainly did occur, it seems likely that it only ever happened in a very small number of cases.

Roman girls were at greater risk of being rejected than boys. This was for similar reasons as in Athens – girls were a greater financial drain on their household because they would not work and they would usually need to be provided with an expensive dowry.

If a baby girl was welcomed by the paterfamilias, the family would put a couch out for Juno (goddess of marriage and queen of the gods). The idea was that this couch invited the goddess into the house and she would watch over the baby in its first days, when it was weakest and at greatest risk of death.

On its eighth day, the family held a naming ceremony for the child. Roman parents did not choose names for their daughters in the same way as today. Girls were simply called a feminine version of their father's clan name. For example, Julius Caesar was a member of the Julian clan, and so his daughter was called Julia. If a couple had multiple daughters, they would all be given the same name.

FIGURE 1.15
This detail from a young boy's grave stele shows him wearing a bulla around his neck. Lucky amulets like this one would have been worn by all Roman children, regardless of their gender.

During the naming ceremony the family would make offerings to the gods in their home and give a party for friends and relatives. The baby would be given gifts, including a **bulla** to ward off evil spirits. The bulla would be worn throughout childhood and only given up when they entered adulthood. For girls, this meant on their wedding day.

Much of a young girl's time would have been spent in the home being cared for by her mother or, for more wealthy families, their household slaves. It was usual for Roman girls to be taught reading, writing and arithmetic from a teacher known as a **litterator**. Wealthy families might also send a slave (usually Greek) to assist with the lessons and report back to the paterfamilias on the child's progress.

bulla a lucky charm in the Roman world

litterator a teacher for primary-aged children in the Roman world

fresco a painting originally done on damp plaster in which the colours become fixed as the plaster dries

The **fresco** (wall painting) in Figure 1.16 was uncovered in the Roman town of Pompeii. Preserved when Mount Vesuvius erupted in AD 79, it shows a young women holding a stylus (writing tool) to her lips. Papyrus (an early form of paper) was an expensive commodity in Rome, so people often wrote using a stylus and a writing board. The board would be covered with a layer of wax, into which a stylus could write. These writing tools allow us to say confidently that she must have been educated. She is also likely to have been rich. The fresco was found in a large villa, and the woman seems to be wearing golden jewellery – a sign of wealth.

FIGURE 1.16
'Sappho' fresco of an educated upper-class Pompeiian woman.

PS

PRESCRIBED SOURCE

'Sappho' fresco of an educated upper-class Pompeiian woman

Date: mid–1st century AD

Ancient location: Pompeii

Current location: National Archaeological Museum of Naples, Italy

Significance: a remarkably well preserved painting from the Roman town of Pompeii

---

Because there was no state education system in Rome, families had to arrange education for their children. This meant that the poorest families would not have been able to afford to have their children educated at all. It is likely that, if money was tight and a family could only afford to educate one child, a son would be educated rather than a daughter. In addition to their basic literacy and numeracy skills, girls would have been instructed in domestic tasks, probably by their mother or a female slave. These tasks included spinning wool, weaving textiles, cooking and managing the house. Girls from poorer families would also often learn a trade so that they could earn money. Evidence from grave inscriptions tells us that Roman girls held jobs such as hairdressers, jewellery makers and bakers.

Advanced subjects, including history, geometry, music, philosophy, law and, most importantly, rhetoric (the art of public speaking) were usually only taught to boys. We do, however, have some evidence of Roman women who were accomplished in these skills. For example, one Maesia was famous for having successfully defended herself in the law courts. In fact, she was found not guilty by a huge majority of votes, so she must have been an impressive speaker. Roman lawyers studied rhetoric for years and crafted careful speeches designed to persuade their audience. It is highly unlikely that Maesia would have been able to win her case if she had not been educated in the art of rhetoric. We should not assume, however, that many women would have been educated in the art of public speaking. Maesia was nicknamed 'Androgyne' because she was thought to have the spirit of a man. It seems, therefore, that Maesia was an exception.

> **Study question**
> What can you learn about the education of Roman girls by studying the Sappho fresco? What is it not possible to tell? What reasonable guesses can you make but not know for sure?

Roman marriage customs

As in Greece, marriage matches in Rome were rarely based on love between the bride and groom. The paterfamilias would select appropriate matches for the unmarried women under his control. What made a man 'appropriate' would have differed, but common reasons included:

- solidifying a business or political relationship between male members of the households
- improving the social standing of one or both of the families
- financial gain for the groom's family thanks to a large dowry.

Betrothal

Having found a potential husband for a young woman in his care, the paterfamilias would agree an acceptable dowry with the groom's family. Both the bride-to-be and the groom-to-be needed to give their consent but, as this section from a poem by Catullus shows, young girls may not have felt able to refuse the wishes of their paterfamilias:

> It's not right to struggle, you, whose father gives you away,
> your father and your mother, who prepare you.
> Your virginity's not wholly yours: part is your parents:
> a third your father's, a third your mother's,
> only a third is yours: don't fight those two,
> who grant their rights to the son-in-law with the dowry.
>
> Catullus, *Poem 62*, 61–66

Indeed, Roman law stated that a young girl was free to reject a fiancé, but only if her father had chosen a man who was of bad character or unworthy. For a young girl (some girls were betrothed as young as seven years old) to place such accusations against a man of her father's choice seems unlikely.

From the moment when both families had agreed to the match and dowry, the couple were betrothed. This was only a formality in Rome and did not change anything legally. The engagement could be freely cancelled at any time.

Wealthier families would usually celebrate an engagement by throwing a party, not unlike today. Friends and family would be invited to the prospective bride's house and her groom-to-be would give her gifts. Often he would present her with a ring to wear on the fourth finger of her left hand. In fact, this custom is where we get the practice of exchanging engagement and wedding rings from. The ring was worn on this finger because the Romans believed, based on a limited understanding of the body, that there was a vein running directly from the fourth finger to the heart.

Cum or sine manu?

The Romans had two distinct types of marriage: **cum manu** (with hand) and **sine manu** (without hand).

Study question
How much power did a Roman girl have in deciding who her husband would be? Refer to Catullus *Poem 62* in your answer.

cum manu a form of marriage – 'with hand'

sine manu a form of marriage – 'without hand'

In a cum manu marriage, the wife legally transferred to her husband's family. Her status in the family was the same as if she had been adopted. She could inherit property from her husband, if he died, and would no longer inherit from her father. Women who married cum manu would be given the title **materfamilias**, if their husband was the paterfamilias of his family unit.

Sine manu marriages were more common, particularly in wealthy families, and the bride remained under the legal control of her original paterfamilias. This form of marriage was probably preferred as it made sure that the woman would be able to inherit from her parents and so kept money within the immediate family. Sine manu marriages did not require a dowry, however, and so could have been a less secure prospect for a woman. The husband could easily choose to divorce her with no dowry to repay (for more on divorce see pp. 49–50).

Children were considered part of their father's family, but not necessarily their mother's. This means that in a cum manu marriage, the children would belong to the same family as their mother and father. However, in a sine manu marriage they would belong to their father's family but not their mother's.

Varieties of wedding ceremony

As well as the difference between cum manu and sine manu marriages, the Romans also drew a distinction between three kinds of wedding ceremony: **coemptio**, **confarreatio** and **usus**.

At coemptio wedding ceremonies the bride was symbolically sold by her pater-familias to her new husband. These ceremonies were recognisable because a man would hold a set

> **materfamilias** mother of the Roman household and wife of the paterfamilias

> **coemptio** a Roman wedding ceremony (resulting in a cum manu marriage) where the bride was symbolically sold to her new husband
>
> **confarreatio** a traditional patrician wedding ceremony. Resulted in a cum manu marriage
>
> **usus** a very popular marriage with no formal wedding ceremony and resulting in a sine manu marriage

FIGURE 1.17
This section from the front of a Roman sarcophagus depicts a wedding ceremony, probably confarreatio. The woman between the couple would be the pronuba, presiding over the ceremony.

MODERN PARALLEL

Many modern countries recognise long-term relationships between couples living together as a 'common-law marriage'. In the UK the term is used informally and cohabiting couples who see themselves as married in 'common-law' actually have no legal connection to each other. Contrastingly, the Israeli government will recognise 'common-law marriages' and even grant benefits provided that the couple can prove that they live as man and wife.

pronuba a Roman citizen woman who had been married only once and was still married to this man

Study questions

1 What was the difference between a cum manu and a sine manu marriage?
2 Explain why usus marriages were popular.

lares the Roman family's household gods, representing the spirits of the family ancestors

of banking scales. The bride's paterfamilias would present a single coin, representing her dowry, in the scales and thus 'sold' her. Because this type of wedding ceremony was all about exchanging property, coemptio ceremonies were only used for cum manu marriages.

The confarreatio wedding ceremony is probably the oldest version of a Roman wedding and was used only by the patrician (noble) class. The central part of the ceremony was an offering made by the bride and groom to Jupiter (king of the Roman gods). The couple offered a ceremonial cake in the presence of Rome's chief priest, the Pontifex Maximus. The ceremony itself was presided over by a woman known as a **pronuba**. This type of marriage ceremony was also used only for cum manu marriages.

The third and final type of wedding did not involve a formal ceremony at all. Marriage by usus was similar to a modern common-law marriage. The couple simply declared that they wanted to be married, and the bride moved into the groom's house. Although there was no formal ceremony, it is likely that usus marriages would have been celebrated in a similar way to coemptio and confarreatio weddings. Usus marriages were the most commonly used, perhaps because it was the only kind that could result in a sine manu marriage. If a wife wanted to remain a member of her paterfamilias' household and not come under the control of her husband, she could be married by usus, but she had to spend three consecutive nights away from her husband's house each year. If she stayed for a whole year without taking a break like this, the marriage became cum manu, and she legally transferred to her husband's family.

Wedding celebrations

Regardless of the type of ceremony, wedding celebrations did not vary much.

On the day before her wedding, the bride-to-be would make sacrifices to the **lares** of her bulla, which had protected her throughout childhood, and her toys.

On the morning of her wedding, the bride would put on her wedding dress and knot a woollen belt around her waist. Only her new husband would be allowed to unknot the belt, once the wedding celebration was complete. She would also wear a flame-coloured veil and wear her hair in six separate locks, like the Vestal Virgins. The bride and groom each wore a wreath of flowers on their head.

The wedding ceremony itself (for coemptio and confarreatio marriages) would take place in the bride's father's house. Afterwards there would usually be a lavish wedding feast and then began the procession to the husband's home. The groom would dramatically grab the bride from her mother in a pretend show of force. The celebrants would escort the married couple through the streets, singing wedding hymns. Friends and relatives might carry with them spindles, to represent the bride's domestic tasks, and the groom would throw small treats (nuts, dried fruits) to the crowds. During the procession the bride would carry three coins. One was dropped during the procession as an offering to **Janus**, one was for her husband to symbolise her dowry, and one was offered to the Lares of her new household.

Janus god of transitions, beginnings and endings

When they arrived at the groom's house, the bride would wrap wool around the door posts, again symbolising her domestic role, and she would be carried across the threshold by her new husband. This tradition survives to this day, and originated in the belief that it would be a terrible **omen** if the bride tripped on her way into the house.

omen sign from the gods

The wife would be led to the hearth, which she would light using a torch from the wedding procession, and the couple would be led to their wedding couch.

This extract from a poem by Catullus illustrates some of the key points of a Roman wedding celebration:

Crown your brow with sweet flowers
of marjoram fragrance,
put on the glad veil, here,
come, wearing the saffron shoes
on your snow-white feet:
summoned to the happy day
singing the nuptial songs
with ringing voice,
strike your feet on the ground, shake
the pine torch in your hand.

Catullus, *Poem 61*, 6–15

PRACTICE QUESTIONS: ROME

1. What was the name of the lucky charm given to Roman children on their naming day? [1]
2. 'A Roman girl's education was not very useful.' Using the Sappho fresco (overleaf) and your own knowledge, discuss how far you agree with this statement. [8]

TOPIC REVIEW

You should be able to:

1. Describe:
   - the upbringing of an Athenian girl, including the kind of education she received
   - customs surrounding betrothal and marriage of Athenian girls
   - the upbringing of a Spartan girl, including the kind of education she received
   - customs surrounding betrothal and marriage of Spartan girls
   - the upbringing of a Roman girl, including the kind of education she received
   - customs surrounding betrothal and marriage of Roman girls.

2. Explain:
- how an Athenian girl's education was meant to prepare her for life
- the significance of the different parts of an Athenian wedding ceremony
- how a Spartan girl's education was meant to prepare her for life
- what Spartan customs surrounding betrothal and marriage imply about the status of girls in Sparta
- how a Roman girl's education was meant to prepare her for life
- why a girl might prefer to be married cum manu
- why a girl might prefer to be married sine manu.

PRACTICE QUESTIONS: COMPARING GREECE AND ROME

Source A (Greek): *Xenophon, Constitution of the Spartans, 1.3–4*

With other people, girls who are intending to become mothers and who are respectable girls are raised on a completely modest diet and with the smallest possible number of delicacies. . . . Other Greeks think that girls ought to sit alone doing their wool-working. . . . How, then, can they expect that girls raised like this will bear strong children? But Lycurgus thought that slave women produced clothing that was sufficient, and thinking that producing children was the most important function of free women he established physical exercise for the female no less than for the male sex. Then he set up competitions in speed and strength just as there were for the men. In this way, he also set up contests for females to compete with one another, thinking that the offspring from parents of two fit parents will be stronger.

Source B (Roman): *'Sappho' fresco of an educated upper-class Pompeiian woman*

Study **Source A** and **Source B**.

1. Explain how these sources convey the different kinds of education received by Spartan and Roman girls. [6]
2. In which society did young girls enjoy the greater freedom, Greece or Rome? [15]

1.3 Women in the Home

The roles and responsibilities of female members of the household, including domestic duties; childbirth; legal rights and property ownership; divorce and adultery; typical duties of female slaves.

Greece

- The kyria and Athenian ideas of wifely virtue
- Athenian domestic slaves
- The experience of a Spartan wife and mother.

Rome

- The matrona and Roman ideas of wifely virtue
- Roman domestic slaves.

The prescribed sources for this topic are:

- Hegeso Stele, attributed to Callimachus, in the National Archaeological Museum, Athens (3624)
- Ampharete Stele, in the Kerameikos Museum, Athens
- *Laudatio Turiae*.

Don't forget that you will be given credit in the exam if you study extra sources and make relevant use of them in your answers.

In this topic you will study the experiences of grown women in Athens, Sparta and Rome, in terms of their contribution to their households. You will consider how much authority they had in their own homes and how the expected roles of women in the domestic sphere can indicate how each society viewed women more generally. You will also consider the roles played by female slaves, and how these differed from the roles of male slaves.

GREECE: ATHENS

The kyria

In one of the most famous speeches from the ancient world (known as *Pericles' Funeral Oration*) the Athenian politician Pericles outlined what made Athens great. Mostly he focused on men and male virtue. But he did make one comment on Athenian female virtue:

> [the] greatest [glory] will be hers who is least talked of among the men whether for good or for bad.

> Thucydides, *History of the Peloponnesian War*, 2.45

An ideal Athenian woman, then, did not involve herself in the public spheres of politics, culture or war. Her place was in the home and her greatest glory could be won by simply avoiding criticism. But this was not the only thing an Athenian woman could aspire to. Once married, an Athenian kyria had a strictly defined set of roles and responsibilities she was expected to fulfil. And, as Pericles implies, she was expected to complete these without drawing any attention to herself.

The duty to bear children

The first and most important duty of an Athenian kyria was producing a male son to be heir to the kyrios' property.

> **parthenos** an unmarried virgin Greek girl
>
> **nymphe** a married Athenian woman who had not yet given birth to a child
>
> **gyne** a married Athenian woman who had given birth to a child

An unmarried girl in Athens was referred to as a **parthenos**. Once married and having lost her virginity she would be referred to as a **nymphe**. It was not until she had given birth to her first child that she would be considered a fully grown woman and then she would be referred to as a **gyne**.

Producing heirs for her husband was of vital importance because it meant that the family and the household could perpetuate itself. If the kyrios died with no legitimate heir, his property would transfer to his closest male relative and his own household would cease to exist.

The number of women's grave markers that reference childbirth show that women were greatly valued for their ability to produce legitimate children. In Classical Athens it

S & C *Pericles' Funeral Oration*

Thucydides was a historian, but his methods of investigation were certainly not up to the rigorous standards of modern historians. He did base his work on research and sources, but Thucydides openly admitted that he would make things up if he could not remember exactly what happened. This was particularly true of speeches – even if Thucydides had heard the speech himself, he admitted to filling gaps in his memory with his own invented phrases. One ancient critic, Dionysius of Halicarnassus, even suggested that he invented *Pericles' Funeral Oration* from scratch.

Discussion question: How does it impact the meaning of the speech if Thucydides wrote it for his history, instead of Pericles making it for the people of Athens?

FIGURE 1.18
Grave stele of
Ampharete.

The grave stele of Ampharete

Date: *c.* 400 BC

Artist: Unknown

Style: relief sculpture, Classical style

Original Location: Athens, Kerameikos, on the Sacred Road

Current Location: Archaeological Museum of Kerameikos

Significance: a stele commemorating the life and death of an Athenian woman

stele (pl. **stelai**) stone slabs, often with patterns or images carved on them, indicating where a body was buried

was common for graves to have either a short carved inscription (an epigram) or a relief sculpture on a **stele**. Grave markers would be placed along the side of the roads near city gates and would invite passers-by to learn about the deceased. As such, they would display virtues and achievements of the deceased. A typical example is the grave stele of Ampharete (see Figure 1.18).

Ampharete sits on a chair, draped in a chiton (long woollen tunic), with a himation (an outer garment) over her head. The scene is framed by walls and a roof, implying that she is inside. All these features emphasise Ampharete's modesty. Despite the fact that the stele appears outside for the public to see, she does not invite the viewer to gawk at her by making a spectacle of herself. She holds a baby and the two seem to be making eye contact in a maternal, caring pose. The stele's inscription identifies the child as Ampharete's grandchild. Ampharete's family were able to choose a single image to convey her nature and achievements in life. The fact that they chose this maternal scene strongly implies that they saw her maternal role as her greatest contribution to the family.

The Athenians had a far less advanced understanding of medicine and pregnancy than we do today. Miscarriages and complications in childbirth were commonplace, and many women and children died in childbirth.

As producing children was seen to be a wife's main duty, many felt a great deal of anxiety around the issue of infertility (which was almost always considered to be a problem with the woman – most Athenians did not believe in male infertility). There were a variety of remedies (potions, ointments, fragrances etc.) that a woman could use to 'combat' infertility. When these failed, it was common to turn to the gods for help, particularly the god of medicine, Asclepius. Women would spend the night at his shrine at Epidauros and, it was believed, divine snakes would visit them and cure their infertility. Archaeologists have found many examples of dedications at the sanctuary thanking the god for having enabled women to become pregnant.

When these measures failed, there is some evidence that women might have traded in a black market in male babies. In one of his comedy plays, Aristophanes depicts an Athenian woman retelling the story of a friend who had been unable to conceive and tricked her husband into believing that she was in labour:

> "I know another, who for ten whole days pretended to be suffering the pains of labour until she had secured a child; the husband hurried in all directions to buy drugs to hasten her deliverance, and meanwhile an old woman brought the infant in a stew-pot. . ."
>
> Aristophanes, *Women at the Thesmophoria*, 501–504

Aristophanes' plays were intended to be comedic, so it would be rash to take this extract as solid evidence for the existence of this practice, but jokes are often rooted in truth, and we might easily imagine the scenario considering the pressure many Athenian women would have felt.

Household duties

As soon as she was married, an Athenian woman became the leading woman of her household. While her husband went out to run a business, make money and participate in the public life of Athens, she was responsible for the smooth running of the household itself.

FIGURE 1.19
Domestic scene of women washing.

One of our best sources for the duties of the kyria within the household is the *Oeconomicus*, a work by the Athenian writer Xenophon. This work is an imagined conversation between the philosopher Socrates and a man called Ischomachus, in which they discuss issues surrounding marriage. Ischomachus states that:

> For the wife it is more noble to remain inside than outdoors, but for the husband it is more shameful to stay indoors than to take care of things outside.
>
> Xenophon, *Oeconomicus*, 7.23

He goes on to explain how the kyrios' responsibility is to bring goods into the household and it is the responsibility of the kyria to manage both these goods and the work of all those inside the house:

> You must receive what is brought into the house and distribute what must be consumed and think ahead what reserves need to be kept and take care of what is intended for a year is not used up in a month. When wool is brought to you, you must see that clothes are made for those who need them, and that the dry corn is in a fit state for making food. One of the tasks that falls to you may seem rather thankless: you must see that all members of the household who fall ill are cared for.
>
> Xenophon, *Oeconomicus*, 7.35–36

So, through careful management of the household's resources, the kyria was able to contribute to the household's **self-sufficiency**. She would also be able to increase the household's wealth through the production of textiles. As all cloth had to be made by hand it could be incredibly expensive, and women throughout the ancient world were expected to produce it within their households.

> **self-sufficiency** supporting a household without relying on outside assistance (an important Athenian value)

As part of managing the work of other members of the household (unmarried girls and slaves), a skilled kyria could improve the wealth of the household by training slaves:

> There are other particular responsibilities belonging to you that turn out to be pleasant: whenever you take a slave who knows nothing about spinning and make her skilled she becomes twice as valuable to you; whenever you take one who doesn't know how to manage housekeeping and serving and she is made a skilled and loyal servant and you then have one who is invaluable . . .'
>
> Xenophon, *Oeconomicus*, 7.41

Although the kyria had authority over certain members of the household, it should not be forgotten that she was under the authority of her husband and had to obey his orders. Any order she gave could also be overturned by the kyrios.

A typical Athenian house would have a room called the **gynaikeion**, in which the female members of the household would work and where women other than the kyria would sleep. This room would often be located at the back of the house or upstairs, out of the way.

Athenian houses would also usually include a room called the **andron**. This was a room reserved for men to relax in and have drinking parties known as **symposia**. Female family members were not allowed to attend these parties, but were expected to help to decorate the room to make a good impression on guests. The andron was usually located

> **gynaikeion** the women's working room in a Greek house, which may have doubled as a bedroom
>
> **andron** the men's socialising room, usually located by the front door
>
> **symposium** (pl. symposia) a drinking party held by Athenian men, which citizen women would not have been allowed to attend

FIGURE 1.20

This mid-fifth-century white-ground pyxis (box) depicts Athenian women in a domestic scene. The wool basket suggests they have been working wool.

Study questions

1 What can we learn from the grave stelae in this topic?
2 How can we tell that women were often anxious about the issue of infertility? Refer to primary sources from this topic in your answer.
3 How much power do you think a kyria had within her own home? Explain your answer.

by the front door of the house so that the men could keep track of who entered and left.

The kyria would not be allowed to leave the house without a male escort. As such, she spent the majority of her life inside her own home. It seems likely, however, that poorer Athenians who needed all members of the household to be working would have ignored this custom. Some poorer kyriae worked as market traders, jewellers and midwives. These women surely must have had the freedom to leave their house unescorted.

When the kyria did leave the house, she was limited by laws that restricted how much money she was allowed to spend. She could not buy anything worth more than a medimnos of barley (this was not much, only enough to buy food to support a family for around a week). She could also not buy or sell land, and could not personally own property of any real value. This meant that she would be unable to do any severe or lasting damage to the household, if she were to act against the kyrios' wishes or make decisions in his absence.

Despite the fact that the kyria rarely went out in public and was not allowed to attend a symposium, we have evidence that Athenian wives took good care of their looks. This can be seen on another commemorative monument: the grave stele of Hegeso (see Figure 1.21).

As with the grave stele of Ampharete, Hegeso is seated in a domestic scene. Like Ampharete she is heavily draped, implying modesty, but she has an elaborate hairstyle. In contrast, her slave girl (standing) has a simple hairstyle. This imparts elegance to Hegeso, which is amplified by the fact that the slave girl is holding out a jewellery box for Hegeso to consider. Hegeso's right hand is tilted up. This sculpture would have originally been painted and it is believed that she was holding a piece of jewellery, which would have emphasised Hegeso's elegance and also the family's wealth.

FIGURE 1.21
Grave stele of Hegeso.

PS

PRESCRIBED SOURCE

The grave stele of Hegeso

Date: *c.* 410–400 BC

Artist: Callimachus

Style: relief sculpture, Classical style

Original Location: Athens, Kerameikos, on the Sacred Road

Current Location: National Archaeological Museum, Athens

Significance: a stele commemorating the life and death of an Athenian woman

Adultery and divorce in Athens

Wives in Athens were expected to be absolutely faithful to their husbands. As one of the main reasons for marriage was to have legitimate heirs, the husband had to know for certain that the children his wife bore belonged to him. Therefore, the laws surrounding adultery were severe. If a man caught his wife having an affair, he was legally allowed to kill her lover. If the adulterous man's life was spared, he could be made to pay a large fine and/or be publicly humiliated. The woman's husband would divorce her immediately and keep her dowry. The woman would also be barred from joining in public religious festivals, for fear that she might corrupt other women by her presence.

Men, on the other hand, were free to engage in sexual activity outside of their marriages, as long as they did not seduce another married woman or the unmarried daughter of an Athenian citizen. One famous Athenian playboy, Alcibiades, apparently spent so much time with prostitutes that his wife tried to do something about it:

> Hipparete was a decorous and affectionate wife, but being distressed because her husband would consort with courtesans, native and foreign, she left his house and

went to live with her brother. Alcibiades did not mind this, but continued his wanton ways, and so she had to put in her plea for divorce to the magistrate, and that not by proxy, but in her own person. On her appearing publicly to do this, as the law required, Alcibiades came up and seized her and carried her off home with him through the market place, no man daring to oppose him or take her from him.

Plutarch, *Life of Alcibiades*, 8.3

This anecdote shows that men were free to seek sexual gratification outside of their marriages, and that women had relatively little power to affect the state of their own marriage. Hipparete shows remarkable initiative to go to the law court to ask for a divorce, but Alcibiades prevents this without encountering any resistance from the government or other citizens of Athens.

Study question

Why were Athenian adultery laws so severe?

Legally, an Athenian woman could divorce her husband by leaving his household and making her way back to her father's house. However, as in the case of Hipparete and Alcibiades, the husband could prevent this relatively easily. The husband was able to divorce his wife by sending her back to her father, or by expelling her from his house. Usually he would have to return the dowry to her father.

Athenian female domestic slaves

Like most ancient societies, Athens kept slaves. In the fifth century BC it is estimated that Athens had a ratio of 3.75:1 free citizens to slaves.

The most common route into slavery was to be captured in war. Piracy was also common in the Classical world and being kidnapped by pirates could lead to a life of slavery. Less commonly, exposed babies might be rescued and raised as slaves. Any children borne by a slave woman would automatically be slaves as well.

Slaves were mostly used as a source of cheap labour by the Athenians. Male slaves would be made to work on their master's farm or in their business. Some educated male slaves would act as tutors for children or as craftsmen if they were skilled. State-owned male slaves had some of the worst jobs, such as maintaining the roads or working in Athens' silver mines.

Female slaves were not usually given such hard manual labour to do. Most female slaves fell into one of two categories: prostitutes (see pp. 55–9) or domestic slaves.

Study questions

1 How did female domestic slaves help to ensure the smooth running of a household?
2 Who was more important to the running of the household – the kyria or the female slaves?

Female domestic slaves would be managed by the kyria, but be under the ultimate authority of the kyrios. They would be able to circulate in public and so would often be used to run errands for the housebound kyria. They would perform a variety of domestic tasks, from answering the door and supervising the children to collecting water.

As they would spend the majority of their time working closely with the kyria, many domestic slaves would develop close bonds with their masters. Xenophon explains how, through kind treatment, a slave girl was made to be loyal:

We also taught her to be loyal to us by making her a partner in all our joys, and by inviting her to share our troubles.

Xenophon, *Oeconomicus*, 9.12

The quality of life of a domestic slave was entirely dependent on the temperament of their masters, and treatment could be very harsh. One slave who was discovered helping her kyria organise an affair was whipped. Slaves were not allowed to marry and it was common for their children to be sold. As the legal property of the kyrios, a slave had little defence against mistreatment. They were able to appeal to the law courts if they felt that they were being unfairly treated, but we have very little evidence that such appeals were ever successful.

Slaves were occasionally freed by their masters, although this was not a common occurrence.

GREECE: SPARTA

As in Athens, Spartan society expected married women to conceive and bear children. As was discussed in the previous chapter, the education received by Spartan girls was designed to prepare their bodies for the pains of childbirth and to ensure that they were healthy and vigorous enough to bear healthy and vigorous babies.

No Spartan woman could be commemorated with a grave marker until she had borne children. This is somewhat like the Athenian practice of referring to a married woman without children by one word and a mother by another. A key difference, however, is that the monuments dedicated to Spartan mothers celebrated their service to the state. The difference between an Athenian nymphe and gyne was a private, family matter.

Spartan polyandry

In Sparta it was usual for a healthy woman to have multiple sexual partners, especially if her husband was much older. Xenophon, in his description of the Spartan system of government states:

> If . . . an old man . . . had a young wife . . . he would bring into his house a man
> whose body and mind he admired, for the purpose of bearing children. And if a man
> did not want to have sex with his wife but desired children in whom he could take
> pride, . . . if he saw a woman who was a good breeder and was of a noble sort he
> could produce children from her, if he could persuade her husband.
>
> Xenophon, *Constitution of the Spartans*, 1.7–8

Similarly, Plutarch reports that in Sparta:

> It was possible for an older man with a young wife, if he was taken with one of the
> handsome and noble young men and approved of him, to introduce him to her and
> adopt the offspring as their own.
>
> Plutarch, *Life of Lycurgus*, 15.7

In Sparta, sex with multiple partners was not really adultery at all. Rather, it was seen as men and women doing their duty to the state to bear healthy children. Spartan society discouraged the accumulation of personal wealth and so most citizens led modest lives.

This meant that there would not be concerns over the inheritance of property and so it did not matter whether a baby was legitimate. All that mattered was that it was healthy enough to serve Sparta, either as a warrior or as a strong, fertile woman.

Duties of a Spartan wife and mother

Women in Sparta were not expected to work wool and stay indoors. The Spartans believed that their slaves should do this work and that free Spartan women should focus on physical training, managing the household and its farm, and upholding the Spartan ethos.

So that she could make the maximum contribution to the Spartan state, a Spartan woman would want to bear children until she was no longer fertile. Spartan women therefore continued to train after they were married so that they could maintain their good health.

Spartan women were also responsible for the management of the family's **kleros** (farm) while the men were living and training in their communal barracks. They would direct slaves to do work and ensure that enough food was produced to support the household and to contribute to her husband's **syssition**. They made decisions about what to grow, when to purchase equipment and how to sell any surplus. It is therefore clear that Spartan women must have had some training in arithmetic in order to manage the farm as well as the household.

Unlike most other Greek women, Spartan women were allowed to inherit property, including land, from their fathers. Nearly two fifths of the property of Sparta was owned by women. As such some Spartan women were very wealthy and powerful enough to decide how to spend this wealth by themselves.

One of the most important roles that Spartan wives and mothers played was to instil a love of Sparta and obedience to its system in their sons. Spartan mothers were expected to send their sons, aged just seven, to the gruelling training in the **agōgē** without hesitation or question. They had to prepare their sons for this daunting experience by making sure that they were brought up loving the Spartan state and willing to give everything to protect it.

The absolute dedication of a Spartan woman to her state is neatly summed up in this anecdote, preserved by Plutarch:

> Another woman was burying her son when a worthless old woman came up to her and said "Oh, Woman, what an awful thing!", "No, not by the gods," the woman said, "a good thing, rather, for I bore him so that he would die for Sparta, and this is exactly what happened for me."
>
> Plutarch, *Sayings of Spartan Women* (*Moralia* 241C)

Spartan wives and mothers were also thought to give the following advice to their sons and husbands when they were about to go to war: *return either with your shield or on it*. This basically means: *return to me victorious, or return to me dead*. There was no honour in Sparta in surviving as a result of cowardice. The women of Sparta were the ones who instilled this value in the menfolk and, in so doing, ensured that Spartan discipline survived.

kleros household farm on a plot of land assigned by the state to a Spartan warrior

agōgē the training school that all Spartan boys attended from the age of seven

EXPLORE FURTHER

Research what happened to a Spartan boy as part of his training in the agōgē to appreciate how important it was that Spartan women instil a love of Sparta in their sons.

Study questions

1 How much freedom did Spartan women have? Make a table to help organise your thoughts: 'Freedoms Spartan women enjoyed', 'Restrictions Spartan women had to bear'.
2 What do you think was the most significant contribution made by a Spartan woman to the Spartan state? Justify your response.
3 Who do you think was more important to the smooth running of the state, the Athenian kyria or a Spartan wife?

PRACTICE QUESTIONS: GREECE

Source A: *Phoclydes, fragment*

The tribes of women originated from these four: one from a she-dog, one from a bee, one from a bristly sow, one from a long-maned mare. The last bears herself well, is swift, a pleasureseeker, and of the finest form. The one from a bristly sow is neither bad nor good. The one from a she-dog is difficult and wild. The one from a bee is a good housekeeper and knows how to work. Pray, dear friend, to obtain delightful marriage with her as your lot.

1. What had to happen before a kyria was referred to as a gyne? [1]
2. Why was it so important for the kyria to produce male heirs? [1]
3. 'The kyria was a valuable and respected member of an Athenian household.' How far do you agree with this statement? Use **Source A** as a starting point, and your own knowledge in your answer. [8]

ROME

The matrona and ideas of Roman wifely virtue

> **matrona** married Roman woman

FIGURE 1.22
This portrait bust of a Roman matrona, with its serious expression and smart, modest hairstyle illustrates how the Romans thought a matrona should look and behave.

> **patronage** a semi-formal association between a richer, more influential Roman patron and a poorer, less influential client, whereby the patron would provide social contacts, advice and perhaps financial support, and in return the client would support the patron in their business or political endeavours

Once a girl had married in Rome she became known as a **matrona**. If she was married to the paterfamilias she would be known as the materfamilias and would have authority over the slaves, children and dependent unmarried women of the household.

The matrona was expected to produce children in order to ensure the continuation of the household and so that the children might advance the status and wealth of the household. Boys could work to earn money, and boys from wealthy families could earn the family status by excelling in areas such as the law, politics or the military. Girls would be useful as they could be given in marriage to allies or business partners, and so solidify relationships between families.

As in Greece, pregnancy and childbirth were dangerous for Roman women and complications were common. Grave epitaphs show that many women died in their teens and early twenties, either in childbirth or shortly after as a result of infections.

The matrona was expected to take an active role in rearing her children, and were well respected for doing so.

Another important role of the matrona was to oversee the day-to-day running of the household. For a poor family, this would mean cooking and cleaning, spinning and weaving wool and looking after any children. She might also work a job to bring money into the household.

A matrona in a wealthy family would live a very different life. She would be able to call on a number of slaves to assist with domestic tasks and so would be able to spend her time in leisure. A wealthy matrona was far more likely to be well educated and might spend time reading books, visiting friends and keeping up with politics. Particularly in the first and second centuries BC (when the Roman empire was expanding and becoming more wealthy), married women enjoyed a good deal of freedom. They were not restricted from leaving the house and were allowed to attend public games, festivals and the theatre.

It was the responsibility of the matrona to organise dinner parties for her husband. Unlike the kyria in Athens, she would be able to attend these dinner parties and so she could help to boost the reputation of the family by presenting herself well and ensuring that the party ran smoothly. Social events such as these were particularly important to the Roman system of **patronage** (client–patron relationships were often made at them), so the matrona's role was important indeed.

When her husband was away from home for extended periods of time (for example on a military campaign, governing a distant province or living in exile), the matrona could take a leading role in managing the public affairs of the household and its businesses.

Despite these powers and freedoms, married women in Rome still had limited rights when compared with their husbands and male relatives. Women could not make a will or sign contracts. She could not sell property, free a slave or bring a lawsuit to court. All of these would have to be done by her husband (if she had been married cum manu) or her father (if she had been married sine manu). Roman women could, however, own land and

FIGURE 1.23
Women in Rome would usually give birth in their homes and preferred, as this relief shows, to recline on a couch with the midwife assisting. It was not common for fathers to be present during the birth of their children.

FIGURE 1.24
Most Roman mothers would breastfeed their own babies, and this relief suggests some fathers even made time to be with their wives as they fed their children.

property, and they could be named as heiresses in a will. As such, some women were responsible for the management of property as well.

The *Laudatio Turiae*

A remarkable written source survives that gives evidence of the opinions of an upper class Roman man on his wife. A funerary inscription, known as the *Laudatio Turiae* ('in praise of Turia'), was made in the first century BC and gives a rare account of a husband's love for his wife. It is written from the perspective of Turia's husband and takes the form of a traditional eulogy that would likely have been delivered at her funeral. Parts of the inscription are fragmentary and other parts have been lost, but what emerges is an image of a truly loving and devoted wife, who was accomplished in the domestic sphere as well as being fearless and effective in the public sphere of politics.

Study questions

1 Who do you think had more influence within her household, a wealthy matrona or a poor matrona?
2 What do you think was the most important role played by a Roman matrona? Justify your response.

FIGURE 1.25
Fragments of the *Laudatio Turiae*.

PRESCRIBED SOURCE

Laudatio Turiae

Date: 1st century BC

Author: unknown upper-class Roman male – the husband of Turia

Genre: eulogy

Original location: unknown

Current location: Museo Nazionale Romano, Rome

Read it here: OCR source booklet

As in Athens, funerary monuments are an excellent source of evidence for ideal female behaviour. Funerary monuments were designed to be seen by the public. They commemorated the deceased and were also intended to promote the image of the family. Therefore, we can assume that the qualities mentioned on these monuments were considered to be positive, and sometimes ideal.

Left hand column

- **1–2** The beginning of the inscription, which addresses the deceased, has unfortunately been lost through damage to the stone. We therefore do not actually know the name of the woman addressed, and the identification of her as Turia is disputed.
- **3–12** The first legible section details how, before Turia was married, her parents were murdered. Through Turia's efforts, the murderers were prosecuted and duly punished. As a woman, Turia would not have been able to bring a case before the law courts, so she must have worked through male relatives to achieve this. During this time, Turia went to live with her future mother-in-law to protect her modesty.
- **13–26** Relatives of Turia's father then made a claim to her inheritance. Turia spoke in defence of her claim to the inheritance herself, which suggests that she was educated in legal matters as well as in the art of public speaking. The claimants relented in the face of Turia's defence and the matter was settled.
- **27–29** The author speaks of how his marriage to Turia was rare, lasting for forty years, unbroken by divorce.
- **30–41** Turia's domestic virtues are listed. They include loyalty and obedience. Her industry in working with wool to make textiles for the household is complimented, as is her modest appearance. A series of rhetorical questions convey that Turia's love and devotion to her family were clear for all to see. The author goes on to say how Turia shared all her property with him, and he shared his with her. This could either imply that they were married cum manu or, if they were married sine manu, that Turia gave her husband the authority to manage both sets of property together.

- **42–51** The next section describes Turia's generosity, always ready to look after members of her family who were in need. Of particular note, she helped to provide dowries for women in her family who would not have been able to afford a dowry large enough to attract a suitable husband. In this way, Turia seems to be behaving as a paterfamilias. Perhaps her wealth allowed her to go beyond traditional gender roles.

Right hand column

- **2a–9a** During the first century BC Roman politics were undergoing massive change, with powerful politician generals fighting for supremacy. It seems as though Turia's husband got caught up in this struggle, and was forced to flee Rome. He recalls how, during his self-imposed exile, Turia looked after the affairs of the household and ensured he lived in a comfortable manner by sending him her golden jewellery to sell, as well as money and provisions. She also went to an unnamed politician and begged for mercy on her husband's behalf. It was because of these pleas that he was able to return safely to Rome. This clearly demonstrates Turia's courage, influence and ability in public speaking.

- **4–21** The next section details how Turia, once again, helped her husband to negotiate the political dangers of Rome. She saved his life by preparing a hiding place for him when thugs came to their house and, on another occasion, was able to repel thugs from their house when it had been seized. Furthermore, she again begged on behalf of her husband for mercy from another prominent politician. On this occasion, she is said to have thrown herself on the floor. She was dragged away like a slave, beaten and insulted, and yet she continued to make her case for her husband. Eventually she was successful and managed to win his safety.

- **22–50** The inscription goes on to describe how, following the previous period of political unrest, the couple began to enjoy peace and stability. That is, until an unforeseen disaster struck them: they were unable to conceive any children. Turia offered to divorce her husband and to help him to find another wife, one of a suitable status, who would be able to produce children for him. Turia's devotion to her husband and her desperation to provide him with heirs is touching, and once again underscores the importance in Roman culture of having children. Turia's husband did not take her up on her offer. Rather, he was horrified that she would suggest ending their marriage. Clearly not all Roman husbands and wives saw their marriages as nothing more than a source of legitimate heirs.

- **51–69** The final section of the inscription expresses the sorrow and genuine grief felt by the author at the death of his beloved wife.

> **Study questions**
>
> 1 Reread the *Laudatio Turiae*. How does this inscription convey the close, loving relationship between Turia and her husband?
>
> 2 How typical was Turia's marriage? Refer to specific sections of the *Laudatio Turiae* and what you have learned about Roman marriages.

Divorce in Rome

Divorce in ancient Rome was easy to organise. All the husband or wife needed to do was to declare that the marriage was over. The woman returned to her original paterfamilias and the man kept custody of any children that had been born during the marriage.

If the man initiated the divorce, the woman was entitled to her whole dowry back. If, however, the woman initiated the divorce, things were more complicated. The man would be able to claim a portion of the dowry for each child that the marriage had produced, and more if the wife had been proven to be adulterous.

Custody battles in Rome were extremely rare. As the children automatically came under the patria potestas of their father as the household's paterfamilias, the mother had little legal claim to the children. It is easy to believe that many women were convinced to stay in unhappy marriages for fear of losing access to their children.

Adultery was a common reason for divorce. Similar to Athenian men, Roman men were free to have sexual partners other than their wives, but they had to be of a certain social class (prostitute, foreigner, slave). If a married man had an affair with the wife or unmarried daughter of another Roman citizen, it was considered adultery. Married women were not allowed to have any extra-marital affairs, again probably due to concerns over the legitimacy of children. If a married woman was found to be having an affair with a Roman citizen, she would almost certainly be divorced and, as mentioned above, forfeit a portion of her dowry. If, however, she was found having an affair with a slave, it was customary to kill the woman and burn the slave alive.

Infertility was also a commonly cited reason for divorce, as can be seen in the case of Spurius Carvilius, a Roman citizen who divorced his wife for just this reason:

> No children were born from her, owing to some defect in her body. . . . Carvilius, as
> the story goes, loved his wife intensely – the one whom he divorced – and valued her
> very highly because of her character, but he gave preference to the sanctity of his oath
> over his inclination and his love, because he had been compelled by the censors to
> swear that he would look for a wife for the purpose of begetting citizen children.
>
> Aulus Gellius, *Attic Nights*, 4.3.2

Study question
What can we tell about Roman attitudes towards marriage based on their laws and customs surrounding divorce?

It was also common for marriages to end in divorce for business and political reasons. In a society where marriages were used to solidify alliances between families, marriages often only lasted as long as was convenient for the men in either family.

Roman domestic slaves

Roman society functioned with the assistance of slave labour. By the first century BC, with the expansion of the Roman Empire, it is likely that around a third of all people living in the city of Rome were slaves. Cities had a higher proportion of slaves than rural areas of the empire.

As in Greece, a common route into slavery was as a captive taken either as a spoil of war or by pirates. Children could be born into slavery if their mother was a slave. In rare situations people could be sold into slavery, and convicted criminals were sometimes made into slaves.

Female slaves in the city of Rome could have had a variety of roles. Many would have been forced into prostitution (see pp. 60–3). Others would have worked in their master's business providing skilled labour. Still others would have worked in the homes of their Roman masters as domestic slaves.

FIGURE 1.26
A Roman matrona aided by two slaves.

Slave children were sometimes given an education alongside the children of the family with a view to making them more useful. Some slave girls would therefore have been able to read and write and do arithmetic to help them manage the family's affairs.

Having many slaves was seen as a status symbol in Rome. It was therefore common for wealthy families to keep a great many slaves, each with a specific job. A satire by the poet Juvenal suggests there might have been a hierarchy within households with numerous slaves. For example, a hairdressing slave would be superior to a kitchen maid or a cleaner, and a wool worker would be superior to the hairdresser.

Perhaps the most well-respected variety of female slave was the **vilica**, who was responsible for the management of the household. Her duties included tending to the family hearth and lararium (shrine for the household gods), grinding flour, preserving fruit and cooking food. In many ways, her role was equivalent to that of the wife of a peasant farmer – one of reasonable authority within the household.

> **vilica** a female slave responsible for managing a household

Many slave dealers and owners would buy slave girls with a view to breeding children and, in so doing, gain a valuable asset: more slaves. There is some evidence to suggest a practice (although we do not know how common or widespread this was) to free a slave woman once she had borne three children, although her children would remain slaves.

Slave men and women were not allowed to be married, but they were allowed to form partnerships known as *contubernium* (which translates roughly as cohabiting). It was common for a male slave, once freed, to purchase the freedom of his partner and then, once free, they would marry.

How well they were treated, as in Athens, depended on their master. Kind masters might develop positive relationships with their slaves, providing them with good food and a comfortable place to live in return for work. They might even agree to pay the slave wages and, as an ultimate reward, give them their freedom. Equally, a cruel master might treat a slave like an animal, or worse. Usually female slaves avoided the most gruelling and dangerous manual jobs, such as working in the mines.

Freeing slaves was relatively common in Rome (certainly more common than in Athens). A freed slave became a second-class Roman citizen, but was still free to live and work as they chose.

PRACTICE QUESTIONS: ROME

Source A: *Relief sculpture*

Source B: *Grave inscription*

Stranger, what I say is modest: stand here and read it through.

Here is the scarcely beautiful burial place of a beautiful woman.

Her parents gave her the name 'Claudia'.

She loved her husband with her heart.

She produced two children. Of these one she left behind

On the earth; the other has been placed under the earth.

She was eloquent of speech, moreover proper in her deportment too.

She looked after the home, she worked the wool. I have spoken. Be on your way.

1. Study **Source A**. What is the relationship between the man and the woman in this image and how can you tell? [2]

2. Using **Source B** as a starting point, outline the roles a Roman matrona was expected to fulfil and describe why they were important. [8]

TOPIC REVIEW

You should be able to:

1. Describe:
   - the daily life of an Athenian kyria, including her duties, freedoms and restrictions
   - laws and customs surrounding adultery and divorce in Athens
   - the duties of female slaves in Athens
   - the daily life of a Spartan wife, including her duties, freedoms and restrictions
   - the daily life of a Roman matrona, including her duties, freedoms and restrictions
   - laws and customs surrounding adultery and divorce in Rome
   - the duties of female slaves in Rome.

2. Explain:
   - how the Athenian kyria contributed to her household's self-sufficiency
   - why punishments for adultery were so severe in Athens
   - why polyandry was encouraged in Sparta
   - which of the Roman matrona's duties was the most important and why
   - how and why different classes of matrona were likely to have lived very different kinds of lives
   - whether you think Athenian and Roman female slaves had a good quality of life and why

PRACTICE QUESTIONS: COMPARING GREECE AND ROME

These questions are based on two stimulus sources, one from Greece and one from Rome. The sources could be extracts from prescribed sources or unseen.

Study both sources and answer the questions that follow.

Source A (Greek): *Black-figure vase depicting Athenian women in a domestic scene*

Source B (Roman): *Plautus, The Merchant, ll.817–823*

Woman: 'Good heavens! Women do live under a harsh law, on terms that are much less reasonable for a woman than for her husband. For if her husband brings home a mistress, kept secret from his wife, and the wife finds out, the husband gets away with it. But if a wife steps out secretly away from the house without her husband knowing it a charge is laid by the husband and she is divorced.'

1. Which of these sources gives a more positive depiction of married life? Support your decision with analysis of both sources. [6]
2. Was the life of a female slave in Athens more or less difficult than the life of a female slave in Rome? Justify your response. [15]

1.4 'Improper' Women

> ## TOPIC OVERVIEW
>
> The legal and social position of women who were unmarried, but had relationships with men, including attitudes towards such women, and ideas about 'proper' female behaviour.
>
> ### Greece
>
> - The roles, laws about and typical portrayal of pornai and hetairai
> - The stories of Neaira and Aspasia.
>
> ### Rome
>
> - The roles, laws about and typical portrayal of the meretrix and lena
> - The stories of Clodia (and her possible identification with 'Lesbia') and Cytheris/Lycoris.
>
> The prescribed sources for this topic are:
>
> - Plutarch, *Pericles*, 1.24
> - Cicero, *Pro Caelio*, 49–51
> - Catullus 7, 8, 83.
>
> Don't forget that you will be given credit in the exam if you study extra sources and make relevant use of them in your answers.

So far, this component has been concerned with attitudes surrounding 'proper female behaviour'. That is, looking at how respectable, citizen women lived their lives. Not all women in antiquity conformed to the models of 'proper female behaviour' that have been discussed in the previous chapters. Here, you will learn about laws and customs surrounding prostitution in both Athens and Rome. You will see how 'improper' prostitutes' lives differed from those of a 'proper' kyria and matrona, and discuss whether their lives could be considered better or worse than their married counterparts. You will also have the opportunity to study some individual women – some prostitutes, some upperclass freeborn mistresses – and ask what the stories of these can teach us about the lives of women in antiquity.

GREECE

Prostitution was legal in Athens. Prostitutes (male and female) and brothel-owners were taxed by the state, as were all businesses. Some brothels were owned and run by the state. There was no stigma attached to visiting a prostitute. A variety of sources written by Athenian men openly discuss their visits to brothels and it seems to have been a normal and accepted part of Athenian life.

There were strict laws in Athens to prevent adultery. But these laws did not consider sex with registered prostitutes to be adulterous. As such, Athenian husbands often visited prostitutes, or even had long-term relationships with them alongside their marriage.

Prostitutes were not subject to the same laws as those that put a kyria under the control of a kyrios and limited the amount of property she could control. A prostitute was allowed to run a business and to buy and sell land. In this way, a successful prostitute could enjoy much more freedom than a traditional kyria. In fact, the Greek historian Herodotus records the story of a prostitute named Rhodonis, who had become so popular and thus so wealthy that she was able to pay for an impressive monument to herself at the religious site of Delphi. Most men in the Greek world would not have had the means to do this.

The Greeks distinguished between different types or classes of prostitute and there were two main categories: the **pornē** and the **hetaira**.

Pornai

A pornē was a general term used to refer to all prostitutes who worked in brothels. The word had a negative connotation and could be used as an insult. Almost all pornai would have been slaves owned by the brothel-keeper.

Despite the fact that prostitution was seen as a reputable business, brothels were often in slum areas of Athens where conditions were unpleasant and unhygienic. A pornē would advertise her services on the streets near to her brothel. Sources suggest that they would commonly expose themselves on the streets to entice potential clients, call to men as they passed by and even grab men and try to pull them into their brothel.

A fragment from a comedy reveals how pornai were viewed by some Athenian men:

> First of all, they care about making money and robbing those nearby. Everything else
> is incidental. They weave traps for everyone. Once they start making a profit they
> take into their house new prostitutes who are novices in the profession. These girls
> they remodel immediately, so that they no longer carry on with the same manners and
> looks. Suppose one of them is small; cork is stitched into the soles of her slippers. . . .
> One of them has no buttocks. The senior one dresses her underneath in a sewn-on
> bottom, so the onlookers shout that she has a fine bum. . . . One has nicely-formed
> teeth. She has to keep laughing perforce, so those present see the mouth she sports so
> beautifully.

Alexis, fr. 103PCG

prostitution a trade where sexual acts are performed in exchange for money

pornē (pl. **pornai**) a low-class Greek prostitute (almost always a slave) who would have worked in a brothel

hetaira (pl. **hetairai**) a high-class Greek prostitute or courtesan who may have lived in her own house, chosen her own clients and charged a high price for her company

This fragment demonstrates some aspects of the difficult life that a pornē would lead. It mentions that all they care about is money. As the vast majority of pornai would have been slaves, the money they earned would not have gone into their own pockets, but the pockets of their master. We can assume a severe punishment if they failed to take enough money. Aside from this, all the focus is on how pornai use makeup, clothing and other tricks to enhance their beauty. This would seem to suggest that the speaker, and perhaps all male clients, were concerned primarily with the women's physical appearance.

Hetairai

As opposed to pornai, who were almost exclusively slaves, the hetaira would usually have been a free woman. She could have been a free Athenian citizen who chose to earn a living as a hetaira, but more commonly would have been a **metic**.

Whereas a pornē would have been hired just for sex, the hetaira could offer a range of talents to her clients, from singing and dancing to intellectual conversation. Hetairai often had long-term relationships with their clients. For this reason, the word 'hetaira' is sometimes translated as 'companion' or 'courtesan' rather than 'prostitute'.

Ancient sources usually mention the hetaira in the context of a symposium. As discussed previously (see p. 39), a symposium was a drinking party, hosted by a kyrios, for his male friends. Often a hetaira would be hired to entertain the guests. She might sing, dance or recite poetry. She would also entertain the group with witty conversation talking about politics, art and philosophy. It seems that the hetaira, unusually for a woman in Athens, must have been educated. She thus offered a unique experience to her clients, who would not experience witty banter with a woman in any other way.

> **metic** a resident foreigner

> **MODERN PARALLEL**
>
> The closest modern comparison to Athenian hetairai would be Japanese geisha of the twentieth century. They were professional performance artists who were paid to entertain men, and occasionally to sleep with them.

> **Study question**
> How can you tell the women in Figures 1.27 and 1.28 are hetairai?

FIGURE 1.27
A hetaira at a symposium. Notice how her figure is visible through her clothing. Her client reclines on a couch, typical of those used at symposia.

It is likely that a young hetaira would have been trained in the performing arts by an older, more experienced hetaira. In order to practise the art of speaking and to keep up with current affairs it is also likely that a hetaira would attend lectures by philosophers and practise discussion alongside the men of Athens.

Some of the most famous women in all of Athens were hetairai. They moved in elite circles, choosing their clients and charging huge sums for their company.

It is relatively easy to recognise the hetaira in Athenian art. She is normally depicted indoors, surrounded by male clients. Because she often worked at symposia, the male clients are often reclining on couches in an andron and holding drinking cups. If an image shows a woman playing a musical instrument or dancing in this situation, she is almost certainly a hetaira, as no other kind of woman in Athens would have possessed these skills. Some scholars have also pointed to clothing as a symbol of the hetaira. Whereas 'respectable' Athenian women are usually shown covered in heavy clothing, hetairai often have form-fitting, suggestive clothing that sometimes seems to be transparent.

FIGURE 1.28
Although the woman here has heavier clothing than the hetaira in Figure 1.27, she can nevertheless be identified as a hetaira by the fact that she is playing a diaulos (double-flute).

Study questions

1 Why do you think prostitution was legal in Athens, but adultery was punished so severely?
2 Who do you think had more freedom, an Athenian prostitute or an Athenian kyria? Justify your response.

ACTIVITY

Make a venn diagram that shows the similarities and differences between a pornē and a hetaira. Which do you think had a better quality of life and why?

Neaira

The story of Neaira demonstrates how difficult the life of a prostitute in Greece could be. Her biography survives to us within a speech given in an Athenian law case against her.

Neaira was born in Corinth where, as a child, she was sold to a female brothel-keeper called Nicarete. She entertained men at symposia, although she was not a free woman. She was a slave hetaira.

Neaira became famous and Nicarete was able to charge a very high price for her company. Eventually two of her regular clients got tired of paying such high fees, and negotiated to buy her. At this stage in her life, Neaira would still have given entertainment at parties, like a hetaira, but she was also the exclusive prostitute of her two owners, like a pornē.

When her two owners were ready to marry, and no longer wanted a full-time prostitute, they sold Neaira to an Athenian named Phrynion. It was not long before she made a plan to escape:

PRESCRIBED SOURCE

Life of Pericles, 24

Date: 1st century AD

Author: Plutarch

Genre: biography

Significance: part of a great biographical project in which two lives are contrasted in pairs: Plutarch's *Parallel Lives*

Read it here: OCR source booklet

Study questions

1 Which woman had the better quality of life, Neaira or Aspasia? Justify your response.
2 What do the stories of Neaira and Aspasia reveal about Athenian attitudes towards 'improper women'?

. . . since she was treated with wanton brutality by Phrynion and was not loved as she thought fit, and since he did not pay attention to what she wanted, she picked up the things from his household and as much as she possessed from him – the clothing and jewellery for adorning her body – and two maid-servants . . . and ran off to Megara.

Demosthenes 59.36

While in hiding, Neaira met another Athenian, Stephanus. He invited her to move back to Athens and live with him pretending to be his wife. He promised that he would protect her from Phrynion, that he would tell everyone she was an Athenian citizen and that he would claim that her three children were his own.

So Neaira moved to Athens to live as Stephanus' wife. Unfortunately, this was not a happy ending for Neaira, as Stephanus rented her out as a prostitute in Athens to make money. He also blackmailed Neaira's clients by 'catching them' with her. As Neaira's 'husband' he could cause a lot of trouble for a man found sleeping with his wife. He would threaten the unsuspecting clients and so extort bribes from them in addition to their payment for Neaira.

Although Neaira was able to live in Athens and enjoy some of the benefits of being an Athenian citizen (for example being able to participate in certain religious festivals), eventually her past was discovered, and a court case was brought against her.

Beyond her false identity as a citizen and Stephanus' wife, Neaira's trial revealed that her daughter Phano had been illegally given in marriage to an Athenian man. The court case did not in any way imply that Neaira had been mistreated. Indeed, Neaira was made to seem a villainess. It was sadly irrelevant that, as a slave and the property of her owners throughout her life, Neaira had very little choice.

Aspasia

One of the most famous women in all of Classical Athens was a brothel-keeper and hetaira named Aspasia. She was originally from the Greek city of Miletus (on the coast of modern Turkey), but lived most of her life in Athens as a metic. She became famous when she moved in with Pericles, the most prominent politician of his day. Pericles had divorced his wife and would live with Aspasia for fifteen years.

Athenian society did not really know what to make of Aspasia. On the one hand, she was greatly admired for her artistic skills and her wisdom in political and philosophical matters. On the other hand, many looked down on her because she was a foreigner and a sex-worker. She was the particular target of comic playwrights, who liked to write bawdy jokes about her in their plays. People certainly believed that Aspasia had a good deal of influence over Pericles and his politics.

The biographer Plutarch considered Aspasia's influence on Pericles, and suggests that he valued her political wisdom and many contacts through the city.

Plutarch begins his consideration of Aspasia by complimenting her ability to please important men and stir up discussion among philosophers. She was clearly notorious in the city, well known for more than just being Pericles' mistress.

Plutarch compares Aspasia to a hetaira named Thargelia, who had influenced her Greek clients to sympathise with the king of Persia, to her own benefit. Perhaps Plutarch is implying that Aspasia was as influential in Athens and had motives that were similarly selfish.

Plutarch goes on to list the people who respected Aspasia's political wisdom:

> [The famous philosopher] Socrates came with his acquaintances, and the wives they lived with, to listen to her, even though she ran a business that was neither decent nor respectful, for she managed youthful prostitutes.
>
> Plutarch, *Pericles*, 24.3

Could Aspasia have been so witty and wise that Athenian men wanted their wives to be more like her?

Plutarch heavily implies that Aspasia was to thank for Pericles' successes in politics but he was writing in the first century AD, hundreds of years after Aspasia's lifetime. He was also less concerned with accurate historical facts and more concerned with writing lives that could illustrate moral lessons. We therefore need to be careful when using Plutarch as a source of evidence for Aspasia's life and Athenian prostitution more generally.

FIGURE 1.29
A modern statue of Aspasia in the Austrian capital, Vienna.

PRACTICE QUESTIONS: GREECE

Source A: *Athenian krater portraying hetairai*

1. What was the name of Pericles' hetaira mistress? [1]

2. Why were hetairai educated? [2]

3. Do you think a kyria would have envied the life of a hetaira? Justify your response referring to **Source A** and your own knowledge. [8]

ROME

As in Athens, prostitution was legal in Rome. It was not seen as shameful for a man to visit prostitutes, no matter his social rank. If a man were to spend too much time with prostitutes, he could be accused of lacking proper moderation or self-control, but paying to have sex with a prostitute was not, in itself, shameful.

Prostitution was overseen by the government, which licenced and taxed prostitutes and brothels. In order to get a licence, a prostitute had to visit the aediles (government officials) and get a 'licence for debauchery'. They would have to state how much they intended to charge clients, and this would be used to tax them appropriately.

Roman prostitutes could be freeborn or they could be slaves. Freeborn prostitutes could charge a higher fee for their services.

Prostitution was considered to be a shameful profession, and so it is likely that any freeperson who became a prostitute did so because of desperate need for money. When a person registered themselves as a prostitute, they became known as an **infamis**. Infamia was a legal status that meant a person lost their rights as a free person. They could be beaten, like a slave. They were also banned from marrying a senator, or the child of a senator, and they could never hold a government job. As well as prostitutes, actors and gladiators were considered to be infames. The Romans believed that it was shameful to allow someone else to control your body – all of the infamis professions required this.

Once one became an infamis, there was no going back. Even a retired prostitute would be considered to have infamia, and would be subject to the same restrictions as during their working life.

In AD 19, it was made illegal for a woman whose family belonged to the class of equites (wealthy families but not necessarily noble) to register as a prostitute. This was probably intended to protect the reputations of these families. It is not clear why a woman from one of these wealthy families would become a prostitute unless in dire need of money. A record survives of a woman named Vistilia who was prosecuted under this law and punished with exile.

> **infamis** literally 'shameful' or 'disgraceful', the very low legal status given to a number of groups in the Roman world, including gladiators, charioteers, actors and prostitutes.

Meretrix

A female prostitute in Rome was known as a **meretrix**. This word could be used to describe any kind of prostitute, from a slave in a low-rent brothel to a freeborn, high-class courtesan. Depending on their status, connections and clientele, prostitutes in Rome could live very well or suffer an extremely difficult life.

Slaves and low-class prostitutes would often work from a brothel, known as a **lupanar**. Many sources describing these establishments paint a grim picture. They seem to have been dirty, cramped and located in the worst parts of town. Other sources suggest that prostitutes worked in taverns, or on busy streets, such as the arches underneath the Circus Maximus.

Roman male poets often wrote about their visits to brothels, and these are a great source of information about the lives and businesses of prostitutes. For example, the

> **meretrix** a technical term for a Roman prostitute, often referred to with euphemisms by their client, e.g. 'puella', which means 'girl' or 'girlfriend'
>
> **lupanar** a Roman brothel

poem *Copa* (said to be by the great epic poet Virgil) tells the story of a prostitute/barmaid luring customers into her tavern:

> The hostess, Syrian woman she, her head
> With Grecian head-band bound and skilled to move
> Her pliant waist beneath the castanet,
> Is dancing lewd and drunken in her inn.
>
> Virgil, Copa, 1–4

This short extract can tell us a lot about prostitution in Rome during Virgil's lifetime. That the woman was a 'hostess' in a tavern suggests that some prostitutes worked as barmaids too. Her 'dancing lewd and drunken' could either suggest that she was wild and uncontrolled, or perhaps that she was putting on a show for her prospective clients, enticing them to join her in drinking and dancing. Finally, her ethnicity is a point of interest: as a Syrian in the city of Rome, this woman would almost certainly have been a slave, a freedwoman or the descendant of slaves.

Some prostitutes, however, were more like the hetairai of Athens, although the Romans did not have a separate word for this. A well-respected, educated prostitute could charge a lot for her company and amass great sums of money. These prostitutes would have arranged long-term contracts with their clients, like a mistress. In one extraordinary example, a prostitute grew so close to one of her clients, a politician named Sulla, that she left him her wealth in her will, and it was this money that allowed Sulla to build a successful career.

A well-known, educated prostitute might be invited to a dinner party as a guest. The Romans did not usually hire women to entertain, like an Athenian hetaira, possibly because their wives were not excluded from attending dinner parties.

Female prostitutes in Rome wore a toga. The toga was normally seen as a badge of honour and only citizen men were allowed to wear it. In the case of prostitutes, it seems to have been used as a badge of shame, separating them from respectable matronae who would have worn a stola. An alternative interpretation of this custom is that it marked the prostitute as being in the 'public sphere'. Men usually wore the toga to public events, such as meetings of the Senate. It is possible that Roman prostitutes wore the toga to symbolise that they were 'public property' and not tied to a husband or paterfamilias.

Despite their infamia, prostitutes could play an important role in certain Roman religious festivals. For example, the festival of Fortuna Virilis (which roughly translates as the 'luck of men') involved prostitutes joining together with respectable Roman matronae to clean and dress a cult statue of Fortuna Virilis.

FIGURE 1.30
This cubicle is all that remains of a prostitute's bedroom in a lupanar in Pompeii. Preserved by the eruption of Mt Vesuvius, along with the rest of the Roman seaside town, the bed is short and narrow. The room has no ventilation or natural light and must have been lit by an oil lamp.

FIGURE 1.31
Limestone amulet depicting a meretrix and her client.

Lena

A **lena** was a female pimp. Because she owned and ran a business, she would have been a freewoman, not a slave.

Being a lena, making profit from forcing others to be prostitutes, was considered to be one of the lowest, most shameful professions in Rome. That being said, it was perfectly legal. Although the lena did not make a living by selling her own body, she was still considered an infamis.

Several ancient sources show a lena referring to one of their prostitutes as 'daughter'. Either some lena forced members of their own families to become prostitutes or the term 'daughter' may have been a trick intended to fool clients into believing that they were paying for the services of a free woman (sources suggest free prostitutes were able to charge higher prices than slaves).

The lena/leno was a popular character in Roman comedy plays. They are usually depicted as stupid and incredibly greedy. It would be common for them to carry a money bag on stage to convey their love of gold.

Cytheris/Lycoris

Study questions

1 What did it mean to be infamis in Rome? Can you think of any modern professions that carry such a social stigma?
2 What can you tell about how Roman men viewed prostitutes based on their laws and customs?

Volumnia Cytheris was born a slave *c.* 70 BC, in the last century of the Roman Republic. She became famous for her work as an actress and a mime. Despite her infamia, Cytheris was a celebrity in the city of Rome, celebrated for her skills on the stage and also her great beauty. Even her name, Cytheris, is linked to love and beauty, as it derives from 'Cythera', one of Aphrodite's many nicknames. The Roman politician Cicero despised Cytheris. We are not sure why this was the case, but his feelings are clear from one of his speeches:

> . . . among whom, on an open litter, was carried an actress; whom honorable men, citizens of the different municipalities, coming out from their towns under compulsion to meet him, saluted not by the name by which she was well known on the stage, but by that of Volumnia.
>
> Cicero, *Philippic*, 2.58

Cicero's tone of voice here, and his use of the word 'forced' suggests that Cytheris was a cause of scandal. A shameful woman, despite her celebrity.

Like many actresses at this time, Cytheris was also a prostitute. She was owned by a wealthy leno called Publius Volumnius Eutrapelus. When she was at the height of her fame, Eutrapelus freed Cytheris. This was a calculated move to make Cytheris more attractive to upper class Roman clients, who would not have paid as much for a slave prostitute.

FIGURE 1.32
This theatrical mask was worn by an actor playing a courtesan.

After being freed, Cytheris had a series of professional relationships with leading politicians, including Mark Antony (see pp. 124–8). Antony kept Cytheris as an official mistress, which would have been expensive. Eventually he was forced to break off this relationship by his mentor, Julius Caesar. Antony had been treating Cytheris like a wife rather than a prostitute. He took her with him when he had to inspect his armies and referred to her by her real name, rather than her professional nickname. This incident is telling about Roman attitudes towards prostitutes. Clearly it was acceptable for a man to have a relationship with a prostitute, but the relationship was supposed to remain professional and private.

After her relationship with Mark Antony ended, Cytheris was hired by the politician, soldier and poet, Cornelius Gallus. He wrote four books of love poetry about her (now mostly lost), referring to her by the pseudonym Lycoris (this was a convention of Latin love poetry, to hide the identity of the addressee).

Throughout her life Cytheris would have been under the authority of her owner. Even after she was freed, she would have been bound to him by a contract and he would have arranged for all her relationships. That being said, she was wealthy in her own right, a welcome guest at the dinner parties of Rome's elite and she was known throughout the city and the Empire.

Clodia/Lesbia

Clodia Metelli is a striking example of a scandalous and improper woman in Rome who was not a professional prostitute. Indeed, she was a noblewoman, and her improper behaviour made her notorious.

Clodia Metelli was from an old, established, wealthy family. She was married to her first cousin, a senator who had held the highest political office in Rome: the consulship. In order to maintain the image of her family, Clodia was expected to uphold the ideals of the traditional Roman matrona. Being very rich, however, Clodia did not have to work or manage domestic duties – she was free to spend her time as she pleased.

Clodia, like so many women in her position, therefore spent much of her time in the company of rich, educated, cultured friends enjoying parties. A new kind of 'high society' emerged: young upper-class Romans rejecting traditional, conservative morals in favour of parties, drinking and gambling.

This life of luxury was enough to raise the eyebrows of some of Rome's most conservative men. No matter how wealthy the family, a respectable matrona was expected to live somewhat modestly. But luxury alone would not have been enough to provoke a real scandal. What really made Clodia a prime example of an 'improper woman' was her love affairs.

Her marriage to her cousin was not a happy one and it was rumoured that Clodia had several affairs with married men and even with slaves. One of Clodia's most famous lovers was the poet Catullus, who immortalised her in his love poetry.

As in the case of Cytheris, Clodia was given a nickname in Catullus' poetry: Lesbia. This nickname gave protection to both Catullus and to Clodia, who would have been punished for adultery if they had admitted the truth. It was, nevertheless, common knowledge in Rome's high society that Clodia was Lesbia.

Latin love poetry was often based on the real-life experiences of the authors. Catullus was inspired by his relationship with Clodia to compose many poems charting the ups and downs of their affair. Some compare Lesbia to the goddesses and claim all other women pale in comparison with her beauty. Others show Catullus as a gibbering wreck, entirely ruined by his love of Lesbia and broken when she rejects him or (even worse) when she takes another lover.

MODERN PARALLEL

The high society of Clodia's time was a Roman version of the British upper classes during the 'roaring twenties', or like the New York socialites of *Gossip Girl*. Clodia was the ultimate 'it girl'.

PRESCRIBED SOURCE

Poems 7, 8, 83

Date: 1st century BC

Author: Catullus

Genre: love poetry (elegy)

Significance: selections from the love poetry of one of Rome's preeminent elegists and assumed lover of Clodia/Lesbia

Read it here: OCR source booklet

EXPLORE FURTHER

Read poems by Catullus beyond those that have been prescribed. How does Catullus talk about the women he associates with? How do these women compare to the traditional model of the good Roman matrona?

In Poem 7 Catullus is completely in love. No amount of kisses from Lesbia will be enough to satisfy him. He calls himself 'mad Catullus', which makes the experience of being with Lesbia seem like the experience of being drunk (the god of madness was also the god of wine).

Poem 8 takes a more restrained tone. Catullus advises himself not to chase after the 'girl' (we have to assume he means Lesbia).

> And now she no longer wants you: and you
> weak man, be unwilling to chase what flees,
> or live in misery: be strong-minded, stand firm.
>
> Catullus, *Poems*, 8.9–11

The fact that Catullus says 'she no longer wants you' shows that Lesbia has all the power in their relationship. He loves her and wants her, but she no longer wants him. This ruins Catullus. It is likely that the amount of power that he suggests Lesbia wields over him would have been shocking to the Roman audience. Catullus ends the poem with a series of rhetorical questions. These give us a glimpse into his relationship with Lesbia because, even though they are asking about the future, they refer back to their relationship.

Poem 83 is rather short and shows us Catullus' frustration. Lesbia has been insulting Catullus to her husband. This reminds the audience that his own relationship was adulterous, but also reveals an issue with this kind of affair. In order to keep herself and her lovers secret, Lesbia might have to pretend to dislike Catullus in public. In the second half of the poem Catullus shows some hope. He suggests that, because she complains, he knows that she loves him. If she truly did not care, then she would be silent. Catullus' use of 'inflamed' in the last line indicates the passion that he is sure Lesbia feels for him.

As tempting as it might be, we should not read Catullus' poems as records of fact. Most scholars agree that Catullus did, in fact, have a relationship with Lesbia and most scholars agree that Lesbia is a pseudonym for Clodia. We cannot, however, be certain that their relationship followed the ups and downs of his poems.

FIGURE 1.33
A nineteenth-century painting of Lesbia by Sir Edward John Poynter.

Clodia and Cicero: the *Pro Caelio*

Catullus was not the only Roman man to write about Clodia. The famous politician and orator Cicero wrote a speech known as the *Pro Caelio*, which viciously attacked Clodia's character.

Pro Caelio means 'In Favour of Caelius' and was a speech to defend Marcus Caelius Rufus from charges that Clodia had brought against him. Clodia had accused Caelius of attempting to poison her. As part of the defence, Cicero took apart Clodia's character, hoping to discredit her argument by showing how scandalous she really was. This has implications for the reliability of the speech. Cicero clearly wants us to see Clodia negatively. He wants his audience to dislike her so much that they have to judge that she lied in the court case as well. So it is possible that Cicero's entire speech could be made up. But if it were entirely false, he could be caught out and his defence of Caelius would fail.

Regardless of how much of Cicero's speech is true, it is a fascinating document for the study of women in Rome. Cicero's intention was to destroy Clodia's character. We can look at his speech, then, as evidence for the most extreme version of improper behaviour.

Throughout his speech, Cicero paints Clodia as dangerous and hyper-sexed. He makes veiled references to relationships and affairs she had with multiple men at parties and banquets, and he accuses her of using her money to buy young men. At one point in the speech (not in the prescribed sections) he even refers to her as a new Medea (see pp. 113–20 for more on the character of Medea). Cicero's assassination of Clodia's character won the case. Caelius was found not guilty of all charges, and Clodia vanished from public view. We do not know what happened to her, but it seems likely that her family put an end to her improper ways, fearing further disgrace.

PRESCRIBED SOURCE

Pro Caelio **49–51**

Date: 56 BC

Author: Cicero

Genre: legal speech

Significance: a famous speech given during a scandalous court case

Read it here: OCR source booklet

Study questions

1 Read through the set sections of the *Pro Caelio*. How does Cicero depict Clodia? Support your ideas with evidence and analysis from the text.
2 What can we tell about Clodia based on her depiction by Cicero and by Catullus?

PRACTICE QUESTIONS: ROME

Source A: *The remains of a room in a Pompeiian brothel*

1. Give any **two** professions that carried with them the status 'infamis'. [2]
2. Why were prostitutes infamis? [1]
3. Using **Source A** and your own knowledge, discuss whether you think it was possible for a Roman prostitute to have a good quality of life. [8]

TOPIC REVIEW

You should be able to:

1. Describe:
   - the main differences between pornai and hetairai
   - the life stories of Neaira and Aspasia
   - the laws surrounding prostitution in Rome
   - the life stories of Cytheris/Lycoris and Clodia/Lesbia.

2. Explain:
   - why sex with a prostitute was not considered to be adultery in Athens
   - how and why the lives of pornai and hetairai differed from each other
   - why prostitution made a person infamis in Rome
   - why the quality of life of Roman prostitutes varied so greatly.

PRACTICE QUESTIONS: COMPARING GREECE AND ROME

Study both sources and answer the questions that follow.

Source A (Greek): *Athenian krater showing a dinnerparty*

Source B (Roman): *Tacitus, Annals, 2.85*

In the same year the senate passed severe provisions to repress women's dissoluteness and prohibited prostitution for granddaughters, daughters, and wives of Roman knights. For Vistilia, a woman of praetorian family, had made public, before the aediles, her practice of prostitution. This was done in keeping with a valid and venerable custom by which it is considered sufficient punishment for unchaste women to admit their shame publicly.

1. Explain how these sources present prostitutes. [6]
2. Do you think that 'improper women' had an easier life in Greece or in Rome? Justify your response. [15]

1.5 Women and Religion

The roles of women in religious rites and what these reveal about the nature and roles of women in their respective societies.

Greece

- Priestesses and prophetesses, including the Pythia
- The roles women played in state cult, including the Panathenaia, Thesmophoria and worship of Dionysus
- The role of women in ritual mourning and preparation of the bodies of the deceased

Rome

- Priestesses, including the rights, responsibilities and punishment of the Vestal Virgins, and the Flaminica Dialis as the wife of the Flamen Dialis
- Prophetesses, including the Sibyl
- The roles women played in state cult, including worship of the Bona Dea, Patricia Pudicitia and Plebeia Pudicitia

The prescribed sources for this topic are:

- The Parthenon Frieze, in the British Museum
- Maenad Cup, in the British Museum
- House of the Vestal Virgins in Rome
- Pudicitia (Pudicizia) statue of a woman in the Vatican Museum (Braccio Nuovo 23)

Don't forget that you will be given credit in the exam if you study extra sources and make relevant use of them in your answers.

Women in both Greece and Rome played a vital role in the religious life of their cities. Both societies had important religious positions that were filled by women as priestesses and prophets, and religious rituals that could only be completed by women. Religion gave women the opportunity to leave their homes and engage with the community beyond their immediate households and, in some cases, could give women influence over the public sphere of government.

GREECE

The ancient Greeks worshipped a **pantheon** of gods and goddesses, each responsible for a different part of the natural world or aspect of daily life. They believed that the gods would only favour a person/city if they had been honoured with proper worship and offerings.

Women could be involved in public religious rituals in a variety of ways. Indeed, religious worship was the most common way for a Greek woman to get out of the house and be involved in the life of the city.

Priestesses

A priestess was referred to as a **hiereia**. As a general rule, goddesses were served by priestesses, whereas male gods were served by priests. There were some notable exceptions – for example, for Dionysus (the god of wine, theatre and madness). Most priests and priestesses would work at a particular **temple** within a particular **sanctuary** in honour of a particular god.

Priests and priestesses in ancient Greece were not like those in modern societies. They had no responsibility for the spiritual and moral wellbeing of their congregation. They did not have to study theology or go through extensive training. Many priesthoods were elected positions, others could be chosen by lottery or inherited from a parent. Priestesses did not have to dedicate their lives to the service of the gods as many priesthoods were held only for a short period of time – often only a year.

The main roles of a priestess were:

- looking after the sanctuary and the buildings inside it
- supervising the work of temple attendants as they washed and clothed the statue of the god
- presiding at sacrifices and certain public festivals.

Being a priestess brought many benefits. These were salaried positions, and some paid very well. The priestess of Athena Nike was paid fifty drachmas a year and she kept the legs and skins of all sacrificed animals (which could be sold for profit). Priestesses had considerable influence and were highly respected throughout Greek society. The historian Herodotus relates an occasion when the priestess of Athena Polias refused to let the Spartan king Cleomenes onto the Acropolis (Athens' most important sanctuary). Cleomenes was forced to turn back, an event that clearly demonstrates the power that a priestess could wield over 'ordinary' men, even if that man were a king (Herodotus, *Histories*, 5.72).

FIGURE 1.34
Greek grave stele from the second century BC of a priestess of Demeter and her husband.

Sacrifice

One of the most important ways that the Greeks honoured their gods was through sacrifice. A sacrifice could be an offering of anything valuable to the god. Common offerings were small figurines or valuable objects left at an altar (votives), liquid offerings poured onto the ground (libations) or food offerings left at an altar. The most important and expensive sacrifices were animal sacrifices, in which a domestic animal like a sheep, pig or cow would be ritually killed and part of the meat burnt as an offering.

The priestess would direct the ritual, and they offered up prayers to the god on behalf of the group. These would normally be either asking for a particular favour or blessing, or thanking the god for something. An animal would be killed at the altar outside the temple, usually by the priestess or one of their attendants, and its blood allowed to cover the altar. The priestess would pray, and then direct the attendants to carve the meat, burning some for the god and cooking the rest. At the moment of death, all female celebrants would shout 'ololyge' – a high-pitched ritual cry that marked the transition from life to death. All celebrants would eat the meat of the sacrificed animal, enjoying a communal feast. This custom was particularly significant for the celebrants, as meat was an expensive luxury in ancient Greece and eaten only occasionally.

Soothsayers and oracles

Another key function of a sacrifice was to receive messages from the gods. After the animal had been killed, a **mantis** would examine the entrails. Based on their colour and texture, the mantis would interpret whether the gods approved of the sacrifice. If the sacrifice had been offered to ask the god a particular question, the mantis would interpret the answer from the internal organs.

> **mantis** (pl. **manteis**) a prophet, seer or soothsayer

S & C

Roles for young girls in Athenian ritual

There were several opportunities for unmarried Athenian girls to participate in religious worship. Two such opportunities were:

- **Arrephoroi ('bearers of secret offerings')** Four girls aged seven to eleven were selected each year from Athens' noble families to live on the Acropolis. During the festival of the Arrephoria, which honoured Athena, the girls would descend into a cavern underneath the Acropolis to fetch baskets containing secret, sacred items. We do not know what these items were. Indeed, the girls themselves never looked inside the baskets.
- **Bears** Every four years a group of Athenian girls, aged five to ten, would be selected as 'bears' to spend time honouring the goddess Artemis at her sanctuary at Brauron (near Athens). Amongst other things, Artemis presided over girls, virginity and the transition towards adulthood and childbirth. Artemis' 'bears' honoured her to prepare for this transition and ask for her protection. Images on pots suggest that the 'bears' spent time exercising and playing sports together. Archaeologists have also uncovered weaving and spinning equipment – perhaps the girls also made textiles as part of their service as bears.

Discussion questions

Why do you think a young Athenian girl would have wanted to take part in either of these religious rituals?

Imagine you are an Athenian girl. Which of these two roles would you prefer to hold?

MODERN PARALLEL

Manteis in the Greek world were quite similar to horoscopes in the modern world. Vague predictions are given, allowing plenty of room for interpretation.

FIGURE 1.35
Diotima's stele.

Pythia priestess of Apollo at Delphi – sometimes called the 'Delphic Oracle'

religious pollution state of uncleanness acquired in a number of ways (e.g. coming into contact with a dead person, having sex, killing outside of war) that offended the gods and prevented participation in religious festivals, and was removed by ritual cleansing

The woman in Figure 1.35 seems to be holding a liver, which would suggest that she is a mantis. The palm tree by which she stands supports this theory; palm trees were traditionally associated with the island of Delos, birthplace of Apollo, god of prophecy (among his many responsibilities).

Other common methods of divining messages from the gods included interpreting the flight patterns of birds and changes in the weather.

The role of mantis did not require any special training. A person could simply claim to have prophetic gifts. Manteis could be men or women, and they became successful by acquiring a reputation for giving accurate prophecies. Prophecies were often vague, probably because by leaving plenty of room for interpretation, manteis could not be proven wrong. Such ambiguity protected their reputation, because they could object that their oracle had been misinterpreted.

A well-respected mantis could wield great political power. Governments would often consult on matters of national importance. For example, Lycurgus, the legendary Spartan lawgiver, consulted an oracle when he needed guidance on his legal reforms. A mantis would also usually be taken on military campaigns and consulted before important tactical decisions were made. It is easy to see how a corrupt soothsayer could give false prophecies and twist situations to their own advantage.

The Pythia

The most important ancient Greek mantis was a woman known as the **Pythia**. The Pythia resided at the sanctuary of Apollo at Delphi. It was common for people to make pilgrimages to visit her from all over the Greek world. As the priestess of the god of prophecy, Apollo, the Pythia was thought to be one of the most reliable in the world.

The Pythia gave advice on a wide range of matters. People would commonly ask her for guidance on how to remove **religious pollution**, how to earn the gods' forgiveness, whether they should move to a different part of the world, or whether the gods were in favour of a given course of action. Essentially, if a decision was important, it was worth asking the advice of the Pythia.

The temple of Apollo at Delphi had two full-time male priests and their attendants, but it was the Pythia alone who dispensed prophecies. The seventh day of each month was consultation day. The Pythia would bathe herself in the nearby Castalian Spring, whose waters were sacred, and garland herself with bay leaves (Apollo's sacred plant). Accounts vary, but the most common version states that the Pythia would then seat herself on a three-legged stool in the innermost room of the temple. In this room was a chasm down into the earth. The Pythia burnt barley and laurel leaves as an offering to Apollo and then breathed deeply. Either the smoke from the sacrificial fire or fumes rising from the chasm would send the Pythia into a state of intoxication. When this state had been achieved, she would be ready to answer questions. It was believed that the Pythia was a conduit through which Apollo would speak. By letting herself become intoxicated, the Pythia was temporarily allowing Apollo to take control of her body.

Inquirers would bring offerings for Apollo and make an animal sacrifice. Once inside, he would ask his question (it was always a man – women were forbidden from asking the

Pythia questions in person) and await the answer. Some reports state that the Pythia would then mumble and groan incomprehensibly. These noises would be interpreted by one of the temple's priests, written down in verse, and given to the inquirer to take away. Other reports state that the Pythia would answer questions in plain, comprehensible Greek. Whichever of these is true, all accounts agree that the Pythia's pronouncements, like those of any mantis, were ambiguous.

We cannot be certain about the identity of the Pythia. Some sources suggest that she had to be a local peasant woman, over the age of 50, who had been born in Delphi and lived a blameless life. Others suggest that the she was a virgin maiden. Sources do generally agree, however, that she served as Apollo's priestess for the rest of her life and that she had to refrain from having sex for this time. When a Pythia died, a woman would be chosen to replace her, although the rituals surrounding this choice are not known.

Religious festivals

The Greek calendar was peppered with religious festivals, some of which lasted a single day whereas others could last as long as a week. These were days when most work would cease and people would come together to participate in acts of collective worship. Different festivals involved very different kinds of rituals. It would be impossible to consider all these festivals, so we will instead focus on three examples that were particularly significant for Athenian women: the Panathenaia, the Thesmophoria and the Dionysian Mysteries.

Study questions

1 Why do you think an Athenian woman would have wanted to be a priestess?
2 How important were prophets and oracles in Greece? Justify your response with specific detail from this topic.

The Great Panathenaia

The Panathenaia was, arguably, the most important festival in the Athenian calendar. It was held every year to honour the birthday of Athena, patron goddess of Athens, and to celebrate the victory of the gods over the titans, known as the Gigantomachy.

Every four years, a much larger, grander festival, called the 'Great Panathenaia' was held. The Great Panathenaia probably lasted for eight days, and comprised a series of games and contests. The festival probably followed a schedule like this one:

Day	Events
1	Poetry reciting and musical competitions
2	Boys' athletic competitions
3	Men's athletic competitions
4	Equestrian competitions
5	Strength, sailing and dancing contests between men of Athens' different tribes
6	All-night torch race, procession and sacrifice
7	Chariot and boat races
8	Prize giving

Women were not allowed to compete in the games, but they were allowed to watch.

The most important role that women played in the festival took place long before the festival itself began. Every year the people of Athens would present the olivewood statue of Athena in the Erechtheon (a temple on the Acropolis) with a new **peplos**. The peplos was woven on a large loom, set up by four Arrephoroi under the supervision of the chief priestess of Athena. The peplos itself was woven by women known as the **Ergastinai**. The peplos was made of thread that had been dyed purple and saffron, two of the most expensive colours available. The Ergastinai wove intricate pictures into the fabric of the peplos, depicting a famous mythological battle between the Olympian gods and the giants (known as the Gigantomachy).

The peplos was paraded through the streets as part of the procession on the sixth day of the festival and then dedicated to the goddess on the Acropolis.

Women also took active roles in the procession on the sixth day. Our evidence for this is a **frieze** from Athens' largest and most significant building, the Parthenon.

The Parthenon Frieze runs around the interior perimeter of the Parthenon and is almost 160 metres in length. Made of imported marble, it was designed to add to the overall impressiveness of the building, serving the dual purpose of honouring the goddess and impressing foreign visitors.

The subject of the frieze is the procession at the Panathenaia. Various scenes are depicted and so the frieze can be read 'in order', like a comic book. The story begins at

peplos a Greek dress made from a long tube of fabric and fastened over the shoulders with brooches or pins

Ergastinai 'female weavers', either Arrephoroi, another group of unmarried girls, or a mix of older and younger women

frieze a horizontal sculptured or painted decoration depicting a scene or number of scenes

Who should have the Parthenon marbles?

The sculptures from the Parthenon have been removed from their original site by various collectors over the years. Many were taken by Lord Elgin in 1801 and brought to England for his personal collection. These were later donated to the British Museum, which is where they are today. Many people believe that the sculptures should be returned to Athens. Others believe that, because Elgin took ownership of them legally, they should stay in England. Still others question whether they should be moved for fear of damaging them. What do you think should be done with the Parthenon sculptures?

PRESCRIBED SOURCE

The Parthenon frieze

Date: 443–438 BC

Sculptor: unknown –
possibly Pheidias

Commissioned by:
Pericles

Style: high relief
sculpture, Classical
style

Original Location:
The Parthenon, the
Acropolis, Athens

Current Location: The
frieze has been divided
between several sites,
including the British
Museum in London
and the Acropolis
Museum in Athens

Significance: sculptural
decoration from the
most important temple
in Athens

the west end, depicting preparations, and continues towards the east end where the final scene depicts the peplos itself. Figure 1.37 explains the frieze as a whole.

The long north and south sides of the frieze are busy, with horses and men filling the space. They are sculpted with dynamism of movement that implies noise and bustle. The east end of the frieze, which portrays the last events of the procession, is much more calm. This section is the only one to depict girls and women.

Figure 1.38 is a slab from the outer edges of the east wall. It depicts small groups of women carrying equipment for the sacrifice. Some carry baskets, one an incense holder, others carry vessels presumably for pouring libations to the gods. These girls are thought to be unmarried maidens. They wear a long **chiton** with a peplos over the top. It is likely that they are wearing peploi in honour of Athena and as a reference to the peplos that has been made for the goddess. The Panathenaia took place in the middle of Summer (our July), so it seems unlikely that this double-layer was worn for warmth!

Figure 1.39 is the focal point of the entire frieze. Originally located in the very middle of the east wall, it depicts the peplos. This scene shows five figures. Two women on the left carry stools to a third woman in the centre. As she seems to be directing the other two women, we can assume that she is the priestess of Athena Polias. The two figures on the right hold the peplos. The one on the left is a man, probably an **archon**. The smaller figure is less clear. Many assume that it is one of the Arrephoroi, presenting the peplos she helped make to the archon, who will assist the priestess in giving it to the statue. Their unbelted peplos, open at the sides, would imply that it is a young girl. However, the hairstyle and musculature seem too masculine. Also, it was not usual to portray citizen girls uncovered to such an extent. The fact that we can see a glimpse of bare skin beneath the peplos implies that this figure is a young man.

chiton a long woollen
dress, popular everyday
clothing throughout the
Classical period

archon a magistrate in
Athens, responsible for
organising civic as well as
religious matters

```
                                           Musicians  Cattle
┌──────────────────────────────────────────────────────┐
│ ┌──────────────────────────────────────────────┐     │  Women
│ │    Riders            Chariots          Sheep  │     │
│ │                                               │     │  Heroes
│ │              ↑                                │     │  Gods
│ │ Riders       N      Elders    Carriers        │     │  Peplos
│ │                                               │     │  Gods
│ │    Riders            Chariots          Cattle │     │  Heroes
│ └──────────────────────────────────────────────┘     │  Women
└──────────────────────────────────────────────────────┘
```

FIGURE 1.37
The layout of the
Parthenon frieze.

FIGURE 1.38
Ergastinoi on the Parthenon, East Frieze, slab 8.

FIGURE 1.39
Parthenon, East Frieze, slab 5.

The Thesmophoria

KEY INDIVIDUALS

Demeter goddess of fertility and the harvest

Persephone Demeter's daughter

Hades god of the Underworld

Zeus king of the Olympian gods

The Thesmophoria was the only Greek annual festival that was exclusively for married women. It was held in the autumn and honoured Demeter. Demeter was the goddess of agriculture, fertility and the harvest, and the primary function of this festival was to ensure the success of the next year's harvest. As corn seed would be sown just after the ritual, it was vitally important that Demeter be properly honoured.

Another significant aspect of Demeter was motherhood. This is most striking in the myth of the abduction of her daughter, Persephone, who was taken from a meadow to the Underworld by its king, the god Hades. Demeter, distraught, searched the whole earth for Persephone. When she was unable to find her, she went into a state of deep grief, which brought an end to all fertility in the world. Without Demeter's influence no crops would grow and all life would perish. Eventually Demeter discovered who had taken her daughter, and she begged Zeus to intervene. Zeus commanded Hades to release Persephone, but it was too late. Persephone had eaten pomegranate seeds from Hades' garden. According to the laws of the Underworld, she was bound to stay forever, having eaten food from the land of the dead. Demeter threatened never to restore fertility to the world. And so Zeus negotiated a compromise. As Persephone had eaten only three seeds (six in some versions of the myth), she would have to spend only a portion of the year with Hades. This is how the seasons came to be. When Persephone returns to her mother, fertility returns to the world as Spring. When it is time for Persephone to leave again, Demeter begins to grieve, ushering in barren Winter.

The Thesmophoria lasted three days and the rituals mirrored the events of the abduction of Persephone.

> **EXPLORE FURTHER**
>
> Our main source for the myth of the abduction of Penelope is the *Homeric Hymn to Demeter*. Read this hymn, noticing how Demeter and Persephone are linked to the idea of fertility and nature's bounty.
>   Read it here: http://www.uh.edu/~cldue/texts/demeter.html.

Day	Event
1	Worshippers would set up temporary shelters near the **Pnyx**. This was significant as, for the duration of the festival, the women symbolically took over the city.
2	Worshippers would fast for this day and sit on the ground, covering themselves in ashes. This was a ritual act of mourning, re-enacting Demeter's grief at the loss of her daughter.
3	Worshippers would pray for blessings related to fertility – for children, future families and bountiful crops.

> **Pnyx** the hill on which the Athenian Assembly met

The rituals also involved making offerings to Demeter and Persephone. Some time before the festival, piglets would be cast down into a chasm and their decomposed remains retrieved during the festival. The chasm represented the Underworld and the piglets represented Persephone's journey into the darkness and back to the light. These remains would be mixed with corn seed and placed on the altar. Later they were scattered on the fields to ensure a good harvest.

This festival was one of an Athenian woman's few opportunities to escape the direct control of her kyrios, to socialise and make new friends. As part of the rituals of the Thesmophoria the women would joke with each other. This joking was supposed to be particularly crude, prompting one ancient author to compare their language to that used in a brothel. The jokes mimicked those said to cheer Demeter when she was grieving for her lost daughter.

The Thesmophoria was a **mystery cult**. We therefore do not know the details for certain and the outline given here is agreed by scholars having compared various sources. The majority of ancient accounts, however, would have been produced by people with no first-hand experience of the rituals and thus based on hearsay and conjecture at best – at worst entirely made up.

The extract below is an example of such a source. It was written by the comic playwright Aristophanes, who would never have attended the festival himself. Moreover, his

> **mystery cult** a kind of religious worship only open to those who had undergone a special rite of passage (initiation), and whose details celebrants were forbidden from sharing with the uninitiated

work is a comedy – intended to entertain other men of Athens. So even if he did have a clear idea of what went on in the Thesmophoria, his intention is primarily to entertain his audience, not to relay accurate facts:

> **Female Herald:** Hearken, all of you! This is the decree passed by the Senate of the Women under the presidency of Timoclea and at the suggestion of Sostrate; it is signed by Lysilla, the secretary: "There will be a gathering of the people on the morning of the third day of the Thesmophoria, which is a day of rest for us; the principle business there shall be the punishment that it is meet to inflict upon Euripides for the insults with which he has loaded us".

Aristophanes, Women at the Thesmophoria

Aristophanes shows the women of Athens using the Thesmophoria as an excuse to meet and plot in secret. In particular, they intend to punish the tragic playwright Euripides for his negative portrayals of women in his plays. Could the Thesmophoria really have been used by women to scheme in this way? Or was Aristophanes finding comedy in poking fun at a serious ritual that men knew little about?

Worship of Dionysus

Dionysus is best known for being the god of wine. But he was also the god of theatre, ecstasy and madness. Essentially, Dionysus was the god of stepping outside yourself and becoming, for a while, someone else. This may seem to be a peculiar concept, but the Greeks knew it well and had a word for it: **ekstasis**.

It should not be surprising, then, that one of Dionysus' main religious cults involved women going out into the countryside, becoming intoxicated, singing and dancing. These women are referred to as **maenads**, and it is believed that the music, dancing and wine/drugs helped them to lose their inhibitions, shake off the constraints of their daily lives and have an ecstatic experience.

Like the Thesmophoria, the worship of Dionysus by maenads was a mystery cult. As such, we do not know the details for certain. Sources could be based on an incomplete idea of what happened at the rituals and/or be tainted by the bias of male authors. When considering sources for mystery cults, remember to consider who made the source, when and for what purpose.

The woman depicted in Figure 1.40 is a maenad. She is identifiable not only by her pose (she seems to be dancing), but by her clothing. She is draped with a leopard skin. Leopards were sacred to Dionysus, and so his worshippers often wore leopard skin cloaks. She is also holding a leopard. In some accounts, maenads chase after wild animals in their ritual madness. She is holding a staff covered in ivy leaves, known as a thyrsus. This was a symbol of Dionysus, and was sometimes shown with a pinecone on the end, although this example does not have this feature. Her loose hairstyle also indicates that this woman is a maenad. Athenian women usually wore their hair tied up – a sign of respectability and self-control. Hair worn down represented wildness and frenzy, and so maenads are almost always depicted in this way. Finally, there is a snake wrapped around the woman's head. This was not part of the standard dress of a maenad, but there are

ekstasis standing outside oneself; the experience of being someone other than yourself

maenad female worshipper of Dionysus, sometimes referred to as a bacchant

FIGURE 1.40
The Maenad Cup.

PRESCRIBED SOURCE

Maenad Cup

Date: 490–480 BC

Artist: Brygos Painter

Style: white-ground painting

Location of discovery: Vulci

Current location: Staatliche Antikensammlungen, Munich

Significance: a remarkably detailed image of a maenad

plausible explanations for its appearance here. As it is wrapped around her head, it could represent her temporary madness. Another possibility is that, because snakes were associated with the Underworld, it refers to another of Dionysus' roles, as a god of death and rebirth. This image is found on the inside of a drinking cup. Cups like this were used mostly at drinking parties for men. The image would only be visible once the drinker had emptied their cup, perhaps a surprise for the drinker. It is possible that the maenad was chosen as the subject of this painting because their association with Dionysus and wine made sense for a drinking vessel.

The most extensive literary source we have for Dionysian rituals comes from the tragic playwright Euripides. The *Bacchae* tells the story of King Pentheus of Thebes and his attempts to stop the worship of Dionysus in the city. The god takes great offence at this and plots Pentheus' downfall. Dionysus arranges for Pentheus to infiltrate the rituals disguised as a woman. The maenads, including Pentheus' own mother Agave, notice Pentheus but in their madness mistake him for a lion cub. The women chase the 'cub', catch it and tear it limb from limb. It is only at the very end of the play that Agave realises what she has done.

This extract from the play is spoken by a herald who has spied the women in the middle of their rituals. Notice how the women seem to be at one with nature and fertility:

> First they let their hair fall to their shoulders, fixed all the clasps and pins of their fawn skin dresses that had become loose and then tied around their waist snakes whose heads came up and licked their beautiful cheeks. Others, who had babies back home and their breasts were bursting with milk held gently in their arms young deer or young wild wolves which they suckled with their own white milk. Others were making garlands of ivy, fir branches and bryony. One of them hit a rock with her

thyrsus and the rock became a spring of gushing clear water. Another digs her reed into the ground and right on that spot the god opens up a spring from where wine rushes out. Those who wanted a drink of milk, all they had to do is scratch the ground with their fingernails and out it would come, all bubbly and white. Sweet honey dripped from the ivy around their thyrsus.

Euripides, *Bacchae*, 695–711

The scene soon changes though, and the herald tells of the maenads' frenzy when they notice the presence of the men:

We just managed to run away and escape the slaughter but they threw themselves, with no spear nor sword, at the calves that were quietly grazing nearby. One of those women tore a poor, tiny calf away from its mother's udder and others ripped calves to bloody pieces with their bare hands and then they began eating them raw.

Euripides, *Bacchae*, 732–737

Study question

Which do you think an Athenian woman would have enjoyed more, the Panathenaia, the Thesmophoria or the worship of Dionysus? Justify your response.

This play gives a vivid account of the rituals of Dionysus, but it is important to remember that Euripides, as a man, would not have had first-hand experience of the rituals of Dionysus. Indeed, as it was a mystery cult, it is doubtful that he could have even spoke to a celebrant to get a reliable account of what went on. Finally, it is important to remember that Euripides was writing a tragic play, not a textbook on the rituals. As such, his account may have sensationalised events for the sake of audience excitement. His work can hardly be called reliable. But it may contain a kernel of truth. It possibly captures some of the anxiety that Greek men may have felt about the rituals of Dionysus and the role of women in them.

Burial rites in Athens

When a relative died, it was the responsibility of the women of the household to prepare the body for burial. Only direct relatives or women over the age of sixty were allowed to be involved. They would first wash the body, taking care to dress any wounds. It was then anointed with perfumed oils and clothed in a white burial shroud. Finally, the body was garlanded with flowers and a coin placed in its mouth. The Greeks believed that, in order to pass into the Underworld, the dead would have to be ferried across the River Styx by the boatman, Charon. This coin would pay for the crossing.

The family then held a wake. The body would be laid out in the house, and friends and relatives would visit to pay their respects. The women of the household would engage in ritual lamentation for the dead. This tradition is extremely old and is described in the oldest literature of the Greeks, Homer's *Iliad*. It involved an excessive show of grief. Women would cut their hair short, dress in tattered clothing and dirty themselves with ashes. They would wail, beat their breasts and scratch at their cheeks until they drew blood. This ritual was less a display of genuine emotion, as a carefully planned ritual pageant, designed to uphold the family's reputation. Some wealthy families even hired professional mourners to create a bigger spectacle. Figure 1.41 depicts a scene of mourning. Notice the women's short hair and dark clothes. Their open mouths may indicate ritual wailing or the singing of mourning songs.

On the third day after death, the body was carried in a procession known as the ekphora. This procession began at the deceased's house and ended at the burial site. The procession would often be accompanied by sombre music, the women of the family singing mourning songs.

When they reached the burial site the body was laid in the ground, sometimes buried with objects of value. For example, a craftsman might be buried with his tools or a child buried with their toys. Poignantly, unmarried girls would be buried in wedding clothes, signifying that they were now 'married to death'. After the burial, the mourners would often pour libations and make food offerings to the shade of the deceased. These were meant to provide sustenance on their journey to the Underworld. Finally, the family would usually offer an animal sacrifice. The meat would be taken back to the family home and enjoyed as part of a feast in honour of the dead.

Study questions

1 What was the most important religious role played by a woman in Athens? Justify your choice.
2 How many similarities can you find between Athenian marriage customs and Athenian burial rites?

FIGURE 1.41
Archaic black-figure loutrophoros (a water carrier used in wedding and funeral rituals), late sixth century BC.

PRACTICE QUESTIONS: GREECE

Source A: *Scene from a Greek loutrophoros*

1. **a.** Describe the Panathenaic peplos. [2]
   b. Why was it important? [1]
2. 'A ritual pageant with no real emotion'. Using **Source A** and your own knowledge, discuss whether you feel this is an accurate description of Athenian burial rites. [8]

ROME

Roman priesthoods

The Romans worshipped a pantheon of gods, very similar to the Greeks. The roles that women could play in Roman religion were, however, significantly different from those in Greece.

Men held the vast majority of priesthoods in Rome. Even the cults of female deities were usually presided over by male priests. Groups of priests known as **colleges** oversaw different aspects of civic religion. Women were excluded from the majority of these colleges, perhaps because priesthoods in Rome were highly political. It was common for a high-ranking priest to also be a leading politician, and women were excluded from being actively involved in politics.

> **college** a group of priests

Some positions in Roman religious life, and some important religious rituals, did require women. It should be noted, however, that these women were always under the direct authority of a man, either the higher-ranking priests of their college or their paterfamilias.

The Vestal Virgins

One of the most important female religious roles was to be a Vestal Virgin. The college of the Vestal Virgins was comprised of six women who were charged with taking care of the temple of Vesta and tending to the ceremonial fire inside the temple. The ceremonial fire was symbolic of the hearth and centre of Rome, so tending the fire was an important job.

The college was one of the oldest in the city, having been installed by Numa, the second king of Rome in 713 BC. Dionysius of Halicarnassus tells the story:

> The fifth [college of priests] he assigned to the virgins who are the guardians of the sacred fire and who are called Vestals by the Romans, after the goddess whom they serve, he himself having been the first to build a temple at Rome to Vesta and to appoint virgins to be her priestesses . . . the custody of the fire was committed to virgins, rather than to men, because fire is incorrupt and a virgin is undefiled, and the most chaste of mortal things must be agreeable to the purest of those that are divine.
>
> Dionysius of Halicarnassus, 2.64–66

The main responsibilities of the Vestal Virgins were:

- to tend to the sacred fire and make sure it never went out accidentally
- once a year to extinguish the fire, clean and purify the temple and relight the fire
- to attend certain public festivals and sacrifices
- to assist with the worship of the Bona Dea (see pp. 86–7) and Vesta by making blood sacrifices at their festivals
- to bake the sacred salt cake used at state sacrifices
- to act as guardians of important documents, including wills and treaties.

FIGURE 1.42
The Temple of Vesta in Rome.

The consequences of failing in any of these duties, in particular for letting the sacred flame go out, were severe. Dionysius of Halicarnassus tells the story of Aemilia, a Vestal who was accused of causing the fire to go out. Normally when a Vestal was negligent and let the fire go out, she would be beaten by the **Pontifex Maximus**. However, on this occasion people suspected that Aemilia had not been negligent, but that she had lost her virginity and so the goddess had made the fire go out.

Pontifex Maximus the chief priest of Roman religion

The punishment for a Vestal Virgin who was found to have been unchaste, like Aemilia, was death. She would be entombed in a cave and die of starvation or dehydration. It is possible that this punishment was supposed to mirror the death of Tarpeia, crushed beneath shields (see pp. 13–15), as the guilty Vestal would be trapped under the weight of stones and earth. If we accept this interpretation, then it would suggest that a Vestal succumbing to temptation and besmirching her chastity was thought of as a kind of betrayal of Rome.

Although punishments for failing in their duties to the goddess were harsh, the Vestal Virgins did enjoy a number of privileges that made them the most powerful women in all of Rome.

- They were free from a paterfamilias. When a girl became a Vestal Virgin, she ceased being under the control of her father.
- They had the right to manage their own property and to write their own will.
- They were the only women in Rome allowed to travel by carriage with a lictor (armed attendant who otherwise guarded senior magistrates).
- They were protected – to harm a Vestal Virgin was sacrilegious and punishable by death.
- If they met a person on their way to be executed, the person could be pardoned.
- Special seats were reserved for them at pubic shows and festivals.
- They lived in a palatial residence known as the House of the Vestal Virgins next to the Temple of Vesta.

At any one time there were six Vestal Virgins in Rome. Two would be in their first decade of service, and they would focus on learning the customs and rituals of the college. Two would be in their second decade of service and they would focus on performing the rituals and tending the fire. The final two would be in their third and final decade of service and they would focus on teaching the customs and rituals of the college to the two least experienced priestesses. After thirty years of service a Vestal Virgin was released from her obligation to the goddess. At this point she was free to leave the house and the temple, and to marry, if she so chose. She did not revert to the control of her former paterfamilias. Sources suggest that many retired Vestals chose not to marry and instead stayed in the House of the Vestal Virgins. It seems likely that, after thirty years of increased power and independence, not many would have been keen to submit to the authority of a husband.

EXPLORE FURTHER

Research the stories of some famous Vestal Virgins, such as Minucia, Cornelia, Fabia Terentia and Posthumia. What can their stories reveal about the status of the college of Vestal Virgins?

When a vacancy came up, twenty eligible girls were selected from amongst the Roman people. In order to be eligible a girl had to be between six and ten years old, have no physical defects, be the child of two parents who were still alive and who were themselves freeborn citizens of Rome. If a girl had an elder sister who was already a member of the college of Vestal Virgins, or if her father was a flamen (a type of priest) then she would be exempt from the selection process. From this pool of twenty girls, one would be chosen by lot. She would immediately be led away from her father by the Pontifex Maximus to the Temple of Vesta. At this point, she ceased to be under the control of her paterfamilias and she belonged to the college of Vestal Virgins.

The House of the Vestal Virgins (Atrium Vestae)

The House of the Vestal Virgins was located right in the civic heart of Rome – in the Forum. The Forum was a rectangular marketplace in the centre of the city – its most popular and important meeting place. It was surrounded by important buildings, such as temples and the senate house. This prominent position within the city indicates the importance of the Vestal Virgins themselves and the respect the Roman people had for them. The house itself is located next to the circular Temple of Vesta, probably for practical as well as symbolic reasons.

The House of the Vestal Virgins was like a palace. A fifty-room, three-storey complex built around a rectangular courtyard with two decorative pools, this house reflected the power and status of the women who resided there. The porticos were decorated with statues of senior Vestals. As well as private rooms for each of the serving Vestals, the house contained a private shrine (lararium) and functional rooms including kitchens, a mill and an oven that the Vestals probably used to bake the ceremonial salt cake.

The House of the Vestal Virgins that stands today was built around AD 113 by the Emperor Domitian. It is on the same site, next to the Temple of Vesta, as it had always been since the cult was started under King Numa. However, although we can still learn about the Vestals from studying the current ruins, we cannot assume everything was the same in earlier periods.

PRESCRIBED SOURCE

The House of the Vestal Virgins (The Atrium Vestae)

Date: AD 113

Architect: unknown

Location: eastern edge of the Roman Forum

Significance: the residence of the most important priestesses in Rome

---

Study questions

1 Imagine you are a young Roman girl at the ceremony for selecting a new Vestal Virgin. Would you want to be chosen? Why/why not?
2 What do you think we can learn about the lives and significance of the Vestal Virgins by studying the House of the Vestal Virgins?
3 Which of the Vestal Virgins' roles and responsibilities do you think was the most important? Justify your response.

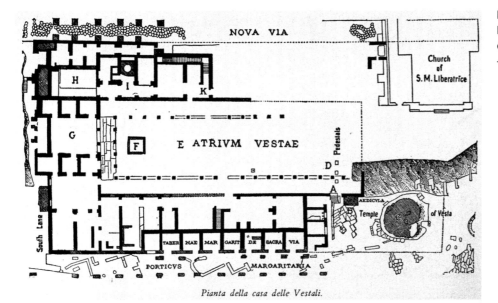

Pianta della casa delle Vestali.

FIGURE 1.43
Plan of the House of the Vestal Virgins.

PS

FIGURE 1.44
The ruins of the House of the Vestal Virgins today.

The Flaminica Dialis

The flamines were a college of fifteen priests. Each priest was associated with the worship of a single deity.

The Flamen Dialis, the priest of Jupiter, was one of the most important flamines. His wife was automatically the Flaminica Dialis, a priestess.

In order to become the Flaminica Dialis, a woman did not need any specific training. The only requirement was that she be married to the Flamen Dialis by the traditional patrician method of confarreatio and that she was a virgin when they were married.

The Flaminica Dialis was not permitted to divorce her husband for any reason, and if she died then her husband was required to give up his post as the Flamen Dialis. If the Flaminica's husband died, then she too would have to give up her position.

Duties of the Flaminica Dialis included:

- sacrificing a ram to Jupiter every eighth day on the market day
- weaving a ceremonial cloak for the Flamen Dialis
- attending certain festivals alongside her husband
- avoiding religious pollution by observing a series of superstitious rules, such as not cutting her hair or nails in June.

DEBATE

There is scholarly debate over which deity the Flaminica Dialis served. Many have assumed that as her husband served Jupiter, she must have served Jupiter's wife, Juno. Others argue, however, that there is no ancient evidence for the Flaminica being associated with Juno. In fact, one of the main religious duties of the Flaminica Dialis was sacrificing a ram to Jupiter. This seems to suggest that she served Jupiter, not his wife.

The cults of Plebeia Pudicitia and Patricia Pudicitia

Roman society greatly valued feminine sexual modesty, known as **pudicitia**. As has been discussed previously, women who demonstrated this virtue were greatly praised and held up as role models for others, like the legendary Lucretia (see pp. 15–17). Those who failed to live up to this standard earned infamy for themselves and their families.

The common explanation for the Romans' concern with pudicitia is that a modest and chaste woman would never have an affair and so her children's parentage would never be called into question. This is certainly part of the picture, but Roman religious belief also drew on the power of feminine sexual modesty. Chaste women (virgins, or matronae who were faithful to their husbands) were believed to be particularly effective at offering prayers and sacrifices, and so were often called upon to worship the gods in times of crisis. The historian Livy provides an example of the power of a chaste woman's prayers, relating how Claudia Quinta prayed to the gods to free a ship which had run aground, if her chastity were pure. According to Livy, the ship immediately broke loose and continued on its voyage. This miraculous story, whether true or not, reveals the Roman attitude towards the power of pudicitia.

The statue shown in Figure 1.45, of an unknown Roman woman, is typical of the 'pudicitia style' of sculpture that first arose in the second century BC and remained popular until the second century AD. She is depicted standing, fully robed and with a hand near to her face. This pose and costume are deliberately restrained. In fact, they are designed to deflect the attention of potential viewers. This reflects the expected behaviour of a chaste Roman woman. Everything about her appearance, dress and mannerisms was expected to convey that she was not sexually available. Having conveyed this message, she would be able to maintain her unblemished pudicitia. There existed, in Rome, a cult dedicated to the personification of feminine virtue, known as the cult of Patricia Pudicitia. This cult worshipped the goddess in a shrine in the Forum Boarium. It was open only to

FIGURE 1.45
Statue of Pudicitia.

PRESCRIBED SOURCE

Pudicitia (Pudicizia) statue of a woman

Date: first century AD

Sculptor: unknown

Material: marble

Original Location: Unknown

Current Location: The Vatican Museum

Significance: a particularly fine example of the pudicitia statue type

univira a Roman woman who has been married only once, either one still married or a widow who chooses not to remarry; derives from the Latin 'unus' for 'one' and 'vir' for 'man'

plebeian class commoners in the Roman world

women of the patrician class (nobility) and the only women allowed to participate in sacrifices to Pudicitia in this cult were matronae who had been married only once. Such a woman was known as a **univira**.

The best way for a woman to maintain her own personal pudicitia was to stay at home, away from prying eyes and temptation. Thus, pudicitia can be seen to restrict women's freedom. However, the cult of Patricia Pudicitia allowed women to worship in public and to remind the politicians and businessmen in the Forum Boarium of the power of feminine virtue. Ironically, by embracing a cult that limited their behaviour, members of the cult were able to make their voices heard in the male-dominated worlds of Roman business, religion and politics.

The historian Livy tells of how, in a time when numerous disturbing omens had been received from the gods, the Senate decreed that extra prayers and sacrifices be made across the city. The cult of Patricia Pudicitia set to making their sacrifices, when a woman named Verginia attempted to join the ritual and was turned away. Verginia had been born into a patrician (noble) family, but had married a **plebeian**. She argued that she was entitled to take part in the ritual owing to her high birth. She said that she was not ashamed of her husband and that she had been chaste and faithful to only him. Still, she was turned away. Livy narrates what Verginia did next:

> In the Vicus Longus, where she lived, she shut off a portion of her house, sufficient to form a moderately sized chapel, and set up an altar there. She then called the plebeian matrons together and told them how unjustly she had been treated by the patrician ladies. "I am dedicating," she said, "this altar to the Plebeian Pudicitia, and I earnestly exhort you as matrons to show the same spirit of emulation on the score of chastity that the men of this City display with regard to courage, so that this altar may, if possible, have the reputation of being honoured with a holier observance and by purer worshippers than that of the patricians." The ritual and ceremonial practised at this altar was almost identical with that at the older one; no matron was allowed to sacrifice there whose moral character was not well attested, and who had had more than one husband.

Livy, *History of Rome*, X.7–9

In this way an argument between members of different classes gave birth to a new cult in Rome. In time, a Temple of Plebeia Pudicitia was built on the Quirinal Hill, showing that it had become a popular institution. However, Livy writes that it was eventually polluted by the presence of unchaste women and it fell out of practice.

Worship of the Bona Dea

Every year a ritual for the Bona Dea (the 'Good Goddess', sometimes known as the 'women's goddess') was carried out exclusively by women. The Bona Dea is a little-known deity who seems to have been associated with fertility, women and healing.

The ritual took place on the first night of May, in the middle of the festival of Flora (goddess of flowers and the season of Spring) in the house of the highest-ranking magistrate in Rome. The wife or mother of the magistrate would preside over the ceremony, which involved the sacrifice of a pig and a feast. Women did not normally take part in blood sacrifices in Rome, but the worship of the Bona Dea seems to be one of very few exceptions to this rule. The Vestal Virgins would attend the ritual also, and sources suggest that they would carry out the sacrifice itself.

Plutarch describes the rites of the Bona Dea in the following extract:

> It is not lawful for a man to attend the sacred ceremonies, nor even to be in the house when they are celebrated . . . Accordingly, when the time for the festival is at hand, the consul or praetor at whose house it is to be held goes away, and every male with him, while his wife takes possession of the premises and puts them in due array. The most important rites are celebrated by night, when mirth attends the revels, and much music, too, is heard.

> Plutarch, *Life of Caesar*, 9.7–8

The exclusion of men from the ritual was absolute. Even male animals had to be removed from the household. However, in 62 BC, a young nobleman named Clodius Pulcher infiltrated the rites and sparked a scandal. In this year the ritual was taking place in the house of Julius Caesar, who was consul. His wife Pompeia was responsible for hosting the ritual, and Clodius wanted to catch her alone so that he might sleep with her. He put on a dress and otherwise disguised himself as a lute-girl so that he could infiltrate the rites. His disguise must not have been very convincing – he was discovered and ejected from the house. The rituals had to be called off and rescheduled with even grander offerings to the goddess, to apologise for the previous presence of a man. Clodius was formally charged with sacrilege. Julius Caesar divorced Pompeia because a rumour had spread that she was having an affair with Clodius. Whether this was true or not we will never know. But Caesar stated that his wife 'should be above suspicion' – a phrase still in use today.

Study question
How do we know that the Romans believed that female chastity was a powerful force?

The Sibyl

Just like the Greeks, the Romans believed in the power of prophets who could divine the will of the gods and pass on messages from them. The Romans called prophetesses **sibyls**.

It is believed that there was once a famous prophetess whose name was Sibyl, who probably lived around the sixth century BC. As the fame of Sibyl grew, more and more towns claimed to have been her birthplace. Multiple stories about Sibyl began to circulate, and eventually the name became a generic term for any prophetic woman.

There are documents recording the presence of a sibyl in Rome from as early as the fifth century, so although the original Sibyl may not have been Roman, she was an old and established part of Roman culture. At times of national emergency, the Romans would consult the **Sibylline Books**. These books were full of prophecies and advice from a famous sibyl who claimed to have been inspired by Apollo, god of prophecy. A group of male priests, known as the **quindecemviri** were responsible for caring for the books and interpreting their messages. The books were written in Greek verse, so these men would have been highly educated. They held their post for life and were exempt from any other civic or religious service.

sibyl prophetess or female mantis
Sibylline Books books held in Rome, full of prophecies
quindecemviri literally 'fifteen men', the keepers of the Sibylline Books in Rome

EXPLORE FURTHER
Read Book 6 of Virgil's *Aeneid*. In this book, the hero Aeneas meets the Sibyl of Apollo. She delivers a prophecy, being possessed by the god himself.

Study question

Who do you think had the greater influence on Rome – the Sibyl or the quindecemviri?

The books did not contain predictions of the future per se. Instead, they described a range of situations and problems that might face Rome and the appropriate religious rituals to perform to appease the gods. There are many examples of the books being consulted throughout Roman history, each time the words of the sibyl were obeyed without question. In 216 BC, when Rome was at war with Carthage and had just suffered a crushing defeat, the books were consulted and on their advice the Romans buried two Greek and two Gallic captives alive in the Forum.

In 83 BC a fire swept Rome's Capitoline Hill, destroying the Temple of Jupiter and the books guarded within. After this disastrous event, the Senate ordered the quindecemviri to make a new collection of prophecies from various reputable sources.

PRACTICE QUESTIONS: ROME

1. List **three** privileges that the Vestal Virgins enjoyed. [3]
2. How did the Flaminica Dialis become a priestess? [1]
3. Why were the majority of Roman priesthoods held by men? [1]

TOPIC REVIEW

You should be able to:

1. Describe:
   - the duties of a hiereia and how a woman could become a hiereia
   - the function of a mantis
   - the role played by women at the Great Panathenaia, the Thesmophoria and in the worship of Dionysus
   - Athenian burial customs
   - the duties and privileges of the Vestal Virgins and the selection process for Vestal Virgins
   - the duties of the Flaminica Dialis and how she was chosen for this role
   - the rites of the Bona Dea.

2. Explain:
   - why a woman might want to be a hiereia
   - why the Pythia was so well-respected
   - how the events of the Great Panathenaia were meant to honour Athena
   - how the Thesmophoria was meant to honour Demeter
   - how the worship of Dionysus gave worshippers an ecstatic experience
   - why Vesta was so important to the Romans
   - the significance of pudicitia in Roman religion
   - the significance of the Sibylline Books to Roman religion.

PRACTICE QUESTIONS: COMPARING GREECE AND ROME

These questions are based on two stimulus sources, one from Greece and one from Rome. The sources could be extracts from prescribed sources or unseen.

Source A (Greek): *Euripides, Bacchae, 732–749*

We just managed to run away and escape the slaughter but they threw themselves, with no spear nor sword, at the calves that were quietly grazing nearby. One of those women tore a poor, tiny calf away from its mother's udder and others ripped calves to bloody pieces with their bare hands and then they began eating them raw. My lord, you could see bits of flesh strewn all around the place. Whole sides of animals, legs, other chunks of animal flesh hanging from the fir trees, dripping blood. Huge bulls, my Lord which only a few minutes earlier stood tall and proud, the sort that if one got them angry they'd tear everything apart with their massive horns, well, now they dropped their bodies to the ground and straightaway countless girls dragged them about with their bare hands and . . . and by the time you blinked your royal eye, my lord, they'd have the skin torn off those massive carcasses of them bulls. And then they went flying about like the wild birds that ruin the proud wheat stalks of Thebes, the ones that fly low next to the rushing waters of Asopos river.

Source B (Roman): *Pudicitia statue of a woman*

Study **Source A** and **Source B**.

1. Explain how these sources show the different roles played by women in religious worship in Greece and in Rome. [6]
2. 'Women played a more important role in religious worship in Greece than they did in Rome.' To what extent do you agree with this statement? [15]

1.6 Women in Power

The political institutions of both cultures, and the extent to which women were able to be involved in the political process or effect political change.

Greece

- The Athenian Assembly, and the exclusion of women
- The story of the *Assemblywomen* of Aristophanes and how the idea of women being involved in politics is presented in the context of farce
- The trial of Agnodice.

Rome

- The structure of the Roman Senate, and the exclusion of women
- The story of the repeal of the Oppian Law
- Sempronia and her involvement in the Catilinarian Conspiracy.

The prescribed sources for this topic are:

- Aristophanes, *Assemblywomen*, 1–240
- Livy, *History of Rome*, 34.1
- Sallust, *Catilinarian Conspiracy*, 24.5–25.

Don't forget that you will be given credit in the exam if you study extra sources and make relevant use of them in your answers.

Both Athenian and Roman societies excluded women from government. They were not allowed to run for public office, nor were they allowed to vote. In this topic you will explore the political systems of Athens and Rome to appreciate how they were governed. You will also examine the stories of individual women who were able to bring about change in their societies.

GREECE

The Athenian Assembly and the exclusion of women

Athens in the Classical Period was not governed by a king, but by the people. Athenian **democracy** was based on the idea that it was the civic duty of all male citizens to be involved in politics, with an equal vote in matters of state.

Matters of political importance were discussed and voted on in the **Assembly** every nine days. At a meeting of the Assembly a herald would introduce topics that had been selected by the **Boule**. All members of the Assembly would have an equal right to speak and try to sway the opinions of those present. However, in practice it was the wealthy, educated citizens who were able to use their polished public speaking skills to sway the crowd. Once the discussion had ended, the members of the Assembly would vote by raising their hand and a designated magistrate would calculate the outcome of the vote.

Athens' model, which valued the opinion of all citizens, was years ahead of its time and is considered to be the world's first democracy. The system was, however, only democratic for a very small portion of the overall population of Athens. In order to be eligible for the Assembly you had to:

- be an Athenian citizen (i.e. be the child of parents who were both Athenian citizens)
- be over eighteen
- have served in the military for at least two years
- not be (and never have been) a slave
- have paid all taxes
- be male.

> **democracy** rule of the people
>
> **Assembly** the central institution of the Athenian system of democracy, in which all adult male citizens were eligible to attend and vote
>
> **Boule** a council of 500 citizens in Athens who decided what issues would be discussed in the Assembly

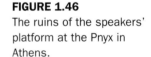

FIGURE 1.46
The ruins of the speakers' platform at the Pnyx in Athens.

With all these restrictions, it is likely that no more than twenty per cent of the overall population of Athens was eligible to participate in the Assembly. Athenian 'democracy' was usually left in the hands of a privileged few.

Women could not attend the Assembly, and so could not participate in political debate, nor could they vote on important matters of state.

All Athens' magistrates and city officials were selected from the pool of adult males who were eligible for the Assembly. As such, no Athenian woman could hold a position of any real political power.

Study questions

1 How effective do you think the Athenian Assembly would have been at making good decisions and governing well?
2 Athenian democracy was direct, not representational (there were no MPs, each citizen voted on each issue). Do you think this system of government was preferable to Britain's current system? Explain your answer.

PRESCRIBED SOURCE

Assemblywomen, 1–240

Date: 391 BC

Author: Aristophanes

Genre: comic drama

Significance: a farcical play depicting women being involved in politics by one of Athens' preeminent comedians

Read it here: OCR source booklet

EXPLORE FURTHER

Browse some political satirical cartoons online at www.punch. photoshelter.com/ gallery-list or www. telegraph.co.uk/news/ matt/. Which is your favourite and why? How does it raise a serious issue through humour?

Aristophanes' *Assemblywomen*

There were two main types of theatrical play in Athens: tragedy and comedy. Aristophanes was famous for writing comedies, including the *Assemblywomen*. These plays were intended to entertain the audience – what good would a comedy be if it did not make the audience laugh? But they also served a more serious purpose. Like modern political satire programmes (such as *Have I Got News for You*, *Mock the Week* and *Saturday Night Live*), Aristophanes' plays critiqued Athenian society by poking fun at it.

How, then, should we treat Aristophanes' work when we want evidence of how the Athenians viewed the issue of women in power? We cannot take everything he writes at face value. But neither should we dismiss what he says completely, assuming it is 'just a joke'. His satire would not work without a grain of truth. We need to find a middle ground, where we can acknowledge that Aristophanes will exaggerate and twist certain features for comic effect but underneath the exaggerations and twists there is a nugget of truth.

The play centres around a kyria named Praxagora and a group of women she has recruited to her cause. Praxagora has devised a scheme to take power from the men of the Assembly (who she thinks are doing a bad job of governing) and to give the power over to the women of Athens.

Aristophanes' comedies almost always involve a main character with an outlandish scheme. For example, in *Wealth* the protagonist plans to find Plutus, the blind god of wealth, and restore his sight so that he can stop giving money to undeserving people. To a modern reader, Praxagora's idea that women should have political power is not outlandish at all. But to Aristophanes' audience, it would have been radical.

The play begins at night, just before the dawn meeting of the Assembly in Athens. Praxagora and her co-conspirators plan to disguise themselves as men and infiltrate the

FIGURE 1.47
A modern performance
of *Assemblywomen*.

S & C Read some of Aristophanes' other plays (or even just summaries of these). What schemes do the main characters come up with? Do you think these main characters were supposed to be taken seriously?

Assembly. There they will force a vote on whether political power in Athens should be taken away from the men and given to the women of the city.

As the women gather, they discuss their husbands. Aristophanes cracks a few jokes, some based around negative stereotypes of women and some at the expense of their husbands.

> **Second Woman**: I have brought this [wool] with me to card during the Assembly.
>
> **Praxagora**: During the Assembly, wretched woman? . . . Think of her wanting to card! whereas we must not let anyone see the smallest part of our bodies.
>
> Aristophanes, *Assemblywomen*, 87–94

Praxagora is bossy and commanding, but her accomplices are more concerned with gossip. They want to talk about their husbands' snoring, farting and obsession with sex.

They also discuss the preparations they have made for their disguises. They have each brought a false beard and male clothing, and some have let their body hair grow out and been out in the sun (a good kyria would stay inside and be less tanned than her husband). In Athens all actors were men, so seeing men dressed as women discussing how they would disguise themselves as men would have been particularly funny.

Although their disguises should be effective, the women face the problem that, in order to win the vote, they will need to convince at least some of the men in the Assembly to vote with them. This will require skills of public speaking, and as Athenian women did not receive this kind of education (see pp. 21–2), they do not look likely to succeed. Praxagora suggests that they practise giving speeches. The women, however, are difficult to control. They are more interested in fixing their disguises and drinking.

Your prescribed lines end with a passionate practice speech by Praxagora herself. She claims that the short-sightedness and self-interest of their menfolk damage Athens. She

EXPLORE FURTHER

Read the rest of *Assemblywomen*. How well do the women run the city? What do you notice about the kinds of reforms that they make to Athens? Do you think Aristophanes really thought women could or should be involved in politics?

proposes that power be given to the women because, as they are experienced in managing the affairs of their own houses, they have the skills to manage the state. The crux of her argument is that women manage their houses in the old, traditional way. Where men are always looking for something new just for the sake of change, women run their houses in a tried and tested way, and this leads to a prosperous household.

And so we reach a nugget of truth behind Aristophanes' comedy. He is criticising the men of the Assembly for being swayed by new, innovative ideas. At the same time, he compliments the women of Athens for sticking to established, traditional methods that have been proven to work.

Study questions

1 Reread the set lines of Aristophanes' *Assemblywomen*. How does Aristophanes present Praxagora's gang of women? Support your judgements with evidence and analysis of the text.
2 Do you think that the women in Aristophanes' *Assemblywomen* are presented positively or negatively? Justify your response.

The trial of Agnodice

Agnodice is famous as the first recorded example of an Athenian doctor for women and midwife. It was against the law for a woman to train as a doctor in Athens, but Agnodice wanted to be able to help women through the dangers of pregnancy and childbirth. She trained as a physician in Egypt and, when she was ready to return to Athens, cut her hair short and disguised herself as a man.

FIGURE 1.48
Nineteenth-century depiction of Agnodice.

Women of Athens preferred Agnodice because (once they knew her true identity) they trusted her more than they trusted male doctors.

Over time, male doctors in Athens became jealous and suspicious of Agnodice. Who was this mysterious doctor and why did their female patients prefer 'him'? Eventually a group of jealous husbands brought a case against Agnodice. They claimed that the reason for Agnodice's popularity was that 'he' was seducing their wives and using medical appointments as a cover for affairs.

During her trial, Agnodice revealed her woman's body to the jury, proving her innocence. This only spurred the accusers on. Instead of accusing her of committing adultery, they accused her of deceit and of practising medicine against the law. The punishment would have been death.

The Roman writer Hyginus tells the story of what happened next:

> The leading women came to the Court and said: "You are not husbands, but enemies, because you condemn her who discovered safety for us." Then the Athenians amended the law, so that free-born women could learn the art of medicine.
>
> Hyginus, *Fabulae*, 274

This is a rare example of the women of Athens involving themselves in the public sphere of politics and law. One might have expected this tactic to have failed. But the men of Athens bowed to pressure from their wives, acquitted Agnodice of any crimes and changed the law.

This episode shows how Athenian women could make their voices heard through the influence they had over their male relatives, despite the limitations placed on them by Athenian law. But it should be noted that the story of Agnodice may not be true. All of our evidence for her life and trial was produced centuries after she lived. Scholars dispute whether she was a real historical woman or merely a legend.

Study questions

1 What can we learn from the story of Agnodice about Athenian male attitudes towards women?
2 What can we learn from the story of Agnodice about the relationship between Athenian women and political power?

PRACTICE QUESTIONS: GREECE

Source A: *Hyginus, Fabulae, 274*

The leading women came to the Court and said: "You are not husbands, but enemies, because you condemn her who discovered safety for us." Then the Athenians amended the law, so that free-born women could learn the art of medicine.

1. Where did the Athenian Assembly meet? [1]
2. List **two** criteria someone had to meet before they were allowed to attend the Athenian Assembly. [2]
3. Using **Source A** and your own knowledge, discuss how women were able to bring about political change in Athens. [8]

ROME

The structure of the Roman Senate and the exclusion of women

> **Senate** Rome's central governing body, formed of men, the majority advanced in years
>
> **magistrate** an elected politician in Rome
>
> **cursus honorum** the ladder of political offices in Rome

Rome's central governing body was known as the **Senate**. The Senate itself was an advisory group, who met to discuss and offer advice on matters of political importance to that year's **magistrates**. Each year the people of Rome would vote for the next year's magistrates. Only men were eligible to stand for office. Once a man had held just one elected position, he was automatically a member of the Senate for life.

The different magistracies of Rome were organised into a 'career ladder' known as the **cursus honorum**. In order to progress up the ladder, a man had to have held each previous position.

Rank	Number per year	Duties
quaestor	20	Managed Rome's finances.
aedile	4	Oversaw public services.
praetor	8	Ran law courts.
consul	2	Co-heads of state in charge of the military, and political relations with other states; passed laws (after consultation with the Senate).

EXPLORE FURTHER

Research the story of Cincinnatus, a man who was given the role of dictator. How does his behaviour uphold Roman values?

The consulship was the highest position on the cursus honorum and the job to which every Roman politician aspired. Having two consuls was meant to be a safeguard against any one man having too much power, as had been seen when Rome was a monarchy. In times of national emergency the consuls could, however, agree to appoint a dictator. A dictator had total authority in Rome, trumping the power of the consuls. He would serve for a maximum period of six months and then would be expected to step down, having dealt with the crisis.

Women were not eligible to stand for public office and they could not therefore be members of the Senate. Women were also not eligible to vote in elections, so they could not choose their representatives.

The only political influence that a Roman woman could hope to wield would have been through the men close to her. Commonly, this was by influencing her husband, but we have evidence of sisters, friends and mistresses manipulating male politicians to their own ends. For example, the historian Plutarch refers to a woman named Praecia who was highly influential in Rome:

> And when Cethegus also, then at the zenith of his fame and in control of the city, joined her train and became her lover, political power passed entirely into her hands. No public measure passed unless Cethegus favoured it, and Cethegus did nothing except with Praecia's approval.

> Plutarch, *Lucullus*, VII

FIGURE 1.49
This sculpture, a fragment of a stone sarcophagus, depicts the Roman Senate. Notice how only men are shown here, since women were excluded.

A similar story of a woman leaning on a powerful male associate is that of Fabia, who was able to (indirectly) change the law to let **plebeian** men apply for the consulship. Apparently, Fabia, who had married a wealthy man of plebeian origin, was jealous of her sister whose **patrician** husband was consul. Fabia's father was so moved by his daughter being upset that he put forward an amendment to the law, which was eventually passed.

The story of the repeal of the Oppian Law

On one notable occasion the women of Rome banded together to make their political opinions known and to spark change that was in their own interests.

In 215 BC, Rome was engaged in a long and costly war against Carthage. This war caused a financial crisis in Rome. It had suffered a costly defeat at the Battle of Cannae and was short on resources to rebuild the army. So the consuls passed a law that forced men to contribute some of the gold and silver from their wives' jewellery to the city treasury. The law also banned women from making public shows of wealth. This was known as the Oppian Law.

Twenty years later, the financial crisis had passed, but the law endured. Livy tells the story of what the women did to draw attention to their cause in his *History of Rome*.

He explains that while a debate was going on over whether or not to repeal the law, a crowd of matronae blocked the streets around the forum, imploring men that they met to repeal the law. This seems to have been a large-scale, multi-day, organised protest, as Livy states that each day more women would come from nearby towns to join the crowd.

Following the women's protest, another debate was held in the Senate. In this debate, those who were against repealing the law accused the husbands of the protesting women of failing to keep a tight enough watch on their wives. They believed that the women should quietly and passively accept the letter of the law. Those who were in favour of repealing the law reminded the Senate that, when the law was passed, the women gladly gave their jewellery for Rome. They also argued that, as they had contributed to the war, they should be entitled to enjoy the wealth and plenty that had been won in that war.

Eventually the Senate voted and the Oppian Law was repealed. The women had, through protest and by putting pressure on their male relatives, achieved political change in Rome.

Sempronia and her involvement in the Catilinarian conspiracy

As the Roman Empire experienced massive expansion in the first century BC, money and slaves started to flow into the city like never before. This meant that women of noble families had far more free time. While many women used this time for leisure activities, others took advantage of the opportunity to better themselves through education. Not unexpectedly, some of these wealthy, intellectual women wanted to have a say in how Rome was governed. Unable to vote or stand for office, they were still able to offer their support to ambitious male politicians.

One such man was called Catiline. From a wealthy family, he had some talent for politics, but had run for the consulship several times and failed. This had been very expensive. By 63 BC he was almost bankrupt.

That year, with the support of some fellow noblemen and some sections of the military, Catiline devised a plot to overthrow the Republic and take power for himself. This is known as the Catilinarian Conspiracy. Many of Catiline's supporters felt dissatisfied with the Roman government. Many had failed to win elections and were not prepared simply to try again. Others had been disgraced in a number of scandals and wanted to oust the current leaders to 'wipe the slate clean' and regain their former status. Many were facing financial problems, similar to Catiline's. One of his most appealing promises was to cancel all debt after his revolution.

The historian and politician Sallust recorded the events of the Catilinarian Conspiracy and in this work he mentions a prominent woman and co-conspirator: Sempronia.

Sempronia was the wife of a prominent senator, Decimus Junius Brutus, who had been consul in 77 BC. She was from a wealthy, influential family and, according to

Sallust, she was highly accomplished. She knew Greek and Roman literature, could sing, play music and dance. Sallust presents her as having the background and the skills to be an ideal matrona: more than able to manage the affairs of her household and to oversee an excellent dinner party.

Although Sallust never outlines exactly what Sempronia did to help the conspiracy, he says that Catiline recruited women to his cause so that they could help him win the support of their slaves and husbands. He even implies that these women would have been asked to murder their husbands if they could not be persuaded.

In reading Sallust's description of Sempronia, it is hard to tell what he thinks of her. He compliments her abilities. But he also accuses her of breaking oaths, being privy to murder and of adultery. Sempronia, then, was a dark mirror of the ideal Roman matrona. She had all the necessary skills and resources, but did not abide by the strict code of chastity and obedience to her husband.

Ultimately, Catiline's conspiracy failed. We cannot know how involved Sempronia was, or what she hoped to achieve. What is clear from this story is that individual Roman women could involve themselves in the male-dominated world of politics.

Sempronia was never prosecuted for her role in the conspiracy. Roman law did not recognise the possibility that a woman could commit treason. Because women were (legally speaking) excluded from the world of politics, they were consequently immune from any of the laws that policed politics.

Study questions

1 What can we tell about Roman attitudes towards women from the fact that they were not allowed to stand for office or vote?

2 Is protest an effective way of being involved in politics? Are there any issues with protests, like the matronae's protest of the Oppian Law?

3 What do you think of the fact that women could not be prosecuted for treason under Roman law? How could you link this law to the story of Tarpeia?

PRACTICE QUESTIONS: ROME

1. What was the highest elected office in the Roman Senate? [1]

2. **a.** Describe how the women of Rome brought about the repeal of the Oppian Law. [2]

   b What does this approach suggest about women's influence in Roman politics? [1]

TOPIC REVIEW

You should be able to:

1. Describe:
   - how the Athenian Assembly worked
   - Praxagora's plan in Aristophanes' *Assemblywomen*
   - the story of Agnodice's life and trial
   - how the Roman Senate worked
   - the story of the repeal of the Oppian Law
   - the Catilinarian Conspiracy and Sallust's account of Sempronia's involvement in the plot.

2. Explain:
   - how Aristophanes characterises Praxagora and her accomplices, the women of Athens
   - how the women of Athens were able to make their voices heard in the law courts
   - what we can learn about women and politics in Rome based on Sallust's account of the Catilinarian Conspiracy
   - why some women (like Sempronia) felt the need to conspire against the Roman government.

PRACTICE QUESTIONS: COMPARING GREECE AND ROME

1. In which society did women wield the most political power, Greece or Rome? Justify your response.   [15]

2. Could women be involved in politics in a meaningful way in the ancient societies of Greece or Rome?   [15]

1.7 Warrior Women

The presentation of maiden warriors in art and literature, and what this presentation can tell us about the position of real women in these cultures.

Greece

- Penthesilea and the Amazons

Rome

- Camilla, as represented in Virgil's *Aeneid*

The prescribed sources for this topic are:

- Bassae Frieze in the British Museum
- Virgil's *Aeneid* 11.532–835

Don't forget that you will be given credit in the exam if you study extra sources and make relevant use of them in your answers.

In this topic you will study representations of warrior women in Greece and Rome. Although female combatants were incredibly rare in either culture, both the Greeks and the Romans told stories about particular women who fought alongside and against men on the battlefield. You will study two: from Greek myth, Penthesilea, a legendary Amazon queen; from Roman literature, Camilla, the Volscian warrior maiden.

GREECE

The Amazons

The Amazons were a mythological race of warrior women who lived on the eastern borders of the Greek world. Interestingly, the Greeks could not decide on one place that they thought the Amazons came from – as they colonised new and broader areas, they located the home of the Amazons further and further away. It did not matter exactly where the Amazons came from – the important thing was that they came from somewhere else.

FIGURE 1.50
An Amazon warrior in armour, bearing a shield with the image of a gorgon.

Amazonian society was matriarchal – governed exclusively by women. Indeed, most versions of the Amazon myths state that Amazonian society was exclusively female. In Amazon society, women governed, farmed and fought – completely rejecting Greek gender norms. Once a year they would visit a neighbouring tribe in order to get pregnant. Any girls that resulted from these unions would be raised as Amazons, whereas any boys would (depending on the version of the story) either be sent to live with their fathers, made into slaves or abandoned and left to die.

The Greek historian Herodotus tells us that the Amazons rode horses, hunted and fought alongside male allies, and he reports a peculiar alternative custom regarding marriage:

> . . . no maiden weds until she has killed a man of the enemy; and some of them grow old and die unmarried, because they cannot fulfil the law.

> Herodotus, *Histories*, 4.117

This extract is revealing of the supposed priorities of Amazonian society. Proving oneself in war was more important than marriage and bearing children. In this respect, the Amazons really were more masculine than feminine. A similar priority can be seen in the Amazons' supposed practice of removing their right breasts, apparently so that they would not be hampered when throwing a spear and so that their right arms would be strengthened:

> They have no right breast; for while still of a tender age their mothers heat strongly a copper instrument constructed for this very purpose, and apply it to the right breast which is burnt up, and its development being arrested, all the strength and fullness are directed to the right shoulder and arm.

> Hippocrates, *Airs, Waters, Places*, 17

Some people have interpreted this practice as being symbolic of the Amazons' rejection of femininity because of their preference for masculinity. They reduce their capability to nurse their babies in order to increase their capability to fight. Not all versions of the Amazon myths agree that they removed a breast. And images in art tend to show them with two (e.g. Figure 1.51, though the detail is badly eroded).

> **hoplite** Greek infantry soldier named after their circular shield, a hoplon.

> **Study question**
> Make a list of the ways that the Amazons depart from the traditional roles and characteristics expected of women studied so far in this component.

The origin of the name 'Amazon' is not certain, but two possible etymologies have been suggested. The most popular is that it comes from the Greek 'a' (meaning 'un-' or 'no') and 'mazos' (meaning breast). An alternative suggestion is that it comes from the Old Persian 'hama-zan', which translates as 'all women'.

Amazonomachy

> **Amazonomachy** a mythological battle against the Amazons

Amazonomachy was a common theme for Greek temple sculpture. The Amazonomachy frieze from the temple of Apollo at Bassae is particularly well preserved and is currently on display in the British Museum.

PRESCRIBED SOURCE

The Amazonmachy Frieze of the Temple of Apollo at Bassae

Date: 420–400 BC

Architect: Unknown

Commissioned by: the Phigalian people, in thanks for the passing of a plague

Style: relief sculpture, Classical style

Original Location: Temple of Apollo Epikourios, Bassae

Current Location: the British Museum

Significance: sculptural decoration from the Temple of Apollo at Bassae, a UNESCO World Heritage Site

The frieze from the temple of Apollo at Bassae ran around the whole interior of the temple – roughly thirty-one metres in length. Much like the Parthenon frieze (see pp. 72–4), the Bassae frieze served to beautify the temple and so honour the god, but also to convey a message to visitors. It displays three myths, two of which are two of the most famous Amazonomachies in Greek myth: the Amazons against the Greeks at the Trojan War, and the Amazons against Herakles and his Greek allies.

Both scenes display the Amazons in a similar style. They are not dressed in armour, but in short tunics that would allow free movement on the battlefield. This style of dress may have been used by Greek women in the few athletic contests they were allowed to attend (for example, the Heraean Games). The fabric drapes over the figures of the Amazons, suggesting sturdy, muscular bodies and dynamic movement. These are not gentle women – they are warriors through and through. And yet the sculptor ensures that the Amazons retain their femininity. Their facial features are soft and feminine, and their

FIGURE 1.52

Heracles (left), recognisable by his characteristic lion skin cloak, fights an amazon, as a wounded or dead Amazon falls from her horse (right). **PS**

FIGURE 1.53

A scene from the Trojan War section of the frieze, the Amazon on the ground is sometimes identified as Penthesilea and the man standing over her, Achilles. **PS**

breasts are visibly exposed – reminding the viewer that these are different from 'average' warriors.

Although the Amazons are depicted as strong and capable on the frieze, they can never defeat the armies of Greek men they fight. This scene plays over and over in Greek mythology. Not just in the Amazonomachies depicted on the Bassae frieze, but in every fight between the Amazons and 'civilised' Greek men. The women fight nobly and well, but are ultimately defeated.

Bassae is in Greece, and so the majority of people viewing the frieze would have been Greek. Many scholars believe that the Amazonomachy motif was intended to inspire a sense of national superiority in the Greek viewers. The Amazons can represent any barbarian race, any system that is alien and unlike their own. By seeing the barbarians defeated, the Greeks are reassured of their own superiority. Indeed, by seeing them fight nobly and well before being defeated serves to further emphasise Greek superiority.

An alternative interpretation of the meaning of the Amazonomachy has to do with the suppression of women by men throughout Greece. The Bassae frieze shows women who have been trained in the arts of war being defeated by their male counterparts. If the mythical Amazons cannot defeat a force of Greek men, then what 'normal' woman would stand a chance? This interpretation suggests that the Amazonomachy celebrates male dominance. This interpretation could explain why Amazonomachies often appear next to Centauromachies. The Centauromachy represents the mythical battle of Greeks and centaurs, thus dominance of Greek men over horses. The two scenes, when read together, celebrate the dominance of Greek men over women and horses.

Study questions

1 Study the Bassae Frieze (Figures 1.52 and 1.53). How do these images convey the strength and power of the Amazons?

2 What do the stories concerning Amazonomachy reveal about the relationship between the Amazons and Greek men?

FIGURE 1.54
The Athenian hero Theseus (left) is abducting Antiope, an Amazon princess, with the help of his allies. Antiope's clothing and weapons show her to be a formidable 'barbarian' warrior, but she has been defeated by the Greek heroes. According to myth, this abduction caused the Amazons to attack Athens, yet another Amazonomachy that ended in defeat for the warrior women at the hands of 'civilised' Greek men.

glorious death in Greek myth, heroes (typically male) often desire a 'glorious death' on the battlefield, which would ensure that their reputation and fame would last forever

EXPLORE FURTHER

Research the stories of Jocasta, Eurydice and Phaedra. Why do they decide to kill themselves? How do they go about doing it? Can you identify any common trends or themes?

Penthesilea

One of the most famous Amazons was the queen Penthesilea, the daughter of Ares (god of war) and Otrera, an Amazon queen. Penthesilea is best known for leading her people during the Trojan War (against the Greeks).

Penthesilea had joined the war in search of a **glorious death**. Before the war she had accidentally killed her sister Hippolyta whilst out hunting and her grief was so great that all she wanted was to die. Women grieving so much that they wish to die is a common theme in Greek mythology. Famous examples include Jocasta (Oedipus' mother), Eurydice (Creon's wife) and Phaedra (Theseus' wife). Each of these women choose to die by committing suicide. So Penthesilea's feelings are not out of the ordinary for a woman in the world of Greek myth. However, she is the only woman to look for death on the battlefield. By doing this, Penthesilea is choosing to die in the way she and the other Amazons lived, blending masculine and feminine qualities.

Penthesilea and her Amazons arrived late to the Trojan War. The conflict had already lasted ten years. The Trojans' best fighter, Hector, had just killed by the Greeks' best fighter, Achilles, and Trojan morale was low. Penthesilea promised the Trojans that she would slay Achilles. The Greek epic poet Quintus Smyrnaeus describes the coming of Penthesilea and her Amazons to Troy, concluding:

> . . . with her followed twelve beside, each one a princess,
> hot for war and battle grim,
> far-famous each, yet handmaids unto her:
> Penthesileia far outshone them all.

Quintus Smyrnaeus, *The Fall of Troy*, 1.33–36

FIGURE 1.55
This black-figure amphora depicts Achilles killing Penthesilea.

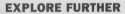

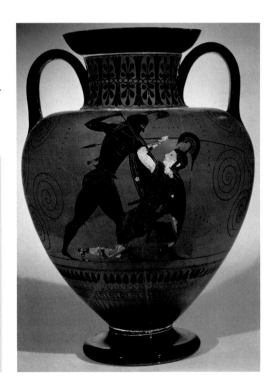

EXPLORE FURTHER

Read the story of Herakles' encounter with the amazon queen Hippolyta (Pseudo-Apollodorus, *Library*, 2.5.9). How typical are the characters and events of this story compared with those of the stories covered in this topic?

On the first day of fighting after the Amazons arrived, Penthesilea killed many Greek men. However, she was unable to fulfil her promise and kill Achilles, for he in fact killed her and 'fell in love with the Amazon after her death' (Pseudo-Apollodorus, *Library*, E.5.1; trans. G Frazer).

> **ACTIVITY**
>
> Modern writers are still making use of the myths of the Amazons in their own characters. Research 'Amazons' in modern pop culture (e.g. Wonder Woman and Xena Warrior Princess) and compare these with the ancient depictions you have seen in this topic.

PRACTICE QUESTIONS: GREECE

Source A: *Greek lekythos portraying an Amazon*

1. Why, according to some stories, did the Amazons remove one of their breasts? [1]
2. 'Men in women's bodies.' Is this a fair assessment of Amazon society? Use **Source A** and your own knowledge in your answer. [8]

catalogue a long list that often features in epic poetry to name warriors in an army or boats in a fleet

PRESCRIBED SOURCE

Aeneid, **11.532–835**

Date: *c.* 18 BC

Author: Virgil

Genre: epic poetry

Significance: the great Roman epic poem – a successor to Homer's *Iliad* and *Odyssey*

Read it here: OCR source booklet

ROME

Camilla

Stories about female warriors were far less common in Roman society than Greek. The Romans did tell stories and produce artworks featuring the Amazons, but these were mostly copies of Greek originals. There is, however, a single example of a warrior woman who was a completely Roman invention: Camilla.

Camilla is a Volscian princess who appears in Virgil's epic poem, the *Aeneid*. She does not appear before this in any existing myth or story, and Virgil may have invented her.

Camilla appears as a supporting character halfway through the epic, as war breaks out between the Trojans (led by Aeneas) and the Latins (led by Turnus). Virgil introduces her to the reader as part of a **catalogue** of warriors, giving her the position of honour at the very end of the catalogue. This is particularly interesting as she is given preference even over Turnus, the warrior who leads the entire army. This draws attention to Camilla, marking her as somehow different or special. Scholars have suggested that this shows how much Virgil himself liked the character of Camilla, and wanted his audience to like her as well. The passage follows:

> Besides all these came Camilla, of the Volscian race,
> leading her line of horse, and troops gleaming with bronze,
> a warrior girl, her hands not trained to Minerva's distaff,
> and basket of wool, but toughened to endure a fight,
> and, with her quickness of foot, out-strip the winds.
> . . . All of the young men flooding from houses and fields,
> and the crowds of women marvelled, and gazed, at her as she went by . . .
>
> Virgil, *Aeneid*, 7.803–13

Virgil is quick to tell us that Camilla was not a typical Roman girl. As we have seen (p. 15, p. 46), Roman girls and women of all social classes were expected to spin and weave, but Virgil sends his readers a clear message that this is not what Camilla has been trained in. She rejects the life of a 'normal' woman. But what kind of life she has chosen for herself is unclear. Her toughness seems masculine but Virgil goes on to stress her feminine beauty, referring to her 'smooth shoulders' and a 'brooch clasped her hair with gold', ensuring that she cannot be understood simply as 'hyper masculine'.

Camilla seems to combine features of the masculine and the feminine. She also seems to be godlike in her abilities. Virgil goes on to describe her running faster than the wind and so light-footed that she can run on water or over ears of corn without damaging them. Could Virgil be saying that a gender identity that combines the masculine and the feminine can make a person godlike? Or is he suggesting that, because Camilla is godlike, she is able to pick and choose her gender? There is no 'correct' answer, of course, and so the reasons behind Camilla's presentation are a matter of personal interpretation.

After she has been introduced, Camilla disappears from the narrative until Book 11. Camilla has been fighting bravely and with great success. The scene then changes to the palace of the heavens and Virgil narrates a conversation between Diana (goddess of the hunt and protector of unmarried girls) and her companions.

Diana explains that Camilla has always been one of her favourite mortals and describes how she came to be her protector. When Camilla had been a baby, her father Metabus was exiled. During their flight, their escape was cut off by a river and, afraid to swim across in case Camilla might drown, Metabus tied the baby to a spear and launched her across the river. As he did so, Metabus offered up a prayer to Diana, promising Camilla's life would be dedicated to the goddess, if she survived. Diana heard his prayer and made sure that the spear made it safely to the other side of the river.

Metabus remained in exile, unable to find a city that would welcome him, and so he raised Camilla in the wilds. She was fed milk from the udders of wild horses and taught how to use a javelin and a bow and arrows as soon as she learned to stand. From Virgil's description, it is clear that Camilla does not just refuse to conform to the norms of feminine behaviour, but rejects 'civilised' city life entirely.

Virgil goes on to say how mothers in the surrounding towns all longed for Camilla to marry their sons. This seems strange. Why would typical, Italian women want to have a girl who lives in the wild as their daughter-in-law? Surely Metabus would not be able to give an attractive dowry. Surely Camilla would never submit to staying indoors and learning to weave. It is possible that Virgil uses this to show how attractive Camilla is. Equally likely, he is challenging assumptions about the 'ideal' Roman wife and whether she was actually as desirable as someone like Camilla.

Regardless of how desirable she might be, Camilla has no intention of marrying. She loves only two things: her weapons and her chastity. We have already seen the importance of virginity in Roman culture. The loss of virginity marks the transition into adult womanhood and so, by choosing to remain a maiden forever, Camilla is choosing a sort of perpetual adolescence. In this way, she matches Diana herself. Diana, as a goddess, was ageless and always depicted (in art) as an adolescent maiden. Diana also made the choice never to lose her virginity and loved hunting in the wild. Is it possible, therefore, that Camilla is merely meant to be a mortal 'version' of Diana?

As Diana finishes telling the story of Camilla's upbringing, she makes it clear that she is destined to die in the battle. Diana is unable to prevent this, but sends Opis, a nymph, down from the heavens to avenge Camilla by killing her killer. Once again, the close bond between Camilla and her patron deity is stressed.

The scene then shifts to the battlefield. Virgil's descriptions of battle are very gory, and right in the middle of the fighting is Camilla. Virgil calls her an 'Amazon' – clearly not meant as a literal description, but meant to make his reader remember famous Amazon warriors from Greek mythology such as Penthesilea and Hippolyta, and think of Camilla as their equal:

> But an Amazon exulted in the midst of the slaughter,
> with one breast bared for battle: Camilla, armed with her quiver.
>
> Virgil, *Aeneid*, 11.648–49

FIGURE 1.56
Metabus and Camilla in a nineteenth-century statue by Francesco Massimiliano.

KEY INDIVIDUALS

Diana Camilla's patron deity; maiden goddess of the hunt and the wild

Metabus Camilla's father

ACTIVITY

Compare Camilla's upbringing with the upbringing of a typical Roman girl. Make a Venn diagram charting the similarities and differences.

Camilla is an impressive fighter – as good as any male hero on the battlefield. She swaps between bow and arrows, spears and a mighty double-axe, using each weapon expertly. She is accompanied by a band of maiden warriors into battle, just like Diana. We do not learn much about these attendants, just that Camilla chose them to be her companions in peace and war. Camilla's **aristeia** lasts for many lines and she is able to cause such fear in her enemies that they turn to retreat. Just like the Amazons of Greek myth, Virgil makes sure that we see how fearsome and deadly Camilla truly is.

Camilla's eventual downfall is her desire for spoils of war. She notices a warrior called Chloreus, wearing fabulous armour made of gold and decorated with purple – the colour of royalty. Virgil states that she burned with a 'woman's passion'. This is possibly a reference to her losing self-control, which Virgil implies is a female weakness. An important feature of Roman masculinity was being able to keep control of emotions and not letting them dictate action.

An enemy soldier named Arruns takes advantage of Camilla's distraction and throws his spear from a great distance. As Camilla lies dying, Arruns flees. Virgil clearly does not want his reader to sympathise with Camilla's killer, and so has Arruns act in a cowardly manner. As Camilla dies, her last act is to give instructions to her companion to call for Turnus. She regains her self-control and ensures that her soldiers will not be left without a leader.

What can we make of Camilla's death? Does she, like the Amazons of Greek myth, need to die to show that women warriors are inferior to men? If this is the case, then why did Virgil not have Arruns defeat Camilla in a fair, one-on-one duel? Perhaps Virgil wanted his reader to feel deep sorrow at the death of the maiden warrior and so has her death be as unfair as possible. A further possibility is that Virgil wanted his reader to understand that, no matter how great the warrior, loss of masculine self-control will lead to defeat. Again, there is no correct answer – we can only discuss different, equally valid interpretations.

---

aristeia a scene in an epic poem in which a great warrior fights with exceptional courage

---

KEY INDIVIDUAL

Arruns a Trojan warrior who stalks and kills Camilla

EXPLORE FURTHER

Research the typical presentation of the goddess Diana in art and literature. How similar is Camilla to Diana?

Study questions

1 Read the prescribed lines of Virgil's *Aeneid* on Camilla and produce a character profile. Include notes on how she looks, what she does, her relationships with other people and what she says.

2 Do you think a Roman man would have wanted Camilla to be his wife? Why/why not?

3 Do you personally find Virgil's presentation of Camilla to be positive or negative? Support your answer with specific detail and analysis of the text.

PRACTICE QUESTIONS: ROME

1. Name Camilla's father. [1]
2. Of which tribe was Camilla a princess? [1]
3. Why was Camilla not raised in a city? [2]
4. Discuss the ways in which Camilla goes against the expected behaviour of a Roman girl. [8]

TOPIC REVIEW

You should be able to:

1. Describe:
   - the key features of Amazonian society
   - at least two separate myths involving Amazonomachy
   - Camilla's upbringing
   - what happens to Camilla on the battlefield.

2. Explain:
   - the significance of the Amazonian custom of removing one of their breasts
   - the significance of the Amazonomachy myth for Greek society
   - how Virgil shows Camilla to be similar to the goddess Diana
   - how Virgil shows Camilla to be fearsome and dangerous.

PRACTICE QUESTIONS: COMPARING GREECE AND ROME

1. Whose story do you find to be more tragic, Penthesilea's or Camilla's? [15]
2. Discuss whether you think we can learn anything about ordinary Greek and Roman women from stories of warrior women. [15]

1.8 Women to be Feared

TOPIC OVERVIEW

The presentation of foreign, powerful women in art and literature, including how they compare to 'respectable' women from each culture, and what makes them so dangerous and threatening to the ancient audience.

Greece

- The story and presentation of Medea by the Greeks, from meeting Jason in Colchis to her escape to Athens

Rome

- The story and presentation of Cleopatra VII by the Romans, including her love affairs with Roman generals (Julius Caesar and Mark Antony), her role in the decisive Battle of Actium, and the political and military threat she was seen to be

The prescribed sources for this topic are:

- The Flight of Medea krater, in the Cleveland Museum of Art
- Euripides, *Medea*, 1–38; 1293–1389
- Virgil, *Aeneid*, 8.671–713

Don't forget that you will be given credit in the exam if you study extra sources and make relevant use of them in your answers.

In this topic you will study the stories of two women that inspired fear and loathing in Greece and Rome. From Greece, the mythological Colchian witch, Medea. From Rome, the historical Egyptian pharaoh, Cleopatra. Concepts of civility and barbarism are central to our understanding of these 'dangerous foreigners', and so you will need to make direct comparisons between these stories and everything you have learned about the societies of Greece and Rome so far in this component.

GREECE

Medea is one of the most independent, powerful and thus dangerous women in all of Greek mythology. She was a **barbarian** princess, descended from the god of the sun and a priestess of Hekate (an Underworld goddess of witches and witchcraft). She was a fearful character to the Greeks because she did not conform to the expectations of female behaviour. She refused to put the needs of her male relatives and husband above her own. She was highly emotional and powerful. Essentially, the Greeks feared Medea because she was a woman who could not be controlled.

In Greek mythology, female characters are rarely protagonists. More often they appear as love interests, mothers or daughters. Medea is no exception. To understand her story, first one must understand the story of the man she loved: a Greek hero called Jason.

> **barbarian** the Greek word for any non-Greek

> **KEY INDIVIDUALS**
>
> **Medea** princess of Colchis
>
> **Jason** Greek hero and leader of the Argonauts

Jason, Medea and the Golden Fleece

Medea met Jason when he was on his quest to find the legendary **Golden Fleece**. The fleece was kept far away in the land of Colchis at the edge of the world, and Jason's half-uncle Pelias, the king of Thessaly, had promised to give up the throne to Jason if he brought it back. So Jason built a ship called the Argo and gathered a crew of the greatest living heroes to help him. These became known as the Argonauts. The Argonauts had many adventures on their way to Colchis, but eventually they arrived on the island at the edge of the world and asked where they might find the Golden Fleece.

Aietes, the king of Colchis, did not want Jason to take the fleece away and so he set a challenge. Jason could take the fleece if he yoked a pair of oxen to a plough, used them to plough a field and then sowed the field with serpents' teeth. The oxen were monstrous beasts of metal whose breath was fire. What was worse, the serpents' teeth, once sown in the earth, would spring up into warriors ready to attack him. Aietes expected Jason to die attempting this task. Even if Jason were successful, the fleece would not be simple to take; it was hung in the branches of a tree, guarded by a ferocious serpent.

Jason was a favourite mortal of the queen of the gods, Hera. She knew that Jason could not hope to succeed in his task alone, and so she arranged for Aietes' daughter Medea fall in love with Jason. With Medea's magical powers to aid him, Hera hoped that Jason would succeed in his quest for the fleece. The Greek epic poet Apollonius narrates the moment when Medea falls in love with Jason:

> **Golden Fleece** the skin of a divine golden ram kept by the Colchians after the ram was slaughtered as a sacrifice; it became the constellation Aries

> **KEY INDIVIDUALS**
>
> **Pelias** the king of Thessaly
>
> **Argonauts** Jason's crew of heroes that accompanied him on his quest for the Golden Fleece (named after their ship, the Argo)
>
> **Aietes** king of Colchis, Medea's father
>
> **Eros** winged god of love, son of Aphrodite, the Greek equivalent of the Roman Cupid

> [Eros] laid the arrow-notch on the cord in the centre, and drawing wide apart with both hands he shot at Medea; and speechless amazement seized her soul. But the god himself flashed back again from the high-roofed hall, laughing loud; and the bolt burnt deep down in the maiden's heart like a flame; and ever she kept darting bright glances straight up at Aeson's son, and within her breast her heart panted fast through anguish, all remembrance left her, and her soul melted with the sweet pain.
>
> Apollonius, *Argonautica*, 3.281–90

The love that Eros inspired in Medea was overwhelming. She longed for nothing else than to use her magic to save Jason's life. But to help Jason take the fleece would go

FIGURE 1.57
This second-century AD fragment depicts Medea (right) distracting the guardian serpent, as Jason (left) retrieves the fleece.

EXPLORE FURTHER

Read Book 3 of Apollonius' *Argonautica* for his version of Medea's dilemma, her betrayal and Jason's theft of the fleece. Do you sympathise with Medea? Why/why not? Do you think that Jason could have survived without her assistance? Why/why not?

directly against her father and her king, Aietes. Apollonius describes how Medea spent a long night debating with herself about what she should do, and that she even considered killing herself to avoid the problem. In the end, Medea chose to follow her heart. She betrayed her father and her country by giving Jason a charm that would make him invulnerable and allow him to complete Aietes' task. She then used a combination of magic chants and drugs to lull the serpent to sleep. Jason stole the fleece and returned to the ship.

Medea begged Jason to take her away with him, knowing that Aietes would be angry when he found out what she had done. In gratitude for her help, Jason promised to take Medea back to Greece with him and to marry her:

> Lady, let Zeus of Olympus himself be witness to my oath, and Hera, queen of marriage, bride of Zeus, that I will set thee in my halls my own wedded wife, when we have reached the land of **Hellas** on our return.'
>
> Apollonius, *Argonautica*, 4.95–98

Hellas the Greek name for the Greek world

Medea thus betrayed her father in favour of a husband. As we have seen (p. 22, p. 26), a Greek woman was not expected to choose her own husband. Rather, she was expected willingly to marry a man of her father's choice. Aietes certainly did not choose Jason for Medea. Indeed, Aietes had been trying to kill Jason by setting an impossible task. Medea refused to play by the rules of Greek society and she got what she wanted. Such defiance could set a dangerous precedent for other women and destabilise Greece's traditional patriarchy.

Jason and Medea return to Greece

The journey of the Argo back to Greece was fraught with dangers, which Medea helped Jason to overcome. These episodes display another of Medea's key characteristics: her cunning (indeed, Medea's name derives from a Greek word that means 'planner' or 'deviser').

The first challenge that the Argonauts faced was the angry Colchians. Aietes sent ships to chase after Jason. When they began their pursuit, Medea thought of an ingenious, but brutal way of slowing them down. She killed her brother Apsyrtus and cut his body into pieces. Every time the Colchian ships got close to the Argo, she threw a piece into the water. This forced the Colchians to stop rowing and spend time retrieving the piece of Apsyrtus. Medea knew that her people would never let their prince go without a proper burial, and so this stratagem bought Jason and the Argonauts all the time they needed to escape.

Medea sacrificed the life of her brother to save the life of her lover. Once again, we see Medea following the passions of her heart rather than a sense of duty to her family. We also see Medea's ruthlessness for the first time. Whereas on Colchis she used her skills to save a life, here Medea becomes a murderer. Worse, she kills a member of her own family. The killing of a family member was particularly polluting in Greek religion and these crimes could be punished by the Furies.

Medea saved Jason and the Argonauts once again when the crew arrived at the island of Crete. The island was home to a metal giant named Talos and only Medea could save the crew. She defeated Talos by summoning Underworld spirits and so brought down a giant that could have easily defeated all the Argonauts.

Thessaly

When the pair arrived in Thessaly and showed king Pelias the Golden Fleece, the king was shocked. He never expected Jason to return from his quest and he refused to give up his throne.

Once again, Medea came up with a plan. She went to the daughters of Pelias and showed them a 'magic ritual' that could reverse the aging process. Medea demonstrated this on an old ram, which she cut into pieces and boiled in a cauldron. While the daughters of Pelias were distracted, Medea pulled a young lamb from under her cloak and pretended that it was the old ram, made young again.

Pelias' daughters were impressed and fooled by Medea's ploy. They eagerly told their father about the ritual and offered to perform it on him, as he was an old man. The girls slaughtered their own father, dismembered his body and boiled it in a cauldron, expecting a young man to emerge from the pot. Of course, this did not happen – they had unwittingly murdered their father.

ACTIVITY

Make a comic strip showing how Jason overcame each of his tasks on Colchis. Where relevant, label the assistance that Medea gave to him.

KEY INDIVIDUALS

Apsyrtus Medea's younger brother

Furies goddesses who avenged 'blood crimes' – the personifications of vengeance

FIGURE 1.58
This fifth-century BC relief depicts Medea demonstrating her false ritual to Pelias' daughters.

The plan succeeded in removing king Pelias, but things did not work out well for Jason and Medea. They were driven out of Thessaly by the angry townsfolk and they had to seek refuge in the Greek city of Corinth. For the first time, Medea suffered negative consequences for her schemes and her violence. Once she had come to the Hellenic world, where people were 'civilised', she was less able to get away with behaving like a 'barbarian'.

Medea's revenge

Jason and Medea settled down in Corinth and lived happily for a while. Medea gave birth to two sons and was content to live with Jason as a resident foreigner. Jason, however, was a little more ambitious. He wanted to be a king. Unfortunately for Medea, she was the reason Jason could not achieve this goal. Her actions in Thessaly had made them both exiles, and her status as a barbarian foreigner meant that they were both unpopular with the local rulers.

Jason left Medea so that he could remarry and improve his position in society. His new bride was a princess of Corinth, a young and beautiful girl called Glauce. Medea was devastated. She had betrayed her father and her country, murdered her brother, travelled to a foreign land where people treated her with fear and suspicion, and she had borne Jason two sons. Without Jason, she was left with nothing.

Medea grieved deeply for her lost marriage. In fact, her lamentation was so extreme that Creon, the king of Corinth, exiled her from the city. He was afraid that, if he let her stay, Medea would exact a terrible revenge on his Glauce. Medea agreed to go, but asked

S & C

The helpful princess trope

The story of Medea's love for and abandonment by Jason fits into the trope of the 'helpful princess'. The helpful princess is a character type who appears in a story about a hero. Typically, she is young, unmarried and related to the ruler of her homeland. She will meet the hero and offer him help in the hope that he will fall in love with her. Usually the help that she gives is against her own interests. Perhaps she will betray her father/homeland or sacrifice her own reputation in order to help the hero. Eventually, the hero will discard the helpful princess once she is no longer useful to him. The earliest example of this motif in ancient literature is princess Nausicaa in Homer's *Odyssey*, but the motif appears in myths from many different cultures.

Research two or more examples of 'helpful princesses' and compare their stories, making note of similarities as well as significant differences. Some examples include Ariadne who helped Theseus in Greek mythology, Dido who helped Aeneas in Virgil's *Aeneid*, the Little Mermaid who helps the prince in Hans Christian Andersen's original story, and Eponine who helps Marius in Victor Hugo's *Les Miserables*.

Creon for a single day to put her affairs in order. Creon agreed. One day was all Medea would need for her revenge.

Euripides' tragic play *Medea* tells the story of Medea's final day in Corinth. The play opens with a speech by the nurse of Medea's children, who summarises the story of how Medea met Jason and came to be in Corinth. Medea's foreignness is a main theme of the play and retelling the story of how Jason and Medea met the nurse reminds the audience that Medea is a barbarian. Nevertheless, the nurse paints a positive image of Medea and Jason's lives in Corinth. They are exiles, but are welcomed by the community.

This image soon turns sour, as she tells of Jason's abandonment of Medea and his marriage to princess Glauce. She describes the power of Medea's pain – she is refusing food, lying on the floor, weeping and refusing to look up at the sky. This behaviour is reminiscent of Athenian ritual grief. But what is Medea grieving for? Her ended marriage? Her lost future with Jason? Her father and country, to which she can never return? Her murdered brother? Perhaps she mourns for all of these.

The audience would surely feel pity for Medea at this point in the play. But the nurse finishes her speech with a disturbing prophecy. She worries what Medea will do next. She reminds us that Medea has a terrible temper and a violent disposition. The nurse suggests that Medea might kill the royal family in revenge. The audience is then left to anticipate and wonder what form Medea's revenge will take.

Throughout the course of the play, Medea gives several passionate speeches. Perhaps the most famous is this passage that outlines the many hardships women were made to suffer in the Greek world:

> Of all creatures that have breath and sensation, we women are the most unfortunate. First at an exorbitant price we must buy a husband and master of our bodies. And the outcome of our life's striving hangs on this, whether we take a bad or a good husband. For divorce is discreditable for women and it is not possible to refuse wedlock. And when a woman comes into the new customs and practices of her husband's house, she must somehow divine, since she has not learned it at home, how she shall best deal with her husband. If after we have spent great efforts on these tasks our husbands live with us without resenting the marriage-yoke, our life is enviable. Otherwise, death is preferable. A man, whenever he is annoyed with the company of those in the house, goes elsewhere and thus rids his soul of its boredom. But we must fix our gaze on one person only. Men say that we live a life free from danger at home while they fight with the spear. How wrong they are! I would rather stand three times with a shield in battle than give birth once.'
>
> Euripides, *Medea*, 230–251

Medea's statement that she would rather serve three times in battle than give birth once is a direct challenge to Greek values that prized the contributions of men over those of women. Moreover, Medea gives voice to the unhappily married women of Athens by outlining all the indignities they are forced to suffer in marriage. It is easy to forget that these words were written by Euripides, an Athenian man, as they so clearly and passionately convey the wrongs done to women throughout the Greek world.

Later in the play, Jason tries to soothe Medea's anger by explaining that she ought to be grateful to him. He argues that, even though he is divorcing her, their marriage was

KEY INDIVIDUALS

Glauce princess of Corinth

Creon king of Corinth

PRESCRIBED SOURCE

Medea, 1–38; 1293–1389

Date: 431 BC

Author: Euripides

Genre: tragic drama

Significance: a famous retelling of the Medea story by one of Athens' preeminent tragedians

Read it here: OCR source booklet

beneficial for Medea because she no longer lives among barbarians (her people), and now understands justice and the rule of law (which the Colchians lacked). This speech clearly demonstrates the prejudice of Jason and indeed of all Greek people against foreigners. Jason believes that their marriage has given Medea the opportunity to better herself by association with civilised people. Unsurprisingly, Medea is not convinced by Jason's speech and she resolves to exact her revenge against all those who have wronged her.

First, she devises a scheme to deal with Glauce and her father Creon. Medea knows that the Corinthian royal family would be suspicious of her and so she pretends to be full of remorse for her angry behaviour. She asks that her sons be allowed to stay in Corinth and not be sent into exile with her. She even sends them with gifts for Glauce on her wedding day to convince the royal family that she is sincere. Glauce happily accepts Medea's gifts, a coronet and a dress.

As soon as the princess puts on the dress, it clings to her body and burns her flesh – Medea had cast a poisonous spell over the garment. In desperation, Creon tries to help his daughter take the dress off, but it sticks to him as well. And so the king and the princess die agonising deaths at the hand of Medea's magic.

Medea's final and worst revenge is reserved for her ex-husband. After much deliberation, agonising over the decision for the majority of the play, Medea resolves to kill her own children to hurt their father.

Lines 1293–1389 are the closing scene of the play. At this point Medea has gone offstage to kill her children. Jason arrives, knowing only that Medea's gifts killed Glauce and Creon – he is worried that the people of Colchis, angry at Medea's actions, will harm his sons. The leader of the chorus speaks with Jason and tells him what has happened.

FIGURE 1.59
This fifth-century red-figure vase shows an alternative version of the story in which Medea gives Glauce the poisoned cloak herself, instead of sending her sons.

At this point Medea appears, triumphant, above the stage in a flying chariot, the bodies of her dead sons with her. Medea explains that she is beyond Jason's reach in the chariot, loaned to her by her grandfather the sun god. Jason gives an anguished speech in which he blames himself for ever bringing a barbarian princess to Greece. He recalls Medea's murder of her own brother and compares her to various animals and monsters, claiming that no Greek woman would or could ever do what Medea has done.

Medea replies, showing no remorse for her actions and blaming Jason and Creon. She acknowledges that the death of her children brings her pain but says that this pain is bearable, as long as Jason cannot mock her. She denies Jason the right to bury his sons, and foretells that Jason will die a miserable death, hit on the head by a piece of the Argo. Such an unheroic death would shame Jason, hoping for a noble death on the battlefield like other Greek heroes.

The play closes with both Jason and Medea flinging insults at each other. Neither comes across as good, noble or sympathetic. At the end, the chorus is left to comment on the unpredictability of life and of the gods.

Euripides' *Medea* shows the destructive power of the title character in a truly terrifying way. She destroys everything around her to hurt Jason and to satisfy her own selfish desire for revenge. And she gets away with it.

The krater in Figure 1.60 depicts the moment when Medea appears to Jason having just murdered their two sons. She is identifiable in the centre of the image surrounded by the rays of the sun (a reference to her grandfather, the god of the sun) and riding in a chariot drawn by serpents. She is dressed in Eastern clothes, a highly decorated robe and tall cap. This clothing marks her out as foreign, as it is unlike the usual dress of a Greek woman and, in fact, is reminiscent of the clothing worn by the barbarian Persians.

The damage Medea has done is clear. To the bottom right her sons lie dead over an altar as their nurse and tutor grieve next to them. Jason is at the bottom left, looking up at Medea. He seems totally powerless against Medea, physically lower than her and unable to reach up to her. His facial expression seems hopeless and his shoulders slump in defeat.

At the top edges, the image is flanked by winged creatures that are probably the Furies. But why are they there? Are they overseeing Medea's revenge or are they present to take vengeance on Medea for committing a blood crime?

Study questions

1 Throughout her story Medea pushes against the expected behaviour of a Greek woman. Find as many examples of this as you can and for each briefly explain how this differs from expected behaviours.
2 Medea committed several murders. Which do you think was the worst crime? Justify your choice.
3 Do you think that Jason deserved the revenge that Medea took?
4 What do you think would have terrified a Greek audience more: Medea's magical powers, her cunning mind, or her independence?
5 Study Figure 1.60. How has the artist represented this scene differently from Euripides?

FIGURE 1.60
Krater showing the
Flight of Medea.

PRESCRIBED SOURCE

The Flight of Medea Krater

Date: *c.* 400 BC

Artist: unknown

Style: late Classical red-figure

Location: The Cleveland Museum of Art, Cleveland, Ohio

Significance: depicts the scene of Medea's escape on a dragon-drawn chariot of the Sun god

---

PRACTICE QUESTIONS: GREECE

1. **a.** Describe why Medea killed her sons. [2]
   b. Give **one** reason why this act made her fearful to a Greek audience. [1]
2. 'Hell hath no fury like a woman scorned.' Using the Flight of Medea Krater (above) and your own knowledge, explain how far the story of Medea agrees with this statement. [8]

ROME

Cleopatra VII was pharaoh of Egypt from 51 to 30 BC, during the final years of the Roman Republic. At this time, Egypt was a **client kingdom** of Rome, and Cleopatra was one of many **client monarchs** that were allied with Rome. Cleopatra became famous throughout the Roman world when she had a love affair with one of Rome's most powerful politicians, Julius Caesar. History has remembered her for her love affair with another Roman politician, Mark Antony.

By the end of her life, Cleopatra was hated and feared by the Romans. How could a client monarch, whose position was subservient to Rome, ever come to inspire such anxiety in the Roman people? Put simply, she was seen to be a threat to the Roman way of life.

> **client kingdom** a state that was allied with, but subject to Rome
>
> **client monarch** the king or queen who was the leader of a client kingdom. A client monarch would be able to rule their own kingdom, but Rome would handle any international relations

Cleopatra comes to power

Cleopatra was born around 69 BC and grew up in the royal household. Her family, the Ptolemies, had ruled Egypt since the death of Alexander the Great in 323 BC and had allied with Rome before Cleopatra's birth, taking on the status of a client kingdom.

FIGURE 1.61
This stele depicts Cleopatra to the right dressed as a pharaoh, presenting offerings to the Egyptian goddess Isis, seated to the left. Not intended as a realistic likeness, the depiction of Cleopatra in male garb is likely meant to represent her power as ruler.

KEY INDIVIDUALS

Cleopatra VII (70/69–30 BC) pharaoh of Egypt, a member of the dynasty of the Ptolemies

Julius Caesar (100–44 BC) very popular Roman politician and general who was elected 'dictator for life' by the Roman Senate, which in effect made him the sole ruler of Rome. Some Senators thought that he was a tyrant who wanted to rule like a king. He was assassinated by a gang of Senators on the 15th March, 44 BC

Mark Antony (83–30 BC) Roman politician and general, one of Julius Caesar's key supporters. After Julius Caesar's assassination, Mark Antony positioned himself as his successor and wanted to take control of Rome for himself

EXPLORE FURTHER

Research the lives of Ptolemy XII (Cleopatra's father) and Berenice (her older sister). What can you learn about the nature of Egyptian government? How did Egyptians feel about female rulers?

Cleopatra became ruler of Egypt jointly with her father, Ptolemy XII in 55 BC. She was only fourteen years old. As she was ruling alongside her father, Cleopatra did not have a great amount of power. Tradition dictated that a man and a woman should rule together, although the female ruler would be subservient to the male ruler. Four years later, Ptolemy XII died, leaving an eighteen-year-old Cleopatra the ruler of Egypt, joint-monarch alongside her younger brother Ptolemy XIII. At this time, Ptolemy XIII was only ten years old. Cleopatra took advantage of her brother's young age, side-lining him and taking the reins of power for herself.

Cleopatra's sole rule was short lived, however, as she was forced to flee Egypt in 48 BC following a palace coup that removed her from power. The conspirators placed Ptolemy XIII on the throne and Cleopatra escaped into exile.

At this time in Rome, a bloody civil war was being fought between two of the leading politician-generals of the age: Pompey and Julius Caesar. Roman politics in the first century BC was characterised by a series of ambitious individuals, each vying for the greatest personal power. Pompey and Julius Caesar had been allies once, but at this point were fighting a war for control of the Roman world.

Following a military defeat, Pompey and his forces fled to the Egyptian capital of Alexandria. Pharaoh Ptolemy ordered Pompey to be killed in an attempt to win the favour of Julius Caesar, who was looking likely to win the war. Pompey was beheaded on the beach in front of his own wife and children on 28th September 48 BC.

Ptolemy's actions backfired, however. When Julius Caesar arrived in Egypt he was not pleased that Pompey had been killed. Pompey had been Julius Caesar's rival in the war, but they had been allies previously. Julius Caesar had wanted to defeat Pompey, but he had not wanted to kill him.

hieroglyphics Egyptian written script

cartouche a rectangle with rounded ends, usually giving the name of a god or king, used in Egyptian inscriptions

FIGURE 1.62
This stone relief depicts Cleopatra wearing a sun headdress – the **hieroglyphics** in the **cartouche** in the top left of the image identify the individual as Cleopatra. Egyptian pharaohs were believed to be divine and typically associated themselves with a particular god or goddess. Cleopatra styled herself as the reincarnation of the goddess Isis. Isis often had a sun headdress in art, hence Cleopatra's headdress in this image.

Pompey had been a prominent Roman politician and Ptolemy, a client monarch, had ordered his death. This could not be allowed to stand, and so Julius Caesar took immediate control of Alexandria. At this point, Cleopatra saw her opportunity to reclaim power. Her younger brother had fallen out of favour with Rome, and so Cleopatra sought to state her case and make her claim to the Egyptian throne directly to Julius Caesar himself.

Cleopatra with Julius Caesar

Cleopatra knew that her best shot at reclaiming the throne of Egypt was to win the support of Julius Caesar, who had taken control of Alexandria and, following the death of Pompey, had been voted dictator of Rome for a period of ten years. But how to get to him? Plutarch tells the story of how Cleopatra gained an audience:

> So Cleopatra, taking only Apollodorus the Sicilian from among her friends, embarked in a little skiff and landed at the palace when it was already getting dark; and as it was impossible to escape notice otherwise, she stretched herself at full length inside a bed-sack, while Apollodorus tied the bed-sack up with a cord and carried it indoors to Caesar. It was by this device of Cleopatra's, it is said, that Caesar was first captivated, for she showed herself to be a bold coquette.

> Plutarch, *Life of Caesar*, 49

Evidently, Cleopatra wanted to meet with Julius Caesar alone and unnoticed. Cleopatra's gambit relied on Julius Caesar preferring her to her brother. By engineering a situation where the two could meet in private, she could work her charm uninterrupted and win him over. We can only surmise what happened between the two on that night, but the meeting ended well for Cleopatra. Julius Caesar declared that Cleopatra should rule jointly with her brother Ptolemy XIII. Cleopatra also became Julius Caesar's mistress (despite the fact that Cleopatra was twenty-one years old at this point in time and Julius Caesar was fifty-two) and, in the following year, gave birth to their son, Ptolemy Caesar (usually called Caesarion).

Just months before Caesarion's birth, Cleopatra's rule was greatly strengthened; in January 47 BC, Ptolemy XIII was killed during a failed attempt to take the throne for himself. In adherence with Egyptian custom, Cleopatra named another brother (Ptolemy XIV) as her co-ruler, but she was essentially in sole control of Egypt from this point. The next year, Cleopatra visited Rome with Caesarion. She was immediately unpopular with the Roman people, as she insisted on being addressed as 'queen'. Romans had an ingrained dislike of monarchs and a Roman citizen would be insulted to be treated as a royal subject.

Moreover, Cleopatra was staying in one of Caesar's country villas. It was plain to see that she was his personal guest and their romantic relationship was well known. As has been discussed in previous topics, it was usual for Roman men to have extra-marital affairs. However, husbands were expected to take mistresses of a low social class so that any children would not have legitimate claim to family power or money. As a foreigner, Cleopatra technically fulfilled this criterion. However, she was one of the most powerful foreigners in the Roman world – queen of a rich state. The people of Rome worried that Cleopatra's influence on Julius Caesar could result in radical changes in Rome.

These worries were somewhat justified. Julius Caesar erected a statue of her in Rome. The statue represented Cleopatra as the Egyptian goddess Isis and was placed in the temple of Venus Genetrix (goddess of motherhood). The Romans did not worship rulers. This statue was seen as symbolic of changes that Julius Caesar was trying to make to Roman culture. The introduction of ruler worship and encouraging Romans to take on the Egyptian custom of identifying rulers with gods was a huge change to Roman religion.

In 44 BC the Roman Senate, eager to curry the favour of Julius Caesar, elected him dictator for life. After taking this post, Julius Caesar was essentially the king of Rome, romantically entangled with the queen of Egypt. Whether this was the result of Cleopatra's influence of Julius Caesar's own ambition is unclear. Regardless of the answer, the fears held by some Romans after Cleopatra's arrival in Rome had come true.

Just a month after his election as dictator for life, Julius Caesar was set upon by a group of conservative Senators on the Ides of March, 44 BC (15th March 44 BC). They stabbed him to death in the Senate House, ending his dictatorship. Cleopatra was still in Rome at this time but, fearful for her life, she returned to Alexandria at the news of her lover's assassination.

Antony and Cleopatra

Shortly after Cleopatra returned to Egypt, in 44 BC, her younger brother Ptolemy XIV died. Some suggested that he had been poisoned by Cleopatra to prevent him from taking power. After Ptolemy's death, Cleopatra made her son Caesarion her co-ruler.

Julius Caesar's assassination had left a power vacuum in Rome. The assassins had hoped that, by removing Julius Caesar, the Senate would reclaim its old, democratic power. But there was no shortage of people who wanted to take Julius Caesar's power for themselves. Soon enough two men rose to prominence: Mark Antony (who had been one of Julius Caesar's political lieutenants) and Octavian (Julius Caesar's young nephew and legal heir). Like Julius Caesar and Pompey before them, these men formed an alliance to help them gain power but, when they found that there was nobody left to overcome, they turned against each other.

In 41 BC, Antony requested Cleopatra to meet with him in Tarsus (in modern day Turkey). He wanted her to ally with him in the upcoming wars. According to Plutarch, Cleopatra went to Tarsus with the intent of not only allying with Antony, but to charm him as she had Julius Caesar:

> She had hopes that she would more easily bring Antony to her feet. For Caesar . . .
> had known her when she was still a girl and inexperienced in affairs, but she was
> going to visit Antony at the very time when women have the most brilliant beauty and
> are at the acme of intellectual power. Therefore she provided herself with many gifts,
> much money, and such ornaments as high position and prosperous kingdom made it
> natural for her to take; but she went putting her greatest confidence in herself, and in
> the charms and sorceries of her own person.

Plutarch, *Life of Antony*, 25

KEY INDIVIDUAL

Octavian (63 BC–AD 14) Julius Caesar's nephew and adopted heir, Octavian positioned himself as his successor and wanted to take control of Rome for himself. After a long period of civil war, in 27 BC he assumed the name Augustus

S
&
C

Cleopatra the great beauty?

Why was Cleopatra so attractive? Modern culture tends to stress Cleopatra's physical beauty as the reason. In the 1920s Cleopatra was used in an advertising campaign by Palmolive™ to sell their soaps. The message of the advert was: this soap will give you beauty like Cleopatra's. Similarly, the 1963 film *Cleopatra* shows the Egyptian queen as a devastatingly beautiful person, whose mere glance can enflame desire. One of the most famous anecdotes regarding Cleopatra is that she bathed in asses' milk to preserve her youth and beauty – again implying that her looks were of great importance.

The fact is, however, that we have no real idea what Cleopatra may have looked like. Ancient images of her are often stylised (as in the case of Figure 1.62 above) and ancient authors do not often mention her beauty.

Plutarch does, however, explain her allure. He does not focus on the physical, but rather compliments her charm in conversation and her ability with languages:

> Converse with her had an irresistible charm, and her presence, combined with the persuasiveness of her discourse and the character which was somehow diffused about her behaviour towards others, had something stimulating about it. There was sweetness also in the tones of her voice; and her tongue, like an instrument of many strings, she could readily turn to whatever language she pleased, so that in her interviews with Barbarians she very seldom had need of an interpreter, but made her replies to most of them herself and unassisted, whether they were Ethiopians, Troglodytes, Hebrews, Arabians, Syrians, Medes or Parthians. Nay, it is said that she knew the speech of many other peoples also, although the kings of Egypt before her had not even made an effort to learn the native language, and some actually gave up their Macedonian dialect.
>
> Plutarch, *Life of Antony*, 27

Cleopatra succeeded in her seduction of Antony and he chose to spend the winter of 41–40 with her in Egypt. The following year Cleopatra gave birth to twins, the children of Antony.

In 36 BC Antony married Cleopatra in Egypt, despite the fact that he was already married to Octavia, a Roman noblewoman. This went directly against Roman customs, which allowed men to have affairs, but did not allow bigamy. Antony setup a household in Alexandria, living with Cleopatra for most of the year. This act caused a scandal in Rome. Now that Antony and Cleopatra were married, any children she had would have a claim to Antony's property and his power. It seemed likely that, if Antony won the war against Octavian, that Rome would be ruled by a foreign queen and, after Antony's death, continue to be ruled by his foreign children.

Roman politicians and writers thought that Antony had lost his senses. He had been a fine, upstanding Roman citizen and Senator. And now he was putting his own interests and his love for Cleopatra first. There was even a rumour that he intended to move the

centre of the Roman Empire away from Rome to Alexandria. Plutarch sums up Roman feeling towards Cleopatra:

> Antony, where now as a crowning evil his love for Cleopatra supervened, roused and drove to frenzy many of the passions that were still hidden and quiescent in him, and dissipated and destroyed whatever good and saving qualities still offered resistance. And he was taken captive in this manner'.
>
> Plutarch, *Life of Antony*, 25

Antony and Cleopatra became symbols of the madness of love, and Cleopatra herself was seen as a corrupting force that robbed Antony of his Roman dignity and masculine self-control.

Donations of Alexandria

In 34 BC Antony and Cleopatra held a public event in Alexandria known as the Donations of Alexandria. This was in celebration of a victory Antony had won over the Parthians the previous year.

The Donations of Alexandria were based on a traditional Roman triumph (a parade given to celebrate a military victory) but with some significant changes. Most importantly, it was held in Alexandria, not Rome. This was seen as proof that Cleopatra had convinced Antony to move the centre of the Empire to Egypt. Cleopatra herself also took a central position in the parade, seated on a golden throne among her people. This implied that she was responsible for the victory as well as Antony. He also named her 'Queen of Kings', a title that clearly conveyed that she was *not* a traditional, subservient Roman matrona and that also suggested that she was more powerful than Antony himself.

At the Donations of Alexandria, Antony named Cleopatra the ruler of Cyprus as well as Egypt. He also gave kingdoms in Syria, Cyrenaica and Armenia to his children by Cleopatra. As a Roman general, Antony should have given these realms to Rome so that the city could govern them and benefit from their riches. By giving them to Cleopatra and his children he was essentially betraying Rome.

Civil war with Octavian

In 33 BC, relations between Antony and his former ally Octavian broke down completely. Octavian convinced the Senate to declare war on Cleopatra. This was a masterstroke by Octavian, as it allowed him to wage war against his political rival Antony, but also played into the hands of popular opinion in Rome, where Cleopatra was viewed as a danger and Antony's downfall.

The decisive battle of this conflict was the Battle of Actium, fought at sea off the coast of Greece. Octavian's forces, backed by the Senate, faced off against Antony's loyal legions and Cleopatra's own fleet. A short time into the battle Octavian's fleet got the upper hand and Cleopatra ordered her own fleet to retreat. This was the turning point that allowed Octavian to claim victory. Both Antony and Cleopatra survived and retreated to Alexandria, but Octavian had won the war and Egypt was his for the taking.

Years later, after Octavian had taken total control of the Roman Empire for himself and renamed himself Augustus, he commissioned the poet Virgil to write an epic poem celebrating the founding of Rome. The hero of the story, Aeneas, is given a shield by the gods and on it are depicted the great people and events that will come to pass once Rome has been founded. In the very middle of the shield, in pride of place, is a depiction of the Battle of Actium. This passage is a piece of propaganda in favour of Octavian and so the depictions of Antony and Cleopatra are not flattering.

Virgil introduces the forces of Antony and Cleopatra by using the word 'barbarian'. This word implies that Antony, Cleopatra and their soldiers were less civilised than Augustus Caesar's Roman forces. This could be seen as a direct insult or it could be read as meaning that Cleopatra and her forces were a dangerous foe because they lacked restraint and civility.

Virgil also suggests that Cleopatra's forces were disordered when he says that the warriors were in 'all different kinds of armour'. Roman legions would all have had similar uniform, identifying them as part of the mighty and organised Roman army. As Antony and Cleopatra's gaggle of Eastern forces are all in different armour, Virgil suggests that they come from different places and that they lack discipline. This seems, again, to be an insult to their leadership and a reference to the popular Roman idea that Antony and Cleopatra spent more time entertaining themselves than they did governing and leading.

ACTIVITY

Imagine you are a Roman citizen at the time of Antony's marriage to Cleopatra. Write a letter to a friend expressing your feelings about the marriage. Try to refer to specific events and aspects of Roman culture.

PRESCRIBED SOURCE

Aeneid, 8.671–713

Date: *c.* 18 BC

Author: Virgil

Genre: epic poetry

Significance: the great Roman epic poem – a successor to Homer's *Iliad* and *Odyssey*

Read it here: OCR source booklet

Virgil does not name Cleopatra in this passage, referring to her only as Antony's 'Egyptian wife', calling her an 'outrage'. This conveys the strength of Virgil and his Roman audience's negative feelings towards Cleopatra. Everyone knows who she is, so she does not need to be named.

She is shown to be directing the warships by shaking her 'timbrels' (similar to a tambourine). As discussed in previous topics, women were not expected to fight on the battlefield and they were certainly not expected to lead men. The fact that she does could suggest that she is personally very commanding and dangerous, having bent the male warriors to her will and made them submit to her.

At line 705, Cleopatra begins her retreat, causing all of the Eastern forces to fall back to Egypt, represented by the Nile, who has been personified as welcoming the defeated forces into his robe.

ACTIVITY

Read the prescribed lines of Virgil's *Aeneid* Book 8. Make a list of words and phrases that Virgil uses to describe Augustus and Agrippa, the Roman generals. For each, briefly comment on the effect that they create (e.g. 'radiant' makes Augustus seem to be shining like a god or like the sun; this conveys him positively and like a hero). Overall, how does Virgil portray Augustus and Agrippa in this scene? Then repeat this process, considering how Virgil has chosen to present Antony and Cleopatra.

Cleopatra's death

Antony and Cleopatra retreated to Alexandria following the battle of Actium. In the following year, 30 BC, Octavian marched on Alexandria and Antony's remaining forces defected to Octavian. After this, Antony killed himself. Cleopatra killed herself shortly afterward. Writers have romanticised this event, suggesting that Cleopatra, like an ancient Juliet, killed herself for love. We know that Octavian had ordered her to be taken alive, so it seems far more likely that Cleopatra killed herself to avoid the humiliation of being taken as a slave and paraded through the streets of Rome as part of Octavian's triumph.

We do not know for sure how Cleopatra died. The most popular version of events is that she allowed an Egyptian asp or cobra to bite her. Plutarch gives various accounts of what happened:

> It is said that the asp was brought with those figs and leaves and lay hidden beneath them, for thus Cleopatra had given orders, that the reptile might fasten itself upon her body without her being aware of it. But when she took away some of the figs and saw it, she said: 'There it is, you see,' and baring her arm she held it out for the bite. But others say that the asp was kept carefully shut up in a water jar, and that while

Cleopatra was stirring it up and irritating it with a golden distaff it sprang and fastened itself upon her arm. But the truth of the matter no one knows; for it was also said that she carried about poison in a hollow comb and kept the comb hidden in her hair; and yet neither spot nor other sign of poison broke out upon her body. Moreover, not even was the reptile seen within the chamber, though people said they saw some traces of it near the sea, where the chamber looked out upon it with its windows. And some also say that Cleopatra's arm was seen to have two slight and indistinct punctures; and this Caesar also seems to have believed. For in his triumph an image of Cleopatra herself with the asp clinging to her was carried in the procession. These, then, are the various accounts of what happened.

Plutarch, *Life of Antony*, 86

After Cleopatra's death, Egypt became an official Roman province under the control of Octavian. He continued to stress the danger that Cleopatra had posed to the Roman people. An extract from the Sibylline Oracles survives and was published after Cleopatra's death:

And thereupon shall the whole world be governed by the hands of a woman and obedient everywhere. Then when a widow shall o'er all the world gain the rule . . . Then all the elements shall be bereft of order . . . There shall flow a tireless cataract of raging fire, and it shall burn the land, and burn the sea, and heavenly sky, and night, and day, and melt creation itself together.

Sibylline Oracles, 3.92–109

Although she is not named, the woman who would govern the world is Cleopatra. This oracle tells what would have happened had Antony and Cleopatra defeated Octavian and taken control of the Roman world. The scene surely could only increase Cleopatra's image as a dangerous, foreign woman.

ACTIVITY

For each of the following stages of Cleopatra's life, rate how much personal power she had on a scale from 1–10:

- Early life as a princess of Egypt
- As co-ruler of Egypt with her father
- As co-ruler with Ptolemy XIII before her exile
- During exile
- For the duration of her relationship with Julius Caesar
- Immediately following Julius Caesar's death
- For the duration of her relationship with Mark Antony.

You might like to chart your decisions on a line graph, to see the overall trend of her power.

PRACTICE QUESTIONS: ROME

Source A: *Dio, Roman History, XLII.34.4–6*

For she was a woman of surpassing beauty, and at that time, when she was in the prime of her youth, she was most striking; she also possessed a most charming voice and a knowledge of how to make herself agreeable to every one. Being brilliant to look upon and to listen to, with the power to subjugate every one, even a love-sated man already past his prime, she thought that it would be in keeping with her role to meet Caesar, and she reposed in her beauty all her claims to the throne. She asked therefore for admission to his presence, and on obtaining permission adorned and beautified herself so as to appear before him in the most majestic and at the same time pity-inspiring guise. When she had perfected her schemes she entered the city (for she had been living outside of it), and by night without Ptolemy's knowledge went into the palace.

1. What was the name of Cleopatra's son with Julius Caesar? [1]

2. Julius Caesar dedicated a statue of Cleopatra in the Temple of Venus Genetrix. Why was this scandalous? [1]

3. Why do you think Cleopatra was so attractive to both Julius Caesar and Mark Antony? Use **Source A** and your own knowledge in your answer. [8]

TOPIC REVIEW

You should be able to:

1. Describe:
   - how Medea met and fell in love with Jason
   - what happened to make Medea turn against Jason and her plot to get revenge on him
   - what happened to remove Cleopatra's brother from power and establish her as the sole ruler of Egypt
   - Cleopatra's relationships with Julius Caesar and with Mark Antony
   - the story of Cleopatra's suicide, according to Plutarch.

2. Explain:
   - why the Greeks thought of Medea as a 'barbarian'
   - how Euripides characterised Medea in his play, *Medea*
   - how Medea's behaviour went against the expectations for a 'good Greek woman'
   - why the idea of being ruled by a foreign monarch would have terrified the Roman people
   - how Virgil presents Cleopatra in the *Aeneid*
   - how Cleopatra's behaviour went against the expectations of a 'good Roman woman'.

PRACTICE QUESTIONS: COMPARING GREECE AND ROME

These questions are based on two stimulus sources, one from Greece and one from Rome. The sources could be extracts from prescribed sources or unseen.

Source A (Greek): *Apollonius Rhodius, 4.1654–72*

"Listen to me," [Medea] said. "I think that I and I alone can get the better of that man, whoever he may be, unless there is immortal life in that bronze body. All I ask of you is to stay here keeping the ship out of range of his rocks till I have brought him down."

They took the ship out of range, as Medea had asked, and rested on their oars waiting to see what marvellous device she would employ. Medea went up on the deck. She covered both her cheeks with a fold of her purple mantle, and Jason led her by the hand as she passed across the benches. Then, with incantations, she invoked the Keres (Spirits of Death), the swift hounds of Hades who feed on souls and haunt the lower air to pounce on living men. She sank to her knees and called upon them, three times in song, three times with spoken prayers. She steeled herself of their malignity and bewitched the eyes of Talos with the evil in her own. She flung at him the full force of her malevolence, and in an ecstasy of rage she plied him with images of death.

Source B (Roman): *Egyptian stele*

1. Explain who seems to be the more powerful woman in these sources, Medea or Cleopatra? [6]
2. Whose 'foreignness' is stressed more by the ancient sources, Medea's or Cleopatra's? [15]

Further Reading

Blundell, S. (1998) *Women in Classical Athens*. Bristol: Bristol Classical Press

Chrystal, P. (2015) *Roman Women: The Women Who Influenced the History of Rome*. Stroud: Fonthill Media

Fantham, E. (1995) *Women in the Classical World: Image and Text*. New York: Oxford University Press

Haward, A. (2006) *Penelope to Poppaea*. Bristol: Bristol Classical Press

Lefkowitz, M. R. and Fant, M. B. (2013) *Women's Life in Greece and Rome: A Source Book in Translation*. London: Bloomsbury

MacLachlan, B. (2012) *Women in Ancient Greece: A Sourcebook*. London: Bloomsbury

MacLachlan, B (2014) *Women in Ancient Rome: A Sourcebook*. London: Bloomsbury

Pomeroy, S. B. (2015) *Goddesses, Whores, Wives and Slaves: Women in Classical Antiquity*. London: Bodley Head

What to Expect in the Exam for Women in the Ancient World

This section aims to show you the types of questions you are likely to get in the written examination. It offers some advice on how to answer the questions and will help you avoid common errors.

THE EXAMINATION

This component of the GCSE examination is designed to test your knowledge, understanding and evaluation (analysis) of the lives of women in the ancient world. The examination is worth 90 marks and lasts 1 hour and 30 minutes. This represents 50% of the total marks for the GCSE.

There are three sections to the paper, one on Greece, the second on Rome and the third on Greece and Rome. Each section is worth 30 marks. The question paper will consist of both short-answer and extended-response questions. You will be required to respond to both literary and visual/material sources, some of which will be from the prescribed material, and some you will not have seen before. In the third section of the paper you will be required to compare two ancient sources, one Greek, one Roman, one of which will be literary, the other visual/material.

There are two Assessment Objectives in your GCSE in Classical Civilisation. Questions will be designed to test these areas. These Assessment Objectives are explained in the table below:

	Assessment Objective	Marks
AO1	Demonstrate knowledge and understanding of: • literature and visual/material culture from the classical world • how sources reflect their cultural contexts • possible interpretations of sources by different audiences and individuals.	58
AO2	Analyse, interpret and evaluate literature and visual/material culture from the classical world, using evidence and producing coherent and reasoned arguments.	32

For AO1 in this component, you will need to demonstrate the following:

- A good range of accurate and relevant knowledge of the lives, roles and representation of women in Greece and Rome.

- A detailed understanding of the prescribed sources, including the ability to discuss different types of sources and their characteristic features.
- An understanding of the cultural contexts of Greece and Rome in relation to the sources and issues raised by the course.
- An understanding of some different possible interpretations of the sources and the various conclusions that can be drawn from these.

For AO2 in this component, you will need to demonstrate that you can analyse, interpret and evaluate the sources you have studied, giving opinions and backing them up with evidence, for example:

- Sound analysis of sources and factual evidence to reach and support reasoned opinions about the lives, roles and representation of women in Greece and Rome.
- Appropriate evaluation of different sources and factual evidence to provide reasoned ideas.
- The ability to compare Greek and Roman sources and ideas and to reach conclusions about the similarity and difference of these two societies.

QUESTION TYPES

All questions, apart from extended-response questions (see pp. 140–3), will be linked to an ancient source. These will be a mixture of literary and visual/material sources. Some will be prescribed sources that you will have studied beforehand and others will be 'unseen' sources, which you will need to study in the exam.

There are five types of questions that will feature in your exam. The question types are listed in the table below, which identifies where in the exam the questions will appear.

They are arranged into two categories: knowledge and understanding, significance, and stimulus questions are all short-answer questions; detailed-response questions and extended-response questions, require a longer answer.

Section	Question type	Number of marks available
Section A: Greece	Knowledge and understanding questions	16
	Significance questions	6
	Detailed-response question	8
Section B: Rome	Knowledge and understanding questions	16
	Significance questions	6
	Detailed-response question	8
Section C: Greece & Rome	Stimulus questions	15
	Extended-response question	15

Knowledge and understanding questions

There will be 16-marks' worth of knowledge and understanding questions (all AO1). The 16 marks will be broken down into a series of short-answer questions, typically worth 1, 2 or 3 marks.

Some questions will require you to show your **knowledge** of an aspect of women's lives, roles and representation or of a prescribed source. Other questions will require you to show **knowledge** and *also* demonstrate an **understanding** of these facts.

There will be a **stimulus** (an extract from a literary source or a visual/material source) to assist you.

For example, you might be shown this image with the following questions:

Question 1: Where did prince Paris come from? [1]

Answer: Troy [1]

Correctly stating that Paris came from Troy is a piece of knowledge. This answer should be brief. There is in fact no need to write full sentences for this type of answer if it seems that only a single word or a phrase is needed.

Question 2: Why was Paris and Helen's love scandalous? [2]

Answer: Helen was already married to Menelaus when she met Paris [1]. Women in ancient Greece were expected to stay faithful to their husbands [1], so Helen's preference for Paris scandalously went against what society expected her to do [1].

Being able to explain why Paris and Helen's affair went against the expectations of ancient Greek society shows your understanding of events and of the context. This sort of developed explanation should usually be phrased in full sentences to make sure that your meaning is clear. Question 2 is worth two marks, so this kind of developed explanation is an appropriate length. An equally good approach would be to give two simple or undeveloped ideas. For example:

Answer: Helen was already married [1]. Paris was a guest in Menelaus' house when he and Helen fell in love [1].

In this case, there is more than one acceptable correct answer, and you will not be penalised for making more points than the number of marks available. However, if you are asked to only give a certain number of facts, or make a certain number of points, you should stick to the instructions. In this type of question, each correct fact or opinion is worth one mark. You will not be asked to evaluate ideas (e.g. whether you think Helen was right to go with Paris, or whether the pot is well painted), so do not waste time in doing so.

Significance questions

There will be two of these questions in both Section A and Section B. Significance questions are split into two parts. You will be asked to give two pieces of information (2 marks AO1) and state why one or both are important or significant, or what this knowledge tells us (1 mark AO2). Examples are given below.

'Sappho' fresco of an educated upper class 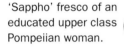 Pompeiian woman.

Question: **a.** List two things a Roman girl would have learned from
a litterator.   [2]
b. Why was the litterator important to a Roman girl's education?   [1]

There are various possible answers for the first part, including reading, writing and/or arithmetic. For the second part, this might lead to the idea that the litterator equipped a girl with the mathematical skills to help with finances and running a family business if she was from a poorer family. Equally valid, you might say that the literator helped a girl to read and this would enable her to enjoy literature, which would help her to seem witty and intelligent at a dinner party. Either of these ideas would gain the mark available.

For part (a) we are looking for knowledge about how a girl was educated. For part (b) we are looking for why she was educated in this way.

Detailed-response questions

You will get one of these questions in both Section A and Section B – with one or more sources to prompt you. This stimulus is meant only as a starting point, and it will be clear from the question that you will need to bring in **extra information and examples**.

Four marks are awarded for your knowledge and understanding (AO1), and four marks given for your analysis, interpretation and evaluation of your facts and understanding (AO2). It is important to remember that for AO1 you will need to show knowledge and understanding of a source's context and the different ways people interpret the sources.

These questions are marked in a different way, however; you are not given one mark for each correct opinion and each piece of evidence, but the answer as a whole is marked using a Levels of Response Grid. A Levels of Response Grid explains to examiners what answers may look like to achieve a certain number of marks. An examiner will read the whole answer and check the grid to work out what level the answer belongs to. It is important to remember that the quality of your answer is more important than the amount you have written. The Levels of Response Grid is included in the mark schemes for exam papers.

Remember that you can examine both sides of an argument. For example, if you are asked whether a Roman wedding would have been enjoyable to attend, there are likely to be arguments on both sides of the question. It may be that it would have largely been an enjoyable event but have some unpleasant aspects, or that you largely do not think it would have been enjoyable but may have had some redeeming features. If you do not examine both sides of an argument, you may have missed some key facts, and your answer may not show a full evaluation.

This question is not meant to be an essay. You are advised not to write an introduction that simply outlines how you will write your response as this will not add anything to your answer and will take up valuable time. You may find you have more to say than time allows, so you might have to be disciplined in moving on. Make your key points at the start, keep to the point, and if you do choose to have a conclusion, keep it brief, as you will ideally have answered the precise wording of the question throughout your answer.

It is not necessary to have a conclusion to gain full marks.

An example of a question is given below.

'The most powerful woman in all of Greece.' How far do you agree with this assessment of the power of the Pythia? Use the source as a starting point and your own knowledge in your answer. [8]

In order to show you know about the Pythia you might include some of these facts:

- Delphi was a panhellenic site sacred to all Greeks.
- She was believed to be the most reliable oracle.
- People would visit from far and wide to ask her questions.
- Prophecies were believed to have come from the god Apollo, after the Pythia was put into a trance by use of fumes and/or drugs.
- The Temple of Apollo was attended by male priests, who may have interpreted the utterances of the Pythia.
- The Pythia had to serve at the Temple of Apollo for the rest of her life.

You then need to explain what you feel this says about her power, with possible ideas being:

- She had great influence because so many people believed in her power.
- She had great influence because of her reputation for accuracy.
- Her influence was limited by the fact that she only answered questions that she was asked.
- If she was intoxicated when she gave prophecies, then she was influential but not powerful, since she did not have control over what she said.
- If the male priests interpreted her utterances, then they were the ones with the power, since they decided what answers would be given.

Half the marks are awarded for AO1 and for AO2, but this does not necessarily mean that you should give four facts and four explanations. Examiners will read your whole response and judge how good they feel it is overall.

Stimulus questions

These questions will only be asked in Section C, the **Greece and Rome** section of the examination. You will be given a series of questions that will ask you to identify something relevant from the stimuli given, and to analyse what you have recognised.

While your Literature and Culture exam also contains stimulus questions, the ones in Women in the Ancient World are slightly different as they have more marks for AO2 than AO1. To indicate this, they all use the command word 'explain'; suggesting that you need to expand a little more on your analysis and explain your ideas more fully.

These questions will add up to a total of fifteen marks, with each question carrying **three** marks; **one** mark for AO1 and **two** marks for AO2. You will be given one literary **and** one visual source from the Greek **and** Roman world. Thus, if you are given a Greek literary source it will be accompanied by a Roman visual source, and vice-versa.

An example of a question is given below.

Source A: *Amazonomachy Frieze, Mausoleum at Halicarnassus*

Source B: *Virgil's* Aeneid, *Book 11*

No city would accept him within their houses or their walls, (nor would he in his savagery have given himself up to them) he passed his life among shepherds on the lonely mountains. Here, among the thickets of savage lairs, he nourished his child at the udders of a mare from the herd, and milk from wild creatures, squeezing the teats into her delicate mouth. As soon as the infant had taken her first steps, he placed a sharp lance in her hands, and hung bow and quiver from the little one's shoulder. A tiger's pelt hung over head and down her back instead of a gold clasp for her hair, and a long trailing robe. Even then she was hurling childish spears with tender hand, whirling a smooth-thonged sling round her head, bringing down Strymonian cranes and snowy swans. Many a mother in Etruscan fortresses wished for her as a daughter-in-law in vain: she, pure, content with Diana alone, cherished her love of her weapons and maidenhood.

Question:	Explain how both sources give a positive portrayal of warrior women. [6]
Answer:	**One** from:

The Amazonomachy frieze shows: An Amazon standing over a male warrior with her weapon raised [1], an Amazon is riding a horse [1], two Amazons shown fighting closely together [1].

Plus one from:

Virgil's *Aeneid* shows: Camilla's close relationship with her father [1], she learned to use weapons from an early age [1], she has a gold clasp in her hair [1], she hunts birds successfully [1], the mothers of Etruscan boys wanted her for a daughter-in-law [1], she has a close relationship with Diana and cherishes her maidenhood [1].

Four from:

The Amazonomachy frieze: Confidently wielding a weapon implies that the Amazon is a skilled warrior [1]. Having control of the horse also implies a level of skill on the battlefield [1]. Also implies she is skilled enough to have trained the horse [1]. The man's cowering position implies that the Amazons are more powerful than him [1]. This is a great compliment to the Amazon, as Greek men viewed themselves as the superior gender and the superior race in their world so it elevates them to (if not above) his level [1].

Virgil's Aeneid: Fathers were highly respected in Roman households so Camilla's close relationship with her father shows that she is appropriately respectful of him [1]. Camilla learning to use weapons from a young age show that she was eager to improve her skills [1]. Camilla and her father lived in the wilds – her learning to wield weapons from a young age show she was willing and able to contribute to her 'household' [1]. Gold clasp in her hair emphasises her beauty [1]. Hunting was a popular pursuit amongst men (and of the goddess Diana) – Camilla's hunting birds likens her to these positive figures [1]. If mothers of Etruscan boys want her for a daughter-in-law then Camilla must have been desirable [1]. The Romans sought to have a close relationship with their gods because they believed that the gods would bless and protect them – Camilla cherishing Diana shows her devotion to the gods [1]. The Romans believed that female chastity was powerful – Camilla prizing her maidenhood maintains her pudicitia – it also likens her to Diana [1].

The question is out of six marks, so your answer needs to contain **two** marks for AO1 and **four** marks for AO2.

The question asks you about both sources, so be aware that you need to give equal attention to both sources. Even if you were to list several correct points focusing only on the Amazonomachy frieze, you could only get four of the available marks.

Extended-response questions

You will only need to do one extended-response question in this exam, and this is in Section C. This type of question is different from all the other questions in two respects: there is no stimulus passage to introduce it, and you will be given a **choice** of questions to answer (there will be two on the paper and you answer **one** of these). However, it is marked using a Levels of Response Grid in the same way as the detailed-response question.

Five marks are awarded for your knowledge and understanding (AO1), and ten marks given for your analysis, interpretation and evaluation of your facts and understanding (AO2). This means more marks are awarded for how good your argument is than for simply what you know. Therefore, you might want to spend a bit of time thinking about the structure of your answer. As for the detailed-response question, it is important to remember that for AO1 you will need to show knowledge and understanding of the literary and historical context of sources and the different ways people interpret them.

Extended-response questions will cover a wider area than detailed-response questions. You will be expected to bring together your knowledge and understanding of both Greek and Roman cultures and will directly compare the societies with regard to a particular aspect of the course, and reach a judgement about them.

The following is an example of a possible extended-response question.

Question: In which society did women wield the most political power, Greece or Rome? Justify your response. [15]

To answer this question you should mention the ways in which women could be involved in politics in both societies. You might include some of these facts:

- In both societies, women were excluded from the main mechanisms of government (Assembly in Greece, Senate in Rome).
- In both societies, women could protest (example of the trial of Agnodice in Athens, or the repeal of the Oppian Law in Rome).
- In both societies, women could have indirect power through their male associates (examples of specific women who held sway over their male associates would be credited).
- In Rome, women were allowed to attend dinner parties and discuss political issues with men.
- In Greece, the idea of women being involved in politics was seen as ridiculous and used as the basis for comedy.
- In Rome, we have evidence of women being involved in political conspiracies (Sempronia).

Throughout your writing you need to analyse which society gave women more room to have political influence. You could make such arguments as:

- Roman women had more influence because being allowed to attend dinner parties gave them the opportunity to convince their male friends and relatives to advocate on their behalf.
- Roman women had more influence because they enjoyed more freedom in their daily lives and so they could more easily be involved in conspiracies to try to influence politics. However, Sempronia's involvement in the Catilinarian Conspiracy shows limited power, since the plot failed.
- Greek women had less influence because the very idea that women could be involved in government was seen, by Aristophanes, as ludicrous. His comedy play the *Assemblywomen* is only funny if the audience believed that women could not be in power.
- Greek women had more influence because their protest at the trial of Agnodice managed to get the woman acquitted straightaway, whereas the Roman women's protest regarding the Oppian Law only managed to inspire a second debate – it was the men who successfully argued to have the law repealed.

Remember that examiners will read your whole response and judge how good they feel it is overall.

Key points

The following applies to both detailed-response questions and extended-response questions:

- Your facts must be **relevant**. Do not merely state everything you know about a particular topic.
- It is a common mistake to over-narrate examples and to retell a whole story. You should instead **summarise** the main points of a story, or focus in detail on one or two parts of it. This is particularly important in your extended-response answer, where five marks are available for your knowledge, but ten marks are given for your evaluation, interpretation and analysis.
- Show that you **understand** things from an ancient point of view wherever possible. For example, people in ancient Greece and Rome had very different views regarding prostitution from ours today. Show that you understand these differences in context through explanation of the facts.
- Evaluation is best done throughout the response. **Keep referring back** to the title in your essay to do this. If you give all your facts, and then give all your opinions, it is easy to miss something out, or to run out of time.
- Try to find a **balance** of ideas as the question will usually require you to argue both for and against an idea.
- Sometimes a piece of evidence can be taken two ways. If so, remember to give **both interpretations** in order to show a high level of understanding.
- You will not have a lot of time to do these questions and so it is always best to make your most important arguments first in case you find yourself running out of time.
- Ultimately make your conclusion **logical**, and supported by evidence from your whole answer, not just one part of it.

Look at these two extracts from an essay.

Question: Whose story do you find to be more tragic, Penthesilea's or Camilla's? [15]

Extract 1

Penthesilea's story is highly tragic. Before the Trojan War she accidentally killed her sister Hippolyta, which made her very upset. She did not want to go on living and so she went to Troy in search of a glorious death on the battlefield. She did not have to wait long – in the first day after her arrival in Troy she met Achilles and he killed her in a one-on-one duel. What happened to her in life and the manner of her death makes her story highly tragic. On the other hand, Camilla's story is not that tragic. She was raised in the forest by her father, who taught her to fight and hunt. She fought alongside Turnus in his war against Aeneas, but ultimately she was killed by a warrior named Arruns. Camilla's patron goddess was Diana, who avenged her death by sending a nymph to kill Arruns. On balance, I think that Camilla had a nicer life than Penthesilea.

Extract 2

Although both Penthesilea and Camilla were killed in battle, Penthesilea's motivation for fighting makes her story more tragic than Camilla's. Before the Trojan war Penthesilea had killed her own sister in a hunting accident. The guilt Penthesilea felt over this act drove her to fight at Troy – she was looking for a glorious death on the battlefield. It is tragic to think that, following her sister's death, Penthesilea felt so guilty that all she wanted was to die herself. This is even more tragic, considering the fact that Hippolyta's death was an accident and Penthesilea was not really to blame. Contrastingly, Camilla was not looking for death on the battlefield. She answered the call from Turnus and willingly went to help him fight against Aeneas' army and to win glory for herself. The tone of Camilla's story is therefore much brighter than Penthesilea's, and it feels less tragic overall. On the other hand, Camilla's story could be seen as more tragic since she did not want to die but Penthesilea did. By being killed in a one-on-one duel by Achilles, Penthesilea won glory for herself, which is what she wanted. Camilla wanted glory, but she also wanted to survive the war – as evidenced by her stopping to take the armour of her defeated enemies. On balance, I still think that Penthesilea's story is more tragic – she may have got what she wanted, but to wish for death is highly tragic.

Notice how the first extract spends more time on presenting the facts than giving opinions, and many of the facts are unnecessary. The evaluation is not developed fully, and the final statement is irrelevant to the question. The second extract is much more balanced. It argues both sides and flows smoothly from one story to another, providing alternative interpretations of episodes.

GENERAL EXAM SKILLS

When you are sitting the examination, read the instructions carefully so that you realise which questions are compulsory and which are optional (the only option you have is which of the two extended response questions you choose to answer). Remember that the examination will have a range of difficulty of questions; some of it is designed to be challenging, and you should not be panicked if you cannot think of an answer immediately. The following pieces of advice may seem obvious, but you should not underestimate their importance:

- The examination lasts 90 minutes and is worth 90 marks. Do not assume this means you should spend a minute per mark: in reality a lot of short questions will take less than a mark a minute and you should spend longer than a mark a minute on the long questions.

- Each section is worth 30 marks. Do not spend too long on whichever you choose to do first, especially if you like the questions that have been set and feel you could say a lot.
- If you see a question that you do not know the answer to, move on quickly to another question and do not waste time thinking. Leave enough time to go back to it as during the examination you might well remember the answer.
- Stick to the question: if you are asked for facts, do not give opinions and vice versa.
- Do not try to answer a slightly different question if you wish another had been set, or if you have practised a similar one before at school.
- For detailed-response and extended-response questions, present different interpretations.
- More marks are available in the paper for opinions than knowledge or understanding. It is vital that you do not over-narrate.

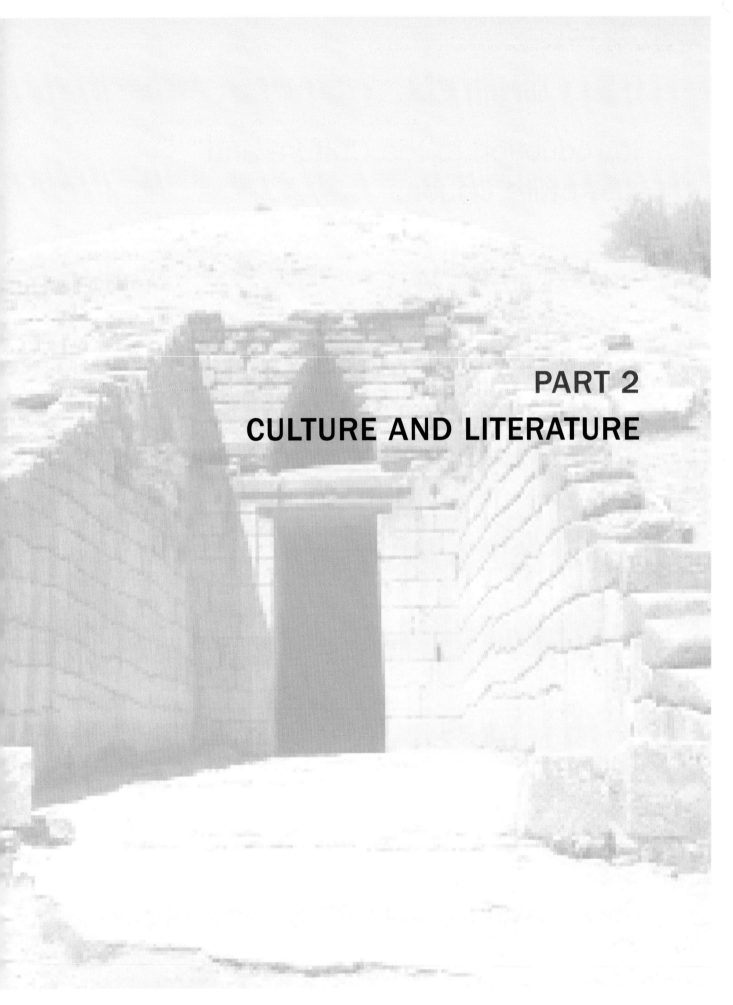

PART 2
CULTURE AND LITERATURE

Introduction to the Culture and Literature Options

Half of your GCSE in Classical Civilisation involves the study of an aspect of ancient culture combining a cultural depth study with reading and analysis of ancient literature in translation.

OCR offers the choice of one of three options:

The Homeric World	J199/21
Roman City Life	J199/22
War and Warfare	J199/23

The following pages of this textbook include all the content needed to study all three of these options, but you will only study one of them.

EXAM OVERVIEW

Your assessment for the Literature and Culture option will be:

50% of the GCSE	1 hr 30 mins	90 marks

50 marks will test AO1: demonstrate knowledge and understanding of:

- literature and visual/material culture from the classical world
- how sources reflect their cultural contexts, and
- possible interpretations of sources by different audiences and individuals.

40 marks will test AO2: analyse, interpret and evaluate literature and visual/material culture from the classical world, using evidence and producing coherent and reasoned arguments.

The Literature and Culture paper is divided into two sections:

Section A	Culture	45 marks
Section B	Literature	45 marks

Each section has five question types:

- knowledge-and-understanding questions
- significance questions
- stimulus questions
- 8-mark detailed-response question
- 15-mark extended-response essay

You can read more about these question types for each component in the three What to Expect in the Exam Chapters, pp. 233, 345 and 453.

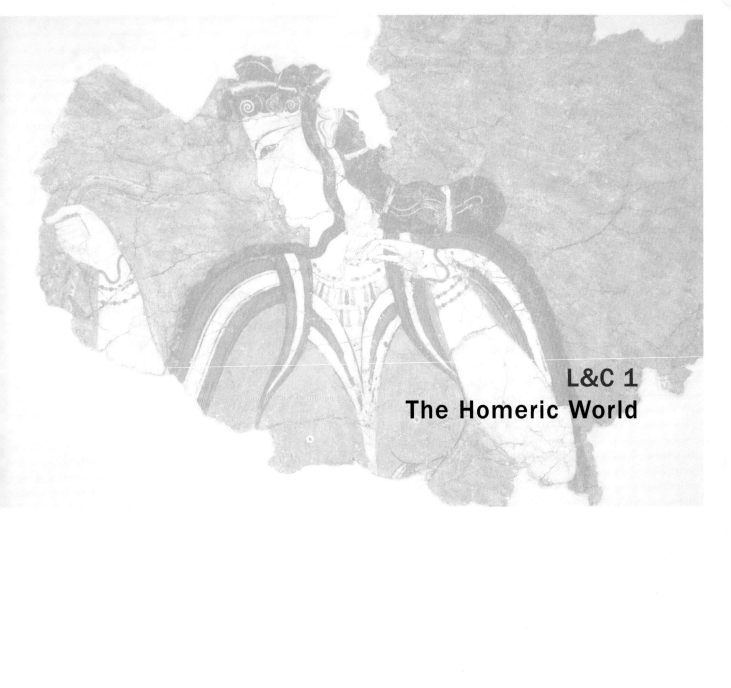

L&C 1
The Homeric World

Introduction to the Homeric World

This component is based around life in ancient Greece just over three thousand years ago. The Culture half of the topic covers the ancient civilisation known as the Mycenaean Age. You will study some of the main Mycenaean sites and the items that made these places so remarkable. From tiny objects like rings, to huge city walls, you will study a variety of source material to find out what life was like at the time.

In the Literature half, you will read five books (the equivalent of modern chapters) from Homer's poem, the *Odyssey*. You will read some of the most important parts of the *Odyssey*, including the stories of the giant Polyphemus and the witch Circe, and Odysseus' encounter with his rivals, the suitors, in his palace. You will look at these characters, and other key figures, and the themes that feature throughout the poem, such as hospitality, civilisation and trickery. You will find out about how Homer composed the poem and the literary style he uses in it, which has influenced many writers throughout history.

EXAM OVERVIEW — J199/21

Your examination will require you to show knowledge and understanding of the material you have studied (AO1) and will require you to analyse and evaluate it (AO2), giving your opinions on areas such as characters in the literature or objects in the culture.

This component makes up 50% of your GCSE. In this component 50 marks will test your AO1 skills and 40 marks will test your AO2 skills.

There will be a distinct section of questions on the Mycenaean Age, and a distinct section on the literature. Neither section will ask questions requiring knowledge of the other: for example, you will not be asked how far the *Odyssey* confirms knowledge of what life in the Mycenaean Age was like.

In both sections you will be asked to answer a series of short factual questions, based around images or around passages from Homer. Some of these will also ask for your opinions. You will be required to write longer answers in each section, worth 8 marks and 15 marks, showing knowledge and giving opinions. There will be 45 marks' worth of questions on Mycenae, and 45 marks' worth on Homer. You will have a choice of longer questions worth 15 marks in each section, but all other questions will be compulsory.

Culture

2.1 Key Sites

Cities in the Mycenaean Age were small by modern standards, often having an area similar to a small village today. However, these cities had a lot of different areas packed into them, including palaces, defences and burial grounds. In this section you will read about some of the major cities of the Mycenaean Age.

THE CONCEPT AND DATING OF THE MYCENAEAN AGE

Mycenaean a civilisation that was powerful from around 1600 BC to 1150 BC, named after the city of Mycenae in southern Greece

The **Mycenaean** Age, named after the city of Mycenae in Greece, is a general term that describes the time when many separate independent cities in the Greek world were powerful. Mycenae was the most famous of these cities. They had a similar culture, buildings and administration, and had palaces at the heart of them. However, it is important to realise that they were totally independent from each other, and the term 'Mycenaean' is a modern one to link cities that had these similarities. There was no concept at the time of all the cities being in any way linked or united. These cities are found in many parts of the Mediterranean, and not only Greece; in fact, the country of Greece did not even exist at the time of the Mycenaeans, and whilst we cannot say how they felt for certain, it would seem very likely that they saw other cities as totally distinct from themselves.

The Mycenaean Age lasted from approximately 1600 BC to 1150 BC. This period is part of what is known as the Bronze Age, because it was in this time that tin and copper were first mixed together to make the alloy bronze, which is a much stronger material than the elements that were combined to make it.

As with many aspects of Mycenae, it is very hard to be more exact about these dates, as nothing can be precisely dated until much later in Greek history. Further complications are caused by the fact that the Mycenaean civilisation is very similar to the **Minoan civilisation**, which came just before it, and it is often hard to distinguish from which of these civilisations objects come.

In order to date the Mycenaean Age, historians look at pottery styles in Greece, comparing them to those in Egypt, where historical records were kept more accurately. Carbon objects, such as wooden objects and timbers, are also beginning to yield clues as scientists can date them using the radioactivity that is present in such materials.

The Mycenaean Age has been divided into three phases by historians:

> **Minoan civilisation** a civilisation based on Crete that influenced neighbouring areas. It lasted from around 3500 BC until around 1400 BC, overlapping in both time and area with the Mycenaean civilisation

- The early period (1600–1400 BC), in which burials were made in shaft graves (see pages 191–192).
- The palatial period (1400–1250 BC), when the great palaces are thought to have reached their peak.
- The later period (1250–1150 BC), when the palaces seem to have come under more attacks before suddenly being abandoned or destroyed.

S & C

Much debate has existed over the collapse of Mycenaean cities. In the final decades of the age, huge changes were happening throughout the Eastern Mediterranean. The kingdom of the Hittites to the east of Greece collapsed around 1200 BC, and written accounts from Egypt tell of 'Sea Peoples' attacking Egypt from the north. Moreover, the site of Troy was also destroyed around this time, although this is probably not the famous Trojan War, which is discussed on pages 161–163. There is evidence that some of the main Mycenaean cities strengthened their walls and defences around this time, presumably in fear of an attack. However, these measures did not prevent the destruction of the cities as there were huge fires in many of the sites, although we do not know what was the cause of these.

After the end of the Mycenaean Age, the Iron Age began. Iron, widely neglected by the Mycenaeans, was used for weapons and tools in this age. We have no written records at all from this period, and it used to be known as the 'Dark Age', as it was felt that we knew little about life at this time. Historians are now able to give more information about the period, and one idea is that the decline that was evident in the Mycenaean Age continued into the Iron Age, with large falls in the populations of some cities.

TIMELINE OF THE MYCENAEAN AGE

Date (BC)	Major events in the Mycenaean Age	Period
1675	First burials in Grave Circle B at Mycenae	Early
1600	First burials at Grave Circle A Destruction of Akrotiri	
1400	Start of major building at Mycenaean sites Treasury of Atreus built Development of the city of Tiryns End of Minoan Age	Palatial
1375	Shipwreck of Ulu Burun	
1350	Tombs of Clytemnesta and Aegisthus built Cyclopean Walls of Mycenae built	
1300	Western wall of Mycenae strengthened Eastern Gate and palace built at Mycenae	
1250	Further strengthening of walls and defences of Tiryns Building of Galleries at Tiryns Lion Gate built Destruction of Troy VIIa Decline of major Mycenaean sites	Later
1200	Destruction of Troy VI Damage to Mycenae from fire	
1075	Final destruction at Mycenae from fire	

THE LOCATION AND IMPORTANCE OF THE KEY SITES, INCLUDING MYCENAE, TIRYNS AND TROY

Mycenae is the most famous city of the Mycenaean Age, and in mythology it was the home of King Agamemnon, who led a Greek army against the city of Troy. The city is built on a hill, which is 40–50m above the plains that it surrounds. It is a small area by modern standards, with a perimeter of around 900m. Hills to the north and south and ravines surround the plains on three sides, and a spring less than 400m away supplied water throughout the year.

An ancient city built on higher ground, and defended by walls, is known as a citadel. The term means 'little city', and these were indeed very small by modern standards, being more like small towns. For the sake of convenience, this chapter will use the term 'city' to describe the sites.

Evidence for the occupation of the site goes back a few thousand years beyond the Mycenaean Age. Archaeologists have traced the first Mycenaean burials to around 1650 BC, and believe the site reached peak prosperity from around 1400 BC to 1200 BC.

ACTIVITY

Imagine you are the person who decided where the city of Mycenae should be built. Explain why you have chosen the site as the location for your city.

FIGURE 2.1 (PS)
View of the archaeological site of Mycenae. You can clearly see the surrounding hills, and some of the huge walls that helped defend the city.

The Greeks believed that the hero Perseus, the man who killed the Medusa, first founded the city. He was given help in building the city by the mythical race of giants called the Cyclopes. The Greeks did not think that any human could have built such huge structures without help. According to legend, Agamemnon became king of Mycenae centuries later. Homer states that Agamemnon led an army gathered together from lots of Greek cities and islands against Troy, although the evidence for Agamemnon's existence and the war itself is debatable.

Mycenae is most famous for the tombs and the treasures that were found there. These tombs, together with the rest of the city, were excavated by a German archaeologist, Heinrich Schliemann, between 1876 and 1878.

Another important Mycenaean site is Tiryns, located around 10 miles from Mycenae. It had strong defensive walls, which were up to 8m high and 13m thick, and is famous for its palace, throne room and a series of arched galleries. Numerous frescoes have been found from Tiryns; one of these shows a youth somersaulting over a bull, which was an activity that was popular in the Minoan Age. The ancients believed that Tiryns was slightly older than Mycenae. It was supposedly founded by Proitos, whose brother was Acrisius. Acrisius' grandson was Perseus, the founder of Mycenae. It was also thought to be the birthplace of the hero Heracles (known as Hercules by the Romans).

Troy, the site of the famous war between the Greeks and the Trojans, is found in northwest Turkey. It is a city that was rebuilt several times in ancient history, with each new version built on top of the previous one. Much debate surrounds which version of the city existed at the time of the Trojan War (see pages 181–183). The city has revealed little evidence of the riches that Homer describes, but it is likely that it was an important site in Mycenaean times.

Study question
Why might the Greeks have wanted to believe that their mythological heroes founded their cities?

KEY PLACE

Mycenae the best preserved site of the Mycenaean Age, containing a significant quantity of gold, pottery, treasure and frescoes (wall paintings). It has huge defensive walls and the remains of a palace. The site also contains several different types of tombs and graves

KEY PLACE

Tiryns a strongly
defended site, famous for
its walls, palace, throne
room and frescoes

megaron the central hall
in the Mycenaean palace,
used for banquets,
worship and meetings

S & C There are a number of other important Mycenaean sites in and around Greece. One of these is Pylos, which is situated in the far southwest of Greece. It has excellent views to the sea to the west, as it is built on a small bank, a few metres higher than the surrounding area. To the west is a natural bay, and to the east are mountains. In Homer's *Iliad*, Pylos is the home city of Nestor, the aged advisor to the Greek army at Troy.

It is different from many Mycenaean sites as it does not show evidence of large perimeter walls, although it does contain a well-preserved palace. There is evidence that this palace was destroyed by a large fire in the thirteenth century BC. During a fire at the palace, hundreds of clay tablets were preserved that showed evidence of a written language known as Linear B (see pages 175–178). Other parts of the site include a **megaron** (see pages 166–167) with a central hearth and four columns. The site also contains a smaller megaron (possibly for the queen), a bathroom with a bathtub, storage rooms with jars sunken into the floor, and an armoury. You can find more information about it at http://www.ancientgreecejourney.co.uk/places/nestors.htm.

Another important site is Akrotiri. Akrotiri is on the island of Santorini, situated in the Aegean Sea. The site is famous for its wall paintings, which show a heavy influence from the earlier Minoan Age. These include paintings of ships, boxers, flowers, birds, priests and worshippers.

THE LAYOUT AND STRUCTURES OF THE SITES OF MYCENAE AND TIRYNS

FIGURE 2.2
Plan of Mycenae.

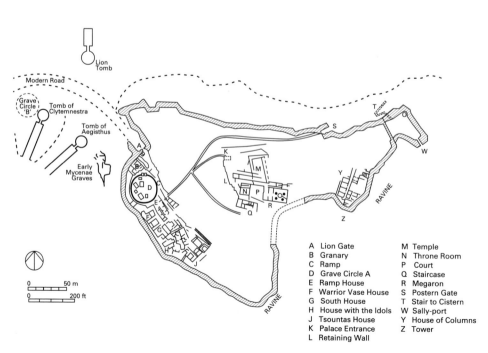

A Lion Gate
B Granary
C Ramp
D Grave Circle A
E Ramp House
F Warrior Vase House
G South House
H House with the Idols
J Tsountas House
K Palace Entrance
L Retaining Wall
M Temple
N Throne Room
P Court
Q Staircase
R Megaron
S Postern Gate
T Stair to Cistern
W Sally-port
Y House of Columns
Z Tower

FIGURE 2.3
Aerial view of
Mycenae.

PRESCRIBED SOURCE

Site of Mycenae

Built: 17th–11th century
BC (approximately)

Location: northeast
Peloponnese, Greece

Materials: limestone and
conglomerate blocks

Significance: contains
important frescos,
tombs and treasure

Find out more here:
http://www.ancient.eu/
mycenae/

The palace of Mycenae is situated at the very top of the hill. The hill did not have a flat top, so the ground had to be artificially levelled. There were large terraces at the sides that would have been used for storage.

The **sally ports** were an important part of the defensive structure of the city. There were two of these; one at the north and one at the south of the city. These have been suggested to have been secret passages from which defenders could rush out and attack unsuspecting enemy soldiers. However, the south sally port is visible from a distance, which might question whether it was a defensive measure, or at least how effective it was, especially as the passage is only 2.5m wide.

The ports use a technique known as **corbelling**, which was a method of spanning a gap between two structures. At the top of both sides of the gap, increasingly larger blocks of stone would be placed one on top of the other until they joined at the top. Examples of this technique are the passage that leads to the underground cistern (see Figure 2.4 on page 156) and the roof of the Treasury of Atreus (see Figure 2.40 on page 193).

Next to the northern sally port is a passage that goes under the perimeter wall and leads to an underground cistern (a tank used to store water). The cistern itself is 18m below ground level. It collected water through a series of clay pipes in the roof. This water came from the natural spring that lay close to the city. If attackers laid siege to the city and tried to cut off the water supply, the Mycenaeans could secretly get to a supply of water to enable them to hold out for a lengthy period.

The walls of Mycenae are an impressive feat of engineering and construction. In the first phase of wall building (from approximately 1350 BC), the walls only surrounded

> **sally port** a gap in the outer wall through which defenders could rush out to surprise attackers

> **corbelling** a technique used to span a gap between two walls by placing increasingly larger blocks of stone onto each other, thereby creating a vaulted roof (see also Figure 2.10 on p. 160)

FIGURE 2.4
Passage leading to the underground cistern at Mycenae. The walls and roof are an excellent example of the corbelling technique.

PS

relief (from the Latin verb 'relevo', 'to raise') a carving that projects from, and is a part of, the same background material; it has the effect of shading and being in 3D

Study question
Why do you think the rulers used a symbol of lions at the entrance to the city?

the top of the city of Mycenae, and little of this survives. The walled area was enlarged a century or so later, until the final perimeter wall was finished around 1200 BC, being around 900m long.

The best preserved section of the wall at the north of the city ranges from 5.5m to 7.5m thick. This thickness is the length of a large room in a house today. None of the walls survives to full height, but it is estimated that they reached around 12m high. The section of wall surrounding the Lion Gate (Figure 2.5) is 8.25m high.

To build these walls was a superhuman feat. Even the ancient Greeks could not work out how any human built them, as each block weighs around 2 tonnes. The ancient Greeks referred to them as the 'Cyclopean Walls', after the giant that Odysseus blinded, believing that only a huge giant could have moved such blocks.

The walls were made out of huge blocks of limestone piled on top of each other; the area around Mycenae is a good source of the stone. Mortar (to join the blocks) was not used, but smaller pieces of limestone filled the spaces between the blocks. Some blocks could have been moved from higher areas of the city by placing them on rollers. Other blocks would have been raised through the construction earth ramps. Larger blocks were used for the visible parts of the wall, while the inner core was made from earth and rubble. The wall generally followed the contours of the hill to make it easier to build.

The Lion Gate is probably the most famous feature of Mycenae and is one of the most impressive pieces of masonry in the Greek world. This was the main entrance to the city and was built in the thirteenth century BC, when Mycenae was at its most powerful. The approach to the gate was along an uphill path. The area surrounding the gate itself is not made of limestone, but of a different rock called conglomerate. This would provide an effective contrast with the limestone around the rest of the site as conglomerate is a shinier and smoother material than limestone.

The opening where the gate would have been is roughly a square whose sides are 3m. The gate has large blocks at either side (the jambs) and above (the lintel). The lintel on its own weighs 20 tonnes. Above the edges of the lintel is a corbel arch. In the lintel and threshold holes are visible for the doors and bar that would have locked the gates.

In the triangle created in the corbel arch is a slab of limestone, carved into the form of two lions in **relief**. The lions have their paws on altars, but their heads have not survived. These would probably not have been made of limestone, as it is very difficult to carve precise details in this medium. The columns above the altars are typically Minoan, being thicker at the top than the bottom. By showing the sides of the lions, but with their heads possibly facing forward, an air of solemnity and majesty was created. The Lion Gate would be an obvious area for attackers to focus on, but defenders on the walls would hurl missiles down to try to prevent enemies breaking through. The only other entrance to the city was through the northern gate, also known as the Postern Gate.

The tombs of Mycenae are the probably the most famous in ancient Greece. This is due to the physical structures of the tombs themselves and the lavish treasures that they contained.

There are several different areas of tombs both in Mycenae itself and a short distance from the city walls. Full details of these tombs and their contents is given on pages 190–195.

The oldest tombs are those that are found in the area known as Grave Circle B (so called because it was discovered in 1952, while Grave Circle A had been discovered and named in 1876). Grave Circle B is an area around 200m to the east of the city walls, and contains twenty-four graves, dated to the seventeenth and sixteenth centuries BC. It is enclosed within a stone wall, which had a diameter of 28m. Just over half of the graves are thought to have been for members of the royal family, owing to the objects that were found within them. Part of the tomb of Clytemnestra was built over Grave Circle B around 300 years later.

FIGURE 2.5
Lion Gate, Mycenae, 13th century BC.

Around thirty-five bodies of men, women and children have been found. The location of some of these are marked with upright stone **stelai**. An uncarved stele indicates the burial of a female, while carved ones indicate male burials.

Grave Circle A, situated in the south west area of the city, is similar in many respects to Grave Circle B. It is also 28m in diameter, and was originally surrounded by a low wall. It is thought to have been a royal burial site since the sixteenth century BC because the rich contents found within it were similar to those that had been dated to this time in Egypt. When the Lion Gate was built next to it, it was rebuilt with a new wall and the level of the ground was raised. At the time of the rebuilding, rulers were being buried in even grander tombs (see pages 192–193), and so it is thought the improvements to Grave Circle A were carried out to honour previous rulers. The original wall of smaller stones can be seen near the top of Figure 2.6, enclosed within the later double perimeter wall.

The area contained six shaft graves (see pages 191–192), in which a total of nine women, eight men and two children were buried at the bottom of shafts. These shafts are deeper and larger than those of Grave Circle B. The dead were buried with a vast quantity of precious objects, including gold objects weighing 14kg, together with silver, amber, glass and ivory. Stelai, often elaborately carved, were set over the burials. Three of these depict chariot scenes. It is not surprising that Homer called Mycenae 'rich in gold' (*Iliad*, 11.25).

Outside the walls of Mycenae are even grander tombs; the 'so-called' tombs of Clytemnestra and Aegisthus and a tomb known as the Treasury of Atreus (treasury in this context means a place where treasure was stored). These were built around the fourteenth century BC. The

> **stele** (plural **stelai**) stone slabs, often with patterns or images carved on them, most commonly used as tombstones

FIGURE 2.6
Grave Circle A, Mycenae.

tholos tomb a large domed tomb in the shape of an igloo, roughly circular in its floor space – also known as a beehive tomb

Study questions

1 What classes of people do you think would be buried in the graves of Grave Circle B?

2 Why do you think the shafts were deeper and larger than the earlier shafts of Grave Circle A?

construction of these is discussed fully on pages 192–193. Such tombs are known as **tholos tombs**, from a Greek word meaning 'domed'.

Despite their names, the tombs of Clytemnestra and Aegisthus never housed these legendary rulers. Clytemnestra was the wife of King Agamemnon in mythology and Aegisthus was her second husband after she had killed Agamemnon. The tombs were given their names in relatively recent times by local villagers. Atreus was the father of Agamemnon. It is possible (though unlikely) that this actually was the tomb of Atreus: it might date from the time when he was supposed to have lived, and there was a tomb with this name in ancient times as the Greek writer Pausanias tells us:

> In the ruins of Mycenae is a fountain called Persea; there are also underground resting places of Atreus and his children. Their treasure was kept in these chambers. There is the tomb of Atreus, and the tombs of those who came back with Agamemnon from Troy.
>
> Pausanias, *The Description of Greece* 2.16.6

The tombs of Clytemnestra and Aegisthus are situated just to the west of the city, with the Treasury of Atreus a little further away. The tombs of Clytemnestra and Aegisthus each have a diameter of around 13m, with the former also being an impressive 13m high. The roof of the tomb of Clytemnestra collapsed in 1951 and the roof that can be seen there now is a reconstruction. No treasure remained in the tombs when they were excavated in the nineteenth century, as they had been robbed of their contents in ancient times.

Like Mycenae, Tiryns is built on a hill. This hill rises 18m above the land that surrounds it. The city is 300m long and is between 45m and 100m wide. The earliest buildings at Tiryns date from around 2500 BC, but the first Mycenaean phase of building occurred around 1400 BC, where the first city walls were built to the south of the site. Around a century later the Eastern Gate was added as the city expanded and the palace was constructed. This was further strengthened in the thirteenth century, and the wall on the western side was added with its curving defence, justifying the description in the *Iliad* of Tiryns being 'surrounded by walls' (*Iliad*, 2.559).

FIGURE 2.7

PS

Entrance to the Treasury of Atreus, Mycenae, 14th century BC. For a view of the interior of the tomb, see Figure 2.40 on page 193.

FIGURE 2.8
Plan of Tiryns:
1 – Cyclopean Ramp,
2 – Gates, 3 – Galleries,
4 – Courtyard,
5 – Palace courtyard,
6 – Megaron and
Palace, 7 – West Gate.

EXPLORE FURTHER

There are other important areas of the city of Mycenae: the area by the western wall contains a number of buildings, thought to be either royal workshops or the houses of noblemen. These houses contain important evidence for what life was like at the time through the frescoes and artefacts found in them, such as religious statues (see pages 187–188) and the Warrior Vase (see p. 169); next to Grave Circle A was a granary, where jars of carbonised wheat have been found.

PRESCRIBED SOURCE

Site of Tiryns

Built: 15th–13th century BC (approximately)

Location: East Peloponnese, Greece

Significance: contains an important palace and throne room, frescoes and treasure

Find out more here: http://www.ancient.eu/tiryns/

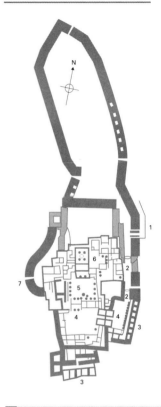

The walls at Tiryns, like those at Mycenae, were thought to have been built by the Cyclopes, whom Proitos had brought in from Turkey to complete the task. They are around 7m high now, but extended to as high as 10m in Mycenaean times. The main approach to the walls was on the east side up a ramp, now known as the Cyclopean Ramp because of its size. Only a small part of this remains, giving little clue as to as its impressive nature in ancient times. From here it was a short walk to the main gate.

The gate was thought to be about 3m high, although it is only half this height now, and is about 3m wide, therefore being of a similar width to the Lion Gate at Mycenae. Pivot holes for the doors can still be seen, together with slots in the gate posts for a bar to lock the gates. Attackers could be trapped in the long, narrow passage between the two gates beyond the entrance. This would have been an ideal area into which defenders could hurl down objects on attackers.

Many of the walls around Tiryns are relatively straight, but the wall on the west of the city has a significant, and very deliberate, curve. There was also a stairway leading to a very narrow corridor.

The palace was built on the highest part of Tiryns, known as the Upper City. This was protected by its own defensive walls. A grand entranceway led to the megaron. The central hearth was surrounded by four wooden pillars, whose stone bases still survive. Towards the east of the megaron was a small platform on which the king's throne would have been. The floor was plastered and had images of octopi and dolphins on it. The walls were also covered with plaster, on which **frescoes** were painted on damp plaster of rich ladies and a hunting scene.

Around the megaron were a series of apartments and colonnades for the rulers, and even a bathroom whose floor was made of a polished limestone slab. Holes were drilled

> **Study question**
> The Cyclopean Ramp at Tiryns was long and uphill. Why do you think it was designed in this manner?

> **fresco** a painting originally made on damp plaster in which the colours become fixed as the plaster dries

FIGURE 2.9
The entrance passage and main gate of Tiryns, 13th century BC, looking outwards from the city towards the Cyclopean Ramp.

Study question
Why do you think the wall on the west was rebuilt in the manner it was?

Study question
What do you think the galleries might have been used for?

FIGURE 2.10
Gallery, Tiryns, 13th century BC.

into the floor for drainage. There is also evidence of at least two staircases, revealing a second level to some of the parts of the megaron.

Some of the most famous features of the city of Tiryns are the galleries, which were built into the outer walls of the city. They used the technique of corbelling to create vaulted roofs. Some of these galleries were up to 30m long. Leading off the galleries were a large number of rooms. At the end of the thirteenth century BC, the site was extended to the north by adding an extra loop to the wall, with the area containing workshops and houses.

Just over half a mile from Tiryns another tholos tomb has been found, built into the side of a hillside. It is about 6m tall and 6m wide, with an entrance 1.5m high. Inside the tomb was discovered a large round stone, which might have been an altar. It has a superb corbelled roof and massive blocks of stone were used to hold up the roof of the entrance.

TROY

Of all the Mycenaean sites, the one that most people are familiar with is Troy. However, the knowledge that people have comes mostly from the *Iliad* of Homer, rather than the site itself. Indeed, some of the evidence from the site itself seems to contradict the impression of Troy in the *Iliad*.

EXPLORE FURTHER

There are some excellent websites on the history of Tiryns. Have a look at http://www.greek-thesaurus.gr/Mycenaean-Tiryns-Acropolis.html for a good description and http://ancient-greece.org/archaeology/tiryns.html for some excellent photographs.

For images of the tholos tomb, look at http://www.megalithic.co.uk/article.php?sid=15099.

The evidence for and against Troy VI and Troy VIIa being the site of Homer's Troy

While people were certainly living in the settlement that many believe was Troy during the Mycenaean Age, it is highly debatable this site formed the historical basis of the Trojan War. We no longer think that there was a Trojan War in the way that the myths of Homer describe. However, these stories may recall an actual historical siege of Troy. We know from archaeology that there were several wars fought at Troy in Mycenaean times, which might have been merged together, but the evidence for each of these does not match in their entirety what is in the myths of Homer. It may be there was no single war as described by Homer, but a series of conflicts over a much longer timespan, which Homer merged into one story.

The oldest settlement at Troy, called Troy I, dates back to 3000 BC, and the Mycenaean period at Troy occurs in the ruins of Troy VI and Troy VIIa (1900–950 BC).

There are several reasons why archaeologists think Troy VI could have been the site of Homer's Troy:

- It was destroyed around 1250 BC, with the Trojan War traditionally dated to 1200 BC.
- It seems to have been a rich city with numerous large houses.
- Its stone walls were over 7 metres high, and the *Iliad* refers to the high walls of Troy.
- These walls seem to have had towers, with towers a feature of Troy in the *Iliad*.
- It extended over quite a large area with a suggested population of 10,000, which would indicate a thriving city as in the *Iliad*.

However, there is also some evidence that seems to contradict the mythological legend, including:

- Archaeologists also believe it was destroyed by an earthquake, not the fire that ancient literature suggests.

It was then succeeded by Troy VIIa, which seems to have been a settlement that existed for only around 30–40 years. There are several pieces of evidence that Troy VIIa could have been the site of the legendary war:

Study question

From the archaeological evidence, do you believe that Schliemann found the site of Troy?

ACTIVITY

Debate whether you would have preferred to have lived in Mycenae or Tiryns.

To extend this idea further, research what life was like in the city of Pylos and add this to the debate.

FIGURE 2.11

Sophia Schliemann wearing some of the treasures excavated from Troy.

- It too had large towers.
- It had single-storey houses, which were relatively crowded together and built in a short period. This would fit in with the idea of emergency housing for the Trojans when the Greeks were attacking the city.
- Storage jars were sunk deep into the ground. Were the people trying to store up food when under siege?
- It was destroyed by a large fire. The writings of the Roman poet, Virgil, describe the fires started by the Greeks when they destroyed Troy.
- Partial human remains of individuals have been found (possibly killed in warfare).
- Three bronze arrowheads have been found.

S & C

Troy was excavated in the late nineteenth century, by the archaeologist Heinrich Schliemann. He had long been fascinated by the legend of Troy. Of the many possible sites in Turkey that might have been Troy, he decided to excavate one near the village of Hisarlik. On excavating, he discovered a walled city, which had been rebuilt many times in history. Not only did he discover this, but he also found treasure, leading him to the conclusion that he had found Troy, and to calling what he had found 'Priam's treasure' (Priam was supposedly the king of Troy at the time of the Trojan War). He later wrote how his wife had smuggled it out of Troy in her clothing, rather than officially declaring what he had found. He even got his wife to model some of the jewellery for publicity. However, other evidence from the site where the treasure was found suggests that it came from over 1,000 years earlier.

Moreover, in digging through the layers of Troy, many later archaeologists believe that Schliemann caused considerable damage to the part that may have been Homer's Troy. This excavation was done quickly, and with very rough methods. Schliemann did not keep detailed records nor map his finds. Yet, in the nineteenth century, these methods were commonplace, and Carl Blegen, a later famous archaeologist at Troy, said that there was probably no other digger who was better than Schliemann in field work.

Troy was part of the kingdom of a people known as the Hittites. Some of their writings refer to a place to the west of their kingdom called Ahhiyawa. This perhaps sounds similar to Achaea, one of the words for Greece, in Homer. Moreover, the Hittite word for Troy, Wilusia, is similar to the Greek word for Troy, Ilion. From this it was generally accepted that where Schliemann had excavated was indeed Troy, although in recent years scholars have become more sceptical about these verbal connections.

As Troy developed as a city, each civilisation destroyed what had been there already, and built on top of the ruins. These layers reached a height of 32m over the surrounding plains. As archaeologists have dug down, they have come across nine different periods of settlement at Troy, during which houses were built, occupied and finally destroyed (usually by a fire or earthquake).

EXPLORE FURTHER **CW**

For further ideas on the levels of Troy and the remains, an excellent source of information is http://www.dartmouth. edu/~prehistory/aegean/? page_id=630#L271.

Another important Mycenaean site is Pylos. Find out information about it at http://www. ancientgreecejourney. co.uk/places/nestors. htm.

All of this, while hardly conclusive, might seem to back up the view that this was the site of the actual war between the Greeks and Trojans. However:

- The houses were crammed together, which suggests the city was not rich, unlike the one described by Homer.
- The sunken jars might not indicate a siege, but simply a lack of space that people had in which to keep food.

All that can be said for sure it that there is no certain answer as to which of the two layers might have been Homer's Troy, although there has been more support from scholars in recent decades in favour of it being Troy VIIa.

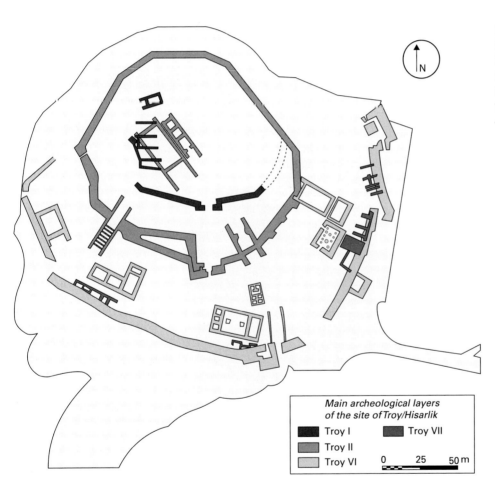

FIGURE 2.12
Plan showing some of the buildings and defences of some of the layers of settlement at the city traditionally called Troy.

Main archeological layers of the site of Troy/Hisarlik

Troy I   Troy VII
Troy II
Troy VI   0   25   50 m

TOPIC REVIEW

You should be able to:

1. Describe:
   - the important stages in the history of the Mycenaean Age
   - the layouts of Mycenae and Tiryns
   - the key features of Mycenae and Tirnys
   - the findings in the different levels of Troy.

2. Explain:
   - why the cities of Mycenae and Tiryns were built in the locations that they were
   - why the cities of Mycenae and Tiryns developed as they did
   - what is particularly impressive about Mycenaean cities
   - the arguments for and against the archaeological levels of Troy VI and VIIa being the site of the Troy of the Trojan War.

PRACTICE QUESTIONS

Source A: *The entrance to Mycenae*

1. What is the name of this entrance to Mycenae? Why is it known by this name? [2]
2. Choose **two** features of the image in this source and say why they might be admired. [4]

2.2 Life in the Mycenaean Age

- Palaces:
  - the typical palace complex and megaron (central hall)
  - their functions and use

- Everyday life; evidence for, and nature of:
  - hunting
  - armour and weapons
  - chariots
  - clothing
  - trade

- Linear B tablets:
  - how the tablets were preserved and what they record
  - the significance of the tablets

The prescribed sources for this topic are:

- Dagger blade showing hunting scene from Grave Circle A, Mycenae
- Mycenaean warrior vase, House of the warrior, Mycenae
- Linear B tablet showing the word 'tripod' in syllabic and ideogram forms, Pylos.

Don't forget that you will be given credit in the exam if you study extra sources and make relevant use of them in your answers.

In this section you will discover what life was like in cities for both rulers and their subjects by looking at the sites themselves and objects that have been found within them. These things tell us what priorities the Mycenaeans had in their daily lives, and show a very precise and advanced civilisation.

PALACES

Mycenaean cities were ruled by kings, and as such they contained palaces. These palaces, although small by modern standards, occupied a large percentage of the city. They

FIGURE 2.13

Plan of a typical megaron:
A – entrance porch; B – front
room; C – hearth.

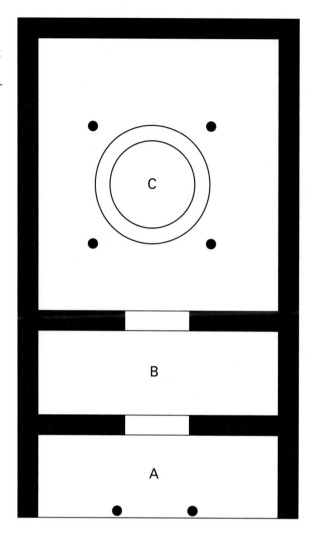

contained numerous pleasant areas, such as colonnades, but were more than just areas for the royal family to relax in. There is evidence that palaces contained rooms for official documents, shrines, potteries, oil press rooms, armouries and storerooms for food.

The most important part of the palace was the megaron. This was often in the highest part of the city, dominating the area. In many ways it had a similar design to later Greek temples as it was usually rectangular in shape, and had an entrance porch with two columns, with another room behind this (known as a vestibule). The megaron usually contained one or more courtyards.

The most important feature of the megaron was a hearth. The hearth was a stone area, usually circular in shape, on which a fire would be lit for religious purposes or cooking. Around this would have been four columns, which supported the roof. A hole in the roof would have allowed smoke to escape from the fire.

This room would also be where the king's throne would have been. The megaron would have been used for feasts, like the one described in the *Odyssey* during which the suitors are killed, and poetry would have been recited there.

FIGURE 2.14
Megaron from Pylos,
showing central hearth and
holes where two pillars
would have been.

HUNTING

Animal hunting was an important activity in the Mycenaean Age. As most of Greece was unsuitable for farmland, and flat land was normally used for growing crops, hunting animals was essential if people were to eat meat. Many of the animals the Greeks liked to hunt lived on mountainous terrain.

Our evidence for hunting comes from frescoes, scenes on daggers and carvings on rings. The most famous piece of evidence comes from a dagger blade showing a lion hunt (lions lived in the wild in Greece in ancient times), widely known as the Lion Hunt Dagger. This was found in Grave Circle A in Mycenae.

The dagger in Figure 2.15 is too intricate and precious to have been used for combat, but is instead an ornamental object. It would have almost certainly belonged to a king as a status symbol. The hunting of a lion was the greatest challenge a hunter could face, and the image on the dagger highlights this as the hunter on the right has been felled by the

PRESCRIBED SOURCE

Dagger blade showing hunting scene

Date: 16th century BC

Location: Grave IV, Grave Circle A, Mycenae

Materials: gold, silver and niello

Significance: inlay technique, use of weapons and armour, evidence of trade and hunting

FIGURE 2.15
Detail of the Lion
Hunt Dagger.

lion. One hunter has a bow and arrow, while the others have long spears. Two types of shield are shown; the ones in a figure of eight shape originate from the earlier Minoan age.

Other precious objects also provide vital evidence for the importance of hunting. Two cups from Vapheio, near Sparta, show the capture of bulls (see p. 186). A signet ring from Grave IV in Grave Circle A in Mycenae shows a miniature scene of a hunter and driver on a chariot, armed with a bow and chasing deer (see p. 170). A fresco from Tiryns shows the use of dogs in hunting.

ARMOUR AND WEAPONS

There is no doubt that battles played a huge part in the lives of the Mycenaeans, judging by the evidence from Homer and numerous objects found in Mycenaean cities. Different styles of armour and weapons have been found, leading to some uncertainty as to the exact nature of warfare, with helmets and shields changing significantly over the period.

It would seem that a major change was happening at the start of the Mycenaean period: the huge figure of eight shields and tower shields that the Mycenaeans used were being gradually replaced by smaller ones. The older style shields are shown on the Lion Hunt Dagger, and Homer describes a tower shield that was used by the Greek hero Ajax, made up of eight layers of leather and one of bronze (*Iliad*, 7.219–223). Painted shields, covering from the neck to the knees are also shown on the frescoes of Akrotiri, and the ones on the Lion Hunt Dagger covered all the way to the ankles, as did Ajax's shield in the *Iliad*. Agamemnon is also said, in the *Iliad*, to have had a shield that could cover a man (although it could be that Homer is inferring that Agamemnon was tall and that his shield would cover a lesser man than him).

FIGURE 2.16
Mycenaean boars' tusk helmet, Chamber tomb 515, Mycenae, now in the National Archaeological Museum, Athens.

S & C

As part of this component, you will read the story of the battle between Odysseus and the suitors, which gives some ideas of the weapons and armour that the Mycenaeans used. More traditional battles are shown throughout the *Iliad*. Read Book 16 of the *Iliad*, where the Greek hero Patroclus arms himself and goes out to fight the Trojans. Below is the passage where Patroclus arms himself. Read the rest of Book 16 and make a list of all the types of weapons and armour used.

At his words, Patroclus began to clad himself in gleaming bronze. First he clasped the shining greaves, with silver ankle-pieces, about his legs. Next he strapped Achilles' ornate breastplate round his chest, richly worked and decorated with stars. Over his shoulder he hung the bronze sword with its silver studs, and then the great thick shield. On his strong head he set the fine horse-hair crested helm, its plume nodding menacingly. Lastly he grasped two stout spears that suited his grip, though not peerless Achilles' own great, long, and heavy spear that alone among the Achaeans he could wield, that spear of ash from Pelion's summit that Cheiron gave to the warrior's dear father Peleus, for the killing of men.

Homer, *Iliad*, 16.131–44

Helmets also changed significantly. The *Iliad* tells of a helmet that Odysseus once wore, made up of a leather cap, covered with felt, onto which boars' tusks were put. This seems to have been used in the early Mycenaean Age, and one of these helmets survives from Mycenae. The tusks are extremely strong and gave good protection, but each helmet would need the tusks of at least ten wild boars, and possibly many more. The hunting of these animals was extremely dangerous, as seen from the story of how Odysseus got badly injured when hunting a wild boar in the *Odyssey* Book 19.

Several other boars' tusk helmets have been found at other sites, suggesting they were used fairly commonly in early Mycenaean times. One from Dendra, near Argos, even has bronze cheek pieces on it. However, most helmets in the *Iliad* are not like these. These are often described as gleaming, and having animal skin liners for comfort and some added protection. They often had throat straps and animal hair plumes on top, presumably simply to look impressive. Mycenaean wall paintings also regularly show plumed helmets.

One of the most famous pieces of pottery from Mycenae shows how far helmets and shields developed over the centuries. The warrior vase, from a house in Mycenae of the same name, depicts a series of soldiers in a battle-line.

On this vase, a group of almost identical warriors are shown marching. They carry long spears (for thrusting rather than throwing) and small round shields. They are dressed in tunics, called **chitons**, and wear breast-plates and greaves for protection. They also carry knapsacks on their spears, perhaps suggesting they have a long journey to make. The helmets have horns coming from them and seem to be relatively light. On the far left of the vase, a woman is shown, presumably saying farewell to the soldiers as they depart for battle. On the other side of the vase are more soldiers wearing spiky helmets (the helmets look like hedgehogs!) and carrying much shorter spears. Noting the similarities in the handles of the vase and the appearance of the soldiers to later depictions, some scholars suggest this vase is not Mycenaean, but is from the eighth century BC.

The Mycenaeans used a variety of weapons. Spears were commonly used, consisting of a wooden handle into which a bronze spearhead would be fitted. By the twelfth century

EXPLORE FURTHER

A detailed study of helmets in the *Iliad*, and drawings of how they may have looked, can be found at http://www.salimbeti.com/micenei/helmets4.htm.

---

chiton a large, loose-fitting, woollen tunic worn in ancient Greece

krater a large bowl used for mixing wine and water

PRESCRIBED SOURCE

Mycenaean warrior vase

Date: 13th century BC

Location: House of the Warrior, Mycenae

Material: clay

Original purpose: krater

Significance: weaponry and armour of Mycenaean soldiers

FIGURE 2.17
The Warrior Vase.

FIGURE 2.18
Sword found in a Mycenaean tomb.

BC spears had become shorter and could have been thrown. Evidence for spears also comes from Linear B tablets (see pages 175–178) from Crete which refer to forty-two bronze tipped spears.

Many swords have been found in Mycenaean tombs, some with elaborate golden hilts (handles). Early swords also often featured a wooden pommel (a rounded end to the handle), covered in gold. They would have been much sharper than they now appear.

The more elaborate the sword, the less likely it was to have been used for actual combat. The sword would have been carried in a holder called a scabbard, and a wall painting from Akrotiri shows tassles on the end of the scabbards. Like spears, swords became shorter through the Mycenaean age, which would have been more useful in close quarter combat.

The earliest suit of armour in Europe comes from a Mycenaean site. A breastplate was found at Dendra, near the city of Argos, from the fifteenth century BC. It was made up of sheets of bronze for the chest and back, which were hinged together using strips of leather. Further plates of bronze protected the shoulders, neck and upper legs. Altogether fifteen separate plates of bronze make up the suit, which differs significantly from the armour shown on the warrior vase, which would probably have been made of leather. Found with this breastplate at Dendra were a boars' tusk helmet, a pair of greaves and a wrist guard. This armour would certainly have been heavy, but the protection it gave was far greater than other types of body armour.

FIGURE 2.19
Signet ring showing a hunting scene, Tiryns, 15th century BC.

Bows were certainly used in Mycenaean times, but were considered a cowardly weapon in the battlefield in the *Iliad*, as they could inflict death from afar with little risk to the archer. Odysseus kept his bow at home in the *Odyssey*, and none of the great warriors used one in the *Iliad*. The Lion Hunt Dagger shows the use of a bow, as does the image on the signet ring from Tiryns shown in Figure 2.19. Arrowheads have been found on several sites and bowmakers are recorded on the Linear B tablets from Pylos (see pages 175–178).

CHARIOTS

Figure 2.19 shows another key aspect of life in Mycenaean times; the use of chariots. Chariots are regularly shown in wall paintings, pottery and even stelai. They were used most often for chasing prey (as in the signet ring in Figure 2.19), or in war. In the *Iliad*, warriors are often driven to the centre of the fighting, before getting off the chariot to fight on foot. Generally, warriors did not fight other warriors from their chariots. After the fighting, the chariot driver would pick up the warrior to drive him elsewhere. Chariots also raced each other as part of funeral contests, as is told in the famous chariot race in *Iliad* Book 23.

The earliest representation of a chariot is from one of the stelai of Grave Circle A at Mycenae (see Figure 2.38 on p. 191). It shows a man on a simple two-wheeled box chariot, chasing down another man, either during a race or in a battle. The wheels on this and other chariots regularly have four spokes.

A fresco from Tiryns shows that chariots were not just used for fighting or competition, but were a mode of transport. Figure 2.20 from Tiryns shows a very different type of chariot from the image on the signet ring in Figure 2.19. The chariot shown below is more spacious and covered in a red fabric or animal hide, and a fresco from Pylos shows a similar, if slightly lighter chariot covered in a yellow material. These chariots would presumably have travelled on roads, but little is known for sure about roads at this time.

FIGURE 2.20
Fresco showing a couple travelling by chariot, Tiryns, 13th century BC, now in the National Archaeological Museum, Athens.

EXPLORE FURTHER

CW

To see the other chariots mentioned in this section, together with a full discussion of Mycenaean chariots, go to http://www.salimbeti.com/micenei/chariots.htm.

Study questions

1 What do you think it would have been like to have travelled in chariots in Mycenaean times?
2 Which class of society would need and use chariots?
3 Why do you think this was the case?

CLOTHING

As clothes are made from materials that decay over time, no actual clothing remains from Mycenaean times, and the descriptions of clothes in Homer's poetry do not give us much helpful information. However, we are able to gain an understanding of what Mycenaean people wore from art, and frescoes in particular (see above, p. 172 and p. 183).

The vast majority of garments in Mycenaean times were made from wool from sheep or goats, or linen, which is made from fibres of the flax plant. These were then dyed with natural products, with the colour being locked in through the addition of a substance such as vinegar or urine, which would preserve the dye when the garment was washed. Some garments were also made from silk, but these would have been rare.

The table below shows the possible origins of some of the dyes used by the Mycenaeans.

COLOUR	SOURCE
yellow	onion skins; saffron (a spice)
red	insect eggs; madder (a plant)
blue	indigo (a plant)
purple	shellfish ink

Some of the colours, such as blue and purple, were likely to have been expensive as they were harder to obtain.

The Linear B tables from Pylos (see pages 175–178) are a valuable source of information on cloth making. They tell us of different workers who prepared, spun, dyed and wove the wool. Some of the workers were given rations from the palace, but whether this means they were slaves or not is unclear.

Women are regularly shown wearing wrap-around skirts. These skirts often had several thin layers, creating a tiered effect. They were often very colourful and would have required great skill to make. They would have been worn with an underskirt. Frescocs from Akrotiri show both longer and shorter versions of this type of skirt, while later versions from Mycenae and images on rings from shaft graves only show the longer garment. Perhaps this shows how fashion changed even in the ancient world?

Blouses were short-sleeved, but may not have covered the breasts: some frescoes show bare-breasted women, and in other ones the clothing seems designed to highlight the breasts. There is also evidence from frescoes that women wore robes, cloaks, shawls, ornate headbands and ankle bracelets. Archaeological discoveries also give us examples of different jewellery.

The most famous original fresco is known as "the Mycenaean Lady". It shows a thoughtful woman in a typically Mycenaean garment holding a necklace. This might have been a gift to her, leading some to believe that she is a goddess. She wears a short-sleeved top over a thin bodice, which has enabled the artist to show off her breasts. She has an intricate hairstyle and is wearing a fine necklace and bracelet. In her hand she holds another bracelet.

PRESCRIBED SOURCE

Fresco of a Mycenaean lady holding a necklace

Date: 13th century BC

Location: Shaft grave IV, Grave Circle A, Mycenae

Significance: fresco colours and styles of female clothing and hairstyle, jewellery

FIGURE 2.21
A Mycenaean lady holding a necklace, 13th century fresco from Mycenae.

EXPLORE FURTHER

Mycenaeans had elaborate hairstyles (at least on their frescoes). Young children seem to have had their heads shaved, except for a lock of hair at the top of their head and a pony-tail. As they reached puberty, they grew their hair more. Women had long hair, intricately tied with ribbons and beads, with strands of hair falling down to their shoulders. In some images headbands were worn on the fringe and the hair was generally short, but more often it seems the hair was allowed to grow long and was plaited. Men too had long hair which was elaborately arranged. The chariot fresco (Figure 2.20) shows a typical male and female hairstyle.

Study question
Why should historians be wary of using the evidence from frescoes about how Mycenaeans dressed?

Men wore a braided, short-sleeved tunic, with a robe over it. There is also evidence that they wore a kilt-like garment, especially if they were soldiers, and a kind of loincloth for underwear. Leather boots were also worn, as shown on the Warrior Vase (see p. 169), but people may well have generally gone about barefoot (see Figure 2.22).

TRADE

The major Mycenaean cities developed strong trades links with many areas around the Mediterranean and beyond. This was essential for the growth and survival of their societies, as Greece does not have a rich supply of the mineral resources and metals that the Mycenaeans used. Much of the trade was done by sea as travel on land was slow due to mountain ranges and probably difficult due to bandits. The roads that existed would have been very basic and little could be carried on animals or chariots in comparison with boats.

FIGURE 2.22
From left to right: male robe, tunic and kilt. Image from *Mycenae: Agamemnon's capital*, Elizabeth French (London: Tempus).

We have evidence from a variety of sources of this trade, including the objects themselves in cities, written records on Linear B tablets, and even shipwrecks (see p. 174). As many of the Mycenaean sites are just a few miles from the sea, and there are many sheltered harbours, it was natural to import and export goods this way. However, such journeys were very hazardous, and a round trip would take many weeks. In ancient times it was only safe to sail for around half the year from early spring to the early autumn, and even then the weather in the Mediterranean could be very unpredictable. Journeys would not usually have been undertaken in one go, as ships were manned by rowers; as there are so many islands dotted around Greece, merchants would 'island hop' to get to mainland Greece from more distant places, and would probably both drop off and pick up cargo on the way. Most of the trade was with areas to the east, such as the islands in the Aegean Sea or Egypt, and the Middle East, but there was some trade with Italy and the surrounding islands. Some historians even believe the Mycenaeans imported amber and tin from Britain. Items were exchanged for other goods in a system known as bartering (in which if a merchant wanted one type of item or service, he would offer something he already had), rather than sold for money, as there is no evidence that money existed at the time.

We can never be sure of exactly where products and raw materials came from, as the Mycenaeans did not keep such records. We have to look at where else was producing these materials and products at the same time and make a reasoned guess about trade. The following table suggests possible areas from which the Mycenaeans imported items.

PRODUCT	PLACE OF ORIGIN
Gold	Macedonia, Egypt, Thasos (Greek island)
Amber (for beads)	Denmark, northern Europe
Ivory	Africa, Syria
Lapis lazuli gemstones	Africa
Silver, lead	Attica (area around Athens)
Copper	Attica, Syria, Cyprus, Sardinia
Ostrich eggshells	Africa
Tin	Britain, Turkey, Afghanistan, Spain
Glass	Egypt

Some of these products are found in small quantities and are luxury items, but copper was perhaps the most crucial import as it is the main metal in the manufacture of bronze. Gold is probably the most famous import as some of the most famous objects in Mycenae were made from it.

It is much more debatable whether people were also imported as slaves. In the *Iliad*, people defeated in war were regularly turned into slaves, especially the women, and there are numerous mentions of workers in the Linear B tablets, though it is not known whether they had slave status or not. However, their native land is often mentioned, and many came from a long way away.

We should remember that trade was a two-way system; the Mycenaeans exported items throughout their known world. Pottery seems to have been their main export, with examples being found in Israel, Egypt, Sicily, Albania and Macedonia, amongst other places. Many pottery vessels would have contained olive oil, and some of these have been found in other parts of Greece. Large mixing bowls for wine, called kraters (such as the Warrior Vase on p. 169), were exported to Cyprus. One of the inhabitants of Mycenae seems to have traded wine and another one oil. Other items include a gold Mycenaean-style dagger found in Romania, and beads found in Egypt.

Around 1375 BC, a Mycenaean ship sunk off the coast of southwest Turkey, near Ulu Burun. We do not know where it was travelling to or from, but its cargo reveals a lot about trade at the time. The ship was carrying 10 tonnes of copper and 1 tonne of tin, which would have been used to make bronze, and is the correct proportion of each metal needed to make it. Around 150 jars of a type found commonly in the Middle East were also on the ship, with the majority filled with resin or olives, and one with glass beads. Other items included wooden logs, elephant tusks, hippopotamus teeth, tortoise shells, oil lamps and pottery, amber, drinking cups, weapons, food (including nuts, olives and spices), a trumpet, wooden tablets (possibly to be filled with wax for writing) and much else besides.

EXPLORE FURTHER

An excellent short video on the Ulu Burun shipwreck, showing numerous items from the wreck can be viewed at https://www.youtube.com/watch?v=7IZWOdY7fEk.

LINEAR B TABLETS

Study question
Why do you think the Mycenaeans used clay to create the Linear B tablets?

The Linear B tablets (there is an even older form of writing known as Linear A, which is yet to be deciphered) are a series of inscribed clay tablets from the Mycenaean Age. They are found at some of the major palace sites of the time, notably Pylos and Knossos on the island of Crete. Over 1,000 tablets have been discovered at Pylos, and even more at Knossos. Scholars have identified different sets of handwriting among the tablets, leading to the conclusion that up to 100 different individuals wrote the tablets at Knossos. Many of the tablets were kept in a special document room, assumed to be an archive room.

The tablets were simply pieces of damp clay on which written records were inscribed with a sharpened tool. These tablets were then left to harden in the sun to provide a semi-permanent record. As the clay was not fired in an oven to become pottery, it would eventually take on moisture from the air, then crack and crumble. In their natural state, it has been estimated that each tablet would last for several months at most.

So how have these tablets survived for over 3,000 years, if they were meant to only last for a few months? It is entirely down to luck: the sites where they have been found suffered major fires, and as a result the tablets were baked as if in a kiln and became hardened.

As other tablets only lasted for a few months, those that we have represent a moment in time, in much the same way as the site of Pompeii provides a snapshot of what life was like when Mount Vesuvius erupted in AD 79. Most have been dated to the end of the Mycenaean period.

It seems that the first stage in recording information was to inscribe the detail on a small piece of clay, designed to be held in the palm of the hand. Some of these are only about 3cm in length. The information on these was then transferred to a larger thin horizontal tablet, known as a leaf tablet, and several of these could then be transferred to a larger document measuring up to 30cm in length. Many of these were extremely fragile on discovery and some crumbled when touched.

There are two main types of symbol used in the Linear B tablets: syllables (parts of a word sounded as a single unit) and ideograms (pictures that represented what the item

FIGURE 2.23
A selection of Linear B syllables.

ACTIVITY

Think of a word or phrase and try to write it using the Linear B script. You may alter the word a little to make it work.

e.g.

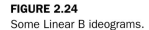
mu si ke

(music)

Give it to a friend to translate.

S & C
For many years, the tablets could not be deciphered. An American, Alice Kober, made vital steps in working out combinations of symbols in words, and after many years of struggle, a Briton called Michael Ventris worked out what the symbols represented. He realised that many of the deciphered words were an early form of Greek whose alphabet developed a few hundred years later.

Investigate further into how Kober and Ventris managed to decipher the symbols.

looked like). Words could be shown using either of these. There were symbols for each of the vowels and a symbol for each consonant and vowel syllable.

In addition to the syllables above, there were also signs known as ideograms, where the picture represented a whole word. These could depict animals (e.g. rams or pigs) or objects (e.g. tripods or swords). Sometimes the syllable form and ideogram form of a word are inscribed next to each other, presumably to aid those reading the signs in Mycenaean times. The gender of the animal was shown by extra strokes on the ideogram, with two small extra horizontal lines indicating a male animal, and an extra vertical, or near vertical, line for a female. For example, look at the difference in the following symbols:

ewe ram
(female) (male)

In addition, there were separate symbols for numbers, weights and measures.

FIGURE 2.24
Some Linear B ideograms.

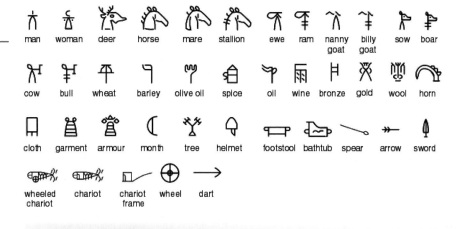

FIGURE 2.25
A Linear B tablet together with a line drawing to show its inscription **PS** more clearly.

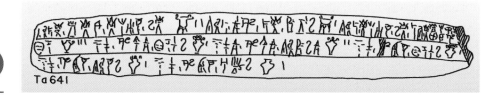
Ta 641

The complete translation of the tablet reads:

2 tripod cauldrons of Cretan workmanship of the Aikeu type, tripod cauldron on one
foot with a single handle, 1 tripod of Cretan workmanship burnt from the legs up,
3 wine jars, larger sized goblet with 4 handles, 2 larger sized goblets with 3 handles,
1 smaller sized goblet with 4 handles, 1 smaller sized goblet with 3 handles, 1 smaller
sized goblet without handles.

PRESCRIBED SOURCE

Linear B tablet showing the word 'tripod' in syllabic and ideogram forms (number 641)

Date: 13th century BC

Material: clay

Original location: Archive room, Palace of Pylos

Current location: National Archaeological Museum, Athens

Significance: shows various syllables and ideograms, including the word for tripod

Ti-ri-po-de (syllable form)   Tripod (ideogram form)

This tablet is typical of those found. Most of the tablets list objects, and are probably best
regarded as a way of keeping records of items that were in the palace, or transactions that
were made.

The tablets are vitally important documents. We have no literature that was written in
this period, and without the tablets we would know nothing of certain aspects of life,
such as how cities were run or where some of the workers came from. The tablets also
shed light on how the Greek language developed, and even some of its beliefs. For
example, the tablets reveal the names of several of the main Olympian gods (Zeus,
Poseidon, Hermes, Hera and Artemis appear on tablets), together with female versions of
Zeus and Poseidon, called Diwia and Posidaia. These female identities of Zeus and
Poseidon did not exist much beyond the Mycenaean age, showing that some, but not all,
aspects of the Mycenaeans survived into later times.

Some of the words survived over the centuries and are found in ancient Greek with
little change in spelling. For example, the word for gold in Greek is chrusos, which was
written in Linear B as kuruso. Some English words derive originally from Linear B, such
as the word pamako. This meant medicine, and has come to be used by us in English
through ancient Greek: it is the origin of our word pharmacy. Tripod, as seen in Fig 2.25
is another example of such a word, being written as tiripode in Linear B. Until the
decipherment of Linear B, it was generally thought that the arrival of later Greeks wiped
out the language of the Mycenaeans.

The tablets tell us a lot about agriculture and food production in Mycenaean times. A tablet from Knossos tells us about wine production, mentioning 420 vines and the storage of 14,000 litres of wine. One tablet records the delivery of 518 litres of oil by Kolakas to Eumedes. Figs, wheat and barley are also mentioned. We read of an official who was in charge of honey production and of honey being used for religious offerings. Spices, such as saffron and coriander, are also mentioned.

Animals are mentioned in the tablets as well. Some plough oxen are even named, for example Dusky, Dapple or Whitefoot. Horses are listed as a part of military equipment, and goats and pigs appear in the tablets.

Some of the tablets record details about how the cities were run. There seems to have been a chieftain or king called a **wanax** at the top of each society. This corresponds to the word 'anax' in Homer, which means 'lord'. This word does not appear in later authors, suggesting that this position may only have existed in Mycenaean times. He had royal lands, special garments (often purple-coloured), and freedom from some taxes. Beneath him was an official called a **lawagetas**, whose estate at Pylos was a third of the size of the wanax. This title might be connected with the later Greek words for people and leader, which might suggest he was a military figure. Beneath both of these are a noble class known at the **hequetai**, who were perhaps followers of the ruler in war and a warrior class. These were landowners who may have owned slaves. Beneath these were the classes who did much of the work.

These workers fulfilled a variety of roles. There is mention of female religious workers and women who ground corn, spun, produced flax (from which the Mycenaeans made linen), and were waitresses and bath attendants. Often these are mentioned as coming from other parts of the ancient world, possibly suggesting that they were slaves. Other workers mentioned include headband makers for horses, musicians, sweepers, bakers, fire-kindlers, perfume makers and stonemasons.

Tablets telling of military organisation exist, and perhaps the details of the struggles of cities to survive. The tablets of Knossos tell us of forty-two bronze-pointed spears, while tablets from Pylos tell us that officials had to provide bronze for spears, arrows and ships, suggesting perhaps a greater focus on producing what would be needed in an attack. The tablets also tell us of chariot parts, such as wheels or frames, with those from Pylos mentioning 117 pairs of wheels. Tablets from Pylos mention 600 rowers and 800 coastal watchmen, which might suggest a major invasion was feared.

Offerings made to gods are mentioned in one tablet. Aside from gold items, some of which were offered at a shrine of Zeus, other offerings were made. There is much controversy about the translation, but many scholars believe that two men and eight women are mentioned as offerings for gods including Zeus, Hermes and Hera, indicating the custom of human sacrifice.

wanax the Mycenaean word for a chieftain or king

lawagetas the leader of the people in Mycenae, who was also probably the leader of the army

hequetai the nobles in Mycenae; they were probably also important troops in the army

---

TOPIC REVIEW

You should be able to:

1. Describe:
   - the appearance of a typical Mycenaean palace
   - how the Mycenaeans hunted animals
   - what Mycenaean chariots looked like and were used for
   - the weapons and armour of the Mycenaean age
   - what Mycenaean men and women wore
   - what items the Mycenaeans imported and the evidence for this
   - the syllables and ideograms of Linear B
   - what the Linear B tablets record and how they were preserved.

2. Explain:
   - the functions and use of a typical Mycenaean palace
   - the difficulties of travelling by chariot and hunting in the Mycenaean Age
   - the strengths and limitations of Mycenaean weapons and armour
   - how practical and comfortable the clothing was that the Mycenaeans wore
   - the difficulties and extensiveness of Mycenaean trade
   - the importance of Linear B tablets to our understanding of the Mycenaeans
   - the strengths and limitations of the evidence for daily life of the Mycenaeans

---

PRACTICE QUESTIONS

Source A: *Linear B tablet*

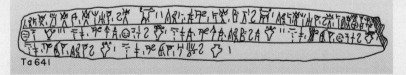

1. 'The Linear B tablets tell us little about the lives of ordinary Mycenaeans.' Using **Source A** as a starting point, how far do you agree with this assessment? [8]
2. What do the Linear B tablets say about religion? [2]
3. Why is this knowledge important to our understanding of how Greek religion developed? [1]

2.3 Decorative Arts

The quality of craftsmanship in Mycenaean objects has been greatly admired. The objects themselves, whether paintings, metalwork, or items of jewellery show very intricate and detailed manufacture. In this section you will find out how these items were made, what they were used for and why they are so admired.

FRESCOES

Some of the most famous pieces of artwork of the ancient world are Mycenaean paintings known as frescoes. These seem to have been influenced by earlier frescoes from Crete in the Minoan Age. Mycenaean frescoes are admired for their use of colour and attention to fine detail. They would originally have adorned palaces, but some are also found at houses, workshops and public buildings. While the grander buildings had frescoes of important individuals or detailed scenes, like the ship fresco from Akrotiri (see Figure 2.27), even small houses had walls where the plaster was painted, although in a much simpler fashion.

Initially a thick layer of lime plaster would have been put on a stone wall to be decorated. Then a finer layer of plaster would have been added. Before this dried, colours would be painted on using natural and manufactured products. String would have been used to set out lines during the composition, and faint lines from this string can be seen at times on the plaster.

A black colour could be gained from carbon, while the famous Mycenaean blue was manufactured from a copper compound. As it did not occur naturally, this blue colour would have been more expensive, and its use would have been designed to impress. Red was obtained from a mineral called haematite, white from lime, yellow from ochre, and green was obtained from mixing blue and yellow, or grinding a mineral called malachite. Some details in lighter colours were added later when the plaster dried, but these have faded over time. A white colour could have been achieved by cutting through to the backing plaster, or by adding more lime plaster.

There seem to have been common uses for these colours. Men are shown with a red skin colour and women with white. Red indicated a tanned skin, and white suggested a person spent more time indoors. Yellow was used for lions and blue for monkeys.

Many different subjects were painted on the frescoes. Those from Akrotiri have been especially admired. Akrotiri was a Minoan site destroyed by fire around the start of the Mycenaean period, so it is debatable how strong the link was between the two societies, but it is not unreasonable to think the Mycenaean frescoes, possibly indirectly, were influenced by those from Akrotiri.

Scenes from nature feature heavily at Akrotiri, such as a spring fresco, which features on three walls of a house. One part of this shows lilies or papyrus growing among colourful

FIGURE 2.26 Fresco of a fisherman with his catch, Akrotiri, 16th century BC, now in the National Archaeological Museum, Athens. Notice the shaved head painted blue, with the elaborate strands of hair, a sign of youth.

FIGURE 2.27
Fresco of a ship procession and a coastal town from Akrotiri, Santorini, 16th century BC, now in the National Archaeological Museum, Athens. The image, part of a longer scene on a river, is tremendously detailed, and notable for its use of colour.

Study question
Why do you think the Mycenaeans chose the subjects for frescoes that they did?

EXAM TIP

If you talk about a particular fresco, do not only talk in general terms about what you can see in it. You will need to explore areas such as the use of colour, the atmosphere of the composition, the realism and the shapes. There is no single correct interpretation, but you must be willing to give your opinions, positive or negative, on it.

ACTIVITY

Research a Mycenaean fresco and give a presentation to the rest of your class on it, stating the dating and location, what it depicts, and your reaction to it. If you are in a group, you could give a presentation on the frescoes from a particular room or house in a site.

rocks with swallows flying overhead. Another house has a fresco of blue monkeys climbing rocks to escape chasing dogs, and two boxers are seen to be fighting in another fresco. Women feature heavily in the frescoes, with some picking saffron in one example.

Perhaps the most famous fresco is the ship fresco shown in Figure 2.27. The full fresco contains eight large ships and three boats being rowed though a town. The ships are decorated with flowers, butterflies, swallows and lilies. Dolphins swim through the water. The town is shown in great detail, with even the clothes of the people individually highlighted. It has been suggested that the high-status clothes and abundance of flowers might show a festival in progress. Others note that helmets hang under the canopies of the ships, suggesting a scene of conflict.

Other common images in frescoes include animals such as octopi, cuttlefish, horses, bulls, lions, dogs, deer, boar and even creatures from myth, such as sphinxes and griffins. In some, men seem to be leaping over bulls, an activity which is shown famously in the earlier Minoan Age in the palace at Knossos.

There are also several examples of processions in frescoes. At Thebes, a fresco shows women carrying a vase, a pyxis and flowers. Images from war are seen too, with figure of eight shields depicted at several cities, including Mycenae. Repeated patterns are also found in some frescoes, such as swirls, spirals or wavy lines.

For all their beauty, the frescoes did have their limitations: the Mycenaeans did not use perspective in their pictures, and sometimes people or objects appeared disproportionately large or small; no attempt was made to give the pictures a three-dimensional feel; faces are shown with eyes looking forward, even if the head is facing to the side. However, all this should not take away from the incredible skill shown for the time in creating such frescoes.

The fresco in Figure 2.28 shows a use of contrasting colours to pick out the details of the woman. There is a significant level of detail, shown by the bracelets on the woman and the varied patterning of the brown fabrics. The blue bracelets are similar to one another, creating a consistency in the picture. Her facial features are very delicate and she gently grasps the saffron. She seems to have a slight smile, which helps create a sense of energy in the picture.

JEWELLERY

The burial sites of Mycenae and Tiryns have revealed a significant amount of jewellery, which may have been worn by men as well as women. Rings and beads have been found at the major graves. Rings are commonly made from gold, and beads were moulded from gold or carved from gemstones, amber, ivory or a form of glass.

Gold rings were often engraved with images on them. These are known as signet rings. Many of these show religious scenes, although the precise meaning of the images is often unclear.

One such ring from Tiryns shows a goddess seated on a folding chair holding a cup, with a hawk or eagle behind her, which may signify power. She is approached by strange lion-headed spirits carrying long-necked jugs perhaps with a drink offering in them. There are ears of wheat, and the sun and moon are also visible, possibly signifying a

FIGURE 2.28
Fresco showing a woman gathering saffron from Akrotiri, Santorini, 16th century BC, now in the National Archaeological Museum, Athens.

FIGURE 2.29
Fresco showing a goddess or priestess holding plants or flowers, Cult Centre, Mycenae, 13th century BC, now in the Archaeological Museum, Mycenae.

ritual connected with crops. Perhaps the most remarkable thing of all is to consider that all this detail could have been put onto a ring.

The details on Figure 2.30 would have been made using a technique known as **repoussé**. Using a hammer and nail, an elaborate pattern could have been worked on to metal to give a sense of depth. Usually the hammering would have been done from the inside of the object so that the scenes would face out. This can be seen from the ring showing a hunt on p. 170, the Vapheio cup on p.186 and the funeral mask on p. 195.

> **repoussé** a technique where a design is hammered onto an object from the inside of it

Many other undecorated rings, gold necklaces and diadems (a kind of royal head-dress) have been found at sites. The beads on necklaces were often worked into imaginative shapes, such as flowers or eagles, and moulds have been found at Mycenae to enable craftsmen to do this. Necklaces of gemstones and rock crystal have also been found. Some of these beads would have been imported, such as amber, ivory, glass and lapis lazuli.

> **Study question**
> What can you find to admire, or criticise, about Figure 2.29? Use the example of the analysis of the saffron gatherer fresco to give you ideas.

MODERN PARALLEL

Many people today wear signet rings. The images on them might show things about the wearer, and the same thing may well have been the case about the images shown on Mycenaean ring, although fewer signet rings today have a religious significance.

FIGURE 2.30
Gold ring, Tiryns, 15th century BC, now in the National Archaeological Museum, Athens.

---

pyxis a box, often with a lid, to hold cosmetics or possibly jewellery

inlay a technique where one metal is put on top of another on an object

cloisonné the soldering of a wire onto metal and then putting glass or gemstones in the soldered pattern

granulation dropping molten metal onto on an object to give a spotted effect

---

A particularly fine example of metalwork is a **pyxis** found in Mycenae. A pyxis is a small storage box. The inner part of this pyxis was a hexagonal wooden box, which is covered in twelve small plates of gold with filigree borders (made by twisting metal wire). The plates show lions chasing deer and antelope among palm trees. Spiral patterns and heads of cattle can be seen, whose bulging eyes stand out in the composition. Aside from the detail of the composition, which shows the use of the repoussé technique, the piece is also a very rare example of a wooden object surviving from the period. The item would have probably been used to contain cosmetics or jewellery.

Another technique used by the Mycenaeans was **inlay**, where one metal was heated and laid over another in an object. This is shown most famously on the lion hunt dagger on p. 167. Swords, too, have been found on which the handle was covered and elaborately patterned with gold. The Mycenaeans also used a technique called **cloisonné** where a fine wire was soldered onto metal and inlaid with gemstones or glass. Tiny beads of gold could also be dropped onto an object to give a spotted effect, a technique known as **granulation**. An example of this is the rhyton on p. 187.

S & C

The ring in Figure 2.30 is thought to have had a religious meaning, although it is not clear what this may have been. The Mycenaeans worshipped many gods and almost certainly made offerings, sacrificed and poured drink offerings, known as libations, to them. Parts of the cities seem to have had a religious function with small shrines dedicated to worship, but there is no evidence of the huge temples of later Greek times.

Research further into the possible religious beliefs of the Mycenaeans and their shrines. Present your findings to your class.

FIGURE 2.31
Gold pyxis, grave V, Grave Circle A, Mycenae, now in the National Archaeological Museum, Athens.

PS

DECORATIVE OBJECTS AND THEIR CREATION

Types of storage vessels and drinking vessels

The Mycenaeans were equally as talented in the manufacture of pottery as they were in the making of jewellery. This is not surprising as early in the period, before developing their own style, they imitated the Minoans, who were also excellent potters. The basic shape was made on a potter's wheel, with patterns then applied. An iron-rich slip (a mixture of water and clay used to give decoration to pottery) was then added. This became various shades from red to black depending on the temperature of the kiln.

The Mycenaeans made many different types of storage vessels. The largest were **pithoi**, which could be over 1.5m high and weighed over 2 tonnes when filled. These would usually contain liquid or food, and could be partially buried in the ground to keep the contents as cool and fresh as possible. As they often contained oil, it is likely that they could become a fire hazard, and many ancient cities suffered greatly from huge blazes.

Another popular vessel were **amphorae**. These differed from pithoi in that they were much smaller, and had a much narrower neck. They often were more elaborately painted with geometric patterns or images from nature.

These amphorae show that the Mycenaeans liked to decorate their pots. A common style of decoration included marine and plant life, while others showed a simpler geometric pattern. In later Mycenaean jars, the neck and lower part of the amphora were painted in lines or a solid block, focusing the eye on the picture in the main part.

The most common form of storage vessel in Mycenaean times would seem to have been the stirrup jar. The jar gets its name from the handle, which resembles stirrups on a horse. Stirrup jars would have been used to store oil or wine. Figure 2.33 shows a stirrup jar decorated with a common form of precise geometric design that had a major influence on later Greek pottery.

In the early Mycenaean Age, double axes, spirals and leaves were commonly shown on vessels. As tastes changed, scenes might include chariot racing, bulls or human figures. The Warrior Vase on p. 169 is an example of such a scene. Other representations on later vessels include flowers, spiralled whorl shells, zigzags and vertical lines.

Other types of storage vessels included large **kraters** for mixing water and wine, squat three-handled jars made from alabaster, and miniature vases for perfumes. Even burial caskets and bath tubs were made from clay by the Mycenaeans.

Many other cups have been found. These often had long stems and two small handles. Such a cup is known as a **kylix**.

Vessels were also made from gold in Mycenaean times, including jugs and cups. Gold cups decorated with beautiful swirls were found in Grave Circle A at Mycenae, whilst two elaborately decorated cups were found at Vapheio, near Sparta.

One cup shows the capture of bulls with a man tying a rope around the bull's leg without any signs of a struggle. In the other cup (Figure 2.34) one bull is caught in a net while another two attack hunters, one of whom flees. It is possible that these cups were originally from Crete and were made in the Minoan times, as their quality surpasses other early Mycenaean cups. Unlike many cups, they are one handled, without stems, and are not curved.

PRESCRIBED SOURCE

Gold Pyxis

Date: 16th century BC

Original location: Shaft Grave V, Grave Circle A, Mycenae

Current location: National Archaeological Museum, Athens

Material: wood and gold

Image: lions chasing animals, heads of cattle (and spirals, not visible in Figure 2.31)

Techniques used: repoussé and filigree

Function: to hold cosmetics or jewellery

Significance: shows techniques in metalworking

---

pithos (pl. **pithoi**) a large clay storage jar

amphora (pl. **amphorae**) a clay storage jar, often containing wine or olive oil, with two carrying handles

kylix (pl. **kylixes**) a drinking cup

Study question
Why do you think amphorae differed in their style and decoration from pithoi?

FIGURE 2.32
Amphorae from Argos, 15th century BC, now in the
National Archaeological Museum, Athens.

FIGURE 2.33
Stirrup jar, Kalkani tomb, Mycenae, 12th century BC, now
in the Archaeological Museum of Mycenae. Note the
precise patterning on the jar using a clay slip.

FIGURE 2.34
Vapheio cup, Laconia, 15th
century BC, now in the
National Archaeological
Museum, Athens.

> **rhyton** (pl. **rhyta**) a vessel,
> either in the shape of a
> cone or animal head,
> probably for pouring liquid,
> and made from either
> pottery or metal

Another famous cup is a golden cup from Mycenae. In the *Iliad*, a Greek leader called Nestor had a famous gold cup, which was four handled and had a pair of golden doves around each handle (*Iliad* 11.632–637). It was so heavy, it could barely be lifted when full. When Schliemann excavated the gold cup at Mycenae, he named it the 'cup of Nestor'. However, although Schliemann's name for it has stuck, it differs significantly in having a single falcon on each of its two handles, and being very easy to lift.

Other striking vessels include **rhyta**, which could have been made from pottery or metal. They are roughly cone-shaped, with many taking the form of animal heads. The liquid was designed to fall through a hole at the bottom or the mouth of the animal head.

The rhyton in Figure 2.35 is in the form of a lion's head, a fitting image for the rulers of Mycenae. It was made from sheets of gold, which were hammered into shape. Liquid would have been poured through the top of the head, with it flowing out through the muzzle. Another notable rhyton from Mycenae is a spectacular silver rhyton in the shape of a bull. This had gold horns, a multi-layered gold rosette on the top of its head, and gold plating on the nose. One hole was between the horns (presumably for filling) and another at the mouth (for pouring). When it was first discovered by the archaeologist Heinrich Schliemann, he thought the hole at the top was for putting flowers in. One pottery rhyton from near Athens was even in the shape of a shoe.

Gold rhyton

Date: 16th century BC

Original Location: Grave IV, Grave Circle A, Mycenae

Current location: National Archaeological Museum, Athens

Material: sheets of gold

Original purpose: container for pouring wine

Image: lion's head

Techniques used: hammering, granulation, repoussé

Significance: shows techniques in metalworking

Study question

Why do you think that most scholars believe that people did not drink out of a rhyton?

FIGURE 2.35
Mycenaean gold rhyton in the shape of a lion's head.

Animal figures, human figures and votive offerings

Many clay **figurines** of animals and humans have been found in private houses and tombs in Mycenaean cities. While some of the human figurines might have been toys, as they were found in children's tombs, it would seem that many had a religious significance, although what this was is unclear. It has been suggested that figurines were used in religious worship, or else were votive offerings to the gods in the hope of the fulfilment of a prayer. These figurines were usually small enough to be held in a hand.

Three particular styles of human figurines are easily recognisable: the phi, psi and tau figurines. They get their names respectively from the Greek letters ϕ, ψ, and τ whose shapes the figurines resemble. It is thought that they may have represented female goddesses, with the phi and psi types usually showing females with prominent breasts. These goddesses were imported from Crete, probably in the Minoan Age.

Other pottery figurines are more recognisable as human and include a number with arms raised or holding implements. Female figurines often are painted wearing fine jewellery and with prominent breasts. Animals figures include numerous coiled snakes, which almost certainly had a religious significance, and miniature pottery cattle.

> **figurine** a small statue of a person, god or animal

Ivory carving

We have already seen how the Mycenaeans used ivory tusks to make helmets (see p. 168), but they also used ivory from elephants, hippopotami and boars to make elaborate works of art. One of the most famous is a sculpture of a child (possibly a young god) with two bare-breasted women (possibly goddesses).

FIGURE 2.36
Left – Phi figurine, Mycenae, 13th century BC, now in the National Archaeological Museum, Athens; centre – Psi figurine, Mycenae, 13th century BC, now in the Ashmolean Museum, Oxford; right – Tau figurine, Mycenae, 13th century BC, now in the National Archaeological Museum, Athens.

FIGURE 2.37
Ivory sculpture showing two women and a child, 14th–15th century BC, Mycenae, now in the Archaeological Museum, Athens.

Other figures include a reclining lion and the head of a youth, both from the House of the Fresco in Mycenae.

Another very intricate piece of ivory carving is a comb from Attica. Above the teeth of the ivory comb are two bands containing sphinxes and a rosette. Ivory was also used to make a pyxis from Thebes, also depicting sphinxes, and a pair of chair legs from Thebes. Other items of furniture included ivory inlays of sphinxes, dolphins, columns, shells and shields.

TOPIC REVIEW

You should be able to:

1. Describe:
   - how frescoes were painted and what they showed
   - the types of jewellery that the Myceanaeans wore
   - the designs on Mycenaean rings and the techniques that were used in making them
   - the types of other metal objects such as storage boxes, cups and rhyta, and the designs on them
   - what the Mycenaeans used ivory for
   - the different types of pottery storage vessels that the Mycenaeans had
   - the appearance of pottery figurines and votive offerings.

2. Explain:
   - why Mycenaean frescoes are generally admired
   - what the designs on frescoes tell us about Mycenaean life
   - what the designs on jewellery and cups tell us about Mycenaean life
   - the different possible uses of rhyta and figurines.

PRACTICE QUESTIONS

Source A: *A gold pyxis from Mycenae*

1. How would an object such as the gold pyxis from Grave Circle A have been made? [2]
2. Give **one** reason why this particular object is unusual. [1]
3. 'We can gain a full understanding of the Mycenaeans from their metalwork?' How far do you agree with this assessment? [15]

2.4 Tombs, Graves and Burial

TOPIC OVERVIEW

- Burial customs
- Structure and use of cist graves
- Structure and use of shaft graves
- Structure and use of tholos and chamber tombs
- The use of funerary objects
- The contents of the graves of Grave Circle A and Grave Circle B at Mycenae

The prescribed source for this topic is:

- Gold death mask of Agamemnon from Shaft grave V, Mycenae

Don't forget that you will be given credit in the exam if you study extra sources and make relevant use of them in your answers.

Honouring the dead was an important part of Mycenaean life. A significant area of Mycenae and the surrounding area is devoted to burial spaces, and the places where bodies were buried could be very grand constructions. In this section you will learn how the Mycenaeans buried their dead, and the types of graves and tombs that they used.

BURIAL CUSTOMS

Although the form of Mycenaean tombs changed, burial customs probably did not differ greatly over the period. We know that the body, if wealthy, would have been adorned with jewellery, as this has been found on the necks and wrists of skeletons. From this we can assume that bodies were clothed for burial too. A drink offering was almost certainly made to the gods as metal cups have been found badly damaged on the floor at the entrance to tholos tombs.

Bones of animals and sea-shells have also been found, suggesting a meal was eaten in honour of the dead. Gifts would have been offered, although these have often either decayed or were robbed in ancient times. A pair of horses was found slaughtered at both Marathon and Dendra, but there is no such evidence from Mycenae to suggest this was a common practice. However, the killing of animals does mirror a scene from the *Iliad* Book 23, where two of Patroclus' dogs were slaughtered at his funeral.

Finally, the earth would have been filled in and a raised mound would then have covered the area so that it was visible from a distance. A stele would have been placed over the tomb, such as the one shown in Figure 2.38.

The mound would be dug again when another burial was made and bodies would be interred in the same area.

There is evidence that some bodies could have been put in a clay burial casket, as remains from Tanagra in central Greece show. The painted scenes on the caskets also tell us a lot about customs as we can see a funeral procession of women, many of whom are in elaborate dresses. Some women also wear an unusual feathered cap, and it is the women, rather than the men who have their hands raised to their heads, perhaps in a sign of grief. Women, not men, are shown near the bodies, all indicating they had the greater role in burial. On one casket, a body lies on a bed and the dead person is wrapped in a short tunic. On another casket a drink offering, known as a **libation**, seems to be poured in honour of the dead. However, these caskets are extremely rare, and it is hard to know whether what they represent was typical of Mycenaean funerals and burials.

FIGURE 2.38
Stone stele (grave marker) showing hunting from a chariot, Grave Circle A, Mycenae, now in the Archaeological Museum, Athens.

---

libation a drink offering poured in honour of the gods

cist grave a grave in the form of a stone-lined pit, dug into the earth, and covered up

Study question
Graves and tombs were reused many times. Why do you think this was the case?

shaft grave a grave in which a deep shaft was dug and a space created at the bottom for a body, often re-used for later burials

STRUCTURE AND USE OF CIST GRAVES

In the Mycenaean Age the most basic type of burial was one in a **cist grave**. These were used before the Mycenaean Age, but continued to be used at sites until the end of the period. In a cist grave, a shallow pit was dug in the earth, and the sides were covered in slabs of stone. A pile of stones was then placed at the bottom for the body to lie on. These pits were so small that the body had to be placed in a curved position.

Before the Mycenaean Age, these tombs were intended only for a single use. At the start of the Mycenaean Age they began to be grouped together with a mound of earth raised on top. The mound was opened up when a new body needed to be buried. These might be placed in pithoi, or in fresh pits, or in re-dug earth beside the original burial.

STRUCTURE AND USE OF SHAFT GRAVES

A second type of grave, known as a **shaft grave**, was also used at the start of the Mycenean Age. Grave Circle B contained fourteen shaft graves, together with ten cist graves.

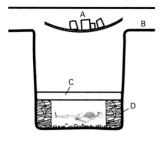

FIGURE 2.39
Diagram of the excavation of a shaft grave at Mycenae.
A = stelai; B = surface level; C = roof support; D = brick.

EXPLORE FURTHER

Skeletons found in the shaft graves of Grave Circle B have been forensically analysed. The one from Grave Sigma was of a large man, aged about 55. He suffered from arthritis and possible problems with gall-stones, but only three of his teeth were diseased. The man in Grave Zeta was aged about 49 when he died, and his skull was notable for deep impressions, an indication that he suffered heavy blows to it. He had lived a violent life as his spine and one of his ribs show evidence of healing after fractures.

One of the five bodies in Grave Gamma was a man aged about 28. He was tall and had strong bones, but he had suffered an injury near the eye and had two fractures in the area. A hole had been drilled at the top of his skull in an operation, possibly to treat his injuries. However, the lack of any evidence of any healing on the bone suggests this failed.

A shaft grave is a natural development of a cist grave, but is larger and deeper. A narrow shaft was dug up to 2.5m deep (the cist graves in Grave Circle B were only dug to up to 0.6m deep). The largest grave (Grave Zeta) measures 3.4 × 3.9m, the size of a typical bedroom today. At the bottom, a chamber with low rubble walls was created with a roof support. The pit of Grave Zeta has four post holes in the corners for beams to hold up the roof, which also rested on a rock ledge. Finally, the shaft that had been previously dug was filled in.

Bodies in shaft graves were usually laid on their backs. Multiple burials in the same chambers were common. When a second body was buried, the first was often pushed aside or moved to a corner to make room for the new one. A new stele might have been placed, but this was not a universal practice. Significant grave goods appear for the first time with the use of shaft graves.

STRUCTURE AND USE OF THOLOS AND CHAMBER TOMBS

After the emergence of Grave Circle A, a new style of burial occurred in the fourteenth century BC, known as the tholos tomb. These derive from an earlier type of tomb, known as a **tumulus**, where a large mound was built over where a group of bodies had been buried. Tholos tombs were different from previous tombs as they were built from stone, rather than dug out the earth. As they are so monumental, they could only have been built for the most important members of a city.

tumulus a raised mound of earth under which bodies were buried

The main part of the tomb consisted of a high-roofed dome (those at Mycenae were the tallest known domes in the world for over a thousand years), which would have been dug down from the top of a hill. A side chamber sometimes was dug to house the body. The stone at the bottom of the excavated area would then have been used to make the walls and roof of the structure, and the excavated earth would then have been placed over the top of the roof. These may have been constructed during the lifetime of the person intended to be

Study question
Why do you think tholos tombs were rarely created after the thirteenth century BC?

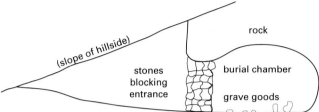

FIGURE 2.41
Drawing of the interior of the chamber tomb.

buried in it, as the construction of these tombs would have been a huge and time-consuming undertaking. Tholos tombs are rarely seen after the thirteenth century BC.

In front of the tholos was a long passageway with stone walls, known as a **dromos**. When a body had been buried, large stones would have been placed at end of the dromos to block off the entrance. Earth would then have been put on the dromos to create an elevated slope.

At the end of the dromos was a richly decorated entrance, although no one could ever have entered it. Some of the entrance from the Treasury of Atreus has survived. There, two green limestone columns with a zigzag pattern framed the entranceway, and about the entrance there would have been a triangle of red stone where a triangular space now exists. This would have relieved the weight on the large block of stone above the doorway.

From the fourteenth century, less important Mycenaean nobles were buried in **chamber tombs** (a tomb dug from rock in which more than one body was buried in a chamber). They were similar to tholos tombs as they had a dromos, with a wall of stones to block the entrance. However, unlike tholos tombs, which were built from stone, chamber tombs were dug out of the earth, using the rock to form the roof of a square or rounded chamber. Several people could be buried in each, often in side chambers, and as such they were probably used as family tombs. These were used right up to the end of the Mycenaean period, but in the final years there is evidence of the resurgence of cist graves, possibly indicating a decline in prosperity in Mycenae.

> **dromos** a passageway leading to the tholos tomb

> **chamber tomb** a tomb, dug from rock, is which a body or bodies would be buried in a chamber

THE USE OF FUNERARY OBJECTS

Many of the shaft graves from Mycenaean cities are found to have contained valuable items, reflecting the importance of the people buried in them. Many ancient societies, such as the Egyptians, believed that the dead would use the items they were buried with in the afterlife. However, as we know virtually nothing of what the Mycenaeans believed happened after death, we cannot be sure that items would have been buried for the deceased to use. The items could have been buried simply to show off the status and wealth of the person during their lifetime.

Pottery items, whether vessels or figurines, are the most common objects found in tombs. These would almost certainly have contained oils, perfumes and other liquids. Military equipment, such as swords and daggers are also commonly found, presumably suggesting the deceased was a warrior. While inlaid weapons, such as the Lion Hunt Dagger, and ones with handles covered in gold are the most famous pieces of military equipment, the vast majority of items were simply made of bronze. Women were often buried with jewellery and sometimes with boxes for cosmetics, combs or bronze mirrors. If tombs were re-used, new items would have been placed in the tomb, with scraps of gold from previous burials found in the shafts.

THE CONTENTS OF THE GRAVES OF GRAVE CIRCLE A AND GRAVE CIRCLE B AT MYCENAE

The contents of Grave Circles A and B included some of the finest grave goods found anywhere in the world. While the goods of Grave Circle B are less spectacular on the whole than those from Grave Circle A, they still contain some remarkable pieces.

This vessel was found in a woman's grave, together with a quantity of jewellery. It is probably to keep cosmetics in. It may have come from Crete, where there are rock crystal quarries, and where there were similar objects in Minoan times. Other items found in graves include gold funeral masks, pottery, jewellery and swords.

The six graves in Grave Circle A contained a vast quantity of treasure. Some of the most famous items come from Grave V and include:

- two gold death masks (see below)
- gold cup with repoussé spirals
- gold necklace
- bronze dagger with the blade inlaid with gold spirals
- amber bead necklace
- wooden pyxis, covered with gold plates
- ostrich-egg rhyton with faience (a glazed ceramic) dolphins applied on to it
- swords with handles decorated with gold
- bronze sword decorated with griffins (a mythical creature)
- gold octopus brooch
- numerous other swords, pottery objects, items of jewellery.

FIGURE 2.42
Rock crystal vessel with a handle in the shape of a duck's head and neck, Grave omicron, Grave Circle B, Mycenae.

The final picture in this section is perhaps the most iconic image from Mycenae, and comes from Shaft Grave V in Grave Circle A. When Schliemann saw the mask, he is alleged to have written 'I have gazed on the face of Agamemnon', believing he had unearthed the death mask of the legendary ruler of Mycenae at the time of the Trojan War, although many dispute if he ever said this. However, as was discussed on p.162, many of the finds come from several centuries before his supposed existence.

A thick sheet of gold would have been heated to make it softer and easier to hammer into shape. This would probably have been done by placing the gold against a wooden background and hammering it to create a representation of the features of the deceased, using the

FIGURE 2.43
The famous death mask found at Mycenae and commonly attributed to Agamemnon.

PS

PRESCRIBED SOURCE

Gold death mask of 'Agamemnon'

Date: 16th century BC

Original Location: Grave V, Grave Circle A, Mycenae

Current location: National Archaeological Museum, Athens

Material: sheets of gold

Original purpose: death mask

Image: face of the deceased

Techniques shown: hammering, repoussé

Significance: shows techniques in metalworking and burial customs

repoussé technique. A sharper tool would have been used for the facial details. Two holes near the ears indicate the mask was fixed over the face with twine when the deceased was buried. It illustrates the dignified and imposing features of a man, with its striking beard and moustache, and closed eyes. Due to the quality of the workmanship, it seems almost certain that it would have been used at the burial of one of the rulers of Mycenae. The mask is 17cm high, 25cm wide and weighs only 168g, indicating the thinness of the gold and, therefore, the skill of the craftsman in being able to create such precise details on such a thin object.

Study question

Do you think Schliemann should be admired or criticised for the way he excavated Mycenae and Troy?

ACTIVITY

Research one of the shaft graves of either Grave Circle A or Grave Circle B, producing either a presentation or wall display. Individuals from a class could produce a booklet, with pages on each of the graves.

EXPLORE FURTHER

Some scholars doubt that this mask is a genuine Mycenaean object, pointing to stylistic differences between it and other masks from Mycenae. This mask has very distinctive facial features and a beard, unlike the other four masks uncovered from Mycenae. Contemporaries of Schliemann said that he planted objects at the site, so that he could later 'discover' them, and that he would make duplicates of objects to pass them off as genuine. He had earlier made an agreement to split his findings with officials in exchange for permission to excavate. He finished excavations three days after finding the mask, which might seem surprising if such a major find was genuinely made. He had left the site a few days earlier, but it was not known where he went. Could he have gone to obtain the mask from elsewhere, possibly Athens, where a relative of his wife was said to have been a goldsmith? The unnatural, upturned effect of the moustache would be very hard to create in Mycenaean times, so would not seem a logical way for a ruler to present himself.

While this may seem convincing, many scholars believe that despite these issues, it is a genuine Mycenaean artefact.

TOPIC REVIEW

You should be able to:

1. Describe:
   - how the Mycenaeans buried their dead
   - the forms of cist graves and shaft graves
   - the forms of tholos and chamber tombs
   - typical objects with which the dead were buried
   - the key objects found in Grave Circles A and B.

2. Explain:
   - why the Mycenaeans buried their dead in the manner that they did
   - the relationships between shaft and cist graves and between tholos and chamber tombs
   - how and why tholos and chamber tombs were constructed
   - what particular funerary objects tells us about the dead.

PRACTICE QUESTIONS

Source A: *Grave circle A at Mycenae*

1. Describe the appearance of a typical shaft tomb in Mycenaean times. [3]
2. 'Tombs and burials raise more questions about the Mycenaeans than they provide answers.' How far do you agree with this assessment? [15]

Literature

2.5 Literary Techniques and Composition

Homer is widely acknowledged as a master story-teller, and his influence on ancient and modern literature has been vast. His poem belongs to a class of literature called Epic Poetry, which you will discover more about in this section.

HOMER AS A STORY-TELLER AND THE IDEA OF EPIC

The *Odyssey* is a poem in twenty-four sections, or books as they are generally known. It tells us of the adventures of the hero Odysseus sailing home after the Trojan War, and how he managed to reclaim his kingdom. This war, between the Greek and Trojans, had lasted 10 years. Odysseus, despite wishing to stay at home with his wife Penelope and new-born son Telemachus, was bound by a promise he had made to go. He tried to back out of his promise by pretending he had gone mad when he was summoned to join the rest of the Greek forces. However, one of the other soldiers sent to fetch him placed his

DEBATE Homer

Homer is widely regarded as one of the greatest and most important authors in history, and yet there is nothing that we know about him for certain. Many stories have arisen about who he was, where he lived, and when he composed his two great poems, the *Iliad* and the *Odyssey*. In fact, even to talk about just one person composing the poems is highly debatable.

If the Trojan War, the setting for the *Iliad*, actually took place, it is thought that it occurred in the twelfth or thirteenth century BC. The *Odyssey* is thought to have been composed a few hundred years later, and the form that we have today was possibly written down in the seventh century BC.

FIGURE 2.44
Marble head of Homer, Palazzo Caetani, Rome, 1st–2nd century AD, now in the Louvre Museum, Paris.

son in front of a plough. Odysseus snatched his son away as he was about to be trampled on, proving that he was sane after all.

During his time at Troy, Odysseus came up with the idea of the Wooden Horse by which the Greeks captured Troy. However, his voyage home from Troy and the reclamation of his kingdom was full of adventure and drama, and you will read some of the key episodes in of these in the *Odyssey*. Together with Homer's other poem, the *Iliad*, the *Odyssey* is considered to be amongst the greatest works of literature ever composed.

THE PLOT OF THE *ODYSSEY*

The plot of the *Odyssey* is a relatively simple one: a man, Odysseus, seeks to return home to the island of Ithaca (see map, Figure 1.10) after twenty years away. In his attempts to sail home, he gets lost and all his crew members die in horrific circumstances. When he eventually gets back, his problems are still not over; he has to reclaim his kingdom from his enemies, and convince his wife that he is the man she married, as he looks like a beggar, rather than her former husband.

You are not expected to know the whole of the *Odyssey*, but to make full sense of the books that you have to read, it is helpful to be aware of what happens in the rest of the story. However, you need to be aware of an added complication in the *Odyssey*; the chronological order of the events is not the same as the order that they occur in the story. This is because Homer uses a flashback technique, and the early books of the Odyssey describe events that occur near the end of Odysseus' ten-year journey home. This flashback is designed to make us to want to read on to find out about these adventures. Odysseus tells these adventures in Books 9–12.

Below is a brief summary of the key events of the *Odyssey* in the order they are written in the text.

S & C Another famous section of the *Odyssey* is Books 5–8, where Odysseus is on an island with the goddess Calypso, and is then entertained by the Phaeacians. These books are particularly worth reading to discover Odysseus' talents as a speaker.

Book 12 is also a famous book, which tells the adventures of Odysseus and his crew. It contains the famous story of Odysseus and the Sirens.

1) Odysseus' son, Telemachus, goes to Pylos and Sparta in search of news of his father, who has not returned home from Troy. It has been 10 years since the war has ended. He does not get any positive information (Books 1–4).

2) At a similar time, Odysseus leaves the island of the goddess Calypso, where he has been stuck for 7 years. He sails to the land of the Phaeacians, despite being hit by a storm sent by Poseidon (Books 5–8).

3) Odysseus tells the Phaeacians about what happened to him after leaving Troy. He tells of adventures with the Cyclops, Circe and various other encounters (Books 9–12).

4) Odysseus reaches home, disguised as a beggar. He bides his time, only revealing his identity to his son and a few slaves. He kills the suitors who wish to marry his wife, before being reunited with her (Books 13–24).

The chronological order of events is somewhat different.

1) After leaving Troy, Odysseus and his crew got lost at sea and had adventures in various places and with various creatures (Books 9–12).

2) After the crew die in a storm, Odysseus gets washed up on Calypso's island. He then sails to Phaeacia and is welcomed (Books 5–8).

3) While Odysseus leaves Calypso's island and is in Phaeacia, his son searches for news of him (Books 1–4).

4) Odysseus reaches home, disguised as a beggar. He eventually kills the suitors and is reunited with his wife (Books 13–24).

THE INDIVIDUAL BOOKS

Book 9

At the start of your selection, Odysseus begins to tell of his adventures since leaving Troy to Alcinous, King of Phaeacia. The king had noticed that Odysseus was crying when a bard (a poet and storyteller) was singing about the Trojan War and questioned Odysseus. As a result Odysseus begins by telling Alcinous who he is, as Alcinous did not know the identity of his guest. Odysseus reveals his identity by saying:

> I am Odysseus, Laertes' son, known to all for my stratagems, and my fame has reached the heavens.

> Homer, *Odyssey*, 9.19–20

Odysseus then goes on to tell of his adventures after Troy in Books 9 and 10, and he is famous for telling tales (and twisting the truth). This might make you wonder if all the stories that Odysseus narrates in these two books are completely or partially made up by Odysseus to create sympathy and gain help from the Phaeacians.

The first of these stories is his attack on the island of the Cicones. His men's insistence on staying an extra day to enjoy the successes of their initial victory result in a counter-attack by the Cicones on the next day and the loss of seventy-two of the crew. After a storm occurs, the crew lose their way and end up on the land of the Lotus-eaters, where a different danger awaits them – the loss of any memory of their home if they eat the lotus fruit. Three crew members do eat the fruit, but Odysseus uses all his strength and bravery to drag crew away, although a deadlier threat is in store.

We find out about the uncivilised land and inhabitants of the island as the suspense is built up by the long introduction to the encounter with the Cyclops, Polyphemus. The actual encounter is possibly the most famous part of the *Odyssey*.

On entering Polyphemus' cave, Odysseus and his men help themselves to his cheese. Polyphemus himself was out shepherding his flocks. His men want to steal the cheese and go, but Odysseus overrules them, staying in the hope of getting gifts from the cave owner. On his return, Polyphemus spots them and questions them about their identity and motives, before suddenly eating two of the men. After four more men are eaten, Odysseus devises a plan to get Polyphemus drunk, and blind him when he is asleep. He makes a huge stake while Polyphemus is out shepherding his flocks, and that evening, he gets Polyphemus drunk, tells him that his name is Nobody, and blinds him. Polyphemus shouts out that Nobody has blinded him, as a result of which the other Cyclopes do not come to help. That night, he and his men then cling on to undersides of his flock until Polyphemus lets his animals out the next morning, not realising that men are clinging on to them. When they have escaped to their boats Odysseus shouts out his name in triumph to Polyphemus, allowing Polyphemus to throw rocks at his fleet and curse him for the rest of his journey.

We are not given all the key information at once: we are not told Polyphemus is one-eyed until his eye is blinded, and whilst Odysseus knows why he is giving Polyphemus strong wine, and giving himself a false name, we do not know.

Book 10

The book starts off with more tales of fantasy with the story of the bag of winds. Aeolus, the keeper of the winds, traps all the winds in a bag, leaving out only the one that will blow Odysseus straight home. As the crew are within sight of Ithaca, Odysseus falls asleep for the first time in many days and his men open the bag, thinking that it is treasure; Odysseus had not told them of the contents, and he was guarding the bag very closely. They are driven back to Aeolus' island, but he refuses to help them a second time. At the next adventure at the land of the Laestrygonians, all of the men except for those on Odysseus' boat get trapped in the harbour and are slaughtered by the inhabitants.

The survivors then sail to Circe's island. Half of them, led by Eurylochus, travel to her home. When they arrive at her house they are seemingly given good hospitality to by Circe, but she slips a drug into their food to turn them into pigs. Only Eurylochus, who had not eaten the food, retains his human form and travels back to Odysseus. Odysseus then sets off on a rescue mission and is given a magic flower by the god Hermes. This ensures that he remains unaffected when he meets Circe, who tries to turn him into a pig.

Study questions

1 Why are the Lotus-eaters such a danger to Odysseus?
2 Why do you think Homer creates them?

KEY INDIVIDUAL

Polyphemus a one-eyed giant belonging to the race of the Cyclopes, who eats six of Odysseus' men

PRESCRIBED SOURCE

Homer's *Odyssey*, Books 9, 10, 19, 21, 22

Date: uncertain (see p. 199)

Author: attributed to Homer

Genre: epic poetry

Read it here: OCR sources booklet

Study question
Why do you think Homer does not give us all the key information earlier in the story than he actually does?

KEY INDIVIDUAL

Circe a witch who turns half of Odysseus' crew into pigs, but ends up being kind and hospitable

She then becomes much more friendly, turning the pigs back into the crew and giving them all hospitality. After a year of relaxation, the crew persuade Odysseus that they must sail for home, and Circe helps with this too, preparing them for the next stage of the journey with gifts and advice.

Book 19

Odysseus is now in Ithaca and has been disguised as a beggar by Athena. Here he is verbally attacked by a maid. His wife, Penelope, comes to his aid, not knowing his real identity, and asks the beggar about his family. Odysseus, not wanting to risk the plans he has been making for revenge on the suitors (a group of men who assume Odysseus is dead and want to marry his wife; see also p. 224), makes up a false tale about his background. He convincingly adds in a few true details from an alleged meeting with Odysseus, which causes Penelope to weep.

Penelope asks Eurycleia, Odysseus' former nurse from his youth, to wash him. She spots a scar that causes her to realise the beggar is really Odysseus. At this crucial moment, Homer stops the story for over two pages while he tells us of how Odysseus got the injury in his youth when hunting a boar.

Odysseus then warns Eurycleia not to reveal his true identity:

> Keep it from all the rest of the house. Otherwise I say, and it shall be so, that if a god delivers the noble Suitors into my hands, I will not spare you, though you nursed me, when I kill the other serving women in the palace.

> Homer, *Odyssey*, 19.486–489

Penelope then tells the stranger of a dream she had. Odysseus interprets this as a sign that her husband will soon return. Finally, she announces the contest that will lead to her marry one of the suitors, as she can hold out no longer against their pressure.

Study questions

1 Why do you think Homer has Odysseus disguised as a beggar during his time in Ithaca?

2 Why does Homer spend so long giving us the details of how Odysseus got his injury?

3 Do you consider Odysseus' reaction to his identity being discovered appropriate? Explain your views.

Book 21

Penelope announces the contest to string Odysseus' bow and fire an arrow through twelve axes. Only Odysseus had been able to string the bow, and so if any suitor can do it, he will be a worthy husband for her. Penelope and Odysseus' son, Telemachus, has the first go, but he cannot quite manage to string it. Odysseus, needing help to put his plan into action, reveals his plan to some of his loyal slaves and to Telemachus. One of the leading suitors, Eurymachus, fails to string the bow, and the other suitors decide to take a break. It is at this moment that Odysseus asks to have a go at it. Despite the outrage of the suitors, Telemachus insists that the beggar is given a go. While this is going on, Eurycleia locks the doors in the palace so that the suitors cannot escape.

At this most tense moment of the whole *Odyssey*, Homer writes:

> So they chattered, but once wily Odysseus had flexed the great bow and checked it all over, he strung it easily, as a man skilled in song and the lyre stretches a new string onto its leather tuning strap, fixing the twisted sheep-gut at either end. Then

Study questions

1 Why do you think Homer uses the simile about the man skilled in song at this point?

2 How are the ideas in the simile developed in the sentence?

grasping the bow in his right hand, he plucked the string that sang sweetly to his touch with the sound of a swallow's note.

Homer, Odyssey, 21.404–411

Book 22

Odysseus shoots the leading suitor, Antinous, who dies is a gruesome manner. Even now, the suitors do not realise who the beggar is, assuming Antinous' death to have been accidental. Odysseus finally reveals his identity at this point. Despite Eurymachus' attempts to avoid his punishment by blaming the behaviour of the suitors on Antinous, he too is slaughtered. A massacre follows when the suitors are unable to escape from the hall, with Athena encouraging Odysseus in the battle. Telemachus and the loyal servants play an active part in the killing of the suitors. When all the suitors are killed, the disloyal maids are hung and the evil slave, Melanthius, also dies in a horrific manner. The loyal slaves are all spared.

HOW THE *ODYSSEY* MIGHT HAVE BEEN COMPOSED AND PERFORMED

So how did the *Odyssey* reach us, if there was such a long gap between the war and its composition? The answer lies in the way that it was composed. At the time of the events of the *Odyssey*, the ancient Greeks did not have a written alphabet, and so it would have been impossible for the story to have been written down at the time that the events might have happened. The *Odyssey* does mention professional singers, known as **bards**, who recited myths. Such singers would have recited tales while playing a stringed musical instrument known as a lyre. This would probably have happened after banquets, and the *Odyssey* itself describes such a situation in Book 8. One part, perhaps equivalent to a book of the *Odyssey*, might well have been recited after a meal. Thus, the *Odyssey* is known as an **oral poem**.

> **bard** a public storyteller who recited vast amounts poetry to the accompaniment of the lyre often during banquets
>
> **oral** poem a poem that is composed and told without the aid of writing

It would seem that this is what happened with the *Odyssey*; someone recited these stories originally, possibly on lots of different occasions, which were passed on through generations of singers and continually adapted. Several centuries later, when the Greeks had developed their written alphabet, the stories were written down.

Narrative and structural features of epic poetry

When people today think of an epic story, perhaps the saga of Beowulf or the Bible come to mind, or in a more modern context, the stories of Harry Potter or the Lord of the Rings. All have elements of epic in them. An epic might be regarded as having some or all of the following elements:

- it is long
- it contains a central figure or hero
- it tells of a quest or mission for the central figure

- it features amazing deeds
- it starts in the middle of the story (known by the Latin phrase 'in medias res')
- it has monsters, magic and gods
- it is set in lots of different places
- it has certain literary features (e.g. epithets and similes) within it.

The *Odyssey* has all these elements.

Descriptive techniques

The *Odyssey* contains over 12,000 lines of poetry and the *Iliad* contains around 3,000 more. We might ask how a bard was able to remember such an extraordinary amount. Part of the answer is that the poems have a number of repetitive elements; in fact, about a third of the lines of the poem are repeated wholly or in part. Moreover, it seems that each poet would develop his own version each time he presented it – he could use the repetitive elements as a starting point, and then insert his own lines around them, or use lines with which he was already familiar. The repetitive elements therefore acted as building blocks for each poet to work from, and allowed him to improvise each time he gave a performance.

Characters are regularly given descriptive phrases, called **epithets**, to highlight key aspects of their character. For example, Odysseus is often called 'noble Odysseus', 'resourceful Odysseus' or 'Odysseus of the nimble wits'.

Sometimes the epithet fits the situation perfectly. For example, when Eurycleia first notices a likeness between Odysseus and the beggar, and reveals this to him, Odysseus replies:

> "Old woman," said the quick-witted Odysseus, "that is what everyone says who has set eyes upon us both."
>
> Homer, Odyssey 19.383–384

> **epithet** an adjectival word or phrase regularly added to a name to denote a personal or physical quality

> **Study question**
> Why is the epithet 'quick-witted' appropriate here?

Different epithets could be fitted it in to different parts of a line simply to fit to the rhythm of epic poetry. Longer phrases, often amounting to a line or more, could also be repeated. These are known as **formulae**.

The most famous example is Homer's description of Dawn, which is always fresh and rosy-fingered. This phrase occurs repeatedly to mark the start of a new day.

One very important feature of epic poetry is the **simile**. This helps the reader to visualise a situation. To analyse a simile properly, you need to consider the individual points of comparison between the simile and story.

Some similes are simple, such as Penelope coming down from her apartment looking like Artemis or Aphrodite in Book 19, but others are more developed like this one about the hanging of the maids:

> **formula** (pl. **formulae**) a section of an epic poem, longer than an epithet, that is regularly used to describe a person, place or object
>
> **simile** a figure of speech whereby one thing is compared to another thing of a different kind in order to make a description more vivid

> The row of women held up their heads, and the rope was looped round their necks so they might die pitiably, like long-winged thrushes or doves, that are caught in a snare as they try to roost in their thicket, and are welcomed to a grimmer nest. For a little while their feet twitched: but not for long.
>
> Homer, Odyssey, 22.468–472

MODERN PARALLEL

Many forms of music use similar techniques in composition. Jazz musicians and rap artists often make up melodies or lyrics on the spot that they insert into their performances. These sections are made up from smaller units in much the same way as Homer used epithets and formulae to create a section.

S & C

Even with these simple little ways to fill in some parts of the story, many people still doubted whether it was humanly possible to memorise all the story, let alone make it fit a particular rhythm. But in the 1930s, studies were made on poets at that time in Bosnia, in eastern Europe, where poems were recited from memory. One illiterate poet was able to recite a 12,000-line poem from memory, proving that what had been done in Greek times in the *Odyssey* was possible with practice.

Find a poem that is at least 10 lines long and learn it. After doing so, consider how long it was compared to the *Odyssey*. What problems did you have, and what helped you to memorise the poem successfully? Think also about learning lyrics to songs. Why are the lyrics of some songs easier to remember than others?

The women, like birds, are caught in a situation they cannot escape from. They had probably been thinking of going to sleep with the suitors (108 local noblemen who wish to marry Penelope, believing Odysseus is dead), just as the birds had been about to roost, before being caught unexpectedly. They twitch in the final moments in the same way as birds in a trap flutter for a while.

Not every element of the simile has to match up: the women are not literally caught in a trap. Perhaps too we feel sympathy for the birds, unlike the women, though trapping birds was a way of life in the ancient world. These differences do not stop the simile being effective, but if there are too many differences, or it is too hard to imagine, you may find it less effective.

There are also longer sections of recurring situations, known as **topoi**, such as welcoming a guest or making a prayer. Many people feel that the repetitive elements add to the charm of the poem and create a sense of familiarity.

We have already seen how Homer uses similes, epithets, formulae and topoi in his narrative, but there are several other ways that he makes his story exciting.

Gory detail features in several books as Odysseus has to show himself to be a great warrior at various points. This is the same kind of appeal that horror and action films have, and the appeal was probably no different in Homer's time. A good example is the death of Antinous:

The point passed clean through the tender throat, and Antinous sank to one side, the cup falling at that moment from his hand, while a thick jet of blood gushed from his nostrils. His foot kicked the table away, dashing the food to the floor, and the bread and meat were fouled.

Homer, *Odyssey*, 22.16–21

In a few lines we can see each separate moment of his death. The twitching of his foot and the kicking of the table are well-chosen details, and the ordinariness of the food on the ground provides a contrast to the blood gushing out.

Dramatic irony is used at various points, especially towards the end of the story. The disguise of Odysseus provides numerous examples, as characters talk to the beggar about Odysseus, without realising his true identity. Examples include the occasion on which

EXAM TIP

If you comment on a simile, do not simply write that 'it helps us to visualise the scene better'. That is the function of similes in general and does not show understanding of a particular simile. If you comment on the exact parallels, as in the quotations on p. 204 and p. 206, you will score more AO2 marks for your evaluation.

topos (pl. **topoi**) a poetic scene that occurs regularly, which is made up of a series of standard elements

dramatic irony when a character does not know the full significance of what is happening or being said, but the readers do

Eumaeus and Philoetius pray that Odysseus returns in a speech to him in Book 21, or when Antinous says that the bow will seal the suitors' fate in Book 22.

Detailed description is also a feature of this scene. It helps the reader to picture the scene completely and get more involved in the story. Look also at the description of the flocks of Polyphemus, the Cyclops. The precise detail that we are given of the separation of the animals and the making of the cheese helps us to see him as something more than just a monster.

Ordinary scenes and objects are raised to a higher status by the way they are described, such as the history of the bow that will seal the fate of the suitors. Homer often uses such descriptions to tell us how important an object is going to be. Sometimes it is not immediately clear why an object is described at length; for example, as Odysseus sets off towards the cave of Polyphemus, Homer tells us about the wine he takes. We are told of where he got it and there is an emphasis on how it is normally diluted heavily with water. When we read these details, we do not realise how the wine will be crucial later in the story, but when we get to the plan to blind Polyphemus, everything fits into place.

At times, detailed description of action creates a sudden dramatic effect:

> "Devoid of pity, he was silent in response, but leaping up laid hands on my crew. Two he seized and dashed to the ground like whelps, and their brains ran out and stained the earth. He tore them limb from limb for his supper, eating the flesh and entrails, bone and marrow, like a mountain lion, leaving nothing. Helplessly we watched these cruel acts, raising our hands to heaven and weeping. When the Cyclops had filled his huge stomach with human flesh, and had drunk pure milk, he lay down in the cave, stretched out among his flocks."

Homer, *Odyssey*, 9.287–298

The sudden action of 'leaping up' comes as a shock after the silence at the start of the passage. It shows Polyphemus' aggression and speed at this point. The simile of the whelps shows the helplessness of the men against the monster, who himself is compared to a lion, highlighting his animalistic behaviour. This is shown as he eats every bit of the men, even the parts such as bones that would seem inedible. The men pray to Zeus as they can do nothing; for battle-hardened soldiers to act in this

---

EXAM TIP

If you are asked what makes a passage exciting or dramatic, try to avoid simply saying there is a detailed description in it. Such comments are too generalised and could apply to most sections of the text. They do not show that you have fully appreciated what Homer is doing. Try instead to focus on what makes something detailed, such as the use of colours in a passage, the appeal to a particular sense, or what the details suggest about characters or objects. If you do this, you will gain more AO2 marks. An example of a dramatic passage, together with analysis of why it is dramatic, is given above.

way shows this is no ordinary enemy. After all this action the passage ends calmly, which provides a strong contrast to the violence of the deaths.

If this were an answer, it would score full marks for AO1 as it demonstrates a detailed knowledge and understanding of the text and full marks for AO2 as each time there is a reference, analysis is given of how it adds to the drama.

The pace of the story is crucial in keeping up the interest of the readers, and Homer changes this regularly. There are times when the pace slows right down with lengthy descriptions of settings, such as Odysseus' arrival on the islands of Polyphemus and Circe. We suspect by the slow build-up that something big is going to happen, so the situation is tense. Clues are given that all is not well, such as the strange animals outside Circe's home, or the introduction to Polyphemus and his home:

> There a giant spent the night, one that grazed his herds far off, alone, and keeping clear of others, lived in lawless solitude. He was born a monster and a wonder, not like any ordinary human.

> Homer, *Odyssey*, 9.187–190

'Lawless' and 'formidable' tell us how threatening Polyphemus will be, but Homer makes us wait to read what Polyphemus does to justify this description. It might seem frustrating to have to wait a few pages to find out, but it allows the reader an emotional breather before the action really gets going.

Everything leads to the climax of the story, which is slowly built up. Odysseus arrives back in Ithaca in Book 13 and we have to wait until Book 19 for Penelope to announce the contest of the bow and we are further made to wait until the end of Book 21 for it to be strung.

Pathos is to be found at various points in the story. When Odysseus' men are killed in the harbour of the Laestrygonians, Odysseus tells us that the groans of his dying men were appalling. We feel sorry for the victims and those who have to witness these events. Just a short while later his men break down in tears remembering what has happened, but get no comfort from Odysseus, although we might well sympathise with them.

But it is not just Odysseus and his crew that readers often feel sorry for. Pathos is a very personal feeling, and many people feel sympathy for the sufferings of Polyphemus (who ends up blind and having lost his flock) and some of the slaves of Odysseus, even though these are generally unlikeable characters. It is a rare skill for an author to make us sympathise with villains in a story.

Use of myth (or stories) is something that features heavily in the stories. Books 9 and 10 are a series of myths, told by Odysseus himself, but other parts feature backstories. When Eurycleia notices the scar on Odysseus' leg, Homer describes how he got this injury. In the same way, when Penelope fetches the bow, we are told how Odysseus got the bow in a myth. We are meant to focus on the history of the bow, just as the bow causes Penelope to reflect on the past. Antinous' tale of the centaur Eurytion is entertaining in itself, but as with many stories in Homer, it is used to give a moral lesson (on this occasion about the dangers of drink). As a story-teller himself, it is perhaps not surprising that Homer gets his characters to tell stories themselves.

ACTIVITY

Choose a passage of about half a page that you think is particularly memorable. Give at least three ways that Homer makes it memorable, using the ideas from the previous pages. Then do the same to say which book is your favourite.

Direct speech makes up a lot of the *Odyssey*. In fact, all of Books 9 and 10 are direct speech as Odysseus retells his tale to King Alcinous, and within this speech are speeches of other characters. It is easy to overlook the power of direct speech as we are so used to it, but it allows us to see the real thoughts of characters. Telemachus, in deciding the fate of the disloyal maids says:

> "These women who poured scorn on my mother's head and mine, while they slept with the Suitors, shall not die cleanly."

Homer, *Odyssey*, 22.462–464

TOPIC REVIEW

You should be able to:

1. Describe:
   - an outline of the events of Books 9, 10, 21, 22 and 23 of the *Odyssey*
   - how the order of the events in the book differs from the chronological order in which they occurred
   - the methods by which the Odyssey was composed
   - common features of oral poetry such as epithets, similes and formulae
   - other story-telling techniques used by Homer.

2. Explain:
   - what is meant by oral poetry and epic poetry
   - how the order of events in the poem affects our appreciation of the story
   - how common features of oral poetry add to our understanding and enjoyment of the text
   - how Homer's story-telling techniques add to our understanding and enjoyment of the text
   - what makes a particular passage interesting, dramatic or exciting.

PRACTICE QUESTIONS

Source A: *Homer, Odyssey, 9.382–388*

"They held the sharpened olivewood stake, and thrust it into his eye, while I threw my weight on the end, and twisted it round and round, as a man bores the timbers of a ship with a drill that others twirl lower down with a strap held at both ends, and so keep the drill continuously moving. We took the red-hot stake and twisted it round and round like that in his eye, and the blood poured out despite the heat."

1. How does this simile help us to understand the situation better at this point of the *Odyssey*? Make **two** points with references to the text. [4]
2. **a.** Give **two** details about the quality of the wine that Polyphemus is given. [2]
   b. Why is the quality of the wine important? [1]

2.6 Themes

There are several key themes that occur throughout the *Odyssey*. Many of these concern values that we are very familiar with today, such as revenge and justice. Others, like having to live away from home (as is the case for refugees) are things that are often in the news.

XENIA (GUEST-FRIENDSHIP)

Odysseus is in a very difficult situation in Books 9 and 10: he is hit by a storm, and soon his boats get lost. Hotels did not exist at this time, and he is forced to depend on the hospitality that strangers might offer for food and accommodation if he is to survive.

The Greeks had a solution to this problem that would encourage hosts to help visitors. They believed in a custom called **xenia**, where travellers would be given a bed, food and other help for as long as they needed it.

> **xenia** in Homer, hospitality given unconditionally to a traveller, involving the giving of any help needed; known as 'guest-friendship'

MODERN PARALLEL

It is very rare today that a complete stranger turn would turn up at a house and be given any form of hospitality, but there are ways in which people today show generosity to those in need. Food banks help many people survive who are in difficult situations. Odysseus too is given food when he desperately needs it on many occasions in the *Odyssey*.

When the traveller wanted to leave, he could be given help for the next stage of his journey, and possibly a leaving present. If the stranger were able, he would give something in return to the host. This was such an important idea in the ancient world that the Greeks decided that Zeus was the god who was in charge of this arrangement. As Odysseus said, when he met Polyphemus:

"Good sir, do not refuse us: respect the gods. We are suppliants and Zeus protects visitors and suppliants, Zeus the god of guests, who follows the steps of sacred travellers."

Homer, *Odyssey*, 9.269–271

Study questions

1 How does Odysseus try to persuade Polyphemus to give him hospitality?
2 Why do you think the Greeks might have made Zeus the god of hospitality?

Such reasoned arguments have no influence over a monster like Polyphemus, who does not follow the normal behaviour of the Greeks. We are not expecting him to follow the custom of xenia, because as soon as he spotted the men, he asked who they were. A key component of the custom of xenia was that you did not ask your questions to your guests before deciding whether to give them help.

Thankfully for Odysseus, other characters are far more helpful. The first example Odysseus experiences of good xenia is given in Book 10 by Aeolus, who fed Odysseus and his crew for a whole month and then gave a gift of a bag of winds to get them home. However, when Odysseus came back a second time, Aeolus refused to help again.

After his travels, Odysseus turned up at his own palace, disguised as a beggar by Athena. The custom of xenia demanded that he should be given help. Indeed, there was already a beggar in the palace whom Odysseus is made to fight as the suitors are only willing to assist one of them. The help that is offered should be unconditional, and not dependent on proving your strength or providing entertainment. The suitors even feel that the food they give, together with the opportunity merely to hear their conversation, should be enough for the beggar.

As we would expect, Penelope is a perfect hostess. After she hears the beggar tell his false tale in Book 19, she offers him a bed, a bath and a seat with Telemachus at breakfast. In Book 21 she says that if he can string the bow, she will give him generous gifts and help him get to his next destination. She realises the importance of helping others when she says:

Study questions

1 Why does Aeolus refuse to help Odysseus when he comes back for a second time? Is he right to do so?
2 Why do you think Odysseus does not get home at this point in his journey?

"But the fame of a good man, with a kind heart, his guests spread far and wide among men, and people sing his praise."

Homer, *Odyssey*, 19.332–334

ACTIVITY

Copy out and complete the table to show which characters offer xenia and which characters do not.

	Food offered	Bath given	Questions asked	Gifts offered
Aeolus	Fed for a month, presumably on the delicacies and roast meat that Aeolus and his family ate	We are not told	Odysseus is questioned on everything about Troy and his journey	A bag of winds when Odysseus leaves the first time, but nothing the second time.
Polyphemus				
Circe				
Penelope				

In some cases, characters offer xenia in a distorted way. In Book 10, the Lotus-eaters had no intention of harming Odysseus, and gave lotus as a gift to the crew. However, the lotus caused the crew members to forget about their home and wish to remain on the island. Circe too offers those who visit her something to eat, but this turns out to change Odysseus' men into pigs. However, when Odysseus proves to be immune to her magic, she turns out to be much more hospitable, entertaining the men for a year. Polyphemus' 'gift' of eating Odysseus last in Book 9 is hardly a gift at all, and shows a total disregard for the concept of xenia.

DECEIT AND TRICKERY

Odysseus was admired in the ancient world for his trickery and lies, and the *Odyssey* is full of examples of him not telling the truth. Indeed, it is impossible to separate truth from reality in the tales of Books 9 and 10 as we only have Odysseus' account of what happened, and he was famous for telling lies. His lies were often told with a view to gaining sympathy or help, and as such might be seen as necessary.

Some of the clearest examples of deceit and trickery come during Odysseus' time in Ithaca. He is turned into a beggar on his arrival by Athena, and he keeps up this pretence until he strings the bow. He even lies to his own wife about where he is from, even claiming to have met Odysseus. His tale makes Penelope weep, which in turn affects Odysseus:

> But though Odysseus pitied his wife's distress, he gazed steadily from beneath eyelids that might have been made of horn or iron, and deceitfully repressed his tears.
>
> Homer, *Odyssey*, 19.209–212

Perhaps the most famous examples of Odysseus' trickery come during his encounter with Polyphemus in Book 9. He lies about what has happened to his ship to prevent Polyphemus destroying it and finding the rest of his crew. Moreover, he is proud of having spotted Polyphemus' attempt to trick him with his questions. He goes on to state his name is Nobody, which results in the other Cyclopes not going to help Polyphemus later in the story. They logically think that if Nobody has blinded him, then he must not need any help.

But it is not just Odysseus that uses deception. Penelope proves a match for him in her tricking of the suitors. We are told in Book 19 that she put off marriage to one of them for years by saying she would only get married when she had finished a funeral shroud for Odysseus' father. Each night she would unpick the work that she had done during the day. This went on for several years until she was caught by her disloyal maids. Even though the trick did not work out, it bought her just enough time to delay her marriage until Odysseus arrived back home.

CIVILISATION AND BARBARISM

One important feature of civilisation that has been mentioned before is the giving of xenia (see pages 209–211). In the same way, those who do not give xenia can be regarded as barbaric. But there is more to characters being civilised than simply whether they give hospitality or not.

The Greeks would have been as horrified as we are today with the idea of eating people. Polyphemus and the Laestrygonians both eat crew members, and Polyphemus does so with the raw savagery of a lion, having bashed his victims' heads on the ground first. The Laestrygonians are no better as they carry off their helpless victims like fish on a spear.

The Laestrygonians' behaviour might come as more of a shock as we are not led to believe they are barbaric when the crew first meet them in Book 10:

> Once ashore, they found a well-worn track down which wagons carried wood to the city from the mountain heights. Near the citadel they came across a girl drawing water, the sturdy daughter of Laestrygonian Antiphates.
>
> Homer, *Odyssey*, 10.103–106

Aside from living in a community, with a reasonable transport system and a ruler who has a palace, they also have an assembly-place. These are all hallmarks of a civilised place, but are overshadowed by the behaviour of the population. Similarly, the skills that Polyphemus shows as a farmer, another sign of civilisation, do not compensate for his brutality.

The Cyclopes in Book 9, as a race, show a lack of civilisation. They have no assembly meetings to help the inhabitants rule in harmony, no laws or communities. To the Greeks,

FIGURE 2.45
Odysseus' men meet the daughter of Antiphates, the Laestrygonian, 1st century BC, fresco, now in the Vatican Museum, Rome. Note the fine jug she holds and her elegant clothing, signs of her civilisation. She appears very tall, even accounting for the slope.

who prided themselves on community life, this must have appeared shocking and primitive. What makes the Cyclopes' lack of civilisation worse is that they had everything they needed for a perfect life. There was a neighbouring island with a seemingly limitless supply of goats. Their island could support agriculture, if only the Cyclopes could be bothered to farm it. The natural, almost magical harbour, could have been perfect for trading opportunities, but the Cyclopes had no contact with any other community and did not bother to make ships. In some respects, they might be simply regarded as independent farmers, but that is not how the Greeks would see it. The people of Homer's time and Odysseus' age had strong trade links and were seafaring people, and would expect any civilised character to be the same.

Ithaca is a far more civilised place; it has a fine palace and command structure, although that seems to have collapsed in the absence of Odysseus; having slaves with clearly defined duties (such as the slaves who look after the swine, cattle and goats) and feasts are things that the Greeks would have expected in their ruling classes; the presence of the bard, Phemius, shows the people value music and song; Penelope also conforms

S & C The Phaeacians are another society in the *Odyssey* which is very civilised. They have a monarchy and decisions are made in a council. Their queen, Arete, can settle disputes, and a princess, Nausicaa, follows all the expected patterns of a good Greek woman, as she is modest, concerned about her reputation and does the traditional female task of washing clothes. They respect the gods, are fine sailors and sportsmen, and are ultimately very hospitable to Odysseus. Find out more about Nausicaa and the Phaeacians by reading Books 6–8 of the *Odyssey*.

to expected Greek standards of behaviour in weaving, which was seen as something a good Greek wife should do.

REVENGE AND JUSTICE

From the moment that Odysseus reveals his name to Polyphemus in Book 9, his crew are doomed to die at sea, and Odysseus is doomed to return to a palace in turmoil. Polyphemus curses Odysseus by raising his hands and praying to the god Poseidon at the end of the book, and as Poseidon is his father, the curse comes true. At the time of the curse, the suitors had not invaded Odysseus' palace, and so we are meant to think that Odysseus brings all his troubles on himself. That is not to say that the crew should not take responsibility for their actions. They have brought about their own downfall by eating sacred cattle in Book 12.

Attitudes to revenge have changed very much over the centuries. Many religions now advise forgiveness and not harming your enemies, but the Greeks would generally not have shared these ideas. The gods regularly punished humans for their wrong-doing, and there was even a goddess of revenge, **Nemesis**, whose name meant revenge in Greek.

> **nemesis** the concept of revenge

Odysseus' and Telemachus' punishments of the maids and suitors would probably not have been questioned by the ancient Greeks. Even begging for forgiveness, as happened with the priest Leodes in Book 22, does not save his life. The severity of the punishments reflect the severity of the wrong-doings.

Eurcyleia felt like crying out in triumph at the death of the suitors, but Odysseus stops her, saying it is wicked to gloat. To him, the Suitors deserved to die, but it is no cause for celebration. He feels that he is acting with justice and divine right, not with feelings of revenge.

However, in the case of Melanthius, the goat-herd, it might be argued that the punishment goes beyond what could be classed as mere revenge. He is subjected to a horrific death in having his nose and ears cut off, and his genitals are ripped away to be fed to the dogs. No doubt such a key slave should be loyal to the ruling family, but the anger of Telemachus and the loyal slaves is clear when Homer says:

PS

. . . lopped off his hands and feet in their deep anger.

Homer, *Odyssey*, 22.477

Likewise, it is not enough that the disloyal maids merely die, as Telemachus declares before hanging them that he is unwilling to give them a decent death. The epithet given to Telemachus before he hangs them is 'wise'. This suggests that he has carefully considered the best course of action under the circumstances.

> ## Study questions
>
> 1 Why do Odysseus and Telemachus kill all the suitors and disloyal slaves?
> 2 Are they right in giving these punishments?
> 3 Do you think an ancient Greek would have shared your views?
> 4 Do Odysseus and Telemachus behave like tyrants in deciding punishments?

NOSTOS

Nostos is the name given to the desire to return home, and is the root of our word nostalgia, which literally means 'the pain felt from missing home'. It is essential for Odysseus to have this goal permanently in his mind to keep him focused on the journey he is undertaking, but things are never simple for him.

In Book 10, the Lotus-eaters may seem harmless, but the danger they present is as great as any monster or witch that Odysseus could face. The easy life that their island offers could be tempting, but at this point his desire to return home is strong and so he overcomes the threat relatively easily. His nostos remains fairly powerful when he is hit by a storm after his men open the bag of winds, as he decides to endure the storm rather than fight, although he did have a moment's hesitation in wondering whether to jump overboard and drown himself.

Later on in the book his determination can be questioned when his men have to ask him to leave Circe's island after spending a year there. When he is told near the end of Book 10 that he has to venture to the underworld, he again feels like giving up. Later in his journey, Odysseus is trapped on the nymph Calypso's island for seven years, and seems to have given up hope of his home before the gods arrange his release. This story is told in Book 5.

> **nostos** the desire to return to your homeland

FATE

We might always feel that Odysseus is bound to get home and reclaim his kingdom, but this is not what is meant by fate. Many Greeks believed that key events in your life were pre-arranged by the actions of the gods, and this does seem to happen to a degree in the *Odyssey*. The key evidence for this occurs in the curse that Polyphemus delivers as Odysseus sails away from his island:

> "If he is destined to see his friends and his fine house in his own country, may he come there late and in sore distress, in another's ship, losing all comrades, and let him find great trouble in his house."
>
> Homer, *Odyssey*, 9.532–535

This all ends up coming true:

- It takes him ten years to get home.
- He suffers hugely on his journey, losing everything.
- All his men die (as told in Books 9–12).
- He gets to Ithaca in a boat provided by the Phaeacians.
- The suitors are competing to marry his wife and are plotting to kill his son.

However, it is important to distinguish between what is fate, and what are the actions of the gods. The gods do ensure that fate happens (such as when Zeus kills the remnants of the crew in Book 12 for eating sacred cattle), but just because they act at other times, this is not usually connected with fate.

Similarly, characters have to take responsibility for their actions. Could Elpenor could blame his death in Book 10 on the curse of Polyphemus, or was it due to his own foolishness and drunkenness. Others die as a result of mistakes they or Odysseus make. At other times we are told what will happen to characters: we are told in Book 21 that Antinous will be the first suitor to die before the contest even started. However, this is not the same thing as him being fated to die.

TOPIC REVIEW

You should be able to:

1. Describe:
   - occasions when Odyssey is given or refused xenia
   - situations where Odysseus and other characters use trickery or deceit
   - barbaric or civilised features in the locations and characters of the Odyssey
   - the ways in which Odysseus seeks justice and gains revenge over the suitors and his attitude to his slaves
   - instances where Odysseus shows a strong desire, or a lack of desire, to return home
   - parts of the story where fated events occur.

2. Explain:
   - what is meant by the concept of xenia
   - why trickery and deceit were acceptable and what they reveal about characters
   - why having certain features made locations and characters civilised or barbaric
   - why Odysseus is keen to gain revenge, and how his actions would have been regarded
   - the importance of the homeland and fame to a hero
   - whether fate is the sole factor in determining what happens to characters.

PRACTICE QUESTIONS

Source A: *Homer, Odyssey, 22.461–473*

Then wise Telemachus spoke: "These women who poured scorn on my mother's head and mine, while they slept with the Suitors, shall not die cleanly."

So saying, he took a cable from a dark-prowed ship, tied it to a tall pillar, high-up, and noosed it over the round house, so that their feet would not reach the ground. The row of women held up their heads, and the rope was looped round their necks so they might die pitiably, like long-winged thrushes or doves, that are caught in a snare as they try to roost in their thicket, and are welcomed to a grimmer nest. For a little while their feet twitched: but not for long.

1. Do you feel any sympathy for the fates of Odysseus' disloyal slaves? Use the passage as a starting point and explain your answer. [8]
2. How civilised are the places that Odysseus visits on his way home to Ithaca? Explain your answer. [15]

2.7 The Character of Odysseus

Odysseus is a very complex character. At times he seems considerate of others, heroic and intelligent, but at other points he seems selfish, weak and foolish. He makes mistakes in the story, but whether you lose sympathy for him is a very personal matter. It is the contradictions in his character that are at the heart of your study of him, and made him such a fascinating character for the Greeks.

To many modern readers, Odysseus is a womaniser. He seems to truly love his wife and be desperate to be with her, but he also has sex with Circe in Book 10 (and with another goddess Calypso earlier in the *Odyssey*). Is he simply thinking that he can get away with his unfaithfulness? Is he too weak to resist temptation when it is offered? As often, it is not as obvious as it may seem.

In the first case Hermes advises him of how he must deal with Circe:

> "When Circe strikes you with her length of wand, draw your sharp sword and rush at her, as if you intend to kill her. She will be seized with fear. Then she'll invite you to her bed, and don't refuse the goddess' favours, if you want her to free your men, and care for you too."

Homer, *Odyssey*, 10.293–298

So it seems Odysseus has no choice in the matter and is forced to sleep with Circe. To refuse her, and go against Hermes' orders, would have been extremely foolish. Homer

FIGURE 2.46
Marble head of Odysseus, 1st century AD, National Archaeological Museum, Sperlonga, Italy.

---

kleos the glorious reputation a Homeric warrior hopes to win

FIGURE 2.47
Odysseus threatens Circe, with Circe's 'animals' looking on, 4th century BC, sarcophagus, Claudio Faina Museum, Orvieto, Italy.

S To fully understand Odysseus' relationships with women, read Book 5 to see
& him with Calyspo. Odysseus is described as a 'cold lover' and it seems he
C gets little pleasure from sleeping with her.

does not tell us if he sleeps with her after this occasion, but he does stay for a year and so it does seem highly probable. He certainly slept with Calypso many times during his seven-year stay.

Moreover, to sleep with a goddess would make him more heroic to the ancient Greeks, as goddesses would not usually sleep with mere mortals. This would increase his fame, or **kleos** as the Greeks called it. Heroes aspired to everlasting fame, and as books did not exist at the time, the only way to achieve this was to ensure that people would talk about you after your death. Odysseus achieved this kind of immortality through his actions, and sleeping with goddesses was one of the things that created his fame.

In Homeric times, it was a key role for a father to provide instruction and inspiration for his son, and Odysseus does all he can to be a good role model. He gives clear instructions to Telemachus about removing the weapons from the hall, even telling him plausible words to say to the suitors to stop their suspicions. The pair of them work together as a team to remove the items, before Telemachus goes to bed on the instruction of his father.

The clearest signs of Odysseus giving his son guidance are in the battle in Book 22. They decide together on Telemachus getting more weapons, and on the strategy for fighting the suitors. When the carnage is complete, Telemachus goes off to fetch Eurycleia when Odysseus tells him to.

Throughout the books that you read in the *Odyssey*, Odysseus always has people to lead: he leads his crew in his journey home in Books 9 and 10; he leads his son and slaves in the preparations for the battle in the hall in Books 19 and 21; and finally he leads them in the battle itself in Book 22. We might expect a great king like Odysseus to show perfect leadership, but this is not always the case, especially during his adventures in Books 9 and 10. Also remember that Odysseus is telling us this part of the story, so he might put a particular spin on the tales to make himself look better.

Odysseus has a very mixed relationship with his crew. At many points in the story the crew do exactly as he says, showing obedience and trust in him as a leader. When he tells them to leave the land of the Lotus-eaters in Book 9, his men immediately obey, and he gets no opposition from his plan to sail over to the island of the Cyclopes later in the book.

The blinding of Polyphemus shows Odysseus and his men working as a team. It is Odysseus that comes up with the plan, but he gives his men specific tasks like smoothing the wood and driving it into Polyphemus' eye. Similarly, the men on his ship obey him when he tells them to sail away from the Laestrygonians in Book 10.

As any good leader should, Odysseus tries to provide for his men. He achieves seemingly superhuman feats, such as killing a huge stag in Book 10 and managing to drag it back single-handedly to his crew on Circe's island. He realises the importance of feeding his men too, when the men eat the flocks of Polyphemus shortly after escaping under them.

In general, Odysseus comes across as a fair leader, even if his crew might disagree with this idea at certain points in the story. The first glimpse of Odysseus with his crew in your reading is in Book 9, on the island of the Cicones, where Odysseus says:

> "I sacked the city and slew the men, and the women and riches we split
> between us, so that as far as I could determine no man lacked an equal share."
>
> Homer, Odyssey, 9.40–42

He also divides up evenly the flocks that they steal from Polyphemus later on in the book. Clearly, he could not eat all the animals himself and his men do need feeding, so we would hardly expect him to do anything else. Even these acts do not stop his men being suspicious about him keeping treasure for himself when they leave Aeolus' island in the next book, but there is little evidence in the text to support their view in other stories that Odysseus is greedy.

Odysseus is often quite sensible in what he does when he gets to a new island. If it is clear that he needs to fight, as is the case in the city of the Cicones in Book 9, then all his men get involved and a battle occurs. If there is no immediate sign of danger, he sends a group to investigate. At the lands of the Lotus-eaters and Laestrygonians, in Books 9 and 10, he sends two men and a messenger or herald to do this and report back (see Figure 2.45 on p. 213). On the island of Polyphemus, where he has only taken his boat across, he selects his twelve best men, whilst on Circe's island, lots are drawn to see whether his group or Eurylochus' should investigate.

(see Figure 2.45 on p. 213)

<table>
<tr><td>

EXAM TIP

When analysing a character, you should always try to start off by considering how the ancient Greeks would have regarded their behaviour. In the case of his treatment of the Cicones, the Greeks might well have admired his strength as a warrior and leader. But often a different, but equally valid, interpretation can be given: on this occasion we might feel he acts brutally and without provocation. It is always best to present both sides of the argument, but if you do not feel there is an alternative viewpoint, don't try to invent one!

</td></tr>
</table>

THE PRESENTATION OF ODYSSEUS AS A WARRIOR AND HERO

Odysseus shows himself to be a traditional Greek hero on a number of occasions. The Greeks would regard a hero as someone who defeats his enemy in a battle, so it is significant he achieves this the first time we see him with his whole crew at the land of the Cicones.

On this occasion there is no investigative group sent, nor any attempt to gain xenia. It is the idea of 'might is right', where the victory justifies the means that is used to achieve it.

Moreover, when Polyphemus spots Odysseus in his cave, he immediately asks him:

> "Where do you sail from over the sea-roads? Are you on business, or do
> you roam at random, like pirates who chance their lives to bring evil to
> others?"
>
> Homer, Odyssey, 9.252–255

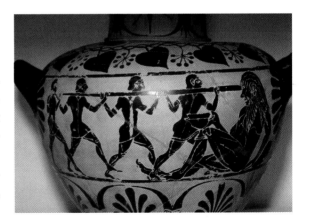

FIGURE 2.48
Odysseus and his men work together to blind Polyphemus, 6th century BC, black figure water-jar, now in National Etruscan Museum of the Villa Giulia, Rome.

Study questions

1 How would you describe Odysseus' feelings for Circe? Should we ignore, excuse or criticise his affairs?

2 What is the significance of Odysseus being allotted the great ram by his crew?

3 Do you think Odysseus was right to send just three of his crew to the Lotus-eaters and Laestrygonians?

4 Look again at the quotation on p. 219. How do you feel about Odysseus' attitude to his victory and achievement?

ACTIVITY

The trial of Odysseus

Imagine Odysseus has been put on trial for being a bad leader and guilty for the deaths of his men. Act out a trial, with people taking the role of the characters of Books 9 and 10, and Odysseus himself. You will also need a prosecution, defence and judge. Will you find Odysseus guilty or not? You could also read Book 12 and find out a bit more about his leadership of the crew.

MODERN PARALLEL

Women and children are still today innocent victims in human conflict situations. In 2014 an extremist group in Nigeria, Boko Haram, kidnapped 276 girls from a school in Chibok. Their leader at the time declared that he intended to sell the girls into slavery, and he later declared that they had been 'married'. Odysseus' behaviour towards the women of the Cicones might be regarded by some as similar, as he takes prisoners from their homeland to use as he sees fit.

In Homer's other work, the *Iliad*, Greek warriors regularly plunder towns near Troy, killing men and taking the women as slaves, and this was seen as normal behaviour at the time. Indeed, Odysseus seems rather proud of doing such a thing to the Cicones in Book 9. Today, piracy has been eliminated from most parts of the world as we see it as unacceptable, but as recently as 2013, pirates captured other ships off the coast of Somalia in Africa, taking the people on board as hostages.

The ancient Greeks would almost certainly have felt admiration for Odysseus for his defeat of the suitors, as they had behaved in an arrogant, greedy and threatening manner in the palace. If Odysseus had not fought them, there is every chance that he would have been killed by them. The opening lines of Book 22, where Odysseus throws off his rags and leaps on to the threshold, reveal a brave and determined hero, and in the battle that follows, he and his men defeat a force of 108 men by a combination of skill and strength.

ACTIVITY

With a partner, improvise a scene between Odysseus and Penelope. One of you should take the role of Odysseus and explain your relationship with Circe, and the other should take the role of Penelope, saying what you think about Odysseus' behaviour.

ODYSSEUS' INTELLIGENCE AND ORATORICAL SKILLS

In the ancient world, Odysseus was most famous for his speaking skills and his clever plans, and your selection of books shows these. There are several occasions where Odysseus gets himself out of trouble with a clever speech. The most famous of these is with Polyphemus in Book 9. When confronted with Polyphemus, Odysseus is the only one who has the courage to answer his questions when the men are spotted, and his answers are designed to make Polyphemus both respect and fear them. In mentioning being part of the victorious Greek forces, Polyphemus should be in awe of them. Odysseus then goes on to tactfully remind Polyphemus of his obligations by reminding them of the rules of hospitality (see the quotation on p. 210).

Later, when Polyphemus tries to get Odysseus to tell him about the rest of his fleet, Odysseus realises a trap that is being laid for him, and convincingly lies about what has happened to his boat. When he gets back to Ithaca, Odysseus is also very careful about what he says. When he speaks to his wife in Book 19, he compliments her fame, and goes on to very tactfully request that she does not ask him about his troubles. He is asked a little later in the book to recount how he (as the beggar) spent time with Odysseus, and then he gives a very detailed story, managing to give Penelope hope by mixing in true facts about Odysseus' appearance and clothing with the lies.

His intelligence is further shown in the events leading up to the battle when he asks his loyal slaves in Book 21 how they would feel about fighting for Odysseus. He is not prepared to reveal his identity until he has very firm support from them. He then goes on to casually request a go at stringing the bow, which would normally be seen as outrageous. Unsurprisingly, the suitors do take offence, but Odysseus convinces Penelope that he is only doing it to test out his strength and has no desire to marry her.

There is no doubt that Odysseus can be a very proud and confident individual. It is a fine line between confidence and arrogance, and you have to decide for yourself which side of the line Odysseus is on at times, such as when he tells Alcinous about himself at the start of Book 9 (see the quotation on p. 200).

Sometimes you might question Odysseus' intelligence. When Polyphemus drank three bowls full of Odysseus' wine, Odysseus refers to him as a fool and he calls him an idiot for not realising they were escaping under the flocks. He also laughs to himself at how the plan of his false name has worked, and goes on to reveal his name during his escape. This is foolish as it allows Polyphemus to be able to identify who has blinded him to Poseidon.

What Odysseus does not say can help us to form opinions of him. When his men are upset by Odysseus' plain assessment of the situation after feasting on arrival on Circe's island in Book 9, Odysseus' reaction is emotionless:

> They groaned aloud, and wept great tears. But all their lamentation did no good.
>
> Homer, *Odyssey*, 10.201–202

The men react similarly later in the book to the news of their journey to the Underworld, with the same lack of comfort given by Odysseus. He had burst into tears when he heard the news and felt suicidal briefly, before pulling himself together. He is tough with his men, and here again it is up to you to decide if you think his approach is right.

ODYSSEUS' RELATIONSHIP WITH ATHENA

Athena is the main source of divine help for Odysseus. This is perhaps not surprising as she is the goddess of wisdom, and Odysseus is a hero who is famed for this quality.

If Athena had not changed Odysseus' appearance into that of a beggar, he would surely have been killed in Ithaca by the suitors before he had a chance to kill them. She helps Odysseus in the battle in the hall, by making the suitors' spears miss and by scaring them when she raises her aegis (a goatskin cloak which was her symbol). During the battle, Homer writes:

Study question

If you were in Odysseus' situation when he is questioned by Polyphemus, what would you have done?

Study questions

1 How do you feel about Odysseus' gloating about his success over Polyphemus?
2 Odysseus stops Eurycleia from gloating over the death of the suitors. Is he right to do so, especially when he gloated over the blinding of Polyphemus?

Study question

Does Odysseus come across as too uncaring towards the sufferings of his men?

Study questions

Odysseus does not mention any help that Athena gave him in Books 9 and 10, although he is in many life and death situations.

1 Why do you think this is the case?
2 If Athena deliberately chose not to help to help Odysseus, why do you this was so?

KEY INDIVIDUAL

Athena the goddess of wisdom and strategy in warfare. She helps Odysseus on numerous occasions in his challenges

Yet despite her words she still withheld from him the power to determine the course of the fight, and continued to test the strength and courage of Odysseus and his noble son.

Homer, *Odyssey*, 22.236–258

This enables us to feel that Odysseus has really earned his victory, rather than being gifted it by the gods.

TOPIC REVIEW

You should be able to:

1. Describe:
   - situations where Odysseus shows good leadership and fighting skills
   - situations where Odysseus shows weaknesses as a leader or hero
   - what Odysseus says to Penelope in Book 19, and what he does with Telemachus during, and after, the battle in the hall
   - parts of the story where Odysseus shows intelligence or an ability to speak effectively
   - instances where Athena appears in the story.

2. Explain:
   - why you might conclude that Odysseus shows good leadership and fighting skills in particular stories
   - why you might conclude Odysseus is a poor leader on occasions
   - how his relationships with Penelope and Telemachus should be regarded
   - what makes Odysseus an affective speaker and a man of intelligence
   - why Athena appears in some of the stories.

PRACTICE QUESTIONS

Source A: *Homer, Odyssey, 19.172–189*

"Out in the wine-dark sea lies a land called Crete, a rich and lovely island. It is filled with countless people, in ninety cities. They are not of one language, but speak several tongues. There are Achaeans there, and brave native Cretans, Cydonians, three races of Dorians, and noble Pelasgians too. One of the ninety cities is mighty Cnossus, where Minos ruled, and every nine years spoke with mighty Zeus. He was brave Deucalion's father, and so my grandfather. Deucalion had two sons, Lord Idomeneus and me. Idomeneus, my older brother, and a better man than I, sailed with the sons of Atreus in the curved ships to Ilium, so I the younger, Aethon is my name, was left behind, there to meet and entertain Odysseus. The wind had driven him to Crete as he headed for Troy, and blew him off course by Cape Malea. He anchored at Amnisus, a tricky harbour, near the cave of Eileithyia, and barely escaped shipwreck."

1. How does Odysseus show himself to be a good storyteller in this passage? Make two points, giving evidence from the passage. [4]

2. Why does Odysseus feel he needs to tell this tale to Penelope at this point in the *Odyssey*? [3]

2.8 The Portrayal of Key Characters

TOPIC OVERVIEW

The portrayal of key characters

- The role of the gods
- The portrayal of the suitors
- The portrayal of the crew of Odysseus
- The portrayal of Polyphemus as a monster and keeper of livestock
- The portrayal of Circe as a witch and host
- The portrayal of Penelope as a host, wife and queen
- The portrayal of Telemachus as a son and hero
- The loyalty of Odysseus' slaves

The prescribed source for this topic is:

- Homer's *Odyssey* Books 9, 10, 19, 21, 22

Don't forget that you will be given credit in the exam if you study extra sources and make relevant use of them in your answers.

There are numerous other key characters in the Odyssey, apart from Odysseus himself. Many of them make life very difficult for him, but there are a similar number that try to help him in his missions. In this section, you will find out more about some of these characters.

THE ROLE OF THE GODS

The gods and goddesses of the *Odyssey* are an intriguing set of characters. Zeus is the god who has the ultimate control over the action, and is held responsible (at least by Odysseus) for some of the problems on the journey. He claimed that the Cicones fought back in Book 9 as Zeus wanted the men to suffer, and just a few lines later he also blames him for the storm which drove the crew off course. This might reflect the typical view of the Greeks in trying to ascribe to the gods events for which they could not find a

KEY INDIVIDUAL

Zeus king of the gods. He has a key role as the god most associated with justice and xenia, and has the final say in the fate of Odysseus and his crew

S
&
C

Some scholars have said that Homer's gods behave like humans.

What do you think is meant by this statement? To what extent do you agree with it?

KEY INDIVIDUALS

the suitors a group of 108 men who wish to marry Odysseus' wife Penelope. They set up permanent residency in Odysseus' palace, abusing the royal family's hospitality and its slaves

rational cause. Zeus is definitely responsible for the storm that killed the crew of Odysseus' boat as a punishment for eating the cattle of the Sun-god, an event referred to in Book 19.

However, he can be equally helpful to Odysseus; as the god most associated with justice, he gives a thunderclap of approval to encourage Odysseus when he strings the bow at the end of Book 21.

Other gods are involved at several points in the story. The goddess Circe has a pivotal role in the story and will be discussed separately, and Athena also features prominently (see pages. 221–222). Hermes too has a minor, but crucial, role in helping Odysseus avoid Circe's magic in Book 10 by giving him the antidote to her drugs.

THE SUITORS

It is difficult to say much that is positive about the suitors: for years they have been pressurising a woman, who is still convinced that her husband is alive, to marry one of them; they seem to have set up camp in the palace; they give orders to the royal family and have sexual intercourse with some of Odysseus' female slaves; they consume food and drink that is not theirs; they plan to murder Telemachus earlier in the story and Telemachus says in Book 2 that they would kill Odysseus if he came back; and they treat the beggar appallingly.

Their ringleader is Antinous. He makes several of the key suggestions in the contest of the bow, such as who should try first, and later proposes a postponement in the contest, both of which the other suitors agree to. He even suggests they can sacrifice some of Odysseus' own flocks to Apollo. He attacks Eumaeus and Philoetius for crying when handing over the bow in Book 21, calling them 'snivelling peasants'. When Odysseus asks for a go, he is threatened with violence by Antinous. Antinous even throws his weight about with the other suitors, abusing Leodes in Book 21 for his weakness and saying the other suitors are better than him at stringing bows.

EXAM TIP

If you are asked why the gods are interesting characters, do not simply state how they help and hinder Odysseus. This will not score highly on AO1 as you will not be showing a full understanding of their roles. Their help towards Odysseus is only one aspect of the issue. Think also about:

- how they are like humans
- their superhuman powers and use of magic
- how they choose to interact with each other and Odysseus. Do they appear in their usual form or disguise? Do they choose to help Odysses or not? If not, what does this show about them?

Eurymachus is the second most important suitor. He seems particularly concerned about his reputation, which is rather ironic as he seems to do everything he can to destroy it by his actions:

> "It's not that I'm bothered about the marriage, though it grieves me. There are plenty of other women in Achaea, in Ithaca's isle, and in other places. No, it's more that our strength falls so short of godlike Odysseus' that we can't even string his bow. It's a disgrace that posterity will hear of."

Homer, Odyssey, 21.251–255

His speech suggests he is more interested in the status of being king, than any genuine feelings for Penelope, or else perhaps he is just trying to appear less bothered at his weakness. He also will do whatever it takes to get out of a tight spot, blaming all the suitors' actions near the start of Book 22 on the dead Antinous. He later attempts to make amends by raising money from taxing the people for all they have eaten and drunk in the palace. This would enable him to keep his wealth and further show his power over people.

One other suitor deserves a special mention: Leodes the priest seems a little out of place with the rest of the suitors. He is certainly no archer, and is the only one to beg Odysseus for mercy in Book 22, claiming to have tried to stop the suitors from their villainy. We see no evidence of this in the story, and so could feel that Odysseus' killing of him is as justified as any of the other suitors. In fact, as a religious figure, some might feel that he should have been more able than anyone to see the wrongs in his actions.

> **Study question**
> Who is the worst of the suitors? Explain your answer.

ODYSSEUS' CREW

Odysseus' crew, rather like the suitors, are a group with a leading individual, while the rest of the men are largely anonymous. This is perhaps not too surprising as there were around six hundred men at the start, fifty on each of twelve boats. Six from each boat get killed on the island of the Cicones, with a further six men in total falling victim to Polyphemus. Later the men from all the boats except his own die in the harbour of the Laestrygonians. Elpenor is the final crew member to die in the prescribed books, leaving Odysseus with forty-three crew members at the end of Book 10.

Eurylochus is the second in command on Odysseus' boat, and he leads the party to Circe's house in Book 10. He shows more suspicion than the rest by not entering, but you might question his leadership in allowing his fellow soldiers to go in while he waits outside. Later he is in tears when reporting the story and asks not to be taken back. Indeed, he suggests they leave the men, half of the crew at the time, with Circe on the island. This can be contrasted with Odysseus who personally drags three men back from the Lotus-eaters in the previous book.

When Odysseus wants to take the rest of the crew to Circe's house, Eurylochus says:

> "Remember how Cyclops too behaved, when our friends entered his cave with reckless Odysseus, this man through whose foolishness they died."

Homer, Odyssey, 10.435–437

FIGURE 2.49
Odysseus (standing) and his men, 3rd century AD, mosaic, now in Bardo Museum, Tunis.

Whether Odysseus' reaction to this is appropriate, and whether there is some truth in the comment, it might be felt that this act of mutiny is not appropriate at a time when Odysseus is seeking to do the right thing in rescuing his men.

The crew as a whole do not always share the same viewpoint as their leader. Their decisions to stay an extra day on the island of the Cicones and to open the bag of winds both result in disaster as seventy-two men are killed in the first instance, and they are blown away from Ithaca in the second. However, they can act more sensibly than their leader, especially when they suggest not waiting for Polyphemus and trying to stop Odysseus from revealing his name. On other occasions, they follow his instructions carefully, and they are called 'loyal' by Odysseus in his adventures with Polyphemus and the Lotus-eaters.

POLYPHEMUS AS A MONSTER AND KEEPER OF LIVESTOCK

The man-eating giant is a standard element of folk tales – think of the giant in the story of Jack and the Beanstalk. But Homer's creation of the Cyclops Polyphemus is more balanced than we might have expected.

Before even meeting him in Book 9, his cave shows an impressive level of organisation and he seems a good farmer. He knows how to make cheese, and does not just kill his animals for meat. All his animals are kept according to age in separate pens, and his vessels and bowls are full of whey (a liquid created in making cheese). He shows genuine tenderness with his flock, milking them efficiently and putting each animal with its mother, all the time leaving the males outside. The affection is shown even more clearly when he talks to the large ram under which Odysseus is clinging, saying:

"My fine ram, why leave the cave like this last of the flock?"

Homer, *Odyssey*, 9.447–448

However, this speech also shows Polyphemus' brutal side, when just seconds later he says he wishes to splatter Odysseus' brains. It is this contradiction in his character that makes him so fascinating.

Perhaps the most brutal part of the story is where Polyphemus kills the first two crew members. See p. 206 for a full analysis of this scene.

His uncivilised nature is shown in numerous other ways in the story:

- He lives alone in a cave, and has no contact with his neighbours, the other Cyclopes.
- He drinks milk rather than wine as a normal drink.
- He thinks his race is better than that of the gods, (even though Zeus is an uncle).
- He has no respect for xenia, and makes a mockery of it by his 'gift' of eating Odysseus last.
- He traps the men in the cave.

- Dung is in heaps in his cave.
- He gets drunk too easily and falls for Odysseus' trap.

As Odysseus says, perhaps with a touch of desperation:

> "why would anyone on earth ever visit you again, when you behave so badly?"
>
> Homer, *Odyssey*, 9.351–352

Homer has created a memorable character, in making the most monstrous individual in the book a figure whom we can also admire and be sympathetic towards.

CIRCE AS A WITCH AND HOST

Circe is a rather odd character. Despite being a goddess, she is a stereotypical ideal Greek mortal woman who weaves and sings. As such, we would expect her to be a rather powerless and gentle figure, but this is hardly the case. She is most famous for her witch-craft in turning Odysseus' men into pigs in Book 10, and has done the same to others, making them the wolves and lions who prowl about her house. Homer gives us no clue as to why she does this, and it is hard to find a reason for her doing so.

Although this is only a small part of the section in which she appears, it is the one thing that everyone remembers about her. She does go on to be the perfect hostess, giving food, a bath, clothes, lodgings, advice and gifts to Odysseus and his crew. Her hospitality is such that Odysseus stays for a year, and would probably have stayed longer had it not been for his crew's request to leave. She represents to Odysseus danger, temptation and relief from his troubles, but ultimately her contribution to Odysseus' mission is huge as she tells him to go to the underworld for advice about his journey.

Study question
'Circe acts like an ordinary mortal woman.' In what ways is this statement true, and in what ways is it false?

PENELOPE AS A HOST, WIFE AND QUEEN

In an age where women were supposed to know their place and be supportive to their husbands, Penelope is the standard that all women in Greece (and those in mythology) were expected to match. Under immense pressure, she has held out against the suitors' imposition of marriage for three years, with all logic suggesting Odysseus has died, and custom suggesting she should remarry. As a good hostess, she is always polite and gener-ous to the suitors. You might feel she should have expelled them from her home earlier. However, a Greek woman would not have the authority to force a group of men out, and her son Telemachus is also too young at the time to make a stand.

That is not to say that she does not speak her mind. When Antinous abuses Odysseus, she declares:

KEY INDIVIDUAL

Penelope the wife of Odysseus, famed for her patience in waiting for her husband to return home from Troy

> "It is neither right nor just, Antinous, to deny his due to a man who came to Telemachus' house as a guest."
>
> Homer, *Odyssey*, 21.312–313

She speaks politely, but with firmness, putting Antinous in his place, and does similarly when Eurymachus tries to save his own reputation shortly after (see the passage on p. 225).

S & C

Many scholars believe Penelope actually realises the beggar is Odysseus. They note that in Book 18 Penelope suggests for the first time that the suitors should bring her gifts. Is it a coincidence that she does this just as the beggar arrives on the scene? She suggests she might be ready to marry one of them. Odysseus is delighted by his wife's attempts to win gifts while 'her heart was set on something quite different' (18.280). Does the phrase 'quite different' really refer to her reunion with the beggar, whom she suspects is Odysseus. This is far from certain, but it is a real possibility. (Read page 246 of the *Odyssey* to see this part of the story in full.)

These scholars also tend to feel that she issues the challenge at this point, knowing only one man could do it. It is a chance for her to test Odysseus, and gives him the opportunity both to reclaim his kingdom in a blaze of glory, and get rid of the suitors. Even if she does not suspect it is Odysseus, she may set the challenge knowing none could possibly do it. This would buy her even more time, further showing her intelligence. Even when the suitors are dead, she tests the beggar's identity further in Book 23 by getting him to reveal a secret that only Odysseus would know about – how one of the posts of their bed was made from a living tree.

Study question

How does Homer suggest that Telemachus is acting reasonably in sending Penelope to her room? What does this suggest about his position in the household?

suppliant a person who begs for something from someone in a position of authority

Penelope tells him that the suitors have already damaged their reputation, and Eurymachus does not answer her back. In the end, Telemachus orders her to her room, and as he is now the leading man in the house, she obeys dutifully.

She is also generous and compassionate. When the beggar tells her his story in Book 19, she is overcome with grief, and her tears are compared to a river in full flood. She also bursts into tears when she fetches the bow in Book 21. This seems to add to her beauty, and her loyalty to Odysseus is touching. She protects Odysseus from the abuse he gets from the slave-girl Melantho in Book 19, and promises him gifts for the tale that he tells and further gifts if he can string the bow. We sympathise with her when she feels she is neglecting her guests, **suppliants** and messengers, which she declares to Odysseus after he has been abused by Melantho.

She knows what she must do, but is too grief-stricken and harassed by the suitors to fulfil her role as queen as effectively as she might wish.

She proves to be a perfect match for Odysseus. She shares his intelligence, and has managed to delay her marriage to any of the suitors for many years by her cunning ploy of unpicking a funeral shroud every night after having worked on it during the day. (It had been agreed that she would decide whom to marry when it had been completed.) Her weaving conforms to the expected behaviour of a Greek woman and she also covers her face when confronting the suitors after crying, highlighting her modesty. She sets the suitors a difficult task to complete, but one that would make them an equal of Odysseus if managed.

TELEMACHUS AS A SON AND HERO

At the time of Odysseus' return, Telemachus is at a key point in his life. He was born shortly before Odysseus left for Troy, and so is now about twenty years old, and as such is beginning to take his first tentative steps as heir to Odysseus' kingdom and reputation.

His newly found assertiveness in Book 21 largely springs from the fact that he knows who the beggar is, and that the plans to kill the suitors have been made. He puts on a show of surprise to Penelope's news of the contest, and invites the suitors to try, confident in the knowledge that none will succeed. He has the first go, after setting up the axes for the contests. Even his arch enemies, the suitors, feel a grudging admiration for how he went about his business.

When he attempted to string the bow, he nearly did it, and might well have done so if Odysseus had not stopped him in his fourth attempt. It would be an anti-climax if anyone other than Odysseus did string it, and it might have ruined the plan, but it does show him as a son in his father's image, and ready to become a great hero himself.

As the contest progresses, he continues to exert his authority:

> It was wise Telemachus who spoke to her then: "Mother, none of the Achaeans – those who rule in rocky Ithaca or in the islands seaward of the horse pastures of Elis – have more right than I to give or refuse the bow to whoever I wish."
>
> Homer, *Odyssey*, 21.343–345

All that remains for Telemachus to be a true hero is to prove himself in battle, and this he does in killing Amphinomus in Book 22. However, he shows that he still has a little bit to learn in leaping back when he hits his victim, leaving the spear in the body, although he might also be seen as sensibly cautious. He also shows his inexperience in leaving the store-room door open later in the book, but he remedies it in sending slaves to stop Melanthius getting more weapons for the suitors.

He proves himself equal to Odysseus, fighting alongside his father, and also proves himself to be his equal in dealing with those who deserve punishment, and in brutally killing the disloyal maids.

THE SLAVES' LOYALTY AND DISLOYALTY

Odysseus' slaves fall into two categories: those who are loyal and those who are not. There is no middle ground.

The loyal slaves that play a significant role in the story are the more experienced ones, and no one seems older or more experienced than Eurycleia, who has brought Odysseus up from his early years. She is the most trusted non-royal female in the palace, and Odysseus asks for her views about which female slaves have been loyal, even though in Book 19 he claimed he did not need her views to pick out the guilty ones. She is equally respected by Penelope who chooses her to wash Odysseus' feet. She is able to keep the secret of Odysseus' identity and is totally obedient to Odysseus; she locks suitors in the hall and later purifies the palace after the battle, both after requests made by him.

Odysseus' swineherd, Eumaeus, and his cowherd, Philoetius, are also very loyal. Eumaeus is the first man in Ithaca to welcome Odysseus in Book 14, and both of them are used by Odysseus and Telemachus to see to practicalities, such as passing the bow to Odysseus in

KEY INDIVIDUAL

Telemachus the son of Odysseus, who is just about ready to step into his father's position. He is strong, if inexperienced, but able to exert some authority over the suitors and household

KEY INDIVIDUALS

Eurycleia Odysseus' nurse, who recognises the beggar from a scar on his leg he gained whilst hunting

Eumaeus Odysseus' swineherd (man in charge of his pigs), who helps Odysseus in the battle both to get the bow and kill the suitors

Study question
Why else do you think that Homer chose to have Phemius spared?

Book 21 and fetching more weapons in Book 22. When the need arises, they both fight in the battle and kill suitors, and together with Telemachus, they later kill Melanthius.

Another slave worth considering is Phemius. He is spared in the aftermath of the battle as he had been an unwilling performer at the banquets of the suitors.

His survival shows that Odysseus and Telemachus are fair in distinguishing between who deserves punishment and who does not.

Homer's disloyal slaves are presented as thoroughly evil; the slave girl Melantho verbally attacks the beggar at the start of Book 19 and is presumably among the twelve maids who are hung for answering Penelope back, and the goat-herd Melanthius provides weapons for the suitors. It is worth noting that both their names come from the Greek word 'melas' that means 'black', and this colour was associated with evil in ancient Greece.

ACTIVITY

Form a group and get each individual to take a different character in the story. Make a 'Top Trumps' card for your character. Find, or draw, a picture of them and give them a score out of 100 for qualities such as strength, beauty, appearance, importance to the story and goodness. If Homer does not tell us all these details about your character, use your imagination.

Then justify the scores you gave to the rest of the group and play the game!

TOPIC REVIEW

You should be able to:

1. Describe:
   - the actions of Zeus and the other immortals in the story
   - what the suitors do in the story
   - the actions of the crew of Odysseus in Books 9 and 10
   - what Polyphemus does and says to Odysseus and his crew, and the consequences of this
   - what Circe does and says to Odysseus and his crew
   - what Penelope says to the beggar, the suitors and Telemachus, and the contest that she proposes
   - what Telemachus does leading up to, during and after the contest
   - what Odysseus' slaves do and say to the beggar before, during and after the contest.

2. Explain:
   - why the gods act as they do in the story, and how this affects our views of characters and events
   - why the suitors' behaviour is regarded as appalling
   - the relationship, and the reasons for it, between the crew and Odysseus
   - the positive and negative qualities that Polyphemus shows
   - the positive and negative qualities that Circe shows
   - the qualities of Penelope as a mother, wife and queen
   - the development of Telemachus as a prince and hero
   - how the actions of the slaves should be regarded.

PRACTICE QUESTIONS

Source A: *Homer, The Odyssey, 10.438–448*

"Those were his words, and I felt like drawing the long sword strapped to my sturdy thigh and striking his head to the ground, though he was a kinsman of mine by marriage, but my friends each checked me with soothing words: 'Scion of Zeus, let's leave him behind, if you will, to stay and guard the ship, while you lead us to Circe's sacred house.'

So we left the ship and shore, but Eurylochus did not stay behind by the hollow hull, he came with us, fearing my stern rebuke."

1. What had Eurylochus just said? [2]

2. Give **one** reason why this had upset Odysseus. [1]

3. How typical is the relationship in this passage between Odysseus and his crew compared to their relationship at other points in the poem? [8]

Further Reading for Literature and Culture 1: The Homeric World

Mycenae

French, E. (2002) *Mycenae*. London: Tempus Publishing

McCabe, R. and Cacouri, A. (2016) *Mycenae*. New York: Abbeville Press

Mylonas, G. (2006) *Mycenae*. Athens: Ektodike Athenon

Wardle, K. A. and Wardle, D. (2013) *The Mycenaean World*. Bristol: Bristol Classical Press

Homer's *Odyssey*

Graziosi, B. (2016) *Homer*. Oxford: Oxford University Press

Griffin, J. (2010) *Homer: The* Odyssey. Cambridge: Cambridge University Press

Jenkyns, R. (2012) *Classical Epic*. Bristol: Bristol Classical Press

Thorpe, M. (2013) *Homer*. London: Bloomsbury

York Notes (2001) *The Odyssey*. London: Longman

What to Expect in the Exam for The Homeric World

This chapter aims to show you the types of questions you are likely to get in the written examination. It offers some advice on how to answer the questions and will help you avoid common errors.

THE EXAMINATION

This component of the GCSE examination is designed to test your knowledge, understanding and evaluation and analysis of the Homeric world. The examination is worth 90 marks and lasts 1 hour and 30 minutes. This represents 50% of the total marks for the GCSE.

There are two sections to the paper, one focusing on the Mycenaean Age (the 'Culture' topics and sources), the other focusing on Homer (the 'Literature'). Each section is worth 45 marks, and is therefore worth 25% of your GCSE. The question paper will consist of both short-answer and extended-response questions.

For the 'Culture' section, you will be required to respond to visual and material sources. Some of these will be the prescribed sources you have studied in class, and some of these you will not have seen before. Sources for the 'Literature' section will only be from the five prescribed books of Homer that you have studied.

There are two Assessment Objectives in your GCSE in Classical Civilisation. Questions will be designed to test these areas. The Assessment Objectives are explained in the table below:

	Assessment Objective	Marks
AO1	Demonstrate knowledge and understanding of: • literature and visual/material culture from the classical world • how sources reflect their cultural contexts • possible interpretations of sources by different audiences and individuals.	50
AO2	Analyse, interpret and evaluate literature and visual/material culture from the classical world, using evidence and producing coherent and reasoned arguments.	40

For AO1 in this component, you will need to demonstrate the following:

Culture

- A good range of accurate and relevant knowledge of the Mycenaean Age.
- How the sites and objects tell us about life at the time.
- An understanding of the way the Mycenaeans lived, why their cities were built and developed in the way they did, and the creative skills that the Mycenaeans had.
- Different interpretations that can be made about the objects from the Mycenaean world, and the different conclusions that can be drawn from these.

Literature

- A good range of accurate and relevant knowledge of the plot of the *Odyssey*.
- Knowledge and understanding of customs and values in the story.
- An understanding of the literary style of Homer, the themes of the Odyssey, and the way characters behaved.
- Different interpretations that can be made about the *Odyssey*, and the different conclusions that can be drawn from these.

For AO2 in this component, you will need to demonstrate the following:

Culture

- A range of reasoned opinions about life in the Mycenaean Age.
- Appropriate evaluation of different sources to provide reasoned ideas.

Literature

- A range of reasoned opinions about the characters, themes and manner of composition of the *Odyssey*.
- Appropriate analysis of the characters, themes and manner of composition of the *Odyssey*.

QUESTION TYPES

There are five types of questions that will feature in your exam. Each type will appear in both the Culture and Literature sections, and together will be worth 45 marks in each section. With the exception of the extended-response questions (see pp. 239–242), each will be linked to a picture of a site or an object from the Mycenaean Age or a passage from Homer.

The question types are listed in the table below. They really fall into two categories: the first three types (knowledge and understanding, significance, and stimulus questions) are all short-answer questions. The final two types (detailed-response questions and extended-response questions) require a longer answer.

The final two types will usually be the final questions of each section. The short-answer questions can come in any order. For example, there could be a two-mark knowledge and understanding question, followed by a four-mark stimulus question, followed by a three-mark significance question.

The questions will not necessarily be in the same order as here, but the extended-response questions will always be at the end of each section.

Question type	Number of marks in each section for each question type
Knowledge and understanding questions	9
Significance questions	3
Stimulus questions	10
Detailed-response questions	8
Extended-response questions	15

Knowledge and understanding questions

There will be 9-marks' worth of knowledge and understanding questions (all AO1). The 9 marks will be broken down into a series of short-answer questions, typically worth 1, 2 or 3 marks.

Some questions will require you to show your **knowledge** of Homer or a Mycenaean object or site. Other questions will require you to show **knowledge** and *also* demonstrate an **understanding** of these facts.

There will be a **source** (a passage or an image) to assist you. For Literature, this will be a passage from Homer. For Culture, it could be a prescribed source you have studied, or it could be one that you have not seen before. For example, you might be shown the figurine on the right with the following questions:

Question:	**(a)** Name this style of figurine	[1]
	(b) Explain why it is known by this name?	[1]
Answer:	**(a)** A phi figurine.	[1]
	(b) It has the same shape as the Greek letter phi.	[1]

Knowing that this is a phi figurine is a piece of knowledge, and the fact that it gets this name from a Greek letter shows your understanding as to how it got this name. This answer should be brief. There is, in fact, no need to write full sentences for this type of answer if it seems that only a single word or a phrase is needed, as in the first part of the answer.

The following represents a typical Homer knowledge and understanding question, together with its answer:

Source A: *Homer, Odyssey 9.272–280*

"Stranger, you are a foreigner or a fool, telling me to fear and revere the gods, since the Cyclopes care nothing for aegis-bearing Zeus: we are greater than they. I would spare neither you nor your friends, to evade Zeus' anger, but only as my own heart prompted.

But tell me, now, where you moored your fine ship, when you landed. Was it somewhere nearby, or further off? I'd like to know."

Question:	**(a)** What did Odysseus tell Polyphemus had happened to his ship?	[2]
	(b) Why do you think he told him this?	[1]
Answer:	**(a)** It had been destroyed [1] by Poseidon	[1]
	(b) to stop Polyphemus going after his crew [1] or to stop Polyphemus destroying it and trapping the men on the island	[1]

The first part is asking for two pieces of factual knowledge concerning the speech and the other mark is for your understanding of why he said this. In this case, there is more than one acceptable correct answer, and you will not be penalised for making more points than the number of marks available. However, if you are asked to only give a certain number of facts, or make a certain number of points, you should stick to the instructions.

In this type of question, each correct fact or opinion is worth one mark. You will not be asked to evaluate ideas (e.g. whether you think the story that Odysseus told was a clever idea, or whether you think the figurine is well made), so do not waste time in doing so.

Significance questions

There will be one of these questions in each section. It will be split into two parts. You will be asked to give two pieces of information (2 marks AO1) and state why one or both are important or significant, or what this knowledge tells us (1 mark AO2). Examples are given below.

Source A: *Homer, Odyssey 21.68–75*

"Noble Suitors, listen to me. You have battened on this house, with its master long gone, eating and drinking endlessly, and you could find no better excuse to offer than the desire to win me as a wife. Well come now, my Suitors, your prize stands here before you, clear to see. Godlike Odysseus' mighty bow is the test."

| **(a)** | What does Homer tells us about the history of Odysseus' bow? | [2] |
| **(b)** | What does this tell us about Odysseus? | [1] |

There are various possible answers for the first part, including that Odysseus was given it by a friend, and he kept it at home in memory of his friend. For the second part, this might lead to the idea that Odysseus regarded the friendship as important or that he was sentimental about it, either of which would gain the mark available.

In the culture section the question might look something like this:

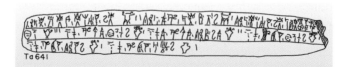

Ta 641

(a) Identify two things that we can learn about Mycenaean written language from the Linear B tablets. [2]

(b) Give one way that Linear B showed a link between the written language and later Greek. [1]

Two marks would be gained for saying that Linear B used ideograms and syllable combinations. The third could be gained for showing that some words came directly into later Greek from Linear B, or that both scripts write the same language.

Stimulus questions

These questions will require candidates to identify something relevant from a stimulus passage or image, and to analyse what you have recognised. Each **relevant** quotation or feature of the image that is picked out will be worth a mark, as will each piece of analysis. Therefore, these questions are each worth equal amounts of AO1 and AO2.

In the culture section, you might be given a picture of a rhyton and asked:

Question: Select **two** features of the design of this vessel, and suggest what each tells us about the Mycenaeans. [4]

Answer: To gain the first two marks (AO1), you might identify any two of the following features: it uses both gold and silver; it is not the most practical container for drinking from; it is made in the shape of a bull; it looks very Minoan in form.

To gain the next two marks (AO2), you might make the following suggestions:

- as gold and silver are not found on Mycenae they must have traded items
- they must have used this for something else, perhaps simply to show off wealth or for a libation
- the bull must have been important in Mycenae
- there were probably links between Mycenae and Crete

Part (a) requires two pieces of knowledge and part (b) asks you to give your opinions of the evidence. You should be careful not to simply show an understanding of how it was used in the second part, but must give your own ideas based on the evidence.

In the Homer section, you will be given a passage and might be asked for your opinions on a character or for how the passage is made exciting. For example, you might be given this passage and asked how Homer makes it dramatic, for 4 marks.

Source A: *Homer, Odyssey, 9.287–295*

"Devoid of pity, he was silent in response, but leaping up laid hands on my crew. Two he seized and dashed to the ground like whelps, and their brains ran out and stained the earth. He tore them limb from limb for his supper, eating the flesh and entrails, bone and marrow, like a mountain lion, leaving nothing. Helplessly we watched these cruel acts, raising our hands to heaven and weeping."

You would be expected to make two points of analysis, giving your opinions. You might say that the victims are helpless and that Polyphemus is totally brutal. Two points of evidence to back this up would be the simile comparing them to whelps and the fact that he ate every last bit of the men.

Look at the number of marks available. If there are two pieces of evidence and two pieces of analysis required, do not give more than this amount. You will be using up time that would be better spent in detailed-response and extended-response questions.

Detailed-response questions

You will get one of these questions in each section with one or more stimulus passages or images to prompt you. This stimulus is meant only as a starting point, and it will be clear from the question that you will need to bring in **extra information and examples**.

Four marks are awarded for your knowledge and understanding (AO1), and four marks given for your analysis, interpretation and evaluation of your facts and understanding (AO2). These questions are marked in a different way, however; you are not given one mark for each correct opinion and each piece of evidence, but the answer as a whole is marked using a Levels of Response Grid. A Levels of Response Grid explains to examiners what answers may look like to achieve a certain number of marks. An examiner will read the whole answer and then check the grid to work out what level the answer belongs to. It is important to remember that the quality of your answer is more important than the amount you have written. The Levels of Response Grid is included in the mark schemes for exam papers.

It is also important to remember that for AO1 you will need to show knowledge and understanding of a source's context and the different ways people interpret the sources. Remember that you can examine both sides of an argument. For example, if you are asked whether you admire a character's behaviour in a particular section of the *Odyssey*, there are likely to be arguments on both sides of the question. If you do not give a balanced argument, you will probably have missed some key facts, and your answer will not show a full evaluation.

This question is not meant to be an essay. You are advised not to write an introduction that simply outlines how you will write your response as this will not add anything to your answer and will take up valuable time. You may find you have more to say than time allows, so you might have to be rigorous in moving on. Make your key points at the start, keep to the point, and if you do choose to have a conclusion, keep it brief, as you will ideally have answered the precise wording of the question throughout your answer. It is not necessary to have a conclusion to gain full marks.

For example, on the paper you might be given a source of a fresco, and then you might be asked the following question:

> What do you think is most impressive about Mycenaean frescoes? Use the source
> as a starting point and your own knowledge in your answer. [8]

In order to show you know about frescoes, you might include some of these facts:

- frescoes were painted on a fine lime plaster
- sometimes on a thicker coarse backing
- mostly done when wet

- a range of colours from natural minerals
- a blue colour was manufactured
- men have red skin colour, women white, lions yellow
- representation of animals, flames, spirals etc.

You then need to weigh up how impressive frescoes were:

- some colours (e.g. blue) were rare and expensive; the use of them was unusual and could be used to show off wealth
- regularity of use of colour creates a very impressive effect
- sense of depth created by overlapping figures
- fine detail in clothing and hairstyle is impressive
- use of friezes is very effective
- use of symmetry/repetition makes the frescoes seem very precise
- division of walls into distinct bands is an impressive feature
- frescoes on floors create a different, interesting effect
- perspective was not always shown effectively
- faces always shown with eyes looking forward, even if the head was facing to the side.

Half the marks are awarded for AO1 and for AO2, but this does not necessarily mean that you should give four facts and four explanations. Examiners will read your whole response and judge how good they feel it is overall.

In Section B, on Homer, a question might ask you about the importance of a theme, or the portrayal of one particular character or episode.

Extended-response questions

This type of question is different from all the other questions in two respects: there is no stimulus passage to introduce it, and you will be given a **choice** of questions to answer (there are two extended-response questions in each section, and you must do **only one**). However, it is marked using a Levels of Response Grid in the same way as the detailed-response question.

Five marks are awarded for your knowledge and understanding (AO1), and ten marks given for your analysis, interpretation and evaluation of your facts and understanding (AO2). This means more marks are awarded for how good your argument is than for simply what you know. Therefore, you might want to spend a bit of time thinking about the structure of your answer. As for the detailed-response question, it is important to remember that for AO1 you will need to show knowledge and understanding of the literary and historical context of sources and the different ways people interpret them.

Extended-response questions will cover a wider area than detailed-response questions and will draw upon material from across topics of either the Literature or the Culture sections. These questions will never, however, cover both Literature and Culture. For example, whereas you might be asked a question, as shown on p. 238 about frescoes in a detailed-response question, an extended-response question might ask about Mycenaean craftsmanship, allowing you to talk about metalwork and pottery too.

The following is an example of a possible extended-response question.

How similar are the characters of Telemachus and Odysseus in the Odyssey?   [15]

To answer this question you should look for evidence where Telemachus and Odysseus can be compared (remember too that you can get credit for introducing material from outside the prescribed sources, so if you have read other books you could draw on these too). You might include some of these facts:

- Both of them plan the murder together.
- Telemachus seems to lead the suitors on in their demise in promoting the challenge. Odysseus does not stop the challenge either.
- Telemachus might have strung the bow the fourth time. Odysseus strung it first time.
- Telemachus orders Penelope to her room as Odysseus had ordered him to go previously.
- Both fight side by side and kill the suitors.
- Odysseus kills Leodes, and Telemachus kills Melanthius and the maids.
- Epithets ('thoughtful Telemachus', 'Odysseus, master of stratagems') suggest both are cunning.

You then need to analyse how similar Telemachus and Odysseus are. You might draw conclusions such as these:

They are similar because:

- Both make cunning plans to defeat the suitors
- Telemachus is almost as strong as his father as he nearly strings the bow
- Both act as master in ordering members of the family to their room
- Both are merciless and merciful as appropriate to the slaves.

They are different because:

- Odysseus does not make mistakes in the fight, but Telemachus does leave the store-room door open
- Odysseus strings the bow with ease, but Telemachus fails in three attempts
- Telemachus leaves a spear in the enemy, through uncertainty, but Odysseus is more experienced and does not
- Odysseus seems arrogant and greedy during his adventures with his crew, but Telemachus does not show such traits.

Key points

The following applies to both detailed-response questions and extended-response questions:

- Your facts must be **relevant**. Do not merely state everything you know about a particular topic.
- It is a common mistake in the literature to over-narrate the plot and to retell a whole story. You should instead **summarise** the main points, or focus in detail on

one or two parts of it. This is particularly important in your extended-response answer, where five marks are available for your knowledge, but ten marks are given for your evaluation, interpretation and analysis.

- Show that you **understand** things from an ancient point of view wherever possible. For example, characters in the Odyssey may have had different attitudes to revenge to modern attitudes, or certain colours that seem to us very ordinary (such as blue), were seen as very luxurious by the Mycenaeans.

- Evaluation is best done throughout the response. **Keep referring back** to the title in your essay to do this. If you give all your facts, and then give all your opinions, it is easy to miss something out, or to run out of time.

- Try to find a **balance** of ideas as the question will usually require you to argue both for and against an idea.

- Sometimes a piece of evidence can be taken two ways. If so, remember to give **both interpretations** in order to show a high level of understanding.

- You will not have a lot of time to do these questions and so it is always best your most important arguments first in case you find yourself running out of time.

- Ultimately make your conclusion **logical**, and supported by evidence from your whole answer, not just one part of it.

Look at these two extracts from an essay:

Question: How important is the theme of justice in the *Odyssey*?   [15]

Extract 1

Justice is very important in the Odyssey. Characters are often punished or rewarded for their actions. Those who help Odysseus are rewarded, while those who hinder his mission often suffer death. An example of someone who is harmed for acting badly is Polyphemus. Odysseus had turned up at his cave and helped himself to cheese. When Polyphemus turned up, he ate two of Odysseus' men who are compared to puppies. Odysseus then made a plan to call himself nobody, and got Polyphemus drunk. When Polyphemus was drunk, Odysseus blinded him and escaped with sheep. Polyphemus clearly deserved his punishment as he had acted in a barbaric fashion. However, I think that other themes, such as hospitality are far more important in the Odyssey.

Extract 2

Justice is first seen in the story of Polyphemus. Clearly Polyphemus pays the penalty for eating six of Odysseus' men by being blinded and losing his flock. However, Odysseus also suffers for his mistakes in being cursed by Polyphemus. His arrogance in calling out his name in triumph could be said to lead to the deaths of his men and him arriving home alone. It might seem unjust that because of his mistake here, a chain of events occurs, causing grief to innocent victims. His wife, son and slaves are harassed by the suitors for years. Some might even suggest that all the men have to die (such as Elpenor in Circe's palace) to fulfil the curse and that there is no justice in this, although Homer does make it clear that they made significant mistakes (no one forced Elpenor to get drunk and climb on a roof).

Notice how the first extract spends more time on presenting the facts than giving opinions, and many of the facts are unnecessary. The evaluation is not developed fully, and the final statement is irrelevant to the question. The second extract is much more concise, and is much more balanced. It argues both sides and flows smoothly from one story to another, providing alternative interpretations of episodes.

GENERAL EXAM SKILLS

When you are sitting the examination, read the instructions carefully so that you realise which questions are compulsory and which are optional (the only option you have is which of the two extended response questions you choose to answer). Remember that the examination will have a range of difficulty of questions; some of it is designed to be challenging, and you should not be panicked if you cannot think of an answer immediately. The following pieces of advice may seem obvious, but you should not underestimate their importance:

- The examination lasts 90 minutes and is worth 90 marks. Do not assume this means you should spend a minute per mark: in reality a lot of short questions will take less than a mark a minute and you should spend longer than a mark a minute on the long questions.
- Both the Culture and Literature sections are worth 45 marks. Do not spend too long on whichever you choose to do first; this is especially tempting if you like the questions that have been set and feel you could say a lot.
- If you see a question that you do not know the answer to, move on quickly to another question. Leave enough time to go back to it; during the examination you might well remember the answer and will not have wasted too much time thinking.
- Stick to the question: if you are asked for facts, do not give opinions and vice versa.
- Do not try to answer a slightly different question if you wish another had been set, or have practised before at school.
- For longer extended response questions, try to find a balanced argument.
- More marks are available in the paper for opinions than knowledge or understanding. It is vital that you do not over-narrate, especially in your Homer answers.

L&C 2
Roman City Life

Introduction to Roman City Life

In this component learners will explore everyday life in Roman cities, with a particular focus on the **Imperial Period** and on popular sites and artefacts from Pompeii, Herculaneum, Ostia and Rome, as well as on four Roman authors who lived during this era.

The Culture section of this component allows you to study a variety of aspects of Roman society. It is sub-divided into the following key topics: Roman Housing, The Roman Home and Family, Society, and Leisure and Entertainment. An examination of topics such as Roman housing, education and citizenship gives us a window into how people in the Roman world lived their lives on a daily basis, and how their society was ordered on a strictly hierarchical foundation, from wealthy aristocrats to lowly slaves. Moreover, the study of Roman entertainment shows both the creativity and the cruelty of the Roman world.

In the Literature section of this component you will read from four authors who offer an insight into life in the Roman world. Two of these, Horace and Juvenal, are poets who wrote satires about the society they lived in. Their satires are quite different in tone from each other, with the light-hearted Horace offering a great contrast to the angry Juvenal. Petronius also satirised the society he lived in, and in particular he focused on the stereotype of the wealthy but vulgar freedman. Finally, Pliny was a successful Roman public official, whose letters to his friends give us a fascinating insight into his life and values.

EXAM OVERVIEW — J199/22

Your examination will require you to show knowledge and understanding of the material you have studied (AO1) and will require you to analyse and evaluate it (AO2), giving your opinions on areas such as characters in the literature or objects in the culture.

This component makes up 50% of your GCSE. In this component 50 marks will test your AO1 skills and 40 marks will test your AO2 skills.

There will be a distinct section of questions on the Culture section of this component, and a distinct section on the Literature material. Neither section will ask questions requiring knowledge of the other: for example, you will not be asked how far the Pliny's Letters confirms knowledge of what you have learnt in the culture section of Roman city life.

In both sections you will be asked to answer a series of short factual questions, based around quotations or images concerning the Culture material, or around passages from the prescribed authors. Some of these will also ask for your opinions. You will be required to write longer answers in each section, worth 8 marks and 15 marks, showing knowledge and giving opinions. There will be 45 marks' worth of questions on the Culture section, and 45 marks' worth on the Literature section. You will have a choice of longer questions worth 15 marks in each section, but all other questions will be compulsory.

Culture

3.1 Roman Housing

TOPIC OVERVIEW

- The layout and decoration of typical Pompeian, atrium-style *domus*
- The design of apartments/blocks of flats (*insula/insulae*)
- Evidence for living conditions of the rich and the poor
- Comparison of the different living conditions in each setting

The prescribed sources for this topic are:

- The Insula of Diana at Ostia
- The House of the Wooden Partition at Herculaneum
- The House of Menander at Pompeii
- The House of Octavius Quartio at Pompeii

Don't forget that you will be given credit in the exam if you study extra sources and make relevant use of them in your answers.

This topic examines two main types of housing in the Roman world – the smart town house and the block of flats. It will cover the typical design features of each, and challenge you to think about the living experience of the inhabitants.

EXAM TIP

Remember that you may be required to answer about the how rich and poor experienced their living conditions, as well as being able to compare the two groups – and indeed to make comparisons between the living conditions of all the types of apartments and houses that you study. While you are studying this topic, therefore, keep asking yourself the question: what would it have been like to live here?

THE INSULA

When people think of Roman houses, they are most likely to think of a large, well-designed house with an internal garden, decorated with beautiful art, and containing plenty of living space and rooms for entertaining guests. However, this type of house, known as a **domus**, was only for the very wealthy, and the number of Romans who lived in such luxurious homes was very small. In fact, in a city such as Rome, the vast majority lived in apartment blocks; the literary sources suggest that these were often cramped and dangerous, although the evidence from nearby Ostia suggests that this was an exaggeration, and that they varied in size and quality. An apartment block was known as an **insula** (the word 'insula' literally meant 'island' in Latin, and presumably the link was that an apartment block was originally a large self-contained building all of its own). One fourth-century AD source records that the city of Rome had fewer than 2,000 domus-type houses but more than 40,000 insulae. To understand the living conditions of the average Roman, therefore, we need to examine what it was like to live in an insula.

Hardly any insulae have survived in Rome itself, and the best evidence can be found in Rome's port town of Ostia, located about twenty miles away. An insula commonly consisted of three to five storeys, although we even hear of insulae six or seven storeys high. Access to the upper floors came from external staircases leading off the street, some of which had impressive doorways, and sometimes from internal staircases as well. From the late first century AD, insulae were usually constructed of brick-faced concrete; roofs were made of wooden beams covered with flat terracotta tiles; at Ostia, examples of large glazed windows have also been found on the upper floors. Ground-floor rooms that faced onto the street tended to be shops, which often had an upper mezzanine level used for storage or even as living space (a **mezzanine** is an intermediate floor of a building, which is open to the floor below).

At Ostia, a few blocks were clearly designed for wealthy occupants: there are some examples of large apartments, which might have two large reception rooms together with a few other smaller rooms, including a kitchen and toilet facilities. However, this was not the standard type, and the city has many more examples of apartments with two to four rooms, both on the ground floor and on upper floors. There is also one interesting example in the Insula of Diana (see below) of small individual rooms in a communal living area.

A number of Roman writers mention how unsafe insulae could be, including Juvenal in a well-known passage discussed on p. 309. Such writers tend to focus on two concerns: that the buildings were poorly constructed and therefore prone to collapse, and that they were likely to catch fire. The wealthy statesman Cicero, who had his own property portfolio in Rome, made the following joke in a letter to a friend:

> Two of my buildings have fallen down, and the rest have large cracks. Not only the tenants, but even the mice have moved out!
>
> Cicero, To Atticus 14.9

domus a large Roman private house in a city or town

insula (pl. **insulae**) the Roman name for a block of flats

mezzanine an intermediate floor of a building, open to the floor below

FIGURE 3.1
The remains of an insula near the Palatine Hill in Rome.

Fire was also a very real hazard. Aulus Gellius, a writer who lived in Rome in the second century AD, here reflects a wealthy man's concern about the dangers of buying property in Rome:

> We were accompanying him home when, while climbing the Cispian Hill, we saw a tall multi-storey block of flats overrun with flames, and all the neighbouring buildings burning in a great fireball. Then one of Julianus' companions said: "The income from urban property is great, but the dangers are far greater. But if some solution could be found to stop houses in Rome from catching fire all the time, by the gods I would sell my country property and buy in the city".
>
> Aulus Gellius, *Attic Nights*, 15.1

PRESCRIBED SOURCE

Insula of Diana

Built: *c.* AD 150

Location: Ostia

Number of storeys: 4

Significance: a very good example of a Roman insula

Reason for name: a relief depicting the goddess Diana on an inner courtyard wall

The Insula of Diana at Ostia

One of the best preserved (and most reconstructed) insulae at Ostia is the Insula of Diana, which takes its name from a relief depicting the goddess Diana on a wall of the inner courtyard. The dimensions of the insula are about 39 × 23 metres; the south and west walls faced out onto the street, while the other two backed onto other buildings, so that they contained no doors or windows. A central, roofless courtyard allowed light into the building, and it contained a cistern which provided water for the inhabitants since individual apartments did not have their own water-supply.

The ground floor contained a number of shops, which opened out onto the street on the south and west sides; they each had mezzanines and some also had a small back room. On the other two sides of the floor were apartments, some of which had elaborate decoration – the remains on one wall still show painted yellow panels divided by borders of red and green. The floor also had its own shared toilet facilities, which were probably available to all the tenants.

FIGURE 3.2

PS

A cut away reconstruction of the Insula of Diana at Ostia.

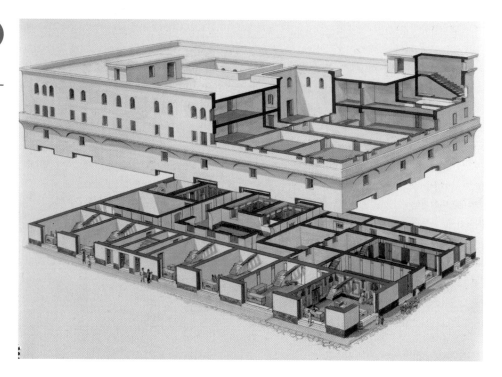

There were three staircases, two external and one internal, which led to the upper floors – the building probably had four storeys in all. On the first floor, only the lowest few centimetres of the walls have survived, but from these we can form a good idea of the layout. On its south and west sides were some fairly large four-roomed apartments, while on the other sides was a communal living area. This consisted of a long corridor off which were small, poorly lit rooms; at one end of the corridor was a larger room that was probably a shared living space. It is also likely that there were communal toilet facilities on this floor too, immediately above the ones below.

It is interesting to speculate as to who might have lived in these apartments. Insulae were mainly rental properties owned by the wealthy (who could make a good profit on the rental income). The four-room apartments may have been rented by people who might be thought of as moderately wealthy, and who may have taken out leases of six months or a year. By contrast, the small rooms in the communal area were perhaps rented by the day or week, most likely to people who were passing through the busy harbour city, or working there for a short period of time.

THE DOMUS

Although the number of large domus-style houses in any Roman city was relatively small, they played a disproportionate role in daily life, since wealthy men used their living space to work, greet friends and clients, and conduct politics – as a general rule, there were no such things as offices where people went to work. Our best evidence for the domus comes from the preserved ruins of Pompeii and Herculaneum, where many such houses have survived. The rooms in these houses have traditionally been given names by archaeologists in the same way that we name rooms in our houses (e.g. kitchen, living room, study, bedroom), but we should be careful not to assume too much about what each room was actually used for: the evidence suggests that many rooms could be used in a variety of ways (in fact, this is not so different from today: a modern living room might be used to work, relax, or eat etc.).

Figure 3.3 outlines the layout of a typical house with its key features. The design is focused around two important areas – the **atrium** (reception hall) and, beyond this, the **peristyle** (colonnaded garden). The atrium was the most public area of the house, and it was here that the owner would meet his visitors and guests, including his clients. The owner of the house might use this room to display signs of his wealth – one Pompeian house had large chests of money in the atrium. In the centre of an atrium was usually an **impluvium** – a rectangular pool into which rain water fell from a specially designed opening in the roof (the **compluvium**). This was a source of water supply for the house since the impluvium was linked to a reservoir below. The atrium might also contain a shrine to the household gods, while according to ancient sources ceremonial wax masks of the family's ancestors could be kept in the open recesses on each side of the atrium. The whole space could therefore be designed to hold the presence of the living, the ancestors and the gods.

The peristyle was a colonnaded garden which aimed to provide a feel of the country. If the atrium was for business, then the peristyle was for relaxation and pleasure. The

Study question
How similar was a Roman insula to the types of apartment blocks we see today?

ACTIVITY
Based on what you have studied of the Insula of Diana, create a drawing of what you think it might have looked like from the outside, and of what you think certain rooms or spaces might have looked like inside.

atrium the main room of the Roman domus, where the family received friends and clients

peristyle a colonnaded garden within a Roman domus

impluvium the pool in the centre of the atrium of a Roman domus that gathered rainwater

compluvium an opening in the roof of the atrium to allow rainwater to fell into to the impluvium

FIGURE 3.3

Plan of a typical domus.

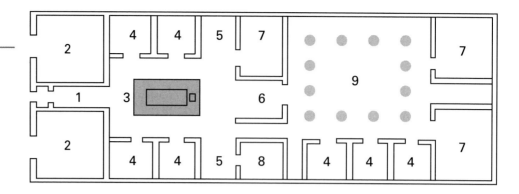

1	entry passage	This led into the atrium, and its walls could be painted ornately; some houses have signs or mosaics in the floor saying 'cave canem' – 'beware of the dog!'
2	shop	External rooms of a house, particularly at the front, were often turned into shops or workshops, either to be rented out to local tradesmen or to be managed by the family itself.
3	atrium	The atrium was the most public and formal part of the house, designed to welcome and impress visitors.
4	bedroom/ private room	These small private rooms could be used for private meetings or for sleeping. Such a room was just big enough for a bed and chair.
5	recess	A small room with one side open.
6	tablinum	This was often located between the atrium and the peristyle. It may have been used as the master's study or the main bedroom.
7	triclinium	The dining room was a key room in a domus: a typical Roman dinner party is described on pp. 262–263.
8	kitchen	This was often quite small and cramped, with a cooking hearth.
9	peristyle	The colonnaded garden was often ornately decorated with a rich variety of flowers, shrubs and trees, as well as fountains and statues.

> **triclinium** a dining room in a Roman domus
>
> **tablinum** a reception room in a Roman domus, often used as the master's study

peristyle may contain an ornate fountain, as well as a variety of flowers, plants and shrubs. The art work on the nearby walls could reflect the theme, with scenes from the countryside carefully painted. Very often rooms used for private hospitality, such as a dining room, known as a **triclinium**, opened onto the peristyle. The other rooms of the house were built around these two spaces. One important room was the **tablinum**, often located between the atrium and peristyle; some ancient sources claim that this was the master's study, where he could conduct private business (although other sources claim quite differently that it was where the matrimonial bed was placed). At the front of the house, rooms giving out onto the street could be converted into shops, which could provide the family with an extra source of income.

A house had a number of small private rooms, which may have been used as bedrooms – but the bedroom was not the important private space that it is in our homes today, it was simply just a place where one slept. Moreover, the activities of a house probably spilled over into a number of places. For example, a kitchen was often too small to cope with the preparations for a dinner party, so slaves might have used the peristyle to prepare food (and probably also to do the washing up afterwards). Similarly, it is unlikely that slaves had their own sleeping space, and so they probably lay down in out of the way corners.

There are some aspects of life in a domus that it is especially hard for us to know about with any certainty. For example, there are only relatively few preserved examples of rooms on an upper floor (the House of the Wooden Partition, described below, is one house where there is evidence). These rooms were typically not grand, and were probably used for sleeping or storage; they may even have been rented out as living accommodation. We can also only guess at how many people lived in a domus, but it would usually have consisted of a family with some close relatives, as well as the attached slaves and perhaps freedmen. The total may, therefore, have been twenty or more.

One feature of a domus that we do know a good deal about is the art and furnishings, thanks to the preservation of houses in Pompeii and Herculaneum. Wall paintings here often come in vivid colours, most commonly red, orange and blue-green, but also yellows, purples and black. Onto these were painted scenes, frequently taken from Greek mythology (a source of great fascination for the Romans, who borrowed much of their own mythology from the Greeks) or country landscapes; still-life scenes such as flowers, fruit and animals. In many houses, painters represented architectural features such as buildings and pillars, giving the images greater perspective and suggesting that the room was more spacious than it really was.

In terms of furnishings, evidence from Pompeii and Herculaneum indicates that houses had many of the items, generally made of wood, which we might use in our homes today: tables, chairs, beds, screens, shelves, chests and cupboards. In one house in Pompeii, the contents of a large cupboard were found in the atrium, including bronze jugs and plates, a bronze basin and cake mould, two bronze signet rings and other pieces of jewellery, nine dice and bits of gaming equipment, as well as some coins made of gold, silver or bronze.

Study question

To what extent are the rooms in homes today used for more than one purpose?

EXAM TIP

The OCR specification for this topic states that 'where houses form part of the prescription it is expected that learners will be familiar with the decoration of these, including examples of frescoes and mosaics'. So make sure you pay attention to the main forms of decoration in each house, and if possible do some further research to learn even more about them.

DEBATE

A Roman writer called Vitruvius, who lived in the first century BC, wrote a book called *On Architecture* in which he defined the characteristics of what he defined as a typical domus. His work has been very influential in the modern era, and for years many books have based their description of a Roman domus on the names, and likely purposes of rooms, on what Vitruvius wrote. However, more recently archaeologists have argued against this approach, stressing that we should not assume that the work of one Roman author speaks for all Roman houses at all times. That is why it is important to remember that rooms in Roman houses often had a variety of functions.

You can read Vitruvius' description of a typical domus in Chapter 6 of his work, an English translation of which can be found on the Companion Website.

The House of the Wooden Partition

House of the Wooden Partition

Location: Herculaneum

Significance: a particularly well-preserved Roman domus with a conventional plan

Name: the house takes its name from the preserved wooden partition that separates the tablinum from the atrium.

This house is a classic example of the atrium-tablinum-peristyle domus. It is also better preserved than many other houses in Pompeii and Herculaneum, and it is a good example of a house where the upper storey has survived. Moreover, carbonised remains – caused by wood being turned into carbon by the intense heat of the eruption of Mount Vesuvius – give us an insight into household design and furnishings.

The house's facade is remarkably well-preserved; indeed, what can be seen today – a two-storey front with roof beams still in place at the top – is probably very similar to what was visible in the first century AD. Outside the front door are the benches for clients; high in the walls above them, small windows look out onto the street from the upper floor, while carbonised wooden beams supporting the roof are still in place. Moving into the house through the entrance way, one walks into an impressive atrium, decorated with red, black and yellow panels. In pride of place was a marble display table in front of the impluvium, while the impluvium itself, with a fountain at its centre, was also lined with marble.

The item of most interest is at the back of the atrium: the 'wooden partition' from which the house takes its name. It is assumed that this was used as a screen to separate the tablinum from the atrium, giving the owner some privacy when required. The partition was originally made of three beautifully panelled sliding double doors, although the middle panel was hacked through by early excavators. Thankfully, the other two panels have survived in carbonised form, together with their hinges and bronze lamp supports, each in the form of a ship's figurehead. Another carbonised relic can be seen in a small room on the west side of the atrium – a bed or couch, which stood on legs shaped by a lathe.

Beyond the tablinum, the peristyle was colonnaded on three sides. There were small family rooms around it, and the house's main dining room lay the other side of it. One of the rooms off the peristyle linked through to one of the various shops bordering the house; these would still have been owned by the owner of the house. At the back of the house was a flight of stairs, which led to a set of rooms above. Steps too can be found in the shop on the front side of the house, and these led up to a small apartment, perhaps the living space of the person who ran the shop – it is unclear if this was attached to the house or not.

FIGURE 3.4
A plan of the House of the Wooden Partition.

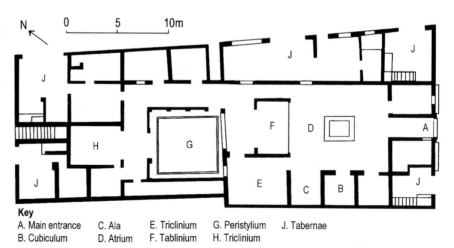

Key

A. Main entrance	C. Ala	E. Triclinium	G. Peristylium	J. Tabernae
B. Cubiculum	D. Atrium	F. Tablinium	H. Triclinium	

FIGURE 3.5
The front of the House of the Wooden Partition from the street. PS

FIGURE 3.6
The wooden partition in place at the back of the atrium.

The House of Menander

This house is one of the largest and most impressive in Pompeii. It is named after a portrait on one of the walls of the peristyle of the Greek comic playwright Menander, who greatly influenced the Roman comic playwrights Plautus and Terence (see p. 286). Scholars are not clear who owned the house at the time of Pompeii's destruction.

The nucleus of the domus had the classic atrium-tablinum-peristyle design, and it seems to have grown out from this core, acquiring neighbouring buildings and incorporating them into an even larger house. From the entrance, one could see right the way through to the back wall of the peristyle. The impressive atrium contained an elaborate household shrine, next to which was a staircase to an upper floor. The recess off the atrium had complementary paintings on its three walls, each one depicting a scene from the Trojan War, including the arrival of the wooden horse at Troy in one of them. The south end of the atrium led into the tablinum, which itself led through to a large peristyle.

The focus of the house was the peristyle and the impressive reception rooms around it. In the north-west corner was a room coloured predominantly in green, with a floor mosaic depicting scenes from the river Nile. In the south-west corner was a suite of baths – only the very wealthiest houses could afford to have their own private set of baths like this. On the south end of the peristyle was a second household shrine, as well as three frescos – one the famous image of Menander, another depicting theatrical masks, and a third another portrait, perhaps of the Greek tragic playwright Euripides. On the east side of the peristyle was a vast dining room, one of the largest reception rooms discovered in Pompeii.

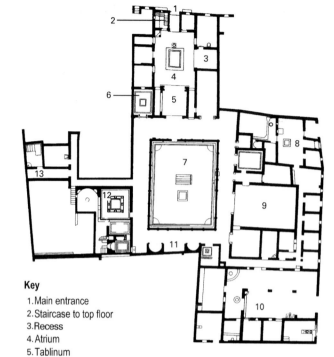

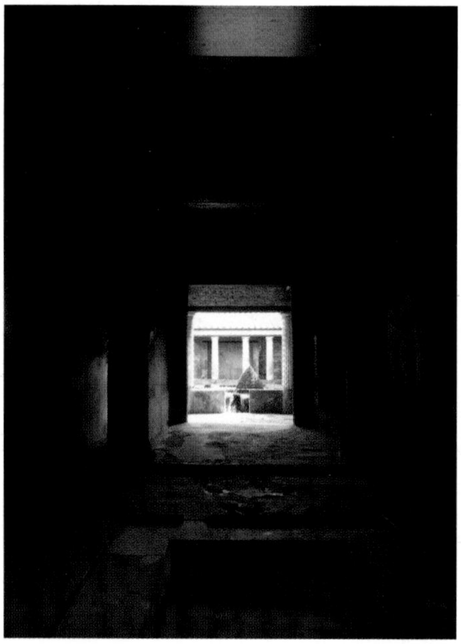

Key
1. Main entrance
2. Staircase to top floor
3. Recess
4. Atrium
5. Tablinum
6. 'Green' reception room
7. Peristyle
8. Second atrium
9. Dining room
10. Service quarters and stable
11. Niche with Menander fresco
12. Small atrium of baths
13. Kitchen quarters

FIGURE 3.7
A plan of the House of Menander.

PS

PRESCRIBED SOURCE

House of Menander

Location: Pompeii

Significance: one of the largest and most impressive houses in Pompeii

Name: the house takes its name from a wall painting of the Greek comic playwright Menander

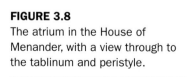

FIGURE 3.8
The atrium in the House of Menander, with a view through to the tablinum and peristyle.

PS

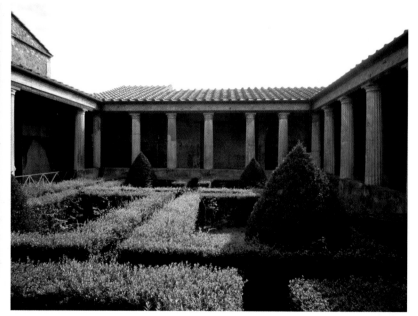

FIGURE 3.9
The peristyle of the House of Menander.

PS

The house was so large that it even had two service areas. To the east side was a long corridor with a number of small rooms; at one end was a large stable, where a wagon, and many amphorae were found, suggesting that the owner may have had a large farming estate as well (agricultural implements were also found in the house). At the other end of the corridor was another small atrium, which may have been the headquarters for the house's steward, or head slave. The other service area, on the west side of the house, consisted of a kitchen, latrine and service rooms, with access to cellars below. It was here that the house's silver service was found by excavators – a large collection of decorated silver vessels, wrapped in cloth and neatly stacked, including plates, trays, spoons, ladles, bowls and cups.

The House of Octavius Quartio

The design of the house of Octavius Quartio shows how, over time, the design focus of a domus could move away from the atrium to the peristyle. The greatest feature of this house was its large and wonderful garden, enhanced by impressive water features, shrines and fountains.

The house is found on one of Pompeii's main streets. Outside the front was stone seating, which may have been used by clients, while the two front rooms opened out onto the street as shops; it is in one of these that a signet ring with the name 'Octavius Quartio' was found, giving the house its modern name. The entrance passage led into a rectangular atrium; its impluvium had a fountain jet and was surrounded by flower boxes, hinting at the beautiful garden that lay beyond. The rooms around the atrium were standard; the south side led directly into a small peristyle, colonnaded on three sides.

The fourth side of the peristyle opened onto a pergola that overlooked the garden. Under the pergola ran a narrow canal, lined with garden statues and probably home to fish; mid-way along was a bridge. Painted on the walls at the west end of the pergola were two scenes from the myth of Diana and Actaeon – Actaeon discovering Diana bathing, and then about to be ripped to death by his own hunting dogs. A large reception room, probably used for dining, opened onto the north side of the pergola; its walls were

FIGURE 3.10 (PS)
A plan of the House of Octavius Quartio, 1 atrium, 2 triclinium, 3 peristyle, 4 outside dining area, 5 pergola, 6 garden pergola.

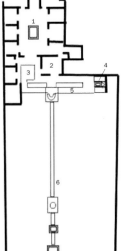

ACTIVITY

Imagine that you have been asked to sell a house in Pompeii (we do not know much about this process in Roman times, but imagine that you are the Roman equivalent of an estate agent). Choose one of the three houses you have studied in this topic, and create a brochure that advertises all its best features for potential buyers.

decorated with scenes from the life of Hercules, as well as from the Trojan War. On the outer north wall of the pergola were painted hunting scenes, and to its east was an outside dining area, with space for two couches rather than the conventional three. Next to the couches on the east wall was a small household shrine flanked by two more paintings – to the left the myth of Narcissus, to the right the story of Pyramus and Thisbe.

The south side of this pergola led off into the garden, which was on a lower level. It was divided by a second, longer pergola and canal. Where the two pergolas met was a fountain shrine dedicated to Diana and Actaeon. The lower canal ran all the way along the garden, about 50 metres in all, and it too was decorated with statues, paintings and crossing bridges. Midway along this lower canal was another fountain, and beyond that a small temple. The garden on either side was planted with ordered rows of acanthus and fruit trees and in the wall at the back was another entrance to the property.

S & C

Find out about the largest domus in Pompeii, the House of the Faun. How does this compare to the houses you have studied?

Study questions

1 How does the layout of a domus compare to that of houses today? How important is it to have personal space within a house?
2 How does the decoration in a typical domus compare to a house today?
3 Which of the houses described in this topic would you have liked to live in and why?
4 How important do you think it was for a house to have outside space for entertaining guests?

FIGURE 3.11
A view down to the garden pergola in the House of Octavius Quartio.

FIGURE 3.12
The outside dining area in the House of Octavius Quartio.

TOPIC REVIEW

You should be able to:

1. Describe:
   - the layout and key features of the Insula of Diana
   - the layout and key features of the House of the Wooden Partition
   - the layout and key features of the House of Menander
   - the layout and key features of the House of Octavius Quartio.

2. Explain:
   - the living conditions for the poor in a Roman city
   - the uses of key rooms in a Roman domus
   - what the art and furnishing in a domus can tell us about the lives of its inhabitants
   - how different you think the lives of the rich and the poor were in a Roman city.

PRACTICE QUESTIONS

Source A: *The house of Menander, Pompeii*

Study **Source A**.
1. Which part of the house is shown in this picture? [1]
2. Identify **three** rooms adjoining this part of the house, and explain how each was important for the inhabitants. [6]

3.2 The Roman Home and Family

- *Paterfamilias,* his rights and duties
- Patrons and clients
- The education of children, including:
  - the role of the *litterator, grammaticus* and *rhetor*
  - subjects taught at each stage
  - preparation for participation in society
  - school equipment (stilus, wax tablet, pen, ink, papyrus)

- The dinner party (*cena*), including organisation, guests, entertainment, purposes

The prescribed sources for this topic are:

- inscription F14 (CIL IV 933)
- inscription H45 (CIL IV 8562)   from Cooley and Cooley, *Pompeii: A Sourcebook*
- inscription D80 (CIL IV 7698a–c)

Don't forget that you will be given credit in the exam if you study extra sources and make relevant use of them in your answers.

This topic examines a variety of subjects related to the household, starting with the role of the male head of the house. It then moves on to focus on the education system such a man would want to put his son through, and then finally explores how he would seek to entertain and impress guests at a dinner party.

THE PATERFAMILIAS

paterfamilias the male head of a Roman family

The **paterfamilias** was the oldest living male in a Roman family, and the head of a Roman household. The term meant 'the father of the family', although the Latin word 'familia' meant more than our concept of 'family', because it also included the slaves and property of the house. The paterfamilias had legal power over his entire household;

in early Roman times, this included the power of life and death, although by the time of the empire, this was only really the case for a new-born child. Indeed, one duty of a paterfamilias was to inspect a new-born baby; if it was unwanted or illegitimate, then the paterfamilias could order for it to be abandoned and exposed (left out to die).

The paterfamilias was responsible for the welfare of his family. He had a duty to raise his children to be good citizens of Rome; he would therefore want to oversee the education of his children, especially his sons, and would normally appoint an educated slave to act as a tutor. When his daughter reached puberty, he was responsible too for arranging a suitable marriage – very often this happened without the girl having any say at all. He would expect his wife to be loyal and hard-working in the home, and would manage the purchase of any slaves for the household. The paterfamilias was also the religious head of the family, and would lead worship at the family's household shrine, where the spirits of the family's ancestors, the **Lares**, were believed to reside. Other religious duties might involve him overseeing suitable offerings to the gods at important moments such as birth, marriage and funerals.

Patrons and clients

If he was wealthy enough, then the paterfamilias might also act as a **patron** to **clients**. Roman society was based around this patron/client relationship. Poorer Romans in need of money would attach themselves as clients to a wealthy man, the patron. Clients were expected to appear at their patron's house at dawn every morning; later, they might be required to accompany him to the forum or to the baths. In the city, they acted as their master's supporters and were expected to vote for him if he ran for political office. In return, clients would hope for a small hand out of money or a gift each day, or perhaps a business opportunity; if they were particularly lucky, they might even be invited to dine with their patron in the evening.

In Roman society, almost everyone seems to have been a patron or a client – indeed, many people were both at the same time, receiving help from those wealthier than them, and providing help to those less wealthy. The system was the oil in the wheels of Roman society.

An inscription of a client supporting a patron

One example of a client publicly supporting his patron can be seen in an election notice carefully painted on the wall of a street in Pompeii, where a man, Thalamus, identifies himself as the client of Publius Paquius Proculus and thereby encourages others to vote for his patron as duumvir, the highest political office in the town:

Thalamus, his client, elects Publius Paquius Proculus duumvir with judicial power.

CIL IV 933

THE EDUCATION OF BOYS

In early Roman times there were no schools as we would understand them. Children simply learnt from their parents – fathers would teach their sons their own trades, as well as some

Lares the Roman family's household gods, representing the spirits of the family ancestors

patron a Roman who gives financial or other such support to a client in return for work and favours

client a Roman who would attach himself to a wealthier patron in order to boost his income and business opportunities

Study questions

1 Is it common for people to have religious shrines or objects at home today?
2 Is there anything similar to the patron/ client system in our society today?

PRESCRIBED SOURCE

Cooley and Cooley, *Pompeii: A Sourcebook*: H45 (CIL IV 8562)

Location: Pompeii, Large Palaestra

Description: an inscription by a teacher referring to being paid

Significance: evidence for the presence of a school at the side of an exercise ground

basic literacy and numeracy, while mothers would teach their daughters how to manage the household. Children were also taught the values of being a good citizen. However, as Rome grew more powerful, it started to be influenced by Greek civilisation, which had a long educational tradition in disciplines such as literature, history, mathematics and philosophy. As a result, the Romans came to model their education system on that of the Greeks.

Schools therefore began to emerge, although not as we would recognise them today – there were no buildings with classrooms, assembly halls and playgrounds. School fees were cheap so a teacher had to find a simple room to hire – perhaps the back room of a shop, with customers coming and going, or a room in a house or apartment building. We even hear of teachers meeting their students in public places, where they would have had to compete with the noise in the streets.

An inscription by a teacher

The following graffito was found scratched on a column on one side of the large palaestra (exercise ground) in Pompeii:

> Whoever has paid me the fee for teaching, let him have what he seeks from the gods.
>
> CIL IV 8562

Besides suggesting that the teacher met his students in a colonnaded part of the palaestra, it is also interesting because the teacher is thanking the pupils who have paid him (or whose parents have) – this of course implies that there were some pupils whose fees were overdue.

In the following passage, the satirist Martial complains about being woken up by a teacher holding an early morning class in the street just outside his block of apartments:

> What do you have against us, spiteful schoolteacher? We know you are hated by all the boys and girls you teach. Before the crested cockerel has even crowed, you shatter the silence with your harsh voice and the lashes of your whip . . . Would you be willing, you old windbag, to accept the same pay for being silent as you now receive for shouting out lessons?
>
> Martial, *Epigrams*, 9.68

FIGURE 3.13
Drawing of a fresco from the Estate of Julia Felix depicting a boy being caned.

It is interesting to note that in this passage school begins before dawn – presumably this allowed the teacher to make the most use of the quietest time of day, before the streets filled up with people conducting their business. The words quoted here also refer to corporal punishment, and this seems to have been common – Horace (see p. 295 ff.) even refers to his old teacher as 'Orbilius the flogger'. Despite this, Orbilius actually had a high reputation as a teacher, but teachers generally must have varied greatly in quality: they did not need any special qualifications, and so in theory anyone could set himself up in the role. They were often poorly paid and drawn from the lower rungs of society – perhaps freedmen or foreigners. It is also very hard for us to know how much progress pupils made in their classes – there were no exams, and therefore no results for us to inspect, and we have no evidence for any other forms of assessment.

The Roman school system in Rome consisted of three stages. The first, between the ages of seven and about eleven, was a type of primary school with a teacher known as the **litterator**; after this, pupils progressed onto a secondary education with the **grammaticus**, followed by tertiary education at the age of sixteen with a rhetoric teacher, the **rhetor**, who taught them the art of public speaking. It is hard to know exactly what proportion of children went to school, and it is likely that it was mainly the preserve of the wealthy; interestingly, it is clear that some girls did attend lessons with the litterator as well as boys. By the age of fourteen, girls were preparing to get married and boys from poorer families had started working. Evidence suggests that the literacy levels amongst the population were very low, although there may have been a higher level of 'functional literacy', whereby people had a limited ability to read and write where they needed to.

The litterator

The first stage of a Roman education was at the school of the litterator. Boys and girls would attend his lessons from the age of seven and learnt reading, writing and some basic arithmetic. The education was very repetitive at this stage – pupils had to practise writing letters endlessly and, once they had mastered the alphabet, they were forced to copy out useful phrases such as 'Seek advice from a wise man'. We even have a diary extract from a Roman schoolboy that tells us about learning at this age:

> My slave who carries my books handed me my waxed tablets, my writing box, and my writing instruments. Sitting in my place, I smoothed over the tablets. I printed the assigned sentence. When I had finished it, I showed it to the teacher. He corrected it, wrote over my errors, and told me to read it aloud. So instructed, I recited it to another student.

> CGL III, pp. 645–647

The boy's words tell us a lot about the equipment used by Roman pupils. They first used wax tablets – thin sheets of wood covered with wax, on which pupils could write with a **stilus**, an implement with a sharp end for marking the wax and a flat end to rub the wax out and smooth

FIGURE 3.14
A relief of a boy arriving late to school.

---

litterator a teacher for primary-aged children in the Roman world

grammaticus a teacher for secondary-aged children in the Roman world

rhetor a teacher for tertiary-aged boys in the Roman world

EXPLORE FURTHER

Fig. 3.13 is a drawing of a wall-painting from a large residence in Pompeii, the Estate of Julia Felix. The whole scene is set under a colonnade in the forum and depicts a pupil being beaten while others get on with their work. What does this painting suggest about Roman education?

---

stilus a pen-like implement used to write on wax tablets

---

it over again. When pupils were competent writers, they would be allowed to move on to write with a pen and ink on a papyrus, thick reed paper invented in ancient Egypt.

Another feature of this passage is that the pupil has a slave to accompany him to school – if a family was wealthy enough, it would appoint an educated slave to supervise a boy's studies and act as his private tutor.

The grammaticus

If parents could afford it, then their sons moved onto the grammaticus at the age of about twelve. The basis of the studies was Greek and Roman literature. The first century BC saw the emergence of some of Rome's greatest writers, such as Cicero, Virgil, Horace and Ovid. In the grammaticus' class writers such as these were studied; in particular, Virgil's *Aeneid*, which told of the escape from Troy to Italy by Aeneas (whom the Romans believed to be their ancestor), was a standard text, much as the works of Shakespeare have been in the English-speaking world. Pupils were taught to learn and recite passages by heart, and to comment on matters such as grammar, figures of speech and the poet's use of mythology. The development of a strong working memory was emphasised at this stage of the curriculum.

In addition, a pupil would start to learn Greek at this time. This was considered the language of educated people, partly because there had been so many great thinkers and writers in the ancient Greek world – poets such as Homer, philosophers such as Plato, historians such as Herodotus, and orators such as Demosthenes. Moreover, it was also important to learn Greek because the eastern half of the Roman empire was predominantly Greek-speaking; Greek was the language of government and law there, and a Roman provincial official would have needed to know Greek fluently.

Other subjects were also studied at this stage too: one source speaks of a curriculum including music, astronomy, philosophy and natural science. However, these subjects were all secondary to the study of literature – for example, astronomy was studied so that a pupil could be better informed when a poet referred to the stars.

The rhetor

At the age of sixteen, the privileged few would move on to lessons with the rhetor. He taught them the art of public speaking, a crucial skill in a world without the various means of communication which we have today, such as newspapers, email, the internet, radio and television; a successful public figure in Rome had to be able to speak well in front of a large crowd of people. Pupils therefore learnt to compose and deliver speeches; one type of exercise required them to debate an event from history or literature, such as 'Should Hannibal have invaded Italy?' or 'Should Dido have committed suicide?' (Hannibal was the great Carthaginian general who almost defeated the Romans in the late third century BC, while Dido was a famous character from Virgil's *Aeneid*

FIGURE 3.15
Roman writing implements.

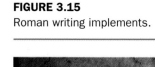

Study questions

1 Are there any similarities between Roman schools and schools today?
2 Why do you think teachers were so undervalued when they played such an important role in society?
3 Do you think that there should be courses in rhetoric today? What would be the advantages and disadvantages of such courses?

who had a doomed love affair with Aeneas.) Another type required them to analyse a specific legal case and argue either for the prosecution or for the defence. Pupils were taught to deliver their speeches with facial expression and hand gestures; their training was therefore similar to a barrister's training today, and it is no surprise that many of Rome's leading politicians were also accomplished lawyers.

In the following passage, the statesman Cicero outlines some of the qualities he feels a pupil should acquire through this training:

> The student must develop his style by careful attention not only to word choice
> but also to sentence construction. He must be thoroughly acquainted with all the
> emotions which nature has given to the human race because he must use all his
> power and ability at speaking to calm or, alternatively, to stir up those that listen to
> him . . . Delivery of speech must be reinforced by bodily movement, gesture, facial
> expression, and by modulation and variation of the voice.
>
> Cicero, *About the Orator*, 1.17–18

cena the Roman word for a dinner

THE DINNER PARTY

A Roman dinner party, known in Latin as a **cena**, was an important social occasion for the affluent. Roman society did not have restaurants as we know them, but merely fast-food bars, which served food of moderate quality. Therefore, a respectable Roman would have eaten at home, and hosting a good dinner party became an important way for a paterfamilias to promote and confirm his social status. He would want to entertain friends and make new business and social contacts, while as a patron he would have been expected to invite his clients and freedmen to dinner from time to time.

FIGURE 3.16
A fresco of a Roman dinner party from Pompeii. The slaves are depicted as smaller in stature than the guests.

A dinner party was full of ritual and formality. It might typically begin in the late afternoon, after the host and guests had spent time at the baths. When the guests arrived at the host's house, wearing formal evening clothes, they might first admire its art and paintings before being shown by a slave into the triclinium. The word triclinium literally meant 'three-couch room', since it contained three long couches laid out in a U-shape. Guests would recline on these couches as they ate, normally with three guests to a couch. Couches were covered in mattresses for comfort and each place was divided by cushions. Guests lay in the reclining position, leaning on their left elbows. They took their food from the central table, which was kept supplied by the slaves, who would also walk round pouring wine and offering basins of water for diners to wash their hands in.

The seating plan was a matter of great precision and a sign of the social status of the guests. The plan in Figure 3.17 shows the layout of the three couches, which were called 'high', 'medium' and 'low'; each of the three seats on a couch was also divided into 'high', 'middle' and 'low', working from the right as you look at the couch. The place of honour was Y, at the low end of the medium couch. This was no doubt because the middle couch faced out towards the entrance to the triclinium and, leaning on one's left elbow,

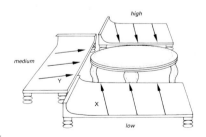

FIGURE 3.17
A triclinium seating plan.

S & C Find out about the Roman cookbook that has survived under the name of 'Apicius'. Are there any recipes there that you would like to try at home?

> **mulsum** a type of Roman wine sweetened by honey

FIGURE 3.18
A fresco from Pompeii of a plate of eggs, dead thrushes and bronze pitchers.

this usually offered the best view of a garden or works of art opposite. Next to the guest of honour normally sat the host at position X, the high position on the low couch, which allowed him to speak with his most important guest. Also on the low couch would likely be the host's clients or freedmen. Other guests would recline on the medium and high couches, with the guest of honour perhaps having his clients or freedmen next to him.

A dinner party typically had three courses. The first might be made up of light appetisers, such as eggs, olives or salads; these were followed by **mulsum**, a type of wine sweetened by honey. The second, the main course, was typically a selection of meats or fish accompanied by vegetables and a variety of sauces. The final course was dessert, which might consist of fruit, nuts or simple sweet-cakes. The host would want to show off throughout by serving a variety of foods and recipes, as well as good quality wine, both red and white.

A number of sources suggest that some hosts served different quality food and wine at the same meal: what you received depended on your social status. You will read one example of this in your prescribed literature (see p. 322), while another famous example comes from the satirist Juvenal, who writes in a poem (Satire 5) of dining with his patron. The dinner party had three categories of guest: the host Virro and his friends; Virro's clients; and the freedmen. Like Pliny, some wealthy Romans clearly disapproved of this practice.

A good host would also put on entertainment during or after the meal. One possibility was an extended session of drinking wine. This was not simply a short-cut to getting drunk, since the Romans always watered down their wine, perhaps by adding as much as four-fifths of water to one-fifth of wine. Other entertainment might include dancers, acrobats and clowns, while we also hear of guests playing games similar to dice and backgammon. Some hosts might organise more intellectual activities, such as a discussion about literature or philosophy. Whatever the case, a host would have hoped that his guests would mix well and behave appropriately.

An inscription by a dinner party host

The following inscriptions found on the wall of the summer dining room of one Pompeian house make clear the standards one host expected from his dinner guests:

PRESCRIBED SOURCE

Cooley and Cooley, Pompeii: A Sourcebook: D80 (CIL IV 7698a–c)

Location: Pompeii, House of Sallust

Description: three inscriptions on the wall of a summer dining-room

Significance: instructions for guests about how to behave at a dinner party

> Let water wash your feet clean and a slave wipe them dry;
> Let a cloth cover the couch, take care of our linens.
>
> Remove lustful expressions and flirtatious tender eyes
> From another man's wife; may there be modesty in your expression.
>
> [. . .] postpone your tiresome quarrels
> If you can, or leave, and take them home with you.
>
> CIL IV 7698a–c

The first inscription refers to the preparations at the start of the dinner party: guests should have their feet washed by slaves and take care not to dirty the furniture. The second inscription warns male diners not to flirt with another man's wife, while the third one tells diners to go home if they are likely to start an argument.

Study questions

1 How common is it for food to be used to denote social status today?
2 What benefits do you think a host would gain from holding a good dinner party?
3 What would you have enjoyed about dining in the Roman style? What would you have found strange?

ACTIVITY

Imagine that you are going to host a Roman dinner party. Design a menu sheet for the occasion (although it should be noted that there is no evidence that the Romans did this, just as it is unusual for us to do this for a private dinner party today).

TOPIC REVIEW

You should be able to:

1. Describe:
   - the powers and responsibilities of a Roman paterfamilias
   - the patron and client system
   - the three stages of the Roman education system
   - the structure and features of a typical Roman dinner party.

2. Explain:
   - how a Roman household was structured
   - why the patron/client system was important for Roman society
   - the strengths and weaknesses of the Roman education system
   - why a Roman dinner party was important for the reputation and social status of the host.

PRACTICE QUESTIONS

Source A: *CGL III, pp. 645–647*

My slave who carries my books handed me my waxed tablets, my writing box, and my writing instruments. Sitting in my place, I smoothed over the tablets. I printed the assigned sentence. When I had finished it, I showed it to the teacher. He corrected it, wrote over my errors, and told me to read it aloud. So instructed, I recited it to another student.

1. What was a waxed tablet and how was it used by school children? [2]
2. Evaluate whether a modern student would have enjoyed studying in a Roman school? Use the source as a starting point **and** use your own knowledge in your answer. [8]

3.3 Roman Society

This topic looks at the different social groups in Roman society, from those at the top rungs, the senators and equites, to those at the other end – the slaves. In between were the ordinary citizens and, below them, freed slaves who are referred to as freedmen.

CITIZENS

Roman society was strongly divided by class and status. All citizens had a wide range of privileges, including protection under Roman law. Full citizenship was only open to men. Women were given a limited form of citizenship and were regarded as minors in Roman law, holding the same status as children; they could not vote and had no say in the Roman political system.

Citizens were entitled to some benefits, including free entry to the public games and free or heavily subsidised use of the public baths; moreover, poorer citizens in the city of Rome were provided with free corn out of public funds. The majority of citizens belonged to the classes beneath the senators and equites described below; many were relatively poor and ill-educated, and engaged in any number of trades and roles to make ends meet. We can learn a great deal about such types of work from surviving paintings and inscriptions, especially in the well-preserved cities of Pompeii and Herculaneum. Moreover, there is also some literary evidence: in the following passage by the comic playwright Plautus, one wealthy character complains about the number of tradesmen he has to pay:

> On your doorstep stand the clothes cleaner, the clothes dyer, the goldsmith, the wool weaver, the man who sells lace and the man who sells underwear, makers of veils, sellers of purple dye, sellers of yellow dye, makers of muffs and shoemakers who add balsam scent to their shoes, linen retailers, bootmakers, squatting cobblers, slipper makers, sandal makers, and fabric strainers. They all demand payment . . . and just when you think you've paid them all, they leave, but others appear, three hundred more, demanding payment – purse makers, weavers, fringe makers, manufacturers of jewellery cases – all cluttering up your atrium!
>
> Plautus, *The Pot of Gold*, 507ff.

In addition to these trades, many men chose to serve in the Roman army.

Above the lower classes, there were two elite classes of Roman society: the senators and the equites.

SENATORS

The highest group in the Roman class structure were the **senators**, who sat in the Senate. For centuries, this was a powerful body within the Roman political structure, although by the time of the emperors its power had been reduced; nonetheless, it continued to influence decisions and had the power to confer the title of emperor. By the first century AD the number of senators was fixed at 600; to qualify, a man had to be born into the senatorial class (meaning that his father had been a senator) or he had to have been elevated to the senatorial class by the emperor. In either case, a senator had to own property worth more than one million sesterces – a vast amount of money in the Roman world. The sons of senators were automatically eligible to be elected to the senate at the age of seventeen, but over time some families fell out of the senatorial class, perhaps through a loss of wealth, perhaps through lack of a male heir, or perhaps through falling out of favour with the emperor. Therefore, in each generation new senatorial families were elevated by the emperor.

Senators had a number of rights and responsibilities. They were not allowed to engage directly in trade and commerce (although evidence suggests that this rule was sometimes ignored), nor were they paid for being senators, and so their wealth came largely from their property. As a result, men of senatorial rank were free to give their time to politics and public service; they were the only citizens who could stand each year for election as **magistrates** – politicians who held the main legal and political offices. The two most important such offices were those of **consul** and **praetor**.

> **senators** members of the highest social class in Rome; a senator had to own property worth at least one million sesterces

> **magistrate** an elected politician in Rome
>
> **consul** the most important public official in Rome after the emperor; two consuls were elected annually
>
> **praetor** the second highest category of public official in Rome, responsible for the law courts and imperial administration

equites members of the second social class in Rome; an equestrian had to own property worth at least 400,000 sesterces

Two consuls were elected each year, and they were the most important officials in Rome after the emperor. In the time of the emperor Augustus, twelve praetors were elected each year, and they were responsible for the legal system and imperial administration. In addition to these positions, the emperor could appoint a senator to a number of other roles, including commanding a legion of the army, governing a province, supervising public services in Rome or holding an important public priesthood. Senators had a number of privileges, including reserved seating at public games and the right to wear a broad purple stripe on the border of their toga to mark their rank.

EQUITES

The second elite group in Roman society was made up of **equites**, or the 'equestrian order'. The word 'equites' literally means 'knights', and in the early days of Rome's history the term applied to those men wealthy enough to own a horse. However, by the first century AD, membership of the equites was open to men who had property worth 400,000 sesterces. The equites were often successful businessmen, since they could engage in trade and commerce where the senators could not. They were also used by the emperor to fill many roles in the civil service in Rome or the provinces, such as managing financial affairs. Equestrians could even be appointed governors of small provinces – one famous equestrian is Pontius Pilate, who was governor of the province of Judaea at the time of the trial and execution of Jesus Christ.

Equites were allowed to signify their rank by wearing a toga with a narrow purple stripe, as well as a gold finger ring. They could also be promoted to the senatorial class if they had enough property wealth and if a vacancy came up.

FIGURE 3.19
A Roman senator wearing a toga.

SLAVES

Slavery was an accepted part of life in the Roman world, as it has been in most societies until recent times. The labour of slaves was central to supporting the Roman economy and it could not have survived without it. There were various ways in which people fell into slavery:

- **Born a slave** This was perhaps the most common route into slavery: any child born to a slave mother automatically held slave status, even if the father was a citizen, as often happened.
- **Captives of war** As the Romans conquered new lands, their victories produced a significant supply of slaves and a great market for slave dealers. However, this supply dried up significantly in the second century AD, by which time the Romans had nearly reached the extent of their conquests.
- **Exposure** Babies abandoned by their parents at birth might be saved and brought up as slaves.
- **Kidnapping** Some were captured by kidnappers or pirates and sold into slavery; some remote parts of the Roman world were particularly dangerous for travellers.

- **Criminals** Some convicted criminals could be condemned to slavery, and sent to train as gladiators or to work in the mines.

Newly captured slaves were taken to a slave-market. There were many of these in the Roman empire, but one or two were particularly large: on the Greek island of Delos, 10,000 slaves could apparently be sold on just one day. At the market, the enslaved people were put on platforms with placards hanging around their necks; these advertised their qualities and characteristics such as age, place of origin, level of education, and state of health.

Once bought, the life a slave lived was somewhat dependent on their skills and talents. There were broadly three groups of slaves in the Roman world:

- **Domestic slaves** It was probably preferable to live in a private household: an educated Greek slave might be highly valued as a tutor for children, while women were bought to help with domestic tasks such as childcare, cooking, weaving and shopping; male domestic slaves would be required to work for the paterfamilias, perhaps doing his accounts, accompanying him to the baths, or running errands.
- **Industrial slaves** Stronger male slaves might be marked down for more challenging or dangerous tasks: working in mines, factories, on large farming estates or as rowers on galleys. In each case, the conditions were grim and life expectancy was relatively short.
- **Public slaves** These were owned by the state rather than a private individual. They could perform a number of roles in a town or city, such as seeing to the upkeep of temples, baths and other public buildings. They might also work on public construction or maintenance projects on public facilities such as roads and aqueducts. Educated slaves could work as scribes in the Roman civil service.

Slaves were legally classified as property and a master had total rights over a slave, including the power of life and death. To stop them running away, some masters branded their slaves. Moreover, some metal identification collars dating to the late Roman period have survived; these would have been fixed around the necks of slaves, and one such collar has the following inscription:

> I have run away. Capture me. When you have returned me to my master, Zoninus, you will receive a reward.

> CIL XV 7194

A slave had no legal or political rights, nor could they marry or own property, and so the quality of their treatment depended heavily on the master's character. Some masters were incredibly cruel, subjecting their slaves to frequent physical and sexual abuse. One example of a cruel master was Larcius Macedo, who you will read about in your prescribed literature (see p. 323). Some of the slaves in his large household conspired to kill him, and after his death the usual punishment was applied – every slave in the house was put to death, whether they were innocent or guilty of the crime.

Nonetheless, we also hear of warm and trusting slave/master relationships. One famous example was Cicero's loyal secretary Tiro, who

KEY INDIVIDUALS
Equites

Total Number: unlimited

Qualification: had to own property worth more than 400,000 sesterces

Work: generally worked in trade and commerce or the Roman civil service

Dress: could wear a narrow purple stripe on their togas

EXAM TIP

If you are asked about the lives of slaves, remember that different types of slaves would have had very different life experiences. Moreover, the quality of life of a domestic slave depended to a great extent on the nature of his or her master. Try not to answer too generally, therefore, about slaves but allow for the fact that there was no doubt a variety of experiences.

FIGURE 3.20
Relief showing slaves working at a wine-press.

was a close adviser of the great statesman, while Pliny, who relates the story of Larcius Macedo's murder with disapproval and horror, admits elsewhere that he could feel great grief at the death of his slaves.

FREEDMEN

Roman society was unusual in that it offered the hope of freedom to slaves. Slaves were able to earn some money, which they could put away to buy their freedom after a long period of service – this was designed to motivate slaves to work hard. In addition, a master might actually choose to free a slave if he had served him well or if he had performed a particularly outstanding act. We even hear of masters who freed slave-girls in order to marry them, especially if they had borne them a child. Some masters had more selfish reasons for freeing slaves: it was often cheaper to free elderly slaves who were too weak to work than to look after them in old age; there was little hope for such ex-slaves being able to support themselves.

Once free, ex-slaves had the status of 'freedmen'; they were allowed to wear a special felt cap to symbolise their liberty. Freedmen were classified as Roman citizens, although they were not allowed to run for public office or to become members of the senatorial or equestrian classes even if they made enough money to do so. However, the children of freedmen had the full rights of citizenship – as we have seen above, Larcius Macedo was the son of a freedman who became a senator. A freedman was still tied to his former master as a client, and required to work for him for a number of days each year, and many would have continued to work for their former master full time as a client.

An inscription by a freedman for an election candidate

In this inscription, Ceratus identifies himself as a freedman and declares his support for Publius Vedius Nummianus as aedile, the second highest political office in Pompeii. Given that he identifies himself as a freedman, it is likely that Nummianus is the former master he still works for:

> Ceratus, freedman, asks for Publius Vedius Numm[ianus] as aedile.
>
> CIL IV 910

However, besides working for their former master, freedmen could also go on to a variety of fields of trade and business, and a few became highly successful. They could also play an important civic role in their city by serving as one of the **Augustales**. Evidence from Herculaneum suggests that these were public officials with a status in the town second only to the magistrates. They could even display the symbols of a magistrate (including a bordered toga), and in return for their status they were expected to repair buildings, erect statues and pay for games. They also performed religious duties, and so have some-times been thought of as priests. A key point about the Augustales was that they were largely drawn from the ranks of freedmen. The term 'Augustalis' came from the emperor Augustus; the Augustales seem to have been connected with preserving the dignity and honour of the emperor of the day. Becoming an Augustalis therefore gave a freedman the opportunity to hold high public office and show their loyalty to the empire which had freed him.

By the late first century AD, it is likely that the vast majority of the citizen population of Rome had some ancestors who had been slaves or freedmen. It was one impressive feature of Roman society that it was able to give hope and opportunity to people who were legally no different from items of property.

The tomb of Naevoleia Tyche

One real-life example of a freedman and freedwoman who became very wealthy can be found in Pompeii. In the AD 60s, the freedman Gaius Munatius Faustus built himself a tomb outside the city for himself and his wife, the freedwoman Naevoleia Tyche. However, after Munatius' death, when Naevoleia seems to have inherited his wealth and property, she soon had another, far grander tomb built outside the other side of the city (burial grounds were always located outside the walls of a city for reasons of public health and religious duty).

Building an elaborate tomb was one way to show off wealth in the Roman world, since it was beyond the means of most Romans. Naevoleia was clearly more determined than her husband to show off both their combined wealth and the influence that Munatius had wielded in the city. The new tomb, made of marble, took the shape of a raised altar and was located within an enclosure. On one side of the tomb was sculpted an image of a ship, on the opposite side a ceremonial seat and footstool. On the front of the tomb was carved a detailed scene showing some sort of public ceremony, with an inscription and an image of Naevoleia above it. The inscription translates as follows:

> Naevoleia Tyche, freedwoman of Lucius, for herself and for Gaius Munatius Faustus, *Augustalis* and Country District Dweller, to whom the town councillors with the consent of the people decreed an honorific chair for his merits. Naevoleia Tyche had this monument in her lifetime for her own freedmen and freedwomen and for those of Gaius Munatius Faustus.
>
> CIL X 1030

We can establish a number of details about the life of Munatius from this tomb. The image of the ship suggests that he made his money through shipping; he clearly became an influential figure in the city, and the public ceremony may even depict a distribution of money or grain that he made to the people of Pompeii. Moreover, he served as an Augustalis, and was awarded a ceremonial seat most probably at public games or performances, for his services to the city.

FIGURE 3.21
A marble relief of two freedmen, Publius Licinius Philonicus and Publius Licinius Demetrius. On the left are the rods and axes used in the ceremony of freeing a slave. The tools of a smith and a carpenter can also be seen.

FIGURE 3.22

A set of drawings showing the sides of the tomb of Naevoleia Tyche and its most important imagery.

FIGURE 3.23

The tomb of Naevoleia Tyche today.

PRESCRIBED SOURCE

The tomb of Naevoleia Tyche, including inscription

Built: AD 60s

Location: Pompeii (outside the Herculaneum Gate)

Name: named after the wealthy freedwoman who had this built for herself and her husband

Significance: a large tomb illustrating how successful freedmen and freedwomen could become in Roman society

Inscription: this identifies the tomb as belonging to Naevoleia and her husband Gaius Munatius Faustus and lists some of his achievements.

It is also important to reflect on the image that Naevoleia projects of herself on the tomb, since it draws attention to her own wealth and status in the city. The inscription itself emphasises that she is the one who has had the tomb built, while an image of her is depicted above the main scene. We learn too that, like her husband, she has other freedmen and freedwomen as her clients; even a freedwoman could play a significant role in Pompeian society.

TOPIC REVIEW

You should be able to:

1. Describe:
   - the nature of citizenship
   - the responsibilties and privileges of the senators and equites
   - the key features of Roman slavery
   - the rights of freedmen.

2. Explain:
   - the importance of citizenship to a Roman
   - the ways in which the senators and equites helped the running of Roman society
   - what life may have been like for different types of slave in the Roman world
   - the extent to which freedmen could be independent and successful.

PRACTICE QUESTIONS

Source A: *CIL IV 910*

Ceratus, freedman, asks for Publius Vedius Numm[ianus] as aedile.

Study **Source A**.

1. What is the relationship between the two men named in this inscription, and how do you know? [2]

2. 'Freedmen could play an important role in Roman society.' To what extent to you agree with this statement? Use the source as a starting point **and** use your own knowledge in your answer. [8]

3.4 Leisure and Entertainment

- The amphitheatre, including:
  - design of amphitheatre buildings, including the *Colosseum*
  - types of shows
  - sponsorship of games by the Emperor or politicians
  - gladiators; their status, training and types
  - audience involvement
- The chariot races, including:
  - design of the *Circus Maximus*
  - teams, colours, charioteers, horses and their status
  - public attitudes and audience involvement
  - the social significance of such events
- The theatre, including:
  - the design of theatre buildings and use of sets, costumes, masks
  - Roman comedy and its stock characters; mime and pantomime
  - actors and actresses; their reputation and social standing
- The baths, including:
  - the reasons people used bath complexes
  - design of bath buildings, and the different types of bath
  - activities at the baths, including the use of the *palaestra*

The prescribed sources for this topic are:

- the Colosseum
- the Circus Maximus
- the Large Theatre at Pompeii
- the Central Baths at Herculaneum
- inscription D51 (CIL X 833, 834) ⎫
- inscription D16 (CIL IV 1189) ⎬ from Cooley and Cooley, *Pompeii: A Sourcebook*

Don't forget that you will be given credit in the exam if you study extra sources and make relevant use of them in your answers.

This large topic examines four different types of leisure and entertainment. Three of them – amphitheatre shows, theatre shows and the chariot races – have a number of similarities, not least in the way that politicians funded them in order to win favour from the people. The fourth, baths, focuses on a central aspect of Roman daily life.

THE AMPHITHEATRE

Design

We first hear of gladiatorial fighting in the third century BC. It grew in popularity and by the late first century BC it was an established and popular part of Roman life. Gladiatorial fights were held in an amphitheatre, a word derived from the fact the stadium was a doubled-up version of a semi-circular theatre (*amphi* meant 'both', so that 'amphitheatre' really meant 'a theatre on both sides'). Today the terms 'theatre' and 'amphitheatre' are often confused – it is simplest to remember that a theatre had a 180-degree viewing area, while in an amphitheatre it was 360 degrees. Amphitheatres were not completely round but rather oval in shape. Most Roman cities of any size had an amphitheatre, and the remains of many more than 200 have been found throughout the Roman world.

The Colosseum

The most famous Roman amphitheatre was of course the Colosseum, situated in the heart of Rome. In fact, Romans never called it by this name (which was first used centuries after the Roman Empire fell). To them, it was the 'Flavian Amphitheatre', from the name Flavius, which was the family name of the emperor Vespasian, who reigned from AD 69 to 79. It was Vespasian who commissioned this enormous building project in the AD 70s, since he wanted to provide a wonderful stadium for the people in order to ensure his popularity. It took about ten years to build, and at its completion his builders had produced easily the largest amphitheatre in the Roman Empire, with its outer walls rising to a height of 57 metres. The capacity is estimated to have been around 50,000 (for comparison, the amphitheatre at Pompeii could hold an estimated 20,000). Its outer dimensions were 188 metres by 156 metres, while the outer wall rose to about 48 metres in height.

The basic design of the Colosseum was based on a series of concentric circles, leading in from a huge outer wall to the arena inside. The outer wall consisted of four storeys: the first three had open archways looking out, while the fourth had small windows. The outer wall was largely built of hard travertine rock, a limestone quarried near Rome. Between the outer wall and the arena at ground level there were four circular corridors, as you can see from Figure 3.24. These had facilities such as water fountains and toilets, while they also led to staircases and the seating above. The whole design was cleverly constructed using archways, since arches provided a very stable support for the weight above. These arches were constructed of bricks and concrete – the Romans had invented concrete, which enabled the construction of a strong arch since the concrete allowed the bricks to stay in place at an angle.

FIGURE 3.24
A cut away reconstruction of the Colosseum.

---

vomitoria the staircases of the amphitheatre, via which people could pour out of the stadium in great numbers

---

PRESCRIBED SOURCE

The Colosseum

Built: constructed in the AD 70s, and opened in AD 80

Location: Rome

Name: called the 'Flavian Amphitheatre' by the Romans, after the emperor Titus Flavius Vespasianus (today commonly known as 'Vespasian')

Capacity: *c.* 50,000

Significance: the largest Roman amphitheatre in the empire

The many staircases and walkways allowed spectators to get in and out of the building quickly and efficiently. Collectively, the staircases were known as **vomitoria**, which is linked to our word 'vomit', since the people could pour out of the seating area in great numbers. The amphitheatre had eighty entrances, with four especially ornate ones on the main axes – the two on the long axis are generally thought to be the performers' entrance and exit, while the two on the short axis were probably the entrances that VIPs used. There is evidence that these two were monumental entrances, beautifully designed with stucco – a type of plaster that it is easy to paint over. In fact, it is likely that stucco was used in many areas of the building, which allowed it to be decorated with beautiful paintwork.

This was not the only impressive design feature – if it became too hot, a huge awning could be pulled over the top of the seating area to protect two thirds of the crowd from the sun. In the seating area, up to the third storey was made of marble, which must have given the stadium a very impressive look. The seats at the level of the fourth storey were of wood, to reduce the downward weight and the pressure on the outer wall. All the seating was steeply tiered so that everyone could get a good view while sitting down. Nonetheless, spectators were seated rigidly according to social class: the more status you held, the nearer to the action you would be. Therefore, on the level podium nearest to the arena was the imperial box for the emperor, special seats for the Vestal Virgins, and seating for the senators. Above that there were three main tiers of seating: the equites sat in the first tier, behind them were the ordinary citizens, and at the top level sat those from society's marginalised groups – women, slaves and the poor.

The arena itself was surrounded by wall of 4 metres in height. Above it was a metal fence, while during the shows archers stood guard to shoot any animal that threatened the spectators. In the arena itself, the ground was covered in sand, which could soak up the blood of victims (in fact, *harena* in Latin meant 'sand', which is where our word 'arena' comes from). Beneath the arena floor was an underground network of tunnels, cages and lifts, where animals were held before being sent into action through trapdoors. This underground area was also linked by a tunnel to a point outside the stadium, so that the spectators would not know what to expect before the animals appeared.

Sponsorship of the games

The gladiatorial games in Rome were closely associated with the power of the emperor. Even before the time of the emperors, senior politicians had campaigned for votes by promising to fund impressive games – it was a fine way to win public popularity. In the time of the emperors, this became a way for the emperor to promote himself and to show off his power. Senior politicians also continued to sponsor gladiatorial shows, although successive emperors passed laws ensuring that they alone could give far more spectacular shows than anyone else. We hear of some remarkable shows – the most extravagant, which was certainly not typical, came early in the second century AD when the emperor Trajan celebrated the military victories he had won by holding games over a 123 day period, during which 10,000 gladiators and 11,000 animals were apparently used.

The link between public shows and political sponsorship also remained strong in the provincial cities of the Roman Empire. Each city had its own council with elected representatives, and the evidence shows that they too paid for impressive shows in order to win public favour from the local population.

FIGURE 3.25
The network of tunnels under the amphitheatre at Puteoli.

An inscription advertising the games in Pompeii

This inscription, which was painted in red on the outside wall of a very large building on one side of the forum, shows a Pompeian politician advertising the games he is soon to put on for the people:

> The gladiatorial troupe of Aulus Suettius Certus, aedile, will fight at Pompeii on 31 May. There will be a hunt and awnings.

CIL IV 1189

The inscription was discovered painted on a wall close to the forum, which faced onto one of Pompeii's largest streets. Clearly Aulus Suettius Certus, who as one of two aediles jointly held the second most powerful position in the city, wanted to advertise his games in a very prominent place. It is also interesting to note that he promised both gladiators and wild beasts (the 'hunt'), as well as an awning to protect spectators from the heat of summer.

Types of shows

There are a variety of references to the gladiatorial games by Roman writers, and so it is possible to piece together the events of a day at the amphitheatre. The action started early in the morning and lasted until evening, so it was vital for the sponsor to make sure that he provided plenty of variety. It seems that the morning events were often dedicated to shows involving animals, while the gladiatorial contests came later in the day. At some point, too, there were often public executions of convicts – one writer refers to these happening at midday on one occasion, although we cannot be sure that this was always the practice. Indeed, we should be careful not to think that a day at the amphitheatre always followed exactly the same pattern.

Wild animals

Wild animals were a key feature of the games. It was a source of pride for an emperor in particular to bring the most exotic and dangerous beasts from all over the Roman Empire

FIGURE 3.26
A Bestiarius fights a tiger.

and beyond to the Colosseum – sources refer to animals such as giraffes, crocodiles and hippopotami. Most spectators would never have seen such animals and must have been amazed at the sight of them. Some were trained to perform tricks, just as circus animals do today. Sources speak of teams of panthers drawing chariots, of a tigress tearing a lion to pieces and then going to lick its trainer's hand, and of elephants bowing in front of the imperial box.

Another form of entertainment was to set two different types of animal against one another, such as a bear and a buffalo, or an elephant and a rhinoceros. Very often, however, a human fighter would line up against such animals. He was known as a Bestiarius ('beast fighter') and his weapons gave him a significant advantage over the animals, despite their ferocity, so that he was expected to dispatch them in a variety of ways. Such slaughter was more than just mere entertainment. By introducing all these animals into the arena, an emperor was able to make two political points – first of all, that the empire had power over nature, just as it did over human beings, and secondly that such a great range of animals demonstrated just how far and wide the Romans had conquered.

ACTIVITY

Imagine that you are a Roman politician about to pay for a day at the amphitheatre. Design an advertisement notice to make the people aware of what you are going to offer.

MODERN PARALLEL

Are there any modern examples of politicians or public figures funding public entertainment in order to win popularity or support from a large number of people?

Executions

During the middle of the day events often took an even more gruesome twist, when convicted criminals were brought out to be executed. Although these executions were presented as entertainment, they also served as a warning to the people to obey the emperor and of the dangers of criminality. The convicts were usually killed by being exposed to the wild animals, either tied to stakes or being made to fight them, but we also hear of criminals being made to fight each other to the death.

Gladiatorial combat

When it was time for the gladiator fights, the proceedings typically began with a procession around the arena, which was accompanied by the music of an orchestra – one mosaic shows musicians playing a water organ, trumpets and horns. When the procession was over, weapons were examined, and the fighters moved off to prepare for their bouts, which were mainly between individual fighters, although it seems that group fights also took place at times. Most bouts were overseen by a referee who also had an assistant on hand; they carried long staffs to separate the fighters if necessary.

A fight between two gladiators might last for as long as fifteen or twenty minutes, but when one man could go on no longer, he signalled defeat by raising a finger. His opponent now stood over him and looked for a signal from the emperor – to kill or to spare. The emperor would listen to the noise of the crowd and make his decision. He indicated this by giving a sign with his thumb – it is not clear if a 'thumbs up' meant 'let him die' or 'let him live'; another theory suggests that if he chose death he put his thumb out sideways to indicate a cutting sword. However, the key point is that at this moment the emperor was seen to engage with his people and to have the power of life and death.

In reality, defeated gladiators were probably not killed that often – evidence suggests that it may only have been one in five. It was very expensive to train gladiators, and a trainer would not have wanted to lose a good one. However, if a defeated gladiator was to be killed, he was trained not to flinch, nor to ask for mercy. Once he was slain, an attendant came out and hit his head with a mallet, while another dressed as Mercury, the god who escorted souls to the underworld, prodded the corpse with a hot rod. It was then removed from the arena, and the throat was cut to make sure that the man was dead. Back in the arena, other attendants raked over the bloody sand.

The gladiators

Gladiators came from a variety of backgrounds. Some would be strong slaves, others prisoners of war, and some convicted criminals; there were even free men who signed up to try to escape poverty. All gladiators had to train in a gladiator school, which was run by a trainer. He would hire out his fighters to a magistrate wishing to fund a gladiatorial show as its sponsor. Training was intensely tough; the men would spend hours practising fighting drills with blunted wooden swords, while they would also be taught how to face death bravely. Much expense was spent on the gladiators: they had access to high quality medical care and were given a high-energy diet of food such as barley, beans, oatmeal and fruit. A trainer had the power of life and death over his trainees, who held a very low social status and did not have the protection of the Roman legal system – a gladiator was regarded as being **infamis**.

The name 'gladiator' comes from the Latin *gladius*, meaning a sword. However, gladiators did not all use the same equipment: there were various types who were distinguished by their armour, their weapons, and their fighting style. The crowds loved to see different fighters pitted against one another, each one using his distinct skills and weapons. Most types of gladiators can be divided into one of two categories: heavily armed and therefore hard to wound, or lightly armed and quick on their feet.

Scholars have examined the evidence carefully for the different types of gladiator – their names and the equipment they used. While we cannot have certainty on these matters, in the box opposite you can see details of what are believed to be some of the most common types of gladiator. Some were heavily armed, others lightly armed, and it seems that it was common for the different types to be pitted against one another in order to watch a clash of styles and weapons. So, for example, a retiarius might be matched against a secutor.

In addition to the normal types of gladiatorial fighting, some sponsors liked to put on shows that were more unusual and strange, and which brought novel interest for the audience. One example comes in the evidence that there were some female gladiators, while another is found in a number of

EXPLORE FURTHER

There is a famous story of a riot in the amphitheatre of Pompeii in AD 59, when rival factions of supporters from Pompeii and a nearby town, Nuceria, broke into a fight with each other. Read the historian Tacitus' account of the riot in Annals 14.17, and examine the details of the wall painting in the House of Actius Anicetus, which seems to depict the event.

infamis literally 'shameful' or 'disgraceful', the very low legal status given to a number of groups in the Roman world, including gladiators, charioteers, actors and prostitutes

FIGURE 3.27
An imagined fight between a secutor and a retiarius.

FIGURE 3.28
A gladiator's helmet.

KEY TERMS Gladiators

Murmillo A gladiator who was heavily armed rather like a Roman legionary soldier. He had a fish-crested helmet without a visor ('murmillo' means 'fish head'), short greaves, the curved rectangular shield of a Roman legionary, and also the legionary's short sword.

Secutor A heavily armed fighter who had a distinctive helmet with a visor containing two small eye-holes, so that his face would be protected from a trident thrust. He also had a greave on his left leg, an arm guard, a legionary-style shield and a short sword. The secutor usually fought against the retiarius.

Hoplomachus A heavily armed fighter who looked like a Greek hoplite, with a large crested helmet with visor, a thigh-length greave on his left leg, a spear and a round shield. He was often pitted against a murmillo in a re-enactment of Rome's wars against the Greeks.

Retiarius The name means 'net-fighter'. He was lightly armed with a large net, a trident, an arm guard, a shoulder guard and a dagger. The retiarius was the most lightly armed gladiator and the only one whose head and face were uncovered.

Thracian A lightly armed fighter who wore a crested, broad-brimmed helmet with a visor, armoured greaves on both legs, a protector on his sword arm and shoulder, a small shield, and a curved short sword designed to slash the opponent's flesh.

Bestiarius A special type of fighter trained to fight wild animals. Technically he was not really a gladiator since he did not carry a sword. He did not usually wear armour, but carried weapons such as whips, spears, or even bows and lances.

references to dwarfs fighting in the arena. In both cases, we can see members of marginalised groups being offered up to the audience as spectator sport.

CHARIOT RACING

Chariot racing was a central part of Roman society, and the Romans themselves liked to believe that it had been introduced to the city by its founder, Romulus, in the eighth century BC. Although today the gladiatorial games are most commonly associated with sporting entertainment in the Roman world, it was really chariot racing which played the same central role in Roman society as sports such as football do in ours today; then, as now, obsessive fans wore their team's colours and became very emotionally involved in the action and the drama of events.

The Circus Maximus

A stadium for chariot racing was known as a **circus**, from where we get the word 'circuit'. There was more than one circus in Rome, but by far the biggest was the Circus Maximus ('The Greatest Circus'), which was located in a small valley in the centre of the city – today

FIGURE 3.29
A reconstruction of
the Circus Maximus

PRESCRIBED SOURCE

The Circus Maximus

Built: first built in the 6th
century BC, rebuilt
a number of times,
particularly by the
emperor Trajan in the
early 2nd century AD

Location: Rome

Capacity: *c.* 250,000 in
the 1st century AD

Significance: the largest
stadium in the Roman
Empire

---

spina the thin dividing
bank down the middle of a
Roman stadium's racing
track

metae the set of three
turning posts located at
each end of the spina

carceres the starting
cages for the chariots –
there were twelve in all

---

the area is a public park, and the outline shape of the track is still visible. In fact, the Circus Maximus was an extraordinarily large stadium, the largest edifice in the Roman Empire; it also remains the largest sporting arena in recorded history. In the first century AD, its capacity was about 250,000, more than twice the size of the largest stadia in the world today.

The track was about 600m long and 150m wide, and down the middle was a narrow dividing bank called the **spina** ('backbone'). The curved turning point at either end of the spina was decorated with three posts, known as **metae**, which were made of gilded bronze. Along the spina were various monuments, including a large red granite obelisk from Egypt, which depicted Rameses II and dated to the thirteenth century BC. The emperor Augustus had this placed there to mark his conquest of Egypt. There were also symbols of the gods, since the chariot races were often put on as part of religious festival holidays; in particular, racing fans would have wanted to honour Neptune, the Roman god of horses. Also on the spina were seven large wooden eggs, which were lowered to indicate how many of the seven laps of a race had been completed; one emperor added seven bronze dolphins to do the same job.

Another important feature of the stadium was the starting cages, known as **carceres** ('cells') which worked in a similar way to the starting gates used in horse racing today. They were constructed to allow a staggered start for chariots, since some cages had a better starting position than others. There were twelve cages, each one with a spring-loaded starting gate; when the signal was given to start the race, all were released at the same time and the chariots flew out.

The substructures of the Circus Maximus were made of brick-faced concrete. Above them, seating wrapped round three sides of the stadium and contained three tiers – the lowest built in marble and the other two in stone. The lowest was reserved for VIPs: state priests, senators and wealthy equites. The next tier was available for anyone – unlike at the amphitheatre, there seems to have been little segregation at the circus, which meant that men, women and children from different sections of society could sit together; the top tier may have been standing room only. On one side of the stadium was the imperial box, built of marble, where the emperor watched the races. This also gave him an important opportunity to be seen by his people in the heart of the city.

The races

As at the gladiatorial games, a day at the Circus Maximus was paid for either by the emperor, or by a senior politician, who would look on this sponsorship as a chance to win popularity. As the sponsor of the games, he led the entry parade that began the day's events. Behind him came the charioteers and horses, as well as musicians and soldiers, who carried images of the gods and goddesses believed to be present at the races. These images were carried to a shrine in the imperial box.

The races would then start: each one consisted of seven laps of the track in an anti-clockwise direction and lasted for about ten to fifteen minutes; there were typically twenty-four races in a day. Chariots were normally drawn by teams of four horses (although we hear of races involving larger teams of horses – the emperor Nero apparently even took part in a ten-horse chariot race in the Olympic Games of AD 67). Before the race, the charioteers were allotted their position in the starting cages. They then lined up and waited for the sponsor to give the starting signal – he did this by dropping a white cloth, at which point the gates sprung open.

Once the race had begun, tactics were all important. A charioteer would wear a tunic, colour-coded to his team, and a leather helmet, and he would also carry a whip. Rather than holding the reins as we would expect, he wrapped them around his body and steered by transferring his weight from one side to another; therefore, if he crashed he was in danger of being dragged along by the reins and so he carried a knife with him to cut himself free. The most difficult section of the circuit was turning around the metae: a charioteer would have to find a balance between not going out too wide, thereby wasting

EXPLORE FURTHER

The fact that men and women could sit together at the Circus Maximus gave some people the chance to try to strike up a romance. The Roman love poet Ovid twice writes about flirting with a woman at the races: read *Amores* 3.2 and *Ars Amatoria* 1.135–162. What can we learn about the chariot races from these poems?

FIGURE 3.30
A chariot race in action.

valuable seconds, and not drawing too close to the spina, so risking a crash. Most accidents happened round the metae, and they could result in appalling injuries to both charioteers and horses.

When the race was over, the sponsor of the games presented the winning charioteer with a palm branch, while the payments to him and his team were made at the end of the day.

Charioteers and horses

A huge amount of time and money was invested in preparing the horses and charioteers to be race-ready. There were only four teams that competed in Rome – the Reds, the Whites, the Blues and the Greens – and since as many as twelve chariots could take part in a race, each team might field up to three chariots. We could therefore compare this system to Formula One racing today, where teams often put out two cars, which might try to work together. Each team was overseen by an owner, who could be compared to a modern football club chairman. He supervised his team's set of stables and employed many staff, including stable-boys, trainers and vets. However, his most valuable employees were the charioteers. As today, owners often paid huge prices to sign up the very best.

Charioteers were usually of low-born origin – either freedmen, or slaves who might be able to pay for their freedom after a few victories; like gladiators, they held the status of being infamis. However, as with exceptional modern sportsmen, an outstanding charioteer was able to win great wealth and fame. Perhaps the most celebrated charioteer in Roman history was Diocles, a Spaniard who competed for twenty-four years and apparently won 1,462 of his 4,257 races, becoming the Roman equivalent of a multi-millionaire in the process. However, Diocles was very much the exception rather than the rule: charioteers could be killed or seriously injured and few won great riches from the sport.

Supporters followed horses just as much as racers, and kept statistics about them, such as their breed and pedigree. Racehorses were purpose-bred on stud farms, which could be found in many parts of the empire, with a particularly high concentration in North Africa and Spain. Many inscriptions have survived on pottery and mosaics that bear witness to the popularity of some horses; for example, one describes a horse called Victor, which won 429 times.

FIGURE 3.31
A charioteer from the Red team holds the palm of victory mosaic.

The spectators

Supporters of chariot racing were just as passionate as many sports fans are today. It was common for fans to wear the colours of their favourite team, while there was also heavy betting on the results. For one obsessed fan, the races were even a matter of life and death: a Roman writer records that at the funeral of a

S Find out more about
& curse tablets in Roman
C Britain by visiting http://
curses.csad.ox.ac.uk/.
What sort of things do
people put curses on?
Are there any modern
comparisons to this
practice?

curse tablet a tablet on
which someone wrote a
prayer to the gods asking
them to put a curse on an
enemy

Red charioteer, a supporter was so devastated that he threw himself onto the funeral pyre. This was an extreme case, but there is no doubt that many fans were overflowing with passion; you will read in your prescribed literature a letter by Pliny describing the behaviour of the spectators at the races (see p. 324). Other evidence for the obsessive nature of fans behaviour comes in the form of **curse tablets** – some supporters even put curses on horses and riders they wanted to lose. This one was found in North Africa:

> I call upon you, o demon, whoever you are, and ask that from this hour, from this day, from this moment, you torture and kill the horses of the Green and the White factions, and that you kill and crush completely the drivers Clarus, Felix, Primulus and Romanus, and that you leave not a breath in their bodies.

> ILS 8753

THE THEATRE

Study questions

1 What similarities can you find between chariot racing and modern horse racing?
2 Why do you think that fans become so passionate about the sports they follow?
3 How does the Circus Maximus compare to a modern sports stadium?

Roman drama was strongly influenced by the drama of ancient Greece, partly because many Greeks had settled in cities of southern Italy, and there was close cultural contact between the two peoples. The Greeks had invented the genre of drama, and their plays were the source of much inspiration for the Romans. In particular, like the Greeks, the Romans often put on plays during religious festivals. They were usually paid for partly out of public funds, and partly by senior politicians responsible for running the festivals – therefore, the funding of plays offered politicians and public figures the opportunity to gain popularity, just as it did with the chariot races and gladiatorial games. Moreover, it was not just the plays themselves that wealthy men funded – there are a number of examples of benefactors paying for the building or upgrading of theatre buildings and facilities.

Theatre buildings

PRESCRIBED SOURCE

Large Theatre

Built: 2nd century BC, renovated at the end of the 1st century BC

Location: Pompeii

Capacity: c. 4,000

Significance: a very good example of a Roman theatre

The first major stone theatre in Rome was not built until the middle of the first century BC, although permanent theatres had appeared much earlier in the cities of southern Italy that had closer contact with the Greeks – Pompeii was one of these. Today, we can learn about the design of Roman theatres both by looking at the remains of those that have survived, and from what Roman writers have said about them.

The large theatre at Pompeii

Pompeii had its own 'theatre district', with two theatres next to each other at the southern end of the city. The larger of the two had an estimated capacity of 4,000 and was first built in the second century BC. It was extensively modified at the end of the first century BC, when two members of very prominent Pompeian family, the Holconii, commissioned major improvements.

FIGURE 3.32
The large theatre at Pompeii.

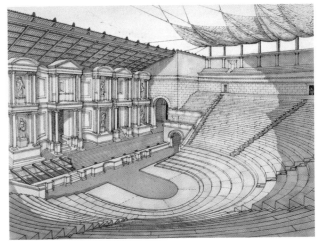

FIGURE 3.33
A reconstruction of the large theatre.

Two inscriptions by the benefactors of the theatre

Two versions of the following inscription were found prominently in the area of the stage:

> Marcus Holconius Rufus and Marcus Holconius Celer (built) at their own expense the crypt, boxes, and theatre seating.
>
> CIL X 833, 834

The two Holconii mentioned here were probably brothers, although it is possible that they were father and son. They clearly wanted to leave no Pompeian in any doubt as to who had paid for the upgrade to their theatre – each inscription was more than six metres long! The inscription refers to three areas that were improved, and these can all be identified in the remains of the theatre today. The main seating area is made of marble, there is a narrow upper section of seating, supported by vaulted passageways, while two marble 'boxes' have been identified above the spectators' entrances at either end of the orchestra (see below) – these may have been reserved for the most privileged spectators or the sponsors of the shows.

Apart from the upper section of seating, the rest of the seating area of the theatre was built into a hillside, following the Greek fashion, although many other Roman theatres were free-standing. The seating area was semi-circular, and there were a number of aisles, which enabled people to reach their seats easily. As at the shows at amphitheatres, there was a clear hierarchy as to who sat where: VIPs sat in the lower rows made of marble; behind them sat other free citizens, and at the back sat freedmen, slaves and women. The theatre had an awning to shade spectators from the sun when necessary.

The spectators looked down onto the performing area, which had three distinct elements: an elaborately decorated back wall, a stage, and a semi-circular area in front of the stage. The back wall was known as the **scaenae frons** (literally meaning: 'front scenery') and usually consisted of two storeys and many columns (the scaenae frons of

scaenae frons the back wall of a stage set in a Roman theatre, usually two or three storeys tall and with elaborate decoration some Roman theatres even had three storeys); it would have been painted and adorned with beautiful statues. It matched the height of the seating area and attached to it on both sides. It also had three doors, each of which led onto the stage by a small set of steps.

The stage itself was made of wood and set on pillars; the area below it would be used to manoeuvre stage machinery and props. The front wall of the stage was normally a little over a metre high and made of elaborate stone. In front of the stage was a semi-circular area, known as the **orchestra**; it seems that this was rarely used for acting in Roman times – it was really a hangover from the era of the Greek theatre, when actors had performed there. In Pompeii, it might have been used for acting if there were revivals of Greek plays, but it seems that most of the time it served as another seating area reserved for VIPs. A further feature of Roman theatres such as this was that there was a curtain that came down at the start of the play, rather than up as we would expect today.

> **orchestra** in a Roman theatre, the semi-circular area in front of a stage normally reserved for VIP seating

Types of plays

There is no conclusive evidence about what types of plays were performed in the Large Theatre of Pompeii. However, drama was clearly popular in the city, since many mosaics, paintings and graffiti relating to the theatre have been found. It is likely that the performances reflected the pattern elsewhere in the Roman world, and this involved great variety.

As the Romans had been influenced so much by Greek theatre, it is no surprise that tragedy and comedy were featured on the Roman stage. However, little has survived of Roman tragedy, and it seems that by the first century BC it had declined in popularity. We have very few surviving texts, and so it is hard to know much about it with any confidence. However, the same is not true of Roman comedy, about which we know a great deal.

Comedy

The two greatest writers of Roman comedy were Plautus and Terence, who both wrote in the first half of the second century BC. Both based their plays on earlier Greek models, and in particular on the plays of Menander – the Greek playwright whose portrait was painted prominently in the Pompeian house that today is named after him (see p. 253). In some ways, the comedies of Plautus and Terence were forerunners to modern sit-coms – their plots were often based around everyday social situations and behaviour. Although the plays have a variety of plots, they have many similar features: love affairs, confusions of identity, conflicts between fathers and sons, or clever slaves who outwit their masters. They contained typical **stock characters**, such as the flatterer, the lecherous old man or the boastful soldier. Music was often composed to accompany the plays.

> **stock character** a character in a work of literature or drama who is easily recognisable as a particular type of person from certain behaviour traits

The comedies of Plautus and Terence were performed in a very similar style to Greek plays. This meant that there were no female actors; rather female parts were played by male actors (as they were even in Shakespeare's day). Actors wore Greek-style costume, often a tunic and cloak for male characters, and a dress and cloak for female characters. A costume and accompanying props could give information about a character type to the audience: for example, an old man might wear white and carry a stick; a cook might hold a knife, spoon or some sort of dish; while a slave-dealer would usually carry a money-bag.

To complete the Greek style of costume, actors wore masks, and these too were designed to indicate a specific type of character – one ancient writer even lists forty-four different types of comic mask. They were all designed to cover the front of the head, while hair was also attached to denote character: for old men, it was white or grey, younger characters were typically given dark hair, while for slave characters the colour was red. Another convenient feature of the masks was that they allowed actors to play more than one part.

Very few comedies were written after the second century BC, but the plays of writers such as Plautus and Terence remained popular for centuries, and scenes from them could be performed or recited at private dinner parties or gatherings as well as in the theatre. One example of this comes in your prescribed literature (see pp. 323–4), when Pliny the Younger writes about the qualities of a favourite freedman, Zosimus, whom he describes as an excellent 'reciter of comedies'.

FIGURE 3.34
A fresco from Pompeii showing actors in a comedy.

Mime and pantomime

By the first century AD, the popularity of both comedy and tragedy had been overtaken by two other forms of dramatic performance: mime and pantomime. Both names can be confusing to a modern reader. Unlike modern mime performances, Roman mime involved actors speaking. Moreover, the Roman pantomime has no similarity or link to modern pantomimes, which are staged during the Christmas period. Both mimes and pantomimes could be presented in the theatre, in other public places, or at a private performance.

Mime originated in Greece and initially was simply a variety show including acrobatics, song and dance, jokes and conjuring based around a simple plot. The subject matter was often obscene, with the emphasis on sex, parody of town and city life, and general silliness; some mimes were political, others presented scenes from everyday life. We hear of plots involving kidnappings, cuckolds and lovers hidden in convenient chests.

FIGURE 3.35
A Roman mosaic showing theatrical masks.

The mime could be presented in a number of settings: on its own, as an interlude to another play, or as part of another public or private form of entertainment.

If mime was similar to comedy, then pantomime seems to have replaced tragedy. A pantomime performance was essentially a form of ballet, but one in which all of the parts were played by a single actor. The actor did not speak or sing, but could be accompanied by musicians or a singer. A pantomime show often performed a scene from a Greek tragedy; the pantomime actor had to show great versatility to play all the roles – male and female, young and old – in a series of solo scenes which might require him to change into and out of a variety of costumes and masks. All the evidence suggests that pantomime was wildly popular in Rome, and that famous pantomime actors attracted a huge fan base.

Actors and audience

Like gladiators, actors held a very low social status and were legally defined as infamis. However, despite their low social status, a few highly successful actors could gain both fame and great wealth; at Pompeii, there are a number of graffiti that refer lovingly to an actor called Paris, including one that refers to him as 'Paris, pearl of the stage'.

Actors were typically organised into a troupe under the charge of a troupe leader. They were usually either drawn from the ranks of slaves or from the lower classes, although of course they had to be skilled enough to act and sing in a variety of different roles. Competition between the troupes seems to have been fierce – prizes were awarded to troupes or individual actors, and sources tell of how they stationed their supporters throughout the theatre with instructions to applaud at the right moment.

Sources suggest that audiences could either be wildly supportive or brutally critical. On the one hand, we hear of spectators learning the songs of the theatre and then singing them by heart; on the other hand, there are stories of actors making mistakes and being hissed or booed off stage. One source speaks of the bad behaviour typical in a theatre audience, with ushers walking in front of spectators, people arriving late, slaves sitting in seats reserved for free men, and mothers bringing crying babies who disturb the performance.

THE BATHS

The baths were a fundamental part of life in any Roman town. In Rome itself, one fourth-century AD source claims that there were nearly a thousand bath complexes. Some of these were absolutely huge; for example, the emperor Caracalla had baths constructed that could hold 1,600 bathers at any one time. However, most bath houses in the city were quite small. Going to the baths was just as popular in other parts of the empire – the well-preserved remains of a huge Roman bath complex can, of course, still be seen in the English city of Bath today.

Going to the baths was a daily routine for free Romans of all classes. Most people did not have bathing facilities at home and so the public baths were vital to keeping the population healthy and warding off disease. For this reason, many baths were subsidised

Study questions

1 How different would it have been to go and watch a play in Roman times?
2 How common is it for private individuals to sponsor the arts today?
3 Which type of performance do you think you would most have enjoyed in the Roman theatre, and why?

by the state, and were very cheap to visit. It seems that men would work in the morning and head for the baths in the afternoon, and it was common for people to stay there until it was time to go home for dinner.

However, the baths were far more than a place where people went simply to keep clean. In fact, they were more like a cross between a modern gym and spa. Many bath houses also had an exercise ground where people could work out or play games, just as people might go to the gym on a daily basis today. Moreover, the baths were a focal point for Roman social life, and a place where people went to see and be seen. Wealthy men would arrive at the baths accompanied by a following of freedmen and slaves in a show of power and status, and it is likely that business meetings were held there. The baths were sometimes also used by the less affluent as a place to latch onto their social superiors, hoping to get an invitation to dinner that day.

Beyond this, the baths were simply just a place to meet up with friends and relax. Bath complexes would normally have shops attached to them where people could buy snacks: scrawled onto the wall of a bar near one set of ancient baths is a list of items for sale, including nuts, drinks, hog's fat, bread, cutlets and sausage.

As there were so many bath houses in the Roman world, no two of them were designed in exactly the same way. However, there were some key rooms and spaces that were common to all. Many baths had separate facilities for men and women, including the Central Baths of Herculaneum, which are featured below. Men's facilities were usually more extensive than those of women. However, if there were no such separate facilities, men and women would typically bathe at different times of the day, with women bathing in the morning and men in the afternoon.

Arriving at the baths, a visitor would first have to pay the entrance fee. This was normally very cheap, perhaps just a quadrans, the smallest coin in the Roman currency system. He would then head to the changing room, or **apodyterium**, where he would leave his clothes in one of the niches along the walls, keeping on some light clothing for the exercise ground. He would then head to the exercise ground to work up a sweat. This area was known as the **palaestra**. Sources speak of various games being played there: one such game was called harpastum ('snatch-ball'), which seems to have been a bit like 'piggy in the middle', in which one player had to seize a ball stuffed with sand from others holding on to it and throwing it around. Some writers speak of men fencing against a post, others of men wrestling with one another, while there even seems to have been a form of tennis played with the hand.

After exercising, the bather would head back to the changing-room and remove the rest of his clothes in preparation for the bathing process. The number of bathing rooms would depend on the size and status of the bath house, but all baths had three fundamental rooms: the **tepidarium** ('warm room'), the **caldarium** ('hot room'), and the **frigidarium** ('cold room'). More extensive bath houses may have had other facilities, a 'sweat-room', which was similar to a modern sauna, or a swimming pool – however, this would not have been used for exercise, since there was no culture of swimming laps in the Roman world; bathers would simply have got in to relax and freshen up.

We cannot be sure about the order in which a bather typically visited these rooms, or even if there was ever a set order. However, a bather would usually head to the tepidarium

---

EXPLORE FURTHER

The Roman writer and philosopher Seneca lived above a bath house and, in a famous letter, complains about the noise, which constantly disturbed him. Read his letter (Seneca the Younger, *Letters* 56.1–2), and make a list of all the different activities he mentions taking place in the bath house.

---

apodyterium changing room in a baths complex

palaestra exercise-ground

tepidarium the warm room in a baths complex
caldarium the hot room in a baths complex
frigidarium the cold room in a baths complex

FIGURE 3.36
The remains of a Roman hypocaust.

---

strigil a curved scraper used to remove oil and dirt from the body

hypocaust underfloor heating system

---

or caldarium first, where he would build up a sweat. At this stage of the bathing process, he would have oil rubbed all over his body (wealthy Romans would bring a slave to do this). Soap was unknown to the Romans, and so olive oil was used to wash the body. The hot atmosphere of the room opened up the pores of his skin, allowing the oil to penetrate thoroughly; the bather might move between any of the warm or hot rooms at this stage. After some time, he ordered his slave to scrape the oil (and dirt) from his body with a curved implement called a **strigil**. He would then head to the cold plunge-pool of the frigidarium, where the cold water closed the pores of his skin, so completing the cleansing process.

The warm rooms of a bath house were heated by a very clever design process that blasted hot air into gaps under the floor and behind the walls. This system of artificial heating was known as a **hypocaust**; the floor was raised above the ground by pillars and spaces were left inside the walls so that hot air and smoke from a nearby furnace (tended by slaves) could pass through these enclosed areas. The caldarium would be located nearest to the furnace, since it required the most heat.

The Central Baths of Herculaneum

We can get a good idea of how a set of baths were laid out from the Central Baths in Herculaneum. They were built in the late first century BC, and located near the middle

FIGURE 3.37
The palaestra of the Central Baths at Herculaneum.

of the town; they have also been known as the Forum Baths, since they are believed to have been located close to the city's forum, which is as yet undiscovered to the north. The baths occupied the southern end of a whole block and opened onto three different streets – this allowed for a number of different entrances. The men's section of the baths is bigger and more extensive than the women's section, but both derive their heat from the furnace room.

The men's apodyterium led off from the palaestra. The apodyterium has a marble bench running along three sides, and above it niches for storing clothes. At one end are two basins – a low one for washing feet, and a grander one made of marble for washing hands. An entrance leads from the apodyterium into the tepidarium. This had marble benches and shelves on all four sides, and the floor has been elevated to allow for the hypocaust – today part of the floor has collapsed and so the hypocaust is visible; the floor contains a black mosaic depicting a Triton (a sea monster) whose legs turn into curling sea serpents, while four dolphins surround him.

A further entrance leads into the men's caldarium. Much of the curved roof here has collapsed, and so it is possible to see hot-air pipes built into the walls. At one end is a large round marble basin, which contained cold water for bathers to splash their faces or bodies if they became too hot and sweaty. At the other end is a hot water bath, which bathers could lie in or sit beside. After completing his bath, a bather would walk back through the apodyterium to the frigidarium, where there was a plunge-pool. On the curved roof are painted various fish and sea-creatures, such as fish, lobsters and even an octopus.

The women's section of the baths has a similar structure, and the apodyterium has a black mosaic of a triton surrounded by dolphins very similar to that in the men's tepidarium.

PRESCRIBED SOURCE

The Central Baths of Herculaneum

Built: late 1st century BC

Location: Herculaneum

Key features: a separate suite of baths for men and women

Significance: a very good example of a bath house with separate bathing areas for men and women, as well as a palaestra

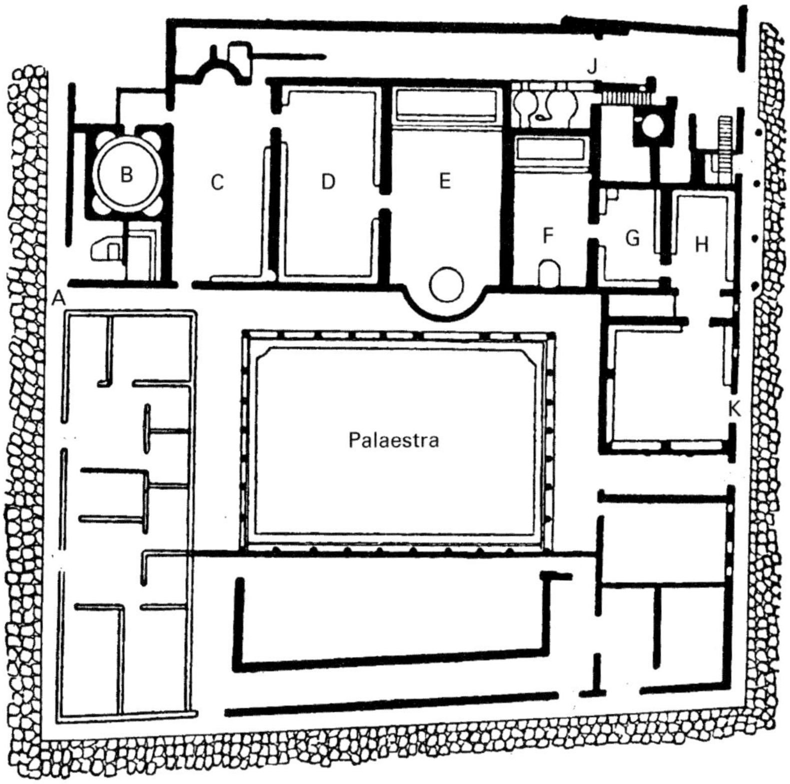

FIGURE 3.38 PS

The Central Baths at Herculaneum: A – Men's entrance; B – Men's frigidarium; C – Men's apodyterium; D – Men's tepidarium; E – Men's caldarium; F – Women's caldarium; G – Women's tepidarium; H – Women's apodyterium; J – Furnace; K – Women's entrance.

FIGURE 3.39

PS

The men's apodyterium in the Central Baths at Herculaneum with the two marble basins clearly visible.

Study questions

1 How do the baths compare to a modern spa or sports club?
2 For what reasons were the baths such an important aspect of Roman city life?
3 What would you have enjoyed, and what would you have disliked about a visit to the baths?

However, one notable point about the women's section is the lack of a frigidarium. Presumably women cooled down by leaving the baths and heading into the open air.

TOPIC REVIEW

You should be able to:

1. Describe:
   - the experience of watching the games at the amphitheatre
   - what it was like to spend a day at the chariot races
   - the experience of watching a play at the Roman theatre
   - a typical visit to the Roman baths.

2. Explain:
   - why the games were important for Roman politicians
   - how society viewed and treated gladiators, charioteers and actors
   - why Romans found these games so entertaining
   - why the baths played such an important role in Roman society.

PRACTICE QUESTIONS

1. **a.** Give **two** details about the content of the inscriptions of the Holconii in the large theatre at Pompeii. [2]
   b. Why was it important for people to see these inscriptions? [1]
2. 'Most Romans would have enjoyed visiting the Circus Maximus more than the Colosseum.' Do you agree with this statement? Give reasons for your answer. [15]

Literature

3.5 Satire and Fiction

TOPIC OVERVIEW

- The origins and purposes of satire
- The style and characteristic approach of each of the authors
  - Horace as the smiling satirist
  - Juvenal as the angry satirist
  - the nature and purpose of Petronius' *Satyricon*

- Narrative and descriptive techniques
- Use of humour and exaggeration
- Choice of themes and examples

The prescribed sources for this topic are:

- Horace, *Satires* 2.2, 2.6, 2.8
- Juvenal, *Satire* 3.190–322
- Petronius, *Satyricon: Dinner with Trimalchio*, 29–33; 37–38; 49–50

Don't forget that you will be given credit in the exam if you study extra sources and make relevant use of them in your answers.

This topic focuses on the literary genre of satire. It will first explore what satire is and how it developed in the Roman world, and then move on to examining three of your prescribed authors, Horace, Juvenal and Petronius, reflecting on how they produced entertaining and interesting works of literature.

THE ORIGINS AND PURPOSES OF SATIRE

> **satire** a form of writing that aims to show up hypocrisy, pretence or other character flaws through the use of humour

What is **satire**? Today, satire often attempts to mock public figures such as politicians and celebrities; usually, this attempt to make fun also has the intention of showing up hypocrisy, pretence or other character flaws in the people being satirised. Therefore, it is not just individuals who can be satirised – satire can focus more generally on social attitudes and everyday behaviour too.

Roman satire was not very different from this – in fact it was the Romans who invented satire as a **genre**. The first satirist we hear of is Lucilius, who lived in the second century BC; he was later recognised by the Romans as the founder of verse satire (satire written as poetry). Lucilius was an angry and outspoken social critic, whose biting verse aimed to show up corruption among the politicians and public figures of his day. One interesting point about him was that he was the first poet we know of from the Roman upper classes – he was a member of the equites. This suggests that it was at this time that writing poetry was first taken seriously by the Roman educated elite, who were Lucilius' target audience and friends.

Lucilius composed in a specific poetic metre, the hexameter. The hexameter might be thought a surprising choice for satire, since it was traditionally the metre of the great epic poems of Homer and others. These poems had a very different tone: where satire was down to earth and focused on everyday life and behaviour, epic poetry recounted great tales of heroism from the mythological past. In some ways, the two genres could not have been more different.

As satire developed after Lucilius, it came to be written in prose as well as in verse – in your prescribed literature, two satirists write in poetry, Horace and Juvenal, and one, Petronius, writes mainly in prose but also in poetry at times. The poetic satirists followed Lucilius by composing in the hexameter. They too were aware of the difference between the two hexameter genres of satire and epic. Horace reflects on this in Satire 2.6 when he describes the genre of satire with the Latin adjective 'pedester', which literally meant 'going on foot'. In other words, while other types of poetry, such as epic, had lofty aspirations of describing noble tales of legendary heroes, satire remained firmly grounded in the day-to-day and the real world.

One key feature of Roman satire was its variety. Indeed, the word 'satire' is probably derived from a Latin phrase, 'lanx satura', which literally means a 'full plate' and referred to a large plate brimming with a wide variety of first fruits offered to the gods (the 'first fruits' were the first agricultural produce of a harvest given to the gods as a thanks offering). The name 'satire' therefore seems to recognise that the genre could focus on any number of different topics and themes, and also that satirists could use a variety of techniques in their poems. Juvenal describes his satires as presenting a whole mixture of vices and immoral behaviours seen in the Rome of his day.

As a result, satire can seem quite gossipy – it is interested in what people are doing, and what they are talking about, in public places such as the forum, the theatre and the sporting arenas, as well as in private places such as dining-rooms and bedrooms.

HORACE

Horace had a remarkable life; he was born the son of a freedman in the small town of Venusia in southern Italy, and yet he grew up to become one of leading poets in the Roman world. He lived during very troubled times; the Roman world was convulsed by

---

genre a category of literature – examples of literary genres might include epic, tragedy, comedy, history and satire

Study questions

1 Who are the best satirists in our society today, in your opinion?
2 What sort of things do they satirise, and what makes them effective?
3 Do they play a helpful role in society?

EXPLORE FURTHER

Find out more about Lucilius. How much do we know about his life and his writings? What do later writers say about him?

S & C The scholar Niall Rudd has identified three key features of Roman satire: attack, entertainment, and preaching. Does this seem to be a good basis of defining satire to you? To what extent does each of these features appear in your prescribed literature?

PRESCRIBED SOURCE

Horace, Satires 2.2, 2.6, 2.8

CW

Date: late 30s BC

Author: Horace (65–8 BC)

Genre: verse satire

Significance: three poems reflecting on life in the town and country, as follows:

- 2.2: A reflection on the virtue of the simple country life, as promoted by the peasant Ofellus.
- 2.6: Horace contrasts his enjoyment of the country life with the stresses of living in the city.
- 2.8: An account of a dinner-party in Rome told to Horace by his friend Fundanius.

Read it here: OCR source booklet

KEY INDIVIDUALS

Octavian/Augustus: (63 BC–AD 14) a leading Roman aristocrat who was Julius Caesar's adopted heir. In 30 BC he became the sole ruler of the entire Roman world, and is regarded as the first Roman emperor

Maecenas: (c. 64–8 BC) a close adviser to Octavian who was appointed his patron of the arts. He welcomed Horace into his circle of poets, and became his mentor and close friend

civil wars for the first decades of his life. In 44 BC, Julius Caesar, the leader of the Roman world, was assassinated, but his assassins were soon hunted down and defeated. Two of Caesar's closest followers, his deputy Mark Antony and adopted heir **Octavian**, tried to share power between themselves and one other, Lepidus. The arrangement soon broke down, and this led to further civil wars during the 30s. Octavian became powerful in Italy and the western Mediterranean and by 30 BC he had become the sole ruler of the Roman world. Soon afterwards, he took the name of Augustus, and he is thought of as the first Roman emperor from this point on.

Although Horace had fought on the side of Caesar's assassins, he benefited from a general amnesty after their defeat at Philippi in 42 BC. He returned to Rome and in 38 he was introduced to **Maecenas**, a close adviser to Octavian who was responsible for promoting his regime. To do this, he aimed to nurture poets who would write poetry sympathetic to Octavian and the regime. Horace had already started writing poetry, and was welcomed into Maecenas' circle of poets. This was a big break for him. It was in the years after this that he composed his satires. Maecenas features in some of them, and is the guest of honour at the dinner-party described in Satire 2.8.

In the mid-30s BC, Maecenas presented Horace with a wonderful gift: a villa and farm in the Sabine Hills, about 25 miles outside Rome. Soon after this, Horace wrote his second book of satires, and it seems that he loved to escape from the city to write, relax and reflect at this country estate. One of the key themes of the book is the contrast between life in the city and life in the country. In two of our poems, 2.2 and 2.6, he reflects on what makes a good life – and seems to conclude that the simple and humble life of the countryside is far richer and more fulfilling than life in the city.

Horace sets himself up as a particular type of satirist; in particular, he distances himself from the aggressive and angry tone of Lucilius. There is an obvious reason for this: while

Lucilius had been very critical of the leading politicians of his day, Horace did not have the scope to do this given that a senior political figure, Maecenas, was his patron. Therefore, he does not attack public figures, but focuses instead on the behaviour and customs of those whom he comes across in his daily life. Even here, he shows little anger or bitterness: his satires are light-hearted, and he makes fun of himself as well as others. In fact, he even claims, in a charming analogy, to use laughter in order to get his point across:

> What stops someone from telling the truth while smiling, as teachers sometimes give children cookies to tempt them to learn the alphabet?
>
> Horace, *Satires*, 1.1.24–5

FIGURE 3.40
A modern statue of Horace in Venosa (ancient Venusia).

His laughter, therefore, recognises that people are all flawed and gently encourages them to do better. As a result, he is sometimes referred to as a 'smiling satirist'. A related message of his satires is that we should remember not to take ourselves too seriously.

A further key feature of Horace's satires is their conversational tone; in fact, he often referred to them as 'sermones', a Latin word that can simply mean 'conversations'. In some of them, the poet appears to be speaking directly to the reader in a chatty tone; others report conversations that have taken place, or are taking place, between characters in the poem. As readers, we might therefore feel that we are listening in on a conversation or discussion.

Who was Horace writing for? It is clear that he was writing to be published, and his satires would have been read on papyrus scrolls. However, it is important to remember that only a small minority of Romans had a high level of literacy, and so we might say that he was writing for the educated elite. Of course, his most immediate target audience was the circle of Maecenas, which was close to the Emperor Augustus. It is quite likely that when Horace first wrote his satires he gave some recitals of them himself. Horace says in Satire 1.10 that he is happy to have a small circle of readers, and does not want his satires to become so popular that they are studied in schools. If we take him seriously in this, then it is ironic that his satires are being studied in schools more than two thousand years after his death!

Satire 2.2

In this poem Horace gives a lecture on the benefits of the simple country life, and this introduces a common theme in his poetry – the contrast between life in the town and life in the country. He credits the ideas he puts forward to Ofellus, a peasant farmer whom he knew from childhood in Venusia. The audience is imagined and the lecture takes place in the morning – Horace specifically rejects discussion of this topic over the dinner table.

A key idea is that it is wrong to seek pleasure through over-indulging in luxurious foods; rather, true pleasure comes from simpler satisfactions. Horace criticises gluttony (eating or drinking far too much), and in particular people who follow the latest fashions in eating expensive food. However, he also emphasises that eating simply does not involve having to be stingy and ungenerous. He gives a sketch of a famously mean character, Avidienus, who represents a character type – the miser. Horace rejects this way of living too – his ideal character lives in balance between being a miser and being a glutton.

EXPLORE FURTHER

Horace's country villa has been identified and excavated. You can find out much more about it on this dedicated website: http://www.frischerconsulting.com/bf3e/horaces-villa/contents.html.

FIGURE 3.41
This ruined villa may be the remains of Horace's Sabine farm.

Epicureanism a philosophy of life that encouraged people to live for simple pleasures and to reduce anxieties as much as possible

Horace goes on to list the benefits of the simple diet: it promotes good health, good sleep and a feeling of wellbeing, and allows for better health in old age. He next suggests that wealth could be spent more profitably on good causes: by giving money to friends in need, or for the upkeep of temples or other public buildings. The poem finishes with Horace quoting Ofellus himself, as he outlines his philosophy of simplicity and self-sufficiency, which still allows for generosity on a special occasion. Even after he loses his farm, Ofellus is still able to live happily.

The ideas of the poem

There are some key themes that emerge in this poem. Central is the question of what is the good life – and Ofellus' recipe is put forward. Despite the fact that he is a simple farmer who is not highly educated, Ofellus represents ideas that can be found in the philosophical school of thought often advocated by Horace, **Epicureanism**. Epicureans believed that the purpose of life was to live for simple pleasures, and to avoid worries as much as possible. An important way to do this, so the thinking went, was to keep life in balance and not to adopt extremes of behaviour; in this poem, such extremes are represented by the glutton introduced at line 21, and the miser Avidienus introduced at line 55. Horace draws out the contrast between the two ways of living, which he believes are equally valueless:

> Ofellus judges that a mean life is different
> From a plain one: so it's foolish for you to avoid
> One fault and steer towards another.

Horace, Satires, 2.2.53–55

Ofellus himself represents the mid-point between the two – in his speech he talks of eating a simple diet, but of being generous in his hospitality to friends or neighbours who pay him a visit. The fact that he keeps his life in balance and that he has learnt to live on little means that he is self-sufficient and so can cope with the loss of his farm.

Speakers and audiences

One of the most impressive techniques used by Horace in this poem is the range of voices speaking to a range of audiences – this is a very conversational satire. You might think about the following:

- **Horace and his friends** The poem starts with Horace directly addressing his friends. We are not told who these friends are, but we can imagine that they are meeting somewhere in Rome. Horace reveals that the conversation takes place in the morning – the best time to think about such matters. In line 7, a new voice is introduced, presumably one of Horace's friends (or more than one), asking what the point of listening to this is – or at least showing his confusion by the look on his face.

- **Horace and the glutton** Horace goes on to outline Ofellus' ideas – notice that he has distanced himself from them so that they do not necessarily represent his own thoughts. In line 21 he reflects on the behaviour of a typical glutton, and in line 23 he moves from talking to his friends to speaking directly to the glutton, as though he was there among them. He questions this imaginary figure, and even calls him a fool in line 33! In lines 39–40, another glutton's own words are even reported, after which Horace seems to return to speaking to his friends again.

- **A rich man and Horace** At line 99, Horace again introduces a new speaker who is clearly another imagined figure and not among his friends. This speaker is a very wealthy man who believes that there is little danger of him falling into poverty. Horace advises him to spend his money for the benefit of others. Then, at line 107, he returns to speaking to his friends again.

- **Ofellus' speech** The poem finishes with Ofellus being given his own speech (lines 116–136), presumably delivered to Horace or anyone else who asks his views. However, in line 128 we learn that he has other company, as he turns to his sons to ask them a question.

How does this variety of speakers and audiences enrich the poem? Two points could be made. First of all, it allows Horace to represent different perspectives. As readers, we are invited the judge the characters through listening to their own words. Secondly, it fosters an atmosphere of debate and discussion in the poem. If you ask the question: 'What is a good way to live your life?' you are likely to have a range of opinions and therefore

---

KEY INDIVIDUAL   Ofellus

Ofellus is presented as a figure of simple common sense in this poem – a countryman who, although not highly educated, has learnt through experience how to live well. We do not know if he was a real person, but it is interesting that his name is very similar to the Latin word 'ofella', meaning a 'small mouthful', which is appropriate to his character.

The poem concludes with Ofellus' speech (lines 116–136). He outlines how his principles have served him well in life and enabled him to survive a reversal of fortune, the confiscation of his farm (lines 128–134). Here Horace is referring to events of his own day – during the civil wars, Octavian rewarded veterans who had served in his army by allotting to them farms in various districts of Italy. He had earlier confiscated these farms and thrown the owners off their land. This must have been an issue close to Horace's heart, since his own family farm had also been confiscated in the aftermath of the battle of Philippi.

> **Study questions**
>
> 1 How does Horace satirise gluttony in lines 21–52? Think about the variety of words and ideas that he uses here to bring his point home.
> 2 How does Horace make his characterisation of the miser Avidienus effective in lines 55–62?
> 3 How does Ofellus come across in lines 116–136? Do you find him admirable?
> 4 How many different types of food and drink are mentioned in this poem? How often does food represent or symbolise a human quality or characteristic?
> 5 Find out about Epicureanism. Does it seem to you to offer a recipe for a life well lived?

agreements and disagreements. Horace's conversational tone allows us to feel that we are part of a debate, rather than simply listening to his own views.

Satire 2.6

This satire was written in 31 BC, a few years after Maecenas had presented Horace with the Sabine Farm. In the poem, he contrasts life in the city with life on the farm; he clearly prefers the latter, since it allows him to live as he wants, comfortably, simply and peacefully, and with the time and space to write poetry.

The poem opens with a prayer of thanks to Mercury, in his role as the bringer of wealth, and Horace explains how grateful he is with his lot in life. He goes on to outline all the unwanted distractions in the city that prevent him from getting down to writing poetry. In particular, because Horace is associated with Maecenas, many people in the city want to speak with him and ask favours. His close friendship with such an important man also arouses envy in others.

Horace then moves on to contrast this with his life in the country. Here, he can live simply, eating and sleeping well. In particular, he contrasts city dinner parties with those in the country, which are relaxed, intimate and full of rich conversation. He concludes by relating a fable that his country neighbour Cervius sometimes tells: the town mouse and the country mouse. While the town mouse has a more luxurious lifestyle, this comes at a cost of losing his freedom and peace of mind. The country mouse, on the other hand, enjoys the simple, self-sufficient life so valued by Horace.

Themes

This satire brings into sharp view two contrasts that often feature in Horace's poetry: city/country and public/private. Horace is the narrator of the first two thirds of the poem, after which he hands over to Cervius. The sentiments he puts forward in the first fifteen lines reflect the views put forward in 2.2 – to be happy with what you have, and not to be envious of others. At line 16, we learn that he is on his Sabine farm, from where he can reflect on the differences between life there and life in the city.

Horace continues by giving a flavour of what his life is like back in Rome, particularly given that he is closely associated with Maecenas. Although Horace does not state this, we can tell from the poem that the events must happen between late 31 and early 30 BC, when Octavian had left Maecenas in charge of affairs in Rome while he was away in the east. As Horace makes his way up to Maecenas' magnificent house on the Esquiline Hill (see map pp. viii) in the heart of the city, he is plagued by the clients and hangers-on who want access to Maecenas. Horace uses a number of different voices in direct speech to communicate the range of these people and their demands. A contrast then comes in lines 40–46, when we are given a private view into Maecenas and Horace's conversations about more trivial things, such as the weather or gladiatorial fights. Yet even these conversations cause problems for Horace, since others are envious of his closeness to such a powerful man.

FIGURE 3.42
A view of the Sabine Hills and the surrounding countryside today.

In line 60, Horace cleverly returns the focus to the countryside again – imagining himself in the city and longing for the country. (But remember that he is actually narrating the poem from the country and thinking about the city!) The theme of simplicity soon emerges as he talks about country dinner parties which do not have the formalities or anxious and envious chatter of those in the city. Once again, the theme of how to live a good life emerges, in relation to food – he and his friends have a philosophical discussion about the meaningful things in life. This is the point at which he introduces the fable told by Cervius, one of his country friends who can be compared to Ofellus in 2.2 – a countryman of simple common sense. We can almost imagine that we are present at one of these country dinner parties where Cervius is telling his tale.

A parody of epic

During Cervius' fable, Horace uses another literary device, **parody**, to make fun of the town mouse. A parody is an exaggerated and comic imitation of the style of a particular writer or genre. Consider the following lines:

> ... His words stirred the country mouse,
> Who scrambled lightly from his house: then the two
> Took their way together as proposed, eager to scurry
> Beneath the city walls in darkness. And now night
> Occupied the zenith, as the pair of them made tracks
> Through a wealthy house, where covers dyed scarlet
> Glowed on ivory couches, and baskets piled nearby
> Held the remains of all the courses of a magnificent
> Feast, that had been celebrated the previous evening.

Horace, *Satires*, 2.6.95–103

The line 'And now night occupied the zenith' would have been immediately recognisable to Roman listeners and readers, since it is typical of an epic poem such as

parody an exaggerated and comic imitation of the style of a particular writer or genre

PS

EXPLORE FURTHER

The story of the town mouse and the country mouse first appears in Aesop's fables, and his version was clearly well known to Horace and his audience. Aesop was a Greek storyteller who is believed to have lived in the seventh or sixth century BC. Are there any other fables or stories you know which have a similar moral message to this one? Why might stories and fables be an effective way to put forward a moral message? Why might using animals to tell a story be a good way of doing this?

EXAM TIP

Literary analysis

Horace makes the following observation about how safe he feels in the country now that he is away from the dangers of Rome:

> I'm not cursed here with ambition, leaden sirocco,
> Or oppressive autumn, deathly Libitina's gain.
>
> Horace, *Satires*, 2.6.18–19

Libitina was the old Roman goddess of burial: Horace is happy to be away from Rome during the autumn when a particular wind blows from the south, the sirocco, bringing cool wet weather to Europe. Even today, people associate it with illness because of the conditions it brings.

These two lines are skilfully written. If you are asked to comment on a passage including lines such as these, think about the following points:

- The lines contain three powerful adjectives, each describing a different noun. Writing a sentence with so many adjectives ensures that it is full of imagery.
- You must explain why a word is powerful, rather than simply saying 'it is powerful'. Therefore, you could say that by describing the south wind as 'leaden', Horace stresses the heaviness of the weather conditions which it brings, as well as the grey skies. Why do you think the adjectives 'oppressive' and 'deathly' might be powerful?
- The sentence concludes with Libitina personifying death. A **personification** is a figure of speech by which something non-human is given human characteristics. We might say that this personification is powerful because it is frightening for a reader to think of what a person representing death might look like (the modern concept of 'the grim reaper', and the imagery which commonly goes with that, is similar). Horace is also clever in leaving his description of Libitina to the end, as this allows him to suggest that ambition, the sirocco and the autumn all lead to death.

personification a figure of speech by which something non-human is given human characteristics

Study questions

1 What are the key differences between satire 2.2 and satire 2.6?
2 Using the example on pp. 298–299, make a list of all the different voices and audiences present in this poem. How does this make the poem interesting and effective?
3 How does Horace bring out the contrast between his life in the city and his life in the country? You could draw up a table listing the advantages and disadvantages of each.
4 What is the main moral message of Cervius' fable? How does the story communicate this message well?
5 Do you think that town and country life today are as different as Horace suggests they were in Roman times?

Virgil's *Aeneid*. Remember that Horace is able to do this successfully since epic and satire share the same poetic metre. The epic tone continues with the description of the luxurious house and the grand banquet in the following lines – it feels as if we are in the palace of a great king or queen.

The point of the humour here is of course that Horace is describing two mice, who are about as far from being epic heroes as it is possible to be! Indeed, their lack of heroism is emphasised in the preceding lines, when they have to creep up to the city walls under cover of darkness so as not to be detected. Moreover, in the house that they arrive at, they are not honoured guests but unwanted intruders who dine on the leftovers. The joke here is surely on the town mouse. He has come across as superior and self-important, and would no doubt like to think of himself as an epic hero, as Horace's parody of epic poetry suggests. Yet Horace's parody also shows up how ridiculous the town mouse's pretensions are.

2.2 and 2.6

Finally, it is worth comparing 2.2 with 2.6. There are a number of similarities and overlaps, including:

- Both place a value on a self-sufficient life in the country.
- Both poke fun at life in the town.
- In both the food eaten reflects the lifestyle of the diners.
- In 2.2 a farm has been lost; in 2.6 Horace celebrates receiving a farm.
- Both end with the quoted words of a simple but wise countryman.

Satire 2.8

This satire describes a dinner party given by **Nasidienus Rufus**, a very wealthy man but one who is desperate to be seen to be a good host and to show off his sophisticated knowledge of food to his guests. Sadly for him, however, the dinner party goes disastrously

FIGURE 3.43
An impressive mosaic such as this from Herculaneum might have greeted the guests of Nasidienus Rufus. It shows the god Neptune with his wife Amphitrite.

wrong, much to the amusement of the other guests. We have no way of knowing if the story is made up or if it really happened, although Maecenas and other real-life characters are mentioned.

The poem starts with a conversation between Horace and his friend Fundanius, who is a comic playwright; Horace asks him how Nasidienus Rufus' dinner party went. The rest of the satire is Fundanius' account of the evening's events. He starts by giving an account of the food, wine and service, and then lists the guests' names and the seating plan. He focuses on the behaviour of Nasidienus and his clients Nomentanus and Porcius, as well as on that of the two clients of Maecenas, Vibidius and Balatro. Nomentanus has been appointed by his patron to explain the food in detail to the guests. However, Vibidius and Balatro soon become fed up with talk about the food and, to Nasidienus' great horror, rudely decide to drink as much of his fine wine as they can as quickly as possible. The other diners follow suit apart from Nasidienus and his clients on the lower couch.

Nasidienus tries to retrieve the situation by giving further detailed description of the lavish foods that are served. However, before the guests have time to taste the fare, disaster strikes: a tapestry that is suspended above their heads falls down onto the food, covering it with dust in the process. Nasidienus reacts as if it is a great tragedy. Nomentanus shows great sympathy, but Balatro plays up to Nasidienus' self-importance by commiserating ironically with him. They try to continue the dinner-party, but it has descended into farce. Vibidius complains that the supply of wine has stopped, while Balatro continues to make fun of the whole situation: both are perhaps drunk. Nasidienus returns, with a new series of dishes, but the guests cannot bear to go through more of the same commentary on the food again and so do a runner.

KEY INDIVIDUAL Nasidienus Rufus

Nasidienus Rufus is obsessed by food. Today, we might call him a 'foodie' – someone who loves food and who loves to talk about food. In his case, however, it goes too far. He wants to make sure that his dinner guests understand just how special their food is, and just how carefully it has been prepared. In part, this is no doubt so that he can also show off just how much he knows about food; this theme reaches its peak in lines 43–53, where Nasidienus is quoted describing the food on the table in great detail. Sadly for him, his attitude only succeeds in boring and irritating his guests, and it is why they find the collapse of the tapestry onto the food so funny.

The names

Horace shows a sense of humour in the names that he gives some of the characters in this satire. We know that some of those present were real people – Maecenas and Fundanius, as well as Viscus and Varius, who are literary friends of Maecenas. However, the other five characters are apparently fictional, and four of them seem to have names that reflect their personalities: Balatro means 'buffoon' in Latin, and he plays the joker; Porcius means 'pig' or 'hog' and he scoffs down his food; the name 'Nomentanus' is linked to the Latin word for 'name', and it seems no coincidence that his job is to name and explain the food; finally, Nasidienus' name is linked to the Latin word for 'nose' – which seems fitting for a host who seems almost to be sniffing the food and wine to confirm their quality.

Themes

After describing dinner parties in the country in 2.2 and 2.6, in this poem Horace turns to satirising a city dinner party. Once again, this satire is rich in dialogue, with a number of different speakers, and it is set up by a conversation between Horace and Fundanius. Fundanius describes a dinner party that goes comically wrong – indeed, it is fitting that the tale is told by a comic playwright. It is also interesting that Horace was not at the dinner party himself – perhaps this is a way for him to distance himself from the events and the behaviour of both host and guests, just as he distances himself in 2.2 and 2.6 by presenting the speeches of Ofellus and Cervius.

The events of the dinner revolve around the behaviour of the host Nasidienus Rufus. Although Maecenas is the guest of honour, he never speaks and is hardly mentioned – all the focus is on Nasidienus and Nomentanus on one side, and Vibidius and Balatro on the other. Nasidienus is clearly very keen to impress such an important guest, and yet his keenness is self-defeating. He is a gourmet who is obsessed by the food and drink he serves, and his desire to explain it in great detail ruins the occasion.

Nasidienus next comes across as a show-off by telling Maecenas that if he is not satisfied with the extremely expensive wines he serves, he has other varieties that he can offer him. This brings an ironic reply from Horace, who claims that it must be tough being so wealthy. Indeed, the wines emphasise the lavishness of the feast. Caecuban was well known as the best Roman wine; it was a white that came from a single vineyard near the coast south-east of Rome. Chian was a red that came from much further afield – the Greek island of Chios in the Aegean Sea – and had long been recognised as one of the finest wines in the Greek world. Thus, when Nasidienus suggests that Maecenas would not enjoy these wines, he is really focusing attention on how good they are. Moreover, he proposed substitutes – Falernian or Alban were the best two Roman wines after Caecuban.

The second half of the satire is defined by the disaster that happens at lines 54–56. It is important to focus on the reactions of the main characters – Nasidienus weeping, Nomentanus trying to console him sympathetically, and Varius and Balatro struggling to contain their giggles. In lines 65–74 Balatro pretends to sympathise with the host, but in fact he is using great **irony** – he thinks the whole thing is highly amusing. However, Nasidienus does not spot Balatro's tone, and thanks him warmly for his kind words – showing just how naïve he is.

> **irony** a way of expressing what you mean by using language that normally suggests the opposite

After this, we get a quick reminder of the start of the satire, as Horace reappears in the narrative to react to what he is hearing – he is finding the story hilarious. Fundanius then finishes the tale, as Nasidienus once again brings in fine food but spoils it by going into a detailed analysis. The satire ends abruptly as the guests run off – we are left to guess how the fragile Nasidienus might have responded to this.

> **simile** a figure of speech whereby one thing is compared to another thing of a different kind in order to make a description more vivid

LITERARY ANALYSIS   Similes

Horace and Fundanius mock Nasidienus' behaviour almost from the start of the satire. One example can be found in Fundanius' description of the entry into the dining room of the two slaves bringing the wine, Hydaspes and Alcon:

> . . . then in came
> Dusky Hydaspes with the Caecuban wine, just like
> An Attic maiden carrying Ceres' sacred emblems,
> And Alcon with a Chian needing no added brine.
>
> Horace, *Satires*, 2.8.14–15

Horace uses a **simile** here to emphasise the pomposity or self-importance of the moment. The slaves' entrance is compared to a solemn religious procession in ancient Athens in which young women carried baskets of offerings to the goddess Ceres. Nasidienus is taking himself – and his dinner party – far too seriously. He will continue to do so when it all goes disastrously wrong – he reacts by weeping as if he had lost his own child.

ACTIVITY

Stage your own short play re-enacting the dinner party hosted by Nasidienus Rufus – you could even write your own script. How many different parts would you need to create? What props would you need? How would you develop each character as he is presented in Horace's poem?

Study questions

1 How much sympathy do you have for Nasidienus in this poem?
2 Do you think that Vibidius and Balatro's behaviour is acceptable in the circumstances?
3 Using the example on pp. 298–299, make a list of all the different voices and audiences present in this poem. How does this make the poem more interesting and effective?
4 What type of behaviour do you think that Horace is satirising in this poem? How successfully does he do this?
5 How does this dinner party compare to the dinner parties described in 2.6? Are there similarities in character between Nasidienus and the town mouse?

JUVENAL

We know very little about the life of Juvenal, although it seems likely that he was a lawyer who lived in Rome between AD *c.* 55 and AD *c.* 130, and who was an excellent public speaker. His sixteen satires are most likely to have been composed between the years 110 and AD 130. Early in the first satire he explains what drives him to write his poems:

> It's not hard to write satire. For who is so long-suffering of this unjust city that, leaden-heartedly, he can hold himself back . . .?
>
> Juvenal, *Satires* 1.30–31

Juvenal's anger with life at Rome is a key theme of many of his poems. In fact, anger and indignation were key features of his writing, and so he rejected the gentler satire of Horace. Juvenal himself recognised this. A few lines after the quotation above, he coins a neat Latin phrase: 'facit indignatio versum', which translates as 'my indignation inspires my poetry'. If Horace was a smiling satirist, then Juvenal was an angry one who looked back to the example of the aggressive Lucilius.

Juvenal seems to have a love/hate relationship with his home city of Rome. While his poetry often savagely criticises life there, it is notable that he never chooses to move away and live elsewhere. Perhaps it was a case of 'I can't live with you, and I can't live without you'. His satires focus especially on the immoral, selfish and hypocritical behaviour of the Roman elite: he seems to believe that traditional Roman values had

PRESCRIBED SOURCE

Juvenal, Satire 3.190–322

Date: sometime between AD 110 and 130.

Author: Juvenal (AD *c.* 55–*c.* 130)

Genre: verse satire

Significance: a poem that relates bitter criticism of the quality of life at Rome.

Read it here: OCR source booklet

S & C

Juvenal has given us two particularly famous Latin phrases that are still quoted in English:

mens sana in corpore sano — a healthy mind in a healthy body
quis custodiet ipsos custodes? — Who will guard the guards?

Find out how these two phrases are used in English today. Do you agree with the sentiments that they communicate?

FIGURE 3.44
The remains of a Roman street alongside Trajan's Market in the heart of Rome.

disappeared from view. The assassinated emperor Domitian (who ruled Rome from 81 to 96) is a particular target. Yet even Juvenal's angry satire has its limits: he explains that he will not name any living individuals for fear of getting himself into trouble.

Since so many details of Juvenal's life are obscure, it is not clear who he was writing for. However, he was writing during a period when Greek as well as Roman orators, thinkers and philosophers were giving popular talks in Rome, and so he may have been in competition with them. As with Horace, he would have been writing for the educated elite, which would have been larger in Juvenal's day, although behaviour was still closely monitored by the emperor's circle. It seems that he was trying to provoke his readers into social change and improvement, and it is interesting that he is so ready to criticise the sort of wealthy men who may have made up much of his audience.

Juvenal's Third Satire

Juvenal's third satire focuses on how difficult life is in Rome. At the beginning of the poem, he addresses the reader directly and explains that his old friend Umbricius has chosen to leave Rome to live in Cumae, a small town near the Bay of Naples. While Juvenal is sad to see him leave, he does not blame his friend for his decision to abandon the capital. After this short opening, Juvenal quotes Umbricius directly – in a long monologue, he outlines the grievances with life in Rome which have driven him away. Therefore, only the first twenty lines of the 322-line poem are in the voice of the narrator – the rest belong to Umbricius. We should immediately be aware, therefore, that the views put forward in the poem are not presented as those of Juvenal, while it is hard to know just how much we can trust Umbricius as a reliable source of information about Roman life – his name even means 'shady'. It may even be that we are meant to laugh at Umbricius and his complaints and prejudices as much as at anything else.

Between lines 20 and 190, Umbricius complains about the difficulties of making a living in Rome. First, he laments the fact that there is no longer a place for an honest man in the city. He goes on to bemoan what he sees as his city overrun with foreigners – claiming that Greeks and Syrians are now everywhere, and presenting them as liars and cheats who have brought their cultural habits with them and taken jobs and opportunities for patronage from local Romans. Finally, Juvenal's departing friend claims that Rome is an awful place to be poor: the law protects the rich and abandons the poor, who are also evicted from their seats in the theatre and struggle to find women willing to marry.

The prescribed lines: 190–322

In these lines, Umbricius turns to listing the discomforts and dangers associated with life in Rome. They can be broken down into four distinct sections as follows:

- 190–231: falling buildings and fire
- 232–267: crowds and traffic
- 268–314: the dangers of the night
- 315–322: Umbricius' farewell.

Lines 190–231

In his attack on the dangers of falling buildings and fire, Umbricius first contrasts the relative safety of buildings in the country with those in the city. The four towns he mentions in lines 190–192 are all in the countryside beyond Rome, and Umbricius brings out a contrast between city and country here – the houses in the city are far more prone to collapse.

Umbricius then moves on to one of his main themes – that there is one rule for the rich, and one rule for the poor. He gives an example of the poor man Cordus, who has a bed so small that the dwarf Procula could not fit into it (an exaggeration to make his point), and who has very little to lose, but loses it nonetheless. At this point he is destitute, but has no support system – this seems to be a criticism of the patron/client system, which was supposed to help poor men support themselves.

LITERARY ANALYSIS

As Horace does in 2.6, Juvenal sometimes parodies epic poetry to further his satire. Consider the following lines:

> The place to live is far from all these fires, and all these
> Panics in the night. Ucalegon is already summoning a hose,
> Moving his things, and your third floor's already smoking.
>
> Juvenal, Satire 3.197–199

These lines only take on their full significance when we understand who Ucalegon is. A Roman reader would likely have spotted the reference to a minor character in Virgil's *Aeneid*, the greatest epic poem of Latin literature. In the *Aeneid* (2.311–12), Ucalegon is a noble Trojan whose house is torched by the Greeks on the night of Troy's sacking. Umbricius chooses to use the name to represent a typical lower class Roman whose apartment block is burning down.

What is the point of this comparison? The Romans liked to believe that they were descended from the Trojans, and so in some sense Virgil's Ucalegon is an ancestor of Juvenal's Ucalegon. Both lose their homes to fire, but that is where the similarity ends. The difference between them is just as important: while Virgil's Ucalegon is a noble Trojan with an impressive house, Juvenal's is a poor Roman living in a cramped apartment block. Therefore, the suggestion is that many of the descendants of the great heroes of Troy have ended up poor and helpless.

Moreover, Juvenal's Ucalegon is seen to be well-prepared to fight the fire and move his possessions, presumably from the ground floor. By the contrast, the imagined person being addressed by Umbricius is on the third floor, where his apartment is already going up in flames. There is a suggestion that Juvenal's Ucalegon has learnt the lesson of his namesake in Virgil's poem, and this time is ready to protect his possessions.

S & C Pliny the Younger, who is introduced on p. 319, also mentions disapprovingly the practice of Romans giving gifts to those who do not need them, while ignoring the poor. Read his letter 9.30 to find out more.

By contrast, if the house of the rich man Asturicus burns down, then important people rush to support him with gifts of new building materials. Umbricius once again uses exaggeration to emphasise how others respond to the news of Asturicus' house: women go dishevelled (a sign of mourning), nobles wear funeral clothes, and the praetor closes his court. Of course, none of these things literally happened – the courts were only closed in a time of national crisis. Umbricius ends this section of his speech by returning to his praise of life in the country, commenting that property is much cheaper there and you can buy a house that comes with a garden and proper quality of life.

Lines 232–267

These lines focus on the crowds, noise and traffic in the streets. Although Juvenal does not state this, we know from other sources that at that time the only vehicles allowed in Rome's streets during a normal day were those carrying materials for public building works, so that at night the streets were full of other traffic. In the poem, Umbricius claims that this prevents people from sleeping properly, and he even uses the comic example of a past emperor, Claudius (whom he refers to as Drusus) who was apparently famous for his drowsiness. Even Claudius would struggle to sleep, he claims! He follows this with a ridiculous parallel: seals – animals the Romans thought were just as drowsy – would also struggle.

At line 239 he gives us a detailed description of a scene in the streets, with a wealthy man being carried in a **litter** at his leisure, completely unaffected by the crowds around him. A litter was a portable taxi carried by slaves that only the wealthy could afford. Here the litter is compared to a **Liburnian galley**, a Roman warship that was more than 33 metres long and 5 metres wide. In these lines is another strong contrast between the experiences of rich and poor – if you are wealthy enough to afford a litter, you can have a relaxing journey through the streets; for the rest, it is an uncomfortable crush. Perhaps out of envy, Umbricius fantasises about a cart load of marble collapsing and crushing a patron and his followers. Back at the patron's house, slaves continue preparations for a dinner-party unawares, while the master lies dead in the mud, unprepared for his journey to the Underworld. This is a reminder of a truth which other Roman sources often mention – that there is no escape from death, whether you are rich or poor. Perhaps this thought gives some comfort to Umbricius.

litter a portable taxi carried by slaves in the Roman world
Liburnian galley a Roman warship

Lines 268–314

Umbricius now starts to focus on other dangers of the city. One of these comes from up above: falling tiles and, amusingly, chamber-pots (bowls used as a toilets) emptied out of windows – perhaps this can be seen to symbolise Umbricius' own ranting and pouring out his views on the problems of life in Rome. He then moves on to discuss the threat posed by a burly drunkard in the streets, joking that he cannot sleep unless he has a fight first. He makes a ridiculous comparison with the great Greek warrior Achilles.

Umbricius goes on to explain why he himself is particularly in danger. The drunkard will avoid picking a fight with a wealthy man (identified by his expensive scarlet cloak) who has an escort of men carrying torches, but as Umbricius is poor – and his only escort

FIGURE 3.45
A drawing showing a Roman litter.

is the moonlight or perhaps a candle he carefully preserves – he is easy prey. Umbricius' poverty is emphasised by the questions the drunkard asks him, suggesting that he has been to a dinner where he has drunk sour wine and eaten beans. Both were signs of a very cheap meal. The episode finishes with another reflection by Umbricius on the lot of the poor man – his only freedom is to plead to be allowed to go home with a few teeth left.

Umbricius' next danger in the streets of Rome at night is the one posed by thieves. He refers to the Pontine Marsh near Rome and the Gallinarian pine-forest near Cumae, both

LITERARY ANALYSIS

Juvenal again parodies epic poetry in lines 279–280. This time the reference is to the *Iliad*, the great poem of the Greek Homer recounting an episode near the end of the Trojan War. At the start of the twenty-fourth and final book of this poem (lines 3–11), Achilles is described mourning his beloved friend Patroclus, who has been killed in battle. Achilles himself feels responsible for his death, since he allowed him to go out to fight dressed in his (Achilles') armour. Achilles is therefore overwhelmed with grief and Homer describes him being unable to sleep, tossing and turning in the night while others slumber. Umbricius compares the situation of the drunkard in the street to that of Achilles – except that in the drunkard's case his mourning and lack of sleep is caused by having no one to fight with. It is a ridiculous comparison!

ACTIVITY

Imagine that you are Umbricius. Write a letter to the magistrate at Rome responsible for the upkeep of roads and streets outlining your complaints and making suggestions for how things could improve.

of which were well known to harbour many robbers and criminals because they were sparsely populated and it was easy to hide there. From time to time Roman troops were sent to clear both areas of criminals, but Umbricius claims that it only has the effect of sending them all to Rome, which is metaphorically described as being 'like a game preserve' for them. In another great exaggeration, Umbricius complains that Rome will soon run out of iron for farm implements as it is all being used to make chains for criminals. Once again, he suggests that Rome was much better in times gone by.

Lines 315–322

He concludes by driving his cattle out of the city, and suggests that when Juvenal himself escapes Rome to his own house in the country at Aquinum, he will come to visit and listen to his satires. This final point illustrates his divorce from life in Rome – he is only prepared to see Juvenal again when he is outside the city.

Study questions

1 Suggest three ways in which Juvenal's style of satire is different from that of Horace.
2 To what extent do you think that Umbricius might himself be being satirised in this poem, as a 'type' who loves to complain about his city?
3 Identify three ways in which Juvenal uses exaggeration in this poem. Do you think that this helps him to get the force of his message across?
4 Juvenal has structured lines 232–314 very cleverly to cover the period of an entire day: 232–238 refer to the nightime, 239–248 to the morning, 249–261 to the main part of the day, 261–267 to the late afternoon, 268–301 to the evening, and 302–314 to the nightime again. How do you think that this structure adds drama and atmosphere to the poem?
5 How accurate a reflection of Roman life do you think these lines give? What elements of the narrative seem to you to be likely?

ACTIVITY

Write two satires of your own, one of which imitates the 'smiling satire' of Horace, and the other the 'angry satire' of Juvenal. If possible, choose a topic or set of characters who you would like to satirise, and base both satires on it.

PETRONIUS

The author of the *Satyricon*, Petronius, was probably an influential aide to the emperor Nero (who reigned from AD 54 to 68), although there is not enough evidence to prove this conclusively. Nonetheless, there are a number of features of the world of this novel that are consistent with this exact period in Roman history. This Petronius is described in some detail by the historian Tacitus. He served as a consul in AD 62, while at the court of the emperor he was Nero's 'judge of taste', a role suggesting that he enjoyed luxurious living. We might even say that he acted as Nero's fashion advisor, in a similar way to how Maecenas had been Augustus' 'Minister of Culture'.

Petronius' novel attempts to show up and satirise social attitudes and pretensions rather than to attack specific individuals. One key difference between his work and the satires of Horace and Juvenal is that it was written largely in prose (although there are sections where poetry is quoted extensively). Moreover, it is a continuous novel with a plot, and so this gives it a very different feel from the poetic satirists. However, it is also clear that Petronius was influenced by the satirists, prose and poetic, who had come before him. When he wrote the account of Trimalchio's dinner party he must have kept in mind, for instance, Horace's account of the disastrous dinner party that he relates in 2.8.

Much of the Satyricon has been lost. It may have been twenty books long (in this sense, a 'book' is what we would think of as a chapter), but sections survive only from books 14, 15 and 16. For this reason, it is hard to reconstruct the outline of the plot, but it clearly centres on the adventures and misadventures of the main character Encolpius, who narrates the story, and his companions, his lover Giton, and Ascyltos, a rival for Giton's affections.

As with Juvenal, it is hard to know exactly who Petronius was writing for, but the novel's language is even more reflective of everyday speech than the language of Horace, and so he was probably aiming at a wider audience than just a small elite. None the less,

EXPLORE FURTHER

You can read Tacitus' account of Nero's aide Petronius in Tacitus' *Annals* 16.17–20.

DEBATE

Scholars do not agree about what genre of literature the *Satyricon* belongs to. While it clearly has strong elements of satire, it also seems to be modelled on a variety of other genres, including Greek romance, epic poetry, comic drama and love poetry. What literary influences can you find in the sections you read?

S & C Modern works of satire

Find out about two works of satire in the modern era: *Gulliver's Travels* by Jonathan Swift and *Animal Farm* by George Orwell. Which groups of people and attitudes were being satirised by each author? How comparable is this to the focus of Petronius' satire?

PRESCRIBED SOURCE

Petronius, *Satyricon*: Dinner with Trimalchio, 29–33; 37–38; 49–50

Date: AD 60s

Author: Petronius (AD *c.* 66)

Genre: prose satire

Significance: a satire of a nouveau-riche freedman who holds an extravagant dinner party

Read it here: OCR source booklet

FIGURE 3.46
A view across the Bay of
Naples towards Mount
Vesuvius.

it is likely that his work was read by Nero and his circle, and may well have raised knowing smiles at a time when wealthy freedmen were prominent in Roman society.

Dinner with Trimalchio

Book 15 of the Satyricon has survived almost completely, and it tells of the dinner party at the house of Trimalchio, a wealthy but extremely vulgar freedman. Encolpius and his companions are citizens of relatively low social status, but have been invited as hangers-on to Agamemnon, a rhetoric teacher they have come to know. Agamemnon is invited as an honoured guest, since he is so intelligent and well-educated. The narrative satirises Trimalchio for his pretensions to high status, but also his inability to get things right. Also satirised, however, is the snobbery of Encolpius as he reacts to what he sees. A reader therefore needs to be alert to the fact that the narrator of the story is flawed too, and his own faults are also on display.

The dinner party takes place in a town somewhere around the Bay of Naples, a fashionable area for wealthy Romans to keep holiday homes. Just before the first prescribed passage (29–33), Encolpius has met Trimalchio for the first time when he finds him relaxing at the baths in the afternoon in preparation for the dinner. Immediately, it is clear that Trimalchio's behaviour is tasteless in the extreme – as he plays a ball game in the palaestra, a slave stands next to him with a silver chamber pot. Encolpius relates a particular incident:

> Trimalchio clicked his fingers. At the signal the eunuch held out the chamber pot for him while he carried on playing. He emptied his bladder, asked for water to wash his hands, splashed his fingers a little and wiped them on a slave's head.

> Petronius, *Satyricon* 27

This episode epitomises the character of Trimalchio throughout the novel – his behaviour is often shocking and disgusting.

Sections 29–33

Section 29 begins with Encolpius arriving at Trimalchio's house and examining the paintings on the wall of the entry-passage: a warning to 'beware the dog', scenes from Trimalchio's career, and scenes from the *Iliad* and the *Odyssey*. The placement of these paintings next to each other is an obvious attempt by Trimalchio to place himself in the same company as the great heroes in the age of the Trojan War.

The guests are then led to the dining room. As they enter the dining room, a slave superstitiously reminds them to cross the doorway with their right feet first. (A similar modern superstition might be refusing to walk under a ladder for fear of bad luck.) Another slave then falls at their feet, begging them to rescue him from the whipping he is about to endure. The irony here is that the whipping has been ordered by a more senior slave: Trimalchio's steward is angry that his valuable clothing, given to him by a client, has been stolen in the public baths. The steward here is overstepping the mark just as

LITERARY ANALYSIS

Trimalchio himself (with hair) was holding Mercury's staff and was entering Rome, led by Minerva . . . Now indeed, where the colonnade was running out, Mercury was carrying him off, lifted by the chin, to a lofty tribunal. Fortune was there with her abundant cornucopia, and the three Fates, spinning their golden threads.

Petronius, *Satyricon*, 29

What can we learn about Trimalchio's character from these lines?

The art described here reflects Trimalchio's enormous sense of self-importance. The goddess Minerva represents wisdom and also military victory, while Mercury is there as the god of trade and profit (although it is ironic that he is also the god of thieves). Trimalchio believes that both are guiding his life. His sense of being divinely blessed does not end there: there are also images of Fortune and the three Fates. In Greek mythology, the three Fates were responsible for choosing the length of a person's life, and they usually appear in literature to warn people that death can come at any time. Here, though, Trimalchio presents them as allies who will allow him to live a long life. This is very arrogant of him, and suggests that he believes that he is immune to ill-fortune.

There is a further sense in which Trimalchio overvalues his achievements here. The reference to the magistrate's platform ('lofty tribunal') means that he has become an Augustalis (see p. 270). While this was the only major civic post a freedman could gain, it was not comparable to one of the major political offices, and so it was not worthy of the great ceremony that is depicted.

much as his master has done – slaves could neither own property nor could they have clients! Nonetheless, the steward decides to let the guilty slave off his punishment.

Once the guests have taken their seats in the dining room, a magnificent first course is presented, which Encolpius describes in detail. The guests are already eating when Trimalchio grandly arrives to the accompaniment of music. He takes his place in the seat reserved for the guest of honour – contrary to the usual custom – and rudely announces that he needs to finish the game he is playing, which has already caused him to be late. At this point, more food is brought in, and the guests witness their first culinary trick.

Sections 37–38

Fortunata, the wife of Trimalchio, is the focus of these sections. Encolpius has turned to another diner to ask about her. He learns that she is now fabulously wealthy, having once been a lowly slave girl and prostitute. Like Trimalchio, she is presented as someone who has come into extraordinary wealth and an extravagant lifestyle – her name, meaning 'Lucky', reflects this.

We then hear more about the extraordinary wealth of Trimalchio. All of his food is home-grown, and he goes to great lengths to import the best raw materials: bees from the region of Attica around Athens (long known for its honey) and mushroom spores all the

LITERARY ANALYSIS Symbolism

Petronius uses symbolism to emphasise Trimalchio's pretensions. As the guests walk into the dining room, they see above the door rods and axes with a miniature ship's beak protruding from the bottom. Rods and axes were symbols of senior magistrates, to illustrate their power to flog or execute. As an Augustalis, Trimalchio was allowed to display them as well, and he makes sure that they are prominently placed. Meanwhile, the ship's beak reflects the beaks that were attached to the main speaker's platform in the Roman forum, from where the city's leading politicians spoke. Again, he wishes to suggest that he is a leading man in the community.

Trimalchio's attire also reflects this desire to show off his status. As an Augustalis, he was allowed to wear a purple-bordered toga and a gold ring. In his case, he draws attention to this privilege by being unconventional: the purple stripe is on his napkin and the ring is gold and bronze.

way from India. The other freedmen at the dinner, while not as wealthy, are still very rich in their own right. As often in Petronius' account, great exaggeration is used to describe the characters, as in this sentence to describe the wealth of one of the freedmen guests:

More wine was poured under the table than another man has in his wine cellar.

Petronius, *Satyricon*, 38

This cannot literally be true, but the narrator (at this point one of the other guests) uses the exaggeration to emphasise just how wealthy this freedman had once been.

Sections 49–50

In section 49, Trimalchio plays another trick on his guests. The pretence that he arranges with his cook – that the cook will pretend not to have gutted the pig – allows Trimalchio to show anger with the cook and threaten to beat him. In turn, the guests beg the master to spare the cook. This episode is all about Trimalchio holding power – he is showing the guests that he has power over his household. More than that, however, the trick allows Trimalchio to have power over the guests, whereby they ask for his mercy almost as if a crowd at the amphitheatre might ask the emperor to spare a fallen gladiator. When they see that they have been fooled, he has power over them again.

In section 50 Trimalchio is shown twice by Encolpius to be uncultured and lacking in class. The first example comes with his play on the term 'Corinthian bronze'. Bronze

FIGURE 3.47
A fresco from Herculaneum showing a dining scene.

EXAM TIP

Similes

Fortunata is described as having a nasty mouth on her and uses bad language, like a 'magpie on his couch'. How is this an effective image?

- A magpie is a bird that squawks loudly – one imagines Fortunata talking loudly and annoyingly.
- A magpie is a bird that collects loose bits of jewellery and takes them to its nest – the suggestion is that Fortunata also loves jewellery, some of which might not match well.
- A magpie is not usually found on a smart couch. This suggests that she does not deserve her current status of having great wealth.

---

tableware from the Greek city of Corinth was regarded as the finest that one could buy, and Trimalchio has some of it at his dinner party. Yet Trimalchio makes a very feeble joke about being the only person who has 'real' Corinthian bronze, since he bought it from someone called Corinthus. It would be one of those moments where the punchline to a joke falls flat, but the guests no doubt had to play along with it.

The second way in which Trimalchio embarrasses himself is in his knowledge of Greek and Roman history and literature. He talks about Troy being captured and looted by Hannibal. Yet the Trojan War – which involved Greeks and Trojans – happened so far back in history that it could not be dated (modern estimates are about 1200 BC), while Hannibal was a Carthaginian who fought against the Romans in the late third century BC. Trimalchio tries to show himself to be an educated man but in doing so proves to be the opposite.

Study question

The nineteenth-century US President Abraham Lincoln once said: 'Better to remain silent and be thought a fool than to speak out and remove all doubt'. Do you think that this sentiment applies to Trimalchio in this passage?

Study questions

1 What can we learn about the design of a Roman house from Petronius' satire?
2 Do you think that the readers of this satire were meant to find the story and its characters recognisable or believable? To what extent are they exaggerated?
3 Which parts of Petronius' satire do you find particularly funny? Do you think that a Roman reader would have found the same things funny as we do today?
4 To what extent do people today use food and dining to show off their wealth or status?
5 What impression do you form of the narrator Encolpius in this satire?

ACTIVITY

What do you think the main characters at Trimalchio's dinner party might have looked like? Choose three characters and draw or paint your own portrait of them. You could even exaggerate their features for comic effect and create a caricature.

TOPIC REVIEW

You should be able to:

1. Describe:
   - an outline of the storylines of Horace's Satires 2.2, 2.6 and 2.8, and their key characters
   - an outline of the storyline of Juvenal's Satire 3 (particularly lines 190–322), and its key characters
   - an outline of the storyline of Petronius' *Satyricon*, 29–33; 37–38; 49–50, and its key characters
   - the cultural context in which each author was writing.

2. Explain:
   - the key themes of each of Horace's satires, and the ways in which he creates humour
   - the key themes of Juvenal's third satire, and the ways in which he creates humour
   - the key themes of Petronius' account, and the ways in which he creates humour
   - the ways in which the style of each author is different.

PRACTICE QUESTIONS

Source A: *Horace, Satires 2.2, lines 112–128*

You'll credit it more if I say that when I was a lad
Ofellus, as I know well, spent no more widely, then,
When his wealth was intact, as now it's reduced.
You can see him there with his sons and herd, a solid
Tenant on his lost farm. 'I was never one,' he says,
'To eat rashly on working days, no more than greens,
A shank of smoked ham, and if friends came to visit
I'd not seen for ages, or if I welcomed a neighbour
On a wet day when I couldn't work, we dined well,
Not on fish from town, but a kid or a pullet: then
Raisins and nuts and split figs graced our dessert.
After it drinking matches with a forfeit for losing,
And with a prayer to Ceres: 'May she raise the stalks high',
She smoothed care from our furrowed brows with wine.
Let Fortune's winds blow, let her stir a fresh tumult:
How can she lessen this? How much worse off have I
Or you been, my lads, since this new landlord arrived?

1. Why has Ofellus lost his farm? [1]
2. How does Horace create a sense of Ofellus' character in this passage?
   Make **three** points. [6]

3.6 Pliny and his Letters

This topic focuses on Pliny the Younger. It will first outline who he was and what he achieved in his career, including his writings. It will then reflect on each of your six prescribed letters in turn, focusing on how his character comes across in them, and what they tell us about Roman life in his day.

THE LIFE OF PLINY

Gaius Plinius Caecilius Secundus was born into a wealthy family in Comum in the north of Italy in AD 61. Today, he is commonly known as Pliny the Younger to distinguish him from his uncle, Pliny the Elder. He was actually brought up by his uncle, and this automatically gave him access to the Roman elite, since Pliny the Elder was an admiral in the Roman navy. One of Pliny the Younger's most famous letters relates the death of his uncle during the eruption of Mount Vesuvius in AD 79, an event to which both men were eye-witnesses.

Pliny the Younger had an excellent education, and as a young man embarked on a career as a lawyer. He soon also rose through the ranks of Roman politics, and was appointed to the senate in the late 80s. Thereafter he held a series of high positions at Rome: most notably, he served as praetor in 93 and consul in 100. In about 111, he was appointed by the emperor Trajan to govern the province of Bithynia-Pontus, a

EXPLORE FURTHER

You can read about the eruption of Mount Vesuvius in AD 79 – including the death of Pliny the Elder and the escape of Pliny the Younger – in letters 6.16 and 6.20.

FIGURE 3.48
A nineteenth-century painting of the eruption of Mount Vesuvius.

FIGURE 3.49
A medieval statue of Pliny on the side of the cathedral at Como (the modern name for Comum).

region roughly corresponding to a large section of northern Turkey today. He apparently died in office there in about 112.

We know a great deal about the life of Pliny through his surviving letters. Since he held so many important posts, they give us a very helpful picture as to what it was like for a senior Roman official to serve under an emperor; we also gain a valuable insight into elements of Roman society such as the patron/client system. However, the letters also give us a helpful lens onto his life away from the public eye; in particular, he writes in 1.9 with great fondness for life on his country estate. He writes in great detail about it in another letter, 2.17; it was a very large estate in Laurentum, about seventeen miles south-west of Rome, and clearly acted as something of a sanctuary for its owner.

PLINY AS A WRITER

Pliny was active as a writer throughout his life. He was a keen poet, although we have only quotations from his verses. He also wrote speeches, one of which has survived. However, Pliny has become best known for his letters, many of which have survived. He published nine books of letters at intervals between about 99 and 109, and they were addressed to a number of friends and acquaintances about many areas of his life, both private and public. A tenth book was published after his death and contains letters to the emperor Trajan while he was governor in Bithynia-Pontus. His letters tend to focus on a single subject or theme, and are relatively short.

Although the letters are centred on Pliny's day-to-day life, it is very important to understand that they are more than simple records of correspondence. In fact, Pliny wrote them to be published as short works of literature; some scholars even credit him with creating a new literary genre, the literary letter. Rather than writing history, it seems that Pliny wished to give a picture of his times through his letters – this obviously allowed him to write about and record the private lives of himself and others in a way which is rarely done by conventional historians. A further key feature of the letters is that they typically have a strong moral tone: Pliny wished to display through his letters how he felt people should behave, and where he felt that society had gone wrong. In this, there is an interesting overlap with Roman satirists, who also aim to point out society's flaws.

When we study Pliny's letters, therefore, we need to think not just about the content of what he is saying, but also how he has structured the letter; how the language he uses brings out his points; and what moral view or idea he is putting forward.

Pliny, Letters, 1.9, 2.6, 3.14, 4.19, 5.19, 9.6

CW

Date: AD *c.* 99–109

Author: Pliny the Younger (AD 61–*c.* 112)

Genre: literary letters

Read it here: OCR source booklet

Significance: letters that reflect on a variety of themes about life at Rome and in the country, as follows:

- 1.9   On the pleasures of spending time on his country estate
- 2.6   On an unkind dinner-party host
- 3.14   On the murder of Larcius Macedo by his slaves
- 4.19   On the excellence of his new young wife
- 5.19   On his concern for the health of his freedman Zosimus
- 9.6   On his dislike of the chariot races

COMMENTARY

In the short commentaries that follow, each letter is summarised along with suggestions for what it might tell us about the following topics:

- the commentary Pliny offers on Roman life
- Pliny's use of language
- the purpose of the letter
- how Pliny reflects his position in Roman society
- the image Pliny projects.

However, it is important to realise that these commentaries are not exhaustive – by no means do they cover everything you could learn about the topics above. Rather, they are meant to give you examples and guide you in your own reading, so that you can develop other arguments and interpretations yourself.

Letter 1.9

Pliny writes this letter to his friend Minicius Fundanus, who was consul in 107. In the letter, Pliny reflects on the contrast between his life in Rome and the life he enjoys on his country estate at Laurentum. In Rome, he finds himself always busy with duties that seem important at the time, but soon seem insignificant. However, on his estate, he has time to relax, he becomes more even-tempered and he can focus on his writing, drawing inspiration from the natural beauty that surrounds him. He therefore encourages Fundanus to leave the city behind too, and summarises his thoughts with a pithy comment by his friend Attilius – it's better to relax than to be busy doing nothing.

Study questions

1 Compare this letter
with Horace's Satire
2.6. What do each find
tiresome in the city?
What do each value
most in the country?
2 What do we learn
about Pliny's emotional
state from this letter?

exclamation a figure of
speech in which a writer
seems to exclaim words
aloud

aphorism a short saying
that communicates a
common truth

This letter presents the city/country contrast in a similar way to Horace in Satire 2.6. Like Horace, Pliny finds time on his country estate to clear his head, and this allows him to read, write and exercise. Pliny shows himself to be very self-aware, as he reflects on his changed emotional state – he does not speak harshly to anyone at his farm, which of course suggests that he does when he is in the city. Indeed, the only person he is harsh on is himself when he does not meet the very high standards he sets himself in his writing.

Pliny uses language carefully to get his point across. Reflecting on his life at Laurentum, he says:

> What a good and honest life! What delightful and virtuous leisure time and more wonderful than almost all business.

Pliny, Letter 1.9

This figure of speech is called an **exclamation** – it is as if we as readers can hear him exclaiming these words out loud, and it serves to draw greater attention to the point he is trying to make.

In the final paragraph Pliny addresses Minicius Fundanus directly again, and the purpose of the letter becomes clear: he is advising his friend to leave the city so that he can rest or study, just as Pliny is doing. We do not know what pressures Fundanus is under, but in another letter Pliny refers to him as a learned man and a philosopher, so he is clearly keen for him to allow more time for this aspect of his character. Pliny finishes the letter by quoting a neat **aphorism** by an old friend, Atilius, who was well known for such sayings. The letter therefore ends in a suitably philosophical tone.

Letter 2.6

This letter is written to Avitius, a younger friend of Pliny. We learn that he had recently attended a dinner party where the host's behaviour left him deeply unimpressed. The guests were divided into three categories: the privileged few, the clients and dependants of the host, and the freedmen. The first group were served excellent food, the rest ordinary fare in small portions; moreover, the wine was arranged and served in three categories by quality. Pliny voices his strong disapproval of the practice of offering different qualities of food at the same dinner party, partly through a conversation he reports with another guest. His own practice is to serve everyone the same, but not to go to great expense. The letter finishes with Pliny speaking as a mentor to Avitius, urging him to follow his own example.

It is clear what the purpose of this letter is – Pliny wishes to offer advice to a younger man about how a Roman of high status should treat those lower than him on the social ladder. We have seen on p. 264 that other writers talk about this practice of serving different foods to guests of varying status at a dinner party; Pliny takes a strong moral line on this, which he wishes Avitius to follow. Pliny therefore sets himself up as a wise mentor who has a clear set of principles.

One important way in which Pliny varies his language is by introducing a reported conversation with another guest half-way through the letter. This serves to magnify the sense of disapproval, since the discussion takes place quietly at the dinner party – there is the sense that the reader is invited to listen in on a confidential chat.

Letter 3.14

The addressee of the letter is Acilius, who is clearly away from Rome and unaware of the city's social problems. Pliny recounts the murder of Larcius Macedo, the son of a freedman who had become a senator. While Pliny admits that Macedo was a cruel master, he is horrified by the killing and approves of the punishment meted out to the slaves. He never says explicitly what this punishment was, but there was a precedent in such situations for every slave in a household – innocent or guilty – to be executed. Towards the end of the letter, Pliny turns to an earlier mishap which had befallen Macedo, when he was slapped by an equestrian at the baths.

It is interesting that Pliny, who is normally so humane, approves of the punishment and suggests that slaves can never be trusted. This attitude is in great contrast to how he speaks about his own household in Letter 5.19. Pliny's language reflects the violence of the murder, with a detailed description of the various parts of his body which were assaulted, followed by his being thrown on a hot pavement to see if he was still alive. During this description, Pliny uses an aside – 'shocking to say' – to illustrate just how repulsed he is by the event.

In the last section of the letter Pliny claims to be filling space left on his paper, but he does give a reason for linking the two stories related to Macedo's ill-fortune. Pliny describes the incident at the public baths as 'portentous' – in other words he believed that it was an omen of what lay in store for him at the hands of his slaves after he had taken a bath at home. Clearly, even this educated Roman believed in signs and omens that foretold the future.

Letter 4.19

This letter gives us an insight into the relationship between Pliny and his new young wife. The person addressed is Calpurnia Hispulla, her aunt (while Pliny does not name his wife in this letter, we know that she was also called Calpurnia). In the letter Pliny reports enthusiastically on her qualities as a new wife, and how they are both thankful for each other. A key point, which Pliny alludes to, is that Calpurnia is Pliny's third wife, and there is a huge age gap between them. She is likely to have been 15 or 16 at the time of their marriage, while Pliny is about 30 years older.

This letter gives a view into the expectations for an upper-class Roman wife. Pliny is pleased that Calpurnia is efficient in running the household, but also that she is a musical and literate young woman. As a consequence, Pliny almost presents her as a star-struck fan, one who memorises his books and listens out of sight when he is giving recitations. It could be argued that he is coming across as rather vain and self-important here.

The final section of the letter reveals its purpose. He wishes to thank Calpurnia Hispulla doubly – once for the role she played in his own upbringing, setting him high standards of behaviour, so that her niece admires him so much; and secondly for bringing them together – in Pliny's eyes, Hispulla is a matchmaker par excellence.

Letter 5.19

Pliny writes to his friend Valerius Paulinus, who was consul in 107, about his concern for the health of his freedman, Zosimus. This letter gives us an insight into the humane way in

Study questions

1 How does Pliny make clear his disapproval of the host's behaviour?
2 Why do you think that it was important to Pliny to act as a good mentor to Avitius?
3 In these first two letters, Pliny has the role of an adviser. What words and phrases from the two letters highlight this fact?

Study questions

1 Pliny admits that Macedo is a cruel master, yet fully approves of the punishment of all his slaves. Does this surprise you? Why do you think that wealthy Romans might have had such attitudes?
2 How does Pliny make his narrative vivid and graphic?

Study questions

1 Does this seem like a loving relationship? How can you tell?
2 What do we learn about Pliny's own upbringing from this letter?

ACTIVITY

Imagine you are Pliny's wife Calpurnia. Write a letter in the style of Pliny to your aunt, Calpurnia Hispulla, outlining what your life is like and how you feel about your marriage.

Study questions

1 Why do you think that Pliny is so keen for Zosimus to be restored to health?

2 Do you think that Pliny's comparison of himself with Odysseus is impressive? What do you think he was trying to say about the way he treats his household?

which Pliny treated members of his household, and so provides a contrast to his comments about slaves in 3.14. We hear about Zosimus' talents, and Pliny's fondness for him. We learn that he has already sent him to Egypt to help him recover from illness once before, and this time he asks Paulinus to host the freedman at his estate at Forum Iulii (modern Fréjus in Provence, France), so that he can relax and recover in the healthy country air.

We learn a great deal about Pliny's literary and cultural world from this letter. Near the start he quotes Homer to illustrate his own approach to the treatment of his household. Two points could be made about the quotation:

- Pliny is seeking to present himself as a cultured man. The two poems of Homer, the *Iliad* and the *Odyssey*, were acknowledged as the greatest works of Greek literature; any educated Roman was expected to know them well and look to them for moral examples.
- The specific words he quotes – 'he was gentle as a father' – are spoken in the *Odyssey* (2.47) by Telemachus, Odysseus' son. At this point Telemachus is referring to the way in which Odysseus, the king of Ithaca, used to treat the other noble men of the island. Pliny therefore compares himself to a king who treats his nobles well.

We can also learn from the letter about the cultured entertainment which Pliny values. Zosimus is highly valued for his skill as a reciter of comedies and other forms of literary performance, as well as for being a gifted musician.

We could reflect too on the presentation of ill-health and its treatment in this letter. Zosimus has already been sent to Egypt for medical attention – a country with a centuries-old tradition of medicine – and this seems to have worked. Now Pliny wishes to send him to southern France. This time, however, there is no tailored medical care on offer, beyond the fresh country air and local milk, which have a restorative reputation. Zosimus is to be sent on a restful retreat in nature to help his health, something which many doctors today would still recommend.

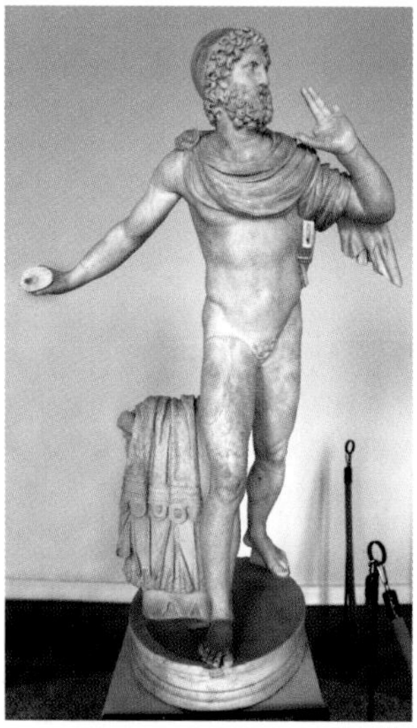

FIGURE 3.50
A statue of Odysseus.

Letter 9.6

In this letter Pliny writes to Calvisius Rufus, an equestrian friend from his home town of Comum, about his disdain for the chariot races, and in particular their fanatical supporters. Pliny seems to come across as quite snobbish in this letter, but he does make some important points about supporters being obsessed about their favoured team winning, rather than actually enjoying the quality of the spectacle – something that would seem to apply equally to many football supporters today.

It is hard not to find Pliny very self-satisfied in this letter. He is disdainful of the behaviour of spectators at the chariot races, and at the start draws a contrast between his own focus on his books and the deranged behaviour of the supporters at the races. This contrast is brought sharply back into view at the end, where he even admits to feelings of superiority over so many of his fellow Romans. The language he uses indicates his scorn and contempt, with words and phrases such as 'pointless', 'tedious', 'low enjoyment', 'wasting' and 'idlest of pursuits'. By contrast, he talks of his own 'utmost delight' at being able to devote his time to literature. Clearly, Pliny intends to place himself far above the crowd by using these words.

Study questions

1 Why do you think that Pliny was happy to publish a letter in which he is so critical of a popular obsession such as chariot racing?
2 Do you feel any sympathy for the views Pliny puts forward here?
3 What impressions do you form of Pliny from all six letters? To what extent would you say that he is wise, or self-satisfied, or arrogant, or humane or inhumane? Would you agree that the letters suggest that he is a complex character?

TOPIC REVIEW

You should be able to:

1. Describe:
   - the key details of Pliny's life and world
   - an outline of each of the six prescribed letters
   - the main characters in each of the letters.

2. Explain:
   - the impression we receive of Pliny and his world from his letters
   - how Pliny uses language to further his ideas
   - what the letters can tell us about Roman city life.

PRACTICE QUESTIONS

Source A: *Pliny, Letter 5.19*

Some years ago, while narrating vigorously and keenly, he began to spit blood, and for this reason was sent by me to Egypt; after a long absence abroad he has recently returned, restored to health. Then, while he was putting too much strain on his voice over several days, he was reminded of his old infirmity by a fit of coughing, and again spat up blood.

For which reason, I decided to send him to your estate which you own at Forum Iulii. For I have often heard you mentioning that there both the air is healthy and the milk is most suitable for this kind of recovery. Therefore, I ask you to write to your household that your estate and house be thrown open for him, even that they cover all expenses, if need be. But the outlay will be modest. For he is so thrifty and abstemious, that he abstains not only from luxuries but also what's necessary for good health by his self-denial. I shall give as much to him for the journey as is enough for him to reach your estate.

1. Who is Pliny talking about in this letter, and what is his relationship to him? [2]
2. To what extent do Roman authors idealise life in the country? Use the source as a starting point, as well as the other Roman literature you have studied. [8]

3.7 Experiencing Roman City Life

TOPIC OVERVIEW

How the authors depict aspects of Roman city life and the attitudes of Romans regarding them, including:

- The dangers of city life
- Life in the city for rich and poor
- Leisure and entertainment
- Food and dinner parties

The prescribed sources for this topic are:

- Horace, *Satires*, 2.2, 2.6, 2.8
- Juvenal, *Satire* 3.190–322
- Petronius, *Satyricon: Dinner with Trimalchio*, 29–33; 37–38; 49–50
- Pliny, *Letters*, 1.9, 2.6, 3.14, 4.19, 5.19, 9.6

Don't forget that you will be given credit in the exam if you study extra sources and make relevant use of them in your answers.

This topic enables you to draw on your knowledge of what you have already studied in the culture section of this component. It is considerably shorter than the previous two topics, since you will already have covered its themes during your reading – so what follows suggests ways in which you can develop your awareness of them.

THE DANGERS OF CITY LIFE

The most obvious passage to think about here will be the prescribed lines of Juvenal. Umbricius himself lists some of the dangers in the city, including falling masonry, fires and collapsing buildings.

However, beyond this, it is important to consider what might be thought of as dangers. You might reflect that both Horace (2.6) and Pliny (1.9) reflect on the stresses the city brings them, and how much better the country seems to be for their wellbeing. Horace even comments that he is glad to be out of the city while the weather conditions bring illness and death. A similar theme seems to emerge in the fable of the town mouse and the country mouse, where a life in the city is portrayed as being fraught with danger and anxiety.

Note that this topic requires you **both** to think about how the authors depict aspects of Roman city life **and** to think about the attitudes of the Romans regarding them. Therefore, you should be alert to both – it is probably much easier to recognise the former than the latter. However, one good example of the latter can be found in Pliny Letter 1.9. Here Pliny reflects on all the activities and responsibilities that he is engaged with on a daily basis in Rome, after which he says:

> On the day you do them, these things seem important; but the same things, if you consider that you have done these every day, seem pointless? much more so when you go to the country. For then comes reflection: How many days have I wasted on such dull things!
>
> Pliny, Letter 1.9

In these lines, Pliny gives us an insight into his attitude towards his own life as a wealthy man in Rome – he concludes that much of it is a waste of time in the grand scheme of things. From this letter, therefore, we learn **both** about the sort of business an important man in Rome would typically attend to, **and** about his attitudes towards this.

LIFE IN THE CITY FOR RICH AND POOR

There are plenty of examples that you can draw on here, including:

- Umbricius' contrast between the reaction of people to the burning of a large house and the burning of an insula.
- Umbricius' portrayal of the street scene, with a wealthy man carried comfortably in a litter, and poor men crushed as they try to make their way.
- Pliny's description of his regular duties in 1.9
- Horace's description in 2.6 of people trying to use him to get access to the wealthy and powerful Maecenas.
- Petronius' portrayal of the excess of Trimalchio, including his lavish house, the food he serves, and the wealth of his freedmen guests.

LEISURE AND ENTERTAINMENT

Of course, a major theme here will be the description of dinner parties, which is explored further below. However, there are other ways in which leisure and entertainment feature in your prescribed reading, such as:

- Horace (2.6) and Pliny talk about using leisure time for reading, study and writing.
- Cervius' fable presumably entertained his companions.
- Pliny's reference to the baths in 3.14, his description of Zosimus' talents as an entertainer in 5.19, and his snobbish disdain for the chariot races in 9.6

• Trimalchio's use of tricks and jokes to try to provide entertainment at his dinner party.

FOOD AND DINNER PARTIES

This is one of the main themes of three of our sources: Pliny (Letter 2.6), all three of Horace's *Satires*, and the *Satyricon*; moreover, even in the Juvenal passage there is reference to the preparations for dinner.

One important idea to reflect on is: what does food symbolise in each source? Do different types of food represent different things? For example, in Satire 2.2, Horace refers to people eating peacock when chicken tastes just as good. It is no coincidence that the peacock is a bird that is known to preen and show off by raising its feathers – perhaps Horace is trying to suggest to us here something of the character of those who eat peacock, that they too are show-offs?

Secondly, we might think about how the authors play with the conventions of dinner parties, which we have learnt about in the culture section. A good example comes in Satire 2.8, when Horace lists the diners at Nasidienus' dinner party:

I was there at the head, and next to me Viscus
From Thurii, and below him Varius if I
Remember correctly: then Servilius Balatro
And Vibidius, Maecenas' shadows, whom he brought
With him. Above our host was Nomentanus, below
Porcius, that jester, gulping whole cakes at a time.

Horace, *Satire* 2.8, 20–24

FIGURE 3.51

A seating plan of Nasidienus' dinner party

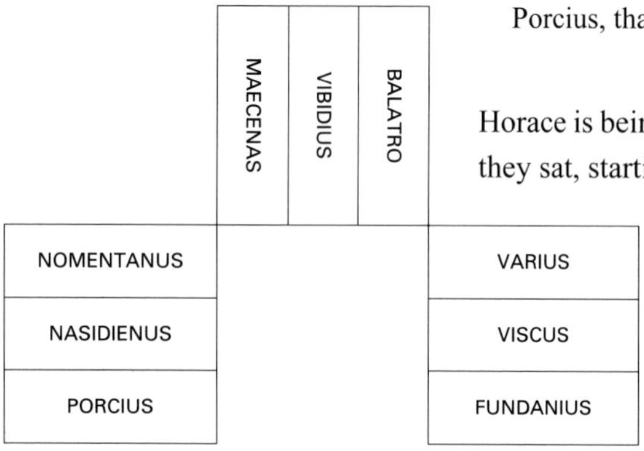

Horace is being clever here – the narrator Fundanius lists the guests in the order in which they sat, starting with himself at the top. However, there is a key point: Maecenas is the guest of honour, but next to him is not the host (Nasidienus) but his freedman Nomentanus, who has been appointed to explain the food to Maecenas. This change in the usual convention allows Horace to emphasise Nasidienus' eagerness to ensure that Maecenas understands all the food that has been prepared for him.

Study questions

1 To what extent do the authors suggest that life in Rome is a danger to physical and mental wellbeing?
2 From what you have read, do you think that there was a greater gap between rich and poor in Rome than there is in our society today?
3 How much can we learn about Roman entertainment from the prescribed literature?
4 To what extent does food represent human character in the prescribed literature?

Moreover, this is not the only example in our prescribed literature of the conventional seating plan being changed: in *Satyricon* 31, Trimalchio arrogantly has the place of honour reserved for himself. In both cases, then, the authors have changed the conventions to say something important about the host of the dinner party.

TOPIC REVIEW

You should be able to:

1. Describe:
   - the various dangers of city life that the authors portray
   - examples of the lives of the rich and the poor from the prescribed texts
   - examples of leisure and entertainment in the prescribed texts
   - examples of food and dinner parties in the prescribed texts.

2. Explain:
   - how dangerous life in a Roman city is depicted to be
   - the way in which the authors portray the differences between the lives of the rich and the poor
   - what we can learn about leisure and entertainment in the Roman city from the prescribed texts
   - what the authors tell us about the importance of food and dinner parties in Roman city life.

PRACTICE QUESTIONS

Source A: *Juvenal, Satire 3, lines 239–250*

When duty calls, the crowd gives way as the rich man's litter,
Rushes by, right in their faces, like some vast Liburnian galley,
While he reads, writes, sleeps inside, while sped on his way:
You know how a chair with shut windows makes you drowsy!
Yet, he gets there first: as I hasten, the tide ahead obstructs me,
And the huge massed ranks that follow behind crush my kidneys;
This man sticks out his elbow, that one flails with a solid pole,
This man strikes my head with a beam, that one with a barrel.
Legs caked with mud, I'm forever trampled by mighty feet
From every side, while a soldier's hobnailed boot pierces my toe.
Do you see all the smoke that rises, to celebrate a hand-out?
There's a hundred diners each followed by his portable kitchen.

1. **a.** Explain what is meant by a 'hand-out' in this passage. [2]
   b. What was the significance of this hand-out for many Romans? [1]
2. In your opinion, how exaggerated are the dangers of life in Rome presented in the sources you have read? Use the source as a starting point, as well as your own knowledge. [8]

3.8 Relationships and Roman Society

The section on this topic is once again shorter than the first two, since it requires you to focus more deeply on the prescribed literature you have already examined. In looking at the relationships between these different groups in Roman society, it is important to be aware that you should reflect **both** on how the authors depict these relationships **and** on how they depict the attitudes the Romans have regarding them.

SLAVES AND MASTERS

Petronius will be one key source for this theme. There are two scenes in which a slave is threatened with a beating (in sections 30 and 49), while in section 29 one of the paintings on the wall of Trimalchio's house portrays a slave-market. This gives us an insight into Roman slave markets, and it is perhaps surprising that Trimalchio wants to acknowledge his own origins as a slave in the paintings that reflect his achievements.

A further notable point comes in section 30, where we can observe the hierarchy of slaves in Trimalchio's household: the steward is his senior slave, who has the power to beat a junior slave for losing his smart clothing; the steward also claims to have a client, something not suitable for a slave. In section 51 we might focus on Encolpius' reaction to the possible whipping of the cook for not having stuffed the pig: he supports the idea that the slave should be whipped for his incompetence, showing little sympathy for him.

A similar lack of sympathy towards slaves can be seen from Pliny in letter 3.14. We might be surprised that he approves of a severe punishment, whereby innocent and guilty slaves are killed alike, but this does give us an insight into the attitude to slaves even by those who are educated and relatively humane.

Finally, we get an interesting insight into slaves preparing the food for a dinner party in Juvenal 3.

PATRONS AND CLIENTS

We get a helpful insight into the attitude of patrons towards clients in Pliny's Letter 2.6 – and here we can also think about how food is used to denote social status. Further examples of the patron/client relationship can be seen as follows:

- The clients of Maecenas trying to get access to him in Horace 2.6, 33–39.
- The behaviour of the clients of Nasidienus and Maecenas at the dinner party in Horace 2.8.
- The fact that Trimalchio's steward himself has a client, even though he is a slave.

MEN AND WOMEN

There are relatively few examples of female characters in your reading. Indeed, Horace's three satires do not feature female characters apart from brief mentions of two divine figures, the muse of satire and Libitina, and one witch, Canidia. However, Fortunata in section 37 of the *Satyricon*, and the two Calpurnias in Pliny's Letter 4.19 are all characters of interest. It is notable that there is a great contrast between the characters of the two wives here, Calpurnia and Fortunata.

Study questions

1 What can we learn about Roman attitudes to slavery in the prescribed literature?
2 How much sympathy is there for clients in the prescribed literature?
3 Compare and contrast Fortunata and Calpurnia as Roman wives.

TOPIC REVIEW

With reference to the prescribed sources, you should be able to:

1. Describe:
   - examples of relations between slaves and masters
   - examples of relations between patrons and clients
   - examples of relations between men and women.

2. Explain:
   - what we can learn about the variety of relations between slaves and masters
   - what we can learn about the nature of relations between patrons and clients
   - what we can learn about how men and women interacted in Roman life.

PRACTICE QUESTIONS

Source A: *Petronius, Satyricon 31*

A very excellent entrée was brought in, for now everyone was reclined except for one man, Trimalchio, for whom a place was saved at the top, in a new fashion. And then, on a large dish, an ass of Corinthian bronze with a double pannier was served up; in one basket there were white olives, in the other black. Over the ass there were two dishes on the edges of which was written the name of Trimalchio and the weight of the silver. Some little bridges soldered onto the plate were even supporting dormice sprinkled with honey and poppy seeds. There were also roasting sausages placed above a silver grill, and below the grill there were Syrian plums along with the seeds of pomegranates.

1. Why is Trimalchio's place at the table described as 'a new fashion'? [2]
2. 'Dining in the Roman world was above all about snobbery'. To what extent do you agree with this statement based on the literature you have studied? Justify your response. [15]

Further Reading for Literature and Culture 2: Roman City Life

Culture

Beard, M. (2010) *Pompeii: the Life of a Roman Town*. London: Profile Books

Beard, M. (2016) *SPQR: a History of Ancient Rome*. London: Profile Books

Beard, M. and Hopkins, K. (2011) *The Colosseum*. London: Profile Books

Berry, J. (2007) *The Complete Pompeii*. London: Thames and Hudson

Connolly, P. (1990) *Pompeii*. Oxford: Oxford University Press

Connolly, P. (2000) *The Ancient City*. Oxford: Oxford University Press

Fagan, G. (2002) *Bathing in Public in the Roman World*. Ann Arbor: University of Michigan Press

Futrell, A. (2006) *The Roman Games: Historical Sources in Translation*. Hoboken, NJ: Wiley-Blackwell

Shelton, J. (1997) *As the Romans Did: a Sourcebook in Roman Social History*. Oxford: Oxford University Press

Treggiari, S. (2001) *Roman Social History*. London: Routledge

Wallace-Hadrill, A. (2012) *Herculaneum*. London: Frances Lincoln

Literature

Braund, S. (ed.) (1992) *Roman Verse Satire*. Oxford (*Greece & Rome* New Surveys in the Classics No. 23)

Braund, S. (2013) *The Roman Satirists and their Masks*. London: Bloomsbury

Courtney, E. (2001) *A Companion to Petronius*. Oxford: Oxford University Press

Courtney, E. (2013) *A Commentary on the Satires of Juvenal*. Berkeley: California Classical Studies

Davie, J. (2011) *Horace: Satires and Epistles*. Oxford: Oxford University Press

Freudenburg, K. (ed.) (2005) *The Cambridge Companion to Roman Satire*. Cambridge: Cambridge University Press

Gibson, R. K. (2016) *Reading the Letters of Pliny the Younger: An Introduction*. Cambridge: Cambridge University Press

Rudd, N. (1998) *Themes in Roman Satire*. London: Bloomsbury

Walsh, P. G. (2009) *Pliny: Complete Letters*. Oxford: Oxford University Press

Walsh, P. G. (2009) *Petronius: Satyricon*. Oxford: Oxford University Press

What to Expect in the Exam for Roman City Life

This chapter aims to show you the types of questions you are likely to get in the written examination. It offers some advice on how to answer the questions and will help you avoid common errors.

THE EXAMINATION

This component of the GCSE examination is designed to test your knowledge, under-standing and evaluation of Roman City Life. The examination is worth 90 marks and lasts 1 hour and 30 minutes. This represents 50% of the total marks for the GCSE.

There are two sections to the paper, one focusing on the 'Culture' topics and sources, the other focusing on the 'Literature' – the prescribed sections from Horace, Juvenal, Petronius and Pliny. Each section is worth 45 marks, and is therefore worth 25% of your GCSE. The question paper will consist of both short-answer and extended-response questions.

For the 'Culture' section, you will be required to respond to visual and material sources. Some of these will be the prescribed sources you have studied in class, and some of these you will not have seen before. Sources for the 'Literature' section will only be drawn from the prescribed sections of Horace, Juvenal, Petronius and Pliny that you have studied.

There are two Assessment Objectives in your GCSE in Classical Civilisation. Questions will be designed to test these areas. These Assessment Objectives are explained in the table below:

	Assessment Objective	Marks
AO1	Demonstrate knowledge and understanding of: • literature and visual/material culture from the classical world • how sources reflect their cultural contexts • possible interpretations of sources by different audiences and individuals.	50
AO2	Analyse, interpret and evaluate literature and visual/material culture from the classical world, using evidence and producing coherent and reasoned arguments.	40

For AO1 in this component, you will need to demonstrate the following:

Culture

- A good range of accurate and relevant knowledge of Roman city life, including sites and inscriptions.
- How the sites and inscriptions tell us about Roman city life.
- An understanding of the way the Romans lived: their housing, their family life, their social structure and their main forms of entertainment.
- Different interpretations that can be made about the sites and inscriptions from the Roman world, and the different conclusions that can be drawn from these.

Literature

- A good range of accurate and relevant knowledge of the prescribed texts.
- An understanding of the relevant genres, and of the historical and literary context in which the prescribed texts were written.
- Knowledge and understanding of the key themes of each text.
- An understanding of the literary styles of each of the authors.
- Different interpretations that can be drawn from the texts, and the conclusions that can be drawn from these.

For AO2 in this component, you will need to demonstrate that you can analyse, interpret and evaluate the sources you have studied, giving opinions and backing them up with evidence, for example:

Culture

- A range of reasoned opinions about Roman city life.
- Appropriate evaluation of different sources to provide reasoned ideas.

Literature

- A range of reasoned opinions about the genres, characters and themes of the prescribed sources, and about what they can tell us about Roman city life.
- Appropriate analysis of the genres, characters and themes of the prescribed sources, and of what they can tell us about Roman city life.

QUESTION TYPES

There are five types of questions that will feature in your exam. Each type will appear in both the Culture and Literature sections. With the exception of the extended-response questions (see below), all questions will be linked to a source. In the Culture section this will be a piece of material evidence such as a picture of a site or an inscription or a literary source. In the Literature section this will be a passage from one of the prescribed texts.

The question types are listed in the table below. They really fall into two categories: the first three types (knowledge and understanding, significance, and stimulus questions) are all short-answer questions. The final two types (detailed-response questions and extended-response questions) require a longer answer.

The final two types will usually be the final questions of each section. The short-answer questions can come in any order. For example, there could be a two-mark knowledge and understanding question, followed by a four-mark stimulus question, followed by a three-mark significance question.

Question type	Number of marks in each section for each question type
Knowledge and understanding questions	9
Significance questions	3
Stimulus questions	10
Detailed-response questions	8
Extended-response questions	15

Knowledge and understanding questions

There will be 9-marks' worth of knowledge and understanding questions in total (all AO1). The 9 marks will be broken down into a series of short-answer questions, typically worth 1, 2 or 3 marks. Some questions will require you to show your **knowledge** of one of the prescribed texts, or of an object or inscription from the Roman world. Other questions will require you to show **knowledge** and **also** demonstrate an **understanding** of these facts.

There will be a **source** to assist you. For literature, this will be a passage from one of your prescribed authors. For culture, it could be a prescribed source you have studied, or it could be one that you have not seen before.

For example, you might be shown the image on the right with the following questions:

Question: What furnishing is seen in this photo? What was it used for?   [2]

Answer: A wooden partition [1]. It was used to separate the atrium from the tablinum in this house. [1]

Knowing that this is a wooden partition is a piece of knowledge, and you can then show further understanding of this object by explaining how it was used. This answer should be brief. There is in fact no need to write full sentences if it seems that only a single word or a phrase is needed, as is the case in the first part of the answer.

The following represents a typical Literature knowledge and understanding question, together with its answer:

Source A: *Juvenal, Satire 3, lines 239–242*

When duty calls, the crowd gives way as the rich man's litter,
Rushes by, right in their faces, like some vast Liburnian galley,
While he reads, writes, sleeps inside, while sped on his way:
You know how a chair with shut windows makes you drowsy!

Question: (a) What was a Liburnian galley?   [1]
                      (b) What is it being compared to here?   [1]
Answer: A Liburnian galley was a Roman warship [1] and it is being compared
                      to a litter being carried through the streets of Rome [1]

The first part is asking for one piece of factual knowledge from the passage and the other mark is for your understanding of what it is being compared to in the passage. Remember, if you are asked to only give a certain number of facts, or make a certain number of points, you should stick to the instructions.

In this type of question, each correct fact or explanation is worth one mark. You will not be asked to evaluate ideas (e.g. whether you think that the wooden partition was a useful furnishing, or if you think that the simile of the Liburnian galley is an effective one), so do not waste time in doing so.

Significance questions

There will be one of these questions in each section. It will be split into two parts. You will be asked to give two pieces of information (2 marks AO1) and state why one or both are important or significant, or what this knowledge tells us (1 mark AO2). Look at the Literature example based on these lines from Horace's Satire 2.6:

O when shall I see you, my farm? When will I be free
To breathe the delightful forgetfulness of life's cares,
Among ancient classics, with sleep and idle hours?
When will they set before me beans, Pythagoras' kin,
And those little cabbages oiled with thick bacon-grease?

(a) Where was Horace's farm, and who had provided it for him?   [2]
(b) Suggest one way in which this farm might have been important to Horace.   [1]

The answers to part (a) are that the farm was in the Sabine Hills outside Rome [1] and that Maecenas had provided it for him [1]. For the second part, this might lead to the idea that it gave him the space and relaxation to write his best poetry for Maecenas [1] or it was a status symbol and acknowledgement of his achievements [1].

In the culture section the question might look something like this:

Source A: *Part of the garden in the House of Octavius Quartio*

Study **Source A**.

(a) Identify two key features of this garden. [2]

(b) Suggest a reason why it was important for the owner of this house to have a garden such as this. [1]

Two marks would be gained in part (a) for saying any two of: there was canal which ran the length of the garden [1], that it was decorated with statues, paintings and crossing bridges [1], that midway along the canal was a fountain [1] and that there was a small temple beyond that. You could also say that the garden was planted with rows of acanthus and fruit trees [1] and in the wall at the back was another entrance to the property [1]. Remember that you only need to make two points to get the marks – it does not help you to make more than two points.

One mark would be gained in part (b) for saying that the owner would be able to provide a beautiful view for dinner guests, or that the garden could give visitors the sense that they had left city life behind and were relaxing in the country, or that it gave the members of the household a shrine where they could worship the gods. Again, remember that you only need to make one point to gain the mark.

Stimulus questions

These questions will ask you to identify something relevant from a stimulus passage or image, and to analyse what you have recognised. Each **relevant** quotation or feature of the image that is picked out will be worth a mark, as will each piece of analysis. Therefore, these questions are each worth equal amounts of AO1 and AO2.

In the culture section, you might be given a picture of a Thracian gladiator figurine and asked:

Question: Select **two** items of Thracian equipment shown in the source, and suggest what each tells us about the combat style of the Thracian. [4]

Answer: To gain the first two marks (AO1), you might identify any two of the following items: a broad-rimmed, full face helmet; a short sword; two thigh-length greaves.

To gain the next two marks (AO2), you might make the following suggestions:

- protected his the entire head, so clearly at risk of heavy blows to it
- implies a close combat fighter
- implies he was at risk of being hamstrung or having leg broken by a heavier opponent.

Part (a) requires two pieces of knowledge and part (b) asks you to give your opinions of the evidence. You should be careful not simply to show an understanding of how it was used in the second part, but instead to give your own ideas based on the evidence.

In the Literature section, you will be given a passage and might be asked for your opinions on a character or for how the passage is made exciting. For example, you might be given the following passage from Satyricon and asked how the character of Trimalchio is portrayed, for 4 marks:

Source A: *Petronius, Satyricon 33*

While he then dug out his teeth with a silver toothpick he said, "Friends, it was not yet agreeable to me to come into the dining room, but so that you might not be delayed any longer by my absence, I have denied myself every pleasure. You will, however, permit me to finish my game." A boy followed him with a board of terebinth wood and crystal pieces, and I noticed the most luxurious thing of all. For instead of counters of black and white he had gold and silver denarii.

You would be expected to make two points of **analysis**, giving your opinions. You might say that Trimalchio is badly-mannered and that he likes to show off how wealthy he is. Two points of **evidence** to back this up would be the fact that he uses a toothpick at the dinner table and the fact that he uses silver and gold coins as pieces on a board game.

Look at the number of marks available. If there are three pieces of evidence and three pieces of analysis required, do not give more than this amount. You will be using up time that would be better spent in detailed-response and extended-response questions.

Detailed-response questions

You will get one of these questions in each section with one or more stimulus passages or images to prompt you. This stimulus is meant only as a starting point, and it will be clear from the question that you will need to bring in **extra information and examples**.

Four marks are awarded for your knowledge and understanding (AO1), and four marks given for your analysis, interpretation and evaluation of your facts and understanding

(AO2). These questions are marked in a different way, however; you are not given one mark for each correct opinion and each piece of evidence, but the answer as a whole is marked using a Levels of Response Grid. A Levels of Response Grid explains to examiners what answers may look like to achieve a certain number of marks. An examiner will read the whole answer and then check the grid to work out what level the answer belongs to. It is important to remember that the quality of your answer is more important than the amount you have written. The Levels of Response Grid is included in the mark schemes for exam papers.

It is also important to remember that for AO1 you will need to show knowledge and understanding of a source's context and the different ways people interpret the sources.

Remember that you can examine both sides of an argument. For example, if you are asked whether you admire the character of Umbricius in Juvenal's third Satire, there are likely to be arguments on both sides of the question. It may be that you largely admire him, but that he has some flaws, or that you largely do not admire him but that he has some redeeming features. If you do not examine both sides of an argument, you may have missed some key facts, and your answer may not show a full evaluation.

This question is not meant to be an essay. You are advised not to write an introduction that simply outlines how you will write your response, as this will not add anything to your answer and will take up valuable time. You may find you have more to say than time allows, so you might have to be disciplined in moving on. Make your key points at the start, keep to the point, and if you do choose to have a conclusion, keep it brief, as you will ideally have answered the precise wording of the question throughout your answer. It is not necessary to have a conclusion to gain full marks.

For example, on the paper you might be given one or more than one sources relating to the baths, and then you might be asked the following question:

'The most important reason to go to the baths was to keep clean.' To what extent do you agree with this statement? Use the sources as a starting point and your own knowledge in your answer. [8]

In order to show that you know about the baths, you might include some of these facts:

- few people had bathing facilities at home, so most Romans went everyday
- people could exercise in the palaestra first
- the tepidarium and caldarium allowed a bather to build up a sweat
- olive oil was rubbed into the body and then scraped off with a strigil
- the process finished with immersion in the cold frigidarium, which closed the pores of the skin – the whole process was very thorough
- the baths were also a social place where people could meet up with friends
- the baths were a place where wealthy Romans went to do business and be seen.

You then need to weigh up the reasons that people went to the baths:

- the fact that there were not baths in most homes meant that people needed to use the baths
- it was vital for public health that people washed properly every day

- however, exercise and keeping fit in the palaestra might be just as important for many people
- meeting up with friends was important but that could take place elsewhere, whereas bathing could not
- wealthy Romans could also do business elsewhere, but often the baths were a very important setting for this – it might be more important for them to go to the baths for this reason than for the rest of the population.

Half the marks are awarded for AO1 and for AO2, but remember this does not necessarily mean that you should give four facts and four explanations. Examiners will read your whole response and judge how good they feel it is overall.

In Section B, on Literature, a question might ask you about the importance of a theme, or the portrayal of one particular character or episode.

Extended-response questions

This type of question is different from all the other questions in two respects: there is no stimulus passage to introduce it, and you will be given a **choice** of questions to answer (there are two extended-response questions in each section, and you must do **only one**). However, it is marked using a Levels of Response Grid in the same way as the detailed-response question.

Five marks are awarded for your knowledge and understanding (AO1), and ten marks given for your analysis, interpretation and evaluation of your facts and understanding (AO2). This means more marks are awarded for how good your argument is than for simply what you know. Therefore, you might want to spend a bit of time thinking about the structure of your answer. As for the detailed-response question, it is important to remember that for AO1 you will need to show knowledge and understanding of the literary and historical context of sources and the different ways people interpret them.

Extended-response questions will be broader than the detailed-response questions, and will draw upon material from across topics of either the Literature or the Culture sections. These questions will never, however, cover both Literature and Culture. For example, whereas you might be asked a question about the baths in a detailed-response question, as shown on p. 339, an extended-response question might ask about Roman entertainment more generally, and also ask you to draw on wider knowledge of Roman city life.

The following is an example of a possible extended-response question:

'Pliny comes across as a very impressive character in his letters'. To what extent do you agree with this statement? [15]

To answer this question you should look for evidence of Pliny's character from your prescribed letters (remember too that you can get credit for introducing material from outside the prescribed sources, so if you have read other letters you could draw on these too). You might include some of these facts:

- 1.9: he is aware of his flaws when he is busy in the city; he realises how much benefit he gets from being in the country.

- 2.6: he takes a moral line about treating freedmen well at dinner and disapproves of those who do not; he gives moral advice on this to a younger man.
- 3.14: he approves of the murder of an entire household of slaves, although he admits that Macedo was cruel and arrogant.
- 4.19: he is very grateful for the excellent character of his young wife, but also talks about how much she admires him.
- 5.19: he wants to be seen as being a master who is 'gentle as a father' and wants to look after his sick freedman Zosimus.
- 6.9: he criticises the behaviour of the crowds at the races and is thankful that he is not like that.

You then need to analyse how impressive a character Pliny is. You might draw conclusions such as:

He is impressive because:

- he is self-aware about his emotional state when in the city, and of his own character flaws – this is a sign of an impressive character
- he is also concerned that people at the top of the social ladder treat those lower down it properly and respectfully
- he wants to act as a moral example to younger Romans
- he is keen for his wife to study and learn, and treats her with respect and admiration
- he shows genuine concern for the members of his household such as Zosimus
- he would prefer to write and study than to go to the races, so he is confident enough to pursue his own interests rather than simply doing what everyone else does.

He is not impressive because:

- he admits that he gets life out of balance in Rome
- he is not prepared to give freedmen his best wine, but only to share lower quality wine with them
- his approval of the murder of all the slaves in Macedo's household, including the innocent ones, seems cruel and lacking in humanity
- his letter about his wife shows that he is vain and wrapped up in his own sense of self-importance
- his letter about those who go to the games shows someone who thinks that he is superior and looks down on other people.

Key points

The following applies to both detailed-response questions and extended-response questions:

- Your facts must be **relevant**. Do not merely state everything you know about a particular topic.
- It is a common mistake in the literature to over-narrate the plot and to retell a whole story. You should instead **summarise** the main points, or focus in detail on

one or two parts of it. This is particularly important in your extended-response answer, where five marks are available for your knowledge, but ten marks are given for your evaluation, interpretation and analysis.

- Show that you **understand** things from an ancient point of view wherever possible. For example, characters in the literature texts may have had different attitudes to slavery than we would today, or Roman baths may have seemed far more luxurious to the Romans than they would do to us today.
- Evaluation is best done throughout the response. **Keep referring back** to the title in your essay to do this. If you give all your facts, and then give all your opinions, it is easy to miss something out, or to run out of time.
- Try to find a **balance** of ideas as the question will usually require you to argue both for and against an idea.
- Sometimes a piece of evidence can be taken two ways. If so, remember to give **both interpretations** in order to show a high level of understanding.
- You will not have a lot of time to do these questions and so it is always best your most important arguments first in case you find yourself running out of time.
- Ultimately make your conclusion **logical**, and supported by evidence from your whole answer, not just one part of it.

Look at these two extracts attempting to answer the question:

Question: How impressive a character does Pliny seem to you from the letters you have read?

Extract 1

Pliny is an impressive character in his letters. He had an interesting life, escaping from Mount Vesuvius and becoming a rich man who had a really big villa in the country. He was also an important person, although he preferred chillaxing in his villa. He treated his slaves well but was happy for other masters to kill their slaves as a punishment. He also treated his wife well, although she was much younger than him. She really rated him as a writer, so he must have been good. He was a bit of a snob though, as he didn't like people who went to the chariot races, which were a bit like football matches today. People could get fanatical about following their chariot teams. Apart from that, Pliny was an impressive character, and he drank cheap wine if he had to.

Extract 2

Pliny is quite an impressive character but he does have flaws. It is impressive that he cares so much for his freedman's health that he is prepared to send him to France to recuperate from illness. He also wishes to be seen as 'like a father' to his household. However, against this he also approves of the execution of all the slaves in Macedo's household, even the innocent ones – this suggests someone who can be very heartless. He treats his wife well, even though she is much younger than him: it is impressive that he encourages her to read and learn and writes a letter to her aunt to say what a good wife she is. However, Pliny can come across as very self-important in the way that he talks of her reading his books, listening to his speeches and singing his music.

Notice how the first extract spends more time on presenting the facts than giving opinions, and some of the facts are irrelevant. The evaluation is not developed fully, and the final statement is not made relevant to the question. The second extract is much more concise, and is much more balanced. It argues both sides and flows smoothly from one example to another, providing a rounded view of Pliny's character.

GENERAL EXAM SKILLS

When you are sitting the examination, read the instructions carefully so that you realise which questions are compulsory and which are optional (the only option you have is which of the two extended response questions you choose to answer). Remember that the examination will have a range of difficulty of questions; some of it is designed to be challenging, and you should not be panicked if you cannot think of an answer immediately. The following pieces of advice may seem obvious, but you should not underestimate their importance:

- The examination lasts 90 minutes and is worth 90 marks. Do not assume this means you should spend a minute per mark: in reality a lot of short questions will take less than a mark a minute and you should spend longer than a mark a minute on the longer questions.
- Both the Culture and Literature sections are worth 45 marks. Do not spend too long on whichever you choose to do first; this is especially tempting if you like the questions that have been set and feel you could say a lot.
- If you see a question that you do not know the answer to, move on quickly to another question and do not waste time thinking. Leave enough time to go back to it as during the examination you might well remember the answer.
- Stick to the question: if you are asked for facts, do not give opinions and vice versa.
- Do not try to answer a slightly different question if you wish another had been set, or if you have practised a similar one before at school.
- For detailed-response and extended-response questions, present different interpretations.
- More marks are available in the paper for opinions than knowledge or understanding. It is vital that you do not over-narrate, especially in your Literature answers.

L&C 3
War and Warfare

Introduction to War and Warfare

In this component learners will explore war and warfare in ancient Greece and Rome, with a particular focus on the Athenian, Spartan and Roman armed forces, as well as on the works of four authors who wrote about warfare, two Greek and two Roman.

The Culture section of this component comprises a study of a variety of aspects of ancient war and warfare. It is sub-divided into the following key topics: Sparta at war in the fifth century; Athens at war in the fifth century; Roman Imperial Military Systems, Tactics and Equipment; and the Romans at war. These topics will enable you to learn about the military systems in each society, and to study four important battles and conflicts: the battle of Thermopylae, the battle of Salamis, the battle of Actium and Trajan's campaigns against the Dacians. You will be encouraged to think about the impact that war and warfare had on wider society.

In the Literature section of this component you will read the work of four famous ancient writers: Homer, Tyrtaeus, Horace and Virgil. All four offer an insight into how war and warfare was viewed in their time. The epic poems of Homer and Virgil are set in the mythological past, while the shorter poems of Tyrtaeus and Horace refer to fighting in their own day. All present a compelling picture of the importance of war and warfare to their societies, and of how ideas of human heroism and dignity were forged through conflict.

EXAM OVERVIEW	J199/23

Your examination will require you to show knowledge and understanding of the material you have studied (AO1) and will require you to analyse and evaluate it (AO2), giving your opinions on areas such as characters in the literature or objects in the culture.

This component makes up 50% of your GCSE. In this component 50 marks will test your AO1 skills and 40 marks will test your AO2 skills.

There will be a distinct section of questions on the Culture section of this component, and a distinct section on the Literature material. Neither section will ask questions requiring knowledge of the other: for example, you will not be asked how far the Virgil's *Aeneid* confirms knowledge of what you have learnt in the culture section about Roman military systems.

In both sections you will be asked to answer a series of short factual questions, based around quotations or images concerning the Culture material, or around passages from the prescribed authors. Some of these will also ask for your opinions. You will be required to write longer answers in each section, worth 8 marks and 15 marks, showing knowledge and giving opinions. There will be 45 marks' worth of questions on the Culture section, and 45 marks' worth on the Literature section. You will have a choice of longer questions worth 15 marks in each section, but all other questions will be compulsory.

Culture

4.1 Sparta at War in the Fifth Century

This topic focuses on the nature of warfare in Sparta during the fifth century BC. At this time, the Greek world was not unified as one political state. Rather, it consisted of hundreds of independent 'city-states', which typically had small territories and just a few thousand inhabitants. Sparta became so powerful partly because it was much larger in size, controlling territory of about 3200 square miles. In all Greek cities, large or

S & C We have no actual evidence for Sparta in the fifth century from Sparta itself, since the city was highly secretive, nor did it produce any historians or poets during this period. Indeed, the most detailed surviving source on Spartan society is Plutarch, who lived from AD 45 to 120. Those who wrote about the city often seem to have presented an idealised picture, and it is likely that by Plutarch's time such an idealised version had grown and developed even more. We should always be aware that few facts about Sparta can be known for certain.

small, it was normal for a large proportion of the citizen body, and other residents, to be conscripted to serve in the military. However, they were only mobilized for the duration of particular campaigns. There was no such thing as a 'professional' army as we have today.

THE STRUCTURE OF SPARTAN SOCIETY

To understand the success of the Spartan army, we must try to understand the sort of society that Sparta had constructed by the fifth century BC. About two centuries earlier, they had conquered and subjugated most of the other peoples in the two regions surrounding the city of Sparta – Laconia and Messenia. When Sparta conquered these new territories, the land was re-assigned to Spartan citizens in allotments. However, these were worked by native Laconians and Messenians, who were obliged to hand over a proportion or a fixed amount of their produce to their Spartan citizen masters. These native inhabitants, now enslaved as agricultural labourers, were known by the Spartans as **helots**.

The allotments of land were designed to be large enough for the Spartan citizen to live off its income. As a result, in Sparta a larger proportion of men than in other Greek cities could afford to dedicate more of their time to warfare. They were still not 'professional' soldiers as we would understand them, since they did not make a living from waging war, nor were they 'full-time' soldiers as they lived at home with their families and were called up only for the duration of a campaign. However, they did spend more time on physical exercise than Greeks elsewhere, and they ate their daily dinners in the company of men who also formed a military unit. Furthermore, they were in principle always available for war, which was not possible for all citizens in other parts of Greece.

> **helots** a large class of enslaved native inhabitants of Messenia and Laconia who worked for their Spartan masters

However, the presence of the helots presented a significant danger for the Spartans, since they were greatly outnumbered by them (perhaps by a ratio of seven to one). Elsewhere in the Greek world, slaves were imported individually or in small groups from foreign parts. By contrast, the Spartans controlled communities of native Greeks who could more easily band together and rebel. (In the 460s, the helots did actually engage in a major revolt after Sparta was hit by an earthquake, and it took many years for the Spartans to suppress this rebellion.) So although the Spartans had a better army than other Greek cities, they needed to use it in part to keep down their enslaved population rather than to fight wars against other Greeks. For a long time, Sparta was able to wage successful external wars, but after the 460s they seem to have become more cautious about sending too many citizens abroad to fight for too long.

There was one other important group within Spartan society. When the Spartans conquered Laconia and Messenia, they left some communities to get on with their way of life, as long as they recognised Sparta's overall control of the region. They knew the people who lived in these communities

FIGURE 4.1
The vale of Sparta.

perioeci a class of people who lived in scattered, less fertile parts of Spartan territory

as the **perioeci**, which meant 'those who live around'. The perioeci tended to live in the less fertile parts of the region, and they were allowed make their living as craftsmen and traders, as well as landowners. The Spartans permitted them to run their own communities themselves, as long as they followed Sparta in matters of war and foreign policy. Therefore, if the Spartans went to war, they would call up members of the perioeci to fight with them. Indeed, by the fifth century the perioeci were an integral part of the Spartan army.

TRAINING AND RECRUITMENT

The main source of information about Spartan education is Plutarch, so there is no way of knowing how accurately he represents the nature of a system from centuries before his time. However, in his view, Spartan education aimed to prepare each Spartan boy to be a highly trained and unquestioningly loyal citizen. This apparently started from the moment of birth. Babies were inspected by a committee of elders and, if considered deformed or too weak, they were left on a mountainside to die of exposure.

agoge the training school that all Spartan boys attended from the age of seven

At the age of seven, a Spartan boy began his training in the school for citizen boys known as the **agoge**, a word which literally meant 'rearing'. The boy was put into a pack, each led by prefects, young men in their late teens. All the boys were under constant supervision and the prefects could whip the boys for any offence. Little reading or writing was taught – only enough to train them for basic literacy. Instead, a great deal of time was spent developing physical strength and obedience. Music was also an important aspect of their education. By learning to sing and dance in choral competitions, the boys were taught the value of precise movement and teamwork.

When they reached their teens, the training became even more intensive. Boys were trained to go barefoot at all times so that they could run faster, scale heights more easily and clamber down cliffs. They had to cut their hair short and were allowed only one cloak for the whole year, whatever the weather. This of course helped foster a sense of equality amongst all boys. Food was deliberately rationed to make them used to doing without it on a military campaign if necessary, and as a result the boys were forced to steal to get more. If they were caught, they were beaten 'for stealing carelessly'. In fact, any offence was punishable by beatings. When walking in the streets, the youths were forced to stay silent and keep their eyes fixed on the ground ahead of them, in order to show respect.

krypteia a period of survival training for the strongest Spartans in their mid-to-late teens

When they were in their late teens, the strongest youths were enlisted into the **krypteia**. It is not clear exactly what this unit was designed to do, but it seems to have been a form of 'survival training' for these young Spartans, during which they were sent out into the countryside of Laconia and Messenia and given minimal rations so that they had to live off the land. Plutarch also suggests that a further purpose of the unit was to kill any helot they thought presented a danger to Sparta.

syssitia dining-clubs of about fifteen Spartan citizens, which met every evening and shared a tent together on campaign

The syssitia

In order for a young Spartan to gain full citizenship after leaving the agoge, he had to be elected into one of a number of dining-clubs, known as **syssitia** (singular: syssition).

Each syssition had about fifteen members who were expected to eat together every night. The food they shared was relatively simple fare, further encouraging equality among the men. When on campaign, the members of a syssition also shared a tent together. The syssition was a key element in the success of Spartan society, since it bred comradeship, and ensured that different generations of Spartans mixed with one another.

EQUIPMENT AND TACTICS

The fully-armed soldier in the Greek world was called a **hoplite**, from the Greek word 'hopla', meaning 'weapons'. The basic item of a Spartan hoplite's uniform was a tunic, over which a cuirass of bronze (later of linen) protected the torso. To protect his legs a hoplite wore bronze greaves (shin-guards), while leather boots were also used in battle. A helmet completed the uniform. Early in the fifth century this was made of bronze and plumed in the Corinthian style. It gave great protection to the head, but did not make vision or hearing very easy. During the fifth century, Spartans stopped wearing this type of helmet and replaced it with a very open-faced, crestless helmet. In addition, Spartan men wore their hair long to make them appear larger in stature and more frightening in battle.

> **hoplite** a heavily-armed Greek infantry soldier who fought in the phalanx

A Spartan hoplite carried three important weapons:

- **Shield** The Spartan shield was two-handled and large (up to a metre in diameter). It was made of wood and bronze and fitted onto the left forearm. It was inscribed with a capital lambda –Λ– the Greek letter L, which stood for 'Lacedaemonians', the collective name of the Spartans and the perioeci.
- **Spear** The spear was made of wood and had an iron head. It was held in the right hand.
- **Sword** If the hoplite lost his spear or fought his enemy at close quarters, he could resort to using a short iron sword, which hung on the right side of a belt around his waist.

The bronze warrior statuette shown in Figure 4.3, about 10 cm in height, was found in Sparta, and shows a heavily armed hoplite of the sixth century. There would originally have been a spear in his right hand, and so the image gives a good idea of the forward thrusting motion a hoplite would have made with his spear during battle. Notice, too, that the hoplite is wearing the Corinthian-style helmet, which would go out of fashion in the following century. It is also interesting that the hoplite is tilting back his shield so as to rest it on his shoulder as well as on his arm. This suggests that it was heavy and offered a lot of protection, but also that it needed a lot of effort to handle it.

The bronze helmet in Figure 4.4 is a good example of a fifth-century hoplite helmet in the Corinthian style. The inscription on it says that the helmet was a spoil of victory for the Argives against the Corinthians, and that the Argives dedicated it to Zeus in his sanctuary at Olympia. It was common for Greeks to dedicate weapons and armour to the gods

FIGURE 4.2
A hoplite.

to thank them for a victory, although such dedications went out of fashion shortly after this one was made.

The Spartans were masters of the **phalanx**, the standard method of fighting in the Greek world during the fifth century. The phalanx was a rectangular formation, a number of rows deep, with soldiers closely packed together in each row. In battle, most Greek phalanxes charged at each other and, when they met, a soldier would thrust at an opponent with his spear, attempting to hit an unprotected area on his body. If a hoplite in the front row fell, the man behind him would step up to take his place. Each hoplite held his shield in his left hand and so often depended on his neighbour's shield to protect his exposed right side. The phalanx was therefore a team effort and soldiers needed to maintain tight discipline. Any disruption to the front line could rip a hole in the formation, at which point the soldiers would have to turn and flee, and the battle would be lost.

The lifestyle of the Spartan citizen ensured that he was in prime physical condition if he needed to fight. The focus and intensity of the Spartans in battle is perhaps suggested by the fact that they were very unusual in the Greek world in approaching an opposing phalanx at a deliberate pace rather than at a run. Another strategy the Spartans employed was a policy of trying not to come up against an enemy too often, so that their tactics would remain a mystery and they would be more difficult to fight against.

---

phalanx a Greek rectangular fighting formation in which men fought in massed ranks and tried to force their way through the enemy phalanx opposing them

---

PRESCRIBED SOURCE

Bronze Warrior Figure

Date: 6th century BC

Location: British Museum; found in Sparta

Significance: a small statuette of a Spartan warrior in armour from the 6th century

---

PRESCRIBED SOURCE

Bronze Helmet of Corinthian Type

Date: *c.* 460 BC

Location: British Museum; found at Olympia

Significance: a good example of a Corinthian-style helmet

FIGURE 4.3
Bronze Warrior Figure from Sparta.

FIGURE 4.4
A Corinthian-type helmet dedicated at Olympia.

THE STRUCTURE AND COMMAND OF THE ARMY

A further key feature of Spartan success was its efficient command structure. The army was led on campaign by one of the two kings who jointly ruled in Sparta. The Spartans believed that their kings were descended from Heracles, and they were also Sparta's religious leaders, so it must have been inspiring to have a king fight in battle with them. The actual divisions of the army seem to have changed during the years of the fifth century, and no source gives an entirely clear picture of how the army was divided up at any one point. However, it seems that the largest sub-division of the Spartan army was a regiment often known in Greek as a **mora**. The smallest unit of the Spartan army was the **enomotia**, which meant the 'sworn-band', it probably consisted of about forty men, similar to a modern platoon. This was a distinctive feature of the Spartan army, as other ancient Greek armies do not seem to have had units this small. It is likely that the enōmotia was in some way linked to the syssition, so that two or three syssitia made up an enōmotia. The enomotia was therefore probably a further way to breed comradeship. It is likely that the members of the enomotia swore the following oath:

> I shall not desert my taxiarch or the leader of my enomotia, whether he is alive or dead, and I shall not leave the battlefield unless our commanders lead us away.

From *The Oath of Plataea*

> **mora** (pl. **morai**) a name for a Spartan army regiment
>
> **enomotia** a 'sworn-band', the smallest unit of the Spartan army

> **taxiarch** a senior commander in the Spartan army

The **taxiarch** mentioned here was a senior officer who was directly responsible to the kings, who are described here as commanders. The fact that with this pledge a Spartan soldier swore not to desert the officers above him illustrates how important loyalty and discipline was to the Spartan army.

The perioeci and helots were also used on campaign. For example, at the battle of Plataea in 479, 5,000 Spartan citizens were joined by 5,000 perioeci and 35,000 helots. Perioeci were used both as hoplite fighters and as craftsmen to repair weaponry and equipment. By the end of the fifth century, when Spartan citizen manpower had declined, the perioeci even fought in the same units as Spartan citizens. Helots carried equipment and supplies, cooked and ran errands for their Spartan owners, but sometimes they also served in much greater numbers as light-armed troops, as they did at Plataea. In order to prevent helots from rebelling while on campaign, Spartan citizens always carried their spears with them in camp and kept a close guard on the weapon store.

THE IDEALISATION OF WAR AND WARFARE

Once again, we are reliant on non-Spartan sources to help us try to understand the extent to which war and warfare was idealised within Spartan society. This makes it difficult, but one thing that other Greek sources emphasise is how highly the Spartans valued a noble death in battle, not least Spartan women. One famous anecdote records that a Spartan mother sent her son off to battle with the words: 'either with your shield or on

EXPLORE FURTHER

Read Thucydides' account (5.64–74) of the battle of Mantinea fought in 418 by Sparta and its allies against an army led by Argos and Athens. What can we learn about Sparta's use of the hoplite phalanx from this passage?

Study questions

1 How did the structure of Spartan society allow its army to have such an advantage over the armies of other Greek cities?
2 Can you think of other societies where a large group of people has been enslaved by a much smaller, militarily stronger group?

it', meaning the one thing for a Spartan soldier to avoid was to return defeated, having deserted in battle and lost his shield. Rather, the son was either to return victorious carrying his shield, or with his dead body carried on it.

Moreover, Spartan women were taught to show no emotion except pride for a fallen relative. One story by the fourth century historian Xenophon, who spent time in Sparta and so knew their society well, illustrates this. In 371, after the news of a defeat to the Thebans at the battle of Leuctra was relayed to Sparta, he reported that:

> On the following day you could see those women whose relatives had been killed going about in public looking bright and happy, while as for those whose relatives had been reported living, there were not many of them to be seen, and those who were to be seen were walking about looking gloomy and sorry for themselves.
>
> Xenophon, *Hellenika*, 6.4.16

Xenophon also gives us interesting information about those Spartans who deserted in battle. They were deprived of citizenship and referred to as **tresantes** instead – tresantes means 'tremblers' and of course implies that they were afraid. Xenophon explains how the tresantes were treated in Spartan society:

> **tresantes** 'tremblers' – Spartans who had deserted in battle and so been deprived of citizenship

> In other cities the coward suffers nothing more than the stigma of cowardice – he goes to the same market-place as the brave man, sits with him and attends the same gymnasium if he wishes. In Sparta anyone would think it a disgrace to take a coward into his mess or be matched against him in a wrestling bout . . . [a coward] must give way to others in the street, and rise even for younger men when seated . . . he must not go about the city looking cheerful, nor must he imitate those who are without reproach; if he does, he must submit to a beating from his betters. When such disabilities are attached to cowardice, I am not surprised that Spartans prefer death to such a deprived and disgraceful existence.
>
> Xenophon, *The Constitution of the Spartans*, 9.4–6

One important point in this passage is that tresantes could be beaten – in other Greek cities, corporal punishment was reserved for slaves alone.

THE BATTLE OF THERMOPYLAE

The battle of Thermopylae, which took place in 480 BC, was the most famous battle in Spartan history, even though it ended in a defeat for the Spartans. Our main source for the battle is the historian Herodotus, who was writing in the third quarter of the fifth century. His account was based on a number of different sources, most of them spoken rather than written. By his day, the battle had entered Spartan folklore, so we might think of his account more as the version of events that the Spartans had chosen to remember and idealise.

KEY INDIVIDUAL

Xerxes the Persian king and leader of the invasion in 480

In 480, the vast Persian Empire to the east of Greece invaded the Greek mainland with a huge force, led by their king **Xerxes**. Only a minority of Greek cities chose to stand and fight the invasion force – about thirty out of several hundred. In fact, some

Greeks even encouraged the Persians to invade and worked with them when they came. As the Persians advanced into northern Greece in the summer of 480 – where they met little resistance – the Greek allies debated what to do. They decided to send an advance party to try to block the Persians in narrow pass in central Greece, where the mountains met the sea, and where it was easy for a small number of men to hold back a large army. The pass was called 'Thermopylae', literally 'hot gates' since the area contained hot springs. Herodotus tells us that this advance party consisted of about 7,000 men. The Spartans contributed 300 men to accompany their king, **Leonidas**; all of the 300 had to be fathers of living sons, so that, if they died, they had provided future warriors for the state.

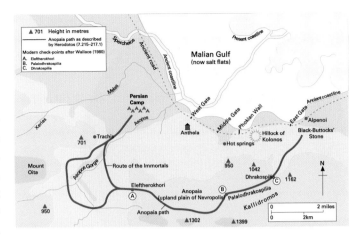

FIGURE 4.5
A plan of the battle of Thermopylae.

The Greek allies reached the pass at Thermopylae before the Persians did. Herodotus tells us that it was very narrow – just wide enough for two wagons to pass between the foot of the mountains and the sea. Led by the Spartans, the Greeks rebuilt an old wall at the narrowest point of the pass, and waited. On the Persian side, king Xerxes did not know what to do, and so he summoned one of his key advisers, **Demaratus**. Remarkably, Demaratus was a former Spartan king who had been deposed, after which he had defected to the Persians. Xerxes had welcomed him as a trusted adviser on Greek affairs. Demaratus had warned Xerxes about the extraordinary courage of the Spartans when he had asked about them:

> First then, they will not under any circumstances accept terms from you which would mean slavery for Greece; secondly, they will fight you even if the rest of Greece submits. Moreover, there is no use in asking if their numbers are adequate to enable them to do this; suppose a thousand of them take the field – then that thousand will fight you, and so will any number, greater than this or less.

Herodotus, *Histories*, 7.102

Xerxes simply laughed at Demaratus when he heard this, but he was soon to learn that he was right. There was a tense stand-off for four days, while the Persian king waited in hope that the Greeks would retreat, terrified by the number of Persian forces facing them. During this time he sent a spy on horseback to survey the Greek camp. He was astonished when the spy reported back that the Spartans were readying themselves for battle by combing their hair. Demaratus explained to Xerxes that the men were preparing themselves for a glorious death in battle.

Day 1

After four days, Xerxes' patience finally gave up, and he sent in his troops. The battle continued all day, and the Persians suffered heavy losses. Even though there were so many of them they did not have the equipment or skill to match the hoplite tactics of

FIGURE 4.6
The site of the pass at Thermopylae today, where the sea is no longer nearby.

FIGURE 4.7
A drinking cup (kylix) showing a Persian and a Greek fighting.

PRESCRIBED SOURCE

Red figure Kylix of a Persian and a Greek fighting, the Triptolemos Painter

Date: *c.* 460 BC

Location: National Museums of Scotland; made in Attica, Greece

Significance: a painting of an imagined scene from the Persian Wars

KEY INDIVIDUAL

Ephialtes a local Greek who told Xerxes about the mountain path to the other side of the pass at Thermopylae

the Greeks, and the narrow space evened up the contest. Late in the day, the Persians decided to send in their elite troops – the King's Immortals – who advanced confidently. However, even they were beaten back and suffered great losses. It was at this point that the Spartans successfully employed the tactic of pretending to withdraw, thereby sucking in more of the enemy, and then turning to fight them suddenly. During the day, Xerxes sat and watched the battle and apparently three times jumped up from his chair in terror for what was happening to his army.

The scene on the inside of the Greek-style drinking cup in Figure 4.7 shows a Greek hoplite poised to kill a fallen Persian soldier. The fact that the two are both using swords may suggest that the hoplite has lost his spear and so has pulled out his sword as a secondary weapon. The scene well illustrates the difference in armour and weapons between the two. The heavily armed hoplite carries a round shield with a Pegasus motif. He towers over the Persian, who is easily recognised from his dress. He wears heavy clothing but no armour.

Day 2

The Persians fared little better on the second day of the battle. The Greeks continued to rotate their front-line troops, so allowing their men to rest, and they suffered few losses. Xerxes had no idea how to resolve the situation, but then he had a stroke of luck. A local Greek, **Ephialtes**, hoping for a huge reward, came to the King and told him of a path over the mountains that could lead his troops to the other side of the pass. That evening, Xerxes sent another band of elite troops up along the mountain path so that they could attack the Greeks from the rear and trap them in the pass. The Persian troops made easy progress. Although a division of Greek troops had been posted to defend the mountain pass, they withdrew when they heard the Persians approaching.

Day 3

As dawn broke on the third day, the Greek forces learnt from scouts returning from the hills that they were about to be surrounded. While Leonidas dismissed most of the Greek forces, it was unthinkable for the Spartans to desert a battle and so they stayed, along with 700 Thespians and 400 Thebans (these Thebans surrendered early in the final engagement), as well as an unknown number of perioeci and helots. The remaining Spartans knew that they would all die that day, but did not flinch from fighting with extraordinary bravery. We are told by Herodotus that when their spears were broken, they fought with their swords, and when these were broken they resorted to fighting with their hands and teeth. Their great courage and resolution was epitomised by one comment from a Spartan warrior called **Dienekes**. Herodotus tells the story as follows:

> Of all the Spartans and Thespians who fought so valiantly the most signal proof of courage was given by the Spartan Dienekes. It is said that before the battle he was told by a native of Trachis [*a local region of Greece*] that, when the Persians shot their arrows, there were so many of them that they hid the sun. Dienekes, however, quite unmoved by the thought of the strength of the Persian army, merely remarked: 'This is pleasant news that the stranger from Trachis brings us: if the Persians hide the sun, we shall have our battle in the shade'. He is said to have left on record other sayings too, by which he will be remembered.

Herodotus, *Histories*, 7.226

KEY INDIVIDUAL

Dienekes one of the 300 Spartans who was remembered for his brave comments before the battle began

Led by the 300 Spartans, the Greek allies again inflicted great losses on the Persians. However, once the allies were surrounded, it was only a matter of time before they were all killed.

King Leonidas was incredibly brave in the face of death. Before the Persians invaded, the Delphic Oracle had informed the Spartans that their city would either be conquered or that they would mourn the death of a king. In short, when Leonidas set out to defend the pass at Thermopylae, he believed that his death would be the necessary price for Sparta's survival. After the battle, the Persians found his body lying amongst those of the other Greeks. Persians normally showed respect to the dead of their enemies, but in his fury Xerxes ordered the body of Leonidas to be decapitated. His head was driven onto a stake, where it rotted in public.

FIGURE 4.8
The modern memorial to the Spartans at Thermopylae.

Even though the Persians won the battle, the example shown by the Spartans at Thermopylae inspired the other Greeks for the coming battles. Although the Greeks had lost this battle, they would go on to beat back the Persian invasion. Herodotus records that an inscription was set up at the spot:

> Go tell the Spartans, you who read,
> we took their orders, and here lie dead.

Herodotus, *Histories*, 7.228

This was one of a number of memorials set up to commemorate the sacrifice of the Spartans at Thermopylae. Herodotus tells us that he was able to learn the names of every one of the Spartan soldiers – as well as their fathers' names. The event was even remembered in Sparta even centuries later. A Greek travel writer called Pausanias who visited the city in the early second century AD, reported that a memorial was still in place with the names of the 300 and their fathers' names.

ACTIVITY

Imagine that you are Leonidas. Write a speech that you will deliver to your men before the battle starts.

S & C Herodotus gives a moving account of the battle of Thermopylae in his *Histories*, 7.198–233. We know that he visited Sparta, and he would have learnt there about the tradition of the battle. What can we learn about the Spartan ideal of military heroism from this account?

For comparison, you can also read an account of the battle by a later historian, Diodorus Siculus, in his *Universal History* 11.5–11. How does his account differ?

Study questions

1 Why do you think that the Spartans remembered the battle of Thermopylae so proudly, despite the fact that it was a military defeat?

2 From what you have learnt about the Spartan army, why do you think that the Spartans were able to hold their ground against the Persians at Thermopylae for so long?

TOPIC REVIEW

You should be able to:

1. Describe:
   - the social structure of Sparta and the training of Spartan soldiers
   - the arms and armour used by Spartan hoplites, and the nature of phalanx fighting
   - the structure of the Spartan army
   - the key events and individuals involved in the battle of Thermopylae.

2. Explain:
   - the importance of the army to Spartan society
   - how Spartan education prepared boys for war
   - why the Spartan army was so successful against its enemies
   - why the battle of Thermopylae became so legendary in Sparta, even though it was a military defeat.

PRACTICE QUESTIONS

Source A: Account of the battle of Thermopylae, Herodotus, Histories, 7.223–224

The Greeks, who knew that the enemy were on their way round the mountain track, and that death was inevitable, put forth all their strength and fought with fury and desperation. By this time most of their spears were broken, and they were killing Persians with their swords.

1. Explain how a Spartan hoplite would use a spear and a sword in battle. [2]
2. In what ways did the Spartans show bravery at Thermopylae? Use the source as a starting point and your own knowledge in your answer. [8]

4.2 Athens at War in the Fifth Century

During the fifth century, Athens grew to become the most powerful Greek city, eventually controlling an empire that consisted of hundreds of other smaller Greek cities. Most of these were dotted around the Aegean Sea. The city's key strength lay in its navy, and it was this that allowed it to gain so much power, although that is not to say that it did not have a strong army. This topic will look first at the Athenian army and it will then focus on the Athenian navy – in each case, the first three bullet points in the topic overview will be treated together as a whole. It will finish with an examination of the famous Athenian-led Greek victory over the Persians in a naval battle at Salamis in 480.

THE ATHENIAN ARMY

One key difference between Athens and Sparta was the way in which the military in each city was funded. In Sparta, while individual hoplites were well-funded by income from land cultivated by helots, there was little money in the public treasury. This meant that it was difficult for the Spartan government to find funds for large endeavours needing a reserve of collective money, such as building fleets and maintaining sieges. In Athens, by contrast, for much of the fifth century the city had a large public treasury that could more easily fund significant campaigns.

As in Sparta, all adult male Athenian citizens were expected to serve in the military when required to do so (although men over the age of sixty were exempt). Those citizens wealthy enough to do so would buy their own sets of hoplite armour. As in the rest of the Greek world, the Athenians fought in the phalanx formation. The armour and weapons used by an Athenian hoplite were very similar to those used by a Spartan hoplite, although the Athenian did not of course have the distinctive 'lambda' on his shield. If a man was not wealthy enough to buy a full set of armour, then he made do with what he could. A shield and spear were the two most essential items. We have little evidence for the training given to Athenian soldiers, but they would not have had the same amount of time to dedicate to physical fitness that the Spartans had.

It is important to be aware that a large number of Athenian citizens were unable to afford any of the equipment required to serve as a hoplite in the army – estimates for the number of hoplites in the Athenian army vary from thirty to fifty per cent of the citizen population, and so somewhere between fifty and seventy per cent of citizens would have fought as light-armed troops. In a battle, a light-armed soldier might throw stones, javelins or arrows from a distance. At the other end of the economic spectrum, the very wealthiest citizens could afford to keep a horse and serve in the cavalry. A cavalryman carried one important weapon, a spear. The cavalry divisions were led by three commanders and divided into ten units based on tribe (see below). While Athens was renowned for its navy, it also had a strong land army and Athenian soldiers had a particularly strong reputation for siege craft.

There is good evidence for the command structure of the Athenian army during the fifth century. It had ten regiments, each one provided by one of the city's ten **tribes** (a tribe was a political constituency). We know the names of these tribal regiments, the areas from which they were recruited, and the fact that they were subdivided into smaller units called **lochoi** (singular, lochos) – although we do not know the size or make-up of these lochoi. Each tribe elected a general, known as a **strategos**, on an annual basis, and collectively the ten generals made the key decisions for the army, voting if necessary to resolve a disagreement. As in Sparta, the second most senior officers in the Athenian army were the taxiarchs, of which there was also one for each tribe.

Figure 4.9 shows a frieze on a temple built on the Athenian Acropolis in the 420s BC. A **frieze** is a sculptured horizontal decoration depicting a scene or a number of scenes, and this one was dedicated to Athena Nike – Athena the goddess of victory – and celebrates scenes from famous Athenian military victories. The south frieze shows hoplites fighting against Persians, some of them on horses. The Persian forces are recognisable from their thick, belted jackets, with long sleeves and tight-fitting trousers. By contrast, the Athenian soldiers are naked apart from their armour – Greek artists often depicted male subjects naked to emphasise the strength of their bodies. This frieze is usually taken to depict an Athenian victory against the Persians, most probably the battle of Marathon in 490.

tribes one of ten political constituencies in Athens. Every Athenian citizen belonged to a tribe, which made up a regiment of the Athenian army.

lochoi units of a tribal regiment in the Athenian army

strategos an elected general in the Athenian army; every tribe elected one each year

frieze a horizontal sculptured or painted decoration depicting a scene or number of scenes

THE ATHENIAN NAVY

The Athenians focused on developing their naval power in the late 480s as they prepared for the Persian invasion. During these years, they greatly expanded their navy so that their fleet came to number about 200 ships. This was comfortably the largest navy in the Greek world, and their decision paid off when in 480 they led their Greek allies to a stunning naval victory over the Persians in the bay of Salamis near Athens (see p. 364).

The Athenian fleet was primarily made up of triremes. A **trireme** was a long, thin ship, typically about 35 metres in length, with a bronze-plated ram extending out from its front. The ship's low centre of gravity gave it stability in the water. It was rowed by 170 men, who sat in three banks, one above the other, on either side of the ship (the name 'trireme' literally meant 'three rowers'). The lower two rows each had twenty-seven rowers on each side; the upper row had thrity-one men on each side. In addition to the rowers, there would be about thirty other men on board, including ten hoplites who served as marines, four archers, a piper who sounded time for the rowers, as well as officers such as a steersman, a quartermaster, and a trierarch (see below). As we have seen, the rowers were normally drawn from the poorer classes of society who could offer their services for pay if rowers were being hired – except in an emergency, service in the fleet was not compulsory. The Athenians usually needed more rowers than they could find from the citizen population, and so their navy often contained a significant number of slaves, as well as mercenaries from other cities.

The navy was largely paid for out of the public treasury, including pay for the rowers and the building of ships. However, this state funding was supplemented by a super-tax on the wealthiest citizens, called a **liturgy**. This required them to pay for something of great civic importance each year (the word 'liturgy' meant 'service to the public'). One of the most prestigious liturgies was payment for the upkeep of a trireme for one year, and the wealthy Athenian who paid for this liturgy was called a **trierarch**. He was responsible for repairs and replacement of anything damaged during the year, while if he

trireme a Greek warship
with three banks of
rowers on each side

liturgy a super-tax on the
wealthiest citizens in
Athens to fund important
civic projects

trierarch a wealthy
Athenian who captained
and paid for the upkeep of
a trireme for one year

FIGURE 4.10
A modern reconstruction of an Athenian trireme.

FIGURE 4.11
Rowers on a trireme.

ACTIVITY
Create your own model, drawing or plan of a Greek trireme.

diekplous a naval manoeuvre whereby a trireme sailed through the enemy line of ships and turned at pace to ram the side of an enemy ship

hypozomata two stretched cables that were tied from one end of a trireme to another and kept it in shape

relief (from the Latin verb 'relevo', 'to raise') a carving that projects from, and is a part of, the same background material, and has the effect of shading and being in 3D

was ambitious he might also offer bonus payments in order to attract the best quality rowers to his ship. It seems that many trierarchs relished taking on this liturgy, since it allowed them to show off their wealth and gain popularity and prestige in the city. On board, the trierarch was technically in command of the ship, although in practice he was likely to allow the more experienced steersman to make the key decisions.

Naval warfare involved two main tactics. Traditionally, a naval battle had been little more than a land battle at sea. Ships would come alongside one another and the marines on deck would try to board and take possession of the other ship, using grappling irons; the rowers simply had to manoeuvre the ships to enable this. However, during the fifth century the practice of ramming became more popular (one of the earliest records of effective ramming is at the battle of Salamis). There was one tactic at sea which needed special skill at sailing and ramming, and this was called the **diekplous**. This involved a ship sailing through a gap in the line of its enemy and then turning at speed to ram the side of an enemy ship from the rear. Ramming from this direction made it slightly easier to withdraw from the damaged enemy ship, which must have been hard to do.

Such a manoeuvre required great skill. Since the Athenians had by far the largest navy in Greece, their regular experience of fighting at sea meant that their rowers were usually experienced, fit and battle ready. Moreover, the Athenians normally factored in a few days at the start of a campaign to practise their rowing. By contrast, most other cities tended not to keep much of a regular navy, so the Athenians had a great advantage on the water, much as the Spartans did on land. There is also some evidence that the Athenians kept improving their triremes so that they gave them advantage over their opponents. For example, they introduced two great cables that stretched down the middle of the hull the whole length of the ship. These were known as the **hypozomata**, and were set at a tension that kept the ship in shape and gave it greater strength when ramming. The hypozomata were considered an important and secret Athenian invention, and it was illegal to export them from the city.

The **relief** shown in Figure 4.12 was dedicated on the Acropolis in Athens, and is one of the very few images of a trireme that has come down to us. The main piece of what

S & C

During the 1980s, a team of archaeologists tried to build a trireme based on ancient records of how they were constructed. The ship was named *Olympias*, and you can read more about it here: http://www.triremeolympias.com/home.html. With an inexperienced crew, the trireme was able to reach a speed of 9 knots (17 km per hour) and to turn through 180 degrees within a minute, in an arc no wider than two and a half ship-lengths. This experiment suggested that the accounts of trireme battles by ancient historians were believable and likely to be accurate.

EXPLORE FURTHER

Read about a naval battle between Athenian and Corinthian ships in 429 in Thucydides 2.83–85. What can we learn about trireme naval tactics from this passage?

FIGURE 4.12
Lenormant trireme relief

PRESCRIBED SOURCE

Lenormant trireme relief

Date: *c.* 410 BC

Material: marble

Location: Acropolis Museum, Athens

Significance: one of very few images of an ancient Greek trireme

survives of the dedication shows a trireme being rowed; there are three banks of oars, with the rowers in the top bank clearly visible. Another surviving piece from the dedication fitted at the top right. This is thought to be the hero Paralos, whom the Athenians believed had invented navigation, and to whom the relief was dedicated. The ship was called the Paralos after him, and was a sacred trireme used for official state business.

THE IMPACT OF THE MILITARY ON ATHENIAN POLITICS AND SOCIETY

As we have seen, being a citizen of Athens was bound up with serving in the military. The Athenians elected their generals on an annual basis, and so the citizen body could choose who would lead them in war. We have also seen that wealthy Athenians could gain prestige in the city through serving as a trierarch.

There were other ways in which the Athenian military impacted on Athenian politics and society. In about 508, the Athenians had established a new political system, which came to be called 'democracy'. This gave extensive power to citizens to vote in the citizens' assembly and serve in the political system. For the first years of the new system, it was unclear whether it would survive, not least because the city was threatened by the

Study question
We have far fewer images of ships than we do of hoplite and cavalry fighters from ancient Athens. Why do you think that land fighting was a more natural topic for Athenian artists to focus on?

Persian Empire. The former tyrant of Athens, Hippias, was now with the Persians and hoped to be restored to power with Persian backing. In 490, the Persians launched an attack on Athenian soil, landing at Marathon on the east coast of Attica. Despite being outnumbered, the Athenians won a remarkable victory with the help of some soldiers from their allies from the city of Plataea. This was a key moment in the development of the Athenian democratic system, since the hoplites were largely drawn from the middle ranks of Athenian society. The traditionally powerful aristocrats realised that they had to depend on their hoplite force for defence, and the later thinker Aristotle commented that the Athenian common people grew in confidence as a result of this victory.

A similar effect seemed to happen ten years later, when the Athenians led the Greeks in a remarkable naval victory at Salamis (described below). During the late 480s, the Athenians had developed a policy of significantly increasing the size of their navy, believing that this was the best form of defence against the Persians. The bulk of the rowers in the Athenian fleet were drawn from the lower classes, as we have seen, and after the victory at Salamis, Athens became a naval superpower in the Greek world for the rest of the fifth century, controlling many other Greek cities. It is often thought that the victory at Salamis helped to establish Athenian democracy in its fullest form, since the Athenian state now relied upon its rowers first and foremost for its defence.

Throughout the fifth century, the topic of warfare was ever present in the Athenian consciousness, something that is clear from the ancient sources. Those who gave their lives in battle were held in great esteem: each year, a prominent Athenian made a speech in the city's main cemetery commemorating those men who had died in war during the previous twelve months. Moreover, the sons of soldiers who had fallen in battle were educated at the expense of the state and given a suit of armour upon reaching manhood. However, there are also other voices more critical of war: the comic playwright Aristophanes wrote a number of plays during the late fifth century in which objections to war and its effect on daily life are made. Perhaps the most celebrated example is his play *Lysistrata*, in which the heroine Lysistrata is an Athenian woman who tries to meet with women from other Greek cities to see if they can put a stop to the Peloponnesian War (by agreeing to a sex strike).

There are many examples of the impact of warfare on wider society and on non-combatants. One famous one comes early in the Peloponnesian War fought between Athens and Sparta, and their respective allies, between 431 and 404. In 431, the Athenians decided to bring all those who lived in the countryside around Athens inside the walls of the city, so that the Spartans would not be able to attack and kill them. This may have been a sound strategic move, but it had devastating consequences for health and hygiene in the city. As a result, a terrible plague broke out in 430 (it may have been typhus), and perhaps as many as 75,000 to 100,000 people were killed – about a quarter of the population.

EXPLORE FURTHER

You can read Thucydides' moving and terrifying description of the effects of the plague on victims at 2.47–55.

EXPLORE FURTHER

Read Herodotus' account of the battle of Salamis in *Histories* 8.40–96.

THE BATTLE OF SALAMIS

As at Thermopylae, Herodotus is our main source for this battle. He lived for part of his life in Athens so he would have known well Athenian folklore about the victory that the city did so much to achieve. Herodotus tells how after Thermopylae the Persians marched south

**S
&
C** Three other accounts of the battle of Salamis have survived for us to read. The first comes in a tragic play, *Persians* (lines 331–461), written by Aeschylus and first performed in 472. Aeschylus probably fought in the battle, and his account is worth reading, even if it is clearly framed within a fictionalised narrative of the Persian response to their defeat. The other two come centuries later, in the *Universal History* of Diodorus Siculus (11.14–18), and in Plutarch's *Life of Themistocles* (9–16). Read these accounts. What are the differences and similarities between them? How does the style of each author differ?

towards Athens. At the same time as the battle at Thermopylae, the Persian and Greek navies had been engaged in a series of skirmishes at the nearby Cape Artemisium. However, when the Persians broke Thermopylae, the Greek ships turned tail to defend southern Greece. The Persian navy did not pursue them, but made their way south at their own pace.

The Persian army marched south through central Greece, brutally sacking those cities that had opposed it, but sparing those that had taken the Persian side. However, the focal point of the Persian march was Athens, the city that had dared to stand up to it since 499, and had administered a humiliating defeat on the Persian army at Marathon in 490. The Persians clearly hoped for revenge. However, when they arrived at the city, they found it almost empty, with just a few people remaining on the Acropolis. What had happened to the Athenians?

FIGURE 4.13
Themistocles.

The Athenian strategy

Long before the Persians had reached Thermopylae, the Athenians debated how to meet the Persian advance. After seeking advice from the oracle of Apollo at Delphi, they debated what to do. Some Athenians wanted to remain in the city, but the leading Athenian politician **Themistocles** persuaded them otherwise. He would go on to be the tactical genius who oversaw the Greek victory. The men of fighting age sailed to the nearby island of Salamis in their triremes, while most of the women, children and elderly took refuge in two allied cities, Aegina and Troezen. The Persians arrived in an empty city, looted the temples of the Acropolis and burnt them to the ground. Archaeology has revealed evidence of this burning of the city, as there is a 'burn-level' that corresponds to this exact period. The Athenians could only watch the smoke rising from nearby Salamis.

KEY INDIVIDUAL

Themistocles the Athenian leader who convinced the Athenians to abandon their city for Salamis, and who then brilliantly commanded the Greek navy in the sea battle against the Persians

Preparations for battle

The Greeks

After withdrawing from Artemisium, the Greek naval commanders brought their ships to harbour on the east side of the island of Salamis. Herodotus lists twenty-one different cities that provided ships for the Greek fleet, which he numbered at 380 in total. Athens provided by far the greatest number of ships, 200 in all. However, there was great division among the Greek commanders as to the best place to meet the Persians. Most of the cities providing ships were from the Peloponnese, and they wanted to move the Greek ships back to the south side of the isthmus, the narrow strip of land separating the Peloponnese peninsula from the rest of Greece (see map, p. ix). This way, they could support their land forces, who were planning to blockade the routes into the Peloponnese by building a wall across the isthmus. When they saw the smoke rising from Athens, some Peloponnesian ships took fright and sailed away, while the council of commanders passed a resolution to sail to defend the isthmus.

This of course did not please the Athenians, nor the other non-Peloponnesian cities, whose lands would be left undefended. Therefore, the cunning Themistocles managed to engineer it that the Greeks had little choice but to fight in the straits of Salamis. First of all, he had a private meeting with Eurybiades, the Spartan admiral of the fleet, and persuaded him to bring the commanders together again. At this meeting he put forward more arguments in favour of fighting at Salamis, in particular that the narrow waters would help them make up for the fact that they had fewer ships than the Persians, and that their ships were heavier and slower. This was a clever plan, since the narrowness of the strait meant that not all the Persian ships could enter it at the same time. Eventually, the Greek commanders agreed to stay at Salamis and join the battle there.

The Persians

Herodotus also reports the deliberations on the Persian side. The Persian navy had been drawn up in Phaleron, which was the harbour of Athens and just a short distance away from the straits between Salamis and the mainland. It is hard to tell how many ships the Persians had. Both Herodotus and Aeschylus give an original number of 1207 ships, but this must have been a wild exaggeration. Scholars offer figures ranging from about 400 to 1200.

Xerxes himself went to Phaleron to consult his naval captains about strategy. Every single one of his captains spoke in favour of fighting at Salamis except one – **Artemisia**, the queen of Halicarnassus, a Greek city on the coast of Asia Minor (many Greek cities fought on the Persian side). Artemisia had come to the throne after her husband's death. As a woman she did not need to fight, since her son was by then old enough to take her place. Nonetheless, she chose to fight for the Persians, believing that an alliance with them was in the best interests of her people.

Ironically, Herodotus portrays Artemisia as the only one of Xerxes' commanders who is 'man enough' to stand up to him and urge him not to fight, saying that he should be prepared for a more long-term and patient approach than an immediate naval action against a more skillful Greek navy. She even says the following words:

> Spare your ships and do not fight at sea: for the Greeks are as far superior to your men in naval matters as men are to women.

> Herodotus, *Histories*, 8.68

Xerxes listened to Artemisia's arguments respectfully and was impressed by her honesty. However, he went with the majority view and ordered his captains to engage with the Greeks in the straits of Salamis.

KEY INDIVIDUAL

Artemisia queen of the Greek city of Halicarnassus, which fought for the Persians

The battle

The Persian fleet put out to sea on the evening after the Greeks last deliberated. The Peloponnesian crews and commanders then started to panic and again planned to withdraw to the isthmus. It was at this point that Themistocles made his next decisive intervention: he ordered one of his slaves, Sicinnus, to journey in a boat across the straits to deliver a message to the Persians. He was to tell them that the Greek commanders were at each other's throats and were planning to sail away. Moreover, he was to say that Themistocles was secretly on Xerxes' side and wished to help him. Sicinnus duly delivered this message, and the Persians believed him. They moved their ships out into the bay of Salamis in order to block the entrance to the straits. When news of this was brought to the Greek commanders, they realised that they had no choice but to fight where they were. They prepared for battle the following morning.

Before the Greeks boarded their ships at dawn, Themistocles delivered a rousing speech. They then lined up according to their cities, with the Athenians on the left and the Spartans on the far right. The Persians moved into the straits towards their enemy. Initially, the Greeks rowed their ships backwards, but then an Athenian ship burst forward and rammed a Persian opponent. The battle had begun. The accounts of both Herodotus and Aeschylus are confusing and do not let us create a coherent picture of what happened. Perhaps this is itself a fitting reflection of the chaos of battle. However, it seems that the Persians had not understood the currents and that many of their ships were turned to one side, making them easy prey for the Greek rams. Fighting in a narrow channel and shallow water gave the advantage to the Greeks, just as Themistocles had foreseen. By contrast, the Persians' superior numbers worked against them: their ships crowded into one another.

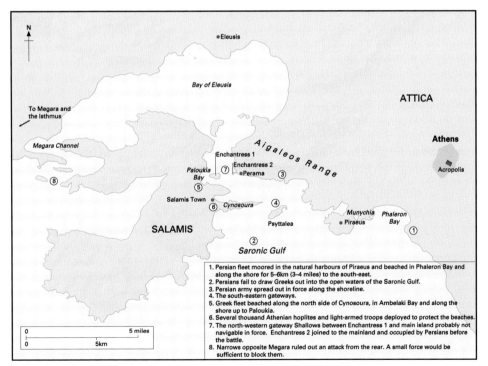

FIGURE 4.14

A map showing the opposing forces in advance of the battle of Salamis.

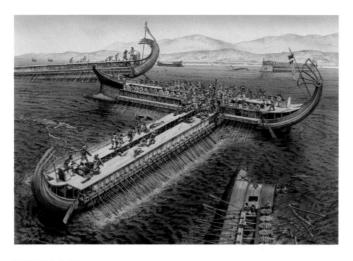

FIGURE 4.15
A Greek ship rams a Persian ship.

Aeschylus gives a vivid picture of the battle as a bloodbath, with one Persian describing his side's losses as follows:

> The shores and reefs were crowded with our
> dead, and every ship that formed a part of the
> barbarian fleet plied its oars in disorderly flight.
> But, as if our men were tuna or some haul of fish,
> the foe kept striking and hacking them with
> broken oars and fragments of wrecked ships.

> Aeschylus, *Persians*, 418–426

Herodotus adds the detail that many of the Persian sailors could not swim and so drowned, whereas the Greek casualties were largely able to swim to safety. Perhaps the most dramatic moment in Herodotus' account of the battle brings Artemisia to the forefront of the action. Her ship was in danger of being rammed by an Athenian ship, and so she deliberately rammed one of her own ships to make it seem as if she had switched sides during the battle. The tactic worked – the Athenian ship backed off, while the ship rammed by Artemisia sank. This was not the only confusion that turned out to her advantage. On the shore, Xerxes' advisers reported to him that Artemisia's ship had rammed another, which they assumed to be from the Greek fleet. Hearing of her supposed bravery, and in despair at the general performance of his navy, Xerxes commented:

> My men have turned into women, my women into men.

> Herodotus, *Histories*, 8.88

Indeed, Xerxes was enraged by what he saw, even ordering the beheading of a group of Phoenician sailors who came to complain about the efforts of some of the Greek ships fighting on the Persian side.

Aftermath

The Greeks won a comprehensive victory and the surviving Persian ships withdrew. The Persian troops headed back to the north of Greece. The following year the Greeks would go on to deliver a final defeat to the Persians on land at Plataea. However, Herodotus, no doubt reflecting the Athenian opinion of his day, argued strongly that it was the Athenians who contributed most to the overall victory in the Persian wars by providing nearly half the ships for the Greek fleet, as well as the belief that victory was possible:

> One is surely right in saying that Greece was saved by the Athenians . . . whichever
> side they joined was sure to prevail. It was the Athenians, too, who, having chosen
> that Greece should live and preserve her freedom, roused to battle the other Greek
> states which had not yet submitted. It was the Athenians who – after the gods – drove
> back the Persian king.

> Herodotus, *Histories*, 7.139

Study questions

1 Why was Themistocles so important to the Greek victory at Salamis?
2 Are there examples today of politicians using religious guidance to help them make major decisions?
3 What plays, films or other works of art are there today which seek to glorify a military victory?

Just eight years after the battle, Aeschylus wrote his play *Persians*, which was performed in front of thousands of his fellow citizens in the city's largest theatre. The play emphasised the Athenian achievement as the leaders of the Greek naval force, and idealised the Athenian citizens as free men fighting against an empire who were slaves to a tyrannical king.

TOPIC REVIEW

You should be able to:

1. Describe:
   - the structure of the Athenian army
   - the structure of the Athenian navy
   - how a trireme was funded and manned
   - the key events and individuals involved in the battle of Salamis.

2. Explain:
   - how the Athenian army and navy were funded
   - the tactics involved in trireme warfare
   - how the army and navy influenced Athenian political life
   - why the victory at Salamis was so important to the Athenians.

PRACTICE QUESTIONS

Source A: *The Old Oligarch, Constitution of the Athenians, 1.2*

It is right that the poor and the ordinary people there [i.e. in Athens] should have more power than the noble and the rich, because it is the ordinary people who man the fleet and bring the city her power.

1. a. How were Athenian rowers recruited and paid for? [2]

   b. What was the significance of this for Athenian politics? [1]

2. Why do you think that the Athenian navy was so effective? Use the source as a starting point and your own knowledge in your answer. [8]

4.3 The Roman Military in the Imperial Period

This topic examines how the Roman army was organised during the time of the Roman Empire, specifically focusing on the first and early second centuries AD. At this point, the Roman Empire controlled much of Western Europe, as well as North Africa and parts of western Asia. This is one way in which the study of the army in the Roman world is very different from studying armies in fifth century Greece, where each relatively small city-state had its own army. A second key difference, which follows on from this, is that the Roman army of the Imperial Period was fully professional in a way the earlier Greek armies never were. The Roman world, therefore, had a clear distinction between its civilians and its professional soldiers.

> **Imperial Period** the period of Roman history from 30 BC, when Rome was ruled by emperors

THE ORGANISATION OF THE ARMY

The Roman army was divided into many divisions and sub-divisions. The largest unit was the legion, and in time of the emperors there were about thirty legions in all; legions were posted all over the empire. Each legion was given a number, although it was not as simple as 1 to 30 because during the time of the civil wars in the first century

BC there had been opposing legions with the same number. When they were brought under the control of the emperor Augustus, the numbering was not changed. This meant that a legion often had a name after it too, which might have been taken from the legion's beginnings or to commemorate a particularly fine achievement by that legion. For example, two of the legions stationed in Britain during the first century AD were II Augusta and IX Hispana; the former took its name from having been loyal to Augustus during the civil wars, while the latter was originally raised and recruited in Spain.

> **S & C** When a legion was wiped out, the number was never used again. Three such Augustan legions were XVII, XVIII and XIX. Research what happened to them in the forests of Germany in AD 9.

The structure of a legion

The legion itself was broken down into a number of different subdivisions. It is perhaps easiest to work from the smallest unit upwards, thinking about how the legionary soldier fitted into his legion.

- **The contubernium** A unit of 8 men who shared the same tent and dealt with their own mess arrangements.
- **The century** Despite the name, this was a unit of about 80 men (although the first cohort consisted of double-sized centuries of 160 men – see below).
- **The cohort** With one exception, each cohort consisted of six centuries; the exception was the first cohort of a legion, which was made up of five double-sized centuries of about 160 men each.
- **The legion** The legion was made up of ten cohorts; the first cohort containing about 800 men, while each of the other nine cohorts was made up of 480 men, a total of about 4,320. In all, therefore, the legion typically had something over 5,000 ordinary legionary soldiers.

In addition to these numbers, there were other members of the legion. Attached to each one were about 120 horsemen, who acted as scouts and dispatch riders. Other numbers were made up by those in the command structure.

> **contubernium** a unit of eight men in a Roman legion, who shared the same tent and dealt with their own mess arrangements
>
> **century** a unit of about 80 men in a Roman legion (there were some double-sized centuries of 160 men)
>
> **cohort** the largest unit of a Roman legion; the first cohort of a legion had five double-centuries; cohorts two to ten each consisted of six centuries
>
> **legion** the largest unit of the Roman army

FIGURE 4.16
A diagram of a legion showing its divisions of cohorts and centuries.

centurion the commander of the century in a Roman legion

primi ordines the collective name for the five centurions of the first cohort of a Roman legion

primus pilus the most senior centurion in the legion

signifer the Roman soldier responsible for the century's standard

standard a Roman war flag, the emblem of a century, a set of medallions hoisted on a pole

optio the centurion's deputy in a Roman legion

tesserarius the Roman soldier in charge of organisation of guards and communication of passwords

cornicen the horn-player in a Roman legion who sounded orders to the soldiers

legatus the commander of the Roman legion

tribunes the six senior officers in a Roman legion after the legatus

tribunus laticlavius the senior tribune of a Roman legion, of senatorial rank

tribuni angusticlavi the five tribunes of equestrian rank in a Roman legion

Command of the centuries

A century was commanded by a **centurion**. The five centurions of the first cohort, known collectively as the **primi ordines** ('those of the first rank'), were the most senior centurions. In turn, they were ranked by seniority, with the most senior known as the **primus pilus** ('the first spearman'); he was a figure of considerable importance in the whole legion. Centurions were responsible for discipline in the army and they were expected to be very tough – they could beat soldiers with a vine cane, often brutally. A centurion would dream of becoming the primus pilus, a position that was usually only open to men over fifty and which lasted for a year. After that, the centurion would retire or be promoted.

Each century had a number of other officials. The **signifer** ('standard-bearer') looked after the **standard** of the century, which was the century's military emblem. It was typically a set of medallions hoisted on a pole, and the signifer carried it into battle. In addition, he was in charge of the century's pay and savings. The **optio** was the centurion's deputy who was also responsible for training. The **tesserarius** organised the guards and communicated the passwords, while the **cornicen** was the horn-player whose main duty was to sound orders to the soldiers.

Command of the legion

The legion as a whole also had a number of senior figures. Some were drawn from the Roman upper classes – the senatorial and equestrian classes (see pages 000–000) – and they served in the army for a much shorter period of time than the regular soldiers. They were therefore really semi-professional soldiers. The **legatus** was the commander of the legion who was of senatorial rank and appointed by the emperor. He was normally a man in his mid-thirties, who had probably served some years previously as a tribunus laticlavius (see below). He would spend about three or four years commanding the legion, and then resume his civilian career, often in politics.

Below the Legatus were six **tribunes**, one of whom held a different and more senior status than the other five. He was the **tribunus laticlavius**, a young man under the age of twenty-five from the senatorial class, the highest class at Rome. He was therefore allowed to wear the broad purple senatorial stripe on his toga ('laticlavius' meant 'broad-striped'). His posting to a legion would be the first in his career, and he would usually do one tour of duty lasting two to three years and then return to Rome, where he would continue a civilian career in financial and legal administration. About ten years later, he might return to the army as a legatus.

The other five tribunes were the **tribuni angusticlavi**. They came from the equestrian class (the second highest social class at Rome), and could therefore wear the narrow purple stripe on their togas ('angusticlavi' means 'narrow-striped'). They were typically wealthy, educated men in their thirties, who served as tribunes for a few years. After that, some returned to civilian life, often in the imperial civil service, while others stayed on in the army as commanders of auxiliary regiments. The main duties of these tribunes were to act as staff officers, doing administrative work and overseeing the welfare and daily routine of the troops.

S
&
C
Agricola

Gnaeus Julius Agricola was born to a senatorial family in AD 40. At the age of eighteen, he was sent to the province of Britain as a tribunus laticlavius, remaining there until he was twenty-two. He then returned to Rome and held various political posts. In 70, at the age of thirty, he was sent to Britain again as the Legatus of the XX Valeria Victrix legion. His command ended in 73, and he became a provincial governor in Gaul. In 77, he was posted back to Britain again – this time as the provincial governor – and remained there until AD 83. He is unique in our records as the only man to have held three military appointments in the same province.

The other senior soldier of the legion was the **camp prefect**. He was the most senior professional soldier in the legion, who was usually a former primus pilus. He was the legatus' right-hand man, responsible for the legion's equipment and transport, much like a quartermaster today.

In addition to these senior officers was the **aquilifer**. His rank was below that of centurion but above that of optio. He was always a soldier of the first cohort, and his role was to protect the legion's **aquila** and carry it into battle. The aquila was the emblem of the legion – it was an eagle, made of gold, with outstretched wings and set on top of a pole. It was the legion's most important possession and symbolised its spirit. Soldiers had an almost religious loyalty to it, and losing it in battle was considered both a terrible disaster and a deep disgrace.

> **camp prefect** the right-hand man to the legatus of a Roman legion

> **aquilifer** the legionary soldier responsible for carrying the aquila
>
> **aquila** the emblem of the legion, an eagle made of gold set on a pole

The legionary fortress

The legionary fortress was the headquarters of the legion. Although no two legionary fortresses were exactly alike, they all shared the same common features; many were originally built in wood, but from the early second century AD they were typically built in stone. A fortress was rectangular in shape with rounded corners, and it was defended all around by a ditch and a wall, while there were towers along the perimeter wall. Each side had a fortified gate, and one of the gates on the shorter side was the main gate. From here one of the fortress' three main streets, the **via praetoria**, led to the main buildings, including the headquarters, the **principia**. At this point, the via praetoria met the main cross-street of the fortress, the **via principalis**, which itself ran from one side gate to the other. The third main street, the **via quintana**, crossed the fortress on the other side of the main buildings.

The principia was the administrative heart of the fortress. It was divided into three parts. At the front lay a large courtyard surrounded by verandas, and notices were often posted here. Beyond lay a large hall known as a **basilica**, where many members of the legion could assemble, to hear the morning report, for example, since it contained a platform for the legatus to address his men. The basilica was usually an impressive and large building – the one at Chester was 73 metres in length. Beyond the basilica lay a range of

> **via praetoria** the road from the main gate to the principia in a Roman fortress
>
> **principia** the headquarters of a Roman fortress
>
> **via principalis** the road crossing the fortress in front of the principia in a Roman fortress
>
> **via quintana** the road crossing the fortress behind the principia in a Roman fortress
>
> **basilica** the large hall used for assemblies of troops in a Roman legionary fortress

FIGURE 4.17
A signifer, a centurion and
an aquilifer.

| **praetorium** the private
quarters of the legatus in a
Roman fortress |

**S
&
C** Chester's name comes
from the Latin 'castra',
which meant 'camp' or
'fort'. There are very
many places in England
today that have the
suffixes '-chester',
'-cester' or '-caster', and
in most cases these
indicate that they were
originally the site of a
Roman camp. In Wales,
exactly the same is true
for the prefix 'caer'.

rooms where the clerks toiled over their documents and pay. The central room was the temple, where the unit's standards were kept, ranged round a statue of the reigning emperor. To one side of the basilica was the **praetorium**, the private quarters of the legatus. This was built like a high status Roman villa, and contained central heating and its own private suite of baths. The legatus was able to receive and entertain important visitors here.

The fortress had a number of other buildings. There was a hospital and workshops, while well-designed granaries kept grain cool and dry in all weather conditions. There was also a set of baths to allow the troops to stay clean and healthy, as well as to socialise. There were of course many barracks, which were split up by cohort, and then by century and contubernium. One contubernium shared two rooms in the barracks – one room was for sleeping, the other contained a hearth and was a living-room and kitchen. A centurion was given his own larger suite of rooms.

Outside the fortress was usually to be found an amphitheatre. This had to be large enough to seat the whole legion, and was used primarily for military purposes: training, assemblies and parades; at times, it could also be used for traditional gladiatorial shows.

One good example of a legionary fortress is the one at Chester, which was initially built in wood in the late AD 70s. The site of its construction was strategically significant since it was located between two areas that the Romans were seeking to subdue: Wales to the west and Brigantia (a large area of northern England) to the east. It was also built at the head of an estuary that was easy to cross, while there was good access for shipping – one of the side gates led straight to the harbour.

Early in the second century, the fortress was rebuilt in stone (by this time the legion garrisoned there was XX Valeria Victrix). Its dimensions were about 591 × 412 metres; its stone perimeter wall was 5 metres in height, with a width of 1.83 metres at the base and 1.37 metres at the top. The surrounding ditch had a width of 6 metres and a depth of 3 metres. The fortress occupied nearly 25 hectares, making it larger than any other in the province of Britain. Three of the fortress' corner towers have been located and one, the south-east tower, has survived. Six other towers have also been identified.

Many buildings have been identified, including the principia. The 73-metre long basilica had a central nave 12 metres wide. Above it was a vaulted roof and on each side columns separated it from an aisle 6 metres wide. Other buildings identified include the praetorium, the baths, the granaries, as well as workshops and barracks. The use of one oval-shaped building near the principia has yet to be properly understood. Today the via praetoria and via principalis have become part of the centre of the modern city of Chester, and are now called Bridge Street and Eastgate. Outside the walls was a very large amphitheatre, which could comfortably seat 8,000. Half of it has survived and can be visited today. It dates to the third century AD, and was built over an earlier version.

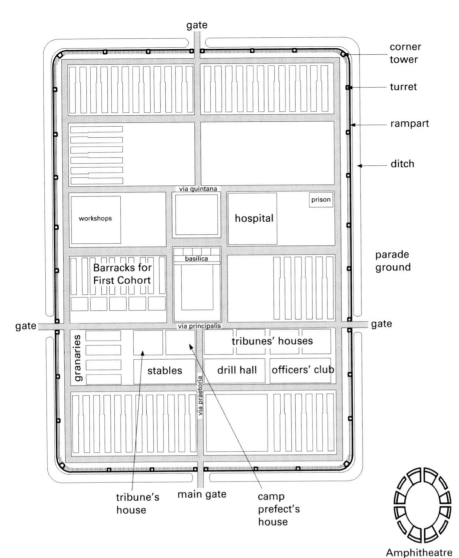

FIGURE 4.18
A plan of a legionary fortress.

PRESCRIBED SOURCE

Roman Fortress at Chester

Date: first built in wood in the AD 70s; rebuilt in stone in the early 2nd century

Location: Chester, England

Significance: the largest legionary fortress in Roman Britain

FIGURE 4.19
A reconstruction of the principia at Novae in the province of Moesia in the Balkans. The room shown in cut-away is the temple.

Auxiliary troops

The auxiliary troops were formed into smaller regiments separate from the legions. Their infantry units were typically 480-strong, but there were some of nearly double-size at 800. They were also called cohorts, and a cohort of 480 was divided into six centuries. All the auxiliary units were commanded by Roman citizens of equestrian rank. They lived in their own forts separate from the legionaries.

Perhaps the most important type of auxiliary unit was the **ala**, a cohort of cavalry. These were 512 strong, and divided up into squadrons of 32 horsemen each; this squadron was known as a **turma**. Each ala had a flag and each turma a standard. A third type of auxiliary cohort was mixed with both infantry and cavalry. Members of the cavalry could also serve as the bodyguard of the legatus.

The auxiliaries played a very important role in the Roman army. Some cohorts offered skills that the legionary army did not have in abundance – horsemen, archers, slingers etc. However, the infantry cohorts often bore the brunt of the fighting in a battle – they were sent in first since it was felt better to lose auxiliary soldiers than the Roman citizens fighting in the legions. Despite this, the numbers fighting as auxiliaries remained strong, no doubt because the men could win Roman citizenship for themselves and their children by serving well.

FIGURE 4.20
Auxiliary cavalryman.

ala a cohort of Roman cavalry, theoretically 512 strong

turma a Roman cavalry squadron of sixteen horsemen

The Roman navy

During the time of the emperors, the Romans faced little threat from any enemy with strong naval power, and so the Roman navy played a less important front-line role than the army did in conquest and defence of the empire. Nonetheless, the emperor Augustus had learnt from his own victory in the civil wars (particularly at the battle of Actium; see p. 385) that it was important to maintain a strong navy. Just as he did with the army, he established permanent professional naval forces, as well as three large naval bases for the fleet: one was at Forum Iulii (modern Fréjus) on the Mediterranean coast of Gaul, and this controlled the coasts of Gaul and Spain; one was at Misenum on the Bay of Naples, which covered the south-west Mediterranean; the third was at Ravenna and this protected the Adriatic coast and the sea crossing to the eastern provinces of the empire. One key responsibility of the navy was to suppress piracy.

Since the fleets were largely drawn from the ranks of non-citizens in the eastern empire, they were given the same status as auxiliary units. A fleet was commanded by a **praefectus**, who would be a man of the senatorial class. Individual ships were captained by trierarchs, while squadrons of ships were led by **navarchs**. The marines who worked alongside the sailors were organised into their own centuries and commanded by centurions and optios. The main duties of the navy were as follows:

praefectus the commander of a Roman naval fleet

navarch the captain of a squadron of Roman naval ships

- To transport land troops.
- To support land campaigns.

- To protect coastal settlements.
- To suppress piracy and support merchant shipping.
- To repel any barbarian incursions into Roman waters.

EXPLORE FURTHER

Perhaps the most famous praefectus of the fleet in Roman history was Pliny the Elder. He was the praefectus at Misenum in AD 79 on the day that Mount Vesuvius erupted so destructively. His nephew, Pliny the Younger, wrote a famous letter (6.16) describing the events of the day and how his uncle had heroically tried to lead a naval rescue mission. However, it was in vain and his uncle died the following day from breathing complications. Read the letter yourself – what can we learn from it about the Roman navy?

EQUIPMENT AND TACTICS

The Roman army

Roman military equipment changed over the centuries, and varied in different parts of the empire, and so any detailed analysis of the equipment used by a Roman legionary should be flexible to reflect this. Nonetheless, the following are the core items of equipment in any era, which the soldier wore over a tunic that reached down to the knees:

FIGURE 4.21
Three Roman soldiers: to the left a centurion, to the right two legionary soldiers.

- **Helmet** From the middle of the first century AD, these were typically made of iron on the inside with bronze plating on the outside; they had cheek and neck guards. A helmet could also have a crest holder – a crest of horse-hair or feathers could be used to indicate the unit a soldier belonged to or his rank.
- **Plate armour** The most common type is known by scholars as lorica segmentata; made predominantly of iron, it covered the chest and shoulders. Both the chest and the shoulder units consisted of overlapping metal strips attached on the inside by leather strips and on the outside by hinges, which made it flexible enough for the soldier to move around. The two units were held together by hooks.
- **The sporran** This was like an apron of leather thongs hanging off the belt (as is often worn with a kilt today). It gave the waist area extra protection but was also decorative.
- **Shield** The shield was rectangular and curved. It was made from three sheets of wood glued together, which was then encased in leather; the front of the shield also had a linen covering. Its rim was normally reinforced with bronze. The handgrip was reinforced by an iron or bronze boss. The front of the

FIGURE 4.22 PS
Bronze statuette of a
legionary.

**Bronze statuette of a
legionary**

Date: 2nd century AD

Location: British Museum

Significance: a statuette
illustrating the
equipment of a
legionary soldier

shield could have a painted design, which perhaps denoted the
soldier's unit.

- **Sword** The legionary's sword was known as a gladius. It was
a key weapon with a blade between 45 and 50cm long. The
soldier used it to thrust at short range. He carried it in a
scabbard on the right side of the body.
- **Dagger**: The dagger was between 20 and 25cm long, and was
attached to the belt. It could be used in battle or for cutting
generally. It went out of use during the second century.
- **Spear** This was typically about 2m long; it was constructed
with a long wooden shaft and then an iron head, which was
typically between 65 and 75cm long. A well-thrown spear
could pierce the shield or armour; even if it did not kill the
enemy, it was then very difficult to remove since the iron
often bent upon impact, so the tactic was to kill or disarm as
many enemy soldiers as possible at the start of the battle. A
legionary often had a second, shorter spear.
- **Leather sandals** Many examples of these have been
discovered. They were heavy sandals with several layers of
sole and held together with hobnails. Leather thongs could
wrap half-way up the shin and could be stuffed with wool or
fur for reinforcement or warmth.

The small bronze statuette shown in Figure 4.22 (height 11.43cm)
dates to the second century AD and gives us an idea of the equipment
of a typical Roman legionary. Visible is: his tunic, over which are the
lorica segmentata and a sporran; his strapped sandals; his crested
helmet.

EXPLORE FURTHER

1. The most complete legionary shield was found in Syria. It has been rebuilt
and is on display at the Yale University Art Gallery. Find out more here:
http://artgallery.yale.edu/collections/objects/5959.
2. The Roman emperor Caligula's real name was Gaius Julius Caesar
Germanicus. However, he was given the nickname Caligula, which means
'Little Boot' after the Latin word for a soldier's sandal, 'caliga'. Find out
how he came to be given this nickname.

Battle tactics

The Romans had a great variety of battle tactics honed over centuries. Generally speaking, once a battle had started the legionary would throw his spear first to kill or disable

opposing soldiers, after this would advance to close combat using his sword and shield. When they needed to, legionaries could use more sophisticated formations during battle. The most famous is the **testudo**, or 'tortoise', whereby a group of soldiers in formation would place their shields over their heads, except for the front row, which would bring them to head height. They would then move forward with strong protection against enemy artillery fire.

The Romans are particularly famous for their artillery, including the following two devices, which were particularly potent in siege warfare:

- **The ballista** This functioned like a crossbow and fired iron darts to great accuracy.
- **The onager** A catapult that fired rocks and large stones at the enemy.

To break down the walls of a city, a battering ram on wheels was often used; to try to breach the walls, siege towers were brought forward.

Naval warfare

During the third to first centuries BC, the Romans had copied the ship construction of those they fought against at sea – in particular, the Carthaginians and the Greeks. As well

FIGURE 4.23
Image of a testudo from Trajan's column.

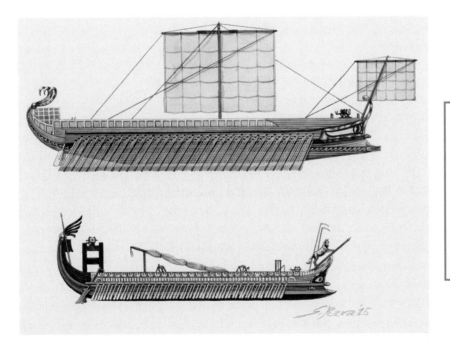

FIGURE 4.24
Drawings of a quadrireme (top) and a quinquereme (below).

> **testudo** a group of Roman soldiers advance in formation with shields over their heads
>
> **ballista** a Roman crossbow that fired iron darts
>
> **onager** a Roman catapult that fired rocks and large stones at the enemy

as using triremes, both these peoples had designed heavier ships with more rowers; the most common were the quadrireme and the quinquereme. The quadrireme had two banks of rowers with two men to an oar, while the quinquereme had three banks of rowers, the top two with two men to an oar, and the lowest with one man to an oar. It is thought that the quinquereme had 300 men on board, 270 of them rowers: 58 two-man oars on the upper level, 54 two-man oars on the middle level, and 46 one-man oars on the lowest level. We also hear of other types of ship, including the 'hexareme', which was often used as a flagship, as well as lighter ships known as **liburnae**, which were swift in the water and were therefore useful for scouting.

> **liburnae** swift Roman
> military ships which were
> used for scouting

Battle tactics for these ships were very similar to those used by the Greeks of the fifth century, based around ramming and boarding. However, after the battle of Actium in 31 BC, the empire faced little naval threat and the navy was generally used to support land troops. Therefore, lighter ships came back into fashion and at this time the trireme was the most common type of ship in the Roman fleet.

RECRUITMENT AND TRAINING

The army

A legionary soldier had to be a Roman citizen (although in the eastern empire, where there were fewer citizens, citizenship was sometimes granted upon enrolment). An applicant, usually a young man, might bring a letter of recommendation, and he would appear before an examining board of experienced officers. Vegetius, an author who writes about the Roman army in the fourth century AD, makes the following recommendations for what to look for:

> A young recruit should keep his eyes watchful and his head upright. He should be broad-chested, with muscly shoulders and strong arms, and his fingers should be on the longer side. He should have a flat stomach and a lean bottom. His calves and feet should not be flabby, but rather full of tough sinews.

> Vegetius, *About Military Matters*, 1.6–7

Vegetius goes on to comment that interviewers should find out about the trade practised by the applicant – carpenters, butchers, smiths and hunters are named as the most suitable kinds. Along with this interview there often came a period of probation, during which the applicant underwent a careful medical examination. If he was finally accepted into the army, he was given some money to pay for his journey to the legionary fortress, the headquarters of the legion. Upon arriving he took the military oath, which he had to renew at the beginning of each year thereafter. He was then dispatched to do a period of training.

The new legionary would need tough and extensive training before he was ready to serve in the army full-time. He would learn first to march, since regular soldiers were expected to be able to complete a route march of around 20 miles in five hours. Marching drill was therefore a key part of training; it helped develop good discipline (armies today still use it for the same purpose), and even a fully trained legionary had to drill once per

ACTIVITY

Imagine that you have just spent your first few weeks as a Roman soldier in training. Write a letter home to your family outlining all that you have experienced since you applied to join the army.

day. In addition, the trainee built up his fitness and skills set by practising swimming, riding, running and jumping, the latter three wearing heavy packs.

The recruit then moved on to weapons training. He would be armed with a wicker shield and wooden sword, each of double weight, and taught to attack a head-high wooden stake. He learnt to thrust with his short stabbing sword, which would inflict more damage on his enemy that the longer slashing sword – an upward thrust would strike into his enemy's vitals. The recruit was also given a wooden javelin which he hurled at the stake, while another training exercise was learning to jump onto and off either side of a horse in full armour. He might also learn to defend himself with his shield, as well as to use it as an offensive weapon to punch an opponent. A final key element in the training was to learn how to construct a camp, a vital task for an army needing to protect itself in hostile territory.

Auxiliaries

Auxiliary soldiers were normally recruited from non-citizens within the empire, although there are records of recruitment from foreign peoples. Therefore, auxiliary soldiers were mainly recruited in the provinces, and service provided a good prospect of employment – upon retirement an auxiliary would be given citizenship. Like the legionaries, they were expected to serve for twenty-five years. It seems that they underwent a similar level of training as the legionaries, since they had similar fighting capabilities.

Some auxiliary soldiers were recruited for their particular capabilities. The auxiliaries provided the backbone of the cavalry squadrons, while certain regions were known for certain skills; for example, archers were often recruited from Syria.

The navy

The Roman fleets were organised very similarly to the auxiliary units of the army. Recruits tended to be non-citizens from parts of the empire with a strong maritime tradition, such as Greece, Phoenicia and Egypt. Sailors were required to serve for twenty-six years and were given Roman citizenship upon honourable discharge, as well as a sizeable cash payment. There is no evidence that slave labour was used, despite the popular belief that the Roman navy relied on 'galley slaves'.

Training for the fleet must have been very standard – learning to row to time and change pace, and learning to follow instructions and engage in naval manoeuvres. Most importantly, a new recruit had to build the required body strength, and the best way to do this would have been to row as much as possible.

PAYMENT

When Augustus became the first Roman emperor in the late first century BC, he created a fully professional, standing army for the first time. This meant that the state paid the salaries of all those working for the army and navy. At this time, the entire Roman army numbered about 300,000. The emperor was the commander-in-chief of all the armed forces, and it was he who appointed senior officers, decided where and when soldiers should fight, and against whom. He also claimed all victories as his own, even if he had not been present.

This was clearly a huge expense for the Roman treasury. In the time of Augustus, the legionary soldier was paid 225 denarii per annum, although in the late first century AD the emperor Domitian raised this to 300 denarii. If a soldier was promoted, he would get a pay rise – a centurion was paid much more than a legionary. However, before pay was handed out a number of deductions were made – the legionary was expected to pay for his own food, clothing and equipment, and would also probably pay into a pension scheme, which guaranteed him a proper burial when he died. Therefore, a soldier's 'take home pay' was much less than the figure given above. Upon completing his service, if he was given an honourable discharge, he was given a lump sum of 3,000 denarii or an allocation of land, although the latter was later phased out.

Auxiliaries and sailors were paid much less – perhaps about a third of the legionary's rate. In their case, however, there was a great incentive to serve and eventually receive an honourable discharge, as this would bring them – and their children – the coveted Roman citizenship.

Study questions

1 How does the command structure of the Roman army compare to the command structure of a modern army today?
2 Why do you think that Roman legionary fortresses were so important and successful in supporting the work of the legion?
3 What are the requirements for new recruits into the army today?

TOPIC REVIEW

You should be able to:

1. Describe:
   - the structure of a Roman legion
   - the plan and main buildings of a Roman legionary fortress
   - how Roman soldiers were recruited, trained and paid
   - the equipment, weapons and tactics used by Roman soldiers and sailors.

2. Explain:
   - how the recruitment and training process produced the soldiers Rome required
   - how the command structure enabled the Roman army to be successful
   - how a Roman legionary fortress was designed to meet the needs of the legion
   - why serving in the army may have been an attractive career for a Roman.

PRACTICE QUESTIONS

Source A: A Roman centurion

1. Give **one** important duty of a centurion. [1]
2. Name **three** pieces of protective armour shown here, and explain why each was effective. [6]

4.4 The Romans at War

- The battle of Actium, including:
  - key events and individuals: Octavian; Marcus Agrippa; Mark Antony; Cleopatra
  - the significance of the battle and how the Romans commemorated it.

- Trajan's campaign against the Dacians, including:
  - reasons for the war
  - presentation of warfare in the material sources
  - the image of Trajan as emperor
  - the pursuit of military glory
  - victims of warfare.

The following are the prescribed sources for this topic:

- Mark Antony Legionary denarius, Obv: galley with banners, Rev: eagle between two standards, likely minted in Patrae 32 BC (example BMC 197, RSC 33, Sear 356)
- Relief commemorating the battle of Actium, Vatican Museum
- Trajan's Column, Rome
- Arch of Trajan, Benevento

Don't forget that you will be given credit in the exam if you study extra sources and make relevant use of them in your answers.

This topic examines two important military campaigns in Roman history. First it focuses on the battle of Actium in 31 BC, the result of which enabled Octavian to become the most powerful man in the Roman world and to become the first Roman emperor, under the name Augustus. The topic then moves to the campaigns of the emperor Trajan against the Dacians in the early second century AD, which illustrate how important it was for the emperor to be successful in war.

THE BATTLE OF ACTIUM

The context

From 91 BC, the Roman world had been convulsed in a series of civil wars. Powerful generals, with soldiers personally loyal to them, vied with each other to win power in Rome. As well as fighting against each other, these men came to challenge the status quo of the traditional Roman system of government, the Republic, which allowed a relatively small number of aristocratic families to keep the main offices of state to themselves. These generals – successful men who had proved themselves in combat – often seemed to want to reform the Republic. Ultimately, however, the civil wars brought the entire system to an end.

The most famous of these generals was Julius Caesar, a remarkable leader who ruled the Roman Empire as dictator between 49 and 44 BC. When he was assassinated in 44, two men closely associated with him aimed to continue his legacy. One was Mark Antony, Caesar's closest ally who had campaigned alongside him as a general; the other was Gaius Octavianus, Caesar's great-nephew who was named as Caesar's adopted son and heir in his will. In 44 Octavian (as he is commonly known) was just 18 years old.

In the year after Caesar's death, the two men joined forces to defeat the conspirators who had organised the assassination. They then set about dividing up the rule of the Roman world between them and one other, Lepidus. However, Lepidus was soon marginalised, and by the mid-30s BC the Roman world had been divided into east and west – with Octavian based in Rome and in charge of the west, and Antony based in Egypt and in control of the east.

Egypt at this stage was a 'client-state' of Rome. This meant that it was not formally part of the empire, but that it needed to follow Rome's lead, acting as a junior ally. Egypt's great attraction to Rome was its fertility, which made it a huge source of grain. The queen of Egypt at this time was Cleopatra, who has gone down as one of the most colourful and remarkable female rulers in history. Egypt had already become embroiled in Rome's civil wars in the early 40s BC, and when Julius Caesar campaigned in the east in 48 BC, he started an affair with the queen. She soon bore him a son, Caesarion, and came to live with him in Rome. After Caesar's assassination in 44, she returned to Egypt.

In 41, Cleopatra was summoned to Asia Minor to meet Antony, now Rome's commander in the east. This was the beginning of one of the most famous love affairs in history, immortalised by Shakespeare in his play *Antony and Cleopatra*. After the two fell in love, Cleopatra bore him twins. However, politics intervened and in 40 Antony was required to return to Italy to seal his pact with Octavian; as part of their alliance, Antony agreed to marry Octavian's sister, Octavia, who bore him two daughters. None the less, in 37 Antony headed east again and renewed his affair with Cleopatra, who bore him another son. Antony now lived permanently with Cleopatra and in 32 he formally divorced Octavia.

There had long been tensions between Antony and Octavian, but this was the moment at which everything came to a head. It was not hard for Octavian to portray Antony as

KEY INDIVIDUALS

Mark Antony Julius Caesar's loyal deputy who came to take charge of the eastern half of the Roman Empire

Octavian Julius Caesar's great-nephew whom he adopted as a son and heir. He would go on to become the first Roman emperor and rename himself Augustus

KEY INDIVIDUAL

Cleopatra the queen of Egypt from 51 to 30 BC, who was the lover first of Julius Caesar and then of Mark Antony

FIGURE 4.25
Cleopatra.

FIGURE 4.26
A denarius of
Mark Antony.

Mark Antony legionary denarius

Date: 32 BC

Material: silver and copper

Obverse: galley with banners at the prow (the front)

Reverse: legionary eagle between two standards

Significance: a coin issued by Antony to his soldiers in the winter of 32/31 BC

KEY INDIVIDUAL

Marcus Agrippa the commander of Octavian's fleet at Actium

someone who had broken his ties with the Roman world and was under the spell of a foreign queen. He obtained and read out a copy of Antony's will, which he claimed named Cleopatra as his heir and main beneficiary (it is unclear how honest Octavian was being in his presentation of the will). At this point, many of Antony's soldiers deserted. Octavian declared war on Cleopatra and Egypt, cleverly portraying it as a war against a foreign rival rather than yet another round in Rome's civil wars.

However, Antony marshalled the rest of his troops to prepare for a showdown. The coin shown in Figure 4.26, called a denarius, was issued to his soldiers in the winter of 32/31 BC and probably minted at his headquarters in Patrae, Greece. Such coins were of a lower silver content than the norm, with copper having been added to the alloy, and so they look like money minted out of necessity for the use of Antony's troops in a time of difficulty.

The reverse of the coin simply shows the legionary eagle flanked by two standards of the type carried by the signifer of a century. The coin is dedicated to the sixth legion, which was fighting for Antony. On the obverse, there is a galley with banners at the prow of the ship. The writing stands for 'Antonius augur' – an augur was a senior priest at Rome, an office that Antony had held. The lower writing stands for 'Triumvir Rei Publicae Constituendae' – 'One of three men for the constituting of the Republic'; this was a reference to his joint rule with Octavian and Lepidus after the death of Julius Caesar – Antony is clearly trying to portray himself as someone who wishes to protect the Republic rather than destroy it.

The battle

Both sides prepared for war. In the east, Antony mobilised all the Roman client states, and gathered his forces at Ephesus in Asia Minor with a total of about 100,000 infantry, 12,000 cavalry and hundreds of warships. In the autumn of 32, they moved to Greece where Antony set up a winter headquarters at Patrae. However, his troops and ships were largely based around the Ambracian Gulf on the west coast – in particular at Actium, the southern promontory at the entrance to the gulf (see map, pages xxx–xxx). Octavian moved his ships and men over to the north-west of Greece, and the two sides spent the winter skirmishing. Octavian had a force of around 80,000 infantry, 12,000 cavalry and about 260 ships. Octavian's fleet was commanded by his close friend and ally **Marcus Agrippa**, who a few years before had gained a reputation as an outstanding admiral by masterminding the defeat of a large pirate fleet that was threatening Rome.

As the spring and summer of 31 wore on, Octavian's forces took the initiative. Agrippa managed to blockade the supply lines of Antony's forces by capturing key locations further south in Greece, including Patrae. Moreover, he also captured the island of Leukas close to the mouth of the Ambracian Gulf, which allowed him to set up a naval blockade at the mouth itself. Antony and Cleopatra were by now with their forces, which were suffering starvation and disease; many deserted. Antony was left with two choices: to abandon the fleet and withdraw his troops to the east of Greece to fight another day, or to try to break out of the blockade by meeting Octavian in battle at sea. Cleopatra urged the latter option, hoping to be able to withdraw back to Egypt to regroup. Antony agreed to fight at sea, and hoped that he would then score a decisive victory over Octavian and secure the west coast of Greece for himself. In preparation for battle, Antony and Cleopatra ordered their war chests of treasure to be loaded on, as well as masts and sails – this was an unusual move for a naval battle, when ships tried to be as light as possible.

The battle itself took place on 2nd September. There is some contradiction in the sources as to the number of ships on each side. Octavian's fleet probably had about 250 ships, consisting of quinqueremes, triremes, liburnae and a few hexaremes. It is harder to put a number on Antony's fleet. One Roman historian gives 500, although this was probably the total number of ships under Antony's command. In the battle, it is more likely that he had about 230, of which 60 were Egyptian ships commanded by Cleopatra. As well as quinqueremes, there seem to have been many heavier ships in his fleet, including hexaremes and even larger ones. Antony's fleet was therefore slower and more vulnerable to ramming. In addition, it was undermanned because of illness and desertions. However, his stronger ships had an advantage when fighting at close quarters.

Antony's fleet moved out into the sea early in the morning, with Cleopatra's fleet of sixty ships remaining behind the main line; Antony himself was commanding on the right. Octavian also commanded his fleet on the right, with Agrippa on the left facing Antony. Octavian ordered his wings to spread out in a crescent formation, from where some ships made to ram Antony's wings. Antony did not wait but engaged in battle. It lasted for a long time without decisive progress; Agrippa moved his ships further north, trying to outflank Antony, and therefore thinned his centre.

By now it was late morning, and the daily breeze from the north-west was starting to blow strongly. Cleopatra's ships had not yet joined the battle; but seeing the centre of Octavian's line thinned, she ordered her ships to raise their masts and sails and to charge through the enemy lines, not stopping to fight. They did so with ease, pulling clear and sailing south. This may not have been Antony's plan, but when he saw this he moved from his own flagship (a 'ten') to a quinquereme, and ordered the rest of his fleet to disengage and follow Cleopatra. Why did he do this? This is one of the great questions of Roman history. Perhaps he simply could not bear to be parted from the woman he loved so much. However, few of his men saw his signal or were in a position to do anything about it. Antony sailed south with some other ships and caught up with Cleopatra. The rest of his fleet fought on manfully through the afternoon, but the survivors eventually withdrew back to Actium, the battle lost. Antony's remaining land troops surrendered to Octavian, who showed them mercy and incorporated many into his own army. The game was nearly up for Antony and Cleopatra.

Aftermath

After his victory, Octavian spent the winter in Greece before sailing to Egypt the next year to finish off Antony. As a result of so many desertions, Antony was beaten again in Alexandria. He heard a false rumour that Cleopatra had been captured and killed, and so he tried to take his own life. Yet his death took days and he died in Cleopatra's arms. Cleopatra then offered Octavian an alliance. When he refused, she pleaded for the life of

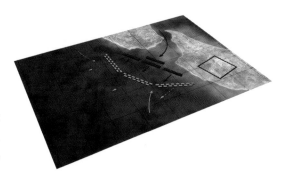

FIGURE 4.27
Battleplan of Actium.

EXPLORE FURTHER

Read the accounts of the battle by Plutarch (*Life of Antony* 60–68) and Cassius Dio (*History of Rome* 50.11–34). How do the two accounts differ?

EXPLORE FURTHER

Read the poetic accounts of Actium by Horace (*Ode* 1.37) and Virgil (*Aeneid* 8.671–713). To what extent does each seem to be propaganda on behalf of Augustus?

Study questions

1 What other naval battles have had a decisive effect on a nation's history? How have they been marked and commemorated?
2 Why do you think that Shakespeare found the story of Antony and Cleopatra such good material for a play?

Caesarion, but it was already too late – Octavian had had him killed. Cleopatra knew that she would be paraded through Rome as a captive, and so she killed herself. One source claims that she did this by having a poisonous snake bite her, although she may simply have taken poison.

Octavian was now master of the whole Roman world. He soon took the title 'princeps' – 'the first citizen' – and changed his name to Augustus. Later Romans and modern historians have regarded him as the first Roman emperor, and the battle of Actium as the day on which the Roman Republic finally died. Augustus himself portrayed Actium as a great moment of liberation for the Roman people. He had a new town built near the battle site, and called it Nicopolis – Greek for 'Victory City'. Nearby a huge monument was set up overlooking the sea, which was decorated with thirty-six battering rams of captured ships. Back in Rome, a number of other monuments to the battle were set up, while two famous poets loyal to Augustus – Virgil and Horace – celebrated the victory in their poetry. Horace (see p. 424) wrote an ode in which he focused on Cleopatra, describing her as a 'fatale monstrum' – a 'deathly monster'. In his *Aeneid* (see p. 429), the poet Virgil gives a vivid description of the battle.

The relief shown in Figure 4.29 was created as part of a monument celebrating Octavian's victory at Actium. It was set up in the town of Praeneste (modern Palestrina) near Rome. The relief seems to show one of Octavian's ships – perhaps the hexareme used as his flagship – with a small tower on deck. It is notable that a crocodile is depicted on the side of the ship. This seems to be a clear reference to Egypt, and perhaps therefore an attempt by Octavian's propagandists to portray the victory at Actium as one against a foreign foe, Cleopatra. This conveniently airbrushes out the fact that the victory at Actium was the final major engagement of a bloody civil war in which Roman had fought against Roman.

FIGURE 4.28
A sixteenth-century painting of Cleopatra killing herself with a snake.

FIGURE 4.29
Relief commemorating **PS** the victory at Actium.

TRAJAN'S CAMPAIGN AGAINST THE DACIANS

Trajan

Marcus Ulpius Traianus (known in English as **Trajan**) was Roman emperor from AD 98 until his death in 117. He was not born in Rome but in Italica, a town in the Roman province of Hispania Baetica, an area corresponding to the southern Spanish region of Andalusia today. Although Trajan was born into a high ranking Roman family and his father served as a consul, it was still remarkable that he progressed to become the most powerful man in the Roman world. Indeed, he was the first Roman emperor born outside Italy.

Trajan made his name as an officer in the Roman army, serving initially as a military tribune. Among his postings at this time was one in Syria during 76–77, while his father was the governor. In about 87 he became the legatus of the Legion VII Gemina in Spain, and in 89 he helped put down a rebellion against the emperor Domitian. In 91, Trajan was made consul for the year. Around this time, he also married Pompeia Plotina, a noble woman to whom he remained married for the rest of his life.

The emperor Domitian was popular with the army, but unpopular with the Roman upper classes. When he was assassinated in 96, he was replaced by the elderly and childless Nerva, who was himself unpopular with the army. In 97, Nerva therefore adopted Trajan as his co-emperor and successor, understanding that Trajan had the respect of the army. It was vital an emperor to have the support of the army in order to survive. When Nerva died in January of the following year, Trajan became the sole ruler of the Roman world.

Trajan is remembered as one of the best Roman emperors. In fact, after his death every new emperor was welcomed by the senate with the wish that he be 'luckier than Augustus and better than Trajan'. Militarily, his reign is remembered for two great wars of conquest; in Dacia between 101 and 106 (see below), and in Parthia (an area equivalent to modern Iran) between 113 and 116. In these years, the Roman Empire reached the largest extent in its entire history. The conquest of Parthia proved to be short-lived, but Dacia was fully incorporated as a province of the Roman Empire. As emperor, Trajan took a great interest in his soldiers, and is on record as describing them as 'my excellent and most loyal fellow-soldiers'. He formed two new legions, and when he was on campaign he marched on foot at the head of his men.

Trajan was also highly respected as emperor in civilian life. He treated the senate and upper classes with respect, and instigated many impressive building projects, including a new forum and grand new baths in Rome, a canal to prevent the river Tiber in Rome from flooding, a new harbour at Ostia (Rome's port), and a new highway in the south of Italy, the via Traiani (see map on page viii). Trajan was also seen to be a generous emperor to the Roman poor. He extended the corn dole, the system by which the poorest Romans received a state handout of corn, while he also developed a state funded welfare programme that helped orphaned and poor children throughout Italy. The scheme was initially funded by the booty won during the Dacian wars, indicating the importance of military conquest for the prosperity of life within the empire.

FIGURE 4.30
The emperor Trajan.

The Dacian wars

During the reign of Augustus, the northern frontiers of the Roman Empire had largely been set along two rivers, the Rhine and the Danube. During the first century AD, the barbarian peoples across the Rhine had proved to be the greater danger, but during the reign of Domitian (81–96) the peoples across the Danube became more hostile. In order to divide these peoples, Domitian chose to make a peace with the Dacians, a people based about half-way along the Danube, in a region today corresponding to western Romania. However, the Dacians had themselves not always been on good terms with the Romans. Indeed, they had raided the Roman province of Moesia to the south twice in living memory, once in 69 and then again in 85/6. When the Romans ventured into Dacia in 87, the barbarian people won a clear victory, led by their new and charismatic king **Decebalus**.

The following year, however, the Romans did win a victory on Dacian soil, and it was after this that the two sides made a peace agreement. Dacia was established as a client-state of Rome, and Decebalus was given a crown to symbolise Roman support for his rule. He was also lent Roman military engineers and given an annual grant to strengthen the outer borders of his region. By the time of Domitian's death, the focus of Roman military defence had moved from the Rhine to the Danube. Whereas earlier there had been eight legions on the Rhine and six on the Danube, those figures were reversed by AD 96.

When Trajan became emperor in 98, he first inspected the entire northern frontier from west to east. He then returned to Rome to win over the upper classes, and it was only in 101 that he launched his first military campaign – against the Dacians. There is a shortage of written evidence as to his motives, but it is clear that the 'official' Roman account – in the written sources and on Trajan's column (described below) – put the war down to the need for frontier security. By this line of reasoning, Trajan was unimpressed with the generous terms given to Decebalus, and particularly with the annual payments being made to him. Moreover, Decebalus was believed to be ignoring the peace terms and seeking to expand his power so that he posed an increasing threat to Rome. He was apparently building alliances with northern peoples, giving refuge to runaway slaves from the Roman Empire, and even recruiting Roman soldiers into his army.

Modern scholars have sought to suggest other reasons for the attack on Dacia in 101, which could be seen either as alternatives or as additions to the official version. One motivation may have been that morale in the legions on the Danube was dangerously low at this time because they still resented the assassination of Domitian. A war would focus their minds and a victory would seal their loyalty to Trajan. Another very plausible reason is that Trajan himself wanted and needed to make his mark as emperor, and that his inspection of the northern frontier when he came to power was an attempt to look for the best place to launch a successful campaign. Another incentive for the war may have been that the outer reaches of Dacia had gold-mines, which would provide ample riches for the Empire.

In the early summer of 101, Trajan launched his first campaign, crossing the Danube and engaging the Dacians in a major battle at Tapae. The Romans won, but there were heavy casualties on both sides. The following year the Romans pursued Decebalus further into Dacian territory close to his capital at Sarmizegethusa and forced him to submit. He was forced to surrender his war-machines, to give back deserters (most of them soldiers or technical experts), to demolish forts and to withdraw from captured territory. Trajan left garrisons behind and returned to Rome in triumph, where he was granted the title Dacicus ('the conqueror of Dacia').

Decebalus should now have been reduced to the role of loyal client-king again, but the Roman sources suggest that he began to break the terms of his surrender and to build an alliance against the Romans. Trajan was left with no choice but to go back to war, this time in order to reduce Dacia to a full province of the Empire. This he did between 105 and 106, first building a huge bridge across the Danube by which his army could cross. After a hard-fought campaign, the Romans emerged victorious. Decebalus was about to be captured when he committed suicide. Dacia became a Roman province and Trajan founded new cities there. It would remain a Roman province for more than 150 years.

Back in Rome, Trajan celebrated his victories with a **triumph**. During the imperial period, this saw an emperor (or member of his family) celebrating a military victory by leading his troops through the city of Rome, with the spoils of war on display and the captive forced to march in chains in the procession.

> **triumph** a grand procession through the streets of Rome to celebrate a military victory

The material sources

We have no detailed written source about Trajan's campaigns in Dacia, although some historians do make reference to it. Therefore, the largest body of evidence comes from the monuments built to commemorate both the victories and Trajan's achievements more generally. It is quite clear that Trajan saw the Dacian conquest as his key military triumph, and wished to promote his achievement in the eyes of the Roman people. Two of your prescribed sources reflect this – Trajan's Column and the Arch of Trajan at Beneventum.

As other emperors had done, Trajan instigated a large building project in the centre of Rome both to improve the city's infrastructure and to commemorate his reign. This project included a new forum with impressive public buildings, the world's first shopping centre ('Trajan's Markets'), two new libraries and Trajan's Column. The whole project was funded by the spoils of the Dacian conquest, and the column sought to give a record of Trajan's victory there.

The column still stands in the centre of Rome today and is one of the ancient city's best known landmarks. However, its original context has all but disappeared. As Figure 4.33 shows, it was originally surrounded on three sides. To the south was the Basilica Ulpia, a multi-purpose building where Romans might do business or where legal cases might be heard. To the east and west were two libraries, one with Greek texts, the other with Latin texts. Their location is significant. Trajan is known to have written his own account of the Dacian Wars, and this was no doubt a major work in the Latin library. Many scholars think that the column is an attempt to record Trajan's written account in art. It is also likely that these buildings had windows on different storeys that gave visitors views of different parts of the column, so they acted as viewing points.

The monument itself consisted of three parts: a large marble pedestal at the base, the marble column, and a bronze statue of Trajan on the top. The statue disappeared centuries ago, probably after an earthquake. (In 1588 Pope Sixtus V had a statue of St Peter

FIGURE 4.31
Trajan's Column on one side of a denarius minted in AD 114.

FIGURE 4.32
Trajan's Column.

PRESCRIBED SOURCE

Trajan's Column

Date: completed in AD 113

Material: marble

Location: central Rome

Significance: a major architectural column in the centre of Rome presenting Trajan's conquests against the Dacians

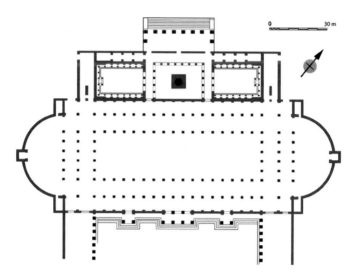

FIGURE 4.33
Plan of the location of Trajan's Column.

FIGURE 4.34
Scene showing Victory writing on a shield, from Trajan's Column.

placed there instead, and this remains today.) The pedestal is about 5 metres in height and became Trajan's tomb. The actual column is about 30 metres in height. It was made from nineteen marble drums and has a diameter of 3.7 metres. On the outside, the frieze depicting the Dacian wars is nearly 200 metres long and winds around the column twenty-three times. Inside the column there is a spiral staircase of 185 steps, which leads to a viewing platform at the top.

The frieze is divided into two halves. The lower half depicts the campaigns of 101–102, the upper half the campaigns of 105–106. The two narratives are separated by a personification of Victory writing on a shield. This was a celebration of the Roman victory in the first campaign. In the 1890s the German historian Conrad Cichorius had plates drawn of every scene on the column. His scheme divided the column into 155 scenes, which he numbered in Roman numerals. This scheme is still used today to refer to the different scenes on the column. The scenes are notable for the relative lack of depictions of fighting or the violence of warfare, and there are no scenes which depict violence towards Dacian women and children. There is much more emphasis on the orderliness of the army, and soldiers are often depicted building camps and forts or enacting ceremonies. The column, therefore, should be seen as propaganda presenting Roman power and rule rather than as an accurate record of the nature of the warfare. Three types of set scenes reappear on the column:

- Trajan addressing his troops.
- Trajan presiding over a sacrifice.
- The army setting out on campaign

In addition, certain specific events from the wars are portrayed. These include the first crossing of the Danube by the Roman army, the Dacian surrender of 102, a sacrifice made at the bridge over the Danube at the start of the second war, and the suicide of Decebalus. In scene 147 his head is displayed to the Roman troops. The presentation of Trajan himself on the column is significant. He appears between 57 and 60 times (three portraits are unidentifiable). He is shown in military armour in about half of these images, although always helmetless so that his head is visible. When he is in the company of officers or advisors he is usually set in the middle of the scene, and slightly taller than the others. He is seen presiding over a sacrifice on six occasions, showing him to be a pious follower of the gods.

The column offers a portrayal of the victims of warfare, which shows the Romans as enlightened conquerors. For example, in scene 30, Dacian women holding their children are shown pleading to Roman soldiers for mercy. The Romans do not kill them but have them taken away to a ship (one particularly aristocratic woman in this scene may be the sister of Decebalus). In scene 146, boys are seen with captive Dacian soldiers, and they may be the sons of Decebalus. Perhaps the most intriguing portrayal of non-combatants, however, is in the so-called 'torture scene' in scene 45. Here, captured Roman soldiers are shown naked and being tortured by Dacian women. The scene is in great contrast to the way in which the Romans treat prisoners of war on the column, and is thought to be a way of promoting Roman civilisation over the barbarism of foreign peoples.

Beneventum was a relatively unremarkable town in southern Italy, and so we might ask why such an impressive ceremonial arch was built there. The answer lies in the fact that the town was the starting point of an important new highway commissioned by Trajan, which would connect Rome to the port of Brundisium in the south-east of Italy.

EXPLORE FURTHER

The Victoria and Albert Museum in London has a plaster cast of the entire column on display in sections. If you are able to, visit the museum and examine the scenes on the column for yourself. Alternatively, you can view every scene with a commentary at http://www.trajans-column.org/.

EXAM TIP

Remember that in your extended response questions you can show off your knowledge, and so doing further research of the scenes on Trajan's Column will give you plenty of interesting information to work with.

FIGURE 4.35
Two scenes from Trajan's Column. To the left, soldiers are engaged in construction, to the right they are tying up Dacian prisoners. Trajan is at the top of the left-hand scene.

FIGURE 4.36
The 'torture scene' on Trajan's Column.

FIGURE 4.37
The Arch of Trajan at Benevento.

Arch of Trajan, Benevento

Date: completed in AD 114

Material: limestone and marble

Location: Benevento (known to the Romans as Beneventum), Italy

Significance: a major triumphal arch set up to commemorate Trajan's achievements as emperor.

Via Appia The traditional highway from Rome to Brundisium.

Via Traiana A new highway from Beneventum to Brundisium, which offered a faster journey than the southern section of the Via Appia.

Brundisium was important to the Romans since it was traditionally the port from which Roman legions sailed to campaign in the east. For centuries, the main highway south from Rome to Brundisium had been the **Via Appia**. Trajan's new route peeled off from the Via Appia at Beneventum and offered a shorter route to Brundisium. It was opened in 109 and known as the **Via Traiana** ('Trajan's Road'). The arch was dedicated by the Senate in 114 to celebrate the opening of the new highway and to commemorate Trajan's rule.

The arch is one of the best preserved triumphal arches in the Roman world. It is built in limestone and covered with marble blocks, on which are reliefs depicting scenes from the reign of Trajan. There was also originally a four-horse chariot with a statue of Trajan riding in it. As a whole, the artwork on the arch may therefore be taken as an attempt to present Trajan's character and achievements as emperor. Scenes depicted include the emperor founding cities and reorganising the corn supply. There are also sacrifices, most notably on the inside of the arch, where Trajan presides over a sacrifice commemorating the opening of the Via Traiana. In another key scene on the inside of the arch, Trajan is seen to hand out money to poor children. Nearby, a personification of Victory crowns Trajan with a laurel wreath, and the emperor is depicted in full military uniform.

This personification of Victory seems to link directly to one of the key scenes on the outside of the arch which portrays the Dacian conquest. This takes the form of a continuous frieze running around the arch at a level just above the top of the central passageway. This is believed to show the triumph held by Trajan in Rome in 107. It portrays a procession that is just reaching the **Capitoline Hill** in Rome, the political and ceremonial heart of the city. The frieze depicts 107 figures: soldiers carrying the spoils of war, chariots carrying chained prisoners, bulls being led to sacrifice, and at the rear Trajan himself is seen riding in a triumphal chariot. Once again, therefore, we see Trajan portraying his victories in Dacia as one of the central achievements of his reign, and using military glory to promote an image of a great conqueror.

> **Capitoline Hill** One of the seven original hills of Rome, it was the political and ceremonial heart of the city.

> **S & C**
> One of the new towns founded by the Romans in Dacia was called Civitas Tropaensium, where today there is the town of Adamklissi. In 109, a large memorial to the Roman victory in Dacia was set up there, Tropaeum Traiani ('Trajan's Trophy'), and it contained fifty-four separate metopes, sculpted scenes of the Roman campaigns. Most of these metopes are now in the site Museum and are therefore referred to as the Adamklissi Metopes. Find out about these metopes – what can we learn about the campaign from them?

TOPIC REVIEW

You should be able to:

1. Describe:
   - the key events of the battle of Actium
   - the key individuals involved in the battle of Actium
   - the key events of Trajan's campaign against the Dacians
   - an outline of the decoration on Trajan's Column and the Arch of Trajan.

2. Explain:
   - why the battle of Actium came to be fought
   - why the battle of Actium was so important in Roman history
   - what Trajan's Column and the Arch of Trajan can tell us about Roman war and warfare
   - how Trajan is portrayed in these monuments.

PRACTICE QUESTIONS

Source A: Relief commemorating Actium

1. Look at this image.
   a. State **two** ways in which this can be identified as a Roman warship. [2]
   b. How did this image seek to glorify Octavian's victory at Actium? [2]
2. 'To the Romans, military discipline was the most important element of a successful army.' To what extent do you agree with this statement? [15]

Literature

4.5 Homer

Literary context

- The genre and author of your set text
- Its composition and aims
- Narrative and descriptive techniques, including:
  - speeches
  - similies and imagery
  - epithets
  - use of emotive language
  - the role of the divine

Characterisation

- The actions of the characters in your selections
- The traits of each of the main characters and how these are depicted
- Interactions and relationships between characters
- The depiction of:
  - leaders and soldiers
  - comrades and enemies
  - non-combatants
  - women

Themes

- Glory, honour and shame
- Comradeship
- Freedom
- Hubris and arrogance
- Love and patriotism
- The horror and glorification of warfare
- Fear and courage
- Family and ancestors
- Military and civilian victims of war

Heroes and Warfare

- How the content of your selections reflects its political or cultural context, including:
  - details of the historical context
  - what constitutes a 'hero'
  - attitudes towards war and warfare
- The possible responses to the text from different audiences

The prescribed source for this topic is:

- Homer, *Iliad*, 5.84–469; 6.118–529; 22.21–409; 24.468–620

Don't forget that you will be given credit in the exam if you study extra sources and make relevant use of them in your answers.

This section will introduce you to the Homeric poems in general, and then move to examine your prescribed passages of Homer's *Iliad*. Throughout, you should keep referring to the topic boxes at the start of the chapter to think about how your prescribed literature includes the themes mentioned.

LITERARY CONTEXT

The *Iliad* and the *Odyssey*, attributed to Homer, are the earliest surviving works of literature from the ancient Greek world, and many would say that they remain its greatest literary achievement. There is no doubt that later Greeks looked to the poems as a deep source of wisdom, inspiration, and entertainment. However, we immediately confront a problem: we have no idea who 'Homer' was, if he ever existed, and (if he did exist) if he composed either or both of the poems. This is often called the **Homeric question**.

We do know that the Homeric poems were probably first written down at some point between 750 and 650 BC, soon after the Greeks had developed a written script (the same one that remains in use today). Since the Greeks had not used writing in the centuries before this, their culture at this time was what is called an **oral culture**. This means that it relied on the spoken word rather than the written word. Anthropologists who have studied oral cultures have noticed some common features in them. Above all, their people have to develop great powers of memory as they do not have books to refer back to. Moreover, in such cultures, song, dance and poetry all become very important, since they make the recording and remembering of stories and information much easier.

All cultures throughout history found ways to tell stories. In our society, we might engage with a story by reading a book, watching television, seeing a film or going to

> **KEY INDIVIDUAL**
>
> **Homer** the name given to the poet who was thought to have composed the *Iliad* and the *Odyssey*

> **Homeric question** the debate about the authorship of the *Iliad* and the *Odyssey* and about the identity of Homer
>
> **oral culture** a society where people rely on word of mouth rather than writing

---

PRESCRIBED SOURCE

Homer, *Iliad*, 5.84–469; 6.118–529; 22.21–409; 24.468–620

Date: probably between 750 and 650 BC

Author: attributed to Homer

Genre: epic poetry

Significance: selections that show aspects of ancient Greek warfare as follows:

- 5.84–469: the prowess and achievements in battle of the Greek warrior Diomedes – 6.118–529: a contrast between events on the battlefield and life inside the walls of Troy
- 22.21–409: Achilles kills Hector and mistreats his corpse – 24.468–620: Priam visits the tent of Achilles to beg for the return of Hector's body for burial

Read it here: OCR source booklet

CW

bard a public storyteller who recited vast amounts of poetry to the accompaniment of the lyre, often during banquets

the theatre. None of these options were of course available to the Greeks who lived before the eighth century BC. Yet one form of entertainment was particularly prominent then – public storytelling by a professional storyteller. In those times, such a public storyteller, known as a **bard**, would recite to an audience very long poems to the accompaniment of a lyre, a musical instrument like a small harp (we might also, therefore, talk of the bard 'singing' his tale). This was the way myths and tales were passed on, and developed and improved over generations. It was also the way people were entertained for centuries.

The *Iliad* and the *Odyssey* centre on events surrounding the Trojan War, a treasure trove of remarkable, wonderful and moving stories. No one believes that the Trojan War happened exactly as described in these poems. However, it is likely that the poems emerged out of the experience of a war or series of wars. The most likely time for such wars was around the twelfth century BC, when we know that the Bronze Age civilisation in the eastern Mediterranean collapsed spectacularly. Many cities were burnt to the ground, and the population declined significantly. Bards presumably started singing about these wars as they were happening. As time went on and the generations passed, the stories were changed by other bards who developed their own interpretations and emphases. Their focus was not on producing factual accounts of the past, but on producing stories with examples of great heroism and nobility.

FIGURE 4.38
This ivory lyre was used by Greek bards in the thirteenth century BC.

When the Greeks started using a written script during the eighth century BC, they had the means to set down these stories for the first time. It is at this point that the figure of Homer emerges. The most common school of thought believes that he was a bard who was literate enough to write down his poems, or who at least dictated them to scribes to write down. In fact, little is known about Homer – he is really a figure of mystery. The best-known tales about him are that he was blind and that he came from the eastern Aegean, possibly the island of Chios. Amongst scholars, there remain wide differences of opinion over his identity. Some think that the two poems were composed by different people, others that 'Homer' is really a term for a group of bards.

We are unlikely ever to be able to answer this Homeric question fully, but what is clear is the huge influence that the poems had on subsequent Greek culture and literature – a huge number of the poetic verses cited by later Greek writers are from Homer, and many Greek writers and artists turned to the Homeric poems for inspiration. Indeed, their influence reaches far beyond the Greek world, since they have inspired countless writers and artists ever since: the *Aeneid* by the first century BC Roman poet Virgil, which you will also be reading, is a notable example. It is for this reason that Homer – whoever he may have been – is regarded as the father of Western literature.

FIGURE 4.39
Although later Greeks did not know what Homer looked like, they created images of him such as this one.

Oral poetry

Although the *Iliad* was written down, it still bears the hallmarks of oral poetry – that is, poetry recited by heart without reference to a written version. Of course, it is much easier to remember poetry than it is prose since poetry has a rhythm and metre (think how lines from a catchy song can easily stay in your head). The Homeric poems were composed in a specific poetic metre, the **hexameter**, which had six 'feet', or metrical units, to each line. Greeks used a word to describe the hexameter line or hexameter poetry – 'epos', originally meaning 'word' or 'utterance'. We therefore call it **epic poetry**.

However, the *Iliad* contains more than 15,000 lines, and so we might ask how a bard was able to remember such an extraordinary amount. Part of the answer is that the poem has a number of repetitive elements typical of oral poetry – in fact, about a third of the lines of the poem are repeated wholly or in part. Moreover, it seems that each poet would develop his own version each time he presented it – he could use the repetitive elements as a starting point, and then insert his own lines around them, or use lines with which he was already familiar. The repetitive elements therefore acted as building blocks for each poet to work from, and allowed him to improvise each time he gave a performance (a comparison could be made with the way in which improvisation is a key feature of jazz music today).

An example of a repetitive element in the *Iliad* is the **epithet**. An epithet is an adjective or adjectival phrase that is repeatedly used to describe a character. When you read the poem, you will notice that the goddess Athena is often referred to as 'bright-eyed' or 'golden-haired', while Diomedes is frequently 'of the loud war-cry', and Hector 'of the gleaming helm'. These phrases neatly made up metrical units and so allowed the poet to fill up part of a line with ease. While each epithet tells us something important about the character being described, it is not always relevant to the exact situation of the poem. Two contrasting examples can be found early in your prescribed literature if we focus on the epithet 'Diomedes of the loud war-cry'.

In the first example, after Diomedes has wounded the goddess Aphrodite at the end of Book 5, section 297–351, the narrative reads as follows:

> Over her Diomedes of the loud war-cry raised a great shout of triumph: "Daughter of Zeus, leave battle and strife to others. Isn't it enough that you snare feeble women? Rejoin the fight and you'll learn to shudder at the name of war!"
>
> Homer, *Iliad*, 5.347–351

Clearly, in this instance the epithet is entirely appropriate to the situation, since Diomedes is shouting triumphantly at Aphrodite on the battlefield.

However, consider the follow example from Book 6, where Diomedes meets an opponent, Glaucus, on the battlefield and learns that he has old family ties with him:

> Diomedes of the loud war-cry rejoiced at these words. Planting his spear in the fertile earth, he spoke to the Lycian general courteously: "You are, then, a friend of long-standing to my father's house."
>
> Homer, *Iliad*, 6.212–215

Here Diomedes' polite speech does not match with him being 'of the loud war-cry'. The poet has used the epithet to fill up a line and to remind us of Diomedes' general character; however, perhaps this also makes his polite conversation with Glaucus even more surprising and remarkable.

hexameter a poetic metre that has six units to a line

epic poetry poetry focusing on great deeds, composed in hexameter verse

epithet an adjectival word or phrase regularly added to a name to denote a personal or physical quality

Study questions

1 How are jazz musicians and rap musicians able to improvise when they perform?
2 Do you think that this adds to an artist's performance?

> **EXPLORE FURTHER**
>
> For a long time it was doubted that was humanly possible to recite such a long poem that had not been written down, especially since each line had to fit the same metre. However, in the 1930s an American scholar called Milman Parry studied poets in Bosnia, where there was a low level of literacy and long poems were still recited by heart. One illiterate poet was able to recite a 12,000-line poem, proving that what had been done in Greek times was indeed possible. What is also interesting about this survey is that Parry noted that each performance was different, even if the storyteller believed that he had produced an exact repetition of an earlier performance. This therefore illustrated that improvisation was a key feature of oral poetry.

There are other examples in the *Iliad* of repetitive poetry besides epithets. Sometimes entire lines are repeated, while there are also longer repeated sections for situations such as making a prayer to a god or a feasting scene. Therefore, when you read the poem, do not be surprised to see this repetition – and remember that it is evidence of the remarkable way in which it came to be composed.

PLOT STRUCTURE

The Trojan War story was well known in ancient times. It tells of a war at Troy in Asia Minor (see map, pages xxx–xxx) between the Greeks and the Trojans over Helen, the wife of King Menelaus of Sparta, and by reputation the most beautiful woman in the world. Helen had been kidnapped by a Trojan prince, Paris, who brought her back to his home city as his wife. In outrage, the Greek chieftains prepared a huge armada of ships to sail to Troy and retrieve her. The ensuing war lasted for ten years, and the Greeks finally won thanks to the trickery of one of their leaders, Odysseus. He came up with the famous idea of ambushing the Trojans by concealing Greek soldiers inside a wooden horse and presenting it to them as a peace offering. The Trojans pulled the horse inside their city and began wild celebrations at what they thought was victory at last. That night, however, the soldiers climbed out of the horse and opened the gates for their comrades, who had returned in secret. The Greeks overran the city, set it on fire, and either killed the Trojans or took them away as slaves.

However, the *Iliad* does not tell this whole story, or indeed anything like it. Instead, it focuses on one short period during the final year of the war; at times, the poet makes mention of other parts of the story, but for the most part he relies on the fact that his audience already knows it well. The poem is divided into twenty-four 'books' – although the word 'book' here really corresponds to what we would understand as a 'chapter', and the name comes from the fact that each book equated to the length of a papyrus scroll, which it was written down on. The whole action of the poem takes place over a fifty-day period. Of this, twenty-two days pass in Book 1; the action of Book 2 through to Book 22 happens over a period of just five days, while twenty-three more days pass during the final two books. Such a short span of time gives the work great intensity.

Plot summary: the anger of Achilles

The central theme of the poem is the anger of the greatest Greek warrior, Achilles. In **Book 1**, Achilles gets into a great quarrel with Agamemnon, the overall commander of the Greek forces. As a result, Agamemnon takes from Achilles a slave girl he has won in battle, Briseis. This is a great dishonour – the concept of honour is very important to Homeric heroes, and it is gained by the award of trophies captured in war, both people and rich possessions (see p. 405). Enraged by his treatment, Achilles refuses to fight for the Greeks any more, and also withdraws his own people, the Myrmidons, from the fight. Moreover, Achilles' mother, the sea goddess Thetis, who is also angered by her son's treatment, travels to Zeus and persuades him to allow the Trojans to get the upper hand so that the Greeks will realise how much they value Achilles. Zeus agrees to allow this, although he says that he cannot alter the fact that Troy is fated to fall to the Greeks.

Books 2 to 7 cover the first day's fighting after this quarrel. Within the poem, these books serve to introduce the main characters and to give the context against which the anger of Achilles will play itself out. In your two prescribed books from this part of the poem, you will read first in **Book 5** about the exploits of a great Greek warrior, Diomedes, as well as about the involvement of the gods in the battle; the focus then shifts in **Book 6** to within the walls of Troy when Hector, the greatest Trojan warrior and the oldest son of Troy's King Priam, returns from battle and meets his mother Hecabe and his wife Andromache, as well as Helen and Paris. At the end of this day's fighting, there follows a day-long truce while each side buries its dead – a theme that will become very important.

Book 8 describes the second day's fighting after the quarrel, and it is at this stage that Zeus actively enables the Trojans to gain the upper hand by forbidding the gods to take part – until now they have been taking sides and balancing out the contest. The Greeks are now alarmed by the fact that the Trojans are camping out on the plain. In **Book 9**, the same evening, Agamemnon concedes that he has made a terrible mistake by insulting Achilles and sends other eminent Greeks to offer him a sincere apology – together with a fabulous collection of prizes and the return of Briseis. However, Achilles will have none of it. He argues that honour is not something that can be valued inconsistently. Despite listening to powerful arguments urging him to return to the fighting, he remains stubborn and even threatens to go home to Greece. At this point we see Achilles unable to let his anger go, something that will have terrible consequences in the coming days.

Book 10 recounts a daring spying mission during the same night into the Trojan camp by two Greek warriors, Odysseus and Diomedes. The action of the third day's fighting takes place between Books 11 and 17. In **Book 11**, the leading Greeks, Agamemnon, Odysseus and Diomedes, are all wounded, while Ajax is forced to retreat. The following book sees the Trojans breach the wall of the Greek camp. In **Books 13** and **14**, the action slows down as Zeus is tricked by Hera into taking his eye off events – the queen of the gods seduces her husband. He falls asleep and so Poseidon helps the Greeks. In **Book 15**, Zeus wakes up and restores the Trojan fortunes – not only have the Trojans breached the

KEY INDIVIDUALS

Achilles the greatest Greek warrior, who refuses to fight after he feels dishonoured

Agamemnon the leader of the Greek forces, who dishonours Achilles

KEY INDIVIDUALS

Hector the greatest Trojan warrior, the son of King Priam of Troy

Priam the King of Troy

Hecabe the wife of Priam and Queen of Troy

Andromache the wife of Hector

wall, but they are now actively threatening the Greek ships, which they intend to burn, so trapping the Greeks without a supply line.

Book 16 is one of the pivotal books of the poem: Patroclus, Achilles' closest friend and one who had also stayed out of the fighting, begs Achilles to let him rejoin battle wearing Achilles' armour; he believes (correctly) that the Trojans are so scared of Achilles that if they believe he is back in battle, they will be intimidated and retreat. Achilles relents but warns Patroclus not to get carried away; he should only drive the Trojans back from the Greek camp and not try to go as far as the walls of Troy. Achilles also sends the Myrmidons back into battle and urges them to fight bravely. Initially, the plan works and Patroclus has great success in driving back the Trojans, including killing a noble Trojan, Sarpedon, a son of Zeus. However, Patroclus becomes overconfident and advances to the walls of Troy where he is killed by Hector; as he lies dying, he prophesies that Achilles will avenge him.

In **Book 17** there is a fierce fight over the body of Patroclus, which the Trojans want to win so that they can keep his armour (which is of course really Achilles' armour) as a

trophy, and then ransom back the body. They manage to strip the armour but eventually the Greeks recapture the body. **Book 18** is set back in the Greek camp, where news is brought to Achilles of Patroclus' death. He is distraught and becomes fixated on taking revenge on Hector, transferring the anger he felt towards Agamemnon onto the Trojan hero. Although he knows that he is fated to die soon after Hector does, he plans to return to the battle to avenge his dear friend. His mother arranges for the blacksmith god Hephaistos to make new armour for him, including a magnificent shield, which is described in detail. In **Book 19**, Achilles and Agamemnon make up their quarrel and the Greeks prepare themselves for battle once more, and then in **Book 20** Zeus allows the gods to rejoin the fighting, and the battle starts; Achilles and Hector inspire their troops, but Hector is warned by Apollo to stay clear of Achilles. The fighting continues in **Book 21**, with the gods coming into sharp focus. Achilles is merciless in his killing.

FIGURE 4.40
A scene from an earlier
stage in the war, where
Achilles tends Patroclus'
wounds.

Book 22 is another central book in the poem, and sees the final showdown between Achilles and Hector. The other Trojans have now retreated inside the walls of Troy but Hector is left outside. From the walls, his mother and father beg him not to fight against Achilles, but he does not listen to them. However, when Achilles comes closer, Hector becomes scared and takes flight; he is chased round the walls of the city three times; eventually, however, he chooses to stop and fight after the goddess Athena tricks him by disguising herself as his brother who has come to help him. He turns and faces Achilles but soon realises that he has been tricked and his time has come. He begs Achilles to return his body for a proper burial – it was believed that without burial a person's spirit could not travel to the Underworld and was in limbo forever. Achilles refuses to do this; he kills Hector, strips his armour and ties his naked body to his chariot, dragging it away to the Greek camp. His anger has led him to ignore all the norms of human behaviour, which are sacred even in a time of war.

In **Book 23**, Achilles holds funeral games for Patroclus. There is a great contrast between the way he treats his friend in death and the treatment given to Hector, whose body is left unburied outside Achilles' tent. **Book 24** begins with Achilles a picture of unresolved grief – his revenge over Hector has brought him no closure; each day, he drags Hector's corpse around the funeral mound to Patroclus. However, most of the gods are horrified by this behaviour, and Apollo protects Hector's corpse from any disfigurement or decay. They send Thetis to tell Achilles to cease from his outrageous behaviour and to accept a ransom for the body of Hector. Zeus then sends Iris, the goddess of the rainbow, to tell Priam to prepare to go to the Greek camp with a fabulous ransom for his son's body.

He is escorted there in secret by the god Hermes, and led to Achilles' tent. He enters and begs Achilles for his son's body back. He asks him to think of his own father, Peleus, who will not now see his son again since Achilles is fated to die soon. Priam even kisses Achilles' hands. Achilles reacts with amazement and compassion to Priam's request, and agrees to return Hector's body, and the two enemies weep together: Priam for Hector and Achilles for Patroclus. They are united in experiencing the tragedy of war and of human life. Achilles has returned to being fully human again; his anger has been resolved as he accepts his forthcoming death and abides by the rules of human decency. He returns the body and agrees to a truce of eleven days to give Priam time to bury and remember Hector. The poem ends with Priam's return to Troy with the body, and the lamentations of the Trojans who see him arrive with it.

The Homeric hero

Even this short outline of the poem forces us to confront how Homeric heroes understood their world and their place in it. A Homeric hero is ultimately preoccupied with two related concepts: his honour and his glory. In Greek, these two words were represented by the words **time** (pronounced 'tim-air') and **kleos**. Closely related to these was the concept of 'shame' or 'respect', as represented by the word **aidos**.

- **time** (honour) Homeric heroes win honour by being awarded highly valued possessions as trophies of excellence: for example, such a trophy could be an enemy's armour, treasure from a conquered city, cattle, or human trophies who serve as slaves having been captured in war.

  > **time** the honour a Homeric warrior hopes to win

- **aidos** (shame/respect) Closely linked to the concept of time is the idea that the people around you show you great respect and choose to give you the trophies of honour – in Greek, the word for such respect was **aidos**. This is often translated as 'shame' but may equally be thought of as showing humility and respect in the face of the honoured person. In Achilles' case, he had been awarded Briseis as a trophy of war by the army, who had showed aidos towards him. Agamemnon's removal of this prize was therefore a great dishonour.

  > **aidos** the shame or respectful modesty a Homeric character feels towards someone who has great time

- **kleos** (glory) The most basic meaning of kleos was 'what people hear said about you' – we might think of it as 'glorious reputation'. To have great honour means that you will be well spoken of and that your memory will live on long after you

  > **kleos** the glorious reputation a Homeric warrior hopes to win

Study questions

1 How is the word 'hero' used in our society today?

2 How would you define a hero?

S Our world has a
& modern set of 'rules of
C war', which are governed by the Geneva Conventions. Find out about these conventions – would you add or change any of their main rules? Do you think that there are any noticeable 'rules of war' in the sections of the *Iliad* that you read?

Achaeans, Argives, Danaans all Homeric terms for the Greeks

have died. This is the way in which a Homeric hero can achieve a form of immortality.

One of the key related themes of the *Iliad* is how a Homeric hero treats the corpse of a conquered enemy. A victorious fighter will try to strip the armour from a man he has killed in battle, and keep it as a trophy. He will also seek to take away the body so that he can ransom it back to the dead man's family for burial. Both Greeks and Trojans believed that a body needed burial in order to reach the underworld, and so denying a man a burial was a terrible thing to do, and one of which the gods generally disapprove.

One other point might be made about the heroic warfare depicted in the *Iliad*. It focuses largely on high-status heroes rather than the soldiers fighting in the ranks. Indeed, there is almost no focus on the common soldier in the poem, and the interest is on the fights between the high-status heroes who lead their men into battle, and who try to defend their people and comrades, and in so doing to win time and kleos.

Greeks and Trojans

In your text, you will notice that the Greeks are often referred to by one of three other names – the **Achaeans**, the **Argives** or the **Danaans**. In fact, these are the only terms that Homer uses for the Greeks, although your translation often refers to them as Greeks instead.

Moreover, even though the Trojans are perceived to be foreigners, they have the same language, customs and gods as the Greeks. This made it much easier for Homer to portray both sides in the conflict, and for the two sides to engage with each other during the poem.

BOOK 5.84–469

KEY INDIVIDUAL

Diomedes one of the greatest Greek warriors, often referred to as the son of Tydeus

aristeia a scene in an epic poem in which a great warrior fights with exceptional courage

The action of Book 5 is largely centred on the great prowess and achievements in battle of the Greek warrior Diomedes. Although not as great a fighter as Achilles, Diomedes is one of the Greeks' finest and it is he who leads the attack against the Trojans in Achilles' absence. The focus on Diomedes in battle begins in Book 4, after Agamemnon insults him about his lack of effort in battle and compares him unfavourably with his father Tydeus. Slighted, Diomedes sets out to prove Agamemnon wrong; there follows the first major battle sequence in the *Iliad*. It is also the poem's first example of a focus on one particular warrior's achievements in battle; such a sequence is commonly known as an **aristeia**, from the Greek word 'aristos' which meant 'best' – an aristeia portrays a great warrior's best moments in battle.

Diomedes is given special strength at the start of Book 5 by the goddess Athena, who wants him to stand out among all the Greeks. We see him rampaging across the battlefield bringing death and destruction, and it is worth focusing for a moment on one short scene:

Astynous and General Hyperion he killed, striking one above the nipple with a throw of his bronze-tipped spear, the other with his long sword on the collarbone, shearing the shoulder from the neck and spine. Leaving them lying there, he chased down Abas and Polyidus, sons of old Eurydamas, interpreter of dreams. They came not back again, whom great Diomedes slew, for their father to tell their dreams. Then he pursued Xanthus and Thoön, Phaenops' dear sons: an old man too weighed down with age to get himself fresh heirs. Diomedes killed both, leaving their sorrowing father to weep when they failed to return, and his surviving kin to inherit.

Homer, Iliad, 5.144–158

In this scene, the poet tries to give very short biographical details about the men Diomedes slaughters. In the cases of Astynous and Hyperion, it is simply the way in which each one dies. For the brothers Abas and Polyidus, we hear of their father Eurydamas, and the poet reflects for a moment on a typical scene from their family life that will happen no more: Eurydamas, an interpreter of dreams, will no longer be able to use his skill for the benefit of his sons. The same theme of fatherhood is seen in the deaths of Xanthus and Thoön; in this instance, it is the age of Phaenops that is emphasised, as he is now too old to have more children. We are left with the image of an old man weeping at the loss of his beloved sons.

These few lines are indicative of the skill of the poet. They portray the mayhem and violence of the battlefield, but also the tragedy surrounding the deaths of some of the men. It would be much less interesting if we knew nothing about them and if Homer simply gave us a list of names of those Diomedes killed – by adding these short biographical details the poet adds great richness to the narrative. We might also note that a key theme in these lines is that of bereaved fathers, something that will come to the fore during the final book of the poem.

Two examples of the *Iliad*'s influence today

The contemporary poet Alice Oswald in 2011 published a poem called *Memorial*. She developed Homer's idea of saying a little about each man who died, and her poem focuses on the more than 200 men who are named as having died fighting at Troy in the *Iliad*. Her poem starts simply by listing the names of the dead, like a war memorial does. Oswald then tries to bring out poetically all that we know from Homer about the dead. The narrative is interspersed with direct translations of some of Homer's similes. Her poem is meant as a tribute to each individual soldier, and so tries to highlight the poignancy of each death.

A second example of how the *Iliad* has been interpreted in modern times is given in the book *Achilles in Vietnam* by Jonathan Shay. Dr Shay is an American psychiatrist who found that reading the *Iliad* in therapy groups with traumatised veterans of the Vietnam War was helpful to their recovery; the veterans found that they could identify with many of the themes and characters in the poem, and with the terrible situations in which they found themselves. In *Achilles in Vietnam*, Shay describes how he used the *Iliad* to work with these veterans.

Why do you think it might be that the *Iliad* continues to have such influence today, nearly three thousand years after its composition?

PS

EXAM TIP

Interpreting similes

One special feature of the *Iliad* is the number of beautiful similes which the poet uses. Your own selection from Book 5 begins with one example:

> As for Diomedes, none could have said which army Greek or Trojan he fought for, since he stormed over the plain like a raging winter torrent that sweeps away the dykes in its swift flood. Close-built embankments and the walls of fertile vineyards fail to hold its onset driven by Zeus' storm and before it the proud works of men all tumble to ruin: so the dense ranks of the Trojans were routed by Tydeus' son, giving way to him despite their numbers.
>
> Homer, *Iliad*, 5.85–94

Homer often draws on the natural world as a source of similes. Here, the poet uses the image of a torrential, overwhelming flood which destroys everything in its path to try to capture the carnage caused by Diomedes' fighting. The warrior is also seen to be elevated above the level of human beings ('none could have said which army Greek or Trojan he fought for'), while he manages to kill vast numbers of men on his own.

In an exam, it is important to explain why a simile is powerful and effective. In this case, the simile presents an image that it is easy for us to conjure up: floodwaters that overrun all before them. Rather than simply giving us facts about the number of men Diomedes killed, the simile allows us to create an image of just how devastating and overwhelming his fighting is. The use of such a simile also has another effect, which is to act as a 'pause button' on action that is happening at breakneck speed: we are allowed to step back from the events of the battle for a moment, and to reflect on them more deeply.

Pandarus and Aeneas

The focus of the episode you first read in Book 5 is the contest between Diomedes on one side, and the Trojan warriors Pandarus and Aeneas on the other:

> **KEY INDIVIDUAL**
>
> **Aeneas** a Trojan warrior who is the son of the goddess Aphrodite

- **Aeneas** became associated in later times with leading surviving Trojans away from the city after its defeat, and bringing them to Italy as settlers – he therefore becomes the main character in Virgil's *Aeneid*, which you will read about on pp. 429–439. However, in the *Iliad*, Aeneas is just one of a number of impressive Trojan warriors, although in his case he receives special protection from his mother, the goddess Aphrodite.

> **KEY INDIVIDUAL**
>
> **Pandarus** a Trojan warrior who is an expert archer

- **Pandarus** is an expert archer who has already made his mark in Book 4; in Book 3 a truce had been agreed between the two sides while Menelaus and Paris fought a duel between themselves to decide the outcome of the war. Menelaus wins, but the gods supporting the Trojans refuse to accept the result, and Athena in disguise persuades Pandarus to break the truce by firing an arrow at Menelaus, which he does, wounding the Greek commander.

In the action in Book 5, Pandarus has once again had success as an archer, managing to wound Diomedes. Unaware of this, Aeneas comes to him and urges him to shoot an arrow at Diomedes; Pandarus reflects that he has already done so, and has not managed to halt the Greek's progress – he concludes (correctly) that a god is helping him. At this point, the poet allows Pandarus to give us some more biographical detail about himself, specifically the reason that he fights with a bow in the absence of horses and a chariot.

This biographical information will make the death of Pandarus more moving, since we know something about his homeland. Aeneas suggests that Pandarus jump into his chariot and they attack Diomedes together, and it is worth reflecting here on the use of chariots in Homeric poetry: the chariot is not a weapon of war to give warriors speed in battle in the way that a horse might – in fact, it only serves the purpose of delivering fighters to the thick of battle; some commentators have even referred to Homer's chariots as glorified taxis.

The involvement of the gods

Athena has already been active supporting Diomedes in Book 5. After the death of Pandarus, the role of the gods in the battle comes into sharper focus; first Aphrodite protects Aeneas from being killed by Diomedes; then Diomedes himself goes after Aphrodite and manages to wound her. She returns to Mt Olympus upset, and is comforted by her mother Dione while other gods also make comments about the situation. Then Apollo intervenes in the battle, rescuing Aeneas and warning off Diomedes, then calling upon Ares to join him in battle. To a modern reader, the involvement of the gods in battle may seem strange, and so we should reflect for a moment on this key aspect of the *Iliad*.

On one level, the gods come across to mortals as powerful, awe-inspiring and at times terrifying. However, they have very human flaws and also take sides in the battle. Apollo, Ares and Aphrodite side with the Trojans, while Athena, Hera and Poseidon side with the Greeks. Zeus, the father of the gods, tries to stay above the fray – although he does of course agree to Thetis' request to help the Trojans. To us, it may seem like cheating to rely on a god's help in battle, but the Greeks did not see it this way: they thought that only great heroes were supported by the gods, and so it was a measure of heroic status to have a god support you.

Moreover, it is interesting is to observe the gods relating to each other on Mount Olympus, as we do in lines 352–430. Here they behave like any other family – both supporting and annoying each other. Dione tries to comfort her upset daughter Aphrodite, but afterwards Hera and Athena – who of course support the other side in the war – try to provoke Zeus with mockery of the situation:

> Bright-eyed Athena was the first to speak: "Father Zeus, I hope you won't be angry at what I say. It seems your Cyprian daughter has been at work luring some Greek girl to chase after those Trojans she loves so deeply, and while fondling this girl and her golden brooch, scratched her own delicate hand."
>
> Homer, *Iliad*, 5.418–425

FIGURE 4.41
Two Homeric warriors fighting.

The joke here is on Aphrodite. Athena pretends that she cannot imagine the goddess of love fighting in battle, so assumes that she must have been encouraging a Greek woman to chase after one of the Trojans Aphrodite is so fond of; in so doing, she must have scratched her hand on the woman's golden brooch as she stroked her. Zeus' only reaction is to smile at the joke and tell Aphrodite that she does not belong in battle.

This episode illustrates something very important about Homer's gods. While they have human qualities and human frailties, in one crucial way they are very unlike human beings: they cannot die. Therefore, their difficulties seem trivial in comparison with human lives. For example, Aphrodite's wound is minor, especially compared to wounds of mortals on the battlefield; neither does she face the possibility of death. However, this also means that the gods cannot display great nobility or heroism by putting their lives on the line in the way that mortals can. The easy, deathless lives of the immortals therefore serve to highlight the risks that mortals must take in battle – as a result, the mortals are far more impressive characters who can face the possibility of death with courage and nobility. This is a key point about the characterisation of the gods in the *Iliad*.

BOOK 6.118–529

At the end of Book 5, Diomedes even manages to wound the war-god Ares with the help of Athena. Although Zeus has promised Thetis that he would let the Trojans have the ascendency, at this point it is the Greeks led by Diomedes who are having the best of it. Therefore Helenus, a son of Priam with prophetic powers, advises his brother Hector to return to the city of Troy and order the women to make offerings to Athena so that she might hold back Diomedes from conquering the city. Hector agrees to do so, and for most of the rest of the book the action takes place inside the walls of Troy.

Diomedes and Glaucus

Before that, however, the focus switches to the battlefield and a meeting between Diomedes and Glaucus, a fighter on the Trojan side from the region of Lycia to the south of Troy. When they first meet, Diomedes asks Glaucus his name and his ancestry, something which might seem strange to us. However, it fits well with the theme of time and kleos – a warrior wants to win significant victories and so it is important to know who he is up against so that he can add to his reputation if he wins (we might think today of the way in which prize-fighters in boxing will speak up about their record before a fight).

Diomedes has been so impressed by Glaucus' fighting that he suspects that he may be a god. He has learnt now not to take on gods (despite having wounded Ares) and uses a myth involving Dionysus to back up his point. In reply, Glaucus also uses a myth – that of Bellerophon – to explain his family lineage and to trace it back to Greece. The two realise that their families have a tradition of 'guest-friendship', in Greek known as **xenia**, a formal relationship between two noble families which carried sacred importance. Diomedes then greets him warmly and suggests they behave as follows:

> **xenia** in Homer, hospitality given unconditionally to a traveller, involving the giving of any help needed; known as 'guest-friendship'

Let us avoid each other's spear in the battle, there are plenty more Trojans and their worthy allies for me to slay, if a god lets my feet overtake them, and many Greeks for you to kill, if you can.

Homer, *Iliad*, 6.226–229

It might surprise us that Diomedes is prepared not to fight an enemy, and even more that he acknowledges that Glaucus will have the chance to kill many of his fellow Greeks. However, many wars have stories of friends on either side of the conflict who try to avoid fighting one another, and so Homer here acknowledges how complex warfare can be.

Inside the walls of Troy

One of the remarkable features of the *Iliad* is that the poet is able to portray both sides of the war – Greeks and Trojans – in a sympathetic light. This is often not the case with war literature, or even with war films in our modern world. In some ways, it is much easier for a writer to create a plot where the 'good guys' take on the 'bad guys' and the reader or viewer has a clear preference for one side over the other. The *Iliad* resists this, something which contributes to its greatness as a poem – it is able to portray sympathetic characters on both sides of the conflict. It is often said that the poet uses great **pathos**, a literary term that describes an appeal to a reader's emotions by inviting them to feel pity and sadness.

This is especially the case in Book 6 when we see Hector withdraw into the walls of Troy. It could be argued that Hector is the most impressive character in the entire poem: while he fights for his time and kleos as the Greek heroes do, he is also defending his city and its people from defeat, which will bring them death or slavery. In Book 6, therefore, we meet him not just as a warrior, but also as a son, a husband, a brother and a father. We are introduced to his mother Hecabe, his wife Andromache and his sister-in-law Helen. This allows the poet to explore and portray the experience of female non-combatants in the war, and the pain that they must endure as they watch on helplessly. At times, the events of the book are almost unbearably moving.

Each of the three women tries to keep Hector away from the battle. First, he meets his mother; he refuses a cup of wine – such is his determination to stay focused for fighting

FIGURE 4.42
Diomedes and Glaucus exchange armour.

> **pathos** literally 'suffering' in Greek, an appeal to the reader's emotions by inviting them to feel pity and sadness

Study question

The episode between Glaucus and Diomedes contains some of the most famous lines in Homer, spoken by Glaucus:

> Like the generations of leaves are those of men. The wind blows and one year's leaves are scattered on the ground, but the trees bud and fresh leaves open when spring comes again. So a generation of men is born as another passes away.
>
> Homer, *Iliad*, 6.146–149

Why do you think that people find this simile so moving? What idea is it putting across?

– and instructs her to make an offering to Athena. He then moves to Paris' home, where he finds his brother with Helen (in Book 3, Paris has been rescued from a duel with Menelaus and brought back into Troy by Aphrodite). Paris is handling his weapons while Helen and her womenfolk are weaving – the comparison portrays Paris as a coward most at home in the company of women, a great contrast to Hector. Hector criticises him for staying out of the fight, a criticism Paris accepts as he agrees to ready himself for battle again. Helen then speaks, full of self-loathing at her situation – she is the cause of the war and all its suffering. It is hard not to pity her. She then invites Hector to sit down and talk with her, an offer he refuses so that he can return to the battle.

Next comes one of the most celebrated scenes in the poem, the meeting of Hector and Andromache at the Scaean gates, the main gates of the city. Andromache runs up to her husband; behind her is a nurse carrying their baby son Astyanax. Andromache begs him to stay out of the fighting; she lists the family members she has already lost in the war, most notably her father and seven brothers. Her plea culminates in the following words:

> Hector you are parent, brother, husband to me. Take pity on me now, and stay here on the battlements, don't make your son an orphan, your wife a widow.

Homer, *Iliad*, 6.429–432

Hector rejects her plea, explaining that he must return to the battle for the sake of his kleos and his people. Yet he acknowledges that he knows deep down that Troy will fall sooner rather than later. What he fears most when this moment comes is not the fate of his people, or his parents, but for Andromache as she is hauled off into humiliating slavery. He concludes his speech with these words:

> May I be dead, and the earth piled above me, before I hear your cries as they drag you away.

Homer, *Iliad*, 6.464–465

The scene is not yet over. Hector stretches out his arms to take his son, but the baby is terrified by his father in full armour and, in particular, by his helmet (remember that a common epithet of Hector is 'of the gleaming helm'), and so he withdraws crying into his nurse's chest. His parents laugh gently at the reaction; Hector removes his helmet and takes his son, moving him lightly up and down in his arms. Beneath the armour of the great warrior emerges the tender and loving father. This paradox between tenderness and ferocity is further brought out in Hector's next speech, where he prays that his son will grow up to be a greater warrior than he is, and bring joy to his mother's heart through his performance in battle.

Having said these words, Hector then returns Astyanax to his mother:

> With this he placed the child in his dear wife's arms, and she took him to her fragrant breast, smiling through her tears. Her husband was touched with pity at this, and stroked her with his hand, saying: 'Andromache, dear wife, don't grieve for me too deeply yet. None will send me to Hades before my time: though no man, noble or humble, once born can escape his fate.'

Homer, *Iliad*, 6.464–465

With this, he tells her to return home while he himself heads back out to war with Paris. This is the last time that Andromache will see Hector alive, something she seems to know instinctively – she returns straight home, where she and her maids mourn for Hector as if he is already dead.

BOOK 22.21–409

Your final two selections of reading come from near the end of the poem. Book 22 describes the death of Hector at the hands of Achilles, and its aftermath. In Book 5 you have read about warfare out on the battle-field and in Book 6 you have read about the situation inside the walls of Troy. Book 22 unites the two, as Hector and Achilles fight on the battlefield while Hector's parents and fellow Trojans look on from the walls of Troy. Once again the poet uses pathos as both Priam and Hecabe appeal to Hector not to stay and fight against Achilles, whom he cannot beat. Hector debates what to do, and he resolves to stand and fight; but when Achilles approaches, he takes fright and runs. Achilles chases him three times around the walls of Troy.

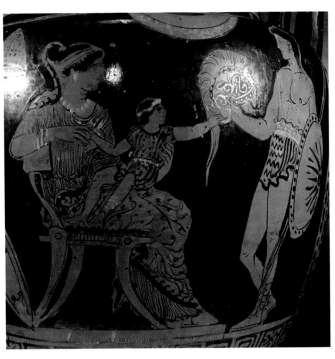

FIGURE 4.43
Hector, Andromache and Astyanax. Astyanax reaches out to touch his father's helmet.

The gods and fate

The poem presents a world in which every mortal has their fated time of death. The concept of **fate** – meaning those events that are destined to happen and cannot be changed – stands apart from the gods. It is not the Olympian gods who decide a person's fate, but three other goddesses, known collectively as the Fates, who spin out the length of a life when someone is born. However, Zeus does have a role as overseer of fate – he has to ensure that what is fated comes to pass, however much it may sadden him.

He is certainly saddened by the impending fate of Hector as he is chased around the walls by Achilles. He even wonders aloud to the other gods if he should try to save him. Athena replies to say that this would not win the support of the other gods, and she implies that it would be wrong for him to do so. Zeus agrees, and Athena heads off to assist Achilles. A few lines later, as the chase continues, Zeus dramatically weighs up the lives of the two men in his golden scales:

> When they reached The Springs for the fourth time, the Father raised his golden scales, and set the deaths of Achilles and horse-taming Hector in the balance, and lifted it on high. Down sank Hector's lot towards Hades, and Phoebus Apollo left his side, while bright-eyed Athena came to Achilles.
>
> Homer, *Iliad*, 22.208–214

> **fate** a set of future events that are destined to happen and cannot be changed

Here, Zeus is seen as the god who upholds fate no matter the situation. As the fight unfolds, the modern reader might be surprised or unimpressed that Achilles needs the assistance and trickery of Athena (who disguises herself as Hector's brother Deiphobus) to make Hector stand and fight him. We might think that a great hero should be able to win unaided. However, it is important to state once more that in the Greek mind the support of a god indicated just what a great hero you were – from this perspective, a victory for Achilles without the help of the gods would be less impressive.

The death of Hector

Before their duel, Hector offers Achilles a pact that the victor will not mistreat the dead body of the loser, but will return it for burial. Once again, it is essential to understand how important this idea is in the Homeric world – to be unburied after death is worse than to die itself, since the spirit can never find peace. Yet Achilles will have none of it, such is his rage towards Hector and what he has done: he says that there can be no treaties between lions and men, or between wolves and lambs.

When Hector realises Athena's trick, and that he is doomed, he accepts his fate, but says:

> But let me not die without a fight, without true glory, without some deed that men unborn may hear.

Homer, *Iliad*, 22.304–305

Hector remains noble to the last, and hopes that his death will add to his kleos. However, he is no match for Achilles, who drives his spear through his enemy's throat, but does not cut the windpipe so that Hector can still just speak before he dies. He begs again for Achilles to return his body to his parents so that he can receive a decent burial. Achilles' reply is chilling:

> Don't speak of my parents, dog. I wish the fury and the pain in me could drive me to carve and eat you raw for what you did, as surely as this is true: no living man will keep the dogs from gnawing at your skull.

Homer, *Iliad*, 22.345–348

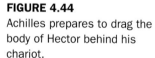

FIGURE 4.44
Achilles prepares to drag the body of Hector behind his chariot.

This is the height of Achilles' rage, and his anger seems to have robbed him of all sense of humanity. He continues like this after killing Hector, piercing holes in his dead foe's ankles and dragging him back to the Greek camp behind his chariot. From the walls of Troy, the people grieve as if the city were on fire – which it soon will be, given that they know the prophecy that Troy will fall after the death of Hector. Soon afterwards, Andromache hears the cries and runs from her home to the walls, where she sees Hector's body being dragged away. She faints at the sight.

BOOK 24.468–620

During Book 23 the Greeks hold funeral games for Patroclus, honouring his memory and giving him a good burial. The contrast with the treatment of Hector's body is stark. At the start of Book 24, the poet describes Achilles' behaviour towards Hector's corpse: he can get no peace or resolution from having killed him, and continues to weep for Patroclus; from time to time, he gets up, climbs into his chariot, and drags Hector's body around the funeral mound that has been raised for his beloved friend.

However, most of the Olympian gods are outraged by Achilles' behaviour. Apollo protects the corpse, while Zeus orders that a resolution be found – Thetis must persuade Achilles to accept a ransom from Priam for Hector's body. Thetis manages to do this, while the messenger goddess Iris travels to Priam to tell him to prepare a ransom and to travel to the Greek camp with it. Despite the misgivings of Hecabe, he agrees to do so. Priam arrives at the tent of Achilles with the aid of the god Hermes who comes to him in disguise as a Myrmidon attendant of Achilles, and guides him through the Greek camp unseen. Here is another example of a god enhancing the status of a mortal by giving him help. Although Priam is an old man who does not fight in the war, he is still worthy of a god's support.

Achilles and Priam

The meeting between the two men is another remarkable scene in the poem (lines 468–620). It starts with silent action as Achilles sits in his tent after finishing dinner, attended by two friends:

> Great Priam slipped in unobserved, and reaching Achilles, clasped his knees, and kissed his hands, the fearful, man-killing hands that had slaughtered so many of his sons. Achilles was astonished at the sight of godlike Priam, as were his friends. They stared at each other, astounded.

> Homer, *Iliad*, 24.477–483

Priam is able to kiss the hands of the man who has killed not just Hector but many other sons of his too. The aged king then appeals for the return of the body with one poignant request – he asks Achilles to think of his own father, Peleus, who is an old man back home in Greece. Achilles is fated to die soon, and so he will never see his father again – Priam appeals to their shared experience and the appeal reminds him that his own father will soon be bereaved in the same way that Priam is. The two men then weep,

Study questions

1 How does the poet create pathos through the speeches of Priam and Hecabe at the start of Book 22?
2 Why do you think that Achilles behaves in this way? Do you think that his anger against Hector is reasonable or understandable given what he has suffered in the war?

PS

Priam for Hector and Achilles for Patroclus. Achilles at this moment is much softened and deeply changed from the moment when he took such savage revenge on Hector.

In reply, Achilles is able to acknowledge how much Priam has suffered. He asks the old man to sit with him, then reflects on how much suffering human life can bring – the two men, although enemies in the war, share the human experience of suffering. Priam replies that he cannot sit until he can see Hector's body and know that he will have it back. Achilles has to hold back anger, and at this point we see that his savage side is lurking just below the surface and that he is straining to hold it in. This theme re-emerges a few lines later, when Achilles leaves the tent to organise the return of the body:

Achilles then summoned two servant-girls and ordered them to wash and anoint the body, first carrying it to a place where Priam could not see his son, lest his grief at the sight provoke his anger and Achilles be angered in reply, and kill him in defiance of Zeus' command.

Homer, *Iliad*, 24.582–586

FIGURE 4.45
Priam kisses the hand of Achilles.

Achilles shows great self-awareness here: he knows that his anger could explode, and yet he takes all precautions to prevent this from happening. The body is prepared, and he returns it to Priam. Achilles then invites the old man to eat with him, reminding him that all must eat, no matter their pain. He tells the story of Niobe to illustrate this: Niobe had boasted of being more fertile than Leto, the mother of Apollo and Artemis. As a result, Niobe had lost all ten of her children, but even she started eating again after nine days of mourning (the exact length of time that had elapsed since the death of Hector). It is also significant that in the story of Niobe the gods bury dead mortals, since they had urged Achilles to release Hector's body for burial at the start of Book 24.

The two men sit down to eat together. Achilles will go on to release the body and offer Priam eleven days' truce so that he can bury Hector and commemorate him suitably. Achilles' anger, which began at the start of the poem, is finally resolved; he has accepted death – that of Patroclus, and his own, soon to come.

TOPIC REVIEW

You should be able to:

1. Describe:
   - oral poetry and epic poetry
   - the overall storyline of the *Iliad*
   - the storylines of your prescribed sections of Books 5, 6, 22 and 24
   - the roles played by the main characters, including the gods, Diomedes, Hector, Andromache, Achilles and Priam.

2. Explain:
   - how the Homeric poems are thought to have been composed
   - the requirements of a Homeric hero
   - the key themes of the *Iliad*, especially heroism and the pathos of war
   - how the key characters are portrayed and how sympathetic you find them.

PRACTICE QUESTIONS

Source A: *Homer, Iliad, 6.297–311*

At the shrine of Athena on the Acropolis, lovely Theano flung open the doors. She, whom Troy had appointed priestess of Athena, was daughter to Cisseus, and wife to Antenor, the horse-tamer. They lifted their hands to Athena, with ecstatic cries, while lovely Theano took the robe, laid it on golden-haired Athena's knees, then prayed to the daughter of Zeus. "Lady Athena, fairest of goddesses, protectress of the city, shatter Diomedes' spear. Topple him headlong before the Scaean Gate, and we will sacrifice in your shrine twelve yearling heifers, unused to the goad. Take pity on the city, the Trojan women and their little ones." So Theano prayed, but Pallas Athena denied the prayer.

1. What sort of a phrase is 'golden-haired'? Why does the *Iliad* contain so many of these phrases? [2]

2. How important is it for characters in the *Iliad* to treat the gods with respect? Use this passage as a starting point, and use your own knowledge in the answer. [8]

4.6 Tyrtaeus

Literary context

- The genre and author of your set text
- Its composition and aims

- Narrative and descriptive techniques, including:
  - similes and imagery
  - use of emotive language

Characterisation

- The actions of the characters in your selections
- The traits of each of the main characters and how these are depicted
- Interactions and relationships between characters

- The depiction of:
  - leaders and soldiers
  - comrades and enemies
  - non-combatants
  - women

Themes

- Glory, honour and shame
- Comradeship
- Freedom
- Love and patriotism

- The horror and glorification of warfare
- Fear and courage
- Family and ancestors
- Military and civilian victims of war

Heroes and warfare

- How the content of your selections reflects its political or cultural context, including:
  - details of the historical context
  - what constitutes a 'hero'

  - attitudes towards war and warfare

- The possible responses to the text from different audiences

The prescribed source for this topic is:

- Tyrtaeus, Fragment 10 – *The Fallen Warrior*

Don't forget that you will be given credit in the exam if you study extra sources and make relevant use of them in your answers.

This topic will examine Tyrtaeus, starting with what we know about his life and the times in which he lived. It will then move on to focus on one of the most famous fragments of his poetry, the 'Fallen Warrior' poem. As with your other authors, you should refer to the topic boxes at the start of the chapter to think about how this poem includes many of the themes mentioned there.

BIOGRAPHY

Although Tyrtaeus was composing poems in the same era that the *Iliad* was first written down, he presents a very different type of war poetry. He was a Spartan writing poetry for other Spartans, urging them on in a war they were fighting against their Messenian neighbours. Whereas the *Iliad* is set in the legendary past, Tyrtaeus is writing about men and fighting of his own day. It is therefore very important to understand the historical context in which he is writing.

We have read on page 00 that by the seventh century BC the Spartans had conquered part of the region of Messenia to the west of Laconia, and that at this time the majority of the Messenian population were enslaved as helots to toil on what were now Spartan lands. At some point during the seventh century, the Messenian helots rose up against their enslaved status, and fought a brutal war against their Spartan masters. The Spartans eventually managed to put down the rebellion, but only after years of hard fighting.

It is thought that Tyrtaeus was composing poetry during the years of this war. Regrettably, only fragments of his work have survived – about 250 lines in all. Apart from what we can glean from his poetry, we know very little about his life, although he may have been a Spartan commander during the war. His poems encourage Spartan warriors to put their lives on the line for their city, and emphasise the glory associated with dying for the city in the front line of battle. The focus of his poetry is very different from that of the *Iliad*, since rather than recounting the deeds of great heroes as they duel on the battlefield, Tyrtaeus emphasises the courage needed by Spartan citizen-soldiers to be victorious in battle. Therefore, it is the brave but nameless soldier who is the hero of Tyrtaeus' poetry.

PRESCRIBED SOURCE

Tyrtaeus, Fragment 10 – *The Fallen Warrior*

Date: mid-7th century BC

Location: Sparta

Genre: elegiac poetry

Significance: a poem urguing young Spartan warriors to fight bravely

Read it here: OCR source booklet

Tyrtaeus' poetry came to epitomise Sparta's warrior ideal. Indeed, later Spartans regarded him as their national poet and for centuries his poems were used to inspire Spartan soldiers. Plutarch, a biographer writing in the second century AD (long after Sparta had ceased to be a power), reports a story in which the famous Spartan king Leonidas (see p. 355) comments on the importance of his poetry to Spartan society:

> There is a story that when the Leonidas of ancient times was asked his impression of Tyrtaeus' quality as a poet, he replied: "A good one for firing the spirits of the young." For the poems filled them with such excitement that they stopped caring for themselves in battle.

Plutarch, *Cleomenes*, 2

GENRE AND COMPOSITION

elegy a genre of poetry that can focus on a number of topics, and where lines have an alternating metre of hexameter followed by pentameter

pentameter a poetic metre with five units to a line

Tyrtaeus' poetry belongs to a genre known as **elegy**. Today, an elegy is a lament for the dead, but it had a much wider meaning in Greek times – such a poem could reflect on one or more of any number of topics, including war, politics, religion, love and friendship. An elegy was composed with an alternating metre – a hexameter line followed by a **pentameter** (five-foot line). Like the *Iliad*, it was designed to be listened to by an audience rather than read by an individual. It could, therefore, be performed on public occasions such as religious festivals or military events, or at private social gatherings. It was either sung or spoken, to the accompaniment of a musical instrument called an aulos, a reed instrument similar to an oboe.

THE FALLEN WARRIOR POEM

EXPLORE FURTHER

You can read all of the fragments of Tyrtaeus' poetry by searching online at www.perseus.tufts.edu or by reading them in M L West's *Greek Lyric Poetry* (see reading list on p. 440).

This poem may actually have been two separate poems, something which is acknowledged in your translation by dividing it into two paragraphs. Each paragraph makes clear what is and is not the ideal for a Spartan warrior. The first paragraph begins with a statement of what a Spartan warrior should be proud to do – fight and die in the front line of battle. The poem then shifts its focus abruptly to the opposite, giving an example of what life would be like for a defeated Spartan warrior. He is described as wandering as a beggar with his entire family, having brought shame on his ancestors; moreover, he is a curse to those he meets. Following on from this image, the poem returns to the theme of the opening line: what is good is to put your life on the line in battle, and to give your life for Sparta if the city requires it.

The second paragraph begins with the poet making a direct appeal to the young men who will fight for Sparta. Again, the message is to be brave and not to fear death in battle. A strong contrast is made with an old man fighting in battle – the message is that the young men should not desert and leave old men to do the fighting; it is the duty of the young men to fight in the front line, and it is, therefore, shameful for an old man to be exposed and to die in battle. One way of reading this poem is as a warning to young men about what will happen to their city if they do not do their duty – old men will be forced to take their place in the front line and to die horribly. The younger men are, therefore, encouraged to take

EXAM TIP

Language and imagery

Tyrtaeus presents a very powerful image of such an old man dying:

> For it is of course shameful for an older man fallen among fighters at the front to lie ahead of the young men, his head already white and beard grey, gasping his stalwart spirit out into the dust, clutching his bloody genitals in his own hands – a shameful thing in one's eyes, a sight to cause outrage – his naked skin exposed.
>
> Tyrtaeus, *Fragment 10*, lines 21–27

We might focus on the language and imagery the poet has used here. The word 'shameful' appears twice, a concept further emphasised by the phrase 'a sight to cause outrage'. There are two senses in which this event would be thought shameful: first of all, it would be shameful for the young warriors who have allowed this to happen; beyond this, it would also be shameful for the wider Spartan community, since it is not producing the sort of brave young men who are prepared to put their lives on the line in battle.

It is not hard for us to conjure up the image, since he communicates it so graphically. The old man's appearance and character are described – his white hair and grey beard, as well as his 'stalwart spirit'; however, the image of an eminent old man is then contrasted with his situation – he is metaphorically 'gasping his stalwart spirit out into the dust', and literally 'clutching his bloody genitals in his own hands'. In this image, he has been killed in battle and stripped of his armour; the reference to his genitals may also suggest that his body has been mutilated. It is a horrifying image of an old man who has died in battle.

PS

S & C The First World War produced some remarkable poets, who reflect different perspectives on the warfare. Read two patriotic poems by British poets: *The Soldier* by Rupert Brooke and *In Flanders Fields* by John McCrae. How do they compare to the fragment of Tyrtaeus that you have read?

their place ahead of the older men, to spare them the greatest danger, and to stand their ground to keep them out of danger. The Spartans revered the elderly and gave them a special place of honour in their society, and so this message is especially powerful.

What might be most surprising to us in the lines that follow is that Tyrtaeus says that such a death is fitting for a young man – the poet is not horrified by the nature of the death itself but by the fact that it is an old man who is suffering it. He therefore concludes the poem by once again encouraging the young men to stand firm in the front line. It is striking in these final lines that he describes a fallen young warrior as 'beautiful', a great contrast from the degraded image of the fallen older man.

Study questions

1 Do you think it is better and nobler for young men to fall in battle instead of older men?
2 Do you think that it is possible for a soldier who has fallen in battle to look beautiful?

ACTIVITY

In class, imagine that you are a group of Spartans who are to listen to the first public performance of this poem by Tyrtaeus. Choose one person to recite the poem, and another to give musical accompaniment (perhaps with an oboe), while the rest of the class are members of the audience. Act out the scene – how do the members of the audience respond to what they hear?

TOPIC REVIEW

You should be able to:

1. Describe:
   - the historical context in which Tyrtaeus was writing
   - the importance of Tyrtaeus' poetry for later Spartans
   - the nature of elegiac poetry
   - an outline of the Fallen Warrior poem.

2. Explain:
   - how Tyrtaeus' historical context influenced his poetry
   - the nature of the heroism that the poem encourages
   - the importance of the concept of shame in the poem
   - the way that young and old Spartans are contrasted in the poem.

PRACTICE QUESTIONS

Source A: Tyrtaeus, *Fragment 10*, Line 1–8

To die is noble when a good man falls among fighters at the front while he defends his fatherland. To leave behind his city and its fertile fields and go begging is the most wretched thing of all, wandering with his dear mother, his elderly father, his tiny children and wedded wife; for he will be hated by the people around him wherever he goes, overcome by need and grim poverty.

1. Which is the 'fatherland' referred to in this poem?   [1]
2. What points do you think Tyrtaeus is making in this passage? Use **two** phrases and suggest what
they tell us about his message.   [4]

4.7 Horace

Literary ontext

- The genre and author of your text
- Its composition and aims
- Narrative and descriptive techniques, including:
  - speeches

  - similes and imagery
  - use of emotive language
  - the role of the divine

Characterisation

- The actions of the characters in your selections
- The traits of each of the main characters and how these are depicted
- Interactions and relationships between characters

- The depiction of:
  - leaders and soldiers
  - comrades and enemies
  - non-combatants
  - women

Themes

- Glory, honour and shame
- Comradeship
- Freedom
- Hubris and arrogance
- Love and patriotism

- The horror and glorification of warfare
- Fear and courage
- Family and ancestors
- Military and civilian victims of war

Heroes and warfare

- How the content of your selections reflects its political or cultural context, including:
  - details of the historical context
  - what constitutes a 'hero'

  - attitudes towards war and warfare
- The possible responses to the text from different audiences

The prescribed source for this topic is

- Horace, *Odes* 3.2

Don't forget that you will be given credit in the exam if you study extra sources and make relevant use of them in your answers.

This topic will examine Horace, starting with his life story and how it influenced his poetry. It will then move on to examining Ode 3.2, a poem that contains one of the most famous lines of Latin poetry. As with your other authors, you should refer to the topic boxes at the start of the chapter to think about how this poem includes many of the themes mentioned there.

BIOGRAPHY

Horace had a remarkable life; he was born the son of a freedman in the small town of Venusia in southern Italy, and yet he grew up to become one of leading poets in the Roman world. He lived during very troubled times, which have been described in some detail (see pp. 295–6). When Julius Caesar was murdered in 44 BC, one of his leading assassins, Brutus, fled to Greece to try to raise an army there. Horace was studying in Athens at the time and he signed up for Brutus' army, fighting in the assassins' final defeat at Philippi in 42 – however, despite fighting on the losing side he survived to live another day. Soon afterwards he returned to Rome, taking advantage of a general amnesty given by Caesar's adopted heir, **Octavian**, to those who had fought against him.

In 38 BC Horace was introduced to **Maecenas**, a close adviser to Octavian who was responsible for influencing public opinion in his favour. To do this, he aimed to nurture poets who would write poetry sympathetic to Octavian and his regime. Horace had already started writing poetry, and was welcomed into Maecenas' circle of poets; this was a huge break for him in his writing career, and indeed in the whole direction of his life.

Horace may have been present at the battle of Actium in 31 BC (see p. 385). When Octavian's victory brought an end to decades of civil wars and left him as the sole ruler of the Roman world, Horace found himself writing poetry for the most powerful man in the known world – the first Roman emperor, who was now referred to as **Augustus**. Horace, therefore, had to be suitably patriotic and praising of his emperor.

THE ODES

Horace published his first three books of odes in 23 BC (a fourth book was published in about 13 BC), and he wrote 103 such poems in all. He consciously looked to the ancient Greek world for his models, and his odes imitate the style of the **lyric poetry** written by a number of Greek poets of the seventh and sixth centuries BC; they had composed personal poems to be sung to the lyre for an audience. However, while Horace drew their inspiration from their style of poetry – and particularly the metres they commonly employed – it is unlikely that he wrote his poems to be sung to musical accompaniment as they did. Instead, he had them published just as a poet might today, although he may have given some recitals himself when they were first published.

His odes focus on any number of themes relevant to his life: some reflect on aspects of his personal life such as love, friendship and social occasions, while others focus on war, politics and religion – we have already seen on p. 388 that he composed a poem to celebrate Octavian's victory at Actium.

ODE 3.2

This ode focuses on war, politics and statesmanship. The poem is divided into eight stanzas of four lines each (a **stanza** is a type of verse in a poem – it has a set metre, which is repeated in every verse of the poem), and these can be divided up thematically as follows:

- **Stanzas 1–4** Young Romans from the highest social classes should undergo tough military training so that they can fight bravely and successfully against Rome's enemies, and so that they are prepared to fight to the death rather than desert in battle.
- **Stanzas 5–6** The courage that such a soldier learns in the army will also be needed in civilian life in Rome. Some exceptional men are examples of this, and such a man does not derive his sense of importance from political status but from his own conduct. This sort of man will be given a place amongst the gods after his death.
- **Stanzas 7–8** Not all Romans can be as great as this, but other men can still serve the Roman state by being loyal and discreet. Those who do not show these qualities are sure to be punished by the gods.

Clearly, one major theme of the poem, therefore, is that the qualities learnt in military life can be transferred across to civilian life, and this suggests how important the army was felt to be for the development of character.

The opening stanza introduces this theme. We know that Augustus established a tough training programme for teenage boys aged 15–18 who came from the top two Roman social classes – the senators and equestrians – so that they were ready to serve in the army as tribunes (see p. 372). Horace therefore opens his poem by approving of this, and then moves on to hope that such a highly trained young man will fight successfully against the Parthians, one of Rome's great enemies. The **Parthian Empire** lay to the east of the Roman Empire and was centred on what is now Iran. In 53 BC, the Romans had suffered

> **stanza** a verse of poetry with a set metre repeated throughout the poem

FIGURE 4.46
A statue of Horace in Venusia today.

> **Parthian Empire** an Empire lying to the east of the Roman Empire, centred on what is now Iran

---

PRESCRIBED SOURCE

Horace, Ode 3.2

Date: published in 23 BC

Author: Horace (65–8 BC)

Genre: lyric poetry

Significance: a poem reflecting on how military training should prepare aristocratic young Romans both for life on campaign and for later civilian life

Read it here: OCR source booklet

CW

EXPLORE FURTHER

You can read about the Roman defeat to the Parthians at Carrhae in Plutarch's *Life of Crassus*, Chapters 24 and 25.

a crushing defeat to the Parthians at Carrhae. However, during the 20s BC, Augustus negotiated a reasonable settlement, which ended in a formal peace being signed in 20 BC.

In stanzas 2 and 3, Horace then imagines a scene from a war in which such a young officer would fight. The poem views the war from the perspective of a young woman and her mother, who is the wife of the local ruler hostile to Rome. The young woman watches from the walls of her city in terror and speaks as follows:

"Alas, don't let my royal bridegroom unskilled in war
provoke the lion that's dangerous to touch,
whom blood-stained anger sends raging
swiftly through the midst of slaughter."

Horace, *Ode 3.2*, lines 9–12

How might this stanza be thought powerful? First of all, we hear from one of the victims of the Roman army in her own words, a young woman who will not herself fight but must watch instead. The terror she feels at the uneven match-up between her beloved and a highly trained Roman soldier gives the impression that even Rome's enemies recognise that Roman soldiers are far better than their own. There is also great pathos at the prospect that the young woman's fiancé will die before their wedding day. Furthermore, in her speech she uses a **metaphor** to describe the ferocity of the young Roman. She does not refer to him as a person but simply as a lion dangerous to touch, an image easy for the reader to form vividly. We might also notice in the stanza two allusions to the *Iliad*, with which Horace would have been very familiar. Lion imagery to describe fighters is common in Homer, while the idea of a non-combatant watching her beloved fighting from the walls of her city echoes the scene at the start of *Iliad* Book 22.

The fourth stanza starts with one of the most famous lines from Roman poetry – in Latin it reads: 'dulce et decorum est pro patria mori'. It is very similar to the first line of Tyrtaeus' 'Fallen Warrior' poem, and some commentators think that Horace may have been consciously imitating it. Moreover, the idea of death in battle being 'sweet' ties closely in with Tyrtaeus' description of such a death as 'beautiful' later in the same poem. In the rest of the stanza, Horace emphasises that death comes to all of us – even to those who flee from battle; they will end up, shamefully, wounded from behind rather than in front. In these lines, Horace uses **personification**, whereby something non-human is given human characteristics to make it more vivid, by suggesting that death literally pursues the fleeing soldier.

The fifth stanza moves the focus from military to civilian life. The key theme is found in the word 'Virtue', and Horace uses a second personification to emphasise this – Virtue is personified both here and in the next stanza. This virtue, which suggests a combination of courage and good character, may have been learnt in the army but should be applied to all areas of life. The man who shows this virtue does not take his sense of self-worth from worldly successes, for example by winning an election (the reference to 'axes' indicates that the poem is talking about senior politicians, since their symbol of power was the **fasces**, a bundle of rods with an axe-head emerging from the top). Such a man is not driven by a need to please the mass of the common people, but instead his character remains constant. Many commentators think that Horace is here referring to the Emperor Augustus, and signalling that he is the great man who can show such virtue.

metaphor a figure of speech in which a word or phrase is used to describe something that it cannot literally be

personification a figure of speech by which something non-human is given human characteristics

fasces a bundle of rods with an axe-head, which were the symbol of the authority of a senior Roman magistrate

This interpretation makes even more sense when we examine the sixth stanza, which continues with the theme of virtue. The poet claims that the virtuous man will journey to the heavens on wings, where he will be given a place among gods. The Romans believed that only the greatest heroes were worthy of becoming divine after death, but Emperors were often included in this category. Once again, this suggests that Horace is describing the Emperor Augustus. A great contrast is made with the common people, who do not have the character to ascend to the gods after death.

In the final two stanzas, the poem changes direction once again. These stanzas focus on the quality of keeping a discreet silence – those who transgress this principle will eventually be punished for their indiscretion. Silence is presented as a sacred duty, not least by the mention of 'those secret **rites of Ceres**'. This is a reference to an ancient Greek religious cult, the Eleusinian Mysteries, which centred on the worship of the goddess of the harvest, Demeter (known to the Romans as Ceres) at Eleusis near Athens. Those who became initiated into the cult took part in its secret rites (religious practices) and were promised a blissful life after death. However, they had to swear to keep the secrets of the cult and were not allowed to divulge what took place during the rites. Those who transgressed this faced the death penalty. Interestingly for our poem, the emperor Augustus himself became an initiate of the Mysteries, and was reportedly well known for his discretion.

In these stanzas Horace says that he will avoid the company of the indiscreet man, and thereby seems to encourage his readers to do the same. He concludes by saying that even if Jupiter sometimes punishes the innocent with the guilty, the guilty never manage to get away with their crimes, even if it takes time for punishment to catch up with them. The point here is that it is best to avoid the company of indiscreet people since Jupiter is likely to bring them to ruin at some point – perhaps by a house falling in or by drowning at sea – and, since Jupiter sometimes allows the innocent to suffer with the guilty, it is advisable to keep out of the way of such people so as not to share their fate. In the final stanza, Horace uses a third personification – this time of Punishment. One could compare the way in which death and punishment both catch up with people who do not live up to Roman ideals in stanzas 4 and 8 respectively.

The last two stanzas are something of a mystery, and seem to represent somewhat of an anti-climax from the previous two. There is no clear way to interpret them, but perhaps one point is that most Romans, even educated ones, cannot aspire to the greatness of Augustus. However, they can serve the Roman state well, and this will involve loyalty and discretion. One way of reading this is to relate it to the growing imperial civil service that Augustus had established. Educated Romans working in this bureaucracy would have needed to keep secrets and to be loyal. There is another way to read this, which is to relate it more directly to Horace himself. By the time of this poem, Horace is no doubt living and working within the Emperor's circle; these final stanzas could therefore be read as the poet talking about himself and his own loyalty to the Emperor – he understands how to behave and who to avoid.

In just thirty-two lines Horace covers a great deal of ground, with a variety of images and themes. The courage learnt by the upper-class soldier will stand him in good stead for his civilian service to the Roman state, a state that looks to the example of the Emperor Augustus as its ultimate role model.

S & C

The line 'dulce et decorum est pro patria mori' was famously used by the First World War poet Wilfred Owen in his poem entitled: *Dulce et Decorum Est*. Read this poem yourself. Why does Owen describe Horace's line as 'the old Lie'? How is the tone of Owen's poem different from that of Horace?

---

rites of Ceres an ancient Greek religious cult, also known as the Eleusinian Mysteries, in which members were sworn to secrecy

---

ACTIVITY

Imagine that you are asked to present the moral messages of this poem in a school assembly. Write an assembly that includes and explains the examples and morals that Horace puts forward.

Study question

How effectively does Horace use imagery in this poem?

EXAM TIP

Explaining personification

In this poem, personification is used of three concepts: death, virtue, and punishment. If you comment on personifications such as these, try not to say simply 'this is effective because Horace uses a personification'. Rather, explain why you think that the personification is effective. For example, you might say that virtue is such a powerful and important quality in the poem that Horace personifies it in order to present it as something that has a way of behaving and a character all of its own.

TOPIC REVIEW

You should be able to:

1. Describe:
   - the historical context in which Horace wrote his odes
   - the outline of Ode 3.2
   - the three different stages of Ode 3.2.

2. Explain:
   - the key themes of the poem, particularly bravery and cowardice
   - the importance of the emperor Augustus in the poem
   - the literary techniques used in the poem to make it powerful.

PRACTICE QUESTIONS

Source A: *Horace, Ode 3.2, lines 25–32*

And there's a sure reward for loyal silence:
I'll forbid the man who divulges the secret
rites of Ceres, to be under the same
roof as me, or to untie with me

the fragile boat: neglected Jupiter often
includes the innocent with the guilty,
but slow-footed Punishment rarely
gives up on the wicked man, despite his start.

1. a. What is Horace referring to by the words 'the rites of Ceres'?   [2]
   b. What is the significance of this reference in the context of this poem.   [1]
2. How does Horace convey the personal qualities expected of a well-trained Roman soldier?
   Make **two** points and support your points with reference to Source A.   [4]

4.8 Virgil

Literary context

- The genre and author of your text
- Its composition and aims
- Narrative and descriptive techniques, including:
  - speeches
  - similes and imagery
  - epithets
  - use of emotive language
  - the role of the divine

Characterisation

- The actions of the characters in your selections
- The traits of each of the main characters and how these are depicted
- Interactions and relationships between characters
- The depiction of:
  - leaders and soldiers
  - comrades and enemies
  - non-combatants
  - women

Themes

- Glory, honour and shame
- Comradeship
- Freedom
- Hubris and arrogance
- Love and patriotism
- The horror and glorification of warfare
- Fear and courage
- Family and ancestors
- Military and civilian victims of war

Heroes and warfare

- How the content of your selections reflects its political or cultural context, including:
  - details of the historical context
  - what constitutes a 'hero'
  - attitudes towards war and warfare
- The possible responses to the text from different audiences

The prescribed source for this topic is:

- Virgil, *Aeneid*, Book 2.268–end

Don't forget that you will be given credit in the exam if you study extra sources and make relevant use of them in your answers.

This topic will examine Virgil and his *Aeneid*, starting with what we know about his life and the context of his famous poem the *Aeneid*. It will then move on to focus on *Aeneid* 2.268 to the end. As with your other authors, you should refer to the topic boxes at the start of the chapter to think about how this poem includes many of the themes mentioned there.

BIOGRAPHY

Since Roman times, Virgil's *Aeneid* has been acknowledged as the greatest work of Latin literature; indeed, for Romans, Virgil held the pre-eminent status that Shakespeare holds for English speakers today. As with all our authors, we must start by finding out something about his life and times.

Publius Virgilius Maro was born near Mantua in northern Italy in 70 BC to a land-owning family. He was therefore able to receive a good education, which culminated with his moving to study in Rome as a young man. In the early 30s, he published his first set of poems, the *Eclogues*, which focused on life in the countryside. At around this time

he came to the attention of Maecenas, whom we have read about on p. 424; like Horace, Virgil was welcomed into Maecenas' circle of poets who wrote poetry supportive of Octavian (Virgil and Horace became very close friends – so close, in fact, that in Ode 1.3 Horace refers to Virgil as 'the other half of my soul').

When Octavian took sole command of the Roman world after the battle of Actium and adopted the name Augustus, he invited Virgil to compose a great poem in praise of his new regime – a national poem for Rome and its empire. Virgil duly spent the remaining years of his life writing the *Aeneid*, which was almost complete when he died in 19 BC. Tradition has it that on his deathbed he asked that the manuscript be burnt, but Augustus forbade this and so the poem survived; indeed, there are still a few lines that are only half-finished – probably evidence that Virgil had not quite completed his task.

FIGURE 4.47
Virgil holds a volume of the *Aeneid*. He is flanked by the muses of history and tragedy, Clio and Melpomene.

LITERARY CONTEXT

Virgil chose to set his great poem in the world of the Trojan War. To understand why he did this, it is important to appreciate the enormous influence that Greek literature had on the Roman world.

Before the third century BC, the Romans had almost no literary tradition – for centuries, Rome had been an agricultural community and its people had developed little love of writing. It was only when the Romans came into contact with the Greek world in the third and second centuries BC that they began to develop their own literature, inspired by the many great Greek writers whom they could now read. Roman poetry therefore came to be heavily influenced by earlier Greek models – something symbolised by the fact that the Romans had no native word that simply meant 'poet', and so borrowed the Greek 'poeta'. It is also worth noting that this is the period in which the Romans started to merge their own native gods with the Greek gods and their accompanying mythology (e.g. the Roman god Mercury became associated with Hermes, the Roman goddess Minerva became associated with Athena, etc.).

The *Iliad* and the *Odyssey* came to be recognised as pre-eminent classics by educated Romans, just as they long had been in the Greek world. We have already met the figure of Aeneas in Book 5 of the *Iliad* – a leading Trojan warrior and the son of the goddess Aphrodite. Later in the poem (20.300–308), Poseidon says that Aeneas is destined to survive the sack of Troy, and also that he and his descendants are fated to rule over the Trojans for generations. Later Greek writers who wanted to continue the saga of Troy therefore wrote of Aeneas' wanderings after the war, and one tradition brought him to Italy. As Romans came to admire Greek civilisation more and more, they became especially interested in this tradition; the idea grew that the Trojans led to Italy by Aeneas were the ancestors of the Romans – indeed, the founder and first king of Rome, Romulus, was said to have been descended from Aeneas himself.

It was this tradition that Virgil worked with. He chose to make Aeneas the central character of his new poem, which was therefore called the *Aeneid*. One appeal of this was that it placed Rome's ancestors in the heroic age of the Trojan War – Romans too could link themselves to that world of admirable and noble fighters. Although Rome's ancestors were the losers of the war, Virgil portrays the sack of Troy as an act of trickery and deceit on the Greeks' behalf – since the Greeks had won through low tactics, the Trojans could keep a sense of the moral high ground. Moreover, Virgil worked with the Homeric tradition that Aeneas was fated to rule over the Trojans by making the hero's journey to Italy an act of destiny, in which he would establish a new race of people who would go on to found the greatest city on earth. Crucially, in the *Aeneid* Aeneas' son Ascanius marries Lavinia, the daughter of a local Italian king, and so Romulus could be said to be descended both from the Trojans and from native Italians – Virgil's tale wove the two peoples together.

Another advantage of Virgil's method was that his poem could seek to emulate the two greatest poems of Greek literature. Virgil chose to write his poem in hexameter so that he could model himself on Homer as closely as possible, thus creating a Roman epic poem, which he hoped would win comparable status in the Roman world. His imitation of Homer takes many forms, not least his use of epithets and of extraordinarily powerful similes. The gods of the *Aeneid* play a similar role to the gods in the *Iliad*, with Venus (the Roman name for Aphrodite) in particular supporting her son Aeneas, while Juno (Hera) opposes the Trojans at every move. As in the *Iliad*, Jupiter (Zeus) must arbitrate between feuding gods and oversee the workings of fate. However, although Virgil seeks to imitate many of the forms of oral poetry, we should remember that his own poem was written down to be read, and he is said to have taken a painstaking amount of time over each and every line.

AN AUGUSTAN EPIC

Although the *Aeneid* is set in the heroic past, Virgil cleverly manages to establish many links and allusions to the Roman world of his own day. Indeed, one of his key aims is to create a national epic that would speak to his fellow Romans who now ruled the world under the command of Augustus. In addition to allusions, the poem contains three direct prophecies of Rome's future. In Book 1 Jupiter unrolls the scroll of fate and speaks to Venus of the future of Rome; he says that he will allow the Romans to have a limitless empire, one which will be well ruled and at peace under Augustus (lines 257–296). In Book 6 Aeneas travels to the Underworld, where his dead father Anchises shows him a parade of great Romans of the future, and Augustus himself is given a prominent place as a glorious conqueror (lines 791–807). Finally, in Book 8 Aeneas is given a new shield (just as Achilles is in the *Iliad*), on which is depicted scenes from later Roman history; in pride of place at its centre is a portrayal of the battle of Actium (lines 675–713, which have already been mentioned on p. 388).

Part of the success of the *Aeneid*, then, is that it can look back to the heroic past as well as speaking about the Roman world of Virgil's day. However, the poet is not blindly patriotic; a key theme of his poem is that creating a Roman Empire will involve great sacrifice and no little tragedy; Aeneas himself suffers greatly, losing amongst others his wife Creusa during the fall of Troy, and being forced by the gods to desert Dido, the woman he loves. Indeed, such is the suffering in the poem that commentators have often wondered just how enthusiastic Virgil felt about Rome's rule of the world, and whether he believed that so much sacrifice was really worthwhile. The poet certainly manages to create great pathos amongst a variety of different characters, some of them in opposition to Aeneas, and the poem allows for no straightforward interpretation. As with the *Iliad*, this is one of its greatest strengths and fascinations.

HEROISM AND PIETAS

We have read about the culture of heroism in the *Iliad*, where warriors were concerned to win time and kleos. In the *Aeneid*, Virgil presents a new type of heroism. It is important to remember that his heroes (and Aeneas in particular) must set an example to Roman readers as to the qualities needed to succeed in ruling the world. In the *Aeneid*, therefore, heroism is not defined simply by one's achievements in battle (although fighting bravely is a key attribute of a hero) but by one's character and temperament in all situations.

> **pietas** the most important heroic quality in the *Aeneid*, a Roman virtue that means 'sense of duty', and applies to a man's duty towards his family, his city and his gods

The most important quality that Aeneas is required to show is **pietas**. This Latin word is hard to translate directly into English (the word 'piety' does not capture it properly), but it might be defined as 'sense of duty', with the understanding that the duty is to your family, to your city and to your gods. Pietas, then, required a Roman to show a sense of responsibility: to his family, for whom he was a role model and provider; to his city and its people, whom he had a patriotic duty to lead or support; and to his gods, whom he was obliged to worship and honour appropriately.

Often, pietas involves great personal sacrifice, since duty must be put before personal desire or happiness. The most famous example of this in the *Aeneid* comes in Book 4, when Aeneas is required to abandon Dido, the queen of Carthage and the woman he loves. The god Mercury comes to tell him that Jupiter commands him to leave Carthage, since he has a duty to found a new race of people in Italy; at this moment, Aeneas must follow the will of the gods, so that he can fulfil his duty to his Trojan people, and also to his young son Ascanius (also called Iulus) who will succeed him. He must therefore put the requirements of pietas before his own interests; Dido is so distraught that, tragically, she takes her own life. It is no wonder that, early in the poem, the founding of the Roman race is described as an enormous struggle.

However, in many ways pietas is an admirable quality, and one episode in Book 2 has provided the most enduring image of this. When Aeneas finally accepts that he must abandon the city of Troy, which is now beyond help after the Greek attack, it is a sign from the heavens which has convinced him. He instructs his elderly father Anchises to climb onto his shoulders so that he can carry him out of the city:

> "Come then, dear father, clasp my neck: I will
> carry you on my shoulders: that task won't weigh on me.
> Whatever may happen, it will be for us both, the same shared risk,
> and the same salvation. Let little Iulus come with me,
> and let my wife follow our footsteps at a distance.
> [. . .]
> You, father, take the sacred objects, and our country's gods,
> in your hands . . ."

Virgil, *Aeneid*, 2.707–711; 717

Here we have a symbolic moment of pietas in action: Aeneas is following the signs of the gods and providing help to his aged father – the man who is actually the head of his family. Anchises himself holds onto the city's holiest images of its gods, which will be brought all the way to Italy and given a new home there. The future of the Trojan race is symbolised in the figure of Iulus, at this time just a small boy who holds his father's hand. Sadly, however, Aeneas' wife Creusa will not survive the escape.

THE CONTEXT OF BOOK 2

The *Aeneid* is divided into twelve books (these books are somewhat longer than the books of the *Iliad*), and thematically the poem is divided into two halves. The first six books describe the sack of Troy and Aeneas' wanderings thereafter; at the start of book 7 he arrives at the shores of central Italy, and the last six books focus on the alliances he makes and wars he must fight to establish his people there. It is often said that the first half of the poem is modelled on the *Odyssey*, in which Odysseus must endure many hardships and adventures before arriving home from Troy, and the second half is closer in spirit to the *Iliad*, as we read of the wars between Aeneas and hostile Italian peoples.

Your prescribed reading in Book 2 is therefore located during Aeneas' travels. The action of the poem begins in Book 1 with the Trojan survivors of the destruction of Troy shipwrecked on the shore of North Africa. They find themselves near Carthage, a new city still being built under the watchful eye of its queen, Dido, who is herself a refugee from her own native city of Tyre in Phoenicia (a region roughly corresponding to modern Lebanon). It is Juno who has caused the shipwreck – she remains as implacably opposed to the Trojans as she is during the *Iliad* (as Hera); an additional concern of hers in the *Aeneid* is that Dido's Carthaginians are her favourite people, and she does not want to see a rival city emerge in Italy. Aeneas and the other Trojans who have survived the storm are welcomed by Dido, and invited to stay with her as honoured guests. Book

PRESCRIBED SOURCE

Virgil, *Aeneid*, Book 2.268–end

Date: 19 BC

Author: Virgil (70–19 BC)

Genre: epic poetry

Significance: an account of the night that the Greeks finally sacked and conquered Troy

Read it here: OCR source booklet **CW**

S & C Artistic representations of Aeneas fleeing from Troy have survived from Roman times, and it has continued to inspire artists ever since, most notably the seventeenth-century Italian sculptor Bernini. Research his sculpture of this scene shown in Figure 4.48, and how art scholars have interpreted it.

FIGURE 4.48
This sculpture of Aeneas leaving Troy with Anchises and Ascanius was created by the seventeenth-century Italian artist Bernini.

1 ends with a banquet in their honour, during which Venus stirs Dido's heart and she begins to fall in love with Aeneas. She asks him to tell them about the day that Troy was finally conquered.

Book 2 opens with Aeneas starting to speak. He opens by saying that he has been given an impossible task, since no words could ever capture the horrors he has seen or the sufferings that his people have endured; still, he promises to do his best. His narrative picks up the story of the Trojan war soon after the *Iliad* finishes; by now Achilles has been killed too. Before line 268, Aeneas' narrative focuses on the arrival of a huge wooden horse on the shore near the city and the disappearance of the Greek army. The Trojans are unsure what to make of it, and want to believe that it is a peace offering from the Greeks who have conceded defeat and sailed away. A Trojan priest, Laocoon, frantically warns them not to trust the Greeks, claiming that the horse is a trick. At this moment, another man appears: Sinon is his name, and he claims to be a Greek deserter; in fact, he is a Greek spy who deceives the Trojans into believing that the horse is a gift to Athena, which they should take into the city and give a place of honour. After he finishes speaking, a terrible event occurs – two huge snakes appear from the sea and make for Laocoon and his two young sons, suffocating them to death.

The Trojans interpret this to mean that they should avoid following Laocoon's advice, and instead honour the horse as Sinon suggests, and so they drag it into the city.

Study question
Virgil could have chosen to tell the story of the sack of Troy in his own words. Why do you think that he decided instead to have Aeneas retell his own experiences in the first person? How might this make the story more moving and more powerful?

EXPLORE FURTHER
To give you a fuller context for lines 268 to the end of Book 2, try to read the opening 267 lines of the book.

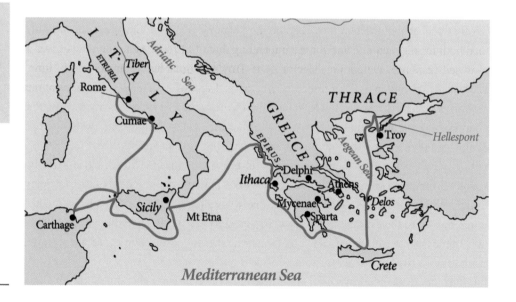

FIGURE 4.49
The journey of Aeneas.

Unknown to them, however, some of the greatest Greek warriors are hidden in its hollow belly – Laocoon was right after all. That night, the Trojans celebrate wildly and then sleep, believing that they have seen off the Greeks at last. As they slumber, the Greek fleet sails back from a nearby island where it has lain hidden. The warriors in the horse climb out and head for the gates, where they kill the guards and open the city to the rest of the Greek army. The scene is set for the final night of the war.

BOOK 2.268–END

Three visions

Your prescribed reading begins with Aeneas telling of a terrifying dream that he has in his sleep that night. This is the first of three important visions that Aeneas will have in the book, and which advise him how to respond to the events around him.

FIGURE 4.50
This Roman sculpture shows Laocoon and his sons being killed by the serpents.

Vision 1 (lines 270–297): Hector

In one of the most famous scenes from the *Aeneid*, the dead Hector appears to Aeneas, his body defiled by its treatment at the hands of Achilles:

> See, in dream, before my eyes, Hector seemed to stand there,
> saddest of all and pouring out great tears,
> torn by the chariot, as once he was, black with bloody dust,
> and his swollen feet pierced by the thongs.
> . . . His beard was ragged,
> his hair matted with blood, bearing those many wounds he received
> dragged around the walls of his city.

> Virgil, *Aeneid*, 2.270–273;277–9

It is a vivid and terrible image, made more poignant by Hector's tears – perhaps they are shed both for his own fate and for the impending fate of his city. Aeneas initially gives a confused response, welcoming Hector as if Troy's saviour has returned just in time. There is great irony in his description of Hector as 'Light of the Troad, surest hope of the Trojans', since Hector can offer no light and no hope. Aeneas' confusion here is symbolic of his struggle throughout the book – he is torn between staying and fighting for Troy, or giving up hope and abandoning the city.

Hector soon sets Aeneas straight: Troy is finished, and Aeneas must flee the city. Moreover, he outlines to Aeneas a new mission: he is to take Troy's holiest religious icons and travel over the seas, after which he will establish a new city. This is a highly symbolic moment in the poem: Hector, the greatest Trojan warrior in the *Iliad*, hands over the leadership of the Trojans to Aeneas and is seen to give him permission to leave their beloved city behind.

Vision 2 (lines 567–623): Venus

After his vision of Hector, Aeneas wakes up and prepares himself to leave his house and gather fellow Trojans to fight – thereby ignoring Hector's advice. He admits that it may be of little use, but fury drives him into battle:

> Frantically I seize weapons: not because there is much use
> for weapons, but my spirit burns to gather men for battle
> and race to the citadel with my friends: madness and anger
> hurl my mind headlong, and I think it beautiful to die fighting.

Virgil, *Aeneid*, 2.314–317

These are noble sentiments, but they will indeed be useless; Hector's words have made no impact yet. Aeneas has some success in battle, and at one point he and his comrades put on the armour of some Greeks they have killed. They then head towards Priam's palace, where the worst horrors of the night are playing themselves out. On their way they see Cassandra, the priestess daughter of Priam, dragged from a temple of Minerva (the Roman name for Athena). Aeneas is keen to emphasise that as he fights for his city, he gives everything to the cause:

> Ashes of Ilium, death flames of my people, be witness
> that, at your ruin, I did not evade the Danaan weapons,
> nor the risks, and, if it had been my fate to die,
> I earned it with my sword.

Virgil, *Aeneid*, 2.431–434

We should remember that Aeneas is telling this story to Dido and her guests at a banquet in Carthage, and he will want to emphasise that he did not abandon his city willingly.

Aeneas' account of the deaths of Polites and Priam in the palace is one of the most moving and tragic episodes in the *Aeneid*. Aeneas watches, perched high above, after which he catches sight of Helen. For a moment, all his fury is transferred onto her, and he resolves to kill her. It is at this moment that he receives his second vision: his mother Venus appears before him. She tells him to control his anger and think instead of his duty to his family, whom she is even now protecting from Greek soldiers. Moreover, she explains that the destruction of Troy is ultimately the work of the gods:

> You do not hate the face of the Spartan daughter of Tyndareus,
> nor is Paris to blame: the ruthlessness of the gods, of the gods,
> brought down this power, and toppled Troy from its heights.

Virgil, *Aeneid*, 2.601–603

After this, Venus alters his sight so that he can see the gods in action in the sack of the city: Neptune, Juno, Minerva and Jupiter are all giving help to the Greeks. Venus sets Aeneas back with his family so that he can protect them. This scene is particularly important since it reinforces to Aeneas what Hector has already said to him – Troy is destined to fall, and there is nothing he can do about it. Aeneas must accept this and follow a new destiny.

Vision 3 (lines 771–794): Creusa

When Aeneas finds himself back home, his father Anchises refuses to leave the city; he is an old man and would prefer death to the life of an exile. Aeneas – showing great pietas – refuses to leave his father behind, and so prepares to return to battle. But his wife Creusa begs him not to leave the family behind. At this moment, the gods intervene once more, sending two omens. First, Ascanius' hair catches fire, although the flame does him no harm. Anchises believes that this is a sign from the gods, and asks Jupiter to confirm it with another; soon afterwards, a shooting star passes through the sky and he is convinced, believing that it is destined for the whole family to leave Troy. It is at this moment that Aeneas lifts his father onto his shoulders, and takes Ascanius by the hand, as we have read on p. 433.

The family make a terrifying escape from the city, with Creusa hanging a little behind them in order to spread the group. It is only when Aeneas reaches the holy mound of Ceres outside the city that he realises that she is no longer with them. In despair, he once again heads back into the city to look for her. He sees own house in flames as he wanders through the city, and even dares to call out Creusa's name. At this moment, Aeneas receives his third vision of the night: his wife has been killed and her ghost appears to him. She explains that her death is fated by the gods, and that Aeneas must move on without her; she predicts his future:

> Yours is long exile, you must plough
> a vast reach of sea: and you will come to Hesperia's land,
> where Lydian Tiber flows in gentle course among the farmers'
> rich fields. There, happiness, kingship and a royal wife
> will be yours.

> Virgil, *Aeneid*, 2.780–784

PS

Hesperia is another name for Italy, while the Tiber is the river which flows through Rome (it is called Lydian since it was believed that some settlers in central Italy came from Lydia in Asia Minor). Aeneas has been given a little more information of the destiny that awaits him. He tries to embrace Creusa, but his hands can only reach through her shadow.

Together, these visions set Aeneas up for his difficult, painful but ultimately triumphant mission after the sack of Troy. They also represent a clever literary device by Virgil, since they allow him to portray his hero in an impressive light, despite his being on the losing side of the war. Indeed, one difficulty for Virgil with his characterisation of Aeneas was how to portray him as a refugee from Troy with his dignity intact. By creating these visions, the hero is seen to have fought as bravely as possible, but to have bowed to the inevitable. He cannot therefore be blamed for abandoning his city – it is the gods' will both that Troy should fall and that Aeneas should survive the night.

Pathos and the horror of war

One of the features of this book is its pathos in portraying the horrors of war. The vision of the dead Hector is an outstanding example of this, as is the tragedy at the end of the book as

Aeneas is widowed. One other profoundly moving episode comes with the death of Priam (lines 526–558). By a great irony, he is heartlessly killed by Pyrrhus, the son of Achilles. Pyrrhus first slaughters Polites, one of Priam's sons, in front of his father's eyes. Priam tells Pyrrhus that he is unworthy of his father, a man who had respected a suppliant's rights. The king tries to fight back but is too old and feeble to do so. In reply, Pyrrhus is heartless:

> Pyrrhus spoke to him: "Then you can be messenger, carry
> the news to my father, to Peleus's son: remember to tell him
> of degenerate Pyrrhus, and of my sad actions:
> now die."

Virgil, *Aeneid*, 2.547–550

Pyrrhus drags the old king to the altar and puts a sword through him. The character of Pyrrhus here embodies the behaviour of the Greeks in Book 2 – they are brutal villains who inspire little sympathy. By contrast, the Trojans are presented as honourable characters and victims of savagery.

Imagery

Another striking feature of the book is the imagery used by Virgil. One prominent image is that of fire representing destruction. Moreover, a number of similes, all of them drawn from the natural world, are woven into the narrative to give mood and context to Aeneas' terrible tale. They can be summarised as follows:

- **The shepherd** (304–309) Aeneas' view of the burning of Troy from his rooftop is compared to a shepherd watching from a peak as fire or a flood attacks his crops (compare the simile at lines 5.85–94 of the *Iliad* mentioned on page 000).
- **The wolves** (355–358) Aeneas and his young companions who head into the city for battle are compared to hungry wolves, desperate to feed their young.
- **The snake (1)** (379–381) Androgeos, a Greek, realises that he has come upon a band of Trojans and recoils in fright like a snake.
- **The winds** (416–419) When Aeneas' Trojan band is attacked from all sides by Greeks, the repeated onslaught of Greek attacks is compared to winds clashing with one another.
- **The snake (2)** (471–475) A second snake simile is used to describe Pyrrhus as he arrives in Priam's palace: he is like a snake with a forked tongue that has fed on poisonous herbs.
- **The river** (496–499) The Greeks bursting into Priam's palace are likened to a river bursting its banks.
- **The doves** (515–516) Hecuba and her daughters seek refuge in the palace like doves trying to find shelter from a storm.
- **The ash tree** (627–631) The sack of Troy is compared to foresters cutting down an ancient ash tree; when it is about to fall it groans in an almost human way.

Just as Homer does, Virgil uses these similes to allow the reader to step back from the fast-paced action for a moment, and to bring to mind an image of what is happening.

ACTIVITY

Choose one or more of the similes on this page, and create a drawing or painting to illustrate the image that you think Virgil is trying to portray.

EXAM TIP

Pathos

If you comment on a literary device such as pathos, remember to explain why it is effective – what emotions might the author be trying to bring out in the reader in lines rich in pathos?

TOPIC REVIEW

With reference to Virgil, *Aeneid* 2.268–end, you should be able to:

1. Describe:
   - the historical context in which Virgil wrote the *Aeneid*
   - the storyline in this prescription, including the context in which Aeneas narrates it.
   - the roles played by the main characters, including Aeneas, Hector, Creusa, Priam and Pyrrhus
   - examples of imagery used by Virgil.

2. Explain:
   - how the politics of Virgil's time influenced the themes of the *Aeneid*
   - the nature of Aeneas' destiny, and the importance of pietas
   - how warfare is depicted, including examples of heroism and of its innocent victims
   - how Virgil's use of imagery lends power to his narrative.

PRACTICE QUESTIONS

Source A: *Virgil, Aeneid, 2.518–525*

And when she saw Priam himself dressed in youthful armour
she cried: "What mad thought, poor husband, urges you
to fasten on these weapons? Where do you run?
The hour demands no such help, nor defences such as these,
not if my own Hector were here himself. Here, I beg you,
this altar will protect us all or we'll die together."
So she spoke and drew the old man towards her,
and set him down on the sacred steps.

1. Give **three** ways that Virgil creates sympathy for Priam and Hecuba in these lines. Support your points with reference to the passage. [6]

2. 'Pathos is an essential part of ancient war poetry'. Based on the texts you have read, to what extent do you agree with this statement? You should refer to at least **two** texts. [15]

Further Reading for Literature and Culture 2: War and Warfare

Culture

Breeze, David (2016) *The Roman Army*. London: Bloomsbury

Cartledge, Paul (2013) *Thermopylae, the Battle that Changed the World*. London: Pan

Connolly, Peter (2016) *Greece and Rome at War*. Barnsley: Frontline

Lange, Carsten (2011) 'The Battle of Actium: a Reconsideration', *Classical Quarterly* 61(2): 608–623

Lepper, Frank and Sheppard Frere (1988) *Trajan's Column*, Stroud: Sutton

Morrison, J. S., Coates, J. F. and Rankov, N. B. (2000) *The Athenian Trireme*. Cambridge: Cambridge University Press

Strauss, Barry (2005) *The Battle of Salamis*. London: Simon & Schuster

van Wees, Hans (2004) *Greek Warfare: Myths and Realities*. London: Bloomsbury

Literature

Camps, W. A. (1979) *An Introduction to Virgil's Aeneid*. Oxford: Oxford University Press

Jenkyns, R. (2013) *Classical Epic: Homer and Virgil*. London: Bloomsbury

Owen, E. T. (1994) *The Story of the Iliad*. London: Bloomsbury

Powell, Barry B. (2007) *Homer* London: Blackwell Introductions to the Ancient World

Silk, M. (2010) *Homer: the Iliad*. Cambridge: Cambridge University Press

West, David (2002) *Horace Odes III: dulce periculum*. Oxford: Oxford University Press

West, M. L. (2008) *Greek Lyric Poetry*. Oxford: Oxford University Press

Williams, R. D. (2009) *The Aeneid*. London: Bloomsbury

What to Expect in the Exam for War and Warfare

This chapter aims to show you the types of questions you are likely to get in the written examination. It offers some advice on how to answer the questions and will help you avoid common errors.

THE EXAMINATION

This component of the GCSE examination is designed to test your knowledge, understanding and evaluation of War and Warfare. The examination is worth 90 marks and lasts 1 hour and 30 minutes. This represents 50% of the total marks for the GCSE.

There are two sections to the paper, one focusing on the 'Culture' topics and sources, the other focusing on the 'Literature' – the prescribed sections from Homer, Tyrtaeus, Horace and Virgil. Each section is worth 45 marks, and is therefore worth 25% of your GCSE. The question paper will consist of both short-answer and extended-response questions.

For the 'Culture' section, you will be required to respond to visual and material sources. Some of these will be the prescribed sources you have studied in class, and some of these you will not have seen before. Sources for the 'Literature' section will only be drawn from the prescribed sections of Homer, Tyrtaeus, Horace and Virgil that you have studied.

There are two Assessment Objectives in your GCSE in Classical Civilisation. Questions will be designed to test these areas. The Assessment Objectives are explained in the table below:

	Assessment Objective	Marks
AO1	Demonstrate knowledge and understanding of: • (literature and visual/material culture from the classical world • (how sources reflect their cultural contexts • (possible interpretations of sources by different audiences and individuals.	50
AO2	Analyse, interpret and evaluate literature and visual/material culture from the classical world, using evidence and producing coherent and reasoned arguments.	40

For AO1 in this component, you will need to demonstrate the following:

Culture

- A good range of accurate and relevant knowledge of war and warfare, including how it is presented in material culture.
- What the material culture tells us about ancient war and warfare.
- An understanding of the way different peoples from Greece and Rome fought: the Spartans, the Athenians and the Romans.
- Different interpretations that can be made about material culture representing Greek and Roman warfare, and the different conclusions that can be drawn from it.

Literature

- A good range of accurate and relevant knowledge of the prescribed texts.
- An understanding of the relevant genres, and of the historical and literary context in which the prescribed texts were written.
- Knowledge and understanding of the key themes of each text.
- An understanding of the literary styles of each of the authors.
- Different interpretations that can be drawn from the texts, and the conclusions that can be drawn from these.

For AO2 in this component, you will need to demonstrate that you can analyse, interpret and evaluate the sources you have studied, giving opinions and backing them up with evidence, for example:

Culture

- A range of reasoned opinions about ancient war and warfare.
- Appropriate evaluation of different sources to provide reasoned ideas.

Literature

- A range of reasoned opinions about the genres, characters and themes of the prescribed sources, and about what they can tell us about ancient war and warfare.
- Appropriate analysis of the genres, characters and themes of the prescribed sources, and of what they can tell us about ancient war and warfare.

QUESTION TYPES

There are five types of questions that will feature in your exam. Each type will appear in both the Culture and Literature sections. With the exception of the extended-response questions (see below), all questions will be linked to a source. In the Culture section this will be a piece of material evidence, such as a picture of a site or a work of art, or a literary source. In the Literature section this will be a passage from one of the prescribed texts.

The question types are listed in the table below. They really fall into two categories: the first three types (knowledge and understanding, significance, and stimulus questions) are all short-answer questions. The final two types (detailed-response questions and extended-response questions) require a longer answer.

The final two types will usually be the final questions of each section. The short-answer questions can come in any order. For example, there could be a two-mark knowledge and understanding question, followed by a four-mark stimulus question, followed by a three-mark significance question.

Question type	Number of marks in each section for each question type
Knowledge and understanding questions	9
Significance questions	3
Stimulus questions	10
Detailed-response questions	8
Extended-response questions	15

Knowledge and understanding questions

There will be 9-marks' worth of knowledge and understanding questions in total (all AO1). The 9 marks will be broken down into a series of short-answer questions, typic-ally worth 1, 2 or 3 marks.

Some questions will require you to show your **knowledge** of one of the prescribed texts, or of an object or site from the ancient world. Other questions will require you to show **knowledge** and **also** demonstrate an **understanding** of these facts.

There will be a **source** to assist you. For Literature, this will be a passage from one of your prescribed authors. For Culture, it could be a prescribed source you have studied, or it could be one that you have not seen before.

For example, you might be shown the image of a trireme on the right with the following questions:

Question: (a) How did a trireme get its name? [1]

(b) How did the design of a trireme make it an effective warship? [1]

Answer: (a) It was named after its three banks of rowers. [1]

(b) The three banks of rowers gave the ship great power and ability to turn or ram into another ship at speed. [1]

Knowing that a trireme has three banks of rowers is a piece of knowledge, and you can then show further understanding of it by explaining how this design made it effective in battle. This answer should be brief. There is in fact no need to write full sentences if it seems that only a single word or a phrase is needed, as is the case in the first part of the answer.

The following represents a typical Literature knowledge and understanding question, together with its answer:

Source A: *Virgil, Aeneid, 2.270–273*

> See, in dream, before my eyes, Hector seemed to stand there,
> saddest of all and pouring out great tears,
> torn by the chariot, as once he was, black with bloody dust,
> and his swollen feet pierced by the thongs.

Question: **(a)** Who killed Hector?   [1]

               (b) Why are Hector's feet described as swollen and pierced by thongs?   [2]

Answer: Achilles [1]. Hector's feet were swollen because after Achilles killed him, he pierced his feet [1] to tie him to his chariot and drag him away [1].

The first part is asking for one piece of factual knowledge. The second part then asks for a combination of knowledge and understanding. Remember, if you are asked to only give a certain number of facts, or make a certain number of points, you should stick to the instructions.

In this type of question, each correct fact or explanation is worth one mark. You will not be asked to evaluate ideas (e.g. whether you think that a trireme was as well designed as it might have been, or if you approve of Achilles' behaviour), so do not waste time in doing so.

Significance questions

There will be one of these questions in each section. It will be split into two parts. You will be asked to give two pieces of information (2 marks AO1) and state why one or both are important or significant, or what this knowledge tells us (1 mark AO2). Look at the Literature example based on these lines from Homer's *Iliad*:

Source A: *Homer, Iliad, 22.331–336*

> "While you were despoiling Patroclus, no doubt, in your folly, you thought yourself quite safe, Hector, and forgot all about me in my absence. Far from him, by the hollow ships, was a mightier man, who should have been his helper but stayed behind, and that was I, who now have brought you low. The dogs and carrion birds will tear apart your flesh, but him the Achaeans will bury."

(a) Why did Achilles stay by the hollow ships and why does he regret not going into battle with Patroclus?   [2]

(b) Why might the Greeks have disapproved of Achilles' decision to remain out of the fighting?   [1]

The answers to part (a) are that Hector stripped Patroclus of the armour he was wearing [1] and that Achilles had refused to fight for the Greeks at this point [1]. For the second part, you could explain that the Greeks expected warriors to show courage in battle and to fight for their people [1].

In the Culture section the question might look something like this:

Look at the outline plan of a Roman legionary fortress.

(a) Identify two ceremonial items on display in the temple of the basilica. [2]

(b) Choose one of these items: why was it important to a typical legionary soldier? [1]

In part (a) you could say that there was a statue of the emperor [1] and that the legion's standards were also on display there [1].

One mark would be gained in part (b) for saying either that the statue of the emperor would be inspiring for a soldier, or that a standard gave a soldier a sense of pride and loyalty to his century. Remember that you only need to make one point to gain the mark.

Stimulus questions

These questions will ask you to identify something relevant from a stimulus passage or image, and to analyse what you have recognised. Each **relevant** quotation or feature of the image that is picked out will be worth a mark, as will each piece of analysis. Therefore, these questions are each worth equal amounts of AO1 and AO2.

In the Culture section, you might be shown an image of the relief commemorating the battle of Actium (right) and then be asked:

Question: Identify two features of this image, and suggest what each might tell us about Roman naval warfare. [4]

Answers: To gain the first two marks (AO1), you might identify any two of the following features:

- it shows a warship with two banks of oars
- you can see a row of small round shields arranged along the length of the ship
- this one has a crocodile emblem on the prow
- soldiers are standing along the ship and it appears packed
- the soldiers are armed with spears and shields.

To gain the next two marks (AO2), you might make any two of the following suggestions:

- The multiple banks of oars must have made the ship fast
- The upper parts of the ship were protected by the banks of shields
- The crocodile shows that ships had important emblems or symbols on them
- the ships carried large amounts of soldiers
- these soldiers must have boarded other ships, or protected against being boarded as they are dressed for close combat.

In the Literature section, you will be given a passage and might be asked for your opinions on a character or for how the passage is made exciting. For example, you might be given the following passage from Tyrtaeus' Fragment 10 and the question below:

Source A: *Tyrtaeus, Fragment 10, lines 15–27*

Do not run away abandoning your elders – agèd men, whose limbs are no longer nimble. For it is of course shameful for an older man fallen among fighters at the front to lie ahead of the young men, his head already white and beard grey, gasping his stalwart spirit out into the dust, clutching his bloody genitals in his own hands – a shameful thing in one's eyes, a sight to cause indignation – his naked skin exposed.

What point do you think Tyrtaeus is making in this passage? Use **two** phrases the passage and suggest what they tell us about his message. [4]

You would be expected to select two phrases and analyse how they communicate Tyrtaeus' message. You might choose the phrase 'his head already white and beard grey' and say that Tyrtaeus is emphasising the old age of the soldier who should not have to be fighting in the front line. You might say that the phrase 'clutching his bloody genitals in his own hands' emphasises the horror and indignity that an old man must suffer when dying in war.

Look at the number of marks available. If there are two pieces of evidence (e.g. choosing two phrases) and two pieces of analysis required, do not give more than this amount. You will be using up time that would be better spent in detailed-response and extended-response questions.

Detailed-response questions

You will get one of these questions in each section with one or more source to prompt you. This source is meant only as a starting point, and it will be clear from the question that you will need to bring in **extra information and examples**.

Four marks are awarded for your knowledge and understanding (AO1), and four marks given for your analysis, interpretation and evaluation of your facts and understanding (AO2). These questions are marked in a different way, however; you are not given one mark for each correct opinion and each piece of evidence, but the answer as a whole is marked using a Levels of Response Grid. A Levels of Response Grid explains to examiners what answers may look like to achieve a certain number of marks. An examiner will read the whole answer and then check the grid to work out what level the answer belongs to. It is important to remember that the quality of your answer is more important than the amount you have written. The Levels of Response Grid is included in the mark schemes for exam papers.

It is also important to remember that for AO1 you will need to show knowledge and understanding of a source's context and the different ways people interpret the sources. Remember that you can examine both sides of an argument. For example, if you are asked whether you admire the character of Diomedes in the *Iliad*, there are likely to be arguments on both sides of the question. It may be that you largely admire him, but that he has some flaws, or that you largely do not admire him but that he has some redeeming features. If you do not examine both sides of an argument, you may have missed some key facts, and your answer may not show a full evaluation.

This question is not meant to be an essay. You are advised not to write an introduction that simply outlines how you will write your response, as this will not add anything to your answer and will take up valuable time. You may find you have more to say than time allows, so you might have to be disciplined in moving on. Make your key points at the start, keep to the point, and if you do choose to have a conclusion, keep it brief, as you will ideally have answered the precise wording of the question throughout your answer. It is not necessary to have a conclusion to gain full marks.

For example, on the paper you might be given the following quotation:

Source A: *Vegetius, About Military Matters, 1.6–7*

> A young recruit should keep his eyes watchful and his head upright. He should be broad-chested, with muscly shoulders and strong arms, and his fingers should be on the longer side. He should have a flat stomach and a lean bottom. His calves and feet should not be flabby, but rather full of tough sinews.

You might then be asked the question:

> How well did the training of a Roman legionary soldier prepare him for life in the Roman army? Use the source as a starting point and your own knowledge in your answer. [8]

In order to show that you know about the training of a soldier, you might include some of these facts:

- recruits had to be physically strong and alert
- they were trained to do drill route marches
- they also practised swimming, jumping, running and riding
- there was offensive weapons training with a wooden sword and javelin
- there was defensive training with a wicker shield
- recruits were also taught to build a camp.

You then need to weigh up how well this training prepared him for life in the Roman army:

- soldiers needed to be physically strong to fight well, build camps etc
- drilling instilled discipline and teamwork, which was vital for military efficiency
- route marches prepared him for marching through a province at speed, particularly at a time of war
- activities such as riding and swimming developed other skills, which could come in useful in times of war or peace
- being able to use both offensive and defensive weapons efficiently was vital to success in battle
- building a camp quickly would enable the legion to move around a province and house itself efficiently.

Half the marks are awarded for AO1 and for AO2, but remember this does not necessarily mean that you should give four facts and four explanations. Examiners will read your whole response and judge how good they feel it is overall.

In Section B, on Literature, a question might ask you about the importance of a theme, or the portrayal of one particular character or episode.

Extended-response questions

This type of question is different from all the other questions in two respects: there is no stimulus passage to introduce it, and you will be given a **choice** of questions to answer (there are two extended-response questions in each section, and you must do **only one**). However, it is marked using a Levels of Response Grid in the same way as the detailed-response question.

Five marks are awarded for your knowledge and understanding (AO1), and ten marks given for your analysis, interpretation and evaluation of your facts and understanding (AO2). This means more marks are awarded for how good your argument is than for simply what you know. Therefore, you might want to spend a bit of time thinking about the structure of your answer. As for the detailed-response question, it is important to remember that for AO1 you will need to show knowledge and understanding of the literary and historical context of sources and the different ways people interpret them.

Extended-response questions will be broader than the detailed response questions, and will draw upon material from across topics of either the Literature or the Culture sections. However, these questions will never cover both Literature and Culture. For example, whereas you might be asked a question about the training of a legionary soldier in a detailed-response question, as shown on p. 447, an extended-response question might ask about life in the Roman army more generally, or even ask you to compare the Roman army with the armies of Athens or Sparta.

The following is an example of a possible extended-response Literature question:

'The willingness to die bravely in battle was the most important quality of an ancient soldier.' Based on the literary sources you have read, to what extent do you agree with this statement?   [15]

There is a great deal of evidence you could draw on from your four sources to answer this question, and you are unlikely to be able to use all of it (remember too that you can get credit for introducing material from outside the prescribed sources, so if you have read ancient authors accounts of war, you could draw on these too). You might include some of these facts:

- *Iliad*: Hector dies bravely, but wishes rather to save Troy.
- *Iliad*: Diomedes and Glaucus put the importance of xenia above risking their lives fighting one another.
- *Iliad*: the women of Book 6 try to keep Hector back from the fighting.
- *Iliad*: Priam and Hecuba beg Hector not to fight Achilles in Book 22.
- Fragment 10: a young man dying in the front line is described as 'beautiful', and it is shameful to be defeated or to let an old man die instead.

- Ode 3.2: dying for one's country is sweet and fitting, but the poem also hopes that the young Roman will defeat the Parthians in battle.
- Aeneid: Aeneas says that it is beautiful to die in battle.
- Aeneid: Aeneas is persuaded to leave Troy and lead the surviving Trojans instead.
- Aeneid: the elderly Priam wants to fight, but is persuaded by Hecuba to wait beside the altar instead.

You then need to analyse whether the willingness to die in battle really was the most important quality for an ancient soldier. You might draw conclusions such as:

It was the most important quality because:

- In the *Iliad*, when Hector knows he is doomed, he chooses to die bravely in order to win a glorious reputation.
- Achilles remembers Patroclus most for the brave way he died in battle.
- There are many examples in Book 5 of warriors dying bravely, and this is sometimes the only times they are mentioned in the poem.
- In Fragment 10, the success of an army and therefore of Sparta itself depends on young soldiers putting their lives on the line.
- Horace's description of a brave death in battle as 'sweet and fitting' shows that it was vital to the success of the Roman army against enemies such as the Parthians.
- Despite being in a hopeless situation, Aeneas is prepared to put his life at risk because he believes it is the right thing to do.

It is not the most important quality because:

- The meeting of Diomedes and Glaucus shows that family ties can sometimes be more important than risking your life.
- Hecuba, Andromache and Helen would all prefer Hector to stay within the walls and not risk his life in Book 6, as would Priam and Hecuba in Book 22.
- Hector would have preferred to have been good enough to defeat Achilles than to die bravely in battle at his hands.
- Horace suggests that the Roman army was a training for civilian life where other qualities, such as virtue and tact, would be the most important.
- Aeneas' duty to lead the Trojan people and their household gods to another land is seen as more important than dying bravely in battle.
- Priam is encouraged to seek refuge at the altars of the gods than to die fighting.

Key points

The following applies to both detailed-response questions and extended-response questions:

- Your facts must be **relevant**. Do not merely state everything you know about a particular topic.

- It is a common mistake in the literature to over-narrate the plot and to retell a whole story. You should instead **summarise** the main points, or focus in detail on one or two parts of it. This is particularly important in your extended-response answer, where five marks are available for your knowledge, but 10 marks are given for your evaluation, interpretation and analysis.

- Show that you **understand** things from an ancient point of view wherever possible. For example, characters in the literature texts may have had different attitudes to slavery than we would today, or Roman baths may have seemed far more luxurious to the Romans than they would do to us today.

- Evaluation is best done throughout the response. **Keep referring back** to the title in your essay to do this. If you give all your facts, and then give all your opinions, it is easy to miss something out, or to run out of time.

- Try to find a **balance** of ideas as the question will usually require you to argue both for and against an idea.

- Sometimes a piece of evidence can be taken two ways. If so, remember to give **both interpretations** in order to show a high level of understanding.

- You will not have a lot of time to do these questions and so it is always best your most important arguments first in case you find yourself running out of time.

- Ultimately make your conclusion **logical**, and supported by evidence from your whole answer, not just one part of it.

Look at these two extracts attempting to answer the question above:

Extract 1

It is very important to be willing to die bravely in battle. In the *Iliad*, Hector dies bravely in battle even though he could have stayed in Troy with his wife. His wife and mother do not want him to fight and offer him some wine instead, but Greek women didn't understand how important it was to be brave. Loads of fighters die bravely when fighting Diomedes so it must have been important to do this. However, Achilles is a wimp and stays out of the fighting, and so does Paris. Tyrtaeus says that Spartans must be prepared to die in battle or else old men will die instead and people will be homeless. Horace also says that it is good to die in battle, although Roman soldiers could be really scary if you were up against them and you hadn't had enough training. But in the Aeneid Aeneas does not think it is important to die in battle and wants to escape from Troy instead.

Extract 2

I believe that the willingness to die in battle was an important quality for an ancient soldier, but not the most important. It is certainly important for Hector to die bravely when he knew that his time had come, but he clearly would have preferred to have been a better fighter so that he would be a match for Achilles. In this case, the most important quality was to be a great fighter. Moreover, the fact that in both Book 6 and Book 22 members of Hector's family urge him not to fight outside the walls suggests that to them it was more important for him to be alive to look after them than to die bravely. Similarly, in the Aeneid, it is clearly an important quality to be willing to die in battle – Aeneas describes such a death as 'beautiful' – but ultimately it is made clear to him in a series of three visions of Hector, Venus and Creusa that his duty to lead the Trojans to a new land is more important.

Notice how the first extract spends more time on presenting the facts than giving opinions, and some of the facts are irrelevant. The evaluation is not developed fully, and the final statement is not made relevant to the question. The second extract is much more concise, and is much more balanced, and it focuses on the issue of whether the willingness to die in battle was the **most** important quality. It flows smoothly from one example to another, providing a rounded view of the answer to the question.

GENERAL EXAM SKILLS

When you are sitting the examination, read the instructions carefully so that you realise which questions are compulsory and which are optional (the only option you have is which of the two extended response questions you choose to answer). Remember that the examination will have a range of difficulty of questions; some of it is designed to be challenging, and you should not be panicked if you cannot think of an answer immediately. The following pieces of advice may seem obvious, but you should not underestimate their importance:

- The examination lasts 90 minutes and is worth 90 marks. Don't assume this means you should spend a minute per mark: in reality a lot of short questions will take less than a mark a minute and you should spend longer than a mark a minute on the longer questions.
- Both the Culture and Literature sections are worth 45 marks. Do not spend too long on whichever you choose to do first; this is especially tempting if you like the questions that have been set and feel you could say a lot.
- If you see a question that you do not know the answer to, move on quickly to another question and don't waste time thinking. Leave enough time to go back to it as during the examination you might well remember the answer.
- Stick to the question: if you are asked for facts, do not give opinions and vice versa.
- Do not try to answer a slightly different question if you wish another had been set, or if you have practised a similar one before at school.
- For detailed-response and extended-response questions, present different interpretations.
- More marks are available in the paper for opinions than knowledge or understanding. It is vital that you do not over-narrate, especially in your Literature answers.

GLOSSARY

Component-specific glossaries can be found on the companion website.

Achaeans Homeric term for the Greeks

agōgē the training school that all Spartan boys attended from the age of seven

aidōs the shame or respectful modesty a Homeric character feels towards someone who has great timē

ala a cohort of Roman cavalry, theoretically 512 strong

Amazonomachy a mythological battle against the Amazons

amphora (pl. **amphorae**) a clay storage jar, often containing wine or olive oil, with two carrying handles

andron the men's socialising room, usually located by the front door

aphorism a short saying that communicates a common truth

apodyterium the changing room in a baths complex

aquila the emblem of the legion, an eagle made of gold set on a pole

aquilifer the legionary soldier responsible for carrying the aquila

archon a magistrate in Athens, responsible for organising civic as well as religious matters

Argives Homeric term for the Greeks

aristeia a scene in an epic poem in which a great warrior fights with exceptional skill

Assembly the central institution of the Athenian system of democracy, in which all adult male citizens were eligible to attend and vote

atrium the main room of the Roman domus, where the family received friends and clients

Augustales Roman public officials connected to preserving the honour of the emperor, largely drawn from the ranks of freedmen

ballista a Roman crossbow that fired iron darts

barbarian the Greek word for any non-Greek.

bard a public storyteller who recited vast amounts poetry to the accompaniment of the lyre, often during banquets

basilica the large hall used for assemblies of troops in a Roman legionary fortress

Boule a council of 500 citizens in Athens who decided what issues would be discussed in the Assembly

bulla A lucky charm in the Roman world

caldarium the hot room in a baths complex

camp prefect the assistant to the legatus of a Roman legion

Capitoline Hill one of the seven original hills of Rome, it was the political and ceremonial heart of the city

carceres the starting cages for the chariots – there were twelve in all

cartouche a rectangle with rounded ends, usually inscribed with the name of a god or king, used in Egyptian inscriptions

catalogue a long list that often features in epic poetry to list warriors in an army or boats in a fleet

cena the Roman word for a dinner

centurion the commander of the century in a Roman legion

century a unit of about 80 men in a Roman legion (there were some double-sized centuries of 160 men)

chamber tomb a tomb, dug from rock, in which a body or bodies would be buried in a chamber

chiton a large, loose-fitting, woollen tunic worn in ancient Greece

cist grave a grave in the form of a stone-lined pit, dug into the earth, and covered up

client a Roman who would attach himself to a wealthier patron in order to boost his income and business opportunities

client kingdom a state that was allied with, but subject to Rome

client monarch the king or queen who was the leader of a client kingdom. A client monarch would be able to rule their own kingdom, but Rome would handle any international relations.

cloisonné the soldering of a wire onto metal and then putting glass or gemstones in the soldered pattern

coemptio a Roman wedding ceremony (resulting in a cum manu marriage) where the bride was symbolically sold to her new husband

cohort the largest unit of a Roman legion; the first cohort of a legion had five double-centuries; cohorts two to ten each consisted of six centuries

college a group of priests

confarreatio a traditional patrician wedding ceremony, resulting in a cum manu marriage

consul the most important public official in Rome after the emperor; two consuls were elected annually

contubernium a unit of eight men in a Roman legion who shared the same tent and dealt with their own mess arrangements

corbelling a technique used to span a gap between two walls by placing increasingly larger blocks of stone on each other, thereby creating a vaulted roof

cornicen the horn-player in a Roman legion who sounded orders to the soldiers

cum manu a form of Roman marriage that was 'with hand'; in this kind of marriage, the wife transferred from her original household to the household of her husband, becoming his legal dependent

curse tablet a tablet on which someone wrote a prayer to the gods asking them to put a curse on an enemy

cursus honorum the ladder of political offices in Rome

Danaans Homeric term for the Greeks

democracy rule of the people

didactic something that is meant to teach or instruct

diekplous a naval manoeuvre whereby a trireme sailed through the enemy line of ships and turned at pace to ram the side of an enemy ship

domus a large Roman private house in a city or town

dowry an amount of money paid to a prospective groom by the bride's family

dramatic irony when a character does not know the full significance of what is happening or being said, but the readers do

dromos a passageway leading to the tholos tomb

ekstasis standing outside oneself; the experience of being someone other than yourself

elegy a genre of poetry that can focus on a number of topics, and where lines have an alternating metre of hexameter followed by pentameter

enōmotia a 'sworn-band', the smallest unit of the Spartan army

epic poetry poetry focusing on great deeds, composed in hexameter verse

Epicureanism a philosophy of life that encouraged people to live for simple pleasures and to reduce anxieties as much as possible

epithet an adjectival word or phrase regularly added to a name to denote a personal or physical quality

equites members of the second social class in Rome; an equestrian had to own property worth at least 400,000 sesterces

Ergastinai 'female weavers', either Arrephoroi, another group of unmarried girls, or a mix of older and younger women

exclamation a figure of speech in which a writer seems to exclaim words aloud

exposure the ancient practice of leaving an unwanted baby outside the city to die

fasces a bundle of rods with an axe-head, which were the symbol of the authority of a senior Roman magistrate

fate a set of future events that are destined to happen and cannot be changed

figurine a small statue of a person, god, or animal

formula (pl. **formulae**) a section of an epic poem, longer than an epithet, that is regularly used to describe a person, place or object

fresco a painting originally done on damp plaster in which the colours become fixed as the plaster dries

frieze a horizontal sculptured or painted decoration depicting a scene or number of scenes

frigidarium the cold room in a baths complex

genre a category of literature, examples of which might include epic, tragedy, comedy, history and satire

glorious death in Greek myth, heroes (typically male) often desire a 'glorious death' on the battlefield, which would ensure that their reputation and fame would last forever

Golden Fleece the skin of a divine golden ram kept by the Colchians after the ram was slaughtered as a sacrifice; it became the constellation Aries

grammaticus a teacher for secondary-aged children in the Roman world

granulation dropping molten metal onto an object to give a spotted effect

gynaikeion the women's working room in a Greek house, which may have doubled as a bedroom

gyne a married Athenian woman who had given birth to a child

helots a large class of enslaved native inhabitants of Messenia and Laconia who worked the land for their Spartan masters

Hellas the Greek name for the Greek world

hequetai the nobles in Mycenae; they were probably also important troops in the army

hetaira (pl. **hetairai**) a high-class prostitute or courtesan who may have lived in her own house, chosen her own clients and charged a high price for her company

hexameter a poetic metre that has six units to a line

hiereia a Greek priestess (masculine: **hiereus**)

hieroglyphics Egyptian written script

Homeric question the debate about the authorship of the *Iliad* and the *Odyssey* and about the identity of Homer

hoplite a heavily armed Greek infantry soldier who fought in the phalanx, named after their circular shield, a hoplon

hypocaust underfloor heating system

hypozomata two stretched cables that were tied from one end of a trireme to another and kept it in shape

impluvium the pool in the centre of the atrium of a Roman domus that gathered rainwater

infamis literally 'shameful' or 'disgraceful', the very low legal status given to a number of groups in the Roman world, including gladiators, charioteers, actors and prostitutes

inlay a technique where one metal is put on top of another on an object

insula (pl. **insulae**) the Roman name for a block of flats

irony a way of expressing what you mean by using language that normally suggests the opposite

Janus the roman god of transitions, beginnings and endings

kleos the glorious reputation a Homeric warrior hopes to win

krater a large bowl used for mixing wine and water

kleros household farm on a plot of land assigned by the state to a Spartan warrior

krypteia a period of survival training for the strongest Spartans in their mid to late teens

kylix a drinking cup

kyria the wife of the kyrios, under the direct control of her husband

kyrios the male head of a Greek household, with responsibility for and authority over his wife, children and any unmarried female relatives

Lares the Roman family's household gods, representing the spirits of the family ancestors

lawagetas the leader of the people in Mycenae, who was also probably the leader of the army

legatus the commander of the Roman legion

legion the largest unit of the Roman army

lena the name for a female brothel-keeper in the Roman world (masculine: **leno**)

libation a drink offering poured in honour of the gods

Liburnian galley a Roman warship

litter a portable taxi carried by slaves in the Roman world

litterator a teacher for primary-aged children in the Roman world

liturgy a super-tax on the wealthiest citizens in Athens to fund important civic projects

lochoi units of a tribal regiment in the Athenian army

lupanar a Roman brothel

lyric poetry personal poetry originally performed to the lyre for an audience

maenad female followers of Dionysus

magistrate an elected politician

mantis (pl. **manteis**) a prophet, seer or soothsayer

materfamilias mother of the Roman household and wife of the paterfamilias

matrona married Roman woman

megaron the central hall in a Mycenaean palace, used for banquets, worship and meetings

meretrix a technical term for a Roman prostitute, often referred to with euphemisms by their client, e.g. 'puella', which means 'girl' or 'girlfriend'

metae the set of three turning posts located at each end of the spina

metaphor a figure of speech in which a word or phrase is used to describe something which it cannot literally be

metic a resident foreigner

Minoan civilisation a civilisation based on Crete that influenced neighbouring areas. It lasted from around 3500 BC until around 1400 BC, overlapping in both time and area with the Mycenaean civilisation

mora a name for a Spartan army regiment

mulsum a type of Roman wine sweetened by honey

Mycenaean a civilisation that was powerful from around 1600BC to 1150BC, named after the city of Mycenae in southern Greece

mystery cult a kind of religious worship only open to those who had undergone a special rite of passage (initiation), and whose details celebrants were forbidden from sharing with the uninitiated

navarch the captain of a squadron of Roman naval ships

nemesis the concept of a downfall or undoing after overconfidence or arrogance

nostos the desire to return to your homeland

nymphe a married Athenian woman who had not yet given birth to a child

omen sign from the gods

onager a Roman catapult that fired rocks and large stones at the enemy

optio the centurion's deputy in a Roman legion

oral culture a society where people rely on word of mouth rather than writing

oral poem a poem that is composed and told without the aid of writing

orchestra in the Roman theatre, the semi-circular area in front of the stage normally reserved for VIP seating

palaestra exercise-ground

pantheon a group of gods and goddesses

parody an exaggerated and comic imitation of the style of a particular writer or genre

parthenos an unmarried virgin girl

Parthian Empire an empire lying to the east of the Roman Empire, centred on what is now Iran

paterfamilias the male head of a Roman family

pathos literally 'suffering' in Greek, an appeal to the reader's emotions by inviting them to feel pity and sadness

patria potestas the power or authority held by the paterfamilias over members of his household

patrician Rome's elite/noble class (determined by family not money)

patron a Roman who gives financial or other such support to a client in return for work and favours

patronage a semi-formal association between a richer, more influential Roman patron and a poorer, less influential client, whereby the patron would provide social contacts, advice and perhaps financial support, and in return the client would support the patron in their business or political endeavours

pentameter a poetic metre with five units to a line

peplos a Greek dress made from a long tube of fabric and fastened over the shoulders with brooches or pins

perioeci a class of people who lived in scattered, less fertile parts of Spartan territory

peristyle a colonnaded garden within a Roman domus

personification a figure of speech by which something non-human is given human characteristics

phalanx a rectangular fighting formation in which men fought in massed ranks and tried to force their way through the enemy phalanx opposing them

piety/pietas the most important heroic quality in the *Aeneid*, a Roman virtue that means 'sense of duty', and applies to a man's duty towards his family, his city and his gods

pithos (pl. **pithoi**) a large clay storage jar.

plebeian class commoners in the Roman world

Pnyx the hill on which the Athenian Assembly met

Pontifex Maximus the chief priest of Roman religion

pornē (pl. **pornai**) a low-class Greek prostitute (almost always a slave) who would have worked in a brothel

praefectus the commander of a Roman naval fleet

praetor the second highest category of public official, responsible for the law courts and imperial administration

praetorium the private quarters of the legatus in a Roman fortress

primi ordines the collective name for the five centurions of the first cohort of a Roman legion

primus pilus the most senior centurion in the Roman legion

principia the headquarters of a Roman fortress

pronuba a Roman citizen woman who had been married only once and was still married to this man

prostitution a trade where sexual acts are performed in exchange for money

pudicitia the Roman idea of sexual modesty shown through a woman's chastity or fidelity to her husband, but also by how she behaved in public and by dressing modestly

Pythia priestess of Apollo at Delphi – sometimes called the 'Delphic Oracle'

pyxis a box, often with a lid, to hold cosmetics or possibly jewellery

quindecemviri literally 'fifteen men', the keepers of the Sibylline Books in Rome

relief (from the Latin verb 'relevo', 'to raise') a carving that projects from, and is a part of, the same background material, and has the effect of shading and being in 3D

religious pollution state of uncleanness acquired in a number of ways (e.g. coming into contact with a dead person, having sex, killing outside of war) that offended the gods and prevented participation in religious festivals, and was removed by ritual cleansing

repoussé a technique where a design is hammered onto an object from the inside of it

rhetor a teacher for tertiary-aged boys in the Roman world

rhyton (pl. **rhyta**) a vessel, either in the shape of a cone or animal head, probably for pouring liquid, and made from either pottery or metal

rites of Ceres an ancient Greek religious cult, also known as the Eleusinian Mysteries, in which members were sworn to secrecy

Roman citizenship a high privilege with various rights and protections, normally reserved for the children of two Roman citizens

Sabine a person belonging to the Italian race of Sabines

sally port a gap in the outer wall through which defenders could rush out to surprise attackers

sanctuary an area of sacred land set apart from the rest of the city

satire a genre of writing that aims to show up hypocrisy, pretence or other character flaws through the use of humour

scaenae frons the back wall of the stage set in a Roman theatre, usually two or three storeys tall and with elaborate decoration

self-sufficiency supporting a household without relying on outside assistance (an important Athenian value)

senators members of the highest social class at Rome; a senator had to own property worth at least one million sesterces

Senate Rome's central governing body, formed of men, the majority advanced in years

shaft grave a grave in which a deep shaft was dug and a space created at the bottom for a body, often re-used for later burials

sibyl prophetess or female mantis

Sibylline Books books held in Rome, full of prophecies

signifer the Roman soldier responsible for the century's standard

simile a figure of speech whereby one thing is compared to another thing of a different kind in order to make a description more vivid

sine manu a form of Roman marriage 'without hand'; in this kind of marriage, the wife remained part of her original household, under the legal protection and control of her original paterfamilias

spina the thin dividing bank down the middle of a Roman stadium's racing track

standard a Roman war flag, the emblem of a century, a set of medallions hoisted on a pole

stanza a verse of poetry with a set metre repeated throughout the poem

stele (pl. **stelai**) stone slabs, often with patterns or images carved on them, most commonly used as tombstones

stilus a pen-like implement used to write on wax tablets

stock character a character in a work of literature or drama who is easily recognisable as a particular type of person from certain behaviour traits

stratēgos an elected general in the Athenian army; every tribe elected one each year

strigil a curved scraper used to remove oil and dirt from the body

suppliant a person who begs for something from someone in a position of authority

symposium (pl. **symposia**) a drinking party held by Athenian men, which citizen women would not have been allowed to attend

syssitia dining-clubs of about fifteen Spartan citizens, which each met every evening and shared a tent together on campaign. Each man had to contribute food to the mess

tablinum a reception room in a Roman domus, often used as the master's study

taxiarch a senior commander in the Spartan army

tepidarium the warm room in a baths complex

temple a building dedicated to one or more of the gods, with a statue of the god kept inside to represent the fact that the temple was a 'home' for the god

tesserarius the Roman soldier in charge of organisation of guards and communication of passwords

testudo a group of Roman soldiers advancing in formation with shields over their heads

tholos tomb a large domed tomb in the shape of an igloo, roughly circular in its floor space, also known as a beehive tomb

timē the honour a Homeric warrior hopes to win

titan the generation of gods before Zeus and the other Olympian gods

topos (pl. **topoi**) a poetic scene that occurs regularly, which is made up of a series of standard elements

tresantes 'tremblers' – Spartans who had deserted in battle and so been deprived of citizenship

tribunes the six senior officers in a Roman legion after the legatus

tribuni angusticlavi the five tribunes of equestrian rank in a Roman legion

tribunus laticlavius the senior tribune of a Roman legion, of senatorial rank

triclinium a dining room in a Roman domus

trierarch a wealthy Athenian who captained and paid for the upkeep of a trireme for one year

trireme a Greek warship with three banks of rowers on each side

triumph a grand procession through the streets of Rome to celebrate a military victory

tumulus a raised mound of earth under which bodies were buried

turma a Roman cavalry squadron of sixteen horsemen

univira a Roman woman who has been married only once, either one still married or a widow who chooses not to remarry; derives from the Latin 'unus' for 'one' and 'vir' for 'man'

usus a very popular marriage with no formal wedding ceremony and resulting in a sine manu marriage

via praetoria the road from the main gate to the principia in a Roman fortress

via principalis the road crossing the camp in front of the principia in a Roman fortress

via quintana the road crossing the camp behind the principia in a Roman fortress

vilica a female slave responsible for managing a household

vomitoria the staircases of the amphitheatre, via which people could pour out of the stadium in great numbers

wanax the Mycenaean word for a chieftain or king

wetnurse woman who looks after and breastfeeds another woman's baby; common in Athens, wetnurses were usually slaves, foreigners or poorer citizens who charged for their services

xenia in Homer, hospitality given unconditionally to a traveller, involving the giving of any help needed; known as 'guest friendship'

SOURCES OF QUOTATIONS

All translations by the authors unless stated below.
*Numbers in **bold** refer to page numbers.*

Thematic Study (Women in the Ancient World)

5 'The bright-eyed . . .' Hesiod, *Works and Days*, 72–79, trans. OCR; **6** 'For from . . .' Hesiod, *Theogony*, 590–608, trans. Hugh G. Evelyn-White (Harvard University Press, 1914), http://www. perseus.tufts.edu/hopper/text?doc=Perseus:abo:tlg,0020,001:597; **8** 'I respect . . .' Homer, *Iliad*, 3.12, trans. A S Kline; **9** 'Three goddesses . . .' Euripides, *Helen*, II.21–26, trans OCR; **10** 'Brother, I . . .' Homer, *Iliad*, 6.343–353, trans. A S Kline; **12** 'This was . . .' Livy, *History of Rome*, 1.9, trans. OCR; **13** 'Some say . . .' Livy, *History of Rome*, 11, trans. OCR; **14** 'If you . . .' Livy, *History of Rome*, 1.13, trans. OCR; **15** '. . . Lucretia was . . .' Livy, *History of Rome*, 1.57, trans. OCR; **16** 'He was . . .' Livy, *History of Rome*, 1.58, trans. OCR; **16** '. . . Collatinus, there . . .' Livy, *History of Rome*, 1.58, trans. OCR; **21** 'a man . . .' Menander, fourth-century BC fragment, trans. S. Jäkel and G. Kock, cited in Lefkowitz and Fant, *Women's Life in Greece and Rome: A Sourcebook in Translation* (Bloomsbury, 1992), p. 31; **22** '[Pataikos] Listen . . .' Menander, *Perikeiromene*, 1012–14, trans. B MacLachlan, *Women in Ancient Greece: A Sourcebook* (Continuum, 2012), p. 57; **25** 'withstand childbearing . . .' Plutarch, *Life of Lycurgus*, trans. B MacLachlan, *Women in Ancient Greece: A Sourcebook* (Continuum, 2012), p. 153; **25** 'With other . . .' Xenophon, *Constitution of the Spartans*, trans. B MacLachlan, *Women in Ancient Greece: A Sourcebook* (Continuum, 2012), p. 151; **30** 'It's not . . .' Catullus, *Poem 62*, ll.61–66, trans. A S Kline; **33** 'Crown your . . .' Catullus, *Poem 61*, ll.6–15, trans. A S Kline; **36** '[the] greatest . . .' Thucydides, *History of the Peloponnesian War*, 2.45, trans. Richard Crawley, http://classics.mit.edu/Thucydides/pelopwar.2.second.html; **38** 'I know . . .' Aristophanes, *Women at the Thesmophoria*, 501–504, trans. Eugene O'Neill, Jr., *The Complete Greek Drama*, vol. 2. (Random House, 1938), http://www.perseus.tufts.edu/hopper/text?doc=Aristoph.%20Thes.%20516&lang=original; **39** 'For the . . .' Xenophon, *Oeconomicus*, 7.23, trans. B MacLachlan, *Women in Ancient Greece: A Sourcebook* (Continuum, 2012), p. 62; **39** 'You must . . .' Xenophon, *Oeconomicus*, 7.35–36, trans. B MacLachlan, *Women in Ancient Greece: A Sourcebook* (Continuum, 2012), p. 63; **39** 'There are . . .' Xenophon, *Oeconomicus*, 7.41, trans. B MacLachlan, *Women in Ancient Greece: A Sourcebook* (Continuum, 2012), p. 63; **41** 'Hipparete was . . .' Plutarch, *Life of Alcibiades*, 8.3, trans. Bernadotte Perrin, *Plutarch's Lives* (Harvard University Press, 1916), p. 4; **42** 'We also . . .' Xenophon, *Oeconomicus*, 9.12, trans. C Brownson, *Xenophon in Seven Volumes*, vol. 4 (Harvard University Press, 1979), http://www.perseus.tufts.edu/hopper/text?doc=Perseus%3Atext%3A1999.01.0212%3Atext%3DEc.%3Achapter%3D9; **43** 'If . . . an . . .' Xenophon, *Constitution of the Spartans*, 1.7–8, trans. B MacLachlan, *Women in Ancient Greece: A Sourcebook* (Continuum, 2012), p. 156; **43** 'It was . . .' Plutarch, *Life of Lycurgus*, 15.7, trans. B MacLachlan, *Women in Ancient Greece: A Sourcebook* (Continuum, 2012), p. 156; **44** 'Another woman . . .' Plutarch, *Sayings of Spartan Women*, 241C #8, trans. B MacLachlan, *Women in Ancient Greece: A Sourcebook* (Continuum, 2012), p. 159; **50** 'No children . . .' Aulus Gellius, *Attic Nights*, 4.3.2, trans. B MacLachlan, *Women in Ancient Rome: A Sourcebook* (Bloomsbury Academic, 2014), p. 53; **55** 'First of . . .' Alexis, fr. 103PCG, trans. B MacLachlan, *Women in Ancient Greece: A Sourcebook* (Continuum, 2012), p. 98–99; **58** '. . . since she . . .' Demosthenes 59.36, trans. B MacLachlan, *Women in Ancient Greece: A Sourcebook* (Continuum, 2012), p. 107; **89** '[The famous

. . .' Plutarch, *Pericles*, 24.3, trans. OCR; **61** 'The hostess . . .' Virgil, *Copa*, 1–4, trans. Joseph J Mooney, *The Minor Poems of Vergil: Comprising the Culex, Dirae, Lydia, Moretum, Copa, Priapeia and catalepton* (Cornish Brothers, 1916), virgil.org/appendix/copa.htm; **62** '. . . among whom . . .' Cicero, *Philippic*, 2.58, trans. C D Yonge, *The Orations of Marcus Tullius Cicero* (George Bell & Sons, 1903), http://www.perseus.tufts.edu/hopper/text?doc=Perseus%3Atext%3A1999.02.0021%3 Aspeech%3D2; **64** 'And now . . .' Catullus, *Poems*, 8.9–11, trans. OCR; **76** 'Female Herald . . .' Aristophanes, *Women at the Thesmophoria*, ll.372–378, trans. Eugene O'Neill, Jr., *The Complete Greek Drama*, vol. 2 (Random House, 1938), http://www.perseus.tufts.edu/hopper/text?doc=Perseus :abo:tlg,0019,008:380; **77** 'First they . . .' Euripides, *Bacchae*, 695–711, trans. George Theodoridis, http://www.poetryintranslation.com/PITBR/Greek/Bacchae.htm; **78** 'We just . . .' Euripides, *Bacchae*, 732–737, trans. George Theodoridis, http://www.poetryintranslation.com/PITBR/Greek/ Bacchae.htm; **80** 'The fifth . . .' Dionysius of Halicarnassus, 2.64–66, trans. Earnest Cary, *Dionysius of Halicarnassus*, vol. 1 (Loeb Classical Library, 1937), http://penelope.uchicago.edu/Thayer/e/ roman/texts/dionysius_of_halicarnassus/2c*.html; **86** 'In the . . .' Livy, *History of Rome*, X.7–9, trans. Rev. Canon Roberts, *Livy. History of Rome* (E P Dutton and Co., 1912), http://www.perseus. tufts.edu/hopper/text?doc=Perseus:abo:phi,0914,00110:23; **87** 'It is . . .' Plutarch, *Life of Caesar*, 9.7–8, trans. Bernadotte Perrin, *Plutarch's Lives* (Harvard University Press, 1916), p.7; **93** 'Second Woman . . .' Aristophanes, *Assemblywomen*, 87–94, trans. Eugene O'Neill, Jr., *The Complete Greek Drama*, vol. 2 (Random House, 1938), http://www.perseus.tufts.edu/hopper/text?doc=Aristoph.%20 Eccl.%20115&lang=original; **95** 'The leading . . .' Hyginus, *Fabulae*, 274, trans. Mary Grant, http:// www.theoi.com/Text/HyginusFabulae5.html; **96** 'And when . . .' Plutarch, *Lucullus*, VII, http:// penelope.uchicago.edu/Thayer/E/Roman/Texts/Plutarch/Lives/Lucullus*.html; **102** '. . . no maiden . . .' Herodotus, *Histories*, 4.117, trans. A D Godley (Harvard University Press, 1920), http://perseus. uchicago.edu/perseus-cgi/citequery3.pl?dbname=GreekFeb2011&getid=1&query=Hdt.%204.117; **102** 'They have . . .' Hippocrates, *Airs, Waters, Places*, 17, trans. Francis Adams, http://classics.mit. edu/Hippocrates/airwatpl.17.17.html; **106** '. . . with her . . .' Quintus Smyrnaeus, *The Fall of Troy*, 1.33–36, trans. A S Way, http://www.theoi.com/Text/QuintusSmyrnaeus1.html; **108** 'Besides all . . .' Virgil, *Aeneid*, 7.803–13, trans. A S Kline; **109** 'But an . . .' Virgil, *Aeneid*, 11.648–51, trans. OCR; **113** '[Eros] laid . . .' Apollonius, *Argonautica*, 3.281–90, trans. R C Seaton, https://books.google. co.uk/books?id=ChqENyZ1iHIC&printsec=copyright#v=onepage&q&f=false; **114** 'Lady, let . . .' Apollonius, *Argonautica*, 4.95–98, trans. R C Seaton, https://books.google.co.uk/books?id= ChqENyZ1iHIC&printsec=copyright#v=onepage&q&f=false **117** 'Of all . . .' Euripides, *Medea*, 230–251, trans. David Kovacs, http://www.perseus.tufts.edu/hopper/text?doc=Perseus:abo: tlg,0006,003:249; **123** 'So Cleopatra . . .' Plutarch, *Life of Caesar*, 49, trans. Bernadotte Perrin, *Plutarch's Lives* (Harvard University Press, 1919) p. 7; **124** 'She had . . .' Plutarch, *Life of Antony*, 25; trans. Bernadotte Perrin, *Lives, Volume IX: Demetrius and Antony. Pyrrhus and Gaius Marius* (Loeb Classical Library, 1920), p. 193; **125** 'Converse with . . .' Plutarch, *Life of Antony*, 27, trans. Bernadotte Perrin, *Lives, Volume IX: Demetrius and Antony. Pyrrhus and Gaius Marius* (Loeb Classical Library, 1920), p. 197; **126** 'Antony, where . . .' Plutarch, *Life of Antony*, 25, trans. Bernadotte Perrin, *Lives, Volume IX: Demetrius and Antony. Pyrrhus and Gaius Marius* (Loeb Classical Library, 1920), p. 191; **128** 'It is . . .' Plutarch, *Life of Antony*, 86, trans. Bernadotte Perrin, *Lives, Volume IX: Demetrius and Antony. Pyrrhus and Gaius Marius* (Loeb Classical Library, 1920), p. 329; **129** 'And thereupon . . .' *Sibylline Oracles*, 3.92–109, trans. Milton S. Terry (1769), cited in L J Taylor, *Extra Canicals II: Christianity's Other Scriptures* (AuthorHouse, 2008).

Literature & Culture 1 (The Homeric World)

168 'At his . . .' Homer, *Iliad*, 16.131–44, trans. A S Kline; **177** '2 tripods . . .' inscription of Linear B tablet from Palace of Pylos, trans. Michael Ventris (1952), https://linearbknossosmycenae.files. wordpress.com/2015/03/linear-b-tablet-pylos–641–1952-translation-drawing-by-michael-ventris–1952.jpg; **200** 'I am . . .' Homer, *Odyssey*, 9.383–384, trans. A S Kline; **202** 'Keep it . . .' Homer, *Odyssey*, 19.486–489, trans. A S Kline; **202–203** 'So they . . .' Homer, *Odyssey*, 21.404–411, trans. A S Kline; **204** 'Old woman . . .' Homer, *Odyssey* 19.383–384, trans. A S Kline; **204** 'The row . . .' Homer, *Odyssey*, 22.468–472, trans. A S Kline; **205** 'The point . . .' Homer, *Odyssey*, 22.16–21, trans. A S Kline; **206** 'Devoid of . . .' Homer, *Odyssey*, 9.287–298, trans. A S Kline; **207** 'There a . . .' Homer, *Odyssey*, 9.187–190, trans. A S Kline; **208** 'These women . . .' Homer, *Odyssey*, 22.462–464, trans. A S Kline; **209** 'Good sir . . .' Homer, *Odyssey*, 9.269–271, trans. A S Kline; **210** 'But the . . .' Homer, *Odyssey*, 19.332–334, trans. A S Kline; **212** 'But though . . .' Homer, *Odyssey*, 19.209–212, trans. A S Kline; **212** 'Once ashore . . .' Homer, *Odyssey*, 10.103–106, trans. A S Kline; **214** '. . . lopped off . . .' Homer, *Odyssey*, 22.477, trans. A S Kline; **215** 'If he . . .' Homer, *Odyssey*, 9.532–535, trans. A S Kline; **217** 'When Circe . . .' Homer, *Odyssey*, 10.293–298, trans. A S Kline; **219** 'I sacked . . .' Homer, *Odyssey*, 9.40–42, trans. A S Kline; **221** 'Where do . . .' Homer, *Odyssey*, 9.252–255, trans. A S Kline; **221** 'They groaned . . .' Homer, *Odyssey*, 10.201–202, trans. A S Kline; **222** 'Yet despite . . .' Homer, *Odyssey*, 22.236–258, trans. A S Kline; **225** 'It's not . . .' Homer, *Odyssey*, 21.251–255, trans. A S Kline; **226** 'Remember how . . .' Homer, *Odyssey*, 10.435–437, trans. A S Kline; **226** 'My fine . . .' Homer, *Odyssey*, 9.447–448, trans. A S Kline; **227** 'Why would . . .' Homer, *Odyssey*, 9.351–352, trans. A S Kline; **227** 'It is . . .' Homer, *Odyssey*, 21.312–313, trans. A S Kline; **229** 'It was . . .' Homer, *Odyssey*, 21.343–345, trans. A S Kline; **231** 'Those were his . . .' Homer, *Odyssey*, 10.438–448, trans. A S Kline.

Literature & Culture 2 (Roman City Life)

247 'Two of . . .' Cicero, To Atticus 14.9, trans. Jo-Ann Shelton, *As the Romans Did* (OUP, 1997) p. 64; **248** 'We were accompanying . . .' Aulus Gellius, *Attic Nights*, 15.1, trans. J. Renshaw; **259** 'Thalamus, his . . .' CIL IV 933, trans. Cooley and Cooley, *Pompeii: A Sourcebook* (Routledge, 2004), p. 116; **260** 'Whoever has . . .' CIL IV 8562, trans. Cooley and Cooley, *Pompeii: A Sourcebook* (Routledge, 2004), p. 171; **260** 'What do . . .' Martial, *Epigrams*, 9.68, trans. Jo-Ann Shelton, *As the Romans Did* (OUP, 1997) p. 105; **261** 'My slave . . .' CGL III, pp. 645–647, trans. Jo-Ann Shelton, *As the Romans Did* (OUP, 1997) p. 109; **263** 'The student . . .' Cicero, *About the Orator*, 1.17–18, trans. Jo-Ann Shelton, *As the Romans Did* (OUP, 1997) p. 119; **264** 'Let water . . .' CIL IV 7698a–c, trans. Cooley and Cooley, *Pompeii: A Sourcebook* (Routledge, 2004), p. 74; **267** 'On your . . .' Plautus, *The Pot of Gold*, 507ff., trans. Jo-Ann Shelton, *As the Romans Did* (OUP, 1997) p. 127; **269** 'I have . . .' CIL XV 7194, trans. Jo-Ann Shelton, *As the Romans Did* (OUP, 1997) p. 177; **270** 'Ceratus, freedman . . .' CIL IV 910, trans. Cooley and Cooley, *Pompeii: A Sourcebook* (Routledge, 2004), p. 116; **271** 'Naevoleia Tyche . . .' CIL X 1030, trans. Cooley and Cooley, *Pompeii: A Sourcebook* (Routledge, 2004), p. 152; **273** 'Ceratus, Freedman . . .' CIL IV 910, trans. Cooley and Cooley, p. 116; **277** 'The gladiatorial . . .' CIL IV 1189, trans. Cooley and Cooley, *Pompeii: A Sourcebook* (Routledge, 2004), p. 52; **284** 'I call . . .' ILS 8753, trans. Jo-Ann Shelton, *As the Romans Did* (OUP, 1997) p. 344; **285** 'Marcus Holconius . . .' CIL X 833, 834, trans. Cooley and Cooley, *Pompeii: A Sourcebook* (Routledge, 2004), p. 67; **297** 'What stops . . .' Horace, *Satires*, 1.1.24–55, trans. J Renshaw; **298** 'Offellus judges . . .' Horace, *Satires*, 2.2.53–55, trans. A S Kline; **301** 'His words . . .' Horace, Satires, 2.695–103, trans. A S Kline, p. 81; **302** 'I'm not . . .' Horace, *Satires*, 2.6.18–19, trans. A S Kline; **306** '. . . then in . . .' Horace, *Satires*, 2.8.14–15, trans. A S Kline; **307** 'It's not . . .' Juvenal, Satires, 1.30–31, trans. J. Renshaw; **309** 'The place . . .' Juvenal, Satire 3.197–199, trans. A S Kline; **314** 'Trimalchio clicked . . .' Petronius, *Satyricon*, 27, trans. J Renshaw; **315** 'Trimalchio himself . . .' Petronius, *Satyricon*, 29, trans. OCR; **327** 'More wine . . .' Petronius, *Satyricon*, 38, trans. OCR; **322** 'What a . . .' Pliny, Letter 1.9, trans. OCR; **325** 'Some years . . .' Pliny, Letter 1.9, trans. OCR; **327** 'On the . . .' Pliny, Letter 1.9, trans. OCR; **328** 'I was . . .' Horace, Satire 2.8, 20–24, trans. OCR; **329** 'When duty . . .' Juvenal, *Satire*, 3.239–311, trans. OCR.

Literature & Culture 3 (War and Warfare)

353 'I shall . . .' From *The Oath of Plataea*, trans. Tod II, GHI 204, lines 25–28; **354** 'On the . . .' Xenophon, *Hellenika*, 6.4.16, trans. Rex Warner, *A History of My Times* (Penguin, 1966); **354** 'In other . . .' Xenophon, *The Constitution of the Spartans*, 9.4–6, trans. J M Moore, *Aristotle and Xenophon on Democracy and Oligarchy* (Chatto and Windus, 1975); **355** 'First then . . .' Herodotus, *Histories*, 7.102, trans. Aubrey de Sélincourt, *Herodotus: The Histories* (Penguin, 1996), p. 404; **357** 'Of all . . .' Herodotus, *Histories*, 7.226, trans. Aubrey de Sélincourt, *Herodotus: The Histories* (Penguin, 1996), p. 445; **357** 'Go tell . . .' Herodotus, *Histories*, 7.228, trans. Aubrey de Sélincourt, *Herodotus: The Histories* (Penguin, 1996), p. 446; **368** 'Spare your . . .' Herodotus, *Histories*, 8.68, trans. Aubrey de Sélincourt, *Herodotus: The Histories* (Penguin, 1996), p. 470; **368** 'The shores . . .' Aeschylus, *Persians*, 418–426, trans. Herbert Weir Smyth; **368** 'My men . . .' Herodotus, *Histories*, 8.88, trans. Aubrey de Sélincourt, *Herodotus: The Histories* (Penguin, 1996), p. 477; **368** 'One is . . .' Herodotus, *Histories*, 7.139, trans. Aubrey de Sélincourt, *Herodotus: The Histories* (Penguin, 1996), p. 415; **380** 'A young . . .' Vegetius, *About Milirary Matter*, 1.6–7, trans. J Renshaw;; **401** 'Over her . . .' Homer, *Iliad*, 5.347–351, trans. A S Kline; **401** 'Diomedes, of . . .' Homer, *Iliad*, 6.212–215, trans. A S Kline; **407** 'Astynous and . . .' Homer, *Iliad*, 5.144–158, trans. A S Kline; **408** 'As for . . .' Homer, *Iliad*, 5.85–94, trans. A S Kline; **409** 'Bright-eyed Athena . . .' Homer, *Iliad*, 5.418–425, trans. A S Kline; **411** 'Let us . . .' Homer, *Iliad*, 6.226–229, trans. A S Kline; **411** 'Like the . . .' Homer, *Iliad*, 6.146–149, trans. A S Kline; **412** 'Hector you . . .' Homer, *Iliad*, 6.429–432, trans. A S Kline; **412** 'May I . . .' Homer, *Iliad*, 6.464 465, trans. A S Kline; **412** 'With this . . .' Homer, *Iliad*, 6.464–465, trans. A S Kline; **413** 'When they . . .' Homer, *Iliad*, 22.208–214, trans. A S Kline; **414** 'But let . . .' Homer, *Iliad*, 22.304–305, trans. A S Kline; **414** 'Don't speak . . .' Homer, *Iliad*, 22.345–348, trans. A S Kline; **415** 'Great Priam . . .' Homer, *Iliad*, 24.477–483, trans. A S Kline; **416** 'Achilles then . . .' Homer, *Iliad*, 24.582–586, trans. A S Kline; **417** 'At the shrine . . .' Homer, *Iliad*, 6.297–311–483, trans. A S Kline; **420** 'There is . . .' Plutarch, *Cleomenes*, 2, trans. Richard J A Talbot, *On Sparta* (Penguin, 2005), p. 99; **421** 'For it . . .' Tyrtaeus, *Fragment 10*, lines 21–27, trans. OCR; **426** 'Alas, don't . . .' Horace, *Ode 3.2*, lines 9–12, trans. OCR; **433** 'Come then . . .' Virgil, *Aeneid*, 2.707–711; 717, trans. A S Kline; **435** 'See, in . . .' Virgil, *Aeneid*, 2.270–273;277–9, trans. A S Kline; **436** 'Frantically I . . .' Virgil, *Aeneid*, 2.314–317, trans. A S Kline; **436** 'Ashes of . . .' Virgil, *Aeneid*, 2.431–434, trans. A S Kline; **436** 'You do . . .' Virgil, *Aeneid*, 2.601–603, trans. A S Kline; **437** 'Yours is . . .' Virgil, *Aeneid*, 2.780–784, trans. A S Kline; **438** 'Phyrrhus spoke . . .' Virgil, *Aeneid*, 2.547–550, trans. A S Kline; Homer, *Iliad*, **439** 'And when . . .' Virgil, *Aeneid*, 2.518–525, trans. A S Kline.

SOURCES OF ILLUSTRATIONS

1.1 Digital image courtesy of the Getty's Open Content Program; **1.2** Trustees of the British Museum; **1.3** Bibi Saint-Pol/Wikimedia; **1.4** Naples Archaeological Museum; **1.5** Jastrow/Wikimedia; **1.6** James Renshaw; **1.7** Filip Maljković/Wikimedia; **1.8** CNG/Wikimedia; **1.9** Rabax63/Wikimedia; **1.10** Marie-Lan Nguyen/Wikimedia; **1.11** Digital image courtesy of the Getty's Open Content Program; **Source A p. 19** Naples Archaeological Museum; **1.12** President and Fellows of Harvard College; **1.13** Μαρσύας/Wikimedia; **1.14, Source A p. 27** DEA PICTURE LIBRARY/Contributor/Getty images; **1.15** rob koopman/Wikimedia; **1.16** Carole Raddato/Wikimedia; **1.17** DEA/A. DAGLI ORTI/Getty images; **Source A p. 34** Carole Raddato/Wikimedia; **1.18** Paweł 'pbm' Szubert/Wikimedia; **1.19** Jastrow/Wikimedia; **1.20** Marie-Lan Nguyen/Wikimedia; **1.21** James Renshaw; **1.22** Marie-Lan Nguyen/Wikimedia; **1.23** Wellcome Library, London; **1.24** Marie-Lan Nguyen/Wikimedia; **1.25** Jastrow/Wikimedia; **1.26** Fabien Dany/Wikimedia; **Source A pp. 52, 53** Marie-Lan Nguyen/Wikimedia; **1.27** Sebastià Giralt; **1.28** Bibi Saint Pol/Wikimedia; **1.29** haknc.1/shutterstock.com, **1.30** Fer.fllol/Wikimedia; **1.31** Caroline Léna Becker/Wikimedia; **1.32** Jastrow/Wikimedia; **1.33** Edward John Poynter; **Source A p. 66** Walters Art Museum (acquired by Henry Walters with the Massarenti Collection, 1902); **1.34** Digital image courtesy of the Getty's Open Content Program; **1.35**; **1.36** James Renshaw; **1.37** Bloomsbury Academic; **1.38** Twospoonfuls/Wikimedia; **1.39** Twospoonfuls/Wikimedia; **1.40** Carole Raddato/Wikimedia; **1.41, Source A p. 79** The Metropolitan Museum of Art, New York, www.metmuseum.org; **1.42** Jebulon/Wikimedia; **1.43** DEA/ARCHIVIO J. LANGE/Contributor/Wikimedia; **1.44** James Renshaw; **1.45** Sailko/Wikimedia; **Source A p. 89** Sailko/Wikimedia; **1.46** James Renshaw; **1.47** LOOK Die Bildagentur der Fotografen GmbH/Alamy Stock Photo; **1.48** Trinquart, 1834; **1.49** Jean-Pol GRANDMONT/Wikimedia; **1.50** Bibi Saint-Pol/Wikimedia; **1.51** Walters Art Museum (acquired by Henry Walters, 1924); **1.52** Athina Mitropoulos; **1.53** Athina Mitropoulos; **1.54** Trustees of the British Museum; **1.55** Leemage/Getty images; **1.56** UniversalImagesGroup/Contributor/Getty images; **1.57** DEA PICTURE LIBRARY/Getty images; **1.58** Danita Delimont/Getty images; **1.59** DEA/G. DAGLI ORTI/Getty images; **1.60** Tim Evanson/Wikimedia; **1.61** Jastrow/Wikimedia; **1.62** Culture Club/Contributor/Getty images; **1.63** Everett Historical/shutterstock.com; **1.64** CNG/Wikimedia; **Source A p. 135** Jastrow/Wikimedia; **Source A p. 136** Jastrow/Wikimedia; **2.1** James Renshaw; **2.2** Bloomsbury Academic; **2.3** Wikicommons; **2.4** Education Images/Contributor/Getty images; **2.5** James Renshaw; **2.6** Dennis Jarvis/Wikimedia; **2.7** Klearchos Kapoutsis/Wikimedia; **2.8** Napoleon Vier/Wikimedia; **2.9** De Agostini/G. Dagli Orti/Getty images; **2.10** siete_vidas/shutterstock.com; **2.11** Time Life Pictures/Contributor/Getty images; **2.12** Bloomsbury Academic; **2.13** Bloomsbury Academic; **2.14** YukioSanjo/Wikimedia; **2.15** Zde/Wikimedia; **2.16** Jebulon/Wikimedia; **2.17** Sharon Mollerus/Wikimedia; **2.18** DEA/G. DAGLI ORTI/Contributor/Getty images; **2.19** Zde/Wikimedia; **2.20** Leemage/Contributor/Getty images; **2.21** Zde/Wikimedia; **2.22** Bloomsbury Academic; **2.23** Bloomsbury Academic; **2.24** Bloomsbury Academic; **2.25a** DEA/G. DAGLI ORTI/Getty images; **2.25b** OCR; **2.26** DEA/G. NIMATALLAH/Contributor/Getty images; **2.27** DEA/G. DAGLI ORTI/Contributor/Getty images; **2.28** Yann Forget/Wikimedia; **2.29** Zde/Wikimedia; **2.30** Zde/Wikimedia; **2.31** Schuppi/Wikimedia; **2.32** Sailko/Wikimedia; **2.33** Zde/Wikimedia; **2.34** Zde/Wikimedia; **2.35** Zde/Wikimedia; **2.36a** Zde/Wikimedia; **2.36b** Zde/Wikimedia; **2.36c** Zde/Wikimedia; **2.37** Zde/Wikimedia; **2.38** Xuan Che/Wikimedia; **2.39** Bloomsbury Academic; **2.40** michael clarke stuff/Wikimedia; **2.41** Bloomsbury Academic; **2.42** Zde/Wikimedia; **2.43** Xuan Che/Wikimedia; **2.44** Hay Kranen/Wikimedia; **2.45** Yorck Project/Wikimedia; **2.46** DEA/S. VANNINI/Getty

INDEX

Page numbers in **bold** refer to figures.